# Lecture Notes in Computer Science 6578

Commenced Publication in 1973
Founding and Former Series Editors:
Gerhard Goos, Juris Hartmanis, and Jan van Leeuwen

Andreas Koch   Ram Krishnamurthy
John McAllister   Roger Woods
Tarek El-Ghazawi (Eds.)

# Reconfigurable Computing: Architectures, Tools and Applications

7th International Symposium, ARC 2011
Belfast, UK, March 23-25, 2011
Proceedings

 Springer

Volume Editors

Andreas Koch
Technische Universität Darmstadt, FB 20 Informatik
Hochschulstraße 10, 64289 Darmstadt, Germany
E-mail: koch@esa.informatik.tu-darmstadt.de

Ram Krishnamurthy
Intel Corp., Hillsboro, OR 97006, USA
E-mail: ram.krishnamurthy@intel.com

John McAllister
Queen's University of Belfast
School of Electronics, Electrical Engineering and Computer Science
Institute of Electronics, Communications and Information Technology
Queen's Road, Belfast, BT3 9DT, UK
E-mail: j.mcallister@ecit.qub.ac.uk

Roger Woods
Queen's University of Belfast
School of Electronics, Electrical Engineering and Computer Science
Institute of Electronics, Communications and Information Technology
Queen's Road, Belfast, BT3 9DT, UK
E-mail: r.woods@qub.ac.uk

Tarek El-Ghazawi
George Washington University, Department of Electrical and Computer Engineering
801, 22nd Street NW, Washington, DC 20052, USA
E-mail: tarek@gwu.edu

ISSN 0302-9743                                          e-ISSN 1611-3349
ISBN 978-3-642-19474-0                              ISBN 978-3-642-19475-7 (eBook)
DOI 10.1007/978-3-642-19475-7
Springer Heidelberg Dordrecht London New York

Library of Congress Control Number: 2011922314

CR Subject Classification (1998): C.2, D.2, I.4, H.3, F.1, I.6

LNCS Sublibrary: SL 1 – Theoretical Computer Science and General Issues

*Typesetting:* Camera-ready by author, data conversion by Scientific Publishing Services, Chennai, India

Printed on acid-free paper

Springer is part of Springer Science+Business Media (www.springer.com)

# Preface

With the number of transistors on a single chip now reaching into the billions for mass-produced devices, answering the question of what to actually *use* them for becomes ever more pressing. Conventional approaches of implementing larger cache sizes and deeper cache hierarchies are no longer efficient when attempting to gain performance, and can even be detrimental when saving power is also a design objective.

Reconfigurable computing (RC) attempts to exploit the growing transistor budgets by mapping part or all of a computation into *dedicated* hardware architectures, instead of executing the application on a general-purpose fixed instruction-set processor. Contemporary configurable devices allow for the definition of specific compute and storage units, adapted to the functions, bit-widths and control structures of a given algorithm. This adaptation can even be performed at run-time, fitting the topology of the underlying architecture to the specific needs of the *current execution*. Looking forward to future nano-scale circuit technologies, the flexibility enabled by reconfiguration can also be seen as a basic technique for overcoming permanent and transient failures of the inherently unreliable device fabrics.

To actually realize the potential of reconfigurable technology, numerous advances in a wide number of research fields are necessary. These include hardware architecture, software tools, operating systems, and design methodologies, as well as algorithmic innovation at the application-level itself. The International Symposium of Applied Reconfigurable Computing (ARC) aims to bring together researchers working on all of these aspects, emphasizing research that shows how RC can benefit specific applications or domains.

With 88 papers, the seventh ARC symposium, held during March 23–25, 2011 in Belfast (UK) had a record number of submissions, up from 66 in 2009 and 71 in 2010. They came from 22 countries, showing the global interest in this field of research: UK (14), Germany (13), France (12), Japan (7), USA (6), Spain (6), Sweden (5), China (4), Ireland (3), The Netherlands (3), India (3), Brazil (2), Canada (1), Denmark (1), Greece (1), Iran (1), South Korea (1), Norway (1), Poland (1), Romania (1), Singapore (1), Vietnam (1).

The submissions were evaluated by three members of the Program Committee. Based on their recommendations, the Chairs selected 24 contributions as full papers for oral presentation (27% acceptance rate) and 15 short papers as posters, giving an overall acceptance rate of 44%. The spectrum of topics addressed by this program reflects a broad part of the research in reconfigurable technology.

We would like to thank all authors for their contributions to ARC 2011. Also, we are grateful for the support of the Program Committee, which shouldered the unexpectedly heavy review load at short notice. Finally, we acknowledge the continued support of Springer in making the ARC symposia series a success.

January 2011

Andreas Koch
Ram Krishnamurthy
John McAllister
Roger Woods
Tarek El-Ghazawi

# Organization

ARC 2011, organized by the Queen's University of Belfast, was the seventh in a series of international symposia on applications-oriented research in reconfigurable computing.

## Steering Committee

| | |
|---|---|
| Hideharu Amano | Keio University, Japan |
| Jürgen Becker | Karlsruhe Institute of Technology, Germany |
| Mladen Berekovic | Friedrich Schiller University Jena, Germany |
| Koen Bertels | Delft University of Technology, The Netherlands |
| João M.P. Cardoso | University of Porto/FEUP, Portugal |
| Katherine Compton | University of Wisconsin-Madison, USA |
| George Constantinides | Imperial College, UK |
| Pedro C. Diniz | Technical University of Lisbon (IST) / INESC-ID Portugal |
| Philip Leong | University of Sydney, Australia |
| Walid Najjar | University of California at Riverside, USA |
| Roger Woods | Queen's University of Belfast, UK |

## Program Committee

| | |
|---|---|
| Jeff Arnold | Stretch Inc., USA |
| Peter Athanas | Virginia Tech, USA |
| Michael Attig | Xilinx Research Labs, San Jose, USA |
| Nader Bagherzadeh | University of California, Irvine, USA |
| Jügen Becker | Karlsruhe Institute of Technology, Germany |
| Mladen Berekovic | Friedrich Schiller University Jena, Germany |
| Neil Bergmann | University of Queensland, Australia |
| Koen Bertels | Delft University of Technology, The Netherlands |
| Christos-Savvas Bouganis | Imperial College London, UK |
| Mihai Budiu | Microsoft Research, USA |
| João M.P. Cardoso | University of Porto/FEUP, Portugal |
| Mark Chang | Olin College, USA |
| Paul Chow | University of Toronto, Canada |
| Katherine Compton | University of Wisconsin-Madison, USA |
| George Constantinides | Imperial College, UK |
| Pedro C. Diniz | Technical University of Lisbon (IST) / INESC-ID, Portugal |

# Reviewers

Jeff Arnold
Peter Athanas
Michael Attig
Samuel Bayliss
Mladen Berekovic
Neil Bergmann
Koen Bertels
David Boland
Christos-Savvas
   Bouganis
Mihai Budiu
João M.P. Cardoso
Paul Chow
Katherine Compton
George Constantinides
Pedro C. Diniz
Tarek El-Ghazawi
Robert Esser
Suhaib Fahmy
António Ferrari
Guy Gogniat

Maya Gokhale
Jim Harkin
Reiner Hartenstein
Roman Hermida
Christian Hochberger
Michael Hübner
Ryan Kastner
Andreas Koch
Adrian Knoth
Ram Krishnamurthy
Philip Leong
Wayne Luk
Terrence Mak
Eduardo Marques
Kostas Masselos
Sanu Mathew
John McAllister
Seda Memik
Saumil Merchant
Fearghal Morgan
Sascha Mühlbach

Peter Müller
Walid Najjar
Vikram Narayana
Horacio Neto
David Neuhäuser
Joon-seok Park
Thilo Pionteck
Joachim Pistorius
Marco Platzner
Bernard Pottier
Tsutomu Sasao
Farhana Sheikh
Pete Sedcole
Lesley Shannon
Florian Stock
Pedro Trancoso
Markus Weinhardt
Stephan Wong
Roger Woods
Thorsten Wink
Peter Zipf

# Table of Contents

## Reconfigurable Processors

## Applications

# Reconfigurable Accelerators II

# Methodology and Simulation

# System Architecture

# Reconfigurable Computing for High Performance Networking Applications

Gordon Brebner

Xilinx

It is now forecast that Terabit Ethernet will be needed in 2015. (A 1 Tb/s data rate means that the estimated memory capacity of a typical human could be transmitted in 24 seconds.) In this talk, Gordon Brebner will give an overview of research which demonstrates that Field Programmable Logic Array (FPGA) devices can be main processing components for 100-200 Gb/s networking, a main event horizon in 2010, and points the way to how techniques might scale (or not) towards a 1 Tb/s transmission rate by 2015. The highly configurable, and reconfigurable, characteristics of such devices make them a unique technology that fits with the requirements for extremely high performance and moreover for flexibility and programmability. Aside from discussing the physical technological properties, the talk will cover work on higher-level programming models that can make the technology more accessible to networking experts, as opposed to hardware/FPGA experts.

**Gordon Brebner** is a Distinguished Engineer at Xilinx, Inc., the worldwide leader in programmable logic solutions. He works in Xilinx Labs in San José, California, USA, leading an international group researching issues surrounding networked processing systems of the future. Prior to joining Xilinx in 2002, Gordon was the Professor of Computer Systems at the University of Edinburgh in the United Kingdom, directing the Institute for Computing Systems Architecture. He continues to be an Honorary Professor at the University of Edinburgh, is a Ph.D. advisor at Santa Clara University, and is a visiting lecturer at Stanford University. Professor Brebner has been researching in the field of programmable digital systems for over two decades, presenting regularly at, and assisting with the organization of, the major international conferences in the area. He has authored numerous papers and holds many patents.

A. Koch et al. (Eds.): ARC 2011, LNCS 6578, p. 1, 2011.
© Springer-Verlag Berlin Heidelberg 2011

# Biologically-Inspired Massively-Parallel Architectures: A Reconfigurable Neural Modelling Platform

Steve Furber

University of Manchester

The SpiNNaker project aims to develop parallel computer systems with more than a million embedded processors. The goal of the project is to support large-scale simulations of systems of spiking neurons in biological real time. The architecture is generic and makes minimal assumptions about the network topologies that will be supported, the goal being to offer a fully reconfigurable platform to test hypotheses of brain function whether they arise from neuroscience, psychology, or elsewhere.

**Steve Furber** BE FRS FREng is the ICL Professor of Computer Engineering in the School of Computer Science at the University of Manchester. He received his BA degree in Mathematics in 1974 and his PhD in Aerodynamics in 1980 from the University of Cambridge, England. From 1980 to 1990 he worked in the hardware development group within the R&D department at Acorn Computers Ltd, and was a principal designer of the BBC Microcomputer and the ARM 32-bit RISC microprocessor. He moved to the University of Manchester in 1990 where his research interests include low-power and asynchronous digital design and neural systems engineering. Steve was awarded a Royal Academy of Engineering Silver Medal in 2003, held a Royal Society Wolfson Research Merit Award from 2004 to 2009 and was awarded the IET Faraday Medal in 2007 and a CBE in 2008. He was a 2010 Millenium Technology Prize Laureate, and was awarded an Honorary DSc by the University of Edinburgh in 2010.

A. Koch et al. (Eds.): ARC 2011, LNCS 6578, p. 2, 2011.
© Springer-Verlag Berlin Heidelberg 2011

# A Reconfigurable Audio Beamforming Multi-Core Processor*

Dimitris Theodoropoulos, Georgi Kuzmanov, and Georgi Gaydadjiev

Computer Engineering Laboratory, EEMCS, TU Delft, P.O. Box 5031,
2600 GA Delft, The Netherlands
{D.Theodoropoulos,G.K.Kuzmanov,g.n.gaydadjiev}@tudelft.nl

**Abstract.** Over the last years, the Beamforming technique has been adopted by the audio engineering society to amplify the signal of an acoustic source, while attenuating any ambient noise. Existing software implementations provide a flexible customizing environment, however they introduce performance limitations and excessive power consumption overheads. On the other hand, hardware approaches achieve significantly better performance and lower power consumption compared to the software ones, but they lack the flexibility of a high-level versatile programming environment. To address these drawbacks, we have already proposed a minimalistic processor architecture tailoring audio Beamforming applications to configurable hardware. In this paper, we present its application as a multi-core reconfigurable Beamforming processor and describe our hardware prototype, which is mapped onto a Virtex4FX60 FPGA. Our approach combines software programming flexibility with improved hardware performance, low power consumption and compact program-executable memory footprint. Experimental results suggest that our FPGA-based processor, running at 100 MHz, can extract in real-time up to 14 acoustic sources 2.6 times faster than a 3.0 GHz Core2 Duo OpenMP-based implementation. Furthermore, it dissipates an order of magnitude less energy, compared to the general purpose processor software implementation.

## 1 Introduction

For many decades, the Beamforming technique has been used in telecommunications to strengthen incoming signals from a particular location. Over the last years, it has been adopted by audio engineers to develop systems that can extract acoustic sources. Usually, microphone arrays are used to record acoustic wavefronts originating from a certain area. All recorded signals are forwarded to processors that utilize Beamforming FIR filters [1] to suppress any ambient noise and strengthen all primary audio sources.

Research on literature reveals that the majority of experimental systems are based on standard PCs, due to their high-level programming support and potential of rapid system development. However, two major drawbacks of these approaches are performance bottlenecks and excessive power consumption. In order to reduce power consumption, many researchers have developed Beamforming systems based on Digital Signal Processors (DSPs), however performance is still limited. Custom-hardware solutions

---

* This research is partially supported by Artemisia iFEST project (grant 100203), Artemisia SMECY (grant 100230), FP7 Reflect (grant 248976).

A. Koch et al. (Eds.): ARC 2011, LNCS 6578, pp. 3–15, 2011.

alleviate both of the aforementioned drawbacks. However, in the majority of cases, designers are primarily focused on just performing all required calculations faster than a General Purpose Processor (GPP). Such an approach does not provide a high-level programming environment for testing the system that is under development. For example, in many cases, the designers should evaluate the Signal-to-Noise-Ratio (SNR) of an extracted source under different filter sizes and coefficients sets. Such experiments can easily be conducted using a standard PC with a GPP, but they would take long time to be re-designed in hardware and cannot be performed on the field at post-production time. The latter problem can be alleviated by introducing reconfigurable hardware and appropriate means to control it.

In our previous paper [2], we have proposed a minimalistic architecture[1] for embedded Beamforming. It supports nine high-level instructions that allow rapid system configuration and data processing control. Moreover, the presented model provides a versatile interface with a custom-hardware Beamforming processor, thus allowing faster system re-testing and evaluation.

The main contribution of this paper is the analytical presentation and evaluation of a Beamforming microarchitecture, which supports the high-level architecture proposed in our previous work [2]. Our microarchitecture is specifically tailored to reconfigurable multi-core implementations. We prove that our proposal combines the programming flexibility of software approaches with the high performance, low power consumption and limited memory requirements of reconfigurable hardware solutions. The architecture implementation allows utilization of various number of processing elements, therefore it is suitable for mapping on reconfigurable technology. With respect to the available reconfigurable resources, different FPGA implementations with different performances are possible, where all of them use the same architecture and programming paradigm. More specifically, the contributions of this paper are the following:

- We propose a microarchitecture of a Multi-Core BeamForming Processor (MC-BFP), which supports the high-level architecture, originally presented in our previous work. The new microarchitecture was mapped onto a Virtex4 FX60 FPGA. The program-executable memory footprint is approximately 40 kbytes, thus makes it a very attractive approach for embedded solutions with limited on-chip memory capabilities.
- We compared our FPGA-based approach against an OpenMP-annotated software implementation on a Core2 Duo processor running at 3.0 GHz. Experimental results suggest that our prototype can extract 14 acoustic sources 2.6 times faster than the Core2 Duo solution.
- Our hardware design provides a power-efficient solution, since it consumes approximately 6.0 Watts. This potentially dissipates an order of magnitude less energy, compared to the Core2 Duo implementation that requires tens of Watts when fully utilized.

---

[1] Throughout this paper, we have adopted the terminology from [3]. According to the book, the computer architecture is termed as the conceptual view and functional behavior of a computer system as seen by its immediate viewer - the programmer. The underlying implementation, termed also as microarchitecture, defines how the control and the datapaths are organized to support the architecture functionality.

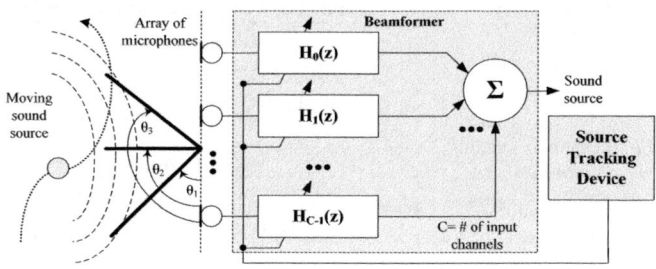

**Fig. 1.** A filter-and-sum beamformer

The rest of the paper is organized as follows: Section 2 provides a brief background on the Beamforming technique and references to various systems that utilize it. In Section 3, we shortly describe our previously proposed architecture. In Section 4 we elaborate on the proposed microarchitecture, while Section 5 presents our hardware prototype and compares it against a software approach and related work. Finally, Section 6 concludes the paper.

## 2    Background and Related Work

**Background:** Beamforming is used to perform spatial filtering over a specific recording area, in order to estimate an incoming signal's direction of arrival. Although there are many approaches to efficiently perform acoustic Beamforming [1], many systems utilize a filter-and-sum approach, which is illustrated in Figure 1. A microphone array of $C$ elements samples the propagating wavefronts and each microphone is connected to an $H_i(z)$, FIR filter. All filtered signals are accumulated, in order to strengthen the extracted audio source and attenuate any ambient noise. The FIR filters are utilized as delay lines that compensate for the introduced delay of the wavefront arrival at all microphones [4]. As a result, the combination of all filtered signals will amplify the original audio source, while any interfering noise will be suppressed.

In order to extract a moving acoustic source, it is mandatory to reconfigure all filter coefficients according to the source current location. An example is illustrated in Figure 1, where a moving source is recorded for a certain time within the aperture defined by the $\theta_2 - \theta_1$ angle. A source tracking device is used to follow the trajectory of the source. Based on its coordinates, all filters are configured with the proper coefficients set. As soon as the moving source crosses to the aperture defined by the $\theta_3 - \theta_2$ angle, the source tracking device will provide the new coordinates, thus all filter coefficients must be updated with a new set. Finally, we should note that in practise, many systems perform signal decimation and interpolation before and after Beamforming respectively, in order to reduce the data size that requires processing.

**Related work:** The authors of [5] present a Beamforming hardware accelerator, where up to seven instances of the proposed design can fit in a Virtex4 SX55 FPGA, resulting in a 41.7x speedup compared to the software implementation. Another FPGA approach is presented in [6]. The authors have implemented an adaptive Beamforming engine,

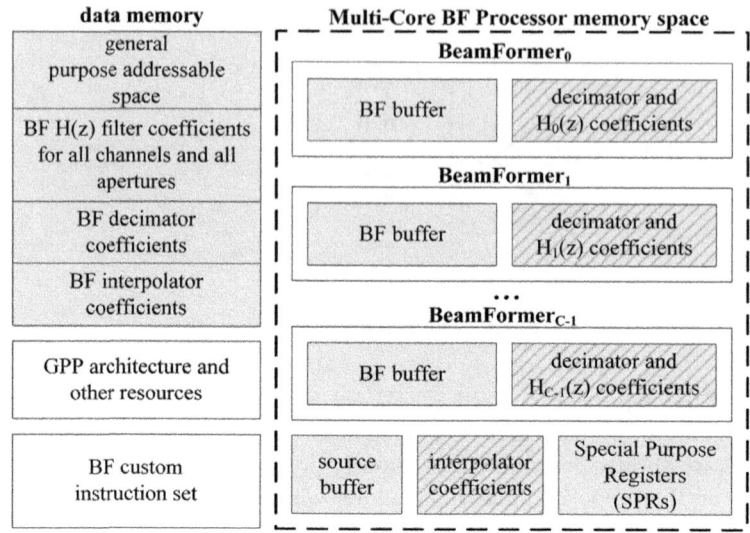

**Fig. 2.** Logical organization of the registers and the memory

which is based on the QR matrix decomposition (QRD), and mapped it onto a Virtex4 FPGA.

A DSP implementation of an adaptive subband Beamforming algorithm, is presented in [7]. The authors utilize an Analog Devices DSP processor to perform Beamforming over a two microphone array setup. An experimental video teleconferencing system is presented in [8] that is based on a Texas Instruments DSP. The authors combine a video camera and a 16-microphone array into a device, which can be placed in the center of a meeting table.

Finally, in [9], the authors describe a PC-based system consisting of 12 microphones. The sound source is tracked through audio and video tracking algorithms. The extracted audio signal is received from a second remote PC that renders it through a loudspeakers array. A similar multiple PC-based system is presented in [10]. The authors have implemented a real-time audio software system that uses the Beamforming technique to record audio signals.

As it can be concluded, DSP and software implementations provide a high-level developing and testing environment, but they lack of adequate performance. Hardware approaches miss a versatile programming environment that would help developing Beamforming systems easier and faster. For this reason, we believe that our solution for reconfigurable Beamformers could combine high-level programmability with improved performance and low power consumption.

## 3    The Beamforming Architecture

As it was mentioned in Section 1, in our previous work [2], we presented a minimalistic high-level architecture tailored to embedded Beamforming applications, which is

**Table 1.** Programming Model for Beamforming applications

| Instruction type | Full name | Mnemonic | Parameters | SPRs modified |
|---|---|---|---|---|
| I/O | Input Stream Enable | InStreamEn | b_mask | SPR0 |
| System setup | Clear SPRs | ClrSPRs | NONE | SPR0 - SPR[9+2·C] |
|  | Declare FIR Filter | DFirF | FSize, FType | SPR1, SPR2, SPR3 |
|  | Set Samples Addresses | SSA | **buf_sam_addr | SPR7, SPR[10+C] - SPR[9+2·C] |
|  | Buffer Coefficients | BufCoef | **xmem_coef_addr, **buf_coef_addr | NONE |
|  | Load Coefficients | LdCoef | **buf_coef_addr | SPR4, SPR8, SPR10 - SPR[9+C] |
|  | Configure # of input channels | ConfC | C | SPR9 |
| Data processing | Beamform Source | BFSrc | aper, *xmem_read_addr, *xmem_write_addr | SPR5, SPR6 |
| Debug | Read SPR | RdSPR | SPR_num | NONE |

**Table 2.** Special Purpose Registers

| SPR | Description |
|---|---|
| SPR0 | InStreamEn binary mask |
| SPR1 | Decimators FIR filter size |
| SPR2 | Interpolators FIR filter size |
| SPR3 | H(z) FIR filter size |
| SPR4 | LdCoef start/done flag |
| SPR5 | aperture address offset |
| SPR6 | BFSrc start/done flag |
| SPR7 | source buffer address |
| SPR8 | interpolator coefficients address |
| SPR9 | number of input channels (C) |
| SPR10 - SPR[9+C] | channel i coefficients buffer address, i=0...C-1 |
| SPR[10+C] - SPR[9+2·C] | channel i 1024 samples buffer address, i=0...C-1 |

briefly described in this section. Figure 2 illustrates the logical organization of the registers and available memory space, assuming that processing is distributed among $C$ *BeamFormer* modules receiving data from $C$ input channels. Memory space is divided into user-addressable and non user-addressable, indicated by the stripe pattern. Off-chip memory is used for storing any required type of data, like various coefficients sets for the decimators, H(z) filters and interpolators, and any other general purpose variables. The host GPP and the Multi-Core BeamForming Processor (MC-BFP) exchange synchronization parameters and memory addresses via a set of Special Purpose Registers (SPRs). Each *BeamFormer* module has a *BF buffer* and memory space for the decimator and H(z) filters coefficients. Finally, the on-chip *source buffer* is used to store the audio samples of an extracted source.

Table 1 shows the nine instructions, originally presented in [2], divided into four categories. The *SPRs modified* column shows the SPR that is modified by the corresponding instruction, which are also provided in Table 2. The functionality of each instruction parameter is explained in Section 4 and in [2].

_InStreamEn_: Enables or disables streaming of audio samples from input channels to the Beamforming processing units.

_ClrSPRs_: Clears the contents of all SPRs.

_DFirF_: Declares the size of a filter and writes it to the corresponding SPR.

_SSA_: Specifies the addresses from where the MC-BFP will read the input samples.

_BufCoef_: Fetches all decimator and interpolator coefficients from external memory to _BF buffers_.

_LdCoef_: Distributes all decimator and interpolator coefficients to the corresponding filters in the system.

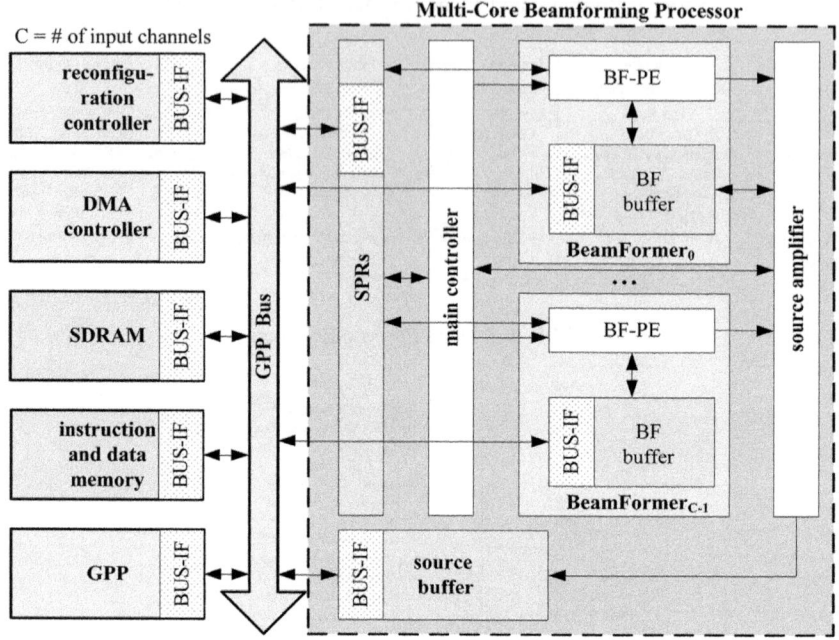

**Fig. 3.** Detailed implementation of the Beamforming system

*ConfC*: Defines the number of input channels that are available to the system.

*BFSrc*: Processes a 1024-sample chunk of streaming data from each input channel that is enabled with the *InStreamEn* instruction, in order to extract an audio source.

*RdSPR*: Used for debugging purposes and allows the programmer to read any of the SPRs.

Note that the *ConfC* configures the number of input channels using a partial reconfiguration module (e.g. Xilinx Internal Communication Access Port). The reason we decided to provide this instruction is for the user to avoid performing the time-consuming implementation process when the number of microphones changes. By having already a set of reconfiguration files for different input setups (e.g. bitstreams), the user can quickly switch among them when conducting application tests.

## 4  The Reconfigurable Beamforming Microarchitecture

**Beamforming system description:** Figure 3 illustrates in more detail the Beamforming system implementation of the architecture from Figure 2. We should note that it is based on our previous Beamforming processor, originally presented in [11], however significant design improvements have been made, in order to support a high-level programming ability. In the following text, $D$ and $L$ represent the decimation and interpolation rates respectively.

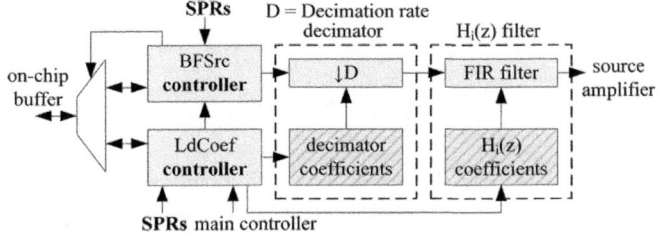

**Fig. 4.** The Beamforming processing element (BF-PE) structure

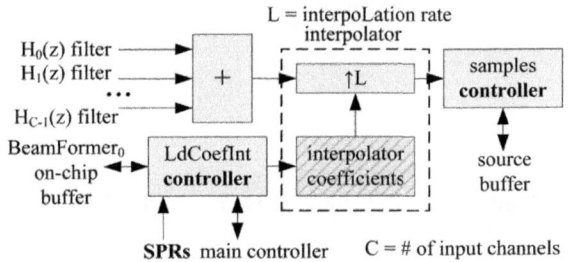

**Fig. 5.** The source amplifier structure

A *GPP bus* is used to connect the on-chip GPP memory and external SDRAM with the GPP via a standard bus interface (BUS-IF). Furthermore, in order to accelerate data transfer from the SDRAM to *BF buffers*, we employ a *Direct Memory Access (DMA) controller*, which is also connected to the same bus. A partial reconfiguration controller is employed to provide the option of reloading the correct bitstreams based on the currently available number of input channels. All user-addressable spaces inside the MC-BFP, like SPRs, *BF buffers* and the *source buffer*, are connected to the *GPP bus*. This fact enhances our architecture's flexibility, since they are directly accessible by the GPP. The *main controller* is responsible for initiating the coefficients reloading process to all decimators and the interpolator. Furthermore, it enables input data processing from all channels, and acknowledges the GPP as soon as all calculations are done.

Each *BeamFormer* module consists of a *BF buffer* and a Beamforming Processing Element (BF-PE), which is illustrated in Figure 4. As it can be seen, there is a *LdCoef controller* and a *BFSrc controller*. Based on the current source aperture, the former is responsible for reloading the required coefficients sets from the *BF buffer* to the decimator and H(z) filter. The *BFSrc controller* reads 1024 input samples from the *BF buffer* and forwards them to the decimator and the H(z) filter.

All *BeamFormer* modules forward the filtered signals to the *source amplifier*, which is shown in Figure 5. The *LdCoefInt controller* is responsible for reloading the coefficients set to the interpolator. As we can see, all $H_i(z)$ signals, where i=0,...,C-1, are accumulated to strengthen the original acoustic source signal, which is then interpolated. Finally, the *samples controller* is responsible for writing back to the *source buffer* the interpolated source signal.

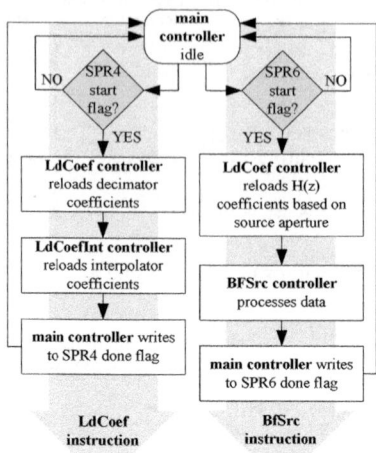

**Fig. 6.** Implementation of the *LdCoef* and *BFSrc* instructions

**Instructions implementation:** All SPRs are accessible from the GPP, because they belong to its memory addressable range. Thus, the programmer can directly pass all customizing parameters to the MC-BFP. Each SPR is used for storing a system config-uration parameter, a start/done flag or a pointer to an external/internal memory entry. For this reason, we have divided the instructions into four different categories, based on the way the GPP accesses the SPRs. The categories are: *GPP reads SPR, GPP writes to SPR, GPP reads and writes to SPR, GPP does not access any SPR*, and they are analyzed below:

*GPP reads SPR*: RdSPR is the only instruction that belongs to this category. The GPP initiates a *GPP bus* read-transaction and, based on the SPR number *SPR_num*, it calculates the proper SPR memory address.

*GPP writes to SPR*: *InStreamEn, ClrSPRs, DFirF, ConfC* and *SSA* are the instruc-tions that belong to this category. When the *InStream* instruction has to be executed, the GPP initiates a *GPP bus* write-transaction and writes the *b_mask* value (a binary mask, where each bit indicates if a channel is enabled or not) to SPR0. Similarly, in *ClrSPRs* the GPP has to iterate through all SPRs and write the zero value to them. In *DFirF* instruction, the GPP uses the filter type *Ftype* parameter to distinguish among the three different filter types (decimator, H(z) filter and interpolator), and calculate the proper SPR address to write the filter size *FSize* to SPR1, SPR3 or SPR2. In *ConfC*, the GPP writes the *C* parameter to SPR9, which is read from the partial reconfiguration con-troller, in order to load from the external memory the bitstream that includes *C* BF-PEs. Finally, in *SSA* instruction, the GPP iterates SPR[10+C] - SPR[9+2·C] and writes to them the *BF buffer* addresses, where 1024 input samples will be written, which are read from an array of pointers to the starting addresses of all *BF buffers*, called *buf_sam_addr*.

*GPP reads and writes to SPR*: *LdCoef* and *BFSrc* instructions belong to this cate-gory. In *LdCoef*, the GPP writes all decimators coefficients addresses to SPR10 - SPR[9+C], and the interpolator coefficients address to SPR8, which are read from an

**Table 3.** Resource utilization of each module

| Module | Slices | DSP Slices | Memory(bytes) |
|---|---|---|---|
| Single BeamFormer | 598 | 2 | 8192 |
| Source Amplifier | 2870 | 0 | 2048 |
| MC-BFP | 14165 | 32 | 133120 |
| System infrastructure | 6650 | 0 | 317440 |
| Complete system with C=16 | 20815 | 32 | 450560 |

array of pointers within the *BF buffers*, where all coefficients are stored, called *buf_coef_addr*. As soon as all addresses are written to the proper SPRs, the GPP writes a *LdCoef start flag* to SPR4 and remains blocked until the MC-BFP writes a *LdCoef done flag* to the same SPR. Figure 6 illustrates the next processing steps within the MC-BFP, in order to reload all decimators and interpolator with the proper coefficients sets. As soon as *LdCoef start flag* is written to SPR4, the *main controller* enables the *LdCoef controller* to start reloading the decimators coefficients. Once this step is finished, the *LdCoefInt controller* initiates the interpolator coefficients reloading procedure. As soon as all coefficients are reloaded, the latter acknowledges the *main controller*, which writes a *LdCoef done flag* to SPR4. This unblocks the GPP, which can continue further processing.

In *BFSrc*, based on the source aperture *aper*, the GPP calculates a *BF buffer* address offset, called *Aperture Address Offset (AAO)*, in order to access the proper H(z) coefficients sets. The GPP writes the *AAO* to SPR5. Furthermore, it performs a DMA transaction, in order to read $C$ 1024-sample chunks from the *xmem_read_addr* memory location and distribute them to *BF buffers* of the $C$ *BeamFormer* modules. As soon as all data are stored, the GPP writes a *BFSrc start flag* to SPR6 and remains blocked until the MC-BFP writes a *BFSrc done flag* to the same SPR. Figure 6 shows the next processing steps inside the MC-BFP. Within each *BeamFormer* module, the *LdCoef controller* reads the *AAO* from SPR5 and reloads to the H(z) filter the proper coefficients set. Once all H(z) coefficients are reloaded, the *LdCoef controller* acknowledges the *BFSrc controller*, which enables processing of input data that are stored to the *BF buffers*. As soon as 1024 samples are processed, the *main controller* writes a *BFSrc done flag* to SPR6, which unblocks the GPP. The latter performs again a DMA transaction, in order to transfer 1024 samples from the *source buffer* to the *xmem_write_addr* memory location.

*GPP does not access any SPR*: *BufCoef* is the only instruction that belongs to this category. The GPP reads all source addresses from an array of pointers to the off-chip memory starting addresses of the coefficients sets, called *xmem_coef_addr*. Also, the GPP reads all destination addresses from *buf_coef_addr*. First, it performs a DMA transaction to transfer all decimator coefficients to the *BF buffers*. Next, based on the total number of source apertures to the system, it performs a second DMA transaction to load all H(z) coefficients and distribute them accordingly to the *BF buffers*. Finally, with a third DMA transaction, the GPP fetches the active interpolator coefficients set to the *BF buffer* of $BeamFormer_0$ module.

## 5   Hardware Prototype

**FPGA prototype:** Based on the above study, we used the Xilinx ISE 9.2 and EDK 9.2 CAD tools to develop a VHDL hardware prototype. The latter was implemented on a Xilinx ML410 board with a Virtex4 FX60 FPGA and 256 MB of DDR2 SDRAM. As host GPP processor, we used one of the two integrated PowerPC processors, which executes the program-executable that requires only 40 kbytes of BRAM. Furthermore, we used the Processor Local Bus (PLB) to connect all peripherals, which are all *BF buffers*, the *source buffer*, all SPRs, and the DMA and SDRAM controllers. For the partial reconfiguration we have used the Xilinx ICAP, which is also connected to the PLB. The PowerPC runs at 200 MHz, while the rest of the system is clocked at 100 MHz. Our prototype is configured with $C=16$ *BeamFormer* modules, thus it can process 16 input channels concurrently. Also, within each BF-PE and the *source amplifier*, all decimators, H(z) filters and the interpolator were generated with the Xilinx Core Generator.

Table 3 displays the resource utilization of each module. The first two lines provide the required resources for a single *BeamFormer* and the *source amplifier* modules. The third line shows all hardware resources occupied by MC-BFP. In the fourth line, we show the resources required to implement the PLB, DMA, ICAP and all memory controllers with their corresponding BRAMs. Finally, the fifth line provides all required resources from the entire Beamforming system. As it can be observed, a single *Beam-Former* requires less than 600 slices, 2 DSP slices and 8 Kbytes of BRAM, which makes it feasible to integrate many such modules within a single chip. Based on the data of Table 3, we estimated that a V4FX60 could accommodate up to 19 channels, while larger chips, such as the V4FX100 and V4FX140, could be used for up to 54 and 89 microphone arrays setups respectively.

**Performance evaluation:** We conducted a performance comparison of our hardware prototype against an OpenMP optimized software implementation on a Core2 Duo processor at 3.0 GHz. In both cases, $C=16$ input channels were tested, with sampling frequency of 48000 Hz. The decimation and interpolation rates were $D=L=4$. Figure 7 shows the results of our experiments. We conducted tests with up to 14 acoustic sources placed inside the same recording area. Recorded audio data of 11264 msec duration, divided into 528 iterations each consisting of 1024 samples, were stored to external memories and used as input to both implementations. Thus, in order to support real-time data processing, all iterations should be done within the aforementioned time window. Furthermore, for all the tests conducted to our hardware prototype, we have included the time spent on SDRAM transactions (HW SDRAM), on the Beamforming calculations (HW BF) and on the PPC (SW-PPC). Thus, the achieved speedup is for the complete application execution.

As we can see from Figure 7, both PC-based (SW-OMP) and FPGA-based systems can support real-time processing when there are present up to four sources. However, when there are five or more acoustic sources, the PC-based system fails to meet the timing constraints, since it takes more than 11264 msec to perform all required calculations. Regarding the hardware prototype, approximately 55% of the execution time is spent on SDRAM accesses, since in each processing iteration, input data from all channels have to be stored to *BF buffers*. This performance degradation could be improved if a faster SDRAM module is available. Even though, our FPGA-based approach can still support up to 14 sources extracted in real-time.

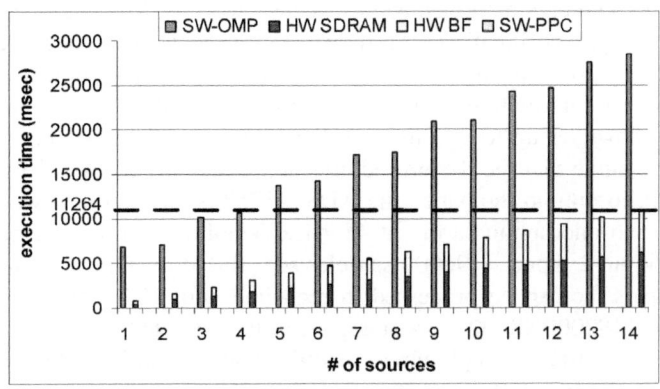

**Fig. 7.** Software and hardware systems execution time

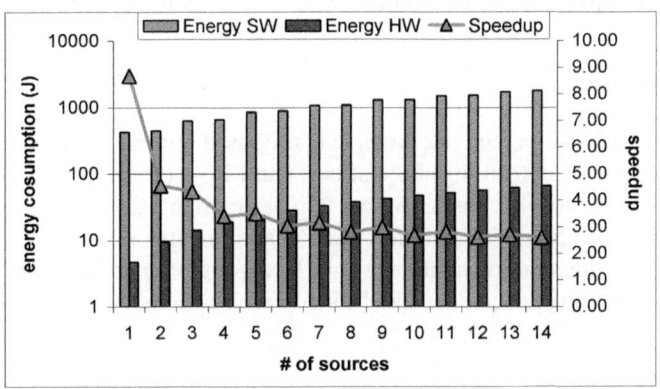

**Fig. 8.** Energy consumption and speedup comparison

**Energy and power consumption:** Based on the Xilinx XPower utility, our FPGA prototype consumes approximately 6.0 Watts of power. This is an order of magnitude lower compared to a contemporary Core2 Duo processor, since the latter consumes up to 65 Watts of power when fully utilized [12]. Based on the power consumption and the execution time of both systems, we calculated the energy consumption using the well-known formula $E = P \cdot t$, where $E$ is the energy consumed during the time $t$, while applying $P$ power. During the software execution, the Core2 Duo was approximately 95% utilized. Thus, we safely assumed that its power consumption during the program execution is approximately 0.95·65 Watts = 61.75 Watts. Figure 8 suggests the energy consumption for the PC-based system (Energy SW), the hardware system (Energy HW) and the achieved speedup against the Core2 Duo software implementation for all conducted tests. As we can observe, because the hardware solution is faster and also requires much less power, it consumes more than an order of magnitude less energy compared to the PC-based system.

**Related work:** Direct comparison against related work is difficult, since each system has its own design specifications. Moreover, to our best knowledge, we provide the first architectural proposal for a reconfigurable Beamforming computer. Previous proposals are mainly micro-architectural ones. In [7], the authors utilize an ADSP21262 DSP, which consumes up to 250 mA. Furthermore, its voltage supply is 3.3 V [13], thus we can assume that the design requires approximately 3.3 V·0.25 A = 0.825 W. In addition, according to the paper, the ADSP21262 is 50% utilized when processing data from a two-microphone array at 48 KHz sampling rate, or alternatively 48000 samples/sec/input·2 inputs = 96000 samples/sec. Based on this, we can assume that 192000 samples/sec can be processed in real-time with 100% processor utilization, which means $\lfloor 192000/48000 \rfloor = 4$ sources can be extracted in real-time. Finally, in [5] the authors use four microphones to record sound and perform Beamforming using an FPGA. They have mapped their design onto a V4SX55 FPGA and, according to the paper, every instance of the proposed beamformer can process 43463 samples/sec, with up to seven instances fitting into the largest V4SX FPGA family. Since the sampling frequency is 16 KHz, $\lfloor (43463 \cdot 7)/16000 \rfloor = 19$ sources could be extracted in real-time.

## 6   Conclusions

In this paper, we implemented our previously proposed minimal architecture as a multi-core processor for Beamforming applications. Our FPGA prototype at 100 MHz can extract in real-time up to 14 acoustic sources 2.6x faster than a Core2 Duo solution. Power consumption is an order of magnitude lower than the software approach on a modern GPP. Ultimately, our solution combines high-level programmability with improved performance, better energy efficiency and limited on-chip memory requirements.

## References

1. Veen, B.V., et al.: Beamforming: a versatile approach to spatial filtering. IEEE ASSP Magazine 5, 4–24 (1988)
2. Theodoropoulos, D., et al.: Minimalistic Architecture for Reconfigurable Audio Beamforming. In: International Conference on Field-Programmable Technology, pp. 503–506 (December 2010)
3. Blaauw, G., Brooks, F.: Computer Architecture: Concepts and Evolution (February 1997)
4. Kapralos, B., et al.: Audio-visual localization of multiple speakers in a video teleconferencing setting. International Journal of Imaging Systems and Technology 13(1), 95–105 (2003)
5. Cedric Yiu, K.-F., et al.: Reconfigurable acceleration of microphone array algorithms for speech enhancement. In: Application-specific Systems, Architectures and Processors, pp. 203–208 (2008)
6. Implementing a Real-Time Beamformer on an FPGA Platform. XCell Journal, Second Quarter, 36–40 (2007)
7. Yermeche, Z., et al.: Real-time implementation of a subband beamforming algorithm for dual microphone speech enhancement. In: IEEE International Symposium on Circuits and Systems, pp. 353–356 (May 2007)
8. Fiala, M., et al.: A panoramic video and acoustic beamforming sensor for videoconferencing. In: IEEE International Conference on Haptic, Audio and Visual Environments and their Applications, pp. 47–52 (October 2004)

9. Beracoechea, J., et al.: On building Immersive Audio Applications Using Robust Adaptive Beamforming and Joint Audio-Video Source Localization. EURASIP Journal on Applied Signal Processing, 1–12 (June 2006)
10. Teutsch, H., et al.: An Integrated Real-Time System For Immersive Audio Applications. In: IEEE Workshop on Applications of Signal Processing to Audio and Acoustics, pp. 67–70 (October 2003)
11. Theodoropoulos, D., et al.: A Reconfigurable Beamformer for Audio Applications. In: IEEE Symposium on Application Specific Processors, pp. 80–87
12. Intel Corporation, http://ark.intel.com/Product.aspx?id=33910
13. Analog Devices Inc., SHARC Processor ADSP-21262 (May 2004)

# A Regular Expression Matching Circuit Based on a Decomposed Automaton

Hiroki Nakahara, Tsutomu Sasao, and Munehiro Matsuura

Kyushu Institute of Technology, Japan

**Abstract.** In this paper, we propose a regular expression matching circuit based on a decomposed automaton. To implement a regular expression matching circuit, first, we convert regular expressions into a non-deterministic finite automaton (NFA). Then, to reduce the number of states, we convert the NFA into a modular non-deterministic finite automaton with unbounded string transition (MNFAU). Next, to realize it by a feasible amount of hardware, we decompose the MNFAU into the deterministic finite automaton (DFA) and the NFA. The DFA part is implemented by an off-chip memory and a simple sequencer, while the NFA part is implemented by a cascade of logic cells. Also, in this paper, we show that the MNFAU based implementation has lower area complexity than the DFA and the NFA based ones.

## 1 Introduction

### 1.1 Regular Expression Matching for Network Applications

**A regular expression** represents a set of strings. **A regular expression matching** detects a pattern written by regular expressions from the input string. Various network applications (e.g., intrusion detection systems [15][8], a spam filter [16], a virus scanning [6], and an L7 filter [10]) use the regular expression matching. The regular expression matching spends a major part of the total computation time. Since the modern network transmission speed exceeds one Giga bit per second (Gbps), the hardware regular expression matching is essential. For the network applications, since the high-mix low-volume production and the flexible support for new protocols are required, reconfigurable devices (e.g., FPGAs) are used. Recently, dedicated high-speed transceivers for the high-speed network are embedded to FPGAs. So, a trend for using FPGAs will accelerate in the future. Although the operation speed for the regular expression matching on the FPGA exceeds one Gbps [5][3][4], these methods require high-end and high-cost FPGAs. In this paper, we realize a low-cost regular expression matching using a low-end FPGA and off-chip memory.

### 1.2 Related Work

Regular expressions can be detected by finite automata. In a **deterministic finite automaton (DFA)**, for each state for an input, a unique transition exists, while in a **non-deterministic finite automaton (NFA)**, for each state for an input, multiple transitions

A. Koch et al. (Eds.): ARC 2011, LNCS 6578, pp. 16–28, 2011.

exist. In an NFA, there exists $\varepsilon$-**transitions** to other states without consuming input characters. Various DFA-based regular expression matchings exist: an Aho-Corasick algorithm [1]; a bit-partition of the Aho-Corasick DFA by Tan et al. [18]; a combination of the bit-partitioned DFA and the MPU [3]; and a pipelined DFA [5]. Also, various NFA-based regular expression matching exist: an algorithm that emulates the NFA (Baeza-Yates's NFA) by shift and AND operations on a computer [2]; an FPGA realization of Baeza-Yates's NFA (Sidhu-Prasanna method) [14]; prefix sharing of regular expressions [11]; and a method that maps repeated parts of regular expressions to the Xilinx FPGA primitive (SRL16) [4].

### 1.3 Features of the Proposed Method

**Lower Complexity than Existing Methods.** In this paper, we compare the NFA, the DFA, and the decomposed NFA with string transition on parallel hardware model. The decomposed NFA is much smaller than conventional methods.

**Efficient Utilization of Embedded Memory.** The conventional NFA based method uses single-character transition [14]. In the circuit, each state for the NFA is implemented by a flip-flop and an AND gate. Also, an $\varepsilon$-transition is realized by OR gates and routing on the FPGA. Although the modern FPGA consists of LUTs and embedded memories, the conventional NFA based method fails to use embedded memories. In contrast, our method can use both LUTs and embedded memory to implement the decomposed NFA with string (multi-character) transition.

The rest of the paper is organized as follows: Section 2 shows a regular expression matching circuit based on the finite automaton (FA); Section 3 shows a regular expression matching circuit based on an NFA with string transition; Section 4 compares complexities on the parallel hardware model; Section 5 shows the experimental results; and Section 6 concludes the paper.

## 2   Regular Expression Matching Circuit Based on Automaton

A regular expression consists of **characters** and **meta characters**. A character is represented by 8 bits. The **length** of the regular expression is the number of characters. Table 1 shows meta characters considered in this paper.

### 2.1   Regular Expression Matching Circuit Based on Deterministic Finite Automaton

**Definition 2.1.** *A deterministic finite automaton (DFA) consists of a five-tuple* $M_{DFA} = (S, \Sigma, \delta, s_0, A)$, *where* $S = \{s_0, s_1, \ldots, s_{q-1}\}$ *is a finite set of states;* $\Sigma$ *is a finite set of input character;* $\delta$ *is a transition function* ($\delta : S \times \Sigma \rightarrow S$); $s_0 \in S$ *is the initial state; and* $A \subseteq S$ *is a set of accept states. In the practical network application,* $|\Sigma| = 2^8 = 256$.

**Definition 2.2.** *Let* $s \in S$, *and* $c \in \Sigma$. *If* $\delta(s, c) \neq \{\phi\}$, *then* $c$ *denotes* **a transition character for the state** $s$.

**Table 1.** Meta Characters Used in This Paper

| Meta Character | Meaning |
|---|---|
| . | An arbitrary character |
| * | Repetition of more than zero or zero (Kleene closure) |
| + | Repetition of more than one or equal to one |
| ? | Repetition of equal and less than one |
| ^ | Pattern to be matched at only start of the input |
| $ | Pattern to be matched at only end of the input |
| () | Specify the priority of the operation |
| [] | Set of characters |
| [^] | Complement set of characters |
| {n,m} | Repetition (more than $n$ and less than $m$) |
| {n,} | Repetition (more than $n$) |
| {n} | Repetition ($n$ times) |
| \| | Logical OR |

To define **a transition string** accepted by the DFA, we extend the transition function $\delta$ to $\hat{\delta}$.

**Definition 2.3.** *Let $\Sigma^+$ be a set of strings, and let the extended transition function be $\hat{\delta} : S \times \Sigma^+ \to S$. If $C \subseteq \Sigma^+$ and $s \in S$, then $\hat{\delta}(s, C)$ represents a transition state of $s$ with respect to the input string $C$.*

**Definition 2.4.** *Suppose that $M_{DFA} = (S, \Sigma, \delta, s_0, A)$. Let $C_{in} \subseteq \Sigma^+$, and $a \in A$. Then, $M_{DFA}$ accepts a string $C_{in}$, if the relation holds*

$$\hat{\delta}(s_0, C_{in}) = a. \tag{1}$$

Let $c_i$ be a character of a string $C = c_0 c_1 \cdots c_n$, and $\delta$ be a transition function. Then, the extended transition function $\hat{\delta}$ is defined recursively as follows:

$$\hat{\delta}(s, C) = \hat{\delta}(\delta(s, c_0), c_1 c_2 \cdots c_n). \tag{2}$$

From Exprs. (1) and (2), the DFA performs the string matching by repeating state transitions.

**Example 2.1.** *Fig. 1 shows the DFA for the regular expression "A+[AB]{3}D".*   ■

**Example 2.2.** *Consider the string matching for an input "AABAD" using the DFA shown in Fig. 1. Let $s_0$ be the initial state. First, $\delta(s_0, A) = s_1$. Second, $\delta(s_1, A) = s_2$. Third, $\delta(s_2, B) = s_5$. Fourth, $\delta(s_5, A) = s_9$. Finally, $\delta(s_9, D) = s_{11}$. Since the state $s_{11}$ is an accept state, the string "AABAD" is accepted.*   ■

Fig. 2 shows the DFA machine, where the register stores the present state, and the memory realizes the transition function $\delta$. Let $q$ be the number of states, and $|\Sigma| = n$ be the number of characters in $\Sigma$. Then, the amount of memory to implement the DFA is $2^{\lceil log_2 n \rceil + \lceil log_2 q \rceil} \times \lceil log_2 q \rceil$ bits[1].

---

[1] Since the size of the register in the DFA machine is much smaller than that for the memory storing the transition function, we ignore the size of the register.

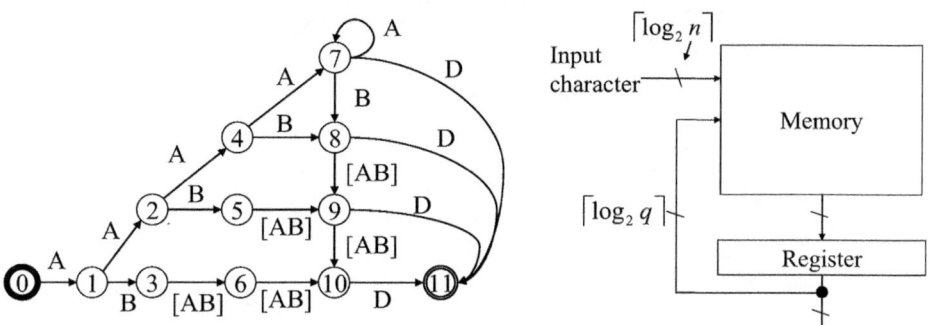

**Fig. 1.** DFA for the regular expression "A+[AB]{3}D"

**Fig. 2.** DFA machine

## 2.2   Regular Expression Matching Circuit Based on Non-deterministic Finite Automaton

**Definition 2.5.** *A non-deterministic finite automaton (NFA) consists of a five-tuple* $M_{NFA} = (S, \Sigma, \gamma, s_0, A)$, *where* $S$, $\Sigma$, $s_0$, *and* $A$ *are the same as ones in Definition 2.1, while the transition function* $\gamma : S \times (\Sigma \cup \{\varepsilon\}) \rightarrow P(S)$ *is different. Note that,* $\varepsilon$ *denotes an empty character, and* $P(S)$ *denotes a power set of* $S$.

In the NFA, the empty ($\varepsilon$) input is permitted. Thus, a state for the NFA can transit to multiple states. The state transition with $\varepsilon$ input denotes **an $\varepsilon$ transition**. In this paper, in a state transition diagram, an $\varepsilon$ symbol with an arrow denotes the $\varepsilon$ transition. Fig. 3 shows conversions of regular expressions into NFAs, where a gray state denotes an accept state.

**Example 2.3.** *Fig. 4 shows the NFA for the regular expression for "A+[AB]{3}D", and state transitions for the input string "AABAD". In Fig. 4, each element of the vector corresponds to a state of the NFA, and '1' denotes an active state.* ∎

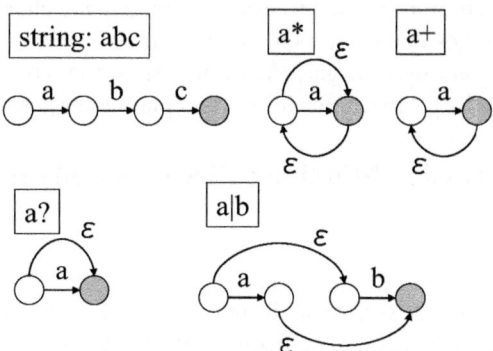

**Fig. 3.** Conversion of regular expression into NFA

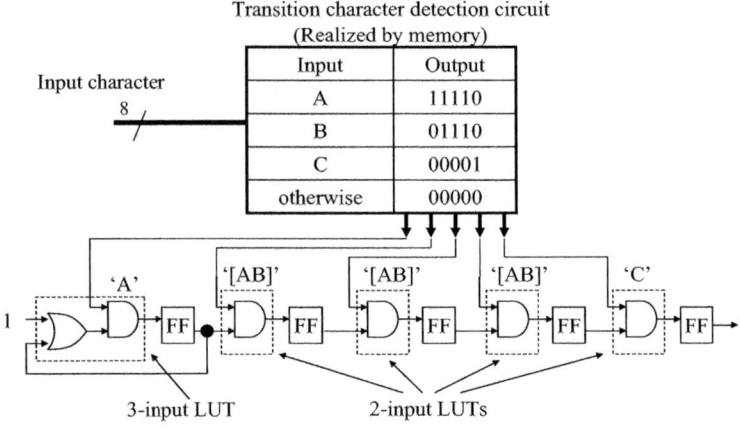

| Initial | 1 | 0 | 0 | 0 | 0 | 0 | |
|---|---|---|---|---|---|---|---|
| Input 'A' | 1 | 1 | 0 | 0 | 0 | 0 | |
| Input 'A' | 1 | 1 | 1 | 0 | 0 | 0 | |
| Input 'B' | 1 | 1 | 1 | 1 | 0 | 0 | |
| Input 'A' | 1 | 1 | 1 | 1 | 1 | 0 | |
| Input 'D' | 1 | 0 | 0 | 0 | 0 | 1 | accept 'AABAD' |

**Fig. 4.** NFA for the regular expression "A+[AB]{3}D"

**Fig. 5.** A circuit for the NFA shown in Fig. 4

Sidhu and Prasanna [14] realized an NFA with single-character transitions for regular expressions [2]. Fig. 5 shows the circuit for the NFA. To realize the NFA, first, the memory detects the character for the state transition, and then the character detection signal is sent to small machines that correspond to states of the NFA. Each small machine is realized by a flip-flop and an AND gate. Also, an $\varepsilon$-transition is realized by OR gates and routing on the FPGA. Then, machines for the accepted states generate the match signal.

## 3    Regular Expression Matching Circuit Based on NFA with String Transition

### 3.1    MNFAU

Sidhu-Prasanna's method does not use the embedded memory[2]. So, their method is inefficient with respect to the resource utilization of FPGA, since modern FPGA consists

---

[2] Their method uses single character detectors (comparators) instead of the memory shown in Fig. 5.

of LUTs and embedded memories. In the circuit for the NFA, each state is implemented by an LUT of an FPGA. Thus, the necessary number of LUTs is equal to the number of states. To reduce the number of states, we propose a regular expression matching circuit based on a **modular non-deterministic finite automaton with unbounded string transition (MNFAU)**. To convert an NFA into an MNFAU, we merge a sequence of states. However, to retain the equivalence between the NFA and the MNFAU, we only merge the states using the following:

**Lemma 3.1.** *Let $S = \{s_0, s_1, \ldots, s_{q-1}\}$ be a set of states, and $S_i \subseteq S$. Consider a partition $S = S_1 \cup S_2 \cup \cdots \cup S_u$, where $S_i \cap S_j = \phi(i \neq j)$. Let $e_r$ be the number of $\varepsilon$ transition inputs and outputs in the state $s_r$. Then, $S_i = \{s_k, s_{k+1}, \ldots, s_{k+p}\}$ can be merged into one state of the MNFAU, if $e_r = 0$ for $r = k, k+1, \ldots, k+p-1$.*

**Definition 3.6.** *Suppose that a set of states $\{s_k, s_{k+1}, \ldots, s_{k+p}\}$ be merged into a state $S_M$ of MNFAU. A string $C = c_k c_{k+1} \cdots c_{k+p}$ is **a transition string** of $S_M$, when $c_j \in \Sigma$ is a transition character of $s_j$ for $j = k, k+1, \ldots, k+p$.*

**Example 3.4.** *In the NFA shown in Fig. 4, the set of states $\{s_2, s_3, s_4, s_5\}$ can be merged into a state of the MNFAU, and its transition string is "[AB][AB][AB]D". However, the set of states $\{s_1, s_2\}$ cannot be merged, since $e_1 \neq 0$.* ∎

**Example 3.5.** *Fig. 6 shows the MNFAU derived from the NFA shown in Fig. 4.* ∎

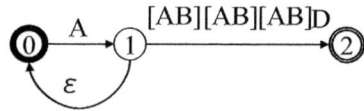

**Fig. 6.** MNFAU derived from the NFA shown in Fig. 4

### 3.2   Realization of MNFAU

To realize the MNFAU, as shown in Fig. 7, we consider **a decomposed MNFAU**, and realize it by the following circuits:

1. The transition string detection circuit
2. The state transition circuit.

Since transition strings do not include meta characters[3], they are detected by **the exact matching**. The exact matching is a subclass of the regular expression matching and the DFA can be realized by feasible amount of hardware [20]. On the other hand, since the state transition part handles the $\varepsilon$ transition, it is implemented by the cascade of logic cells shown in Fig. 5.

**Transition String Detection Circuit.** Since each state of the MNFAU can merge different number of states of the NFA, the lengths of the transition strings for states of the MNFAU can be also different. To detect multiple strings with different lengths, we use **the Aho-Corasick DFA (AC-DFA)** [1]. To obtain the AC-DFA, first, the transition

---

[3] However, a set of characters "[]" can be used.

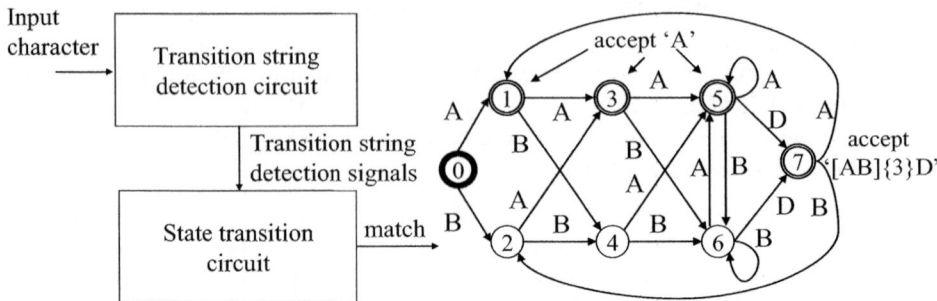

**Fig. 7.** Decomposition of the MNFAU

**Fig. 8.** AC-DFA accepting strings "A" and "[AB][AB][AB]D"

strings are represented by a text tree (Trie). Next, the failure paths that indicate the transitions for the mismatches are attached to the text tree. Since the AC-DFA stores failure paths, no backtracking is required. By scanning the input only once, the AC-DFA can detect all the strings represented by the regular expressions. The AC-DFA is realized by the circuit shown in Fig. 2.

**Example 3.6.** *Fig. 8 illustrate the AC-DFA accepting transition strings "A" and "[AB] [AB][AB]D" for the MNFAU shown in Fig. 6.*  ∎

**State Transition Circuit [13].** Fig. 9 shows the state transition circuit for the MNFAU. When the AC-DFA detects the transition string ("ABD" in Fig. 9), the detection signal is sent to the state transition circuit. Then, the state transition is performed. The AC-DFA scans a character in every clock, while the state transition requires $p$ clocks to perform the state transition, where $p$ denotes the length of the transition string. Thus, a shift register is inserted between two states in the MNFAU to synchronize with the AC-DFA. A 4-input LUT of a Xilinx FPGA can also be used as a shift register (SRL16) [19]. Fig. 10 shows two LUT modes of a Xilinx FPGA.

Fig. 11 shows the circuit for the decomposed MNFAU. We decompose the MNFAU into the transition string detection circuit and the state transition circuit. The transition function for the AC-DFA is realized by the off-chip memory (i.e., SRAM), while other parts are realized by the FPGA. In the AC-DFA, a register with $\lceil log_2 q \rceil$ bits shows the present state, where $q$ is the number of states for the AC-DFA. On the other hand, $u$-bit detection signal is necessary for the state transition circuit, where $u$ is the number of states for the MNFAU. We use the decoder that converts $\lceil log_2 q \rceil$-bit state to $u$-bit detection signal. Since the decoder is relatively small, it is implemented by the embedded memory in the FPGA.

**Example 3.7.** *In Fig. 11, the address for the decoder memory corresponds to the assigned state number for the AC-DFA shown in Fig. 8. The decoder memory produces the detection signal for the state transition circuit.*  ∎

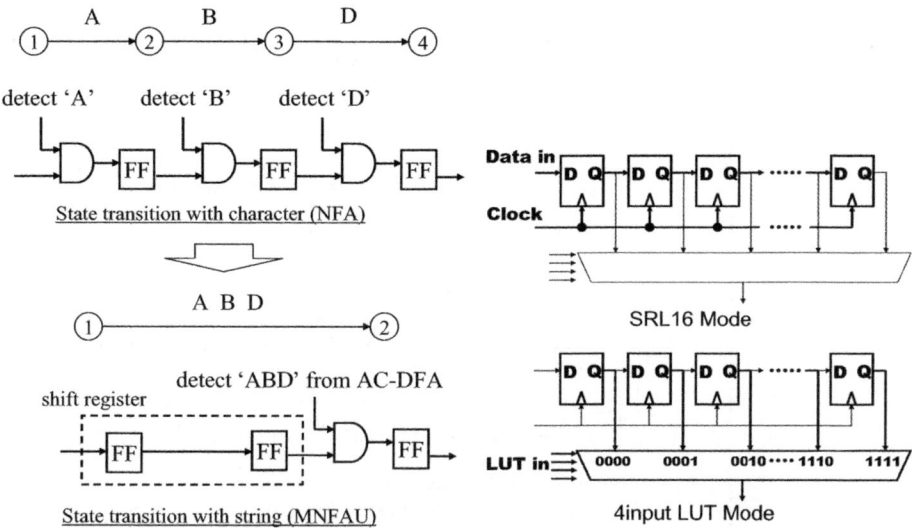

**Fig. 9.** State transition with the string    **Fig. 10.** Two LUT modes for Xilinx FPGA

## 4   Complexity of Regular Expression Matching Circuit on Parallel Hardware Model

For the Xilinx FPGA, **a logic cell (LC)** consists of a 4-input look-up table (LUT) and a flip-flop (FF) [17]. Also, the FPGA has embedded memories. Therefore, as for the area complexity, we consider both **the LC complexity** and **the embedded memory complexity**.

### 4.1   Theoretical Analysis

**Aho-Corasick DFA.** As shown in Fig. 2, the machine for the DFA has the register storing the present state, and the memory for the state transition. The DFA machine reads one character and computes the next state in every clock. Thus, the time complexity is $O(1)$. Also, since the size of the register is fixed, the LC complexity is $O(1)$. Yu et al. [20] showed that, for $m$ regular expressions with length $s$, the memory complexity is $O(|\Sigma|^{sm})$, where $|\Sigma|$ denotes the number of characters in $\Sigma$.

**Baeza-Yates NFA.** As shown in Fig. 5, the NFA consists of the memory for the transition character detection, and the cascade of small machine consisting an LUT (realizing AND and OR gates) and a FF. Thus, for $m$ regular expressions with length $s$, the LC complexity is $O(ms)$. Since the amount of memory for the transition character detection is $m \times |\Sigma| \times s$, the memory complexity is $O(ms)$. The regular expression matching circuit based on the NFA has $s$ states and performs $\varepsilon$ transitions at a time in every clock. By using $m$ parallel circuits shown in Fig. 5, the circuit can match $m$ regular expressions in parallel. Thus, the time complexity is $O(1)$.

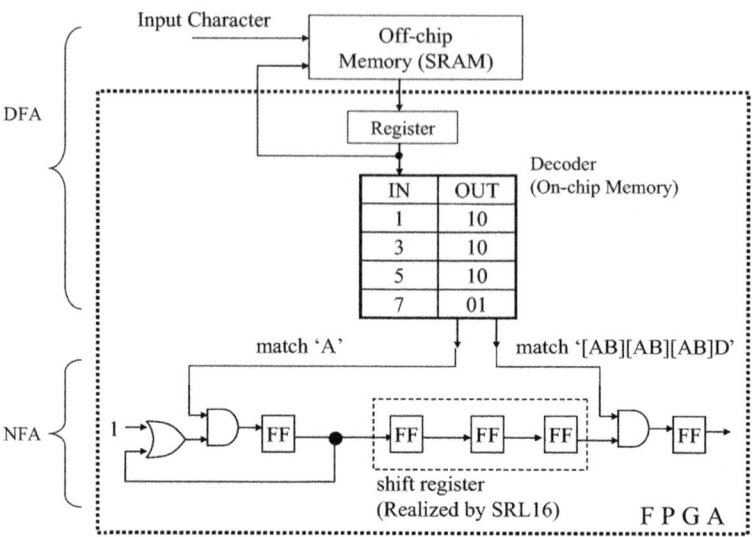

**Fig. 11.** An example of the circuit for the MNFAU

**Decomposed MNFAU.** As shown in Fig. 7, the decomposed MNFAU consists of the transition string detection circuit and the state transition circuit. The transition string detection circuit is realized by the DFA machine shown in Fig. 2. Let $p_{max}$ be the maximum length of the regular expression, and $|\Sigma|$ be the number of characters in a set of $\Sigma$. From the analysis of the DFA [7], the memory complexity is $O(|\Sigma|^{p_{max}})$, while the LC complexity for the AC-DFA machine is $O(1)$. The state transition circuit is realized by the cascade of LCs shown in Fig. 11. Let $p_{ave}$ be the average number of merged states in the NFA, $s$ be the length of the regular expression, and $m$ be the number of regular expressions. Since one state in the MNFAU corresponds to $p_{ave}$ states in the NFA, the LC complexity is $O(\frac{ms}{p_{ave}})$. By using $m$ parallel circuits, the circuit matches $m$ regular expressions in parallel. Thus, the time complexity is $O(1)$.

Note that, in most cases, the amount of memory for the MNFAU is larger than that for the NFA. The memory for the NFA requires $sm$-bit words, while the memory for the MNFAU requires $\lceil log_2 q \rceil$-bit words[4]. For the NFA, off-chip memories are hard to use, since the number of pins on the FPGA is limited. Thus, the NFA requires a large number of on-chip memories. On the other hand, the MNFAU can use off-chip memory, since the required number of pins is small. From the point of the implementation, although the MNFAU requires larger amount of memory than the NFA, the MNFAU can use off-chip memory and a small FPGA.

Table 2 compares the area and time complexities for the DFA, the NFA, and the decomposed MNFAU on the parallel hardware model. As shown in Table 2, by using the decomposed MNFAU, the memory size is reduced to $\frac{1}{|\Sigma|^{ms-p_{max}}}$ of the DFA, while the number of LCs is reduced to $\frac{1}{p_{max}}$ of the NFA.

[4] For example, in the SNORT, the value of $sm$ is about 100,000, while $\lceil log_2 q \rceil = 14$.

## 4.2   Analysis Using SNORT

To verify these analyses, we compared the memory size and the number of LCs for practical regular expressions. We selected 80 regular expressions from the intrusion detection system SNORT [15], and for each regular expression, we generated the DFA, the NFA, and the decomposed MNFAU. Then, we obtained the number of LCs and the memory size. Fig. 12 shows the relation of the length of the regular expression $s$ and the number of LCs, while Fig. 13 shows the relation of $s$ and the memory size. Note that, in Fig. 12, the vertical axis is a linear scale, while, in Fig. 13, it is a logarithmic scale. As shown in Fig. 12, the ratio between the number of LCs and $s$ is the constant. On the other hand, as shown in Fig. 13, the ratio between the memory size and $s$ increases exponentially.

Therefore, both the theoretical analysis and the experiment using SNORT show that the decomposed MNFAU realizes regular expressions efficiently.

**Table 2.** Complexities for the DFA, the NFA, and the decomposed MNFAU on the parallel hardware mode

|  | Time | Area | |
|---|---|---|---|
|  |  | Memory | #LC |
| Baeza-Yates's NFA | $O(1)$ | $O(ms)$ | $O(ms)$ |
| Aho-Corasick DFA | $O(1)$ | $O(|\Sigma|^{ms})$ | $O(1)$ |
| Decomposed MNFAU | $O(1)$ | $O(|\Sigma|^{Pmax})$ | $O(\frac{ms}{p_{ave}})$ |

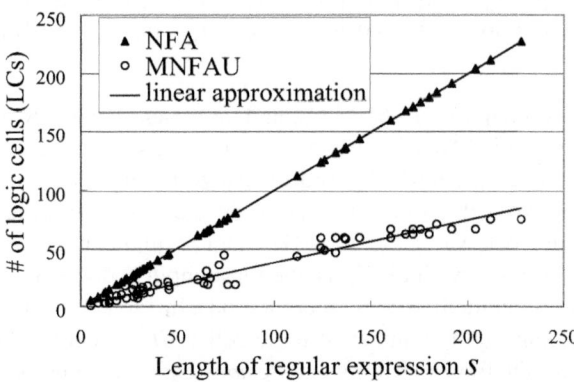

**Fig. 12.** Relation the length $s$ of regular expression and the number of LCs

## 5   FPGA Implementation

We selected the regular expressions from SNORT (open-source intrusion detection system), and generated the decomposed MNFAU. Then, we implemented to the Xilinx Spartan III FPGA (XC3S4000: 62,208 logic cells (LCs), total 1,728 Kbits BRAM). The total number of rules is 1,114 (75,633 characters). The number of states for the MNFAU is 12,673, and the number of states for the AC-DFA for the transition string is 10,066.

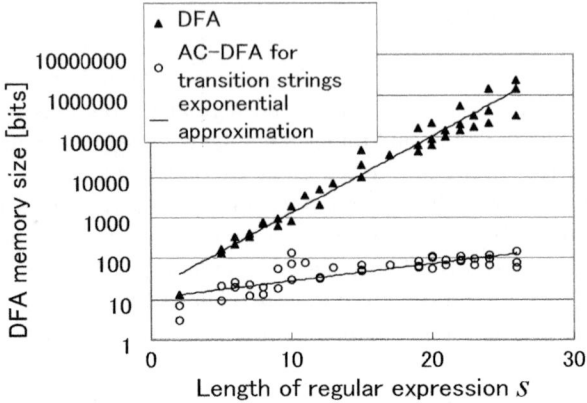

**Fig. 13.** Relation the length $s$ of regular expression and the memory size

**Table 3.** Comparison with other methods

| Method | FA Type | FPGA | Th (Gbps) | #LC | MEM (Kbits) | #Char | #LC/ #Char | MEM/ #Char |
|---|---|---|---|---|---|---|---|---|
| Pipelined DFA [5] (ISCA'06) | DFA | Virtex 2 | 4.0 | 247,000 | 3,456 | 11,126 | 22.22 | 3182.2 |
| MPU+Bit-partitioned DFA [3] (FPL'06) | DFA | Virtex 4 | 1.4 | N/A | 6,000 | 16,715 | N/A | 367.5 |
| Improvement of Sidhu-Prasanna method [4] (FPT'06) | NFA | Virtex 4 | 2.9 | 25,074 | 0 | 19,580 | 1.28 | 0 |
| MNFA(3) [12] (SASIMI'10) | MNFA($p$) | Virtex 6 | 3.2 | 4,717 | 441 | 12,095 | 0.39 | 37.3 |
| MNFAU (Proposed method) | MNFAU | Spartan 3 | 1.6 | 19,552 | 1,585 | 75,633 | 0.25 | 21.4 |

This implementation requires 19,552 LCs, and an off-chip memory of 16 Mbits. Note that, the 16-Mbit off-chip SRAM is used to store the transition function of the AC-DFA, while 1,585-Kbit on-chip BRAM is used to realize the decoder. The FPGA operates at 271.2 MHz. However due to the limitation on the clock frequency by the off-chip SRAM, the system clock was set to 200 MHz. Our regular expression matching circuit scans one character in every clock. Thus, the throughput is $0.2 \times 8 = 1.6$ Gbps.

Table 3 compares our method with other methods. In Table 3, *Th* denotes the throughput (Gbps); *#LC* denotes the number of logic cells; *MEM* denotes the amount of embedded memory for the FPGA (Kbits); and *#Char* denotes the number of characters for the regular expression. Table 3 shows that, as for the embedded memory size per a character, the MNFAU requires 17.17-148.70 times smaller memory than the DFA method. Also, as for the number of LCs per a character, the MNFAU is 1.56-5.12 times smaller than the NFA method.

## 6    Conclusion

In this paper, we proposed a regular expression matching circuit based on a decomposed MNFAU. To implement the circuit, first, we convert the regular expressions to an NFA.

Then, to reduce the number of states, we convert the NFA into the MNFAU. Next, to realize it by a feasible amount of the hardware, we decompose the MNFAU into the transition string detection part and the state transition part. The transition string detection part is implemented by an off-chip memory and a simple sequencer, while the state transition part is implemented by a cascade of logic cells. Also, this paper shows that the MNFAU based implementation has lower area complexity than the DFA and the NFA based ones. The implementation of SNORT shows that, as for the embedded memory size per a character, the MNFAU is 17.17-148.70 times smaller than DFA methods. Also, as for the number of LCs per a character, the MNFAU is 1.56-5.12 times smaller than NFA methods.

## Acknowledgments

This research is supported in part by the grant of Regional Innovation Cluster Program (Global Type, 2nd Stage).

## References

1. Aho, A.V., Corasick, M.J.: Efficient string matching: An aid to bibliographic search. Comm. of the ACM 18(6), 333–340 (1975)
2. Baeza-Yates, R., Gonnet, G.H.: A new approach to text searching. Communications of the ACM 35(10), 74–82 (1992)
3. Baker, Z.K., Jung, H., Prasanna, V.K.: Regular expression software deceleration for intrusion detection systems. In: FPL 2006, pp. 28–30 (2006)
4. Bispo, J., Sourdis, I., Cardoso, J.M.P., Vassiliadis, S.: Regular expression matching for reconfigurable packet inspection. In: FPT 2006, pp. 119–126 (2006)
5. Brodie, B.C., Taylor, D.E., Cytron, R.K.: A scalable architecture for high-throughput regular-expression pattern matching. In: ISCA 2006, pp. 191–202 (2006)
6. Clam Anti Virus: open source anti-virus toolkit, http://www.clamav.net/lang/en/
7. Dixon, R., Egecioglu, O., Sherwood, T.: Automata-theoretic analysis of bit-split languages for packet scanning. In: Ibarra, O.H., Ravikumar, B. (eds.) CIAA 2008. LNCS, vol. 5148, pp. 141–150. Springer, Heidelberg (2008)
8. Firekeeper: Detect and block malicious sites, http://firekeeper.mozdev.org/
9. Kohavi, Z.: Switching and Finite Automata Theory. McGraw-Hill Inc., New York (1979)
10. Application Layer Packet Classifier for Linux, http://l7-filter.sourceforge.net/
11. Lin, C., Huang, C., Jiang, C., Chang, S.: Optimization of regular expression pattern matching circuits on FPGA. In: DATE 2006, pp. 12–17 (2006)
12. Nakahara, H., Sasao, T., Matsuura, M.: A regular expression matching circuit based on a modular non-deterministic finite automaton with multi-character transition. In: SASIMI 2010, Taipei, October 18-19, pp. 359–364 (2010)
13. Nakahara, H., Sasao, T., Matsuura, M.: A regular expression matching using non-deterministic finite automaton. In: MEMOCODE 2010, Grenoble, France, July 26-28, pp. 73–76 (2010)
14. Sidhu, R., Prasanna, V.K.: Fast regular expression matching using FPGA. In: FCCM 2001, pp. 227–238 (2001)
15. SNORT official web site, http://www.snort.org
16. SPAMASSASSIN: Open-Source Spam Filter, http://spamassassin.apache.org/

17. Spartan III data sheet, http://www.xilinx.com/
18. Tan, L., Sherwood, T.: A high throughput string matching architecture for intrusion detection and prevention. In: ISCA 2005, pp. 112–122 (2005)
19. Using Look-up tables as shift registers (SRL16),
    http://www.xilinx.com/support/documentation/
    application_notes/xapp465.pdf
20. Yu, F., Chen, Z., Diao, Y., Lakshman, T.V., Katz, R.H.: Fast and memory-efficient regular expression matching for deep packet inspection. In: ANCS 2006, pp. 93–102 (2006)

# Design and Implementation of a Multi-Core Crypto-Processor for Software Defined Radios

Michael Grand[1], Lilian Bossuet[2], Bertrand Le Gal[1], Guy Gogniat[3],
and Dominique Dallet[1]

[1] IMS Lab., University of Bordeaux
firstname.lastname@ims-bordeaux.fr
[2] Hubert Curien Lab., University of Lyon
lilian.bossuet@univ-st-etienne.fr
[3] Lab-STICC Lab., University of Bretagne Sud
guy.gogniat@univ-ubs.fr

**Abstract.** This paper deals with the architecture, the performances and the scalability of a reconfigurable *Multi-Core Crypto-Processor* (MCCP) especially designed to secure multi-channel and multi-standard communication systems. A classical mono-core approach either provides limited throughput or does not allow simple management of multi-standard streams. In contrast, parallel architecture of the MCCP provides either high encryption data rate or simultaneous use of different ciphers. Up to eight cores can be used at the same time to reach a maximum throughput of 3460 Mbps. Moreover, our architecture targets FPGA platforms to enable its evolution over the time by using hardware reconfiguration.

## 1 Introduction

Multiplicity of wireless communication standards (UMTS, WiFi, WiMax) needs highly flexible and interoperable communication systems. Software based solutions such as *Software Defined Radio* (SDR) are used to meet the flexibility constraint. Independently, most of radios have to propose cryptographic services such as confidentiality, integrity and authentication (secure-radio). Therefore, integration of cryptographic services into SDR devices is essential.

However, the use of cryptographic functions in secure systems tends to limit their overall throughput. Usually, in order to meet the system constraints (i.e. security, throughput, ...), cryptographic services are provided by cryptographic accelerators or programmable crypto-processors. While cryptographic accelerators provide the highest throughputs, they are often dedicated to only one algorithm [12], [10]. In contrast, programmable crypto-processors are flexible, but they also provide lower encryption data rates [7], [5] than accelerators.

To improve the throughput/flexibility trade-off, VLIW (*Very Long Instruction Word*) crypto-processor [15] or multi-crypto-processor [17] architectures have been designed. However, to the best of our knowledge, there is no published studies about multi-crypto-processor scalability. This paper presents a

A. Koch et al. (Eds.): ARC 2011, LNCS 6578, pp. 29–40, 2011.

reconfigurable *Multi-Core Crypto-Processor* (MCCP) especially designed to secure multi-standard and multi-channel communication devices. It also presents
the MCCP scalability and the task allocation problem.

The paper is organized as follows: Section 2 presents previous works on high
throughput cryptographic cores. Section 3 presents the architecture of the proposed MCCP. Its operation is explained in sections 4 and 5. Section 6 presents
some results related to the implementation and the operation of the MCCP.
Finally, section 7 draws a conclusion of this paper.

## 2   Previous Works

The highest data rates are obtained using highly pipelined cryptographic accelerators. In such cores, encryption algorithm is fully unrolled to produce an
efficient pipelined design. For example, AES-GCM (*Galois Counter Mode* [1])
is especially designed to take profit of pipelined cores. There are several works
dealing with hardware implementations of AES-GCM core [12], [14], [16]. These
cores allow throughput of tens of gigabits per second, but this kind of architecture has several drawbacks.

Firstly, algorithm unrolling leads to high hardware resource consumption.
Secondly, data dependencies in some block cipher modes (i.e CCM for *Counter
with CBC-MAC Mode* [3]) make unrolled implementations unusable. Finally,
complex designs are needed when multiplexed channels use different standards.
In consequence, pipelined cores are better suited for mono-standard radio than
for multi-standard ones.

In fact, multi-standard systems often embed programmable crypto-processors.
Such crypto-processors are highly flexible but commonly provide lower throughput than dedicated accelerators. Cryptonite [5] is a programmable crypto-
processor which supports AES, DES, MD5 and others cryptographic algorithms.
It is built around two clusters. Each cluster provides cryptographic functions
used by block cipher algorithms. This implementation targets ASIC platform
and reaches a throughput of 2.25 Gbps at 400 MHz for the AES-ECB algorithm.
Celator   [7] is composed of several *Processing Elements* (PE) which are connected together to form a matrix like a block cipher state variable. According
to PE configuration, cryptographic functions are applied on the grid at each
clock cycle. Celator is able to compute AES, DES or SHA algorithms, providing
for example a throughput of 46 Mbps at 190 MHz when computing AES-CBC
algorithm.

Another approach is to use multi-core architectures in order to achieving
high data rates while remaining flexible. Such architecture is composed of several *Cryptographic Cores* and at least one controller acting as a task scheduler.
Independent cores may process messages from same channel or from different
channels. By this way, high throughputs can be reached on multi-channel radios whatever the operation mode. Basically, multi-core approach for crypto-
processors has almost the same benefits and drawbacks as multi-core general
purpose processor approach (MPSoC issue). CryptoManiac [17] is based on a

multi-core architecture, it achieves a throughput of 512 Mbps on ASIC platform at 360 MHz. The next part presents a crypto-processor architecture which is intended to improve the throughput/flexibility trade-off in the case of the authenticated symmetric encryption.

# 3 Multi-Core Crypto-Processor Architecture

## 3.1 Proposed Approach

Our work focuses on secure and high throughput SDR base-stations. Basically, the MCCP can be used as a cryptographic boundary which secures data streams. It provides most of the necessary cryptographic services needed by an SDR [2].

Such base-station has no resource-restriction which allows to use multi-core architectures. In this paper, MCCP scalability has been studied and up to eight *Cryptographic Cores* have been embedded into one MCCP processor.

While architectures presented above target ASIC platforms, our architecture targets FPGA platforms in order to be as flexible as software components embedded in SDR. By this way, our Multi-Core Crypto-Processor (MCCP) can be updated by using hardware reconfiguration for security or interoperability reasons. The MCCP architecture is presented in the following section.

## 3.2 General Architecture

Our MCCP is embedded in a much larger platform [8] including one main controller and one communication controller which manages communications going through the radio. MCCP does not generate session keys itself. Keys are generated by the main controller and stored into a dedicated memory. MCCP architecture is scalable; the number of embedded crypto-core may vary from two to eight per step of two. As said above, the maximum number of cores is fixed to eight. A four-core architecture is illustrated in Figure 1. On this schematic, dashed lines represent control signals.

The proposed MCCP embeds one *Task Scheduler* which distributes cryptographic tasks to *Cryptographic Cores*. The *Task Scheduler* implementation uses a simple 8-bit controller which executes the task scheduling software. It manages the *Key Scheduler*, the *Cross Bar* and the *Cryptographic Cores*. *Task Scheduler* receives its orders from a 32-bit *Instruction Register* and returns values to the communication controller through the 8-bit *Return Register*. Some signals (*Start* and *Done*) are used to synchronize the instruction execution.

Each *Cryptographic Core* communicates with the communication controller through the *Cross Bar*. It enables the *Task Scheduler* to select a specific core for I/O access. The *Key Scheduler* generates round keys from the session key stored in the *Key Memory*. Before launching the key scheduling, the *Task Scheduler* loads the session key ID into the *Key Scheduler* which gets the right session key from the *Key Memory*. To improve system security, the *Key Memory* cannot be accessed in write mode by the MCCP. In addition, there is no way to get the secret session key directly from the MCCP data port.

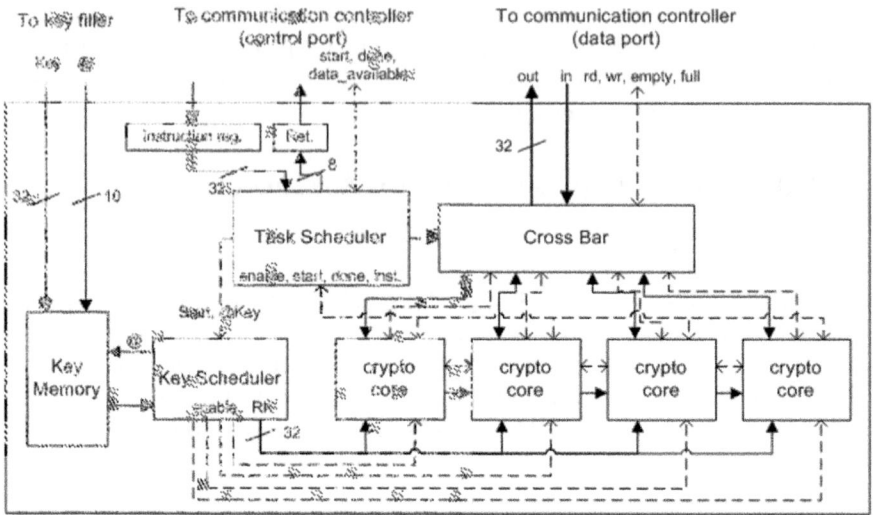

**Fig. 1.** Four-core MCCP Architecture

## 3.3 Cryptographic Core Architecture

Architecture of *Cryptographic Core* is presented in figure 2. On this schematic, dashed lines represent control signals. Each *Cryptographic Core* communicates with the communication controller and other cores through two FIFOs (512 × 32bits) and one *Shift Register* (4 × 32bits). Cryptographic functions are implemented in the *Cryptographic Unit* and they can be used through the *Cryptographic Unit Instruction Set Architecture*. *Cryptographic Unit* provides supports for AES encryption algorithm and several modes of operation (CCM, GCM, CTR, CBC-MAC). However, the AES cipher can be exchanged with any 128-bit block cipher at design step or during processor life using FPGA reconfiguration. AES round keys are pre-computed and stored in the *Key Cache*.

The *Cryptographic Core* have to handle several block cipher modes of operation which may lead to complex control state machines. A more flexible approach is to use a controller to generate instruction flows executed by each *Cryptographic Unit*. Such architecture allows us to simplify execution of loop conditions for packet encryption/decryption. Because this controller does not perform heavy computations, we use an 8-bit controller providing a simple instruction set. This processor communicates with the *Task Scheduler* to receive orders and return execution results. At prototyping step, a modified 8-bit Xilinx PicoBlaze controller [6] has been used. To save resources, it shares its instruction memory with its right neighbouring *Cryptographic Core*.

In the case of AES-CCM, the MAC value returned by the AES-CBC-MAC algorithm needs to be encrypted using the AES-CTR mode. To improve performances, AES-CCM needs to be computed in a concurrent way with two cores. The first one executes AES-CTR algorithm, while the second one executes

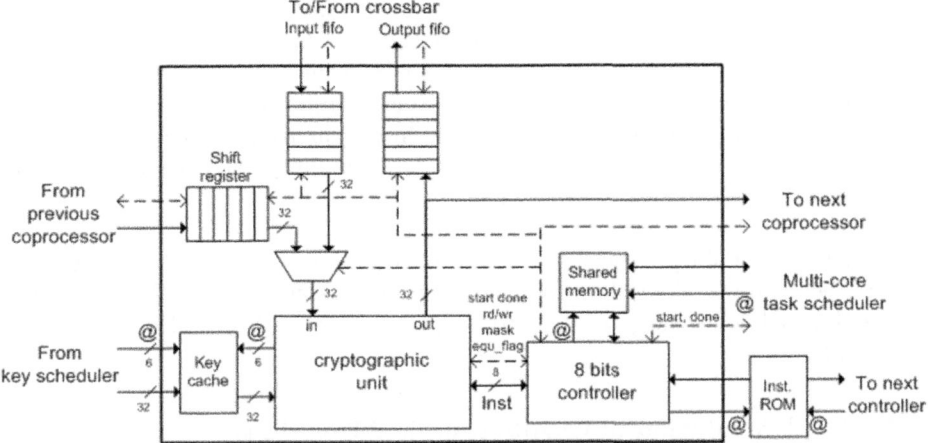

**Fig. 2.** Cryptographic Core Architecture

AES-CBC-MAC algorithm. Inter-*Cryptographic Core* ports are used to convey temporary data, such as the MAC value, from a core to another.

## 4   MCCP Operation

### 4.1   Packet Processing

Incoming packets are processed in the following way:

1. The *Task Scheduler* sends an instruction to the selected *Cryptographic Core* through the shared memory and triggers a *start* signal.
2. The *8-bit Controller* starts pre-computations needed by the selected algorithm and loads data from the input FIFO once they are available.
3. Data are processed by blocks of 128 bits and filled into the output FIFO.
4. When all data have been processed, the *8-bit Controller* sends a *done* signal to the *Task Scheduler*. In order to protect the *Communication Controller* from software attacks (e.g. eavesdropping, spoofing, splicing ), output FIFO is re-initialized if plaintext data does not match the authentication tag. Each FIFO can store a packet of 2048 bytes.

Packet processing is made according to several modes of operation described in the following section.

### 4.2   Available Modes of Operation

MCCP can execute AES-GCM, AES-CCM, AES-CTR, AES-CBC-MAC or any other block cipher mode of operation which only uses a 128-bit block cipher, XOR operators and counter values. Available modes of operation are described below:

- Packets from a same channel can be concurrently processed with different *Cryptographic Core* using the same channel configuration.
- Packets from different channels can be concurrently processed with different *Cryptographic Core* using different channel configurations .
- Any single packet can be processed on any *Cryptographic Core*.
- Using inter-core communication port, any single CCM packet can be processed with two *Cryptographic Cores*.

The right mode of operation is selected by the *Task Scheduler* according to the requested channel algorithm and the available resources. The *Task Scheduler* algorithm, which is used to allocate tasks on the MCCP cores, is described in section 5.

### 4.3   Implementation of Cryptographic Algorithms

ENCRYPT/DECRYPT MCCP instructions are used to launch packet processing. Once such instruction has been received by the MCCP, the communication controller sends data into the input FIFOs. Data must be sent in a specific way to be correctly interpreted by the cores. At first, *Initialization Vector* must be filled into the FIFO, then data must be filled. To finish, communication controller may append a message authentication tag. *Cryptographic Unit* only embeds basic operators in addition to AES core and GHASH core (GCM mode [1]). Therefore, it cannot be used to format the plain text according to the specifications of block cipher modes of operation. In consequence, the communication controller must format data prior to send them to the *Cryptographic Cores*.

In practical terms, the block cipher modes of operation have been developed using *8-bit Controller* assembler and *Cryptographic Unit* assembler. At lowest level, overall performances are limited by AES core computation delays. But, at higher level, performances are limited by the main loops of block cipher modes. The computation time of these loops may be used to approximate the maximum throughput of the implemented ciphers. The measured loop computation times, in number of clock cycle, for 128-bit AES-GCM and AES-CCM are equal to:

$$T_{GCMloop} = T_{CTRloop} = T_{AES} = 49$$
$$T_{CCMloop\_2cores} = T_{CBCloop} = T_{AES} + T_{XOR} = 55$$
$$T_{CCMloop\_1core} = T_{CTRloop} + T_{CBCloop} = 104$$

Eight cycles must be added to these values for 192-bit keys and sixteen cycles must be added for 256-bit keys. Also, pre and post loop invariant computations must be taken into account. Given computation times are measured from HDL simulations:

$$T_{GCMinv128} = 337$$
$$T_{CCMinv\_2cores128} = 354$$
$$T_{CCMinv\_1core128} = 710$$

In addition, packet processing delay must include I/O access delays. Write delays into a *Cryptographic Core* can be neglected because packet processing starts as soon as one 128-bit word is available in the input FIFO. In contrast, read delays cannot be neglected (see item 4 in Section 4.1). The following formulae allows computation of packet processing delays for a specific algorithm:

$$T_{total} = T_{loop} * packet\_size + T_{inv} + packet\_size/bus\_size \qquad (1)$$

## 5 Task Allocation on MCCP

### 5.1 Channel Modelling

In order to evaluate MCCP performances, cryptographic channels have to be modelled. In general, packets pass through a channel in an aperiodic way. However, there is a fixed minimum delay between the arrival of two packets due to the limited bandwidth of underlying physical channels. Indeed, the processing of packets belonging to a channel $C_i$ can be modelled as a sporadic task $\tau_i = (e_i, p_i)$ using the *sporadic task model* [13] where:

- $e_i$ is the processing delay of one packet belonging to $C_i$.
- $p_i$ is the minimum delay between the arrival of two packets belonging to $C_i$.

### 5.2 Hypothesis and Constraints

MCCP architecture does not enable to delay the processing of a specific packet. In consequence, packets are processed in their order of arrival. However, future works will deal with the implementation of scheduling algorithms in order to reduce system latency.

To remain as general as possible, this article propose to evaluate the performances of our MCCP processor under an unscheduled load. Also, in the remainder of this article, we only consider the worst case where sporadic tasks always behave as periodic tasks.

In this work, a set of tasks $\tau$ is *allocable* under the previous hypothesis if and only if the processor load does not exceed the MCCP capacity. Such condition is equivalent to (2) for a MCCP processor which implements $m \geq 1$ cores and handles $n$ concurrent channels.

$$\sum_{i=1}^{n} e_i/p_i \leq m \qquad (2)$$

### 5.3 Task Allocation Algorithm

MCCP release implements a simple task allocation algorithm represented in Figure 3. It is noteworthy that this algorithm gives a higher priority to incoming packets to optimize the crypto-processor activity. Also, it does not try to allocate a specific channel to a core in order to save time needed by round key

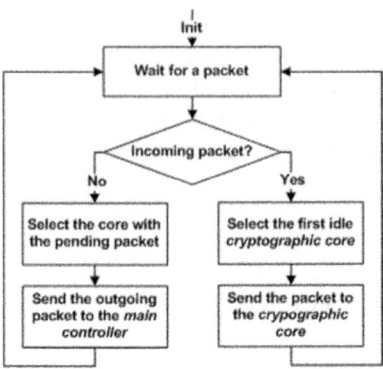

**Fig. 3.** Task Allocation Flow Chart

computations. In fact, keys are computed on the fly, so round key generation delays can be neglected. In addition, this algorithm gives the same priority to each channels. Currently, this algorithm does not support allocation of two cores per packet in the case of the CCM mode.

### 5.4   Performance Estimation of the Task Allocation Algorithm

Let studying the impact of $n$ channels on the maximum *maintainable* throughput when our task allocation algorithm is used. For a fixed number of channels $n$ and a fixed number of processors $m$, we have:

$$\alpha = \sum_{i=1}^{n} e_i / p_{min_i} \qquad (3)$$

Where $p_{min_i}$ is the physical minimum delay between the arrival of two packets of the channel $C_i$. According to (2), the set of channels $C$ is *allocable* if $\alpha \leq m$. If it is not the case and if we assume that all packets have the same priority, then, a *allocable* set of tasks can be obtained by increasing each $p_{min_i}$ by a factor $\alpha/m$. Therefore, the actual *minimum arrival delay* of channel $C_i$ must be equal to:

$$p_i = \frac{\alpha}{m} * p_{min_i} \qquad (4)$$

Unfortunately, this analysis does not take into account I/O accesses over the MCCP *Cross Bar*. In fact, the delay needed to forward a packet to a processor is not null and MCCP *Cross Bar* remains locked while a packet forwarding is in progress. This phenomenon must be taken into account to obtain realistic throughput estimations.

Section 6.3 gives experimental results in order to estimate the effects of the *Cross Bar* congestion on the maximum *maintainable* throughput.

# 6   Results

## 6.1   Implementation Results

The proposed MCCP has been described with VHDL and synthesized using Xilinx ISE 12.1 tool. For MCCP hardware implementation, we use a Xilinx Virtex 4 SX35-11 FPGA. Implementation results are detailed in Table 1 (no DSP block is used).

Results show that the use of resource increases linearly with the number of implemented cores. In addition, maximum frequency remains stable whatever the number of implemented cores. The six-core MCCP version exhibits slightly lower performances than others implementations. But, small change in MCCP architecture may improve performance to reach 190 MHz. To conclude, MCCP architecture is well scalable.

Nevertheless, *Cross Bar* bandwidth may be a bottleneck for MCCP scalability. A 64-bit version of the *Cross Bar* has been implemented to prevent bus congestion when eight cores are used. Section 6.3 provides more details regarding the performances of each of these implementations.

**Table 1.** MCCP Resource Consumption

| Nb of cores | Bus size | Slices | BRAM | Max. Frequency (MHz) |
|---|---|---|---|---|
| 2 | 32 | 2071 | 15 | 192 |
| 4 | 32 | 4055 | 26 | 192 |
| 6 | 32 | 6026 | 37 | 185 |
| 8 | 32 | 7760 | 48 | 192 |
| 8 | 64 | 8714 | 64 | 192 |

## 6.2   Cryptographic Core Performances

This section details raw performances of MCCP cryptographic cores. Actual *Cryptographic Core* throughput depends on packet size (see Section 4.3) and higher throughput are obtained from larger packets. Table 2 summarized these results. For each column, the first value denotes the theoretical throughput calculated from loops computation time, while the second value corresponds to the processing time of a 2 KB packet measured from HDL simulations.

**Table 2.** Cryptographic Core Throughputs at 190 MHz (Theoretical/2KB)

| Key Size (bit) | AES-GCM (Mbps) | AES-CCM (Mbps) | |
|---|---|---|---|
| | 1 core per packet | 1 core per packet | 2 cores per packet |
| 128 | 496 / 437 | 233 / 214 | 442 / 393 |
| 192 | 426 / 382 | 202 / 187 | 386 / 348 |
| 256 | 374 / 337 | 178 / 171 | 342 / 313 |

Table 2 shows that, in the case of AES-CCM, packet processing on one core is more efficient than packet processing on two cores. Indeed, $2\times$ *[1 core per packet]* configuration provides a better throughput than *[2 cores per packet]* configuration. However, latency of the first solution is almost two times greater than latency of the second solution. As a consequence, designers should make their choices according to system needs in terms of latency and/or throughput.

## 6.3   MCCP Performances

To estimate performances of our architecture under an heavy load, a *transaction level model* of the MCCP processor has been developed in Java. This high level model takes into account the packet processing delays and the I/O access delays to provide an accurate estimation of the *maintainable* throughput. In this section, it is assumed that:

- Packets are not scheduled (i.e. they arrive in a random order).
- Channels use CCM and GCM algorithms with 128-bit keys.
- Maximum throughput per channel is given by: $p_{min_i} = e_i$.

For each number of channels, all combinations of channel configuration have been simulated and the worst case has been picked to obtain the maximum *maintainable* throughput whatever the channel combination. Figure 4 shows the simulation results where $\alpha$ is the parameter defined in (3) and $n$ the number of channels.

Figure 4 shows that curves follow, as expected, an $1/x$ law. Also, we can see that bus size does not limit the throughput when less than eight cores are implemented. However, due to bus congestion, the 32-bit version of the eight core MCCP provides worst performances (-8% on average) than the 64-bit version.

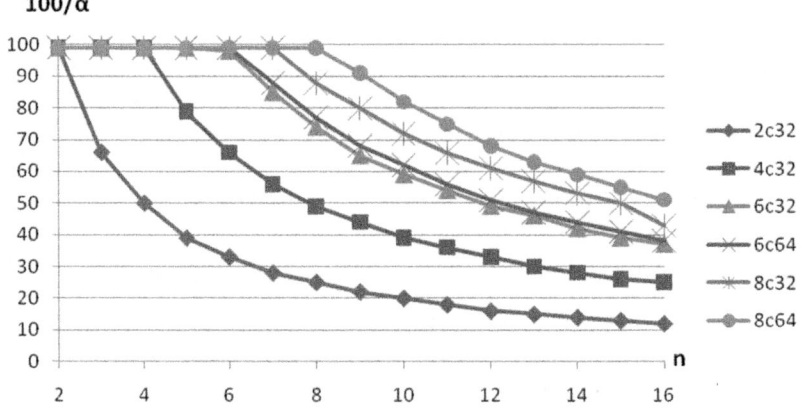

**Fig. 4.** $100/\alpha = f(n)$

This drawback will become a serious issue for MCCPs which implement an high number of cryptographic cores. In this case, others architectures like *Network on Chip* may be more suited. To conclude, the maximum *maintainable* throughput on an eight cores 64-bit MCCP is around 3460 Mbps when just one channel is active.

## 7   Conclusion and Future Works

This work shows that the scalable multi-core architecture presented in this paper provides a good trade-off between flexibility, performances and resource consumption. Its 3.4 Gbps maximum throughput makes it particularly suitable for high throughput multi-channel communication systems. Proposed MCCP supports the commonly used CTR, CBC-MAC, CCM and GCM block cipher modes. Also, AES core may be easily replaced by any other 128-bit block cipher (such as Twofish) thanks to the FPGA hardware reconfiguration. To conclude, last section shows that the scalability of our architecture is limited by the *Cross Bar* congestion. In further works, the use of *Network on Chip* architectures may be a solution to overcome this problem.

## References

1. Special publication 800-38a (2001), http://csrc.nist.gov/
2. Security supplement to the software communications architecture specification (April 30, 2004), http://sca.jpeojtrs.mil/
3. Special publication 800-38c (2004), http://csrc.nist.gov/
4. Baruah, S.: The non-preemptive scheduling of periodic tasks upon multiprocessors. Real-Time Systems 32, 9–20 (2006),
   http://dx.doi.org/10.1007/s11241-006-4961-9
5. Buchty, R., Heintze, N., Oliva, D.: Cryptonite – A programmable crypto processor architecture for high-bandwidth applications. In: Müller-Schloer, C., Ungerer, T., Bauer, B. (eds.) ARCS 2004. LNCS, vol. 2981, pp. 184–198. Springer, Heidelberg (2004)
6. Chapman, X.K.: Picoblaze user resources, http://www.xilinx.com
7. Fronte, D., Perez, A., Payrat, E.: Celator: A multi-algorithm cryptographic co-processor. In: Proc. International Conference on Reconfigurable Computing and FPGAs ReConFig 2008, pp. 438–443 (December 3-5, 2008)
8. Grand, M., Bossuet, L., Gogniat, G., Gal, B.L., Dallet, D.: A reconfigurable crypto sub system for the software communication architecture. In: Proceedings MILCOM 2009 (2009)
9. Guan, N., Yi, W., Gu, Z., Deng, Q., Yu, G.: New schedulability test conditions-for non-preemptive scheduling on multiprocessor platforms. In: Proc. Real-Time Systems Symp., pp. 137–146 (2008)
10. Hodjat, A., Verbauwhede, I.: Area-throughput trade-offs for fully pipelined 30 to 70 gbits/s aes processors. IEEE Transactions on Computers 55, 366–372 (2006)
11. Jeffay, K., Stanat, D.F., Martel, C.U.: On non-preemptive scheduling of period andsporadic tasks. In: Proc. Twelfth Real-Time Systems Symp., pp. 129–139 (1991)

12. Lemsitzer, S., Wolkerstorfer, J., Felber, N., Braendli, M.: Multi-gigabit gcm-aes architecture optimized for fpgas. In: Paillier, P., Verbauwhede, I. (eds.) CHES 2007. LNCS, vol. 4727, pp. 227–238. Springer, Heidelberg (2007)
13. Mok, A.K.: Fundamental design problems of distributed systems for the hard-real-time environment. Tech. rep., Cambridge, MA, USA (1983)
14. Satoh, A., Sugawara, T., Aoki, T.: High-speed pipelined hardware architecture for galois counter mode. In: Garay, J.A., Lenstra, A.K., Mambo, M., Peralta, R. (eds.) ISC 2007. LNCS, vol. 4779, pp. 118–129. Springer, Heidelberg (2007)
15. Theodoropoulos, D., Siskos, A., Pnevmatikatos, D.: Ccproc: A custom vliw cryptography co-processor for symmetric-key ciphers. In: Becker, J., Woods, R., Athanas, P., Morgan, F. (eds.) ARC 2009. LNCS, vol. 5453, pp. 318–323. Springer, Heidelberg (2009)
16. Wang, S.: An Architecture for the AES-GCM Security Standard. Master's thesis, University of Waterloo (2006)
17. Wu, L., Weaver, C., Austin, T.: Cryptomaniac: a fast flexible architecture for secure communication. In: ISCA 2001: Proceedings of the 28th Annual International Symposium on Computer Architecture, pp. 110–119. ACM, New York (2001)

# Application Specific Memory Access, Reuse and Reordering for SDRAM

Samuel Bayliss and George A. Constantinides

Department of Electrical and Electronic Engineering,
Imperial College London, South Kensington Campus,
London SW7 2AZ, United Kingdom
s.bayliss08@imperial.ac.uk, g.constantinides@imperial.ac.uk

**Abstract.** The efficient use of bandwidth available on an external SDRAM interface is strongly dependent on the sequence of addresses requested. On-chip memory buffers can make possible data *reuse* and request *reordering* which together ensure bandwidth on an SDRAM interface is used efficiently. This paper outlines an automated procedure for generating an application-specific memory hierarchy which exploits reuse and reordering and quantifies the impact this has on memory bandwidth over a range of representative benchmarks. Considering a range of parameterized designs, we observe up to 50x reduction in the quantity of data fetched from external memory. This, combined with reordering of the transactions, allows up to 128x reduction in the memory access time of certain memory-intensive benchmarks.

## 1   Introduction

On-chip memory hierarchies improve the performance of the memory system by exploiting *reuse* and *reordering*. Reusing data retained in an on-chip memory hierarchy reduces the number of requests made to the external memory interface. Where those data requests can be safely reordered, often the control overhead of servicing the requests can be reduced and hence bandwidth on the external interface is used more efficiently.

On general purpose computers, the sequence of memory requests generated by the CPU is generally unknown at design time, and the cache is able to reuse and reorder data without a static compile time analysis of the program to be executed. Complex dynamic memory controllers in modern CPUs also buffer and dynamically reorder requests to external memory. Both the cache and memory controllers therefore contain memory and associative logic to buffer and dynamically select and service memory requests.

However, when a specific application is targeted for hardware acceleration on an FPGA, it can often be broken into computation kernels for which static analysis is tractable. More specifically, for such kernels, the sequence of memory requests can often be determined at compile time. This makes possible the development of a custom application-specific memory system which exploits reuse and reordering of data requests to maximize bandwidth and reduce the average

A. Koch et al. (Eds.): ARC 2011, LNCS 6578, pp. 41–52, 2011.

request latency. This work describes a methodology for developing such a system and benchmarks demonstrating its efficacy. The key contributions are:

- A representation of the memory accesses contained within a loop body as a parameterized set.
- A methodology which uses parametric integer programming techniques to find a monotonic function which loads each set member only once.
- An implementation of that function as a state machine within an FPGA.
- An evaluation of the SDRAM bandwidth efficiency improvements achieved by such an approach.

## 2  Background

### 2.1  SDRAM Memory

Synchronous Dynamic Random Access Memories (SDRAMs) are used as the external off-chip memory in most general purpose computers. They are designed for high yield and low cost in manufacturing and have densities which exceed competing technologies. However, the design trade-offs needed to achieve these characteristics means much of the burden of controlling SDRAM memories falls on an external memory controller.

SDRAM memories store data as charged nodes in a dense array of memory cells. An explicit 'activate' command sent to the memory selects a row within the array before any reads or writes can take place. This is followed by the assertion of a sequence of memory 'read' or 'write' commands to columns within the selected row followed by a 'precharge' command which must be asserted before any further rows can be activated. The physical structure of the memory device determines the minimum time that must elapse between the issuing of 'precharge', 'activate' and 'read' / 'write' commands.

The memory controller is responsible for ensuring these minimum constraints are met. When reading consecutive columns within a row, SDRAM memories can sustain two word per clock cycle data-rates. With a 200MHz DDR2 Device, this means 400Mbytes/s. However the overhead of 'activate' and 'precharge' commands and the delays associated with their respective timing constraints means that achieving this peak bandwidth is difficult. In the worst case where a single 32-byte word is requested from memory from different alternating rows within the same bank, memory bandwidth is reduced to 72Mbytes/s.

### 2.2  Previous Work

High performance memory systems are a goal across the spectrum of computing equipment and a large body of work exists which seeks to improve cache performance, for which [8] provides a basic review. Most of the work in the literature assumes the sequence of data is randomly (but not necessarily uniformly) distributed, and describes optimizations of the dynamic on-chip structures which exploit data locality. Where scratchpad memories have been used within a memory hierarchy, there are examples of static analysis to determine which specific memory elements are reused. Of particular note is the work of Darte et al. [5] and Liu et al. [12]. These two works both explore data-reuse using a polytope model. One develops a mathematical framework to study the storage reuse-problem, and the other is an application of the techniques within the context of designing a custom memory system implemented on an FPGA.

Prior work focused more specifically on SDRAM controllers can also be divided into work which seeks to optimize the performance of random data streams using run-time on-chip structures and those which use static analysis techniques on kernels of application code. A review of different dynamic scheduling policies for SDRAM controllers can be found in [15] showing that none of the fixed scheduling policies is optimal across all benchmarks. This is justification for the pursuit of an application-specific approach. The approach presented in [1] describes a memory controller designed to guarantee a minimum net bandwidth and maximum latency to many requestors in a complex SoC. A set of short templates are defined which optimize bursts of data and time-slots are allocated using a credit-controlled static priority arbiter to guarantee allocated bandwidth and bounded latency.

Static compile time approaches to improving SDRAM efficiency can be found in [10] where different data-layouts are used to exploit efficiency in a image-processing application. They propose a block-based layout of data within a data array rather than more traditional row-major or column-major layouts and develop a Presberger arithmetic based model to estimate the number of 'precharge' and 'activate' commands required in the execution of a video benchmark under different parameterizations. Their results show a 70-80% accuracy compared to simulation results and achieve up to 50% energy savings. Energy savings are considered specifically in [14] where an algorithm is developed for maximizing the number of possible concurrent memory accesses through a careful allocation of arrays to different banks.

Some work exists which considers the fine grained sequence of SDRAM commands. Dutt et al. [9] break with the traditional approach of treating loads and stores as atomic operations in a high level synthesis system and introduce fine grained SDRAM control nodes into their CDFG based synthesis flow.

None of the work mentioned above tackles the issue of data reuse (reducing the number of transactions issued to the external memory system) and reordering (reducing the latency associated with each transaction) in a comprehensive framework. The approach taken in this paper seeks to address this. We propose using on-chip memory to reuse data accessed within the innermost loops of a loop nest. Our methodology ensures that only the referenced data items are fetched into on-chip memory buffers and that the sequence of addresses on the external memory interface increases monotonically whilst filling those buffers. This final point ensures that the minimum number of 'precharge' and 'activate' commands are required, ensuring optimal SDRAM bandwidth efficiency.

## 3    Example

As a 'toy' illustrative example, consider the code shown in Figure 1(a). Two dimensional iteration vectors $[i, j]$ represent each iteration of the statement within
the loop nest. Figure 1(c) shows how each of these vectors generates a memory
address. The iterations $[0, 1]$ and $[2, 0]$ both access the same memory address.
This data reuse by different iterations can be exploited by only loading the data
at address 4 once. Furthermore the example contains 'holes'; the items $1, 3, 5$ and
$7$ are never accessed and need not be loaded. Finally, the access order implied by
the ordering of the loop iterations implies that a non-monotonic sequence of addresses is generated by this code. Such a sequence implies that in the presence of
page breaks, unnecessary 'precharge' and 'activate' commands are generated to
swap between rows. Enforcing monotonicity on the address generating function
minimizes the number of 'precharge' and 'activate' commands needed, improving
overall bandwidth efficiency.

## 4    Problem Description

### 4.1    Polytope Model

We will restrict our scope to considering memory access sequences which are
generated by references within a nested loop body.

A nested loop body such as the example in Figure 1(a) is made up of a number
of different levels, each with an associated induction variable. The 2-level nested
loop body shown in Figure 1(a) contains two induction variables ($i$ and $j$). In the
general case, an $n$-level nested loop can be represented by induction variables
$x_1, x_2 \ldots x_n$ with the inner-most loop arbitrarily labelled with the highest index.
Each execution of the statement(s) within the innermost loop is associated with
a unique vector $x \in \mathbb{Z}^n$. If the loop nest is restricted further by the requirement
that the bounds of each loop are affine functions of the induction variables which
exist higher in the loop nest, the set of vectors, which we refer to as an iteration
space is given by the set of integral points in a convex polytope. The loop bounds
define this polytope and can be expressed in the form $Ax \leq b$. The loop bounds
in Figure 1(a) can be expressed as $A = \begin{bmatrix} 1 & 0 \\ -1 & 0 \\ 0 & 1 \\ 0 & -1 \end{bmatrix}$ and $b = \begin{bmatrix} 2 & 0 & 1 & 0 \end{bmatrix}^T$.

The loops will contain memory addressing functions ($f : \mathbb{Z}^n \rightarrow \mathbb{Z}$) mapping induction variables to memory locations, $e.g.$ in Figure 1(a), the function
$f(i, j) = 2i + 4j$ describes memory accesses which load elements of the $A$ array.
In the case of an affine function $f(x)$, we may write $f(x) = Fx + c$ and describe
the set of memory addresses accessed as (1).

$$S = \{Fx + c \mid Ax \leq b\}. \tag{1}$$

```
int A[9];
for  (i = 0 ; i <= 2 ; i++) {
  for  (j = 0 ; j <= 1 ; j++) {
      func(A[2i + 4j]);
  }
}
```

(a) Source Code

```
if (-i - 2*j + 1 >= 0) {
  k = (2*i + 3) / 4;        /* Note: integer division */
  if (j + k - 1 >= 0) {
    R' = 2*i + 4*j + 2;
    i' = i - 2*k + 1;
    j' = j + k;
  }
  else {
    R' = 2*i + 2*j - 2*k + 2;
    i' = i + j - k + 1;
    j' = 0;
  }
}
else {
  if (-i - j + 3 >= 0) {
    R' = 2*i + 4*j + 2;
    i' = i + 2*j - 1;
    j' = 1;
  }
  else {
    // No Solution.
  }
}
```

(b) Output Code

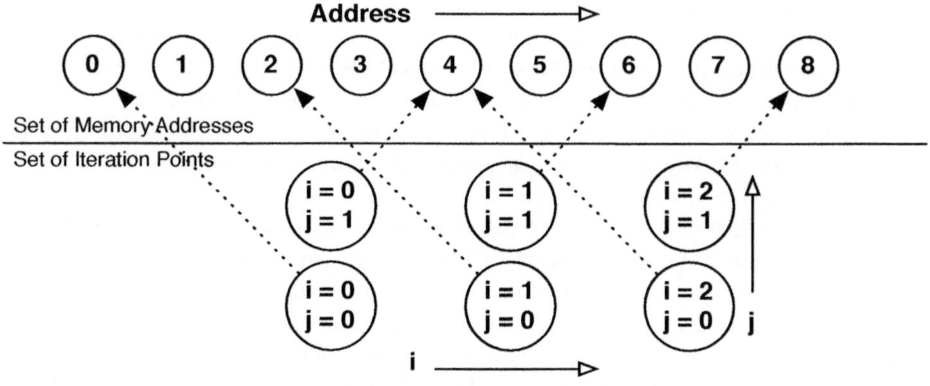

(c) Mapping Diagram for source code

**Fig. 1.** (a) Source code for example (b) Output code listing solution for example (c) Mapping from $(i, j)$ iteration space to memory addresses for code (a)

The memory referencing function $(f : \mathbb{Z}^n \rightarrow \mathbb{Z})$ can be non-injective, which means different iterations within the loop nest can access the same item in memory.

Many common image processing and linear algebra problems can be expressed in this polytope framework. Scheduling and loop transformations which alter the execution order within this polytope framework have been extensively studied [11,7,4] either to expose parallelism by eliminating loop carried dependencies, or to reduce the communications cost when partitioning code across many processors in a HPC system.

## 4.2   Memory Buffering and Reordering

While the work in [11,7,4] considers reordering the statements within a loop nest, we propose a different approach; preserving the original execution order, we propose the introduction of memory buffers (reuse buffers) at levels within the loop body. Unlike caches, which are filled by an implicit hardware mechanism, these memories are explicitly populated with data using code derived from the original problem description. External memory references in the innermost loop are replaced by references into the reuse buffers. The memory buffer can be introduced at any level within the loop nest, we define a parameter $1 \leq t \leq n$ which describes the placement of the buffer within a $n$-level loop nest. A buffer introduced outside the outermost loop and explicitly populated with all the data referenced within the loop-nest is referred to as $t = 1$ while a buffer inserted at $t = 2$ must be refilled every time the outermost loop index is incremented and contains only data accessed within that iteration of the outer loop.

Because such an approach does not alter the *execution* order of statements, introduction of memory buffers can be done without specifically considering data dependencies within the code. Prior work using explicitly populated memory buffers in this way can be found in [13] and [2].

The novelty of our work is derived from the reordering of the memory requests used to populate the reuse buffers. The reordering considers the most efficient access pattern for SDRAM, both exploiting the reuse of data elements with a loop nest *and* rearranging the data accesses so that all the data that lies within a SDRAM row is accessed consecutively, thus minimising the overhead of 'precharge' and 'activate' commands.

The most efficient ordering for transferring data between the external memory and internal buffer is by visiting each row only once, minimizing the number of row swaps necessary. If the function describing the scheduling of loads and stores to the memory is strictly monotonic, this property will hold. The property ensures that memory reuse is exploited (strictly increasing functions are injective, therefore each data item can be loaded only once) and that the minimum overhead of row swaps is incurred.

## 5    Parametric Integer Linear Programming Formulation

Integer Linear Programs are optimization problems which seek to minimize an objective function subject to a set of linear constraints while forcing only integer assignments to the optimization variables. This is illustrated in the formulation in Equation 2. This concept has been extended to parametric integer programming (Equation 3) where the constraints can be described in terms of some parameter $q$ thus producing $p$ as an explicit *function* of $q$ rather than as an integer vector as in ILP. We can use parametric integer linear programming to derive an address generating function for populating reuse buffers within our proposed application specific memory subsystem.

$$\min_{p} k^T p \quad s.t. \quad Ap \leq b \tag{2}$$

$$\min_{p} k^T p \quad s.t. \quad Ap \leq b + Cq. \tag{3}$$

### 5.1    Constraints

Our objective is to derive a function which generates a sequence of memory addresses populating a reuse buffer. We propose a method which produces an address generating function directly from the polytope problem definition using parametric integer linear programming with embedded constraints which ensure that the strict monotonicity property holds. The solution takes the form of an iterative function which generates an address $(R')$ and $n + 1 - t$ state variables which are used to generate subsequent addresses. This is illustrated in Figure 2.

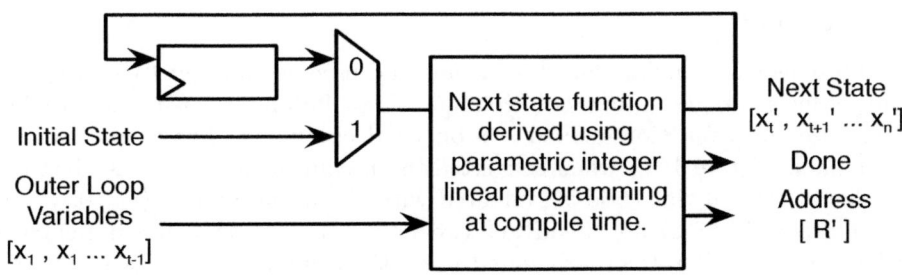

**Fig. 2.** Diagram showing how the Piplib derived addressing function is implemented

For a reuse buffer introduced at a specific level $t$ in the loop structure we define the parametric integer linear program in terms of the variable $p = [R', x'_t, x'_{t+1}, \ldots, x'_n]^T$, representing the next address and inner loop iterators and parameterized in terms of variables $q = [x_1, x_2, \ldots, x_n]^T$. Given the current value $q$ of the loop iterators, our objective is simply to find the first address accessed in the code after $Fq + c$, the current address. This corresponds to minimizing $R'$ subject to the constraints we outline below. In explaining these constraints, we make reference to the example in Figure 1(a) and assume that a reuse buffer is inserted at the outermost level (outside the loop nest). Therefore for this example $p = [R', i', j']^T$, $q = [i, j]$ and $t = 1$.

The first constraint is an inequality constraint which ensures strict monotonicity, i.e. that the next address will be one more than the current address.

$$R' \geq Fq + c + 1 \tag{4}$$

In our example code, this corresponds to the constraint $R' \geq 2i + 4j + 0 + 1$.

The second constraint is an equality constraint that ensures that the new address $(R')$ can be generated by the memory access function $f(x) = Fq + c$ through a linear combination of the domain variables $x_t, x_{t+1} \ldots x_n$. Where $F = [F_1 \ F_2]$:

$$R' - (F_1[x_1 \ldots x_{t-1}]^T + F_2[x'_t, x'_t, \ldots, x'_n]^T) = c \tag{5}$$

In our example, this corresponds to the constraint $R' - 2i' - 4j' = 0$.

The remaining constraints ensure that the combination of the instantiation of the variables $x'_t, x'_{t+1}, \ldots x'_n$ and the parameter variables $x_1 \ldots x_{t-1}$ lie within the iteration space. Where $A = [A_1 \ A_2]$:

$$A_1[x_1 \ldots x_{t-1}]^T + A_2[x'_t, x'_{t+1}, \ldots x'_n]^T \leq b \tag{6}$$

For our example, the constraints $i' \leq 2$, $-i' \leq 0$, $j' \leq 1$ and $-j' \leq 0$ ensure this.

The variables $q = [x_1, x_1 \ldots x_n]^T$ are constrained by the constraints implied by the original polytope. In our example code, this means $i \leq 2$, $-i \leq 0$, $j \leq 1$ and $-j \leq 0$.

## 5.2   Output

The problem is formulated at design time and used as an input to a parametric integer linear programming tool Piplib [6]. The solution returned by the tool is a piecewise linear function defined as a binary decision tree. The output from the example in Figure 1(a), when converted to an equivalent C code, is illustrated in Figure 1(b). If this code is evaluated with the initial indices $(i = 0, j = 0)$, an address $(R' = 2)$ and a further two indices $i' = 1, j' = 0$ are generated. When these are iteratively evaluated using the same function, the sequence of addresses (2,4,6,8) is generated. This is exactly the memory addresses touched by the original input code, presented in a strictly increasing order and with all repetition removed. This ensures no unnecessary row-swaps are incurred and the minimum number of 'precharge' and 'activate' commands are generated.

## 6   Hardware Implementation

The output from the parametric integer linear programming solver implicitly defines a state machine with state defined by $(x'_t, x'_{t+1}, \ldots x'_n)$, a single output $(R')$

and $t - 1$ inputs $(x_1 \ldots x_{t-1})$. Using Handel-C [3] we formed a direct implementation of that state machine within an FPGA and used the address generated to drive the Altera High Performance DDR2 Memory Controller. Verilog code generated from Handel-C was synthesized using Quartus II for a Stratix III target device.

## 7 Results and Discussion

Three benchmarks are presented to measure the effectiveness of our proposed technique in improving memory bandwidth.

**Matrix-Matrix Multiply (MMM).** In this benchmark two 50x50 dense matrices of 64-bit values are multiplied using a classic 3-level loop nest implementation. One matrix is accessed in a column-wise fashion and the other in a row-wise fashion.

**Sobel Edge Detection (SED).** This benchmark is a 2D convolution of a 512x512 matrix of 32-bit values with a 3x3 kernel. Because each iteration requires pixels from three consecutive rows of an image *and* three consecutive pixels in each row, neither row or column major storage of the input array can mitigate poor data locality.

**Gaussian Back-Substitution (GBS).** This benchmark optimizes the memory pattern in a blocked back-substitution kernel. It illustrates that the methodology presented is equally applicable to non-rectangular loop-nests and where not all data in a (square) input array need be accessed.

Each design is parameterized by inserting reuse buffers at different levels within the loop nest (where $t = 1$ implies a reuse buffer inserted outside the outermost loop of the benchmark code). The designs were simulated using a memory controller running at 240MHz with the address generation logic running at the post-fit reported $F_{max}$ frequency.

Synthesis results giving area and speed for the derived address generators are given in Table 1 and reflect the fact that as $t$ is decreased, the conditions evaluated at each clock cycle require more terms (and more multipliers) and a longer critical path. The $F_{max}$ clock speeds of each implementation fall significantly below the peak rated performance of the embedded hardware resources on which they are implemented. The long critical paths in the arithmetic functions used to generate next-state variables for our state machine implementation prevent higher clock rates. Since the parameters calculated in one cycle are used to generate those in the next, pipelining cannot be used without reducing the overall throughput of the address generator.

Yet in spite of this reduction in achievable clock frequency as $t$ is decreased; the wall clock time taken to load data in each benchmark reduces as $t$ is decreased. A comparison of parameterization with $t = 1$ and the original code shows reduction of $128\times$, $29\times$ and $7\times$ in the wall clock time of the three benchmarks respectively. This significant performance improvement occurs because our methodology increases opportunities for reuse *and* reordering as $t$ decreases

**Table 1.** Area Consumed by address generation logic (post synthesis and P&R), breakdown of memory cycles and total wall clock time for memory accesses in each benchmark

| Benchmark | Reuse Level | LUTs | 18-bit DSPs | Clock Speed | Read/Write Cycles | 'Pre'&'Act' Cycles | Other Cycles | Wall Clock Time |
|---|---|---|---|---|---|---|---|---|
| MMM | t = 1 | 1504 | 0 | 55MHz | 29992 | 878 | 22597 | 229 μs |
| MMM | t = 2 | 831 | 0 | 56MHz | 520000 | 15802 | 394988 | 2874 μs |
| MMM | t = 3 | 310 | 0 | 145MHz | 1009954 | 571448 | 59946 | 6952 μs |
| MMM | Orig. | 242 | 0 | 145MHz | 1499952 | 3789438 | 1649683 | 29365 μs |
| SED | t = 1 | 1951 | 112 | 40MHz | 2088988 | 46378 | 2288487 | 18440 μs |
| SED | t = 2 | 1314 | 80 | 43MHz | 4192180 | 106258 | 4550859 | 36880 μs |
| SED | t = 3 | 930 | 68 | 52MHz | 19767560 | 13202772 | 1741317 | 144639 μs |
| SED | t = 4 | 482 | 28 | 107MHz | 21848356 | 16772328 | 1182698 | 174148 μs |
| SED | Orig. | 462 | 24 | 117MHz | 28090752 | 70959548 | 30795889 | 535623 μs |
| GBS | t=1 | 2948 | 128 | 35MHz | 35048 | 5178 | 32881 | 318 μs |
| GBS | t=2 | 1501 | 76 | 46MHz | 35812 | 9038 | 28046 | 309 μs |
| GBS | t=3 | 526 | 36 | 120MHz | 67536 | 168992 | 45364 | 1175 μs |
| GBS | Orig. | 356 | 16 | 75MHz | 165078 | 310758 | 98622 | 2341 μs |

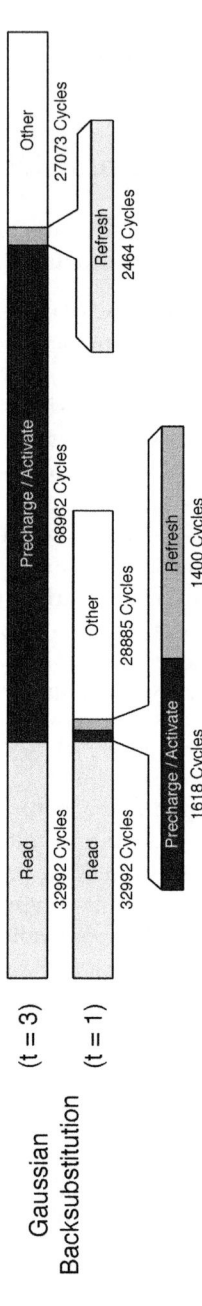

**Fig. 3.** Figure showing SDRAM bandwidth allocation by command type within a single reference in the Gaussian Backsubstitution benchmark

(with buffers inserted at the outermost levels of the loop nest). Three mechanisms can be identified which contribute to this.

1. The first mechanism we can observe is the reduction in the number of read requests through the exploitation of data reuse. Data reuse means some data held in the on-chip reuse buffer is accessed by more than one different iteration within the loop nest. On-chip buffering means that only a single request to external memory is made for each reused item. Table 1 shows how the number of read cycles to external memory decreases as the reuse buffer is instantiated in the outer levels of the loop nest (*i.e.* as $t$ decreases).
2. The second mechanism for the reduction in overall wall clock time is better locality within each memory reference. Figure 3 shows a proportional breakdown of the SDRAM commands generated by a single 'read' reference within the GBS benchmark. When parameterized at $t = 1$ and $t = 3$, the number of memory accesses is constant, however the monotonic order in which they are accessed when $t = 1$ reorders those accesses. This eliminates the large overhead of 'precharge' and 'activate' cycles which in turn means a greater than 2× reduction in total loading time is seen over parameterization at the the innermost level ($t = 3$).
3. The third observable mechanism is the reduction in the interleaving of accesses to different arrays. In general, when bursts of memory access to different arrays are serialized, the inevitable interleaving of accesses to different arrays introduces row-swaps. Under our approach, when parameterization is at the outer levels of the loop nest, the bursts of addresses are longer and there are fewer total interleavings thus the overhead of 'precharge' and 'activate' commands is reduced.

# 8    Conclusions and Future Work

In this paper, we have presented a novel methodology for generating application-specific address generators which exploit data reuse and reorder data accesses. In selected benchmarks, data reuse allows a 50x reduction in the number of memory accesses. The constraints which ensure the sequence of memory addresses requested by each access function is strictly increasing ensure an efficient use of SDRAM memory bandwidth. When exploited together, these two aspects provide up to 128× reduction in overall wall clock time in memory intensive benchmarks.

We are actively investigating methods for compactly representing the solutions produced by the parametric integer programming tool with the aim of increasing the achievable $F_{max}$ clock speed. There remains scope for even more efficient bandwidth utilization by considering application specific *command* generation within an SDRAM controller alongside the proposed address generation scheme and extending our formulation to optimize the scheduling of memory refresh accesses.

# References

1. Akesson, B., Goossens, K., Ringhofer, M.: Predator: A Predictable SDRAM Memory Controller. In: CODES+ISSS 2007: Proceedings of the 5th IEEE/ACM International Conference on Hardware/Software Codesign and System Synthesis, Salzburg, Austria, pp. 251–256 (2007)
2. Baradaran, N., Diniz, P.C., Way, A., Rey, M.: Compiler-Directed Design Space Exploration for Caching and Prefetching Data in High-level Synthesis. In: FPT 2005: Proceedings of the IEEE International Conference on Field Programmable Technology, Singapore, pp. 233–240 (2005)
3. Celoxica Ltd. DK4: Handel-C Language Reference Manual (2005)
4. Claßen, M., Griebl, M.: Automatic code generation for distributed memory architectures in the polytope model. In: IPDPS 2006: 20th International Parallel and Distributed Processing Symposium, Rhodes, Greece, pp. 243–250 (2006)
5. Darte, A., Schreiber, R., Villard, G.: Lattice-Based Memory Allocation. IEEE Transactions on Computers 54(10), 1242–1257 (2005)
6. Feautrier, P.: Parametric Integer Programming. RAIRO Recherche Opérationnelle 22(3), 243–268 (1988)
7. Feautrier, P.: Automatic Parallelization in the Polytope Model. In: The Data Parallel Programming Model: Foundations, HPF Realization, and Scientific Application, pp. 79–103 (1996)
8. Hennesey, J., Patterson, D.: Computer Architecture: A Quantitative Approach, 6th edn. Morgan Kaufmann, San Francisco (2006)
9. Khare, A., Panda, P.R., Dutt, N.D., Nicolau, A.: High-Level Synthesis with SDRAMs and RAMBUS DRAMs. IEICE Transactions on Fundamentals of Electronics, Communications, and Computer Sciences E82A(11), 2347–2355 (1999)
10. Kim, H.S., Vijaykrishnan, N., Kandemir, M., Brockmeyer, E., Catthoor, F., Irwin, M.J.: Estimating Influence of Data Layout Optimizations on SDRAM Energy Consumption. In: ISLPED 2003: Proceedings of the 2003 International Symposium on Low Power Electronics and Design, Seoul, South Korea, pp. 40–43 (2003)
11. Lengauer, C.: Loop Parallelization in the Polytope Model. In: Best, E. (ed.) CONCUR 1993. LNCS, vol. 715, pp. 398–417. Springer, Heidelberg (1993)
12. Liu, Q., Constantinides, G.A., Masselos, K., Cheung, P.Y.K.: Automatic On-chip Memory Minimization for Data Reuse. In: FCCM 2007: Proceedings of the 15th Annual IEEE Symposium on Field-Programmable Custom Computing Machines, Napa Valley, CA, USA, pp. 251–260 (2007)
13. Liu, Q., Masselos, K., Constantinides, G.A.: Data Reuse Exploration for FPGA based Platforms Applied to the Full Search Motion Estimation Algorithm. In: FPL 2006: 16th International Conference on Field Programmable Logic and Applications (2006)
14. Marchal, P., Bruni, D., Gomez, J., Benini, L., Pinuel, L., Catthoor, F., Corporaal, H.: SDRAM-Energy-Aware Memory Allocation for Dynamic Multi-Media Applications on Multi-Processor Platforms. In: DATE 2003: Proceedings of the Design, Automation and Test in Europe Conference and Exhibition, Munich, Germany, pp. 516–521 (2003)
15. Rixner, S., Dally, W.J., Kapasi, U.J., Mattson, P., Owens, J.D.: Memory Access Scheduling. In: ISCA 2000: Proceedings of the 27th Annual International Symposium on Computer Architecture, Vancouver, BC, Canada, vol. 28, pp. 128–138 (2000)

# Automatic Generation of FPGA-Specific Pipelined Accelerators

Christophe Alias, Bogdan Pasca, and Alexandru Plesco

LIP (ENSL-CNRS-Inria-UCBL), École Normale Supérieure de Lyon
46 allée d'Italie, 69364 Lyon Cedex 07, France
Firstname.Lastname@ens-lyon.fr

**Abstract.** Recent increase in the complexity of the circuits has brought high-level synthesis tools as a must in the digital circuit design. However, these tools come with several limitations, and one of them is the efficient use of pipelined arithmetic operators. This paper explains how to generate efficient hardware with floating-point pipelined operators for regular codes with perfect loop nests. The part to be mapped to the operator is identified, then the program is scheduled so that each intermediate result is produced exactly at the time it is needed by the operator, avoiding pipeline stalling and temporary buffers. Finally, we show how to generate the VHDL code for the control unit and how to link it with specialized pipelined floating-point operators generated using the open-source FloPoCo tool. The method has been implemented in the Bee research compiler and experimental results on DSP kernels show promising results with a minimum of 94% efficient utilization of the pipelined operators for a complex kernel.

## 1 Introduction

Application development tends to pack more features per product. In order to cope with competition, added features usually employ complex algorithms, making full use of existing processing power. When application performance is poor, one may envision accelerating the whole application or a computationally demanding kernel using the following solutions: (1) multi-core general purpose processor (GPP): may not accelerate non-standard computations (exponential, logarithm, square-root) (2) application-specific integrated circuit (ASIC): the price tag is often too big, (3) Field Programmable Gate Array (FPGA): provide a balance between the performance of ASIC and the costs of GPP.

FPGAs have a potential speedup over microprocessor systems that can go beyond two orders of magnitude, depending on the application. Usually, such accelerations are believed to be obtained only using low-level languages as VHDL or Verilog, exploiting the specificity of the deployment FPGA. However, designing entire systems using these languages is tedious and error-prone.

In order to address the productivity issue, much research has focused on high-level synthesis (HLS) tools [25,2,10,1,7], which input the system description in higher level language, such as C programming language (C). Unfortunately, so

A. Koch et al. (Eds.): ARC 2011, LNCS 6578, pp. 53–66, 2011.

far none of these tools come close to the speedups obtained by manual design. Moreover, these tools have important data type limitations.

In order to take advantage of the hardware carry-chains (for performing fast additions) and of the Digital Signal Processing (DSP) blocks (for performing fast multiplications) available in modern FPGAs, most HLS tools use fixed-point data types for which the operations are implemented using integer arithmetic. Adapting the fixed-point format of the computations along the datapath is possible, but requires as much expertise as expressing the computational kernel using VHDL or Verilog for a usually lower performance kernel. Keeping the same fixed-point format for all computations is also possible, but in this case either the design will overflow/underflow if the format is too small, either will largely overestimate the optimal circuit size when choosing a large-enough format.

For applications manipulating data having a wide dynamic range, HLS tools supporting standard floating-point precisions [10], or even custom precisions can be used [1]. Floating-point operators are more complex than their fixed-point counterparts. Their pipeline depth may count tens of cycles for the same frequency for which the equivalent fixed-point operator require just one cycle. Current HLS tools make use the pipelined FP operators cores in a similar fashion as for combinatorial operators, but employing stalling whenever feedback loops exists. This severely affects performance.

In this paper, we describe an automatic approach for synthesizing a specific but wide class of applications into fast FPGA designs. This approach accounts for the pipeline depth of the operator and uses state of the art code transformation techniques for scheduling computations in order to avoid pipeline stalling. We present here two classic examples: matrix multiplication and the Jacobi 1D relaxation for which we describe the computational kernels, code transformations and provide synthesis results. For these applications, simulation results show that our scheduling is within 5% of the best theoretical pipeline utilization.

The rest of this paper is organized as follows. Section 2 presents related approaches and their limitations. Section 3 presents FloPoCo, the tool used to generate efficient floating-point pipelined operators. Then, Section 4 shows how to compile a kernel written in C into efficient hardware with pipelined operators. For this, Subsection 4.2 studies two important running examples. Then, Subsections 4.3 and 4.4 provide a formal description of our method. Section 5 provides experimental results on the running examples. Finally, Section 6 concludes and presents research perspectives.

## 2   Related Work

In the last years, important advances have been made in the generation of computational accelerators from higher-level of abstraction languages. Many of these languages are limited to C-like subsets with additional extensions. The more restrictive the subset is, the more limited is the number of applications.

For example, Spark [22] can only synthesize integer datatypes, and is thus restricted to a very narrow application class.

Tools like Gaut [25], Impulse-C [2], Synphony [7] require the user to convert the floating-foint (FP) specification into a user-defined fixed-point format. Other, like Mentor Graphics' CatapultC [5], claim that this conversion is done automatically. Either way, without additional knowledge on the ranges of processed data, the determined fixed-point formats are just estimations. Spikes in the input data can cause overflows which invalidate large volumes of computations.

In order to workaround the known weaknesses of fixed-point arithmetic, AutoPilot [10] and Cynthesizer [1] (in SystemC) can synthesize FP datatypes by instantiating FP cores within the hardware accelerator. AutoPilot can instantiate IEEE-754 Single Precision (SP) and Double Precision (DP) standard FP operators. Cynthesizer can instantiate custom precision FP cores, parametrized by exponent and fraction width. Moreover, the user has control over the number of pipeline stages of the operators, having an indirect knob on the design frequency. Using these pipelined operators requires careful scheduling techniques in order to (1) ensure correct computations (2) prevent stalling the pipeline for some data dependencies. For algorithms with no data dependencies between iterations, it is indeed possible to schedule one operation per cycle, and after an initial pipeline latency, the arithmetic operators will output one result every cycle. For other algorithms, these tools manage to ensure (1) at the expense of (2). For example, in the case of algorithms having inter-iteration dependencies, the scheduler will stall successive iterations for a number of cycles equal to the pipeline latency of the operator. As said before, complex computational functions, especially FP, can have tens and even hundreds of pipeline stages, therefore significantly reducing circuit performance.

In order to address the inefficiencies of these tools regarding synthesis of pipelined (fixed or FP) circuits, we present an automation tool chain implemented in the Bee research compiler [8], and which uses FloPoCo [17], an open-source tool for FPGA-specific arithmetic-core generation, and advanced code transformation techniques for finding scheduling which eliminates pipeline stalling, therefore maximizing throughput.

# 3   FloPoCo - A Tool for Generating Computational Kernels

Two of the main factors defining the quality of an arithmetic operator on FPGAs are its *frequency* and its *size*. The frequency is determined by the length of the *critical path* – largest combinatorial delay between two register levels. Faster circuits can be obtained by iteratively inserting register levels in order to reduce the critical path delay. Consequently, there is a strong connection between the circuit frequency and its size.

Unlike other core generators [3,4], FloPoCo takes the target frequency $f$ as a parameter. As a consequence, complex designs can easily be assembled from subcomponents generated for frequency $f$. In addition, the FloPoCo operators are also optimized for several target FPGAs (most chips from Altera and Xilinx), making it easy to retarget even complex designs to new FPGAs.

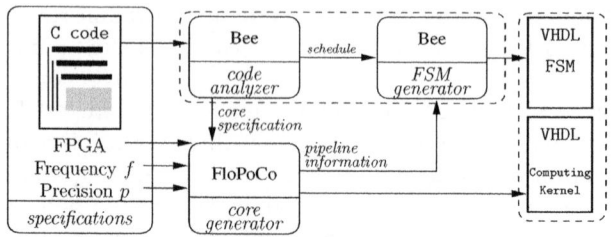

**Fig. 1.** Automation flow

However, FloPoCo is more than a generator of frequency-optimized standard FP operators. It also provides:

- operators allowing *custom precisions*. In a microprocessor, if one needs a precision of 10bits for some computation it makes sense using single-precision (8-bit exponent, 23-bit fraction) for this computation. In an FPGA one should use custom operators (10-bit fraction), yielding smaller operators and therefore being able to pack more in parallel.
- *specialized operators*, as: squarers, faithful multipliers[1], FPGA-specific FP accumulators [19].
- *elementary functions*, as: square-root [16], logarithm [15], exponential [18] which are implemented in software in processors (and are thus slow).
- dedicated architectures for *coarser operators* which have to be implemented in software in processors, for example $X^2 + Y^2 + Z^2$, and others. [17].

Part of the recipe for obtaining good FPGA accelerations for complex applications is: (a) use FPGA-specific operators, for example those provided by FloPoCo (b) exploit the application parallelism by instantiating several computational kernels working in parallel (c) generate an application-specific finite state machine (FSM) which keeps the computational kernels as busy as possible.

In the following sections we present an automatic approach for generating computational-kernel specific FSMs. Figure 1 presents the automation datapath.

## 4      Efficient Hardware Generation

This section presents the main contribution of this paper. Given an input program written in C and a pipelined FloPoCo operator, we show how to generate an equivalent hardware accelerator using cleverly the operator. This process is divided into two steps. First, we schedule the program so the pipelined operator is fed at every cycle, avoiding stalls. Then, we generate the VHDL code to control the operator with respect to the schedule. Section 4.1 defines the required terminology, then Section 4.2 explains our method on two important examples. Finally, Sections 4.3 and 4.4 present the two steps of our method.

---

[1] Have and error of 1ulp, while standard multipliers have 0.5ulp, but consume much less resources.

## 4.1   Background

**Iteration domains.** A *perfect loop nest* is an imbrication of `for` loops where each level contains either a single `for` loop or a single assignment $S$. A typical example is the matrix multiply kernel given in figure 2(a). Writing $i_1, ..., i_n$ the loop counters, the vector $i = (i_1, ..., i_n)$ is called an *iteration vector*. The set of iteration vectors $i$ reached during an execution of the kernel is called an *iteration domain* (see figure 2(b)). The execution instance of $S$ at the iteration $i$ is called an *operation* and is denoted by the couple $(S, i)$. We will assume a single assignment in the loop nest, so we can forget $S$ and say "iteration" for "operation". The ability to produce program analysis at the *operation level* rather than at *assignment level* is a key point of our automation method. We assume loop bounds and array indices to be an *affine expression* of the surrounding loop counters. Under these restrictions, the iteration domain $\mathcal{I}$ is an invariant polytope. This property makes possible to design a program analysis by means of integer linear programming (ILP) techniques.

**Dependence vectors.** A data dependence is *uniform* if it occurs from the iteration $i$ to the iteration $i + d$ for every valid iterations $i$ and $i + d$. In this case, we can represent the data dependence with the vector $d$ that we call a *dependence vector*. When array indices are themselves uniform (*e.g.* $a[i-1]$) all the dependencies are uniform. In the following, we will restrict to this case and we will denote by $\mathcal{D} = \{d_1, ... d_p\}$ the set of dependence vectors. Many numerical kernels fit or can be restructured to fit in this model [11]. This particularly includes stencil operations which are widely used in signal processing.

**Schedules and hyperplanes.** A *schedule* is a function $\theta$ which maps each point of $\mathcal{I}$ to its execution date. Usually, it is convenient to represent execution dates by integral vectors ordered by the lexicographic order: $\theta : \mathcal{I} \to (\mathbb{N}^q, \ll)$. We consider *linear schedules* $\theta(i) = Ui$ where $U$ is an integral matrix. If there is a dependence from an iteration $i$ to an iteration $j$, then $i$ must be executed before $j$: $\theta(i) \ll \theta(j)$. With uniform dependencies, this gives $Ud \gg 0$ for each dependence vector $d \in \mathcal{D}$. Each line $\phi$ of $U$ can be seen as the normal vector to an affine hyperplane $H_\phi$, the iteration domain being scanned by translating the hyperplanes $H_\phi$ in the lexicographic ordering. An hyperplane $H_\phi$ *satisfies* a dependence vector $d$ if by translating $H_\phi$ in the direction of $\phi$, the source $i$ is touched before the target $i + d$ for each $i$, that is if $\phi.d > 0$. We say that $H_\phi$ *preserves* the dependence $d$ if $\phi.d \geq 0$ for each dependence vector $d$. In that case, the source and the target can be touched at the same iteration. $d$ must then be solved by a subsequent hyperplane. We can always find an hyperplane $H_\tau$ satisfying all the dependencies. Any translation of $H_\tau$ touches in $\mathcal{I}$ a subset of iterations which can be executed in parallel. In the literature, $H_\tau$ is usually refereed as a *parallel hyperplane*.

**Loop tiling.** With loop tiling [23,27], the iteration domain of a loop nest is partitioned into parallelogram tiles, which are executed atomically. A first tile is executed, then another tile, and so on. For a loop nest of depth $n$, this requires to generate a loop nest of depth $2n$, the first $n$ *inter-tile* loops describing the different tiles and the next $n$ *intra-tile* loops scanning the current tile. A *tile slice* is the 2D set of iterations described by the last two intra-tile loops for a given value of outer loops. See figure 2 for an illustration on the matrix multiply example. We can specify a loop tiling for a perfect loop nest of depth $n$ with a collection of affine hyperplanes $(H_1, \ldots, H_n)$. The vector $\phi_k$ is the normal to the hyperplane $H_k$ and the vectors $\phi_1, \ldots, \phi_n$ are supposed to be linearly independent. Then, the iteration domain of the loop nest can be tiled with regular translations of the hyperplanes keeping the same distance $\ell_k$ between two translation of the same hyperplane $H_k$. The iterations executed in a tile follow the hyperplanes in the lexicographic order, it can be view as "tiling of the tile" with $\ell_k = 1$ for each $k$. A tiling $\mathcal{H} = (H_1, \ldots, H_n)$ is *valid* if each normal vector $\phi_k$ preserves all the dependencies: $\phi_k.d \geq 0$ for each dependence vector $d$. As the hyperplanes $H_k$ are linearly independent, all the dependencies will be satisfied. The tiling $\mathcal{H}$ can be represented by a matrix $U_{\mathcal{H}}$ whose lines are $\phi_1, \ldots \phi_n$. As the intra-tile execution order must follow the direction of the tiling hyperplanes, $U_{\mathcal{H}}$ also specifies the execution order for each tile.

**Dependence distance.** The *distance* of a dependence $d$ at the iteration $i$ is the number of iterations executed between the source iteration $i$ and the target iteration $i + d$. Dependence distances are sometimes called *reuse distances* because both source and target access the same memory element. It is easy to see that *in a full tile*, the distance for a given dependence $d$ does not depend on the source iteration $i$ (see figure 3(b)). Thus, we can write it $\Delta(d)$. However, the program schedule can strongly impact the dependence distance. There is a strong connection between dependence distance and pipeline depth, as we will see in the next section.

## 4.2   Motivating Examples

In this section we illustrate the feasibility of our approach on two examples. The first example is the matrix-matrix multiplication, that has one uniform data dependency that propagates along one axis. The second example is the Jacobi 1D algorithm. It is more complicated because it has three uniform data dependencies with different distances.

**Matrix-Matrix Multiplication.** The original code is given in Figure 2(a). The iteration domain is the set integral points lying into a cube of size N, as shown in Figure 2(b). Each point of the iteration domain represents an execution of the assignment S with the corresponding values for the loop counters i, j and k. Essentially, the computation boils down to apply sequentially a multiply and accumulate operation $(x, y, z) \mapsto x + (y * z)$ that we want to implement with a specialized FloPoCo operator (Fig. 4(a)). It consists of a pipelined multiplier with $\ell$ pipeline stages that multiplies the elements of matrices a and b. In order to eliminate the step initializing c, the constant value is propagated inside loop k. In other words, for $k = 0$ the multiplication result is added with a constant value 0 (when the delayed control signal S is 0). For $k > 0$, the multiplication result

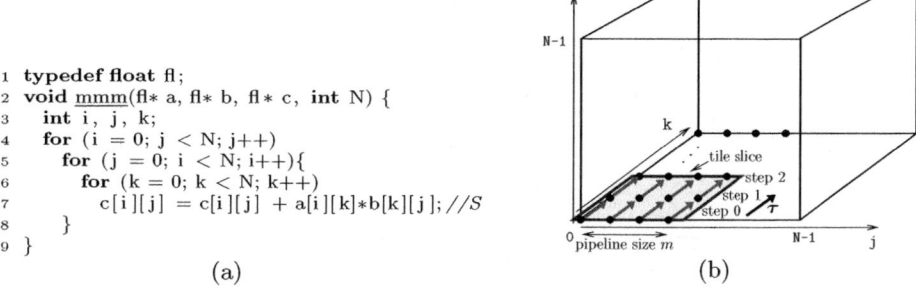

```
1  typedef float fl;
2  void mmm(fl* a, fl* b, fl* c, int N) {
3    int i, j, k;
4    for (i = 0; j < N; j++)
5      for (j = 0; i < N; i++){
6        for (k = 0; k < N; k++)
7          c[i][j] = c[i][j] + a[i][k]*b[k][j]; //S
8      }
9  }
```

(a)                                    (b)

**Fig. 2.** Matrix-matrix multiplication: (a) C code, (b) iteration domain with tiling

is accumulated with the current sum, available *via* the feedback loop (when the delayed control signal S is 1). This result will be available $m$ cycles later ($m$ is the adder pipeline depth), for the next accumulation.

There is a unique data dependency carried by the loop k, which can be expressed as a vector $d = (i_d, j_d, k_d) = (0, 0, 1)$ (Fig. 2(b)). The sequential execution of the original code would not exploit at all the pipeline, causing a stall of $m - 1$ cycles for each iteration of the loop k due to operator pipelining. Indeed, the iteration $(0, 0, 0)$ would be executed, then wait $m - 1$ cycles for the result to be available, then the iteration $(0, 0, 1)$ would be executed, and so on.

Now, let us consider the parallel hyperplane $H_\tau$ with $\tau = (0, 0, 1)$, which satisfies the data dependency $d$. Each iteration on this hyperplane can be executed in parallel, independently, so it is possible to insert in the arithmetic operator pipeline one computation every cycle. At iteration $(0, 0, 0)$, the operator can be fed with the inputs $x = $ c[0][0]=0, $y = $ a[0][0], $z = $ b[0][0]. Then, at iteration $(0, 1, 0)$, $x = $ c[0][1]=0, $y = $ a[0][0], $z = $ b[0][1], and so on. In this case, the dependence distance would be $N - 1$, which means that the data computed by each iteration is needed $N - 1$ cycles later. This is normally much larger than the pipeline latency $m$ of the adder and would require additional temporary storage. To avoid this, we have to transform the program in such a way that: between the definition of a variable at iteration $i$ and its use at iteration $i + d$ there are exactly $m$ cycles, i.e. $\Delta(d) = m$.

The method consists on applying tiling techniques to reduce the dependence distance (Fig. 2(b)). First, as previously presented, we find a parallel hyperplane $H_\tau$ (here $\tau = (0, 0, 1)$). Then, we complete it into a valid tiling by choosing two hyperplanes $H_1$ and $H_2$ (here, the normal vectors are $(1, 0, 0)$ and $(0, 1, 0)$), $\mathcal{H} = (H_1, H_2, H_\tau)$. Basically, on this example, the tile width along $H_2$ is exactly $\Delta(d)$. Thus, it suffices to set it to the pipeline depth $m$. This ensures that the result is scheduled to be used exactly at the cycle it gets out of the operator pipeline. Thus, the result can be used immediately with the feedback connection, without any temporary buffering. In a way, the pipeline registers of the arithmetic operator are used as a temporary buffer.

```
1  typedef float fl;
2  void jacobild(fl a[T][N]){
3    fl b[T][N];
4    int i,t;
5    for (t = 0; t < T; t++){
6      for (i = 1; i < N−1; i++)
7        a[t][i] = (a[t−1][i−1] + a[t−1][i] + a[t−1][i+1])/3;
8  }}
```

(a)

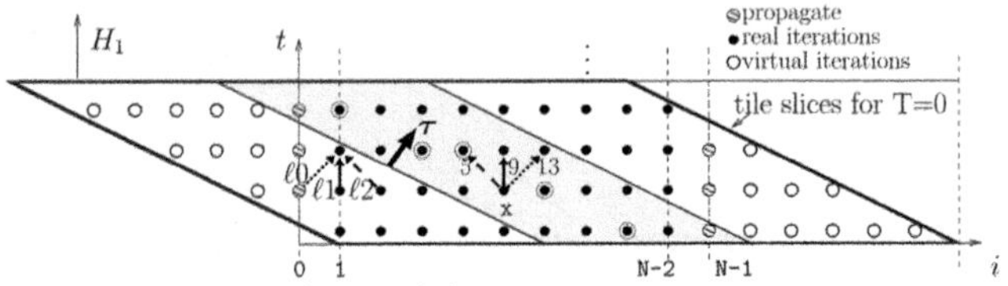

(b)

**Fig. 3.** Jacobi 1D: (a) source code, (b) iteration domain with tiling

**Jacobi 1D.** The kernel is given in Figure 3(a)). This is a standard stencil computation with two nested loops. This example is more complex because the set of dependence vectors $\mathcal{D}$ contain several dependencies $\mathcal{D} = \{d_1 = (-1,1), d_2 = (0,1), d_3 = (1,1)\}$ (Fig. 3(b)). We apply the same tiling method as in the previous example. First, we choose a valid parallel hyperplane $H_\tau$, with $\tau = (t_\tau, i_\tau) = (2,1)$. $H_\tau$ satisfies all the data dependencies of $\mathcal{D}$. Then, we complete $H_\tau$ with a valid tiling hyperplane $H_1$. Here, $H_1$ can be chosen with the normal vector $(1,0)$. The final tiled loop nest will have four loops: two inter-tile loops T and I iterating over the tiles, and two intra-tile loops tt and ii iterating into the current tile of coordinate (T,I). Therefore, any iteration vector can be expressed as (T,I,tt,ii). Figure 3(b) shows the consecutive tile slices with T=0. The resulting schedule is valid because it respects the data dependencies of $\mathcal{D}$. The data produced at iteration $i$ must be available 5 iterations later *via* the dependence $d_1$, 9 iterations later *via* dependency $d_2$ and 13 iterations later *via* the dependence $d_3$. Notice that the dependence distances are the same for any point of the iteration domain, as the dependencies are uniform. In hardware, this translates to add delay shift registers at the operator output and connect this output to the operator input *via* feedback lines, after data dependency distances levels $\ell_0$, $\ell_1$ and $\ell_2$ (see Fig. 3(b)). Once again, the intermediate values are kept in the pipeline, no additional storage is needed on a slice.

As the tiling hyperplanes are not parallel to the original axis, some tiles in the borders are not full parallelograms (see left and right triangle from Fig. 3(b)). Inside these tiles, the dependence vectors are not longer constant. To overcome this issue, we extend the iteration domain with virtual iteration points where the pipelined operator will compute dummy data. This data is discarded at the border between the real and extended iteration domains (propagate iterations, when $i = 0$ and $i = N - 1$). For the border cases, the correctly delayed data is fed via line Q (oS=1).

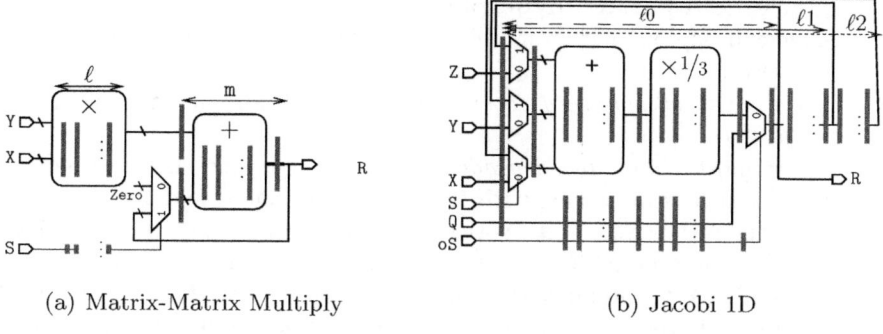

(a) Matrix-Matrix Multiply   (b) Jacobi 1D

**Fig. 4.** Computational kernels generated using FloPoCo

The two next sections formalize the ideas presented intuitively on motivating examples and presents an algorithm in two steps to translate a loop kernel written in C into an hardware accelerator using pipelined operators efficiently. Section 4.3 explains how to get the tiling. Then, section 4.4 explains how to generate the control FSM respecting the schedule induced by the loop tiling.

### 4.3 Step 1: Scheduling the Kernel

The key idea is to tile the program in such a way that each dependence distance can be customized by playing on the tile size. Then, it is always possible to set the minimum dependence distance to the pipelined depth of the FloPoCo operator, and to handle the remaining dependencies with additional (pipeline) registers in the way described for the Jacobi 1D example.

The idea presented on the motivating examples is to force the last intra-tile inner loop $L_{par}$ to be parallel. This way, for a fixed value of the outer loop counters, there will be no dependence among iterations of $L_{par}$. The dependencies will all be carried by the outer-loop, and then, the dependence distances will be fully customizable by playing with the tile size associated to the loop enclosing immediately $L_{par}$, $L_{it}$.

This amounts to find a parallel hyperplane $H_\tau$ (step a), and to complete with others hyperplanes forming a valid tiling (step b): $H_1, \ldots, H_{n-1}$, assuming the depth of the loop kernel is $n$. Now, it is easy to see that the hyperplane $H_\tau$ should be the $(n-1)$-th hyperplane (implemented by $L_{it}$), any hyperplane $H_i$ being the last one (implemented by $L_{par}$). Roughly speaking, $L_{it}$ pushes $H_\tau$, and $L_{par}$ traverses the current 1D section of $H_\tau$.

It remains in step c to compute the tile size to fit the fixed FloPoCo operator pipeline depth. If several dependencies exist, the minimum dependence distance must be set to the pipeline depth of the operator, and the other distances gives the number of extra shift registers to be added to the operator to keep the results within the operator pipeline, as seen with the Jacobi 1D example. These three steps are detailed thereafter.

## Step a. Find a parallel hyperplane $H_\tau$

This can be done with a simple integer linear program (ILP). Here are the constraints:

- $\tau$ must *satisfy every dependence*: $\tau \cdot d > 0$ for each dependence vector $d \in \mathcal{D}$.
- $\tau$ must *reduce the dependence distances*. Notice that the dependence distance is increasing with the radius between $\tau$, and the corresponding dependence vector $d$. Notice that the radius $(\tau, d)$ is decreasing with the dot product $\tau \cdot d$, and thus increasing with $-(\tau \cdot d)$. Thus, it is sufficient to minimize the quantity $q = \max(-(\tau \cdot d_1), \ldots, -(\tau \cdot d_p))$. So, we build the constraints $q \geq -(\tau \cdot d_k)$ for each $k$ between 1 and $p$, which is equivalent to $q \geq \max(-(\tau \cdot d_1), \ldots, -(\tau \cdot d_p))$.

With this formulation, the set of valid vectors $\tau$ is an affine cone and the vectors minimizing $q$ tends to have an infinite norm. To overcome this issue, we first minimize the coordinates of $\tau$, which amounts to minimize their sum $\sigma$, as they are supposed to be positive. Then, for the minimum value of $\sigma$, we minimize $q$. This amounts to look for the *lexicographic minimum of the vector* $(\sigma, q)$. This can be done with standard ILP techniques [21]. On the Jacobi 1D example, this gives the following ILP, with $\tau = (x, y)$:

$$
\begin{aligned}
\min{}_{\ll} & \;(x + y, q) \\
\text{s.t.} & \;(x \geq 0) \wedge (y \geq 0) \\
& \wedge (y - x > 0) \wedge (y > 0) \wedge (x + y > 0) \\
& \wedge (q \geq x - y) \wedge (q \geq -y) \wedge (q \geq -x - y)
\end{aligned}
$$

## Step b. Find the remaining tiling hyperplanes

Let us assume a nesting depth of $n$, and let us assume that $p < n$ tiling hyperplanes $H_\tau, H_{\phi_1}, \ldots, H_{\phi_{p-1}}$ were already found. We can compute a vector $u$ orthogonal to the vector space spanned by $\tau, \phi_1, \ldots, \phi_{p-1}$ using the internal inverse method [12]. Then, the new tiling hyperplane vector $\phi_p$ can be built by means of ILP techniques with the following constraints.

- $\phi_p$ must be a *valid tiling hyperplane*: $\phi_p.d \geq 0$ for every dependence vector $d \in \mathcal{D}$.
- $\phi_p$ must be *linearly independent* to the other hyperplanes: $\phi_p.u \neq 0$. Formally, the two cases $\phi_p.u > 0$ and $\phi_p.u < 0$ should be investigated. As we just expect the tiling hyperplanes to be valid, without any optimality criteria, we can restrict to the case $\phi_p.u > 0$ to get a single ILP.

Any solution of this ILP gives a valid tiling hyperplane. Starting from $H_\tau$, and applying repeatedly the process, we get valid loop tiling hyperplanes $\mathcal{H} = (H_{\phi_1}, \ldots, H_{\phi_{n-2}}, H_\tau, H_{\phi_{n-1}})$ and the corresponding tiling matrix $U_\mathcal{H}$. It is possible to add an objective function to reduce the amount of communication between tiles. Many approaches give a partial solution to this problem in the context of automatic parallelization and high performance computing [12,24,27]. However how to adapt them in our context is not straightforward and is left for future work.

## Step c. Compute the dependence distances

Given a dependence vector $d$ and an iteration $x$ in a tile slice the set of iterations $i$ executed between $x$ and $x + d$ is exactly:

$$D(x, d) = \{i \mid U_{\mathcal{H}}x \ll U_{\mathcal{H}}i \ll U_{\mathcal{H}}(x + d)\}$$

Remember that $U_{\mathcal{H}}$, the tiling matrix computed in the previous step, is also the intra-tile schedule matrix. By construction, $D(x, d)$ is a finite union of integral polyhedron. Now, the dependence distance $\Delta(d)$ is exactly the number of integral points in $D(x, d)$. As the dependence distance are constant, this quantity does *not* depend on $x$. The number of integral points in a polyhedron can be computed with the Ehrhart polynomial method [14] which is implemented in the polyhedral library [6]. Here, the result is a degree 1 polynomial in the tile size $\ell_{n-2}$ associated to the hyperplane $H_{n-2}$, $\Delta(d) = \alpha \ell_{n-2} + \beta$. Then, given a fixed input pipeline depth $\delta$ for the FloPoCo operator, two cases can arise:

- Either we just have *one dependence*, $\mathcal{D} = \{d\}$. Then, solve $\Delta(d) = \delta$ to obtain the right tile size $\ell_{n-2}$.
- Either we have *several dependencies*, $\mathcal{D} = \{d_1, \ldots, d_p\}$. Then, choose the dependence vectors with smallest $\alpha$, and among them choose a dependence vector $d_m$ with a smallest $\beta$. Solve $\Delta(d_m) = \delta$ to obtain the right tile size $\ell_{n-2}$. Replacing $\ell_{n-2}$ by its actual value gives the remaining dependence distances $\Delta(d_i)$ for $i \neq m$, that can be sorted by increasing order and used to add additional pipeline registers to the FloPoCo operator in the way described for the Jacobi 1D example (see figure 4(b)).

### 4.4   Step 2: Generating the Control FSM

This section explains how to generate the FSM that will control the pipelined operator according to the schedule computed in the previous section. A direct hardware generation of loops, would produce multiple synchronized Finite State Machines (FSMs), each FSM having an initialization time (initialize the counters) resulting in an operator stall on every iteration of the outer loops. We avoid this problem by using the Boulet-Feautrier algorithm [13] which generates a FSM whose states are assignments and whose transitions update the loop counters. The method takes as input the tiled iteration domain and the scheduling matrix $U_{\mathcal{H}}$ and uses ILP techniques to generate two functions: First() and Next(). The function First() is actually a constant function, returning the initial state of the FSM with initialized loop counters. The function Next is a transition function which updates the loop counters and gives the next state.

The functions First() and Next() are directly translated into VHDL if conditions. When the conditions are satisfied, the corresponding iterators are updated and the control signals are set.

The signal assignments in the FSM do not take into account the pipeline level at which the signals are connected. Therefore, we use additional registers to delay every control signal with respect to its pipeline depth. This ensures a correct execution without increasing the complexity of the state machine.

## 5   Reality Check

Table 1 presents synthesis results for both our running examples, using a large range of precisions, and two different FPGAs. The results presented confirm that precision selection plays an important role in determining the maximum number of operators to be packed on one FPGA. As it can be remarked from the table, our automation approach is both flexible (several precisions) and portable (Virtex5 and StratixIII), while preserving good frequency characteristics.

**Table 1.** Synthesis results for the full (including FSM) MMM and Jacobi1D codes. Results obtained using using Xilinx ISE 11.5 for Virtex5, and Quartus 9.0 for StratixIII.

| Application | FPGA | Precision $(w_E, w_F)$ | Latency (cycles) | Frequency (MHz) | REG | (A)LUT | DSPs |
|---|---|---|---|---|---|---|---|
| Matrix-Matrix Multiply N=128 | Virtex5(-3) | (5,10) | 11 | 277 | 320 | 526 | 1 |
| | | (8,23) | 15 | 281 | 592 | 864 | 2 |
| | | (10,40) | 14 | 175 | 978 | 2098 | 4 |
| | | (11,52) | 15 | 150 | 1315 | 2122 | 8 |
| | | (15,64) | 15 | 189 | 1634 | 4036 | 8 |
| | StratixIII | (5,10) | 12 | 276 | 399 | 549 | 2 |
| | | (9,36) | 12 | 218 | 978 | 2098 | 4 |
| Jacobi1D stencil N=1024 T=1024 | Virtex5(-3) | (5,10) | 98 | 255 | 770 | 1013 | |
| | | (8,23) | 98 | 250 | 1559 | 1833 | |
| | | (15,64) | 98 | 147 | 3669 | 4558 | |
| | StratixIII | (5,10) | 98 | 284 | 1141 | 1058 | |
| | | (9,36) | 98 | 261 | 2883 | 2266 | |
| | | (15,64) | 98 | 199 | 4921 | 3978 | |

The generated kernel performance for one computing kernel is: 0.4 GFLOPs for matrix-matrix multiplication, and 0.56 GFLOPs for Jacobi, for a 200 MHz clock frequency. Thanks to program restructuring and optimized scheduling in the generated FSM, the pipelined kernels are used with very high efficiency. Here, the efficiency can be defined as the percentage of useful (non-virtual) inputs fed to the pipelined operator. This can be expressed as the ratio $\#(\mathcal{I}\setminus\mathcal{V})/\#\mathcal{I}$, where $\mathcal{I}$ is the iteration domain, as defined in section 4 and $\mathcal{V}\subseteq\mathcal{I}$ is the set of virtual iterations. The efficiency represents more than 99% for matrix-multiply, and more than 94% for Jacobi 1D. Taking into account the kernel size and operating frequencies, tens, even hundreds of pipelined operators can be packed per FPGA, resulting in significant potential speedups.

There exists several manual approaches like the one described in [20] that presents a manually implemented acceleration of matrix-matrix multiplication on FPGAs. Unfortunately, the paper lacks of detailed experimental results, so we are unable to perform correct performance comparisons. Our approach is fully automated, and we can clearly point important performance optimization. To store intermediate results, there approach makes a systematic use of local SRAM memory, whereas we rely on pipeline registers to minimize the use of local SRAM memory. As concerns commercial HLS tools, the comparison is made difficult due to lack of clear documentation as well as software availability to academics.

## 6 Conclusion and Future Work

In this paper, we have presented a novel approach using state-of-the-art code transformation techniques to restructure the program in order to use more efficiently pipelined operators. Our HLS flow has been implemented in the research compiler Bee, using FloPoCo to generate specialized pipelined floating point arithmetic operators. We have applied our method on two DSP kernels, the obtained circuits have a very high pipelined operator utilization and high operating frequencies, even for algorithms with tricky data dependencies and operating on high precision floating point numbers.

It would be interesting to extend our technique to non-perfect loop nests. This would require more general tiling techniques as those described in [12]. As for many other HLS tools, the HLS flow described in this paper focuses only on optimizing the performances of the computational part. However, experience shows that the performance is often bounded by the availability of data. In future work we plan to focus on local memory usage optimizations by minimizing the communication betweeen the tiles. This can be obtained by chosing a tile orientation to minimize the number of dependencies that crosses the hyperplane. This problem has been partially solved in the context of HPC [24,12]. However, it is unclear how to apply it in our context. Also, we would like to focus on global memory usage optimizations by adapting the work presented in [9] and [26] to optimize communications with the outside world in a complete system design. Finally, we believe that the scheduling technique can be extended to apply several pipelined operators in parallel.

## References

1. Forte design system: Cynthesizer, http://www.forteds.com
2. Impulse-C, http://www.impulseaccelerated.com
3. ISE 11.4 CORE Generator IP, http://www.xilinx.com
4. MegaWizard Plug-In Manager, http://www.altera.com
5. Mentor CatapultC high-level synthesis, http://www.mentor.com
6. Polylib – A library of polyhedral functions, http://www.irisa.fr/polylib
7. Synopsys: Synphony, http://www.synopsys.com/
8. Alias, C., Baray, F., Darte, A.: Bee+Cl@k: An implementation of lattice-based memory reuse in the source-to-source translator ROSE. In: ACM SIGPLAN/SIGBED Conference on Languages, Compilers, and Tools for Embedded Systems, LCTES (2007)
9. Alias, C., Darte, A., Plesco, A.: Optimizing DDR-SDRAM communications at C-level for automatically-generated hardware accelerators. An experience with the Altera C2H HLS tool. In: IEEE International Conference on Application-specific Systems, Architectures and Processors, ASAP (2010)
10. AutoESL: Autopilot datasheet (2009)

11. Bastoul, C., Cohen, A., Girbal, S., Sharma, S., Temam, O.: Putting polyhedral loop transformations to work. In: Rauchwerger, L. (ed.) LCPC 2003. LNCS, vol. 2958, pp. 209–225. Springer, Heidelberg (2004)
12. Bondhugula, U., Hartono, A., Ramanujam, J., Sadayappan, P.: A practical automatic polyhedral parallelizer and locality optimizer. In: ACM International Conference on Programming Languages Design and Implementation, PLDI (2008)
13. Boulet, P., Feautrier, P.: Scanning polyhedra without Do-loops. In: IEEE International Conference on Parallel Architectures and Compilation Techniques, PACT (1998)
14. Clauss, P.: Counting solutions to linear and nonlinear constraints through Ehrhart polynomials: Applications to analyze and transform scientific programs. In: ACM International Conference on Supercomputing, ICS (1996)
15. de Dinechin, F.: A flexible floating-point logarithm for reconfigurable computers. Lip research report RR2010-22, ENS-Lyon (2010), http://prunel.ccsd.cnrs.fr/ensl-00506122/
16. de Dinechin, F., Joldes, M., Pasca, B., Revy, G.: Multiplicative square root algorithms for FPGAs. In: Field Programmable Logic and Applications. IEEE, Los Alamitos (2010)
17. de Dinechin, F., Klein, C., Pasca, B.: Generating high-performance custom floating-point pipelines. In: Field Programmable Logic and Applications. IEEE, Los Alamitos (2009)
18. de Dinechin, F., Pasca, B.: Floating-point exponential functions for DSP-enabled FPGAs. In: Field Programmable Technologies. IEEE, Los Alamitos (2010), http://prunel.ccsd.cnrs.fr/ensl-00506125/
19. de Dinechin, F., Pasca, B., Creţ, O., Tudoran, R.: An FPGA-specific approach to floating-point accumulation and sum-of-products. In: Field-Programmable Technologies. IEEE, Los Alamitos (2008)
20. Dou, Y., Vassiliadis, S., Kuzmanov, G.K., Gaydadjiev, G.N.: 64-bit floating-point fpga matrix multiplication. In: ACM/SIGDA symposium on Field-Programmable Gate Arrays, FPGA (2005)
21. Feautrier, P.: Parametric integer programming. RAIRO Recherche Opérationnelle 22(3), 243–268 (1988)
22. Gupta, S., Dutt, N., Gupta, R., Nicolau, A.: Spark: A high-level synthesis framework for applying parallelizing compiler transformations. In: International Conference on VLSI Design (2003)
23. Irigoin, F., Triolet, R.: Supernode partitioning. In: 15th ACM SIGPLAN-SIGACT Symposium on Principles of Programming Languages, POPL (1988)
24. Lim, A.W., Lam, M.S.: Maximizing parallelism and minimizing synchronization with affine transforms. In: 24th ACM SIGPLAN-SIGACT Symposium on Principles of Programming Languages, POPL (1997)
25. Martin, E., Sentieys, O., Dubois, H., Philippe, J.L.: Gaut: An architectural synthesis tool for dedicated signal processors. In: Design Automation Conference with EURO-VHDL 1993, EURO-DAC (1993)
26. Plesco, A.: Program Transformations and Memory Architecture Optimizations for High-Level Synthesis of Hardware Accelerators. Ph.D. thesis, École Normale Supérieure de Lyon (2010)
27. Xue, J.: Loop Tiling for Parallelism. Kluwer Academic Publishers, Dordrecht (2000)

# HLS Tools for FPGA: Faster Development with Better Performance

Alexandre Cornu[1,2], Steven Derrien[2,3], and Dominique Lavenier[1,4,5]

[1] IRISA, Rennes, France
[2] INRIA, Rennes, France
[3] Université de Rennes 1, Rennes, France
[4] CNRS
[5] ENS Cachan Bretagne

**Abstract.** Designing FPGA-based accelerators is a difficult and time-consuming task which can be softened by the emergence of new generations of High Level Synthesis Tools. This paper describes how the ImpulseC C-to-hardware compiler tool has been used to develop efficient hardware for a known genomic sequence alignment algorithms and reports HLL designs performance outperforming traditional hand written optimized HDL implementations.

**Keywords:** ImpulseC, High Level Synthesis Tool, Hardware Accelerator, FPGA.

## 1 Introduction

FPGA density is increasing exponentially in such a way that the number of gates is approximately doubling every two years. Consequently, very complex designs can consequently be integrated into a single FPGA component, which can now be considered as high computing power accelerators. However, pushing processing into such devices leads to important development time and design reliability issues. Recently, many efforts have been done to help FPGA-targeted application designers to deal with such huge amount of resources. In particular, Electronic System Level tools provide higher levels of abstraction than traditional HDL design flow. Several High Level Languages (HLL) for modeling complex systems, and corresponding High Level Synthesis (HLS) Tools to translate HLL-designs into HDL synthesizable projects are now available.

Most of them are based on a subset of C/C++ [1] generally extended with specific types or I/O capabilities. This paper focuses on ImpulseC [3] and its associated design flow proposed by Impulse Accelerated Technologies. It also gives feedback in the context of high performance hardware accelerator design.

Experimentations have been conducted on a specific family of algorithms coming from bioinformatics and which are known to have highly efficient parallelization on FPGA. More specifically, in this work, genomic sequence comparison algorithms are considered. As a matter of fact, many efforts have been done to parallelize these algorithms, providing many optimized implementations which can be used as references [6,9,7,5].

A. Koch et al. (Eds.): ARC 2011, LNCS 6578, pp. 67–78, 2011.

In this paper, we detail how ImpulseC has been used to quickly implement parallel systolic architectures. Even if here, only a single application is considered (genomic sequence comparison), the methodology we followed can obviously be extended to many other algorithms with efficient implementation on systolic array, or more generally, implementation on massively parallel architectures. To achieve reasonable performance, standard optimizations such as loop pipelining or process splitting need however to be done. The use of HLL provides an easy way to perform these optimizations, together with a fast development cycle time. However, to obtain high performance, designers have to bypass ImpulseC restrictions and perform complex program transformations.

The experiments presented in this paper show that an HLL-designed accelerator can outperform optimized HDL designs. This can be first achieved by rapidly exploring several architectural variations without great efforts compared to HDL specifications. Second, this is also achieved by the use of high level code transformations allowing the designer to generate code which better fit to HLS tool input.

The paper is organized as follows: the first section briefly describes the HLS tool we have used : ImpulseC and gives some background on the parallelization scheme used for our target genomic sequence comparison algorithm. Section 3 presents our design strategy. Performances are finally detailed in section 4, in terms of code transformation efficiency, hardware accelerator performance, and design process.

## 2    HLS Tool, Algorithm and Parallelization

### 2.1    ImpulseC

ImpulseC is a high level language based on ANSI C. It has a few restrictions, mainly on structure and pointer usage. On the other hand, it includes libraries to define constructor functions, bit-accurate data types and communication functions.

Two levels of parallelism are available: (1) coarse grain parallelism, by implementing several ImpulseC processes that can communicate through streams, signals or registers; (2) fine grain operator parallelism, within one process or one process loop, through the use of instruction pipelining and data flow parallelism.

Each process can be set as hardware process, meaning it will be hard-wired, or as software process, meaning its sequential code will be executed on a processor. Implementation of streams between hardware and software processes are managed by specific PSP (Platform Support Package). Here, two different PSP have been used : the Nios2 softcore and the XD2000i development platform.

The development environment (IDE) is called CoDevelopper. Designer can perform software simulation, generate HDL for a specific platform through the use of ImpulseC compiler, analyze ImpulseC compiler report through the Stage Master Explorer tool or generate HDL simulation testbench with the CoValidator tool.

## 2.2   Algorithm

The goal of genomic sequence comparison algorithms is to identify similarities
between genomic sequences for discovering functional, structural or evolutionary
relationships. Similarities are detected by computing sequence alignments which
generally represent the main time consuming part. A score is attached to each
alignment and represents the number of matches between 2 sequences. The exact
method for computing alignments between 2 sequences is based on dynamic programming (DP) algorithms. These algorithms have been abundantly described
in the literature and we just give the main idea. Basically, DP algorithms consist
in computing a matrix of size $N \times M$ where $N$ and $M$ are respectively the sizes
of the genomic sequences. The following recurrent equation explains how to fill
the matrix:

$$S(i,j) = max \begin{cases} S(i-1, j-1) + sub(x_i, y_j) \\ S(i-1, j) - gap\_penalty() \\ S(i, j-1) - gap\_penalty() \end{cases}$$

$1 \leq i \leq N, 1 \leq j \leq M$

$x_i$ and $y_j$ are respectively elements of sequences $X\{x_1 \ldots x_N\}$ and $Y\{y_1 \ldots y_M\}$;
$sub()$ refers to a substitution cost. The final score is given by $S(N, M)$. From this
basic equation many variations can be elaborated to compute different types of
alignments. But, the main structure remains and the same parallelizing scheme
can be applied to all.

## 2.3   Parallelization

Data dependencies are illustrated in figure 1. Note that computation of cells that
belong to the same diagonal are independent and can be computed in the same
time. This very regular and fine grained parallelization leads to a systolic array
architecture: each Processing Element (PE) is affected to a sequence character
$X$; then sequence $Y$ crosses the array, character by character; after $M$ steps,
all $N \times M$ values have been computed. Again, a large literature is available on
this topic. Interested readers can refer to the work of Lavenier[2] for a complete
overview of systolic architectures for genomic sequence comparison.

Using systolic architectures requires two separate phases: a initialization step
and a computational step. The first step pushes a query sequence into the systolic
array in such a way that one PE store one character. The second step pushes
several sequences from a bank, character by character, to the systolic array.

# 3   Design Methodology and Architecture Description

The overall architecture is based on very simple two-processes structure
(Figure 2(1)): A first ImpulseC process (Server) generates sequences; the second
process (Master) computes alignments. Both processes exchange data through

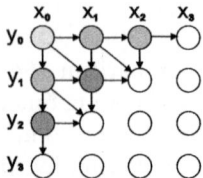

**Fig. 1.** Data Dependency for Similarity Matrix Computation

two streams: one carrying sequences, and the other sending back the scores related to the alignments.

The Server process has been first hardwired (release 1), then implemented on the Nios2 softcore processor (release 2, 3) and, latter on, to the XtremeData Xeon processor (cf. subsection 4.1).

The initial Master process has been split into two entities: a systolic array and a controller entity (still called Master), which has been iteratively split into many simple but optimized processes. Finally, as implementing too many small independent processes was leading to a waste of resources, PEs have been clustered. This architecture evolution is detailed in the following subsections.

## 3.1   Systolic Array Design

Processing Element (PE) have been designed to constitute a 1-D systolic array. Each PE is described as an independent ImpulseC process and performs computation of one column of the matrix (one cell per PE per loop iteration). The Master process feed the first PE of the array and get results from the last one (Figure 2(2)). A PE has 3 pairs of stream interfaces, allowing it to read values from previous PE and forwarding values to the next one. Streams $score_i$, $score_o$, are carrying scores from previous PE and to next PE. Both sequence stream pairs $x_i$, $x_o$ and $y_i$, $y_o$ are carrying sequences, character by character. For sake of clarity, two different streams are shown. Actually, a single time-sharing stream is implemented as there are no concurrent read/write operations.

To compute one cell (current score : $score_C$), one PE need to have: the upper cell's score ($score_U$), the left cell's score ($score_L$), the upper-left cell's score ($score_{UL}$), and the two characters $X_C$ and $Y_C$.

Algorithm 1 describes PE behavior. This description is the input of the ImpulseC compiler to provide an FPGA implementation. Timing isn't specified and is automatically deduced by the ImpulseC compiler from data dependencies. Actually, real code is a little bit more complex, as it contains initialization (not represented here) and it considers more complex alignment computation.

## 3.2   Design Optimizations

This section explains the various optimizing steps which have been done to reach the final architecture.

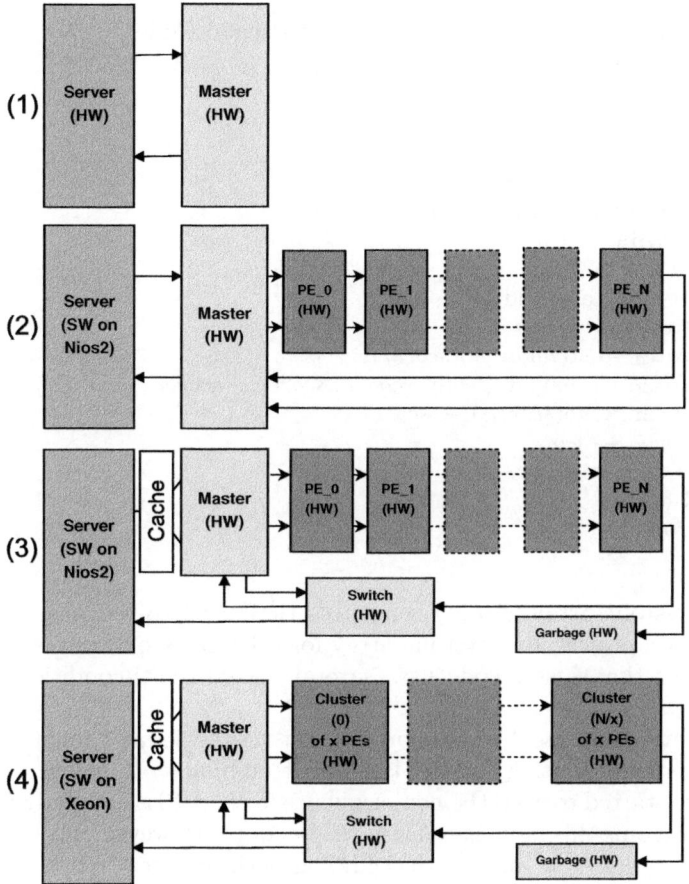

**Fig. 2.** Design Releases

**Speeding-Up Processes.** Once the overall multi-process system has been functionally validated, each process has been separately optimized. This has been done through simple source code transformations or by adding compiler directives (pragmas) such as the CO PIPELINE pragma, which will lead to a pipelined execution on the most inner loop. For example, in Algorithm 1, both inner loops are important loops to pipeline. In addition, code transformations may be necessary to help the ImpulseC compiler to provide better efficient scheduling. In our case, both loops have a rate of 1, meaning that one loop iteration can be started every clock cycle.

**Splitting Slow Processes.** In some cases, processes exhibits codes which are too complex to achieve efficient schedule or pipeline. For example, Master in figure 2(2) must perform all the following tasks: reading 32-bit data on incoming streams from host; serializing these data to push them character by character

**Algorithm 1.** Simple Processing Element Pseudo-Code

```
ProcessingElement(x_I, x_O, y_I, y_O, score_I, score_O)
loop
    x_C ← stream_read(x_I)
    while x_TMP ≠ EOS do
        x_TMP ← stream_read(x_I)
        stream_write(x_TMP) → x_O
    end while
    for n = 1 to N do
        y_C ← stream_read(y_I)
        stream_write(y_C) → y_O
        score_L ← stream_read(score_I)
        score_C ← compute_score( score_L, score_UL, score_U, , x_C, y_C )
        stream_write(score_C) → score_O
        score_U ← score_C
        score_UL ← score_L
    end for
end loop
```

into the systolic array; storing sequences that need to be compared to multiple sequences; controlling systolic array for different sequences; etc. To execute these tasks, the Master code uses several nested multi-conditional controlled loops.

One of the ImpulseC restrictions is that nested loops cannot be pipelined. While Master is waiting for the last result coming from the systolic array, it could have started to send the next sequence, as first PEs are ready to work. One way to overcome this issue is to merge these loops. However, this transformation leads to complex code and poor scheduling performance.

Then, splitting processes with loops that can be executed in parallel can help to improve the overall system efficiency. In the accelerator system, many processes have been created to simplify the Master process code (Figure 2(3)). A garbage process reads useless data from the systolic array. A switch process, configured by the Master, carries results either to the server software process or to the Master when needed for the next computation. A cache system reads alignment structure coming from the Server, stores sequences which need to be sent again, and does the sequence serialization. This splitting mechanism provides an efficient electronic system, minimizing process idle periods and generating simple code which is better suited for ImpulseC scheduler capabilities.

**Minimizing Resources.** As the systolic array represent the major resource utilization, a lot of efforts have been done to minimize individual PE and stream resources. Streams are implemented as FIFOs and have been reduced to their minimal size, allowing memory block FIFOs to be advantageously replaced by register FIFOs. PE arithmetic has been limited to 14 bits which is the theoretical upper bound of score values. Some operators have also been transformed to simple ones when possible. All these optimizations can easily be specified at ImpulseC level and do not generate additional complexity in the design process.

## 3.3 Clustering PEs

Specifying one PE by one process provides efficient hardware (cf. section 4.2): the architecture is fully distributed. Signals (control and operand) remain local, leading to small fanout and easy synthesis. Nevertheless, it uses a lot of resources: each PE duplicates identical control logic and several intermediate streams.

Reducing the duplication of control logic (and streams) resources would enable a larger systolic array (section 4.2). A way to achieve this objective is to cluster PEs. At ImpulseC level, this is done by specifying the behavior of several PEs in a single process (Figure 2(4)). As an example, algorithm 2 shows the code of one cluster of 2 PEs.

**Algorithm 2.** Dual Processing Element Cluster Pseudo-Code

**ProcessingElement**($x_I$, $x_O$, $y_I$, $y_O$, $score_I$, $score_O$)
**loop**
    $x_{C1} \leftarrow$ stream_read($x_I$)
    $x_{C2} \leftarrow$ stream_read($x_I$)
    **while** $x_{TMP} \neq$ EOS **do**
        $x_{TMP} \leftarrow$ stream_read($x_I$)
        stream_write($x_{TMP}$) $\rightarrow x_O$
    **end while**
    **for** $n = 1$ to $N$ **do**
        #pragma CO PIPELINE
        $y_C \leftarrow$ stream_read($y_I$)
        $score_L \leftarrow$ stream_read($score_I$)
        $score_{C1} \leftarrow$ compute_score( $score_{L1}$, $score_{UL1}$, $score_{U1}$, $x_{C1}$, $y_{C1}$)
        $score_{U1} \leftarrow score_{C1}$
        $score_{UL1} \leftarrow score_{L1}$
        $score_{L2} \leftarrow score_{C1}$
        $y_{C2} \leftarrow y_{C1}$
        $score_{C2} \leftarrow$ compute_score( $score_{L2}$, $score_{UL2}$, $score_{U2}$, $x_{C2}$, $y_{C2}$)
        $score_{U2} \leftarrow score_{C2}$
        $score_{UL2} \leftarrow score_{L2}$
        stream_write($y_{C2}$) $\rightarrow y_O$
        stream_write($score_{C2}$) $\rightarrow score_O$
    **end for**
**end loop**

Clustering PE doesn't decrease loop rate, nor increases critical path length (max unit delay), at least for datapath. However it may increase control signals fanout as one state machine has to control more operators.

Reducing the number of FIFO stages decreases the systolic array latency, but increases cluster latency. A small systolic array latency is adapted to process sequences larger than the systolic array size: computation are done in several

**Table 1.** Impact of clustering PEs on Resources and Performances

| Design | HLL(1) | HLL(2) | HLL(3) | HLL(4) |
|---|---|---|---|---|
| Cluster size (x) | 1 | 2 | 4 | 8 |
| 8 PEs ALM util. | 4336 | 3680 | 2246 | 1578 |
| 8 PEs M9K util. | 8 | 4 | 4 | 4 |
| Design Logic Util. | 88 % | 88 % | 74 % | 81 % |
| Max number of PE (N) | 224 | 256 | 288 | 384 |
| BCUPS | 20.5 | 23.7 | 30.5 | 38.4 |

passes and results of the last PE are needed as soon as it is possible for the next computation. On the other hand, a small PE cluster latency is preferable when the query size fit the systolic array size: the first character of a bank sequence can be pushed as soon as the cluster has processed the last character of the previous bank sequence.

Depending of applications, a tradeoff between the size of the query sequence, the total number of PEs and the size of a PE cluster need to be found.

## 4    Performances

### 4.1    Platform Description

The platform used for our experiments is the XD2000i Development platform from XtremeData, Inc. [4]. This hardware holds a dual processor socket motherboard where one of the initial processor chip has been replaced by a XD2000i module. This In-Socket Accelerator embeds 2 Altera EP3ES260 FPGA components.

### 4.2    Design Variations Comparison

Clustering PEs had two goals: (1) share control logic and (2) decrease the number of inter-PEs FIFOs. Table 1 shows FPGA resource utilization (Adaptive Logic Module and M9K memory blocks) equivalent to 8 PE stages for different sizes of clusters. As the number of PE per ImpulseC process increases, resource utilization of equivalent partition of the design is reduced by 2.5, allowing the systolic array to be larger. For each size of clusters, we tried to fit as many PEs as possible on the FPGA, provided the design could sustain a frequency of 200MHz. Measured BCUPS (Billion Cells Updates Per Seconds) are also reported in table 1. This unit represents the number of matrix cells (cf. section 2.2) which are computed in one second, and is the standard unit to measure genomic sequence comparison algorithm performance.

It could be interesting to investigate if better performance could be reached by increasing the cluster size over 8, but, at this point, manually writing the code becomes too complex. This situation reveals the current tool limits.

**Table 2.** HLL versus HDL design performance

| Design | HDL | HLL(1) | HLL(4) |
|---|---|---|---|
| Systolic Array Size | 300 | 224 | 384 |
| BCUPS | 9 | 20.5 | 38.4 |

## 4.3 Comparison with Hand-Written HDL Code

In [7] the authors present a Smith & Waterman HDL-implementation on the same platform. The Smith & Waterman algorithm is one of the most popular genomic sequence comparison and is usually used as reference. In this hand-written code implementation, performance reaches 9 BCUPS. Table 2 summarizes performance of this implementation (HDL), of the first ImpulseC optimized release (HLL(1)) and of the highly-optimized ImpulseC release (HLL(4)).

Our final design, HLL(4), is 4.2x more powerful than HDL-implemented design.

## 4.4 State of the Art

While lots of paper show great speed-ups of genomic sequence comparison over sequential processor, it still remains very difficult to provide fair comparisons. Hardware platforms and algorithms are constantly evolving leading to huge design differences. Thus, we restrict our comparison to the well known Needleman & Wunsch and Smith & Waterman algorithms managing protein sequences and affine gap penalty. As in our implementation, these algorithms compute every cells of the matrix and don't make any optimization such as the diagonal-band-limited optimization which limits computation near the main diagonal of the matrix.

In [6] and [9], both design targets Virtex II XC2V6000 FPGA and respectively get 3.1 GCUPS and 10.54 GCUPS. XC2V6000 are now outdated FPGAs that contain only 33K slices. It would be interesting to see how the proposed architectures scale with current devices.

Two more recent designs, [7], on XD2000i platform, and [8], on XD1000 platform, exhibit respectively 15 GCUPS theoretical performance (9 GCUPS actually measured) and 25.6 GCUPS pick performance. These implementations seems currently to be the best references.

On conventional processors, Farrar [10] holds actually the best performance (up to 3 GCUPS) with the use of SIMD processor instruction set. A multi-threaded implementation on a 4 core Intel Xeon processor (as the processor available on the XD2000i platform) would achieved 12 GCUPS. Our hardware accelerator could also benefit from multi-threaded opportunity. Currently, only half of the FPGA resources of the XD2000i platform is used. As our architecture is not bandwidth limited, using both FPGAs shouldn't alter the design efficiency, providing up to 76.8 GCUPS, or a x6 speed-up over optimized multi-threaded SIMD software.

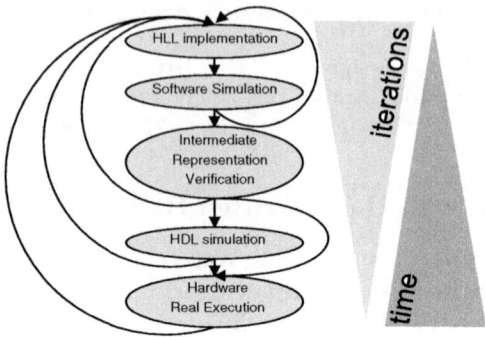

**Fig. 3.** ImpulseC design flow

# 5   Discussion

## 5.1   Fast and Reliable Design Process

Designing hardware accelerator with High Level Language significantly speeds up design process. In this experiment, a first systolic array has been created from scratch within a few hours, while it could have taken days in HDL. First of all, using HLL allows designers to have a behavioral description at a higher level compared to HDL, avoiding lots of signal synchronization problems that occur when dealing with low level signals (data_ready, data_eos and data_read for example). Instead, the use of ImpulseC stream read and write functions allows the designer to specify identical behavior in a very safe way. Inside a process, operation scheduling are deduced from ImpulseC code and from data dependencies. No other timing constraint need to be specified. With ImpulseC, changing operation order, for example, is thus quickly done, while it can be error-prone, or at least time consuming, in HDL.

Working with HLL makes implementation step faster, as shown in figure 3. Software simulation is even faster and is sometimes a sufficient test to pass to the next design process iteration, skipping HDL simulation which can be a more difficult way of debugging. In the same way, an intermediate model is generated during HDL generation, that can be explored with the *Stage Master Explorer* tool and from which designer can have a view of process performance (scheduling, pipeline rate,... ).

Finally, this fast design methodology allows designers to try several design options, or add extra features that can be simply crippling with HDL languages. For example, in the design considered in this paper, adding features such as variable sequence length management or dynamic load of substitution matrix is much easier than it could be with HDL.

## 5.2   Reusable and Portable Design

HLL makes design specification more understandable, easier to maintain and also easier to reuse. Using corresponding Platform Support Package to port an

ImpulseC design from a platform to another one means that application designers would not have to manage architecture dependent issues. This role is devoted to API level and to the platform designers.

Unfortunately, the PSP we experimented is still in its early development stage and was not able to provide all standard features. We had to rewrite part of our software and slightly adapt hardware processes, when moving from Nios2 to the host Xeon processor. We can expect that the future PSP releases will make this transition transparent.

However, moving an accelerated application from an FPGA architecture to a very different one (with different RAM block size or a higher memory bandwidth for example), could require design modifications in order to get maximum performance. Unchanged design should at least provide functional designs and technology modification would be easier to do within HLS tool environment.

### 5.3 Obtaining Real Performance

One typical claim against HLS tools is that the reduction of design time comes at the price of a loss of performance, as these tools prevent designers from optimizing the details of the architecture. We believe such claims do not hold when it comes to the parallelization of high performance computing applications on FPGAs. As a matter of fact, we even believe that using HLL can actually help designer improving performance as it allows designers to abstract away all non critical implementation details (ex: optimizing the RTL datapath of a Processing Elemenent [7]) and instead focus on performance critical system level issues (ex: storage/communication balance).

Indeed, thanks to the expressivity of HLL, designers effectively explore a much larger design space, leading them to optimal architectural solutions they would have never considered in the first place. Even though such system level optimizations could also be implemented at the RTL level using HDLs, it turns out they rarely are so. The explanation is quite straightforward : the impact of these optimizations on performance is often discovered at posteriori (or too late in the design flow) and reenginnering the whole design at the HDL level would require too much effort.

Last, thanks to the drastic reduction in design time to get an efficient implementation, designers can afford to implement several non critical design optimizations. Even if the impact of one of such optimization alone is generally limited (often 10%-30% performance gain), their combined effect on global performance is generally multiplicative/cumulative and ultimately boosts global performance, for very little design effort.

### 5.4 Toward User Assisted Source to Source Transformation Tools

It is clear that HLS do not provide a direct algorithmic to gate design path. In a similar way high performance architecture programmer do, designers need to modify and rewrite their source code so as to get the tool to derive the hardware architecture they actually want for their application. Even though such a rewrite process is much easier to carry with a HLL, it still leaves a lot of burden to the designer.

As a consequence, we feel that there is a need for HLS oriented source to source refactoring tools, which would help designers re-structuring their programs by providing them with a code transformation toolbox tailored to their needs. Such a toolbox would of course encompass most of the transformations that can be found in semi automatic parallelizing source to source compilers (loop and array layout transformations for example), but should also provide domain-specific code transformations specifically targeted at HLS tools users (process clustering could be one of them).

## Acknowledgment

We would like to thank Impulse Accelerated Technologies for their valuable help. This work has been supported by the French ANR BioWIC (ANR-08-SEGI-005).

## References

1. Holland, B., Vacas, M., Aggarwal, V., DeVille, R., Troxel, I., George, A.D.: Survey of C-based application mapping tools for reconfigurable computing. In: Proceedings of the 8th International Conference on Military and Aerospace Programmable Logic Devices (MAPLD 2005), Washington, DC, USA (September 2005)
2. Lavenier, D., Giraud, M.: Bioinformatics Applications, in Reconfigurable Computing: Accelerating Computation with Field-Programmable Gate Arrays. In: Gokhale, M.B., Graham, P.S. (eds.), ch. 9. Springer, Heidelberg (2005)
3. Pellerin, D., Thibault, S.: Practical FPGA Programming in C. Pearson Education, Inc., Upper Saddle River, NJ (2005)
4. http://old.xtremedatainc.com/
5. Aung, L.A., Maskell, D., Oliver, T., Schmidt, B.: C-Based Design Methodology for FPGA Implementation of ClustalW MSA. In: Rajapakse, J.C., Schmidt, B., Volkert, L.G. (eds.) PRIB 2007. LNCS (LNBI), vol. 4774, pp. 11–18. Springer, Heidelberg (2007)
6. Oliver, T., Schmidt, B., Nathan, D., Clemens, R., Maskell, D.: Multiple Sequence Alignment on an FPGA. In: Proceedings of 11th International Conference on Parallel and Distributed Systems, July 22-22, vol. 2, pp. 326–330 (2005)
7. Allred, J., Coyne, J., Lynch, W., Natoli, V., Grecco, J., Morrissette, J.: Smith-Waterman implementation on a FSB-FPGA module using the Intel Accelerator Abstraction Layer. In: International Parallel and Distributed Processing Symposium, pp. 1–4. IEEE Computer Society, Los Alamitos (2009)
8. Zhang, P., Tan, G., Gao, G.R.: Implementation of the Smith-Waterman algorithm on a reconfigurable supercomputing platform. In: Proceedings of the 1st International Workshop on High-Performance Reconfigurable Computing Technology and Applications: Held in Conjunction with Sc 2007, HPRCTA 2007, Reno, Nevada, November 11-11, pp. 39–48. ACM, New York (2007)
9. Yilmaz, C., Gok, M.: An Optimized System for Multiple Sequence Alignment. In: International Conference on Reconfigurable Computing and FPGAs, pp. 178–182. IEEE Computer Society, Los Alamitos (2009)
10. Farrar, M.: Striped Smith-Waterman speeds database searches six times over other SIMD implementations. Bioinformatics 23, 15661 (2007); A Smith-Waterman Systolic Cell

# A (Fault-Tolerant)$^2$ Scheduler for Real-Time HW Tasks

Xabier Iturbe$^{1,2}$, Khaled Benkrid$^1$, Tughrul Arslan$^1$,
Mikel Azkarate$^2$, and Imanol Martinez$^2$

$^1$ System Level Integration Research Group, The University of Edinburgh
King's Buildings, Mayfield Road, Edinburgh EH9 3JL, Scotland, UK
{x.iturbe,k.benkrid,t.arslan}@ed.ac.uk

$^2$ Embedded System-on-Chip Group, IKERLAN-IK4 Research Alliance
Arizmendiarrieta 2, Mondragón 20500, Basque Country (Spain)
{xiturbe,mazkarateaskasua,imartinez}@ikerlan.es

**Abstract.** This paper describes a fault-tolerant scheduler that uses the Area-Time response Balancing algorithm (ATB) for scheduling real-time hardware tasks onto partially reconfigurable FPGAs. The architecture of the ATB scheduler incorporates fault-tolerance by design features; including Triple Modular Redundancy (TMR), parity protection of its memories and finite state machines, as well as spatial and implementation diversity. Additionally, it is able to *scrub* soft-errors and circumvent the permanent damage in the device. Besides the scheduling circuit is itself fault-tolerant, ATB is aware of the occurring faults in the silicon substrate of the chip, leading to a very reliable "fault-tolerant square scheduling".

**Keywords:** Real-Time Scheduling, Fault-Tolerance, Reconfigurable Computing, Hardware Virtualization.

## 1 Introduction: The R3TOS Approach

Xilinx FPGAs incorporate Dynamic Partial runtime Reconfiguration (DPR) capability, which permits to modify the functionality implemented by a part of their computational elements while the rest of them are still performing active computation. This establishes the basis for a new computation model in time and space which combines the speed of hardware with the flexibility of software. Computation-specific circuits ('hardware tasks') can be online swaped in and out of the FPGA on demand. Moreover, radiation induced upsets can be fixed (e.g. *Scrubbing* SEUs [2]) and damaged resources can be circumvented (e.g. [3]). In order to make these improvements exploitable by commercial applications, the R3TOS approach has been recently launched [4]. R3TOS stands for Reliable Reconfigurable Real-Time Operating System and aims at creating an infrastructure for coordinately and reliably executing hardware based applications upon a dynamically reconfigurable FPGA which works under real-time constraints. Hence, R3TOS exploits FPGA's reconfiguration opportunities with two main objectives:

- Achieve the *temporal correctness* by appropriately scheduling the hardware tasks so that all computation deadlines are met.
- Achieve the *computation correctness* by conveniently allocating the tasks onto the available non-damaged logic resources at all times.

A. Koch et al. (Eds.): ARC 2011, LNCS 6578, pp. 79–87, 2011.

Although there are several research efforts reported in the technical literature related to scheduling hardware tasks in FPGAs (e.g.[5,6,7]), to our best knowledge, no previous work has considered the impact that occurring faults in the device's substrate entail in terms of schedulability. Aimed at filling this gap, the Area-Time response Balancing scheduling algorithm (ATB) has been recently presented in [8]. It has been specifically designed to be used in R3TOS with the objective of increasing the allocatability of the hardware tasks in partially damaged FPGAs and thus maintain as much as possible the real-time performance as the device is degraded by faults. Nevertheless, there is no point in using a fault-tolerant scheduling algorithm if there is no guarantee that the scheduling decisions it defines are made in a reliable way. Hence, reliability is the first requirement when designing the architecture of the ATB scheduler. Moreover, ATB is a quite complex algorithm that, however, must make the scheduling decisions at high speed in order to allow real-time behavior. Thus, execution speed is the second requirement.

This paper presents an ad-hoc fault-tolerant architecture for the ATB scheduler that meets the algorithm execution speed requirements as well. After explaining the basis of the ATB scheduling algorithm in Section 2, the developed architecture is described in Section 3, making special emphasis on the fault-tolerance features it incorporates. In Section 4 the measured performance and reliability results are presented and finally, concluding remarks are listed in Section 5.

## 2    ATB: Area Time Response Balancing Scheduling Algorithm

FPGAs open the door for more sophisticated and powerful computation systems in which the available resources can be dynamically utilized in order to efficiently execute several concurrent hardware tasks. However, the fact there is a single reconfiguration port in an FPGA (e.g. Internal Configuration Access Port - ICAP) and the fact reconfiguring a hardware task takes a non negligible amount of time, in the order of milliseconds, introduces a bottleneck that restricts the intensive exploitation of hardware parallelism [9]. Moreover, the limited amount of resources available in the device constrains the number of hardware tasks that can be executed in parallel. Hence, a computation deadline is missed if (i) the occupation of the reconfiguration port delays too much the allocation of a task, or (ii) in case the logic resources required by the task are not available before its deadline expires. This can occur because either there are not sufficient free resources on the FPGA or because the resources are not available in a sufficiently large contiguous region due to fragmentation. While it is possible to deal at design time with the fragmentation provoked by the continuous allocation of hardware tasks with different sizes (Offline scheduling), the unpredictable fragmentation provoked by spontaneous faults and data-dependant computation can only be considered at runtime.

### 2.1    Real-Time Hardware Task Model

A hardware task is the basic unit of computation that R3TOS manages. It is defined in both time and area domains as follows (See Fig. 1a and 1b). In the area domain, a task $\theta_i$ is defined by the amount of resources it requires along $x$ and $y$ dimensions, $h_x$ and $h_y$, respectively. In the time domain, the task is characterized by the amount of time

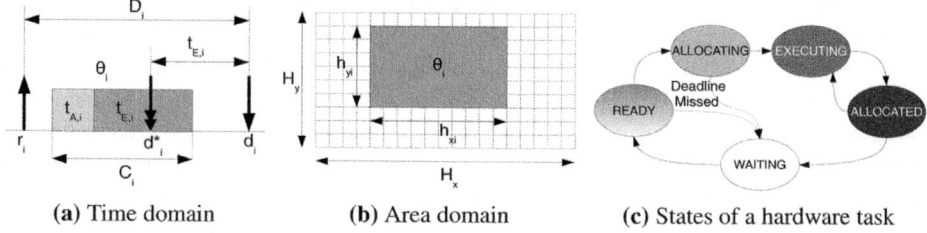

**(a)** Time domain    **(b)** Area domain    **(c)** States of a hardware task

**Fig. 1.** Real-Time hardware task model

needed for configuring it onto the FPGA (allocation time - $t_{A,i}$) and the period of time it needs to finish the computation (execution time - $t_{E,i}$). Hence, the total amount of time a hardware task uses the assigned resources (computation time - $C_i = t_{A,i} + t_{E,i}$). The real-time constraint of R3TOS involves the existence of a relative execution deadline for each task $D_i$, that represents the maximum acceptable delay for that task to finish its execution. The absolute deadline for task execution $d_i$ is computed by adding the task arrival time $r_i$ to the relative execution deadline. Even more important are the relative deadline for task allocation $D_i^*$, that represents the maximum acceptable delay for a task to be placed in the device in order to meet its execution deadline, and the associated absolute allocation deadline $d_i^*$.

Due to existing technological constraints in current reconfigurable FPGAs, we assume that hardware tasks are not preemptive in their execution phase. Preemption involves that the values of all the registers included in a task must be saved and later resumed. Besides the high storage resources this would require, the resuming of registers' state is a tedious and high time-consuming task in which they must be first configured as asynchronous, then updated with the desired value and finally set to the desired behavior (synchronous or asynchronous). Preemption is only allowed during the reconfiguration phase, when the computation has not started yet and no context saving is needed. ATB preempts the allocation of a task $\theta_i$ only when another ready task $\theta_j$ misses its deadline in case it is not immediately allocated ($t = d_j^* - t_{A,j}$). Likewise, in order to improve the performance, the tasks are kept allocated in the FPGA when they finish the execution. They are removed only when the resources they use are needed for allocating other ready tasks. Hence, a hardware task goes through a series of states until it finally finishes its execution: *Waiting, Ready, Allocating, Executing* an *Allocated* (See Fig. 1c).

### 2.2 Scheduling Real-Time Hardware Tasks with ATB

The ATB scheduler coordinates the access to the reconfiguration port and assigns the appropriate allocation starting times to the ready hardware tasks. On the contrary to scheduling software tasks, the area-time duality makes the ATB scheduler deal with area considerations when scheduling the hardware tasks in light of a better performance. In [8] it is reported that considering both time and area domains reduces the amount of missed computation deadlines by over 20% with regard to traditional approaches that only consider the time domain (e.g. EDF). Analyzing the area domain permits to address the fragmentation introduced by faults as well. Furthermore, ATB makes the scheduling decisions at runtime. Besides dealing with the unpredictable degradation provoked by spontaneous faults, this also enables data-dependant computation.

ATB uses an intuitive fragmentation reduction technique. Based on the fact that several small tasks can be mapped to the adjacent resources that are released when large area tasks finish their execution, ATB prioritizes the execution of great area tasks at the expense of delaying the system response time. In order to ensure that the early execution of large tasks do not provoke any deadline missing, ATB evaluates a feasibility test when making the scheduling decisions. This test consists in "looking into the future" for estimating the consequences (both in time and area) that the execution of a given task would involve. We name this task as Task Under Test (TUT) and it is selected starting from the greatest area tasks and ending with the lowest area ones.

For estimating the area implications, a time window equal to the computation time of the TUT is considered. In case the TUT is selected to be allocated, it must be ensured that there are still enough free adjacent resources to be used by the $j$ ready tasks that must be allocated within this time ($d_j^* - t_{A,j} < t + C_{TUT}$, when $t$ is the current time). ATB keeps track of device's area state (occupation and fragmentation) by means of the Maximal Empty Rectangle (MER), which is given by the allocator at each time. It is assumed that in the worst-case, the tasks must be placed on the MER and thus, its size is progressively reduced as the area-based feasibility test is performed. This test does not apply to the tasks that can be allocated out of the considered time window based on the fact that the early execution of the TUT ensures the largest possible MER will be available for them. On its part, the time-based feasibility test progress through a time reference $t_R$ which is gradually updated based on the allocation times of the $j$ ready tasks ($t_R = t_R + t_{A,j}$). Thus, both the exclusiveness of the ICAP access and the reconfiguration time overhead are addressed. ATB checks that after having allocated the TUT ($t_R = t + t_{A,TUT}$) there is still sufficient time for allocating the rest of ready tasks before their respective allocation deadlines expire. Additionally, ATB is able to predict contention situations due to the lack of available resources. Then ATB goes forward to the instant when the resources used by the TUT are released ($t_R = t + C_{TUT}$).

## 3   The Fault-Tolerant Architecture of the ATB Scheduler

Fig. 2 shows the developed fault-tolerant ATB scheduler, which is divided into four main parts: (i) A Task State Memory (TSM), (ii) a Finite State Machine (FSM) that controls the (iii) Data-Path and a (iv) Reconfiguration Manager (RM). The parts are separately floor-planned within the FPGA in order to reduce the probability that a single fault make the scheduler fail (Spatial Diversity). The FSM and the data-path are defined as reconfigurable modules. This brings three benefits: (i) The reconfiguration-*scrubbing* speed is improved by using compressed partial bitstreams, (ii) The parts are self-contained within the reconfigurable slots (components but also routes), improving the fault isolation and, (iii) Different implementations can be configured for each part, being possible to cope with permanent damage in the chip (Implementation Diversity).

The centerpiece of the scheduler is the *Task State Memory* (TSM), which stores the information of the tasks required by the scheduler when making the scheduling decisions (e.g. size, deadlines, allocation and execution times, etc.). The TSM can store

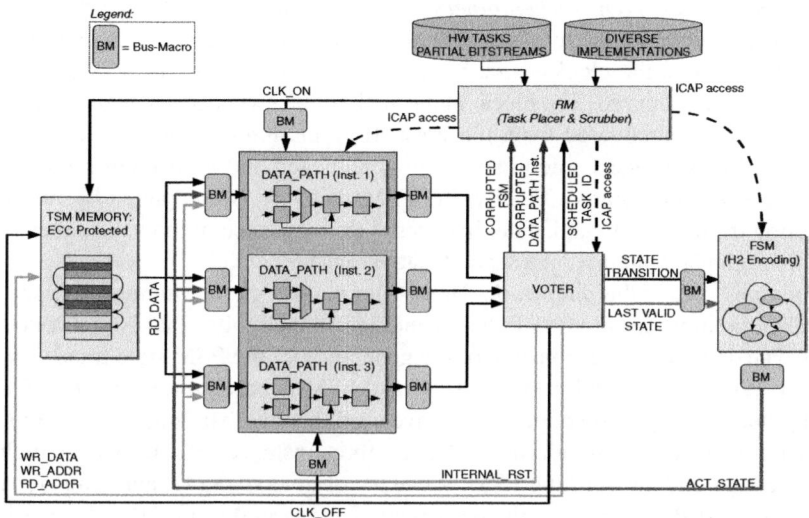

**Fig. 2.** The fault-tolerant architecture of the ATB scheduler

information for up to 253 different tasks. The tasks are dynamically organized in queues based on their state at each time (Ready, Executing and Allocated). There is no need to include a queue for tasks in *allocating* state since there can only be a maximum of two tasks in this state at each time (active and preempted allocating tasks). Furthermore, the stored information for every task includes two timers, *q_time*, which is used for keeping the record of the amount of time the task has been queued in a ready queue and, *allo_exe_time*, which is shared at *allocating* and *executing* states for keeping the record of the amount of time the task has been in each state. As required by ATB, the ready queue is sorted by both decreasing task sizes ($h_{x,i} \cdot h_{y,i}$) and increasing task allocation deadlines ($d_i^* - t_{A,i}$). Two pointers are used to maintain the suitable order in the ready queue, *Pointer_A* (area-based order) and *Pointer_T* (time-based order). Pointer based queues not only allows to maintain the tasks sorted as required by the ATB scheduling algorithm, but also permits to easily modify the state of a task, that is, to move a task from one state queue to another.

The TSM is implemented as a 512 x 64 bit wide Block-RAM, protected with Hamming Error Correction Codes (Xilinx RAMB32_S64_ECC). Based on these codes a periodic diagnostic test is carried out, which is aimed at detecting and correcting upset bits in the TSM, ensuring the correctness of the stored information at all times.

The second part is the *Finite State Machine* (FSM), which coordinates the functioning of the scheduler, managing the timing and state transitions of the tasks. The FSM selects the operation to be performed by issuing the associated state code at each time. In order to achieve high-reliability, we have followed the recommendations of the NASA Jet Propulsion Laboratory (JPL) [10]. Every state code is Hamming distance 2 (H2) from every other and thus, the FSM runs through states that are guaranteed to be different by 2 bits. Hence, from any state a single fault will give an illegal state that is covered with the HDL's *when others* directive to take the FSM to a defined state in which an *scrubbing* procedure is activated (*Corrupted FSM* signal). In order to prevent error propagation, the clock signal is switched off in the rest of the scheduler while the FSM is reconfigured. The clock signal will not be switched on again until the FSM has successfully recovered from the error. If *scrubbing* does not fix the problem, it is assumed that device's silicon substrate is damaged and a different implementation for the FSM is configured. Finally, the FSM recovery is completed by resuming its execution from the last valid state. In order to do so, a trace of the valid states the FSM runs through is maintained in a separate state register.

The third part is the *data-path*. This is the most logic consuming part and hence, it is also the most sensitive to faults. It includes the circuitry that is controlled by the FSM. The data-path is responsible of the generation of the FSM state transition signals as well. While the reliability of the TSM and FSM is based on diagnosis (ECC codes and H2 state coding, respectively), we have used the fault handling strategy reported in [11] for making the data-path robust. Hence, three instances of it have been included in the scheduler and, as with the FSM, a battery of diverse implementations for each of them is provided to cope with the permanent damage in the chip. Besides masking the fault effect, TMR allows for diagnosis as well. We use a majority voter able to identify the instance which produces a distinct output (*Corrupted data-path ID* signal). This activates the *scrubbing* procedure on the corrupted data-path instance, aiming at recovering the triple redundancy and thus, preventing the accumulation of faults that could eventually make the scheduling fail. The small footprint of the voter not only reduces the probability of being corrupted by a fault, but also the amount of time needed for accessing its configuration through the ICAP. Moreover, as it is a pure combinational circuit, its configuration can be periodically *scrubbed* without interfering its functioning. This permits to correct dormant faults, without significantly reducing the ICAP throughput for hardware task allocation, before they manifest in the functioning. Based on the high amount of signals the voter processes, we resort to individually *scrubbing* its configuration frames instead of using modular reconfiguration, which would lead to 45% resources overhead (and footprint increase) due to bus-macros.

Finally, a *Reconfiguration Manager* (RM) controls the ICAP while the tasks are configured in the FPGA. Moreover, this part plays a major role in the reliability of the system as it also controls the *scrubbing* operations and manages the clock signal when the FSM is recovering from an error. At this stage, for simplicity we use a MicroBlaze processor and the ICAP controller provided by Xilinx. However, since this is a crucial part, we plan to use a simpler, faster and fault-tolerant custom solution in the future.

The functioning of the scheduler is shown in Fig. 3. In order to improve the performance, ATB is executed again when a new task is passed to the allocator. Hence, in case the allocator is unable to find a placement for that task, another one can be immediately scheduled. The system has been implemented on a Xilinx XC4VLX160 part. Excluding the RM, it requires 3,808 Slices (6%) and 2 RAMB16s (1%), running at 100 MHz. In the coming years, when the main challenge for designers will move from how to optimize the area usage to how to deal with the (ever increasing) huge amount of on-chip resources, these requirements will definitely be affordable considering the benefit in terms of design automatization and reliability improvement the scheduler brings.

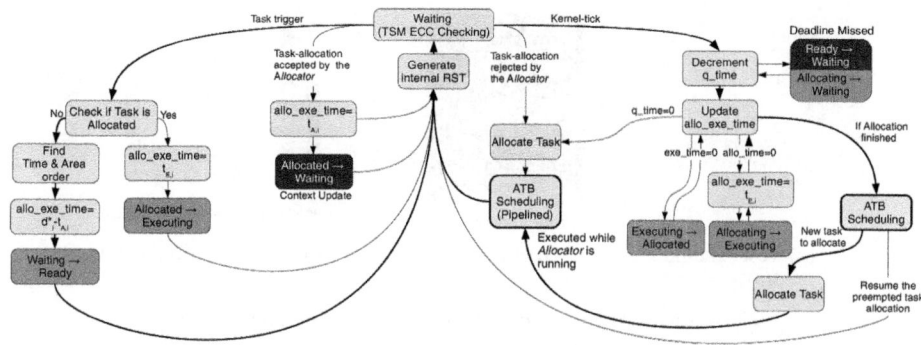

**Fig. 3.** ATB scheduler's flow diagram and task state transitions

## 4   Reliability and Performance Results

Table 1 shows the measured performance results for the developed ATB scheduler; where $R$, $E$ and $A$ refer to the number of tasks buffered in the ready, executing and allocated queues at a given time, respectively. When the scheduler works in standard conditions (with some tens of ready tasks) the scheduling decisions are made in some microseconds and in the worst-case scenario ($R = 252$), it takes less than $9.52\ ms$. As these values are in the same order of magnitude of typical tasks' allocation times [9], we conclude that our scheduler meets the execution speed requirement. The longest loop of the scheduler's functioning (marked with thick line in Fig. 3) must be completed within a single kernel-tick $t_{KT}$. This constraint defines the maximum number of hardware tasks usable in a given application: $N \leq 253$ & $N \leq \lfloor 0.057 \cdot \sqrt{t_{KT}[ns]} \rfloor$, with $t_{KT} = min\{t_{A,i}, t_{E,i}\}$.

**Table 1.** Performance results of the ATB scheduler

| Operation | Definition [$ns$] | Worst-Case Value |
|---|---|---|
| Find a task in the Allocated queue | $40 \cdot A$ | $10.12\ \mu s$ |
| Task State Transition (Light gray in Fig. 3) | 190 | $190\ ns$ |
| Task State Transition (Dark gray in Fig. 3) | $190 + 40 \cdot (R, E \text{ or } A)$ | $10.31\ \mu s$ |
| ATB Execution Time | $150 \cdot R^2$ | $9.52\ ms$ |
| Update $q\_time$ and $allo\_exe\_time$ | $80 \cdot (R + E + 1)$ | $20.24\ \mu s$ |
| Find Time & Area order in the Ready queue | $80 \cdot R$ | $20.16\ \mu s$ |

In order to test the robustness of the ATB scheduler, we have floor-planned two instances of it in different positions of the FPGA and we have injected random faults directly into the architecture of one of them (Scheduler Under Test - SUT), while the other acts as the "*golden*" scheduling model. Since the golden scheduler is not subject to faults, it does not include any fault-tolerance features. We consider the SUT fails when either (i) it schedules a different task than the golden model does or (ii) it gets stuck, without detecting any fault situation. So that to compare the behavior of both parts, the

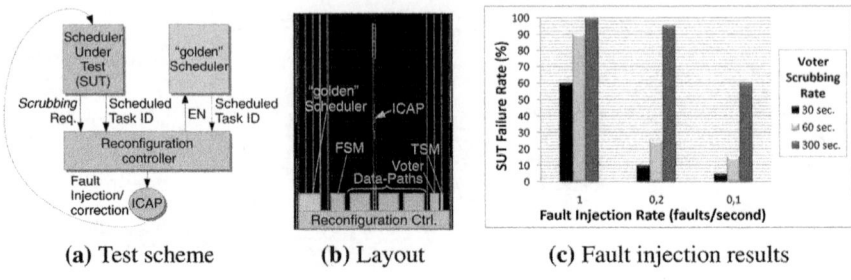

(a) Test scheme          (b) Layout          (c) Fault injection results

**Fig. 4.** Measuring the reliability of the developed ATB scheduler

golden scheduler is stopped when any part of the SUT is being reconfigured (*EN* signal). The used test scheme and floor-planning is depicted in Fig. 4a and 4b, respectively. Since the injection of faults requires to use the ICAP, we have taken the reconfiguration manager out from both scheduler instances. Hence, there is a single ICAP controller in the test system which performs the fault injection and, upon request from the SUT, the consequent fault *scrubbing*. Additionally, it keeps track of the failures of the SUT. We have measured that no more than $3.58\ ms$ are needed for *scrubbing* a data-path instance, $1.95\ ms$ for *scrubbing* the voter and, $4.03\ ms$ for *scrubbing* and resuming the normal operation of the FSM from the last valid state (These values only include the required time for downloading the bitstreams through the ICAP port). Likewise, the diagnostic test on the TSM is completed in less than $40.96\ \mu s$. The percentage of SUT failures for different fault injection rates within 10 minutes observation time are shown in Fig. 4c. Based on these results, we conclude that it is possible to make the scheduler virtually immune to faults by choosing an appropriate *scrubbing* frequency on the voter.

## 5    Conclusions

We have described a fault-tolerant architecture for the ATB scheduler. By using hardware components, we achieve the required speed for the execution of the ATB scheduling algorithm, which is able to reliably schedule hardware tasks onto dynamically and partially reconfigurable Xilinx FPGAs in the presence of permanent damage in the chip. We have validated the robustness of the developed scheduler by directly injecting faults into it and measured its performance.

## References

1. Constantinescu, C.: Trends and Challenges in VLSI Circuit Reliability. IEEE Micro Journal 23(4), 14–19 (2003)
2. Berg, M., Poivey, C., Petrick, D., Espinosa, D., Lesea, A., Label, K., Friendlich, M.: Effectiveness of Internal versus External SEU Scrubbing Mitigation Strategies in a Xilinx FPGA: Design, Test, and Analysis. IEEE Transactions on Nuclear Science 55(4) (2008)
3. Montminy, D.P., Baldwin, R.O., Williams, P.D., Mullins, B.E.: Using Relocatable Bitstreams for Fault Tolerance. In: The Proceedings of the NASA/ESA Conference on Adaptive Hardware and Systems, pp. 701–708 (2007)

4. Iturbe, X., Benkrid, K., Erdogan, A.T., Arslan, T., Azkarate, M., Martinez, I., Perez, A.: R3TOS: A Reliable Reconfigurable Real-Time Operating System. In: The Proceedings of the NASA/ESA Conference on Adaptive Hardware and Systems, pp. 99–104 (2010)
5. Lu, Y., Marconi, T., Bertels, K., Gaydadjiev, G.: Online Task Scheduling for the FPGA-based Partially Reconfigurable Systems. In: The Proceedings of the Reconfigurable Computing: Architectures (2009)
6. Dittmann, F., Frank, S.: Hard Real-Time Reconfiguration Port Scheduling. In: The Proceedings of the Design, Automation and Test in Europe Conference and Exhibition (2007)
7. Danne, K., Muehlenbernd, R., Platzner, M.: Executing Hardware Tasks on Dynamically Reconfigurable Devices under Real-time Conditions. In: Proceedings of the International Conference on Field Programmable Logic and Applications, pp. 541–546 (2006)
8. Iturbe, X., Benkrid, K., Arslan, T., Martinez, I., Azkarate, M.: ATB: Area-Time Response Balancing Algorithm for Scheduling Real-Time Hardware Tasks. In: The Proceedings of the International Conference on Field-Programmable Technology (2010)
9. Liu, M., Kuehn, W., Lu, Z., Jantsch, A.: Run-Time Partial Reconfiguration Speed Investigation and Architectural Design Space Exploration. In: The Proceedings of the International Conference on Field Programmable Logic and Applications (2009)
10. NASA: Fault-Tolerant Coding for State Machines. NASA Tech Briefs NPO-41050 (2009)
11. Iturbe, X., Azkarate, M., Martinez, I., Perez, J., Astarloa, A.: A Novel SEU, MBU and SHE Handling Strategy for Xilinx Virtex-4 FPGAs. In: The Proceedings of the International Conference on Field Programmable Logic and Applications (2009)

# A Compact Gaussian Random Number Generator for Small Word Lengths

Subhasis Das and Sachin Patkar

Indian Institute of Technology Bombay,
Mumbai - 76, India
subhasis@ee.iitb.ac.in, patkar@ee.iitb.ac.in

**Abstract.** The architecture for a compact Gaussian Random Number Generator based on the inversion of the gaussian cdf for word lengths less than 8 bits is discussed. The generator occupies $< 10\%$ of area of conventional 16 or 32 bit GRNG implementations and thus can be useful in cases where a gaussian random number of small word length will suffice and area is at a premium.

**Keywords:** Random Number Generator, Gaussian Random Number, FPGA based Random Number Generator, Channel noise simulation.

## 1 Introduction

Random numbers sampled from a Gaussian distribution are necessary in several areas such as simulation of a noisy channel, Monte-Carlo simulations etc. Random Number Generators (RNG) implemented in the hardware platform itself is preferable because of their speed and inherent parallelism as compared to software implementations.

The Gaussian RNG described here is suitable for generating small length i.e. less than 8 bits wide random numbers. This may be needed as the final output of the noisy channel under consideration may be quantized to 3 or 4 bits only (e.g. [3], [4]), or even not quantized at all when soft information is not needed. Under such circumstances, a 16 or 32 bit random number may not be necessary and instead a lower area implementation will result in a proportionally higher simulation speed in hardware as more units can be packed in the same device.

## 2 Current Algorithms

Various approaches to this problem include the Box-Muller method, Ziggurat method and the inversion of the cdf of the gaussian distribution.

A class of current algorithms used to generate gaussian random numbers accept one or more uniform random variates and generate one or more gaussian variates by applying some transformation on them. The IGCDF method and Box-Muller method belong to this class.

Another class of algorithms use a rejection sampling method, i.e. generate a gaussian variate if a generated uniform variate falls inside a region, otherwise try again. The Ziggurat algorithm employed in [2] falls in this category.

A. Koch et al. (Eds.): ARC 2011, LNCS 6578, pp. 88–93, 2011.

# 3   Algorithm

The current algorithm employed is unique in the sense that it doesn't require any multiplication or polynomial interpolation, which results in a much simpler and smaller circuit implementation. This also has the added advantage that it can be much more easily ported to FPGA platforms with much less available resources.

The algorithm generates the successive bits of the output in successive stages. We have used a 7 bit fixed point notation with 1 bit sign, 3 bits of integer and 3 bits of fractional precision. Thus, the range of the random numbers is $\pm 7.875$. Let $Z$ denote the standard normal random variable quantized in the manner discussed, and let $b = b_6 b_5 \ldots b_0$ be a possible output of the RNG. Also, let $Z_i$ denote the $i^{th}$ MSB of $Z$. First of all, we observe that $Z_6$, the sign bit is independent of all the other bits and is 0 with probability $1/2$ and 1 with probability $1/2$. Thus, this can be generated independently of the other bits.

Then, we observe that

$$P(Z = b) = \bigcap_i P(Z_i = b_i)$$

$$= P(Z_6 = b_6) \prod_{i=0}^{5} P(Z_i = b_i | Z_5 = b_5, \ldots Z_{i+1} = b_{i+1}). \tag{1}$$

This suggests that in order to generate the $i^{th}$ MSB, we can generate the $6^{th}$, $5^{th}$, $\ldots (i+1)^{th}$ MSB, and then generate a bit according to the conditional probability $P(Z_i = b_i | Z_5 = b_5, Z_4 = b_4 \ldots Z_{i+1} = b_{i+1}) = q_i(\bar{b}_i)$ (say), where $\bar{b}_i = b_5 b_4 \ldots b_{i+1}$.

In order to do this, we generate a uniform random number $U_i$ from an Linear Feedback Shift Register (LFSR) with XNOR feedback, independent of all $U_j$, $j > i$. Let the width of $U_i$ be $L_i$. Thus it takes all the values in the range 0 to $2^{L_i} - 1$ uniformly. Thus, we can set a threshold $T_i = \lfloor q_i(\bar{b}_i)(2^{L_i} - 1) \rfloor$, and decide $Z_i = 1$ when $U_i \leq T_i$, 0 otherwise. This will approximate $q_i(\bar{b}_i)$ with

$$\hat{q}_i(\bar{b}_i) = (\lfloor q_i(\bar{b}_i)(2^{L_i} - 1) \rfloor + 1)/(2^{L_i} - 1).$$

This introduces some errors into the methodology which is detailed in section 5.

The different $T_i$'s corresponding to different $q_i(\bar{b}_i)$, are stored in a ROM of size $2^{5-i}$, each corresponding to a different value of $\bar{b}_i$. Thus, the overall memory usage of the architecture is $\sum_{i=0}^{5} 2^{5-i} = 2^6 - 1$. In general, for an architecture of output bit width $L$, the memory usage is $2^L - 1$. Thus, this architecture becomes infeasible for bitwidths $> 13$, due to the large amounts of BRAM needed ($>$ 8KB).

# 4   Architecture

As suggested in the previous section, the bits starting from MSB are generated at each output stage by comparing an uniform random number to a threshold, which in turn depends on the bits already available. Due to the extremely fast decay of the Gaussian PDF, we observe that the values $P(Z_6 = 1)$ and $P(Z_5 = 1|Z_6 = 1)$ are extremely low ($\sim 10^{-6} = 2^{-20}$). Thus, the MSB and second MSB require $\geq 24$ bit uniform random numbers in order to get a good approximation to the actual probabilities (with error $\leq 1\%$). The probability values for the other bit positions are however $\geq 10^{-3}$. Thus they can be approximated with much lower number of bits. The designed RNG uses 24 bit uniform random numbers for both $Z_6$ and $Z_5$. For the remaining ones, it uses 12 bit random numbers.

Each uniform random number is generated by a LFSR with appropriate periodicity considerations as elaborated next.

The requirement for our design is the generation of independent pseudo-random numbers for the random variables $U_i$. We have chosen the length of each LFSR coprime to each other. This generates independent pseudo random numbers as is evident from the following two lemmas.

**Lemma 1.** *If $LFSR_i$ and $LFSR_j$ have coprime periods, say $P_i$ and $P_j$ respectively, then $U_i$ and $U_j$ are independent, i.e. $P(U_i = u|U_j = v) = P(U_i = u)$.*

*Proof.* As periods of $LFSR_i$ and $LFSR_j$ are coprime, hence the total period of $LFSR_i$ and $LFSR_j = P_iP_j$. Within this period, each possible output $u$ of $U_i$ occurs exactly once for every possible output $v$ of $P_j$. Thus, $P(U_i = u|U_j = v) = \frac{1}{P_i} = P(U_i = u)$.

**Lemma 2.** $2^i - 1$ *and* $2^j - 1$ *are coprime if and only if $i$ and $j$ are coprime.*

*Proof.* Say $gcd(i,j) = d$. Then, $2^i - 1 = 2^{d\frac{i}{d}} - 1$ and thus $2^d - 1|2^i - 1$, and similarly $2^d - 1|2^j - 1$, thus $gcd(2^i - 1, 2^j - 1) \neq 1$.

On the other direction, let $p|2^i - 1$ and $p|2^j - 1$, where p is a prime. Let $r = \text{index}(2) \mod p$. Then $r|i$ and $r|j$. Thus, $gcd(i,j) \neq 1$, and hence $i$ and $j$ are not coprime.

Thus, two LFSR's with coprime lengths $l_i$ and $l_j$, and thus coprime periods $2^{l_i} - 1$ and $2^{l_j} - 1$, generate independent pseudo random numbers.

In the designed architecture, we used a 17 bit LFSR for generating the sign bit, 29 and 39 bit LFSR's for generating $Z_5$ and $Z_4$, and 22, 23, 25 and 31 bit LFSR's to generate $Z_3$, $Z_2$, $Z_1$, $Z_0$ respectively. The sign bit was generated independently as the gaussian distribution is symmetric. Thus, the overall period of the GRNG comes out to be $\prod_i(2^{l_i} - 1) \simeq 10^{56}$, where $l_i$ is the length of the $i^{th}$ LFSR.

The overall architecture is pipelined to ensure the generation of one random number per cycle. The pipeline is six-stage, and thus the design has a latency of 6 clock cycles. Figure 1 shows the architecture adopted.

## 5  Statistical Tests

Statistical tests are always necessary in order to rigorously evaluate the performance of a random number generator. In order to evaluate the quality of

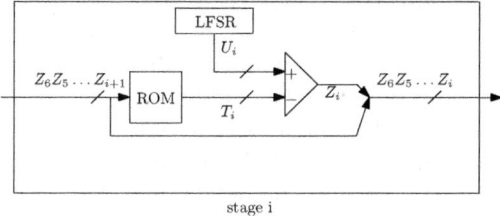

**Fig. 1.** Designed architecture

the generated random numbers, we ran some statistical tests on an observed sequence of $10^9$ numbers. These tests are described next.

In order to make sure that the generated sequence indeed follows $N(0, 1)$, we ran a $\chi^2$ goodness of fit test with the bins centered at the quantized points output by the RNG, and thus a total of 127 bins.

This test uses the statistic $\chi = \sum_{i=0}^{K} \frac{(E_i - O_i)^2}{E_i}$, where $E_i$ = expected number of occurences of a particular event by the theoretical distribution, $O_i$ = observed number of occurences of that event and $K$ is the total number of bins. This value of $\chi$ is compared to a threshold $\chi_\alpha$ which is chosen such that we make the mistake of rejecting a valid sequence with probability $\alpha$, called the significance level.

The value of the $\chi^2$ statistic with 126 d.o.f. for the sequence was 119.7 with p-value $= P(\chi^2_{126} > 119.7) = 67\%$. This shows that the sequence passes the test at 10% level of significance.

In order to evaluate the goodness of fit of the tail alone, we applied the $\chi^2$ test to the extreme half of the distribution alone containing $5 \times 10^7$ samples and 63 bins. This gave a test statistic of 33.98, with p-value $= 99.9\%$. Thus, the tail of the sequence also passes the test at 10% level of significance.

We also tested the whiteness of the generated sequence. For being a white gaussian sequence, the autocorrelation function must be $\delta(t)$. For statistically testing this hypothesis, we took N point Discrete Fourier Transform (DFT) of blocks of N consecutive random numbers from the sequence. If the output was indeed white, the expected DFT would be the same at every point. Thus, we tested the null hypothesis

$$H_0 : E(|F[n]|^2) = N, \qquad \forall\, n = 1, 2, 3, \ldots N$$

versus the alternative hypothesis $H_1 : E(|F[n]|^2) \neq N$ for some $n$. For each n, the hypothesis can be tested by a t-test.

The test is done on a sequence of total $2^{24}$ random number outputs of the generator, for different values of N. Note that the overall null hypothesis consists of N independent null hypotheses which are being tested. Thus, for the overall test to have a significance level of $\alpha$, the significance level for each of these tests, $\alpha_0$ should be such that $(1 - \alpha_0)^N = 1 - \alpha$.

The tests done on this sequence could not reject the hypothesis at an overall significance level of 10% for all N $\leq 2^{14}$. This confirms that the generated sequence is indeed white atleast upto a blocklength of $2^{14}$.

As discussed in Section 3, an error is introduced by approximating each $q_i$ by $\hat{q}_i$. However, the actual probabilities of each possible outcome can be exactly derived from $\hat{q}_i$, as each uniform random number is completely independent of another over a complete period. Such probabilities were calculated and their percentage deviations from the ideal distribution obtained. Figure 2 shows the plot of the deviation against $x$, the RNG output in the positive half of the distribution only. We observe that the percentage errors are always $< 7\%$.

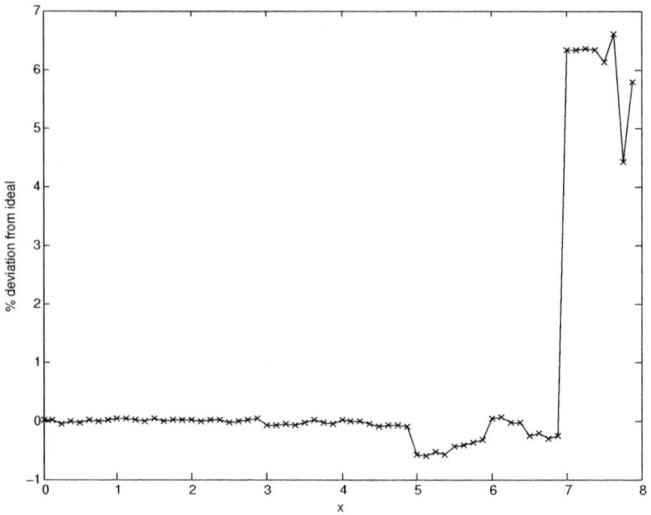

**Fig. 2.** Percentage deviation of the actual distribution from the theoretical one

We also tested a Low Density Parity Check Code (LDPC) decoder with this RNG and found extremely good conformance between the bit error rates obtained by a floating point simulation done on software and the hardware testbench. This further supports the correctness and accuracy of this generator.

## 6    FPGA Implementation

The discussed design was synthesized, placed and routed using Xilinx ISE tools and was put on a Virtex-5 LX110T board. Simulations showed a maximum speed of 220 MHz can easily be achieved. Thus, the overall design has a throughput of 220 million random numbers/s.

The small lookup tables for the thresholds were generated using logic only. The overall design uses only 51 slices, without using any special resources such as BRAM or DSP48E. Table 1 compares and contrasts this implementation with other reported designs and software implementations. We observe that our design uses $< 10\%$ resources of other designs. We were able to fit upto 80 instances of the RNG on an LX110T in addition to a LDPC decoder so as to run a hardware based simulation of the decoder design.

**Table 1.** Comparison with other designs

|  | Slices Used | Speed (MHz) | Throughput | Range ($\sigma$) | Bit Width |
|---|---|---|---|---|---|
| Xilinx module | 653 | 168 | 168 MSamp/s | 5 | 16 |
| Zhang[2] | 891 | 170 | 168 MSamp/s | N/A | 32 |
| Lee[1] | 585 | 232 | 232 MSamp/s | 8.2 | 16 |
| Proposed | 51 | 220 | 220 MSamp/s | 7.8 | 7 |

# 7   Conclusion

We have presented an area-efficient design for generating Gaussian random numbers. Extensive statistical tests on the randomness and distribution of the output numbers has been done in order to confirm the quality of the output. The design can be readily adapted to slightly higher bit lengths ($\leq 14$ bits), but after that the design becomes impractical due to high memory requirements. The small area requirement can translate to higher parallelism.

Lastly, the approach outlined above can be readily modified to generate random numbers from any arbitrary probability distribution, not only normal distribution.

**Acknowledgments.** The authors are grateful to Tata Consultancy Services for funding the research project under project code no. 1009298.

The authors are also grateful to the anonymous reviewers for their comments for improving this paper.

# References

1. Lee, D., Cheung, R., Villasenor, J., Luk, W.: Inversion-Based Hardware Gaussian Random Number Generator: a Case Study of Function Evaluation via Hierarchical Segmentation. In: IEEE International Conference on Field-Programmable Technology, pp. 33–40 (2006)
2. Zhang, G., Leong, P., Lee, D., Villasenor, J., Cheung, R., Luk, W.: Ziggurat Based Hardware Gaussian Random Number Generator. In: IEEE International Conference on Field-Programmable Logic and its Applications, pp. 275–280 (2005)
3. Zarubica, R., Wilson, S.G., Hall, E.: Multi-Gbps FPGA-Based Low Density Parity Check(LDPC) Decoder Design. In: IEEE Globecom, pp. 548–552 (2007)
4. Darabiha, A., Carusone, A., Kschischang, F.: A 3.3-Gbps Bit-Serial Block-Interlaced Min-Sum LDPC Decoder in 0.13-$\mu$m CMOS. In: Custom Integrated Circuits Conference, pp. 459–462 (2007)

# Accurate Floating Point Arithmetic through Hardware Error-Free Transformations

Manouk V. Manoukian and George A. Constantinides

Imperial College, London
{mm3309,gac1}@ic.ac.uk

**Abstract.** This paper presents a hardware approach to performing accurate floating point addition and multiplication using the idea of error-free transformations. Specialized iterative algorithms are implemented for computing arbitrarily accurate sums and dot products. The results of a Xilinx Virtex 6 implementation are given, area and performance are compared against standard floating point units and it is shown that the time×area product can be improved by a factor of 4 and 6 over software error-free addition and multiplication. Furthermore, it is illustrated that a number of area and performance trade-offs can be made when calculating vector sums and dot products.

## 1 Introduction

FPGA based designs offer great flexibility to applications modeled using floating point data processing. Designers can choose highly optimized IP cores or customisable and exotic operations [1,2]. The accuracy of floating point operations has always been a major concern and is dealt with in a variety of ways, both in software and hardware [3]. Traditionally, increased precision in hardware floating point operations is achieved by committing to large floating point units. However, if maximal accuracy is required in a calculation, very long fixed point registers have to be used. These registers can be upward of 600 bits in length for IEEE 32 bit standard floating point numbers [4,5].

This work migrates a method known in software to an FPGA context. It is known to be possible to represent the result of an atomic floating point addition or multiplication without any error by using only *two* registers of standard size [6]. The input pair is transformed into an output pair, where one output corresponds to the traditional result and the other to the error present in the calculation. Such error-free operations are very costly in software [6]. However, in hardware the cost is easily reduced, as we show in this paper. Error-free addition and multiplication have been recently used in a number of projects to develop accurate arithmetic algorithms, mainly for sums and dot products [7,8]. Distillation, one of the most popular among these algorithms, is well suited for FPGA implementation. By using the hardware accelerated atomic operations, as well as exploiting parallelism in the algorithm's structure, we can create high throughput circuits for vector sums and dot products.

A. Koch et al. (Eds.): ARC 2011, LNCS 6578, pp. 94–101, 2011.

# 2    Atomic Operations

## 2.1    Accurate Addition/Subtraction

Error-free floating point addition algorithms have been known since the mid 1960s. Two of the most well known algorithms are 2Sum which is due to Møller [9] and Knuth [10] and Fast2Sum which was created by Kahan [11] and later formalised by Dekker [6] in 1971. Both algorithms produce the same results but Fast2Sum is arguably simpler to understand. Algorithm 1 transforms the precise unrounded sum of two floating point numbers $a + b$ into the sum of two floating point numbers $x + y$. Number $x$ is equal to the rounded-to-nearest floating point sum $RN(a+b)$ and $y = a+b - RN(a+b)$ which is the exact error in the sum due to roundoff error and insufficient precision. Other rounding modes can be used but only with round-to-nearest it is possible to guarantee no loss of information.

**Algorithm 1.** The Fast2Sum Algorithm

**if** $|a| < |b|$ **swap** $a$ and $b$
$x \leftarrow RN(a + b)$
$z \leftarrow RN(x - a)$
$y \leftarrow RN(b - z)$

The algorithm requires 6 FLOPs (floating point operations) in total, 3 additions/subtractions, 2 absolute values and 1 comparison [6]. The absolute values and the comparison are used to check whether $|a| \geq |b|$ and swap the numbers if this is not the case. This branch can be especially problematic in heavily pipelined CPUs. Furthermore, the 3 additions exhibit data dependencies and cannot be executed in parallel. In a FPGA, however, we do not have to abide with the limitations of standard floating point adders. It is possible to modify a regular adder to provide both outputs $x$ and $y$. Such a circuit has been created before [12]; in that work the operation provides the error information on demand, by stalling the pipeline and thus greatly reducing the throughput. In this work the process has been fully incorporated into the design of the adder, maintaining the standard adder pipeline structure.

The logic behind the circuit is straightforward, see Figure 1. When two floating point numbers $a, b$ with $|a| \geq |b|$ are added, the significand of $b$, $sig_b$, has to be aligned with $sig_a$. After the operands have been aligned, some or all of the least significant digits of $b$ can be outside the range of the result mantissa. These "residual" bits that are normally discarded, constitute the error in the addition. The error calculation, besides the isolation of residual digits, needs to account for rounding in the result, for the possibility of subtraction as well as for overflow and cancellation in the fraction addition.

## 2.2    Accurate Multiplication

Similar to addition, an error-free transformation can be achieved with floating point multiplication as well. The aim is to transform the product of two floating

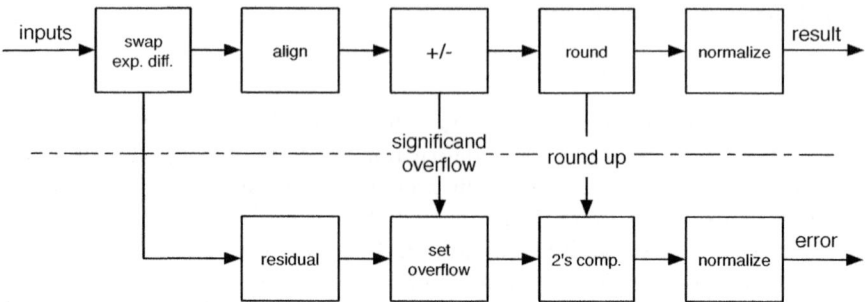

**Fig. 1.** The error calculation flow diagram on the bottom incorporated with the standard FP adder diagram on the top

point numbers $a \cdot b$ to a sum of two floating point numbers $x + y$, where $x = RN(a \cdot b)$ and $y = a \cdot b - RN(a \cdot b)$. The best known way to achieve this is Dekker's product [6]. This algorithm in software requires 17 FLOPs in total, 7 multiplications, 10 additions/subtractions and has a dependency depth of 8, allowing for parallel execution of multiple operations.

A hardware implementation of error-free multiplication can be considerably more cost effective. When two floating point numbers of precision[1] $p$ are multiplied, the infinitely precise result can only be $2p$ or $2p - 1$ digits wide. The most significant half of that is output once rounded as the significand of the result. The second, least significant half, is normally truncated but it can be used instead to calculate the error in the product. The error calculation circuit has to account for potential rounding in the result as well as set the sign of the error. Unfortunately, the error output needs to be normalised whereas the product output does not need any normalisation. This does create the need for a large normalisation unit and introduces a noticeable delay in the calculations as will be discussed in the conclusions.

## 3    Accurate Vector Sums and Dot Products

When calculating the sum of multiple floating point numbers with $p$ digits of precision each, often more than $p$ digits are needed to represent the result with maximal accuracy. To achieve this, two major types of algorithms exist in the literature, multiple-digit [4] and multiple-term algorithms [13].

Multiple-digit algorithms use very long accumulators and require some bit manipulation to position the results in the right slot of the accumulator.

Multiple-term algorithms use error-free transformations to produce results that are expressed as expansions $x = x_n + x_{n-1} + ... + x_2 + x_1$. Each component of the expansion has $p$-digits of precision and is sorted by magnitude $\forall i. |x_{i+1}| \geq |x_i| \wedge (|x_{i+1}| = |x_i| \rightarrow x_i = 0)$. The most important property of the multiple-term

---

[1] Precision is the length of the floating point number's significand including the often suppressed MSB in radix 2.

result is that the terms are non-overlapping[2]; this means that the result will have the smallest possible number of non-zero terms. The sign of the result is the sign of the largest component since $|x_i| > \sum_{j=0}^{i-1} |x_j|$. Thus, crude approximation of the result can be made from the component with the largest magnitude [7].

This work is focused on error-free transformations and more specifically on a commonly used multiple-term algorithm often referred to as the distillation algorithm [7,8]. Distillation is used to transform an input vector of $n$ floating point numbers into an output vector that holds the exact sum $S = \sum_{i=1}^{n} d_i$ expressed as a multiple-term expansion.

**Algorithm 2.** The Distillation Algorithm

**repeat**
    **for** $i \leftarrow 1$ to $n - 1$ **do**
        $(d_{i+1}, d_i) \leftarrow$ Fast2Sum$(d_i, d_{i+1})$
    **end for**
**until** $d_i$ non-overlapping with $d_{i+1}$

Distillation (Algorithm 2) is achieved by sweeping repeatedly through the input data and applying the error-free addition algorithm (Fast2Sum) until the vector is transformed into the expansion of the accurate sum. The algorithm terminates when all the non-zero elements of the vector are non-overlapping. The number of iterations needed for termination is not predefined and depends not only on the input data, but also on the order the data appears. In the worst case scenario the algorithm would take $n$ iterations to complete. In practice considerably fewer iterations are needed. For example, for large random test vectors (millions of inputs) using the IEEE 754 32-bit floating point format, the number of iterations never exceeds nineteen.

Distillation is not only useful for calculating completely accurate sums. When used with a fixed number of iterations $K$, then the most significant component of the result (the first element of the vector) is actually the same as if the sum was computed in K-fold precision and then rounded back to working precision [8]. Therefore, distillation can be used for both accurate multi-term results as well as accurately rounded single-term results.

The error-free adder that has been developed can be utilised to replace the Fast2Sum algorithm to accelerate the accumulation (Figure 2). Further acceleration of the accumulation can be accomplished by unrolling the loop and skewing the iterations. In Figure 3 three iterations have been unrolled, and so three different adders can be used in a pipelined fashion. If the number of elements to be added is much larger than the number of adders, then the iterations are executed in parallel. Another benefit of using multiple accurate adders is minimization of the memory traffic, since it is no longer necessary to temporarily store the results of the intermediate calculations. It is likely that the number of iterations needed is not a multiple of the available adders. This means that more iterations

---

[2] Two floating point values $x$ and $y$ are non-overlapping if the least significant nonzero bit of $x$ is more significant than the most significant nonzero bit of $y$, or vice-versa.

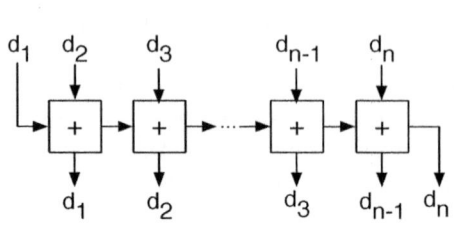

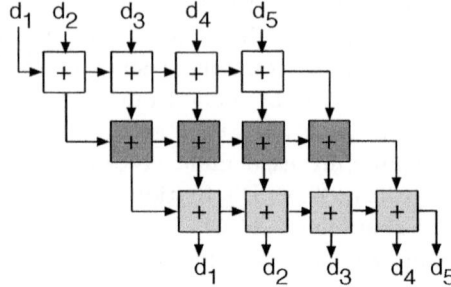

**Fig. 2.** Single distillation iteration, using a single error-free adder

**Fig. 3.** Three unrolled distillation iteration, using separate adders

might be executed than is necessary. Fortunately extra iterations do not corrupt the result and since iterations are executed in parallel there is no performance disadvantage.

Computing dot products does not pose a difficult task. Consider the dot product $\sum_{i=0}^{n} a_i \cdot b_i$. Dekker's product (error-free multiplication) can be used to transform the products $a_i \cdot b_i$ to the sums $x_{2i} + x_{2i+1}$. Then only the accurate sum $\sum_{i=0}^{2n} x_i$ needs to be calculated. This can be achieved by using an error-free multiplier to convert the input products into sums and then simply apply distillation.

## 4   Results

For this work the FloPoCo framework [2] was used to develop all of the accurate operations mentioned. Although the VHDL generated is not parametric, we can generate operations of arbitrary size. The most important operation implemented is the error-free adder. If the error output is ignored then the accurate adders generated are indistinguishable from a standardised adder of the same size, both in terms of results, pipeline depth and latency. This means that the developed unit can replace the 6 FLOPs of the Fast2Sum algorithm with effectively one standard addition at only somewhat increased area cost. In Table 1 a 32 bit adder implemented on a Xilinx Virtex 6 FPGA is compared with a error-free adder. The error-free adder has the same latency - it was possible to maintain the same critical path - and requires a 47% larger area for the error calculation circuit. Therefore, the sixfold decrease in FLOPs and the 1.47 increase in area means an improvement in the time×area product by a factor of $\frac{6}{1.47} \approx 4$, compared to software libraries. An adder with double the precision, 47 bits (56 bit in total) instead of 23 bits, is also compared (1). The longer adder does offer increased accuracy but by no means is it error free. The error-free adder can give more accurate results faster and uses significantly less area.

The multiplication comparison metrics in Table 2 show significantly different results. When comparing a standard 32-bit multiplier with the error-free implementation, a large increase in area and latency is apparent. Both of these are due to the fact that we need to use a normalisation unit for the residual.

**Table 1.** Adder Comparisson on the Virtex 6 FPGA

| Adder Type | Number of Slices | Increase | Latency | Increase |
|---|---|---|---|---|
| 32-bit | 177 slices | – | 20ns | – |
| 32-bit error-free | 260 slices | 47% | 20ns | 0% |
| 56-bit | 392 slices | 121% | 33ns | 65% |

The normalisation unit requires a large number of slices and has a long pipeline that increases the overall latency. On the other hand there is no need for a normalisation unit in the standard design, because the multiplication of numbers will need at most one bit of alignment. The doubling of the area shown in Table 2 refers only to the number of slices used; note that all the multipliers in the table also use the same number (4) of DSP blocks. Software libraries require 17 FLOPs for a single error-free multiplication, our implementation therefore outperforms software alternatives in time×area product by a factor of $\frac{1}{2.02} \times \frac{17}{1.4} \approx 6$.

In a flexible FPGA environment it is possible to have multipliers with standard inputs that produce wider and more accurate results. For example if we opt for a 47-bit precision for the output the result is infinitely precise without any cost in area and with smaller latency. The absolute accuracy is possible because in every floating point multiplier the infinitely precise result is at most $2p$ bits wide and is calculated anyway. The seemingly strange reduction in latency is actually expected since an accurate result does not require any rounding circuitry.

**Table 2.** Multiplier Comparisson on the Virtex 6 FPGA

| Multiplier Type | Number of Slices | Increase | Latency | Increase |
|---|---|---|---|---|
| 32-bits in 32-bits out | 60 slices | – | 20ns | – |
| 32-bit error-free | 121 slices | 102% | 28ns | 40% |
| 32-bits in 56-bits out | 61 slices | 2% | 11ns | -45% |

The accurate summation and dot product algorithms are not only accelerated by the aforementioned atomic operations but can also be accelerated by using multiple adders to exploit the parallelism between consecutive iterations. The area consumed increases linearly with the number of adders utilised. The performance increase however, is not linear and is slightly dampened because the design's maximum frequency drops as the FPGA becomes more saturated. Besides the number of adders, another parameter that can be adjusted is the adder width. If the input precision is kept constant, increasing the adder precision will reduce the number of iterations needed to converge to the precise result, but will also make the adder slower. We used random test cases with 32 bit floating point numbers uniformly distributed in the entire floating point range and studied how the accumulator behaves. Figure 4 illustrates that increasing the adders' precision over the original 24 bits, reduces the iterations needed for the algorithm to complete.

If both the number of adders as well as the adders' precision are varied, then the design space for the accurate accumulator is illustrated in Figure 5.

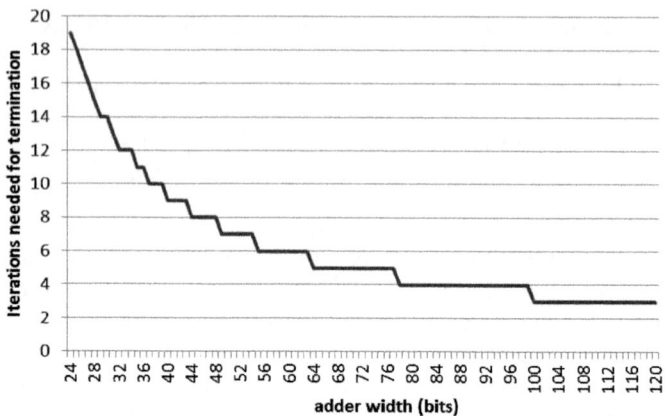

**Fig. 4.** Effect of the adder precision on the number of iteration required to terminate with a fixed specified accuracy level, independent of adder width

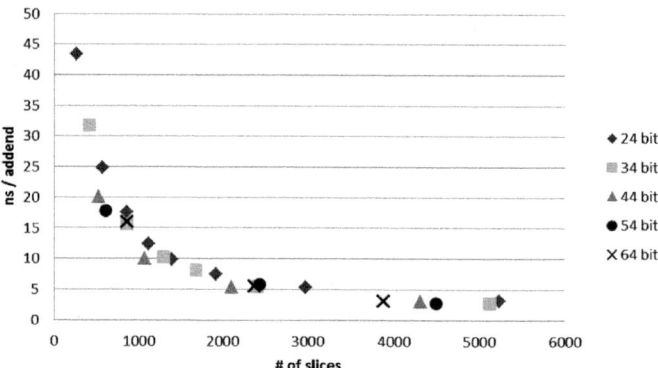

**Fig. 5.** The design space of a 32 bit accurate accumulator, considering alternative conditions of adder width and iteration count to achieve the same accuracy

The vertical axis illustrates the time increase in the accumulation for every extra addend. The horizontal axis illustrates the area resource and reflects the increasing number of adders from left to right. It is clear that for high throughput applications we will have to sacrifice area to accommodate more adders in the design. However, if we use wider adders it is possible to achieve the same level of performance with a smaller footprint. The benefit of using wider adders is also noticeable but not as prominent in small area designs. By using a wider adder we can more than double the throughput with a reasonably small area investment. Near the performance×area sweet spot the adder width does not play a vital role; the level of performance is dictated mainly by the total area committed to the design.

# 5    Conclusion

In this work circuits were developed that can replace software based error-free addition and multiplication. The need for such circuits is apparent to researchers working on error-free transformation and they have expressed their wish for hardware support for their applications [8].

Our error-free adder implementation can be used to accelerate algorithms that already use the software versions and can outperform them in time×area product by a factor of 4×. Our implementation is also a viable method for executing accurate addition in general.Results are produced faster, less area is consumed and greater accuracy is achieved compared to adders that are wider than the inputs. On the other hand, although the error-free multiplier implementation can surpass its software counterpart by a factor of 6× as we have shown, it is not useful as a general purpose accurate multiplier. If accurate multiplication is the main design goal then customised standard multipliers offer a better design choice.

Finally, we have shown how the accurate atomic operations can be combined to calculate precise multi-term or accurately rounded single-term sums and dot products. These algorithms are well suited for FPGA implementation because of their inherent parallelism, and we have illustrated the performance-area trade-offs that can be achieved by varying both the number of floating point units utilised, as well as units' word length.

# References

1. VFLOAT, http://www.ece.neu.edu/groups/rpl/projects/floatingpoint/
2. Flopoco project, http://www.ens-lyon.fr/LIP/Arenaire/Ware/FloPoCo/
3. Muller, J., Brisebarre, N., de Dinechin, F., Jeannerod, C.P., Vincent, L., Melquiond, G., Revol, N., Stehlé, D., Torres, S.: Handbook of Floating-Point Arithmetic. Springer, Heidelberg (2010)
4. Kulisch, U.W.: Circuitry for generating scalar products and sums of floating-point numbers with maximum accuracy. United States Patent 4622650 (1986)
5. Kulisch, U.W.: Advanced Arithmetic for the Digital Computer: Design of Arithmetic Units. Springer, New York (2002)
6. Dekker, T.J.: A floating-point technique for extending the available precision. Numerische Mathematik 18, 224–242 (1971); 10.1007/BF01397083
7. Shewchuk, J.R.: Adaptive precision fp arithmetic and fast robust geometric predicates. Discrete and Computational Geometry 18 (1996)
8. Rump, S.M.: Error-free transformations and ill-conditioned problems. In: International Workshop on Verified Computations and Related Topics (2009)
9. Møller, O.: Quasi double-precision in floating point addition. BIT Numerical Mathematics 5, 37–50 (1965); 10.1007/BF01975722
10. Knuth, D.: The Art of Computer Programming: Seminumerical Algorithms, vol. 2. Addison Wesley, Reading (1969)
11. Kahan, W.: Pracniques: further remarks on reducing truncation errors. Commun. ACM 8(1), 40 (1965)
12. Dieter, W.R., Kaveti, A., Dietz, H.G.: Low-cost microarchitectural support for improved floating-point accuracy. IEEE Comput. Archit. Lett. 6 (2007)
13. Ogita, T., Rump, S.M., Oishi, S.: Accurate sum and dot product. SIAM J. Sci. Comput. 26(6), 1955–1988 (2005)

# Active Storage Networks for Accelerating K-Means Data Clustering

Janardhan Singaraju and John A. Chandy

Department of Electrical and Computer Engineering,
University of Connecticut, Storrs, Connecticut, USA
{jas03023,chandy}@engr.uconn.edu

**Abstract.** High performance computing systems are often inhibited by
the performance of their storage systems and their ability to deliver data.
Active Storage Networks (ASN) provide an opportunity to optimize storage system and computational performance by offloading computation
to the network switch. An ASN is based around an intelligent network
switch that allows data processing to occur on data as it flows through
the storage area network from storage nodes to client nodes. In this
paper, we demonstrate an ASN used to accelerate K-means clustering.
The $K - means\ data\ clustering$ algorithm is a compute intensive scientific data processing algorithm. It is an iterative algorithm that groups
a large set of multidimensional data points in to $k$ distinct clusters. We
investigate functional and data parallelism techniques as applied to the
K-means clustering problem and show that the in-network processing of
an ASN greatly improves performance.

## 1 Introduction

Clustering algorithms are used to group input data into a set of clusters in such
a way that all the elements belonging to a cluster are very closely related. K-
means data clustering is a popular clustering algorithm used in a wide variety
of applications including data mining. The amount of data and floating point
computations involved in K-means algorithm make real time data processing of
this algorithm virtually impossible even on high end workstations. While parallelism is often used to address large scale data processing, there are limitations to
the scalability because of disk and network I/O shortcomings. In this paper, we
present the use of an FPGA within a network switch as a mechanism to address
I/O limitations and improve overall K-means clustering algorithm performance.

Large scale data processing is heavily I/O dependent. On the data storage
side, parallel I/O systems [1] provide one of the approaches to address this issue.
However, these systems do not scale well when a single client reads data from
many storage nodes. In such cases, with high performance storage nodes, we can
easily saturate the network connection to the client.

On the other hand, network switches have a global view of the distributed
data. Embedding computational capabilities in these switches is the core of what
we call an active storage network (ASN). In-network processing can improve the

A. Koch et al. (Eds.): ARC 2011, LNCS 6578, pp. 102–109, 2011.

performance of applications by moving compute intensive parts of data processing to a network switch where computational elements can perform parallel computations.

We have implemented several data processing kernels in an FPGA based ASN switch. In this paper, we discuss the FPGA based k means clustering algorithm built into a network switch. We also show how performance improvements can be made by offloading processing from the storage node to the network.

## 2   K-Means Data Clustering Algorithm

Given N multidimensional data points each having D dimensions, the algorithm starts by selecting $k$ initial cluster centroids using a heuristic. The data point is then assigned to the closest cluster having the least Euclidean distance. After all data points have been assigned to a cluster, new cluster centroids are calculated from the arithmetic mean of data points in the new cluster. The algorithm terminates if the number of points crossing over to a new cluster at the end of the iteration is below a threshold.

The floating point operations in Euclidean distance calculations take a varied number of cycles for completion depending on the type of implementation. They are also expensive in hardware due to the amount of area occupied on the chip/FPGA. For this reason initial hardware implementations have tried to reduce the cost of Euclidean distance calculations by replacing them with Manhattan distance and max distances [2]. Other implementations have taken a hardware/software approach where the cluster assignment part of the algorithm was implemented in software [3].

## 3   FPGA-Based K-Means Implementation

We implemented the K-means clustering algorithm using a gigabit Ethernet switch in a NetFPGA board development board. Fig. 1 shows the reference switch pipeline in the NetFPGA package [4].

### 3.1   User Data Processing Stage

Our FPGA-based K-means clustering application is based on an architecture that allows multiple data processing functions to be performed on data as it flows through the network in the form of Ethernet packets. In order to perform in-stream network data processing, we have added an extra stage between the output-port-lookup and output queues stages in the reference NetFPGA switch shown in Fig. 2. These data processing modules can include reduction operations like min/max, search etc. and transformational operations like sort, K-means clustering. The header processing module is responsible for verifying the contents of the incoming packet and the packet generator constructs new packets with the processed data from the application modules.

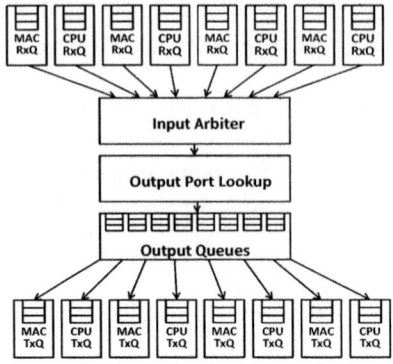

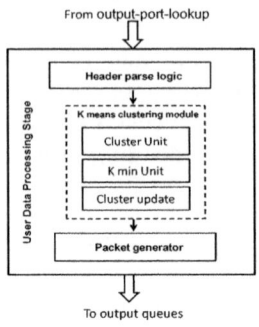

**Fig. 1.** NetFPGA Switch Pipeline [4]

**Fig. 2.** User Data Processing stage containing the K-Means module

## 3.2   K-Means Implementation

The primary K-means clustering components are the *cluster*, *cluster_update*, and *kmin* units. A *cluster* computes the distances between the cluster centroid and the given data point. It is implemented with floating point subtracter, multiplier and adder units as shown in Fig. 3. Each *cluster* also saves cluster centroid information in a register for every $d$ dimensions of the data point. This register is updated at the end of each iteration with the new cluster centroid calculated by the *cluster_update* unit. An array of $k$ such clusters concurrently receives data points from the data FIFOs and calculating the distances in parallel.

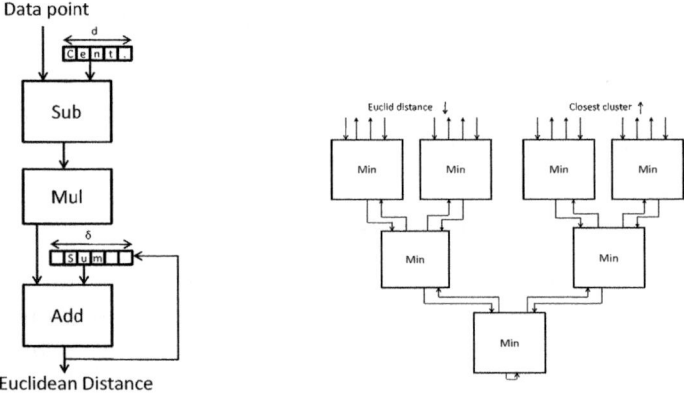

**Fig. 3.** K-means cluster unit

**Fig. 4.** Kmin unit

The *Kmin* unit computes the closest cluster from the Euclidean distance. It has a binary tree structure as shown in Fig. 4 with $\log K^*$ stages where $K^*$ is the extension of $k$ to the nearest power of 2. The given data point is then assigned to the new closest cluster center by updating the embedded header field of the data point. The header field for each data point contains $\log k$ bits at minimum for cluster assignment. The *cluster_update* unit is responsible for header update operations. Any changes in the cluster assignments will increment the crossover count register in the *cluster_update* unit. A data point is latched in the data FIFO until the cluster assignment, after which it is removed from the data FIFOs and and sent to the packet generator where multiple such points are assembled in to new packets and transmitted to the output queues.

At the end of the iteration, the cluster centers required for the subsequent iteration are calculated by the *cluster_update* unit from the average of the data points inside cluster. The crossover count register and the iteration count register are verified to terminate the algorithm. The crossover count register is reset after the completion of a iteration. If the crossover count is less than a threshold value, it means that there are only a few data points that were assigned to new clusters in the current iteration and current assignment is closer to the optimal assignment. The *cluster_update* unit contains a floating point adder, divider, $K$ $d$-dimensional registers to hold the sum and $k$ registers to hold the count of number of elements per cluster as shown in Fig. 5.

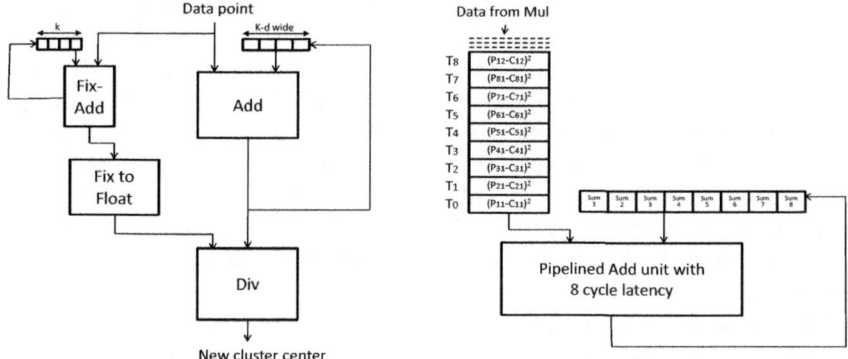

**Fig. 5.** Cluster update unit          **Fig. 6.** Data interleave optimization

## 3.3   Optimization

Pipelined floating point add/subtract and multiplication units on an FPGA have latencies up to 13 and 8 cycles respectively. On an FPGA, floating point implementations have a trade off between the area and latency. A straightforward implementation of Euclidean distance calculations with a floating point adder unit would stall every dimension of the data point for the duration of the latency in the adder circuit. An optimization strategy would be to interleave the dimensions of different points together in such a way that the latency is hidden. An interleaving optimization for hiding eight cycle latency is shown in Fig. 6. Data point $P_{ij}$ (where $i$ is the point number and $j$ the dimension), sent to the *cluster* unit shown in Fig. 3 is interleaved in such a way that , $i \bmod \delta$ (floating point add latency) varies from 1 to $\delta \; \forall \; j$. The floating point add unit in Fig. 6 receives the interleaved $|P_{ij} - C_{ij}|^2$ from the floating point multiplication unit in Fig. 3. The result of the partial sum $\sum |P_{ij} - C_{ij}|^2$ for a dimension $j$ of the data point $i$ will be ready after $\delta$ cycles. This result will be ready just in time for the add unit to perform another partial sum $\sum |P_{ij+1} - C_{ij+1}|^2$.

## 4    Parallelization Techniques

K-means algorithm on a single FPGA exhibits *cluster* level parallelism by performing Euclidean distance calculations belonging to all the *cluster* units in parallel. For higher values of $k$, the amount of resources available on a single FPGA will be insufficient to fit all $k$ *cluster* units. For such cases, the number of cluster units on the FPGA is reduced to a fraction. The remaining *cluster* units are computed in multi steps with $\frac{k}{n}$ *cluster* units per step. The original *Kmin* unit is modified to find the minimum of Euclidean distances from of all the steps. In a multi FPGA environment, the additional FPGA resources can be either used in two ways. **1) Data level parallelism:** Each FPGA can operate on separate data points thereby perform cluster assignments in parallel. Data level parallelism on a multi FPGA system is possible if each of the FPGAs implement all $k$ *cluster* units. The data is uniformly partitioned across all the FPGAs, and each data partition is sent to separate boards where Euclidean distances and cluster assignments are done in parallel. Each FPGA board calculates the local cluster centroids based on the portioned data and at the end of the iteration, the local cluster centroids are broadcast to the other boards for new centroid calculations. The subsequent iteration proceeds upon cluster update acknowledgment from all the FPGAs. Data level parallelism extracted this way would have higher performance but with the limitation on the number of clusters that can be fitted on each of the FPGA.

    **2) Cluster level parallelism:** The second approach would be to partition the $k$ clusters among the multiple FPGAs. This approach is intended for higher values of $k$. Each FPGA operates in parallel on the entire data set calculating the distances between data points and the FPGA's subset of $k$ *cluster* units. The local minimum of the Euclidean distances is broadcast to the other FPGAs where the global minimum is computed for use in resolving cluster assignment.

## 5    Results and Discussion

Several sets of experiments were run on a single FPGA and with a combination of multiple FPGAs. The sequential and parallel versions of the software algorithm [5] were run to evaluate the performance improvements made by implementing k means algorithm on a network switch. All the machines used in the setup run Linux on a dual core AMD Opteron 1.8Ghz processor with a 40GB SATA drive and a gigabit NIC. A client-server program in C handles the data transfer operations. Test data up to 1GB is generated at random as an input to the algorithm and is distributed across several hosts for parallel software and hardware implementations. The time for data partitioning is not timed in all the experimental results. All the host machines are connected through an FPGA based network switch in a low cost 2-dilated flattened butterfly network [6].

The base NetFPGA switch design consumed 15572 slices taking up 65% of the available Xilinx Virtex II Pro FPGA slices. Due to the limited resources available on the FPGA, we were able to fit only eight cluster units. For more than eight clusters, we used the multi step approach discussed in Section 4.

**Single FPGA:** In a single host scenario, one of the machines is used as both the host and server with the NetFPGA board as a co-processor. Data from the client is sent to the NetFPGA through a gigabit interface. The NetFPGA performs the k means clustering assignment and returns the data back to the host. Upon termination, the NetFPGA returns a packet to the host. Results for a single host system in Fig. 7 show the speedup for various cluster sizes and dimensions. The results show speedups 2-10 times over the software. Since the FPGA can calculate several clusters in parallel, the speedup improved with increase in the number of clusters. The runtime per iteration of the algorithm in hardware roughly remained the same with a slight increasing slope towards. However the software runtime software grew non-linearly after 8 clusters. This resulted in the super linear speedups for cluster sizes beyond 8. The FPGA has a limit of 8 clusters, so for 16 and 32 clusters, we used a multi step approach. However for higher number of clusters, the multi-step approach adds a sequential bottleneck in hardware. The results also show speedups independent of the number of dimensions.

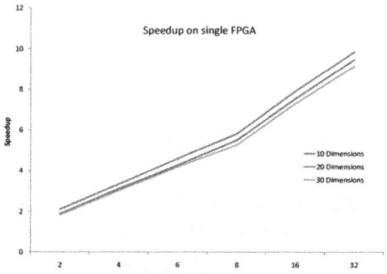

**Fig. 7.** Speedup on a single FPGA     **Fig. 8.** Speedup on multiple FPGAs

**Multiple FPGAs:** Multiple FPGA boards were connected in a 2-dilated flattened butterfly network to implement parallel K-means algorithm. Sets of experiments with two, four and eight FPGA boards were conducted. An equivalent number of hosts act as storage nodes. A client server program on the hosts perform the data transfer operations on the partitioned data in the same manner as on a single FPGA system.

Equivalent parallel versions of the software program were run to compare the performance. During software implementations the the host nodes act as processing nodes and are connected in the same network as in the hardware implementations. The software algorithm utilizes MPICh2 for message parsing. The results for the speedup due to the two parallelism techniques in hardware compared to the parallel software algorithm are shown in Fig. 8.

**Parallelism by data:** Speed up grew linearly with increase in clusters. Results show a speedup of around 9 times over software implementation [5]. As the data is distributed across multiple nodes, the bandwidth scaled with the number of FPGAs and the speed over parallel software implementation remained constant with increase in FPGAs.

**Parallelism by cluster:** The results show an increase in speedup with the number of clusters. The speedup however declined with increasing the number of FPGAs as the bandwidth did not scale with the number of FPGAs. The bandwidth of data coming in to the multi FPGA system remained at constant 1 Gbps for all the FPGAs. The benefit of cluster level parallelism will be evident as we increase the number of clusters. Figure 9 shows the runtime per iteration of execution for different $k$. The results show the data parallelism outperformed cluster level parallelism and a parallel implementation in software based on work in [5]. However for larger values of $k$ the cluster level parallelism should catch up with data level parallelism.

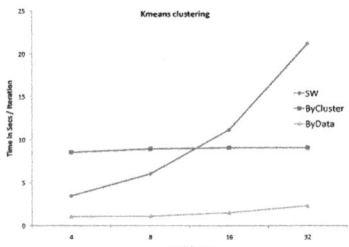

**Fig. 9.** Run time per iteration of K-means algorithm

One of the issues with data level parallelism is the limit on the maximum number of clusters $(k)$ that can be accommodated on the FPGA. A maximum of eight clusters units can fit on the XC2VP50 FPGA. For a given set of available FPGA resources, cluster level parallelism offers maximum choice in terms of the number of cluster units that can be computed. For an an eight FPGA network, using cluster level parallelism a maximum of 64 clusters can be computed before having to resort to the multi step approach.

## 6   Conclusions

In this paper, we have presented a case for the use of FPGA-based data processing in a network switch fabric. In particular, we implemented a scalable K-means clustering application built in to an FPGA switch and showed how performance improvements can be made by moving application data processing to the FPGA network switch. We presented different parallelization techniques useful in building applications on ASN. The performance of the K-means clustering algorithm can be improved by taking advantage of the hardware processing on an ASN. Two different parallelizing techniques, cluster level parallelism and data level parallelism offer different strategies in a multi FPGA in a network. A trade-off in the degree of clusters and performance affect the choice of the technique to be employed. K-means clustering is just one of many applications that can take advantage of this idea. We believe that the use of intelligence at the network could enhance the performance of parallel applications that use reduction or transformation operations on large amounts of data.

## Acknowledgment

This work was supported in part by a National Science Foundation grant (award number CCF-0621448). Any opinions, findings and conclusions or recommendations expressed in this material are those of the authors and do not necessarily reflect those of the National Science Foundation.

## References

1. Gibson, G.A., Meter, R.V.: Network attached storage architecture. Commun. ACM 43(11), 37–45 (2000)
2. Estlick, M., Leeser, M., Theiler, J., Szymanski, J.J.: Algorithmic transformations in the implementation of k- means clustering on reconfigurable hardware. In: Proceedings of the 2001 Ninth International Symposium on Field Programmable Gate Arrays, FPGA 2001, pp. 103–110. ACM, New York (2001)
3. da Filho, A.G., Frery, A.C., de Araújo, C.C., Alice, H., Cerqueira, J., Loureiro, J.A., de Lima, M.E., das Graças, M., Oliveira, S., Horta, M.M.: Hyperspectral images clustering on reconfigurable hardware using the k-means algorithm. In: Proceedings of the 16th Symposium on Integrated Circuits and Systems Design, SBCCI 2003, p. 99. IEEE Computer Society, Los Alamitos (2003)
4. http://www.netfpga.org
5. Son, S.W., Lang, S., Carns, P., Ross, R., Thakur, R., Ozisikyilmaz, B., Kumar, P., Liao, W.K., Choudhary, A.: Enabling active storage on parallel I/O software stacks. In: Proceedings of 26th IEEE Conference on Mass Storage Systems and Technologies, MSST 2010 (2010)
6. Thamarakuzhi, A., Chandy, J.A.: 2-dilated flattened butterfly: A nonblocking switching network. In: 11th International Conference on High Performance Switching and Routing, HPSR 2010, Texas, USA (2010)

# An FPGA Implementation for Texture Analysis Considering the Real-Time Requirements of Vision-Based Systems

Mario-Alberto Ibarra-Manzano and Dora-Luz Almanza-Ojeda

University of Guanajuato; DICIS; Departamento en Electrónica y Comunicaciones
Carretera Salamanca-Valle de Santiago Km. 3.5+1.8
Comunidad Palo Blanco, Salamanca, Guanajuato, Mexico
{ibarram,luzdora}@ieee.com
http://www.ingenierias.ugto.mx/

**Abstract.** This article presents an architecture based on FPGA for the calculation of texture attributes using an adequacy of the technique of sum and differences of histograms. The attributes calculated by this architecture will be used in a process of classification for identification of objects during the navigation of an autonomous robot of service. Because of that, the constraint of real-time execution plays an essential role during the architecture design. So, the architecture is designed to calculate 30 dense images with 6 different attributes of texture for 10 different displacements. Exploiting the reuse of operations in parallel on the FPGA and taking into account the requisites in the time of calculation, it is possible to use the resources in an efficient and optimised way in order to obtain an architecture with the best trade off between resources and the time of calculation. Thanks to the high performance of this architecture, it can be used in applications like medical diagnosis or target detection.

## 1 Introduction

In the autonomous navigation of a robot the identification of objects is a very important task which allows the interpretation of the images by a robot in order to make the decisions [1]. This process can be used in the detection of obstacles during the planning of the movement of the robot. Texture is one of the most used characteristic in image processing and pattern recognition for detecting or identifying reliable objects in a scene. The texture is defined as a particular and usually repeated patron in the surface of a given object which is essentially considered as a neighbourhood property [2]. Nevertheless, dense texture analysis is a very expensive computational time process, therefore to simplify and optimise this process, a complementary segmentation method based on colour is commonly used. However, in some cases, segmentation information based on colour is unreliable or insufficient, e.g. in mobile robotic platforms or medical applications. Furthermore, applications such as robotic platforms, auto-guided

A. Koch et al. (Eds.): ARC 2011, LNCS 6578, pp. 110–117, 2011.

vehicles or medical applications require real-time performances that can not be accomplished by conventional computers [4].

In this article we present an architecture for the dense analysis of the texture in real-time using the adequacy of the sum and difference histograms algorithm (ASDHs). This architecture efficiently reuse certain texture attribute modules in order to enrich the model and at the same time keeping a global high performance in the architecture. The next section briefly describes the ASDHs technique used to design our architecture. The technique used to enrich the number of the attributes and the details of the architecture design is given in the section 3. In section 4, we discuss the performance of the proposed architecture and the comparison among other architectures found in the literature. Conclusions and perspectives are presented at the end of this document.

## 2    Overview of Texture Analysis

The texture is principally represented by means of attributes which describe this property. These attributes of the texture are generally calculated from an image in gray-scale. In order to obtain these attributes, the most common used approach is the co-ocurrence matrices from which diverse attributes in a statistical way can be derived, nevertheless this type of attributes has the problem of not being independent moreover this approach needs a high quantity of memory. A second option consists in using the approach of sum and difference histograms (SDH). The attributes obtained by this approach are more independent, nevertheless, the cost in memory for storing the histograms and for calculating the attributes is as well high that results in a high cost of resources for real-time applications. A possible solution consists in using an adequacy of sum and difference of histograms (ASDHs) which keeps the properties of the texture attributes and drastically reduces the necessary resources. This reduction in resources comes from the direct calculation of the attributes and from the development of the operations in a parallel way, which facilitates its implementation on parallel-processing systems. The ASDHs technique was presented in [3]. This technique is highly interesting because it analyses the texture attributes and obtains the essential information about it in a simplified and optimised way.

The texture is the discrete intensity pattern in a neighbourhood defined by a rectangular grid of size $K \times L$ that contains the discrete texture image denoted by $I(k, l)$, where ($k \in [0, K - 1]$; $l \in [0, L - 1]$). Each pixel $I(k, l)$ is quantified in $N_g$ grey levels. The texture pattern is given by the change in the intensity of the current pixel with co-ordinates $(k, l)$ and a relative displacement of $(\delta_u, \delta_v)$ from the group of $M$ displacements around it. The change in the intensity is represented by the sum and difference images, $I_S$ y $I_D$ respectively, which are defined as:

$$
\begin{aligned}
I_S(k, l) &= I(k, l) + I(k + \delta_k, l + \delta_l) \\
I_D(k, l) &= I(k, l) - I(k + \delta_k, l + \delta_l)
\end{aligned}
\tag{1}
$$

Therefore, the rank of the image $I_S$ is $[0, 2(N_g - 1)]$, and for the image $I_D$ is $[-N_g + 1, N_g - 1]$. The table 1 shows the equations to calculate the attributes of

**Table 1.** Texture attributes computed from adequacy of SDHs (ASDHs)

| Texture attribute | Adequacy of sum and difference histograms |
|---|---|
| mean | $\frac{1}{2N} \sum_k \sum_l I_S(k,l)$ |
| variance | $\frac{1}{2N} \left( \sum_k \sum_l (I_S(k,l) - 2\mu)^2 + \sum_k \sum_l I_D(k,l)^2 \right)$ |
| correlation | $\frac{1}{2N} \left( \sum_k \sum_l (I_S(k,l) - 2\mu)^2 - \sum_k \sum_l I_D(k,l)^2 \right)$ |
| contrast | $\frac{1}{N} \sum_k \sum_l I_D(k,l)^2$ |
| homogeneity | $\frac{1}{N} \sum_k \sum_l \frac{1}{1+I_D(k,l)^2}$ |
| cluster shade | $\frac{1}{N} \sum_k \sum_l (I_S(k,l) - 2\mu)^3$ |
| cluster prominence | $\frac{1}{N} \sum_k \sum_l (I_S(k,l) - 2\mu)^4$ |

the texture using $I_S$ and $I_D$ images. These attributes are defined in a rectangular window of size $K \times L$, where $N$ is the number of pixels in the window and it is used to normalise the attributes, this parameter is defined like

$$N = K \times L \qquad (2)$$

The global algorithm of dense texture analysis based on ASDHs is presented in figure 1. The $I_S$ and $I_D$ images with respect to relative displacements are calculated from the input grey image. Next, only mean and contrast texture features are calculated because they are independed from the others. In other hand, homogeneity, variance and correlation features must be calculated after the mean and the contrast because they depend of mean and contrast. Each feature will be represented as an image. The relative displacements most frequently used by the image processing community are the distances 1, 2, 3 and 4 pixels with $0°$, $45°$, $90°$ and $135°$ as directions, that we also use in this work.

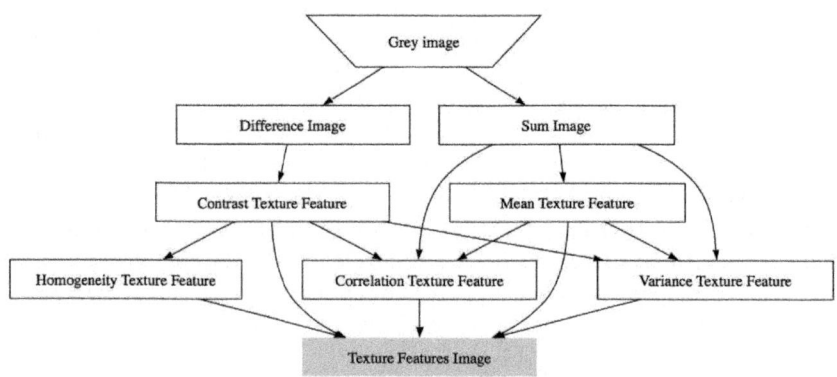

**Fig. 1.** Dense texture analysis algorithm

# 3  Hardware Implementation

One of the essential problems in hardware implementation (like ASIC, FPGA, GPU, DSP, multi-cores or many-cores) is the adequacy of the algorithms. Frequently, the optimisation of the algorithm according to the used technology is enough for solving the problem. However, when real-time processing is a critical and essential constraint in the design then the algorithm development needs a deeper analysis. Thanks to the ASDHs technique it is possible to obtain a good performance because this technique was designed to be implemented on hardware. The architecture presented in this article was designed and implemented on an FPGA device, which is used as an interesting engine for high-speed image processing. Our architecture is mainly focused to solve the navigation problem of a service robot. To accomplish that, first the architecture calculates the texture attributes of the environment, then these attributes are used to identify obstacles.

Usually, the robot moves a slow velocity during its navigation in indoor environments, however, this not avoid the requirement of a high processing performance in the algorithms. A minimal performance of 30 dense texture-images per seconds is needed in order to guaranty the object identification and the object interaction with the robot. A first solution is proposed in [5], this architecture uses a texture model defined by only one single displacement. This texture model is enough when only one class must be detected. In the case of an environment cluttered with several objects, it becomes essential to increase the number of texture attributes and therefore the number of displacements. In the architecture presented in [5], the modules to calculate texture attributes like the mean, the contrast and the homogeneity can be executed to higher performance than the pseudo-variance attribute. This last attribute limits the global performance in the architecture. However, it is possible to take advantage of this delay in the performance to calculate the mean, the contrast and the homogeneity for different displacements. That is, the faster modules are reused during the pseudo-variance attribute execution thus different displacements of the attributes can be obtained for only one distance in the pseudo-variance attribute. The architecture depicted in the figure 2 is proposed in this work to enrich the texture model without increasing the calculating resources. The architecture for each texture module is the same that [5] but in this case the mean, the contrast and the homogeneity modules have been adapted for calculating different attributes which highly increase our information about the environment without the necessity to add new modules.

The calculation of the $I_S$ and $I_D$ images is the first task executed during the dense texture analysis. Addition and subtraction operations are carried out between the current pixel and the displaced pixels. Sixteen displacements are used in total for four ratios and directions, such that (1, 2, 3 and 4 pixels) and ($45°$, $90°$, $135°$ and $180°$) respectively. The $0°$ direction is replaced by $180°$ in order to avoid an additional waiting time caused by the pixel located at right, (i.e. at $0°$) reducing, in this way, the latency time. The multiplexer located between the $I_S$ and $I_D$ image modules selects the ten most important displacements

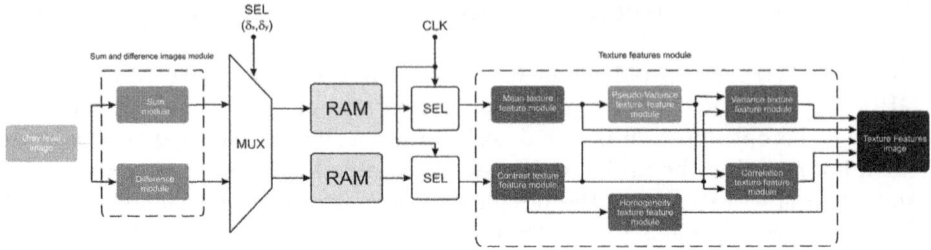

**Fig. 2.** Diagram of dense texture analysis algorithm

depending on the particular conditions of the environment under test. These displacements are predefined into the FPGA because they are obtained by a statistical analysis developed out of line. At each pixel clock, a new pixel from the image is used to calculate $I_S$ and $I_D$ images for the ten most important displacements and stored in the RAM memory. This information corresponds to a processing window of size $17 \times 15$ pixels for each displacement, that will be used to obtain the texture attributes. The frequency of execution for the mean, the contrast and the homogeneity modules achieves until 300 fps. Based on the aforementioned, these three modules calculate ten different displacements for their corresponding attributes against only one of the pseudo-variance module. In this way the selector sent sequentially the ten displacements found in the RAM therefore the texture modules can calculate the corresponding attributes without increasing the resources. To summarise, the architecture is able to obtain 10 different attributes for the mean, the contrast and the homogeneity and 1 for the pseudo-variance, the variance and the correlation attributes, we watch that this displacement gives the best information in according to the object model. This architecture calculates 33 texture attributes in total with a maximal performance of 30 dense texture feature images per second.

## 4   Results

Our architecture was prototyped using VHDL, Quartus II and ModelSim. After, it was synthesized for a EP3C120F780C7N Cyclone III family device of Altera. Some synthesis results of the FPGA device are: the implemented architecture requires $15,676$ combinational functions and $12,591$ dedicated logic registers, both combined represent $19,766$ logic elements, required memory is $1,842,880$ bits, and the number of embedded multipliers is 120. The quantity of logic elements uses only the 17% of total capacity in the device, whereas memory size and embedded multipliers represents the 47% and 42% respectively. These requirements directly depend of the image size, the number of displacements, the distance and the direction in displacements and the size of processing window used by texture features. Essential values used to test our architectures has been given in section 3, with those parameters, our architecture successfully calculates 30 dense texture feature images per second.

**Table 2.** Comparative table from different architectures

|  | Our Design | Design 2 [3] | Design 3 [6] | Design 4 [7] | Design 5 [8] |
|---|---|---|---|---|---|
| Algorithm | ASDHs | ASDHs | GLCH | GLCM | GLCM |
| Image size $[U \times V]$ | $640 \times 480$ | $640 \times 480$ | $512 \times 512$ | $352 \times 288$ | $512 \times 512$ |
| # of band $[B]$ | 1 | 1 | 1 | 4 | 1 |
| Window size $[K \times L]$ | $17 \times 15$ | $17 \times 15$ | $32 \times 32$ | $16 \times 16$ | $128 \times 128$ |
| # of gray Levels $[N_g]$ | 256 | 256 | 32 | 64 | 32 |
| # of features $[f]$ | $3 + 3$ | 6 | 1 | 4 | 6 |
| # of direction $[d]$ | $10 + 1$ | 4 | 4 | 4 | 16 |
| Performance $[p]$ (fps) | 30 | 30 | $25 - 30$ | 133 | 27 |
| Processing performance [pp] (bps) | 72 Gbps | 52 Gbps | 19 Gbps | 617 Mbps | 405 Mbps |
| Latency ($\mu s$) | 449.8 | 449.8 | − | − | − |
| Technology | FPGA | FPGA | FPGA+DSP | FPGA | FPGA |
| L. E. (Altera) | 19, 766 | 73, 021 | − | − | − |
| Emb. mult. | 120 | 480 | − | − | − |
| Slices (Xilinx) | − | − | − | 16, 158 | 5, 740 |
| Memory(I+E) | 1.75Mb+− | 720Kb+− | − + 2Mb | 160Kb+8Mb | 900Kb+− |

Our architecture is compared among other four architectures found in the literature. The table 2 shows the main characteristics and parameters for each compared architecture. The performance of our design is shown in first column, the rest of the columns show four selected designs labelled as Design 2 to 5, respectively. These designs has been presented by different authors (refers respectively to [3], [6], [7] and [8] for technical details of implementation). All of them are FPGA implementations that calculates texture attributes by ASDHs, Grey Level Co-occurence Histograms (GLCH) or GLCM techniques. Our design can be directly compared with the Design 2 and the Design 3 because they use a technique based on the Sum and Difference Histograms also they use an overlapping processing window that moves at each pixel in the image. In the Design 4 and the Design 5 a non-ovelaping window lets to save a big amount of operations then to increase the performance of the architectures. Contrary to the Design 2, our architecture use more efficiently all the texture modules, (see the processing performance value in the table). An efficient reuse of the modules lets to reduce the computation resources moreover to improve the quantity of information. However, this implies the use of more internal memory because the

$I_S$ and $I_D$ images needs to be stored during the computation process for each displacement. The Design 3 is a "heterogeneous" system, (that is FPGA+DSP) in which the DSP store and handle the histograms then the FPGA calculate in parallel the texture attributes. In order to reduce the memory resources due to the histograms, the authors limit the number of grey levels. From the Design 4 we note that it has the best development of the 5 designs but this value is biased by all the tuning parameters. In order to compare in a more unbiased way, we compared directly with the data that each architecture processes. That is, we calculate the amount of information processed by each architecture considering the different parameters that define the architecture. We call this measure the processing performance value in which we note that our architecture has the highest value thanks to the pertinent trade off among the size of the image and processing window, the number of bands, the grey levels in the image, the number of attributes and directions. In other hand, the Design 5 has the highest number of directions thought this architecture and the Design 4 calculate a smaller attribute image than the original image size. Consequently, the position of the identified objects is only approximative because the pixel position was drastically sub-sampled with respect to its original position (i.e.. for Design 5 original image size is $512 \times 512$ and the resulted attribute images are $4 \times 4$ pixels).

## 5   Conclusions and Future Works

The proposed architecture shows a correct use of the resources in order to enrich a model during the object identification task. Thanks to the use of the ASDHs technique the processing time, the latency and the resources are notably reduced. Furthermore, the reuse of the modules with highest development allows to increase the number of directions used in the previous version of the architecture thus defining an object model with richer information.

Every input pixel is codified to 8 bits that corresponds to number of bits used in most of the algorithms developed in computer vision. Nevertheless this decision directly affects the number of multipliers required in the pseudo-variance and the homogeneity modules. That is, these modules use two multipliers during the power operation because every pixel at the outputs of the $I_S$ and $I_D$ image modules are coded in 10 bits. So, it is possible to use only one multiplier if we only consider 7 bits from the input pixel. Thanks to the reuse of certain modules it is possible to implement two more texture attributes to complement our current texture data. These additional attributes are the prominence and the shade clusters, both attributes let to delimitate more efficiently the object contours.

**Acknowledgments.** This work was supported by the Consejo Nacional de Ciencia y Tecnología, the Secretaria de Educación Pública, and the Mexican Government.

# References

1. Avina-Cervantes, J., Estudillo-Ayala, M., Ledesma-Orozco, S., Ibarra-Manzano, M.: Boosting for image interpretation by using natural features. In: Seventh Mexican International Conference on Artificial Intelligence, MICAI 2008. pp. 117 –122 (October 2008)
2. Haralick, R.: Statistical and structural approaches to texture. Proceedings of the IEEE 67(5), 786–804 (1979)
3. Ibarra-Manzano, M.A., Almanza-Ojeda, D.L., Lopez-Hernandez, J.M.: Design and optimization of real-time texture analysis using sum and difference histograms implemented on an fpga. In: Electronics, Robotics and Automotive Mechanics Conference, pp. 325–330 (2010)
4. Ibarra-Manzano, M., Almanza-Ojeda, D.L., Devy, M., Boizard, J.L., Fourniols, J.Y.: Stereo vision algorithm implementation in fpga using census transform for effective resource optimization. In: 12th Euromicro Conference on Digital System Design, Architectures, Methods and Tools, DSD 2009, pp. 799–805 (August 2009)
5. Ibarra-Manzano, M.A., Devy, M., Boizard, J.L.: Real-time classification based on color and texture attributes on an fpga-based architecture. In: Ahonen, T. (ed.) Conference on Design and Architectures for Signal and Image Processing, DASIP 2010, October 26-28, pp. 53–60. ECSI - Electronic Chip and Systems design Initiative and IEEE, Playfair Library Hall, Old College, University of Edinburgh, South Bridge, Edinburgh, Scotland, United Kingdom (2010)
6. Ibarra Pico, F., Cuenca Asensi, S., Corcoles, V.: Accelerating statistical texture analysis with an fpga-dsp hybrid architecture. In: FCCM 2001: Proceedings of the the 9th Annual IEEE Symposium on Field-Programmable Custom Computing Machines, pp. 289–290. IEEE Computer Society, Washington, DC (2001)
7. Maroulis, D., Iakovidis, D.K., Bariamis, D.: Fpga-based system for real-time video texture analysis. J. Signal Process. Syst. 53(3), 419–433 (2008)
8. Siéler, L., Tanougast, C., Bouridane, A.: A scalable and embedded fpga architecture for efficient computation of grey level co-occurrence matrices and haralick textures features. Microprocess. Microsyst. 34(1), 14–24 (2010)
9. Tahir, M.A., Bouridane, A., Kurugollu, F.: An fpga based coprocessor for glcmand haralick texture features and their application in prostate cancer classication. Analog Integr. Circuits Signal Process 43(2), 205–215 (2005)

# CReAMS: An Embedded Multiprocessor Platform

Mateus B. Rutzig, Antonio Carlos S. Beck, and Luigi Carro

Universidade Federal do Rio Grande do Sul – Porto Alegre/Brazil
{mbrutzig,caco,carro}@inf.ufrgs.br

**Abstract.** As the number of embedded applications is increasing, the current strategy of the companies is to launch a new platform within short periods of time to execute them efficiently with low energy consumption. However, for each new platform deployment, new tool chains come along, with additional libraries, debuggers and compilers. This strategy implies high hardware redesign costs, breaks binary compatibility and results in a high overhead in the software development process. Therefore, focusing on area savings, low energy consumption, binary compatibility maintenance and mainly software productivity improvement, we propose the exploitation of Custom Reconfigurable Arrays for Multiprocessor System (CReAMS). CReAMS is composed of multiple adaptive reconfigurable systems to efficiently exploit Instruction and Thread Level Parallelism (ILP and TLP) at hardware level, in a totally transparent fashion. Assuming the same chip area of a multiprocessor platform, the proposed architecture shows a reduction of 37% in energy-delay product (EDP) on average, when running applications with different amounts of ILP and TLP.

## 1 Introduction

Embedded systems are getting increasingly heterogeneous in terms of software. A current high end cell phone has a considerable number of applications, most of them being installed during the product lifetime. As the current embedded systems have hard design constraints, the applications must be efficiently executed to provide the lowest possible energy consumption. To support such demands, current embedded platforms (e.g. OMAP) comprise one or two simple general purpose processors that are surrounded by several dedicated hardware accelerators (communication, graphics and audio processors), each one of them with its particular instruction set architecture (ISA).

The foreseen scenario for the current strategy of embedded platform development is not favorable for future embedded products since it is expected that 600 different hardware accelerators will be needed in the year 2024 [1]. Although such a strategy is energy efficient, it covers only software with a restricted behavior in terms of ILP and TLP. Every release of such a platform will not be transparent to the software developers, since together with a new platform, a new version of its tool chain with particular libraries and compilers must be provided. Besides the obvious deleterious effects on software productivity and compatibility for any new hardware upgrade, there will also be intrinsic costs of new hardware and software developments for every new product.

On the other hand, multiprocessing systems that are conceived as the replication of the same processors, in terms of architecture and organization, are employed in

A. Koch et al. (Eds.): ARC 2011, LNCS 6578, pp. 118–124, 2011.

general purpose platforms where performance is mandatory. However, energy consumption is also getting relevant in this domain (e.g. it is necessary to reduce energy costs in datacenters). In order to cope with this drawback, the homogeneous architecture and heterogeneous organization has been emerging to provide better energy and area efficiency than the other two aforementioned platforms, with the cost of higher design validation time, since many different processors organizations are used. However, it has the advantage of implementing a unique ISA, so the software development process is not penalized: it is possible to generate assembly code using the very same tool chain for any platform version, and still maintain full binary compatibility for the already developed applications. Unfortunately, since there is a limit of TLP for most applications [13], all the above strategies do not provide the energy and performance optimization required with the software productivity necessary in the constrained embedded systems domain.

Alternatively, dynamic reconfigurable architectures have already shown to be very attractive for embedded platforms based on single threaded applications, since they can adapt the fine grain parallelism exploitation (i.e. at instruction level) to the application requirements at run-time [2][3]. However, the applications also exhibit limits of ILP. Thus, gains in performance when such exploitation is employed tend to stagnate even if a huge amount of resources is available in the reconfigurable architecture, so a single accelerator does not provide an advantageous tradeoff between area and performance if one needs to reach high performance levels in single thread execution.

In this work we propose a platform based on Custom Reconfigurable Arrays for Multiprocessor System (CReAMS). With CReAMS it is possible to emulate the desired heterogeneous behavior with a homogenous platform. In a software environment composed of parallel, embedded and general purpose applications, CReAMS achieves better performance than a homogeneous architecture, occupies the same chip area, and consumes less energy. Different from heterogeneous architectures, CReAMS provides the software productivity of a homogeneous multiprocessor device, in which a single tool chain can be used for the whole platform. This paper is organized as follows. Section 2 presents the CReAMS architecture. Results of the proposed architecture considering different instruction- and thread- level parallelism are shown in Section 3. Section 4 concludes this work.

## 2   CReAMS Architecture

A general overview of the CReAMS platform is given in Figure 1(a). The thread level parallelism is explored by replicating the number of Dynamic Adaptive Processors (DAPs) (in the example of the Figure 1(a), by four DAPs) that communicate through an on-chip unified L2 shared cache.

We divided DAP in four blocks to better explain it, as illustrated in Figure 1(b).

*a)   Processor Pipeline (Block 2)*
A SparcV8-based architecture is used as the baseline processor to work together with the reconfigurable system. Its five stage pipeline reflects a traditional RISC execution flow (instruction fetch, decode, execution, data fetch and write back).

*b)  Reconfigurable Data Path Structure (Block 1)*

Following the classification presented in [4], the reconfigurable data path is coarse grained and tightly coupled to the SparcV8 pipeline, which avoids external accesses to the memory, saves power and reduces the reconfiguration. As illustrated in Figure 1(b), the data path is organized as a matrix of rows and columns. The number of rows dictates the maximum instruction level parallelism that can be exploited, since instructions located at the same column are executed in parallel. For example, the illustrated data path (Block 1 of Figure 1(b)) is able to execute up to four arithmetic and logic operations, two memory accesses (two memory ports are available in the L1 data cache) and one multiplication without read after write dependences. The number of columns determines the maximum number of data dependent instructions that can be stored in one configuration. Three columns of arithmetic and logic units (ALU) compose a level. A level does not affect the SparcV8 critical path. Therefore, up to three ALU instructions can be executed in the reconfigurable data path within one SparcV8 cycle, without affecting its original frequency (600 MHz). Memory accesses and multiplications take one equivalent SparcV8 cycle to perform their operations.

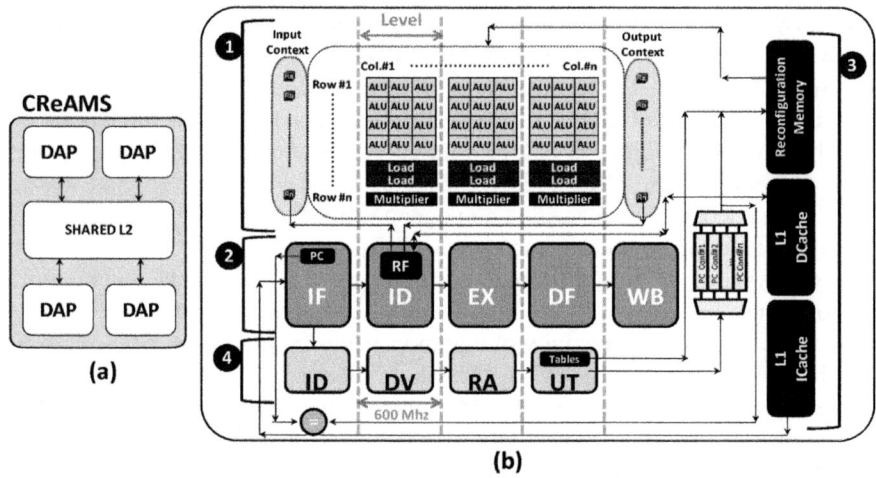

**Fig. 1.** (a) Example of a CReAMS Platform (b) DAP blocks

The entire structure of the reconfigurable data path is totally combinational: there is no temporal barrier between the functional units. The only exception is for the entry and exit points. The entry point is used to keep the input context, which is connected to the processor register file. The fetch of the input operands from the SparcV8 register file is the first step to configure the data path before actual execution. After that, results are stored in the output context registers through the exit point of the data path. The values stored in the output context are sent to the SparcV8 register file on demand. It means that if any value is produced at any data path level (a cycle of SparcV8 processor) and if it will not be changed in the subsequent levels, this value is written back in the cycle after that it was produced. In the current implementation, the

SparcV8 register file has two write/read ports. The interconnections among the functional units, input and output contexts are made through multiplexers.

We have coupled Sleep Transistors (ST) [5] to switch power on/off of each functional unit in the reconfigurable data path. The dynamic reconfiguration process is responsible for the ST management. Their states are stored in the reconfiguration memory, together with the reconfiguration data. For a given configuration, idle functional units are set to the off state avoiding leakage and dynamic power dissipation, since the incoming bits do not produce switching activity in the disconnected circuit.

### c)  Dynamic Detection Hardware (Block 4)
The hardware responsible for code detection, named Dynamic Detection Hardware [12] (DDH), was implemented as a 4-stage pipelined circuit to avoid the increase of the critical path of the original SparcV8 processor. These four stages are the following: *Instruction Decode* (ID), *Dependence Verification* (DV), *Resource Allocation* (RA), *Update Tables* (UT). They are responsible for decoding the incoming instruction and allocating it to right functional unit in the data path, according to the dependences with the already allocated instructions. At the end of the process, the configuration bits are updated in the reconfiguration memory.

### d)  Storage Components (Block 3)
Two storage components are part of the DAP acceleration process: address cache and reconfiguration memory. The address cache holds the memory address of the first instruction of every configuration built by the dynamic detection hardware. It is used to verify the existence of a configuration in the reconfiguration memory. The reconfiguration memory stores the routing bits and the necessary information to fire a configuration, such as the input and output contexts and immediate values. In addition, the current DAP implementation has a private 32 KB 4-way set associative L1 data cache and a private 8 KB 4-way set associative L1 instruction cache.

## 3   CReAMS Evaluation

In all experiments we have compared the CReAMS to a multiprocessing platform built through the replication of standalone SparcV8 processors, named MPSparcV8. Both CReAMS and MPSparcV8 have an on-chip unified 512 KB 8-way set associative L2 shared cache.

Benchmarks from different suites were selected to cover a wide range of behaviors in terms of type (i.e. TLP and ILP) and levels of existing parallelism. The scope is to mimic future complex embedded applications that will run in portable devices that will mix parallel [6] [7] (*md, jacobi* and *lu*), general purpose (*apsi, equake* and *ammp*) [8] and embedded applications (*susan edges, susan smoothing, susan corners* and *patricia*)[9][14]. The benchmarks were parallelized using OpenMP and POSIX.

The base platform is Simics [10], an instruction level simulator. The Synopsys Design and Power Compiler tools, using a CMOS 90nm technology, were employed to synthesize the VHDL descriptions of the both approaches to standard cell and gather data about power, critical path and area. Data on memory was obtained with CACTI 6.5 [11].

In addition, we have considered CReAMS setups with different numbers of DAPs (4, 8, 16 and 64 DAPs). The same was done with the MPSparcV8 system (4, 8, 16 and 64 SparcV8s). Each DAP has a reconfigurable data path (Block 1 of the Figure 1(b)) composed of 6 arithmetic and logic, 4 load/store and 2 multipliers units per column. The entire reconfigurable data path has 24 columns. A 46 KB reconfiguration memory, implemented as a DRAM memory, is able to store up to 64 configurations. They are indexed by a 64-entries 4-way set associative Address Cache.

Figure 2 shows the speedup (y-axis), varying the number of processors (x-axis), provided by the MPSparcV8 and CReAMS over a standalone SparcV8 processor. Analyzing only the MPSparcV8 speedups (striped bars), the applications that contain massive TLP (*md, jacobi* and *susan_s*) scale almost linearly as the number of processors increases. For these applications, the mean performance of the 64-MPSparcV8 grows 46 times. On the other hand, small performance gains are obtained in those applications that contain small TLP (*equake, apsi, ammp, susan_e, susan_c, lu* and *patricia*). In this case, with the 64-MPSparcV8 platform, performance improvements of only 2.3 are obtained, which reinforces the need for an adaptable ILP exploitation mechanism to achieve balanced performance in future embedded systems, since they will mix many applications from different domains and amounts of ILP and TLP.

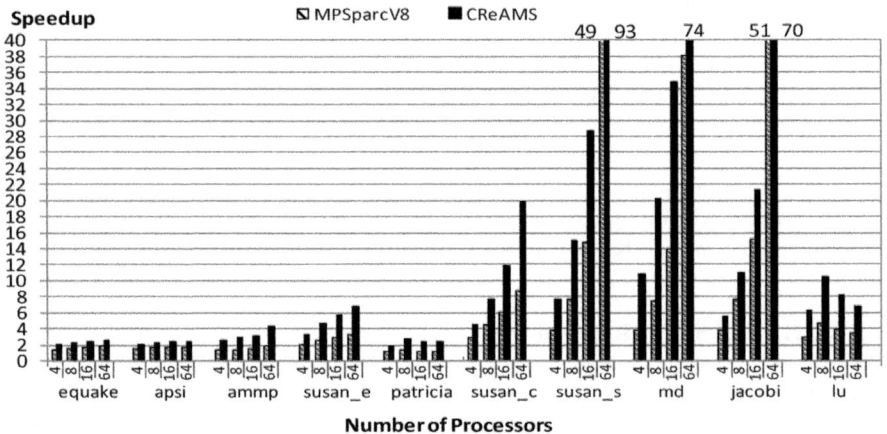

**Fig. 2.** Speedup of CReAMS and MPSparv8 over a standalone SparcV8

CReAMS (solid bars) presents better performance than the MPSparcV8 with the same number of processors, even for those applications that present massive TLP. However, a DAP is almost four times bigger than the SparcV8 processor. Therefore, let us compare both architectures with equivalent area occupation: the CReAMS composed of 4 DAPs against the MPSparcV8 composed of 16 SparcV8s; and the CReAMS composed of 16 DAPs against the MPSparcV8 composed of 64 SparcV8s. As it can be observed, the 4 DAPs outperforms the 16 SparcV8s execution time in six benchmarks (*equake, apsi, ammp, susan edges, patricia* and *lu*), even when applications that present high TLP is considered, such as *lu* and *susan edges*. *ammp* is the one that benefits most from CReAMS: it presents an execution time 41% smaller than the MPSparcV8.

**Table 1.** Energy-Delay product, in J*1e-3s, of the MPSparcV8 and CReAMS (lower is better)

|  | MPSparcV8 | | | | CReAMS | | | |
|---|---|---|---|---|---|---|---|---|
|  | 4 SparcV8 | 8SparcV8 | 16SparcV8 | 64SparcV8 | 4 DAPs | 8 DAPs | 16 DAPs | 64 DAPs |
| equake | 293 | 305 | 287 | 343 | 169 | 175 | 162 | 149 |
| apsi | 10768 | 10386 | 10169 | 10282 | 6361 | 6143 | 6023 | 5355 |
| ammp | 19698 | 22155 | 20764 | 12814 | 5452 | 6282 | 5761 | 2984 |
| susan_e | 7.97 | 7.15 | 6.55 | 6.12 | 3.46 | 2.85 | 2.43 | 2.12 |
| patricia | 2.91 | 1.96 | 2.54 | 2.65 | 1.47 | 0.77 | 1.02 | 1.06 |
| susan_c | 1.0296 | 0.8134 | 0.6274 | 0.4624 | 0.5160 | 0.3761 | 0.2600 | 0.1600 |
| susan_s | 177.2 | 102.5 | 59.8 | 18.7 | 41.7 | 24.9 | 14.7 | 4.7 |
| md | 0.000282 | 0.000171 | 0.000098 | 0.000039 | 0.000066 | 0.000042 | 0.000026 | 0.000013 |
| jacobi | 35.1 | 20.7 | 11.3 | 3.6 | 17.4 | 10.3 | 5.7 | 1.9 |
| lu | 0.000124 | 0.000091 | 0.000127 | 0.000215 | 0.000041 | 0.000028 | 0.000043 | 0.000076 |

Table 1 shows the energy-delay product of both platforms. In this Table, the designs with equivalent area are highlighted with the same color. Let us consider the 4-DAPs CReAMS setup running *ammp*: it saves 32% of energy consumption and improves in 41% the performance compared to the 16-SparcV8 MPSparcV8. Therefore, CReAMS provides a reduction in the energy-delay product in a factor of almost four times in this case. The average reduction in energy-delay by using CReAMS, and considering the whole set of benchmarks, is of 33%; while the energy is reduced in 82% and performance is improved in 4% on average when the same chip area is considered. The main sources of CReAMS energy savings are: fewer memory accesses for instructions; shorter execution time and the use of sleep transistors.

# 4   Conclusions

In this work, we have proposed CReAMS, aiming to offer the advantages of a heterogeneous multiprocessor architecture and to improve software productivity, since neither tool chains nor code recompilations are necessary for its use. Considering designs with equivalent chip areas, CReAMS offers considerable improvements in performance and in the energy-delay product for a wide range of different applications, compared to a homogeneous multiprocessor environment.

# References

1. International Technology Roadmap for Semiconductors,
   http://www.itrs.net/links/2009ITRS/2009Chapters_2009Tables/
   2009_SysDrivers.pdf
2. Clark, N., Kudlur, M., Park, H., Mahlke, S., Flautner, K.: Application-Specific Processing on a General-Purpose Core via Transparent Instruction Set Customization. In: MICRO-37, pp. 30–40 (2004)
3. Lysecky, R., Stitt, G., Vahid, F.: Warp Processors. ACM Transactions on Design Automation of Electronic Systems, 659–681 (July 2006)
4. Compton, K., Hauck, S.: Reconfigurable computing: A survey of systems and software. ACM Computing Surveys 34(2), 171–210 (2002)

5. Shi, K., Howard, D.: Challenges in Sleep Transistor Design and Implementation in Low-Power Designs. In: Proceedings of Design Automation Conference, vol. 43, pp. 113–116 (2006)
6. Dorta, A.J., Rodriguez, C., Sande, F.D., Gonzalez-Escribano, A.: The OpenMP Source Code Repository. In: Proceedings of the 13th Euromicro Conference on Parallel, Distributed and Network-Based Processing, pp. 244–250. IEEE Computer Society, Washington, DC (2005)
7. Woo, S.C., Ohara, M., Torrie, E., Singh, J.P., Gupta, A.: The SPLASH-2 programs: characterization and methodological considerations. In: Proceedings of the 22nd Annual International Symposium on Computer Architecture, ISCA 1995, pp. 24–36. ACM, New York (1995)
8. Dixit, K.M.: The SPEC benchmarks. In: Computer benchmarks. Elsevier Advances In Parallel Computing Series, vol. 8, pp. 149–163 (1993)
9. Guthaus, M.R., Ringenberg, J.S., Ernst, D., Austin, T.M., Mudge, T., Brown, R.B.: MiBench: A Free, Commercially Representative Embedded Benchmark Suite. In: 4th WWC, Austin, TX (December 2001)
10. Magnusson, P.S., Christensson, M., Eskilson, J., Forsgren, D., Hållberg, G., Högberg, J., Larsson, F., Moestedt, A., Werner, B.: Simics: A Full System Simulation Platform. Computer 35, 50–58 (2002)
11. Wilton, S.J.E., Jouppi, N.P.: CACTI: an enhanced cache access and cycle time model. IEEE Journal of Solid-State Circuits 31(5), 677–688 (1996)
12. Beck, A.C.S., Rutzig, M.B., Gaydadjiev, G., Carro, L.: Transparent Reconfigurable Acceleration for Heterogeneous Embedded Applications. In: DATE 2008, March 10-14, pp. 1208–1213 (2008)
13. Blake, G., Dreslinski, R., Mudge, T., Flautner, K.: Evolution of thread-level parallelism in desktop applications. SIGARCH Comput. Archit. News 38(3), 302–313
14. Hanawa, T., Sato, M., Lee, J., Imada, T., Kimura, H., Boku, T.: Evaluation of Multicore Processors for Embedded Systems by Parallel Benchmark Program Using OpenMP. In: Müller, M.S., de Supinski, B.R., Chapman, B.M. (eds.) IWOMP 2009. LNCS, vol. 5568, pp. 15–27. Springer, Heidelberg (2009)

# Dataflow Graph Partitioning for Optimal Spatio-Temporal Computation on a Coarse Grain Reconfigurable Architecture

Ratna Krishnamoorthy[1], Keshavan Varadarajan[2], Masahiro Fujita[1],
Mythri Alle[2], S.K. Nandy[2], and Ranjani Narayan[3]

[1] Dept. of Electronics Engineering, The University of Tokyo, Tokyo, Japan
{ratna@cad,fujita@ee}.t.u-tokyo.ac.jp
[2] CAD Lab, SERC, Indian Institute of Science, Bangalore, India
{keshavan,mythri,nandy}@cadl.iisc.ernet.in
[3] Morphing Machines, Bangalore, India
ranjani.narayan@morphingmachines.com

**Abstract.** Coarse Grain Reconfigurable Architectures(CGRA) support Spatial and Temporal computation to speedup execution and reduce reconfiguration time. Thus compilation involves partitioning instructions spatially and scheduling them temporally. We extend Edge-Betweenness Centrality scheme, originally used for detecting community structures in social and biological networks, for partitioning instructions of a dataflow graph. Comparisons of execution time for several applications run on a simulator for REDEFINE, a CGRA proposed in literature, indicate that Centrality scheme outperforms several other schemes with 2–18% execution time speedup.

## 1 Introduction

Reconfigurable Processors are composed of an interconnection of compute units, which help exploit a higher degree of spatial computation[1] than what is available in General Purpose Processors (GPP). This hardware organization helps exploit parallelism better than in a GPP [3]. However, this necessitates changes in the compilation process, which needs to address both spatial and temporal aspects of computation. Compilation for temporal computation involves identifying a total order among instructions, such that it satisfies all program dependences. For spatial computation, the compiler needs to allocate different instructions to different compute units available on the reconfigurable fabric, such that the overall computation and communication time is minimized. As mentioned in [6], this involves use of several VLSI CAD algorithms, viz. circuit clustering and partitioning, which were previously used for hardware synthesis. In this paper, we propose a new partitioning algorithm based on Edge Betweenness Centrality

---

[1] In temporal execution instructions are sequenced and executed one at time. In spatial computation the number of instructions to be executed is equal to the number of hardware units that are available and the results from one operation to another is conveyed through dedicated wires or an interconnection [3].

A. Koch et al. (Eds.): ARC 2011, LNCS 6578, pp. 125–132, 2011.

[5] for partitioning instructions of an acyclic dataflow graph. Recently Edge Betweenness Centrality has been proposed for detecting community structure in social and biological networks [5], and to the best of our knowledge, this is the first time it is applied to partitioning of programs for CGRA. While the proposed partitioning algorithm is generic, its practical evaluation is possible only when applied on a CGRA. The impact of this algorithm is explored in the context of a CGRA called REDEFINE [1] and it achieves a 6–20% speed up over the other partitioning schemes. A brief introduction to the architecture and partitioning scheme currently used in REDEFINE is provided in the subsequent section.

## 1.1    REDEFINE

The architecture of REDEFINE [1] is presented in figure 1. The core computation engine of REDEFINE is the reconfigurable hardware fabric, which is an interconnection of tiles, where each tile includes a compute element (CE) and a router. The CEs are connected to the router. The routers are interconnected in a honeycomb topology, which forms a Network-on-Chip (NoC). The use of the NoC helps reduce the configuration information needed to determine the communication. Like other CGRAs, it employs a *Spatio-Temporal* execution paradigm, i.e. diverse multiplicity of CEs can be employed for spatial execution. Each CE can enqueue several instructions, which are executed in dataflow order. Applications coded in C language is compiled into an executable by the REDEFINE compiler [2], which generates the Control Flow Graph from the Static Single Assignment form. Several basic blocks are combined to form an application substructure, referred to as a HyperOp. A HyperOp is a vertex-induced subset of an application's dataflow graph such that they are acyclic, pairwise disjoint, and satisfy the convexity condition [2]. A HyperOp is partitioned into *p-HyperOps*, where each p-HyperOp is mapped to a CE.

Each CE can hold $c$ instructions (we assume $c = 16$ in this paper) in the reservation station, which forms the first pipeline stage. An instruction whose operands are available is selected for execution. A priority encoder logic performs arbitration when more than one instruction is ready to be executed simultaneously. The ready instruction along with the opcode and operands are transferred to the ALU. Apart from elementary operations the ALU supports custom function units (CFU) which are very specific to a certain problem domain. The ALU after performing the computation forwards the results to point of consumption through the NoC. In some cases the consuming instruction may be present within the same CE where the data was produced. In this case the data is sent on the bypass channel. The CE is pipelined and its latency is 3 clock cycles. If the path through the router is taken to the destination then an additional latency is incurred based on the traffic at the router and the hop distance of the destination. Instructions of a HyperOp are distributed across various CEs. One instruction in each CE of a HyperOp can execute in parallel (spatial execution) and several instructions placed within the same CE execute sequentially (temporal execution). Hence this is referred to as "spatio-temporal" execution. For efficient spatio-temporal execution, the compiler must be able to *partition* the instructions into different groups so as to minimize the total execution delay. HyperOp is a single schedulable entity. The scheduling of HyperOps and their launching is handled by the Support Logic (refer figure 1). The structural details of two modules are relevant to us: Compute Element and HyperOp Launcher. The HyperOp Launcher is responsible for loading the configuration and the CE performs the computation.

When a HyperOp is ready for execution, the HyperOp Launcher transfers instructions to the fabric. It is connected to the reconfigurable fabric through twelve routers present along the periphery. The HyperOp Launcher reads the instructions from the five instruction memory banks and chooses the closest router to the destination to transfer the instructions and constants. The HyperOp Launcher has five submodules which allow independent handling of instruction stream from an instruction memory bank. Each HyperOp Launcher sub-module transfers instructions, constants and input operands of a single p-HyperOp. In order to support a peak transfer rate of 5 instructions every clock cycle, the 5 instructions must belong to different p-HyperOps. This design choice favours the use of more p-HyperOps. For any given number of instructions in a HyperOp, say $n$, it is beneficial to use more p-HyperOps in order to reduce the transfer latency. However, increasing the number of p-HyperOps increase the number of control packets such as those which mark the beginning and end of the p-HyperOp.

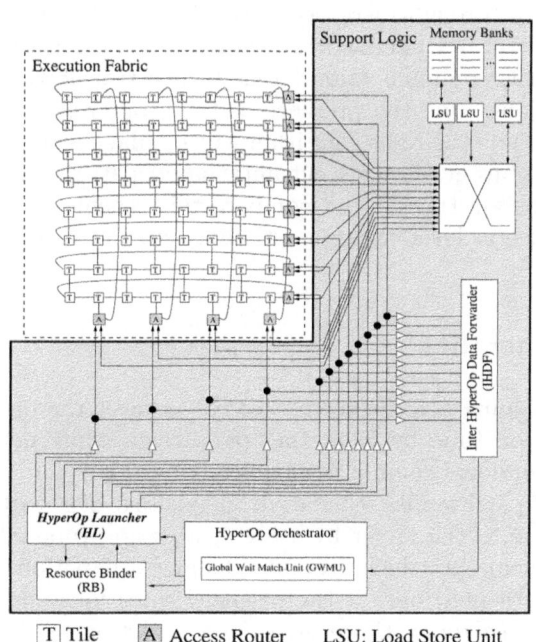

**Fig. 1.** Architecture of REDEFINE

## 1.2 Partitioning the HyperOp

While partitioning the HyperOp into p-HyperOps (recall that a each p-HyperOp is assigned to a CE), several factors need to be considered:

- Parallel instructions are best mapped to different CEs, since this helps exploit parallelism and hence reduce the overall time taken to execute a HyperOp.

– Dependent instructions are best mapped close together, potentially within the same CE. Even when the hop count is one (i.e. instruction is placed in the neighbouring CE) the time to transfer the data may be more than one clock cycle.

While these obvious factors to partitioning the HyperOp's dataflow graph appear to be non-conflicting, they do work as opposing forces. Two parallel instructions consuming data from the same parent instruction need to be placed in different p-HyperOps for exploiting more parallelism, but communication latency is minimized if they are placed in the same p-HyperOp and executed sequentially.

In summary, increasing the number of p-HyperOps (in a HyperOp) helps improve the overall execution latency through increased parallelism exploitation and exploiting higher instruction transfer bandwidth. However, increasing the number of p-HyperOps increases the communication latency when transferring data between dependent instructions. Due the presence of these opposing requirements it is necessary to determine the right algorithm which balances these requirements. We present an adaptation of edge centrality based partitioning scheme for acyclic dataflow graphs (section 2) and compare this scheme with several other popular heuristics such as level based partitioning and Kernighan-Lin (section 3).

## 2   Edge betweenness Centrality

As stated in section 1, the partitioning algorithm must strive to meet the opposing goals of improving execution time by exploiting parallelism while not degrading performance through non-local communication.

The use of network Flow based partitioning schemes in the context of netlist partitioning was made possible due to the paper by Yang et al. who proposed the Flow based bi-partitioning scheme [9] which generates balanced partitions. In this scheme a min-net cut is accepted only if the resulting partitions generated after the edge removal is *r-balanced*. However, the construction of the flow network requires the addition of several nodes and edges and the resulting partitions need to be reconverted back to the original form prior to generating the executable. The edge centrality based technique is similar in nature to this scheme, but more amenable to graphs without edge weights viz. dataflow graphs and social networks. This technique was first proposed by Girvan et al. [5] in the context of social and biological networks. Edge betweenness centrality is a measure that determines how "between" is the edge; it measures the number of shortest paths between vertex pairs that pass through that edge. If more than one shortest path exists between the considered pair of vertices then equal weight is assigned to all paths such that they all add up to 1. The edge betweenness is higher if the edge connects two clusters since several vertices's shortest paths pass through that edge. In our specific context, it means that there exists two groups of nodes or clusters, which have less communication and this communication can be performed over the network. The clusters are closely interacting nodes which are best placed within the same compute element to minimize communication

**Algorithm 1.** Partitioning based on Edge betweenness Centrality

```
if number_of_nodes(G) > maxInstruction then
    compute the edge betweenness centrality for G
    e ←edge with the highest centrality
    flag ← true
    while there exists at least one connected component with more nodes than allowed do
        Remove edge e from G
        H ← convert G to an undirected graph
        graphList ← list of connected components of H
        for g in graphList do
            if number_of_nodes(g) > maxInstruction then
                compute the edge betweenness centrality for g
                e ←edge with the highest centrality
                break
            end if
        end for
    end while
end if
```

latency. The algorithm proposed in [5] involves computing the edge betweenness centrality followed by removal of the edge with the highest betweenness. This is followed by recomputation of the edge betweenness for the graph and removal of the edge and so on. This scheme helps identify edges which are "most between" two clusters. Elimination of this edge from the graph, partitions the graph into two components which are tightly coupled. In the context of dataflow graphs:

- Low centrality points to the existence of a set of vertices with high interaction.
- High centrality points to the edge being a bridge between two clusters, hence an ideal candidate for removal (since cost of communication reduces).

Our adaptation, shown in algorithm 1, has the following changes over the original algorithm [5]:

- Edge Centrality on Subgraph: Removal of an edge causes the graph to be disconnected. Instead of recomputing the Edge betweenness centrality on the whole graph, it is computed on a connected component. A connected component is chosen if it has more than the maximum number of nodes (i.e. $c = 16$, the maximum number of instructions that a CE can hold).
- The algorithm terminates when no connected components has more than the maximum number of nodes.

## 3   Experiments and Observations

We compare the performance of the proposed partitioning scheme with other schemes presented in literature. These include *a*) Parent Affinity Based Schemes: Parent Affinity based scheme was proposed by Gajjala Purna et al. [4]. We derived three variants of this scheme which is referred to as Non-Interleave Parent Affinity-Compute (NIPA-C), Non-Interleaved Parent Affinity-Memory (NIPA-M) and Interleaved Parent Affinity (ILPA). The details of these schemes can be found in [8]. *b)* Kernighan-Lin Scheme (KL): This is based on the original scheme proposed by Kernighan and Lin [7]. *c)* Current Algorithm implemented in REDEFINE: The HyperOp graph is broken into individual threads of sequential instructions. The inter-thread interaction is measured and two threads with the highest interaction are interleaved together. Each of these interleaved components forms a p-HyperOp. If the interleaved component has more instructions than what is allowed in a p-HyperOp then it is horizontally split into two components and so on. This scheme is akin to the ILPA scheme with $m = 2$.

To evaluate the performance of the various partitioning schemes, we have chosen a set of kernels from various application domains. These kernels are so chosen such that they test various aspects of the partitioning algorithms. The kernels are classified into two types, viz. compute-centric and memory-centric. The kernels can also be classified into large kernels and small kernels. In the context of large kernels and compute intensive kernels, use of more CEs helps reduce the overall execution time. Also, if the application has a lot of instruction level parallelism, increasing the number of CEs helps reduce the fabric execution time. Even in the absence of a lot of parallelism, since compute intensive kernels tend to have large HyperOps, the use of higher number of CEs helps reduce the HyperOp launch latency. The various kernels chosen and their characteristics are explained in table 1.

To evaluate the performance of the partitioning scheme, we have performed a full simulation of the generated p-HyperOps on the REDEFINE System-C based simulator. The process of evaluation involves compiling applications listed in table 1 written in C language into HyperOps. The compiler outputs the dataflow graphs of all the HyperOps. Different partitioning schemes are used to generate the p-HyperOps. These are then compiled into binaries which are executed on the simulator. The partitioning schemes are evaluated with respect to the overall execution time.

## 3.1   Results

Comparison of the execution time obtained for the applications are listed in table 1.Centrality based scheme shows 2–18% overall improvement in execution time when compared to the existing scheme implemented on REDEFINE. This is significant since (1) 44% improvement in execution time has already been reported in [2] on account of several dataflow optimizations and use of larger HyperOps (2) REDEFINE architecture and compiler are in an advanced stage [1, 2] and achieving an average 10% improvement in execution time by a mere change in partitioning algorithm is noteworthy. All other schemes have an improvement in the range 1-2% over the existing scheme. *Centrality based partitioning scheme outperforms all other partitioning schemes, by achieving a 10% speedup.* It gains primarily on account of use of higher number of p-HyperOps and appropriate choice of terminal edges (i.e. edges between p-HyperOps).

*Centrality vs. Kernighan-Lin*: The Kernighan-Lin (KL) heuristic has the lowest execution time (lower than centrality) for 2 out of 20 applications: Deterministic Finite Automaton (DFA) and Field Squarer (without CFU). In the case of DFA

**Table 1.** Table showing the overall execution time achieved by various partitioning algorithms for various applications

| Application | Characteristics | Current | NIPA-C | NIPA-M | ILPA | KL | Centrality |
|---|---|---|---|---|---|---|---|
| Deterministic Finite Automaton | Memory Intensive | 21557 | 19123 | 19690 | 19225 | *18060* | 19371 |
| Finite Impulse Response | Memory intensive and Small | 1883 | 1911 | 1908 | 1940 | 1769 | *1586* |
| Matrix-Vector Multiplication | | 4917 | 4728 | 4732 | 4991 | 4751 | *4536* |
| Linear Search | | 864 | 876 | 871 | 881 | 866 | *843* |
| Matrix-Matrix Multiplication | | 5473 | 5410 | 5215 | 5512 | 5344 | *5059* |
| Newton-Raphson Algorithm | Compute Intensive | 1392 | *1214* | 1240 | 1227 | 1601 | 1231 |
| Runge-Kutta Numerical Algorithm | | 1506 | 1529 | 1522 | *1504* | 1786 | 1564 |
| Faddeev's algorithm–computes schur complement | | 17441 | 18129 | 18457 | 18398 | 17973 | *16824* |
| Field addition performed over 163 bit | | 199 | 196 | 204 | 203 | 189 | *163* |
| Barrett Reduction over 163 bit field (with CFU) | | 221 | 230 | 238 | 238 | 219 | *186* |
| Field Squarer over 163 bit field (with CFU) | Small | 282 | 264 | 258 | 253 | 288 | *235* |
| Field Multiplication over 163 bits | | 640 | 637 | 587 | 622 | 608 | *524* |
| Elliptic Curve Point Addition | | 3810 | 3696 | 3626 | 3728 | 3559 | *3233* |
| Elliptic Curve Point Doubling | | 2443 | 2432 | 2409 | 2422 | 2364 | *2103* |
| Pseudo Random Number Generator | | 2723 | 2686 | 2680 | 2716 | 2755 | *2558* |
| Barrett Reduction over 163 bit field (without CFU) | | 2744 | 2668 | *2568* | 2660 | 2804 | 2570 |
| Field Squarer over 163 bit field (without CFU) | Large | 18383 | 18429 | 18362 | 18633 | *15447* | 16741 |
| Secure Hashing Algorithm | | 65361 | 67476 | 64543 | 66215 | 69329 | *62235* |
| Advanced Encryption Standard - 128 bit | | 11791 | 11574 | 11469 | 11615 | 11525 | *10152* |
| Cyclic Redundancy Check - 16 bit | | *26041* | 27822 | 28582 | 27833 | 26811 | 26781 |

even though both the schemes used the same number of p-HyperOps on an average, KL scheme incurred 12% lower instruction execution time for the HyperOps involved in a loop, thus gaining in overall execution time. KL scheme also had the 5% lower HyperOp launch latency than Centrality scheme, due to the use of balanced partitions. A similar trend is observed in Field Squarer Application. Centrality scheme, similar to network flow based scheme, does not produce balanced partitions. These may suggest ways to improve Centrality based partitioning algorithm, which will be our future work. In other applications, such as Matrix multiplication, Field Addition and Barrett Reduction (with CFU) KL heuristic has the least instruction execution time, but incurs a higher HyperOp launch latency due to the use of very few p-HyperOps. In all these applications the Centrality scheme makes up for the increased instruction execution time, by a commensurate decrease in HyperOp Launch latency, thus achieving the lower execution time than the KL scheme. The KL scheme incurs higher HyperOp launch latency with most compute-intensive kernels primarily on account of lower number of p-HyperOps.

*Centrality vs. Parent Affinity*: Each of the parent affinity scheme and the existing scheme performs well in one application each. In the case of Newton-Raphson NIPA-C has a 7% lower HyperOp launch latency due to use of lesser number of p-HyperOps. In the case of Runge-Kutta, the ILPA scheme has a 16% lower instruction execution time than the centrality scheme. We surmise this is due to the lower communication overhead incurred in ILPA due to the use of lesser p-HyperOps than centrality. NIPA-M scheme performs marginally better than centrality in Barrett Reduction. In general, the NIPA-M scheme incurs the least hyperOp launch latency among all the schemes. However, it experiences a high instruction execution overhead, since this class of algorithms don't choose the terminal edge with care.

## 4   Conclusion

Higher degree of spatial computation exploited in CGRAs necessitate spatial partitioning of instructions. Partitioning involves maintaining: (1) a balance between decreasing instruction execution time through ILP exploitation and reducing the communication time, by placing dependent instructions closer. (2) a balance between reducing reconfiguration overhead through better use of available bandwidth while not incurring higher control overheads. We presented an extension of edge betweenness centrality scheme for partitioning the dataflow graph, which achieved the lowest execution time through reduction in both instruction execution time and reconfiguration overhead. The execution time is improved on an average by 10%, which is significant in the context of the highly optimized REDEFINE compiler. Our results indicate that this scheme performs almost always better than several other schemes and outperforms all the partitioning schemes, viz. Kernighan-Lin and parent-affinity based schemes, by 8-9%.

## References

1. Alle, M., Varadarajan, K., Fell, A., Ramesh Reddy, C., Joseph, N., Das, S., Biswas, P., Chetia, J., Rao, A., Nandy, S.K., Narayan, R.: Redefine: Runtime reconfigurable polymorphic asic. ACM Trans. Embed. Comput. Syst. 9(2), 1–48 (2009)
2. Alle, M., Varadarajan, K., Fell, A., Nandy, S.K., Narayan, R.: Compiling techniques for coarse grained runtime reconfigurable architectures. In: Becker, J., Woods, R., Athanas, P., Morgan, F. (eds.) ARC 2009. LNCS, vol. 5453, pp. 204–215. Springer, Heidelberg (2009)
3. DeHon, A., Wawrzynek, J.: Reconfigurable computing: what, why, and implications for design automation. In: DAC 1999: Proceedings of the 36th Annual ACM/IEEE Design Automation Conference, pp. 610–615. ACM, New York (1999)
4. Gajjala Purna, K.M., Bhatia, D.: Temporal partitioning and scheduling data flow graphs for reconfigurable computers. IEEE Trans. Comput. 48(6), 579–590 (1999)
5. Girvan, M., Newman, M.E.J.: Community structure in social and biological networks. Proceedings of the National Academy of Sciences of the United States of America 99(12), 7821–7826 (2002)
6. Hartenstein, R.: A decade of reconfigurable computing: a visionary retrospective. In: Proceedings of Design, Automation and Test in Europe, DATE, pp. 642–649 (2000)
7. Kernighan, B.W., Lin, S.: An efficient heuristic procedure for partitioning graphs. The Bell System Technical Journal 49(1), 291–307 (1970)
8. Krishnamoorthy, R.: Compiler Optimizations for Coarse Grained Reconfigurable Architectures. Ph.D. thesis, Department of Electronics Engineering, University of Tokyo (2011)
9. Yang, H., Wong, D.F.: Efficient network flow based min-cut balanced partitioning. In: ICCAD 1994: Proceedings of the 1994 IEEE/ACM International Conference on Computer-aided Design, pp. 50–55. IEEE Computer Society Press, Los Alamitos (1994)

# A Pipeline Interleaved Heterogeneous SIMD Soft Processor Array Architecture for MIMO-OFDM Detection

Xuezheng Chu*, John McAllister, and Roger Woods

Institute of Electronics, Communications and Information Technology (ECIT),
Queen's University Belfast, Belfast, Northern Ireland, UK
{xchu01,j.mcallister,r.woods}@qub.ac.uk
http://www.ecit.qub.ac.uk

**Abstract.** The most promising way to maintain reliable data transfer across the rapidly fluctuating channels used by next generation multiple-input multiple-output communications schemes is to exploit run-time variable modulation and antenna configurations. This demands that the baseband signal processing architectures employed in the communications terminals must provide low cost and high performance with run-time reconfigurability. We present a softcore-processor based solution to this issue, and show for the first time, that such programmable architectures can enable real-time data operation for cutting-edge standards such as 802.11n; furthermore, by exploiting deep processing pipelines and interleaved task execution, the cost and performance of these architectures is shown to be on a par with traditional dedicated circuit based solutions. We believe this to be the first such programmable architecture to achieve this, and the combination of implementation efficiency and programmability makes this implementation style the most promising approach for hosting such dynamic architectures.

**Keywords:** FSD, SIMD, softcore, interleave, FPGA, MIMO.

## 1 Introduction

The use of multiple antennas at both the transmitter and receiver ends of next generation Multiple-Input Multiple-Output (MIMO) wireless communication systems enables higher rate data transfer and spectral efficiency [1]. However, the channels across which these systems communicate fluctuate rapidly, and as such future MIMO detectors will require the ability to efficiently support variable modulation schemes (QPSK, 16-QAM and 64-QAM, etc.) and antenna configurations to enable reliable signal transmission. This places stringent demands on the baseband signal processing architectures of the terminals in these

---

* The author acknowledges the support from the EPSRC Islay Project (Research Grant EP/F031017/1) and Chengwei Zheng, Sujit Bhattacharya and Matthew Milford for their valuable suggestions in this work.

A. Koch et al. (Eds.): ARC 2011, LNCS 6578, pp. 133–144, 2011.

systems since these not only have to enable real-time performance of the computationally complex algorithms employed for MIMO transmission and reception,
but must also incorporate the flexibility to adapt their behaviour to support
these different system configurations and behaviour.

This is not possible in current MIMO detector architectures. These have generally been custom circuit architectures [2,3,4,5] to meet the real-time performance requirements of state of the art MIMO standards; these, however are
not sufficiently flexible to enable the required dynamic behaviour. An FPGA
presents an ideal platform with which to solve this problem, since its ability to
host massively parallel networks of programmable processors [6,7] promises this
required flexibility with high performance through creation and customisation of
application specific architectures. Unfortunately, to date, FPGA-based softcore
processor architectures [8] have proven incapable of providing the necessary real-
time performance, or cost when compared to dedicated circuits for cutting edge
MIMO standards such as 802.11n. It appears a completely new approach to soft-
core processor based design for FPGA DSP is required to resolve this disparity
between high performance, low cost and flexible processing architectures.

In this paper, with application to a Fixed-Complexity Sphere Decoding (FSD)
MIMO detection algorithm, we present such an approach and show that:

(i) by using heterogeneous Single Instruction Multiple Data (SIMD) soft-
processor arrays, we can achieve real-time implementation of an FSD decoder architectures for 802.11n MIMO.
(ii) by employing deep processing pipelines and task interleaving, the throughput of such architectures can be increased by 20 Mbps whilst saving 29.4%
and 31.7% in DSP48E and LUTs resources, leading to implementations
with 42% less equivalent resources than even traditional dedicated circuit-
based solutions.

These contributions mark important breakthroughs in the area of softcore-based
implementation of FPGA DSP, and offer the potential to radically rethink the
FPGA implementation problem for high performance DSP applications. The
remainder of the paper is organized as follows. Section 2 describes the FSD algorithm and previous implementation approaches. Section 3 describes the SIMD
softcore processor architecture and its use for FSD in 802.11n systems. Section 4
shows how deep pipelines and task interleaving can enable higher performance,
lower cost implementations.

## 2   Related Work and Motivation

A MIMO system with $M$ transmit and $N$ receive antennas may be represented
mathematically as (1), where s is the $M$-element transmitted data vector, y
is the $N$-vector received signal, and **H** is the $N \times M$ complex channel matrix
with additive Gaussian noise **v**. Typically, the communication channel is used
as a set of parallel flat fading subchannels via Orthogonal Frequency Division
Multiplexing (OFDM), with each subcarrier decoded separately at the receiver.

$$\mathbf{y} = \mathbf{H}\mathbf{s} + \mathbf{v} \qquad (1)$$

Embedded MIMO decoders encounter problems resulting from either optimal performance with exponentially huge complexity, non-deterministic data-dependent behaviour [9,2], or high complexity when close-to-optimal performance is required [4]. FSD is highly attractive since it overcomes these problems, achieving near ideal decoding performance, as well as having a fixed, highly parallel structure well suited to high performance implementation [3]. It employs a three step tree decoding scheme, as illustrated in Fig. 1.

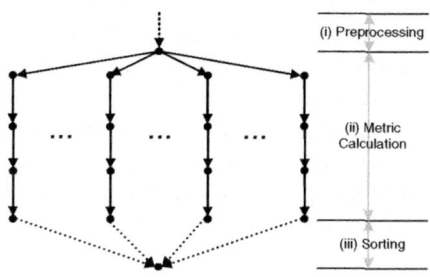

**Fig. 1.** An FSD Tree Search Structure

(i) *Preprocessing* involves generating an upper triangular version **r** of the channel matrix **H**, and initialising the centre of the FSD detection sphere using Zero Forcing (ZF) detection.

(ii) *Metric calculation*, launches a series of iterative *Data Slicing* (DS) (Equation (2)) and *Accumulated Partial Euclidean Distance* (APED) (Equation (3)) calculations on each candidate detected symbol.

$$s_i = \hat{s}_i - \sum_{j=i+1}^{M} \frac{r_{ij}}{r_{ii}}\left(s_j - \hat{s}_j\right) \qquad (2)$$

$$D_i = r_{ii}^2\|s_i - \hat{s}_i\|^2 + \sum_{j=i+1}^{M} r_{jj}^2\|s_j - \hat{s}_j\|^2 = d_i + D_{i+1} \qquad (3)$$

(iii) *Sorting* includes determining the most likely of the candidate detected symbols from each branch of the FSD tree by selecting that with the lowest APED value.

In (2) and (3), $r_{ij}$ refers to an entry in **r**, $\hat{s}_i$ is the center of the constrained FSD sphere, $D_{i+1}$ can be considered as APED in the tree level $j = i + 1$ and $d_i$ is PED in level $i$. Thus, the APED in (3) can be recursively obtained by starting from level $i = M$ (where $\mathrm{APED}_i$ is zero) and working backwards until level $i = 1$. The intriguing aspect of the FSD algorithm is its structural change with varying channel conditions, i.e. there are simple mathematical links between the radix of the modulation scheme and the number of antennas, and the number of branches in the decoder tree and number of APED calculations in each [3]. When configured as 16-QAM for $4 \times 4$ MIMO, the tree has 16 branches of 4 APED calculations each.

This static (with respect to a specific combination of configuration parameters) and highly parallel algorithm structure lends itself well to high performance dedicated circuit implementations [3,5], but these can only realise specific configurations, whilst alternative programmable solutions, such as dedicated DSP processors [8,10] and GPU [11] cannot achieve real-time behaviour. By exploiting FPGA-based softcore processors, it should be possible to combine both programmability and high real-time performance. However, whilst some work has investigated the use of Xilinx Microblaze for such applications [8], these processors have proven too performance-restricted and resource expensive to support real-time processing, such as the 480 Mbps uncoded data rate required in $4 \times 4$ 16-QAM MIMO in 802.11n [12]. Whilst accelerators such as VIPERS [6] or VESPA [7] boost the performance of these processors, they quickly experience performance and cost bottlenecks which restrict their applicability. As such, whilst these architectures offer flexibility, they cannot support high performance and low cost implementations and until they can, their potential to support the dynamic behaviour of next generation MIMO decoders will go unrealised.

In this paper we present a softcore processor based solution which overcomes this problem, enabling cost and performance equivalent to current circuit-based implementations for MIMO 802.11n. In Section 3, we describe the proposed softcore processor architecture.

## 3   SIMD Array Architecture for FSD

We propose to use configurable networks of SIMD processors for implementation of FSD, where the number of SIMD network elements, their interconnectivity and the specific configuration of each element are configurable to suit the processing characteristics of the algorithm being implemented. We have chosen to exploit many-core SIMD architectures for two reasons:

(i)  SIMD is used for realising high performance FSD, since FSD is a highly regular, repetitive arrangement of identical APED behaviours - i.e. it consists of the same task operating on several different data streams; furthermore, the large number of parallel FSD operations (one for each of the 108 subcarriers in 802.11n OFDM MIMO) is ideally suited to implementation on parallel processors.

(ii) FPGA is an excellent platform for constructing such architectures, offering rich on-chip resources such as abundant datapath elements (e.g. DSP48E on Xilinx FPGA [13]), small, high bandwidth memories in the FPGA programmable logic, and the high communications bandwidth offered in the programmable interconnect.

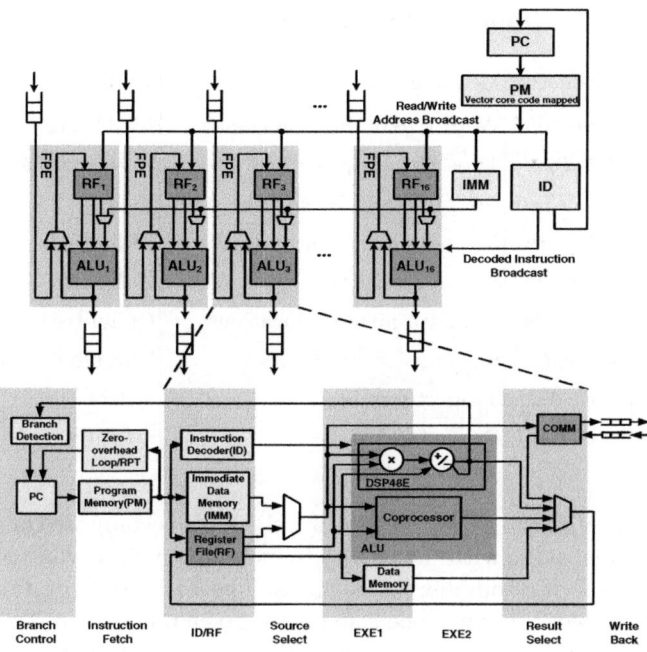

**Fig. 2.** SIMD Architecture

## 3.1   FPGA-Based SIMD Processor Element Architecture

The SIMD architecture that we employ is composed of an array of high performance, resource efficient processing units known as FPGA Processing Elements (FPEs) as shown in Fig. 2. Each FPE consists of *Register File* (RF), *Arithmetic Logic Unit* (ALU), *Communication Adapter* (COMM) and FIFO components, whilst the SIMD includes centralised program control (the *Program Counter* (PC)), instruction (*Program Memory* (PM) and *Instruction Decoder* (ID)) and data (*Immediate Data Memory* (IMM)) memory. The SIMD is both *configurable* (i.e. its architecture can be customised to an application in a set of pre-defined ways, as in Table 1) and *programmable* (i.e.it can mimic any given functionality by issuing sequences of instructions to the ALU) to maximise its flexibility. The configurable aspects of the SIMD processor are given in Table 1.

**Table 1.** SIMD Processor Configuration Parameters

| Parameter | Meaning | Values |
|-----------|---------|--------|
| *SIMDways* | No. parallel FPE elements | Unlimited |
| *Pipeline* | Instruction broadcast pipeline tree breadth | Unlimited |
| *IMMDepth* | No. immediate date memory locations | Unlimited |
| *IMMWidth* | Size of immediate data memory | Unlimited |

**Table 2.** FPE Configuration Parameters

| Parameter | Meaning | Values |
|-----------|---------|--------|
| $DataWidth$ | Word size of data processed | 16/32 bits |
| $DataType$ | Type of data processed | Real/complex |
| $ALUWidth$ | No. DSP48E slices in the ALU | 1 - 4 |
| $PMDepth$ | No. program memory locations | Unlimited |
| $PMWidth$ | Size of instruction word | Unlimited |
| $DMDepth$ | No. data memory locations | Unlimited |
| $RFDepth$ | No. registers in RF | Unlimited |
| $TxCOMM$ | Tx port number | $\leq 1024$ |
| $RxCOMM$ | Rx port number | $\leq 1024$ |

In the Xilinx Virtex 5 FPE architecture, the ALU is composed of a DSP48E for MAC calculation, along with the facility to include a customisable coprocessor for application of specific complex instructions. The FPE configuration parameters are listed in Table 2, having been identified to maximise the flexibility of the processor in terms of arithmetic (i.e. complex or real), word size, number of computational units, and memory requirements.

### 3.2 SIMD-Based FSD

Cutting edge MIMO standards such as 802.11n employ $4 \times 4$ 16-QAM OFDM MIMO with 108 subcarriers. As such there are 108 FSD operations to be performed (one per subcarrier), and each FSD tree has 16 branches of 4 APED nodes. Fig. 3 shows how this may be mapped to a two-stage architecture.

Stage 1 consists of 12 of 16-way SIMD processor, where the FSD metric calculation stage (stage (ii) in Fig. 1) of all 108 subcarriers are combined into twelve groups, and each group mapped to one of the Stage 1 SIMD processors. Within each group, each subcarrier is decoded in turn, with each branch processed by one way of the SIMD, before processing begins on the next subcarrier. The resulting candidate decoded symbols and their associated APED values are then output via LUTs-based FIFOs to Stage 2 of the architecture. Stage 2 consists of a single 12-way SIMD which performs the sorting for all 108 subcarriers (stage (iii) in Fig. 1), with one way of the FSD dedicated to sorting the results from a single Stage 1 SIMD processor.

The measurements in [3] indicates that 16 bit data is sufficient for reliable decoder performance, and as such this is chosen as the ALU unit of both types of the SIMD processors, which exploit a real-valued datapath. Both processors employ respectively 256 and 32 locations in their PM and RF. The 16-way SIMD processors are configured with coprocessor accelerators to speed up the slicing operation, whilst the 12-way SIMD processor incorporates a coprocessor to accelerate the sort operation in each of its FPEs.

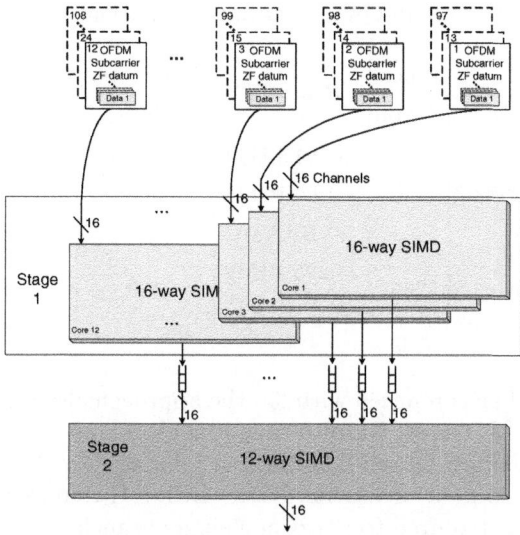

**Fig. 3.** SIMD Processor Array for FSD

The behaviour of each Stage 1 SIMD has three main phases.

1. At the beginning of each OFDM frame, the channel coefficient matrix **r**, and the ZF data values are loaded into the centralized IMM of each SIMD.
2. Each of the mapped OFDM subcarriers is processed in turn, before the next begins. A single branch of each subcarrier is implemented on one FPE. For each symbol, the ZF data values used to initialise the centre of the decoding sphere are loaded into the FPE RFs, which then perform the metric calculation stage of the FSD algorithm, with the APED and detected symbols output into the output FIFOs. This repeats for each subcarrier implemented on the SIMD.
3. The process reverts to either 2 to load new ZF data for the next symbol, or to 1 to reload new channel coefficient if the end of a frame has been reached.

Each way of the Stage 2 SIMD sorts the results from one of the Stage 1 SIMDs; it reads the APED values and detected symbols from its input FIFOs and retains the symbol corresponding to the lowest value.

When this architecture is implemented on a Xilinx Virtex 5 VSX240T using Xilinx ISE 12.2, the implementation metrics are achieved as described in Table 3. We compare the performance of this implementation to a comparable dedicated circuit implementation presented in [3] in terms of the equivalent LUT measure proposed by [14].

Table 3 shows that this SIMD-based solution can enable real-time performance in excess of the 480 Mbps required for 802.11n. This is the first programmable implementation to demonstrate this capability, overcoming the limitations of other softcore detectors [8].

**Table 3.** 4 × 4 16-QAM FSD Implementations Comparison

| Ref | Device | Clock (MHz) | Resource | Throughput (Mbps) | Program-mability | Equivalent LUTs [14] |
|-----|--------|-------------|----------|-------------------|------------------|----------------------|
| [3] | Virtex 5 | 150 | 13,197 LUTs<br>160 DSP48Es<br>49 BRAMs | 600 | No | 168,039 |
| SIMD Array Decoder | Virtex 5 | 265 | 24,295 LUTs<br>204 DSP48Es | 480 | Yes | 140,371 |

Furthermore, when compared with [3], the approach also offers a 16.5% reduction in equivalent LUT cost. Despite this, it is clear that this implementation is expensive in terms of LUTs and DSP48Es as compared to [3]. This extra expense can be attributed to poor utilisation of the DSP48E resources. For instance, of the 151 instructions required to perform a single branch of the FSD tree, 29% is composed of NOPs, reducing the datapath utilisation to 71%. This leads to the requirement for more FPEs to enable real-time performance, which in turn drives up resource cost. In Section 4, we present a solution which significantly reduces this inefficiency.

## 4   Interleaved SIMD-Based FSD

The multi-SIMD FSD in Section 3.2 suffers from high LUT and DSP48E cost as a direct result of inefficient use of the processor datapaths. To overcome this inefficiency, we examine the effect of task interleaving on the real-time performance and cost of this softcore based solution in this section.

In the current implementation, each branch of the 4 × 4 16-QAM FSD tree is mapped to a separate FPE in one of the Stage 1 SIMDs, with the processing for an entire subcarrier completing before that for the next subcarrier begins. As such, the program flow for each FPE resembles that shown in Fig. 4(a), where NOP instructions are represented as gaps in the instruction schedule. These NOPs represent wasted cycles since they serve no useful function.

We propose to interleave the execution of two branches on a single FPE to overcome the inefficiency represented by these NOPs - Fig. 4(b) illustrates the effect of this interleaving. Since the branches of the FSD tree are parallel and all perform the same functions, we can interleave the operations for two branches to fill the NOP cycles exactly to produce a program flow like that depicted in Fig. 4(b). As this shows, the length of program is extended, but from the perspective of each branch, there are no data hazards since the original delays between useful operations for each branch are still observed, but the NOP instruction gaps are filled with useful operations for the other branch. The effect of this interleaving on the program length and efficiency is shown in Table 4. As this shows, although the program length has increased to 214 instructions, we have eliminated 90% of

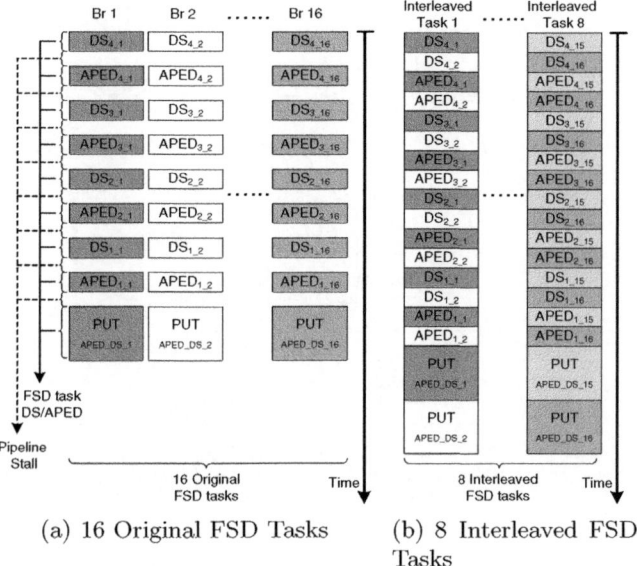

(a) 16 Original FSD Tasks          (b) 8 Interleaved FSD Tasks

**Fig. 4.** Processor Efficiency for Two Branches Without/With Interleaving

**Table 4.** Efficiency Breakdown

| Type | Total Inst. | NOPs Inst. | % of Efficiency |
|---|---|---|---|
| 2 Uninterleaved Branches | 214 | 62 | 71% |
| 2 Interleaved Branches | 151 | 6 | 96% |

the NOP instructions, and the processing efficiency of each FPE has increased to 96%.

As a result of this increased processing efficiency, each FPE can now perform more useful operations in the same time period; thus the number of FPEs to implement the FSD algorithm may be reduced. In this case, we can eliminate 33% of the Stage 1 SIMD processors. Fig. 5 shows the resulting architecture, and mapping of OFDM subcarriers to processor groups. In this case, Stage 1 is composed of only 8 16-way SIMD processors for the metric computation stage (the 108 subcarriers mapped to these as shown in Fig. 5) and Stage 2, a 16-way SIMD processor to perform the sorting.

Each of the Stage 1 SIMDs operates in three phases.

1. At the start of each OFDM frame, each SIMD loads the channel coefficient matrix **r** and ZF data to IMM.
2. Each FPE loads the ZF data representing the centre of the decoding spheres to RF, and processes two branches of each subcarrier FSD in round-robin interleaved fashion; the resulting APEDs are then directed to the output FIFOs, along with the detected symbol values.

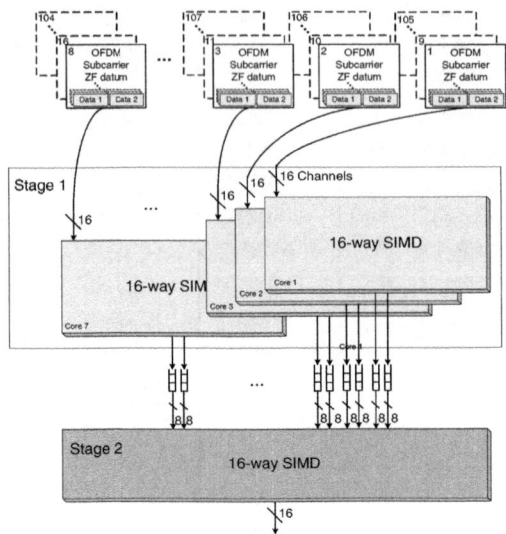

**Fig. 5.** Interleaved SIMD Processor Architecture

3. If the end of a frame has not been reached, the processor reverts to 2 to process the next symbol, otherwise it starts again at 1 for the new channel coefficients required for each new OFDM frame.

Each way of the 16-way Stage 2 sorting SIMD is responsible for sorting the data from one of the Stage 1 SIMD processors in a manner similar to that outlined for the standard SIMD operation in Section 3.2.

# 5    Results and Discussion

Table 5 summarizes the throughput ($T$) and resource cost in conventional and equivalent LUTs (ELUTs [14]) of the multi-SIMD architecture when the interleaving outlined in Section 4 is employed. The architecture is implemented on a Virtex 5 VSX240T using Xilinx ISE 12.2. As Table 5 shows, it offers 502.5 Mbps throughput - an increase of 22.5 Mbps on the uninterleaved architecture. Table 5 compares the cost of this interleaved implementation with that from [3] and the original, uninterleaved architecture (although [3] was implemented on Virtex II, and is retargetted to Virtex 5 here for the purpose of fair comparison.) Table 5 shows that, despite the increased throughput, the implementation employing interleaving consumes 29.4% and 31.7% less DSP48E and LUT resource respectively, leading to a reduction of 30% in ELUT cost, and a 49.1% increase in throughput per ELUT over the uninterleaved version. Further, when compared with [3], the interleaved implementation not only costs 42% less in terms of ELUTs and 10% less in terms of DSP48Es, it also offers a 42.8% increase in throughput per ELUT with comparable absolute LUT cost. These results seem to indicate that this pipeline interleaved softcore-based array offers lower

**Table 5.** Comparison of $4 \times 4$ 16-QAM FSD Implementations

| Ref | Device | Clock (MHz) | Resource | T (Mbps) | Program-mability | ELUTs [14] | T/ ELUT |
|---|---|---|---|---|---|---|---|
| [3] | Virtex II | 150 | 16,119 LUTs 160 Multipliers 82 BRAMs | 600 | No | 216,055 | $2.77 \times 10^{-3}$ |
| [3] | Virtex 5 | 150 | 13,197 LUTs 160 DSP48Es 49 BRAMs | 600 | No | 168,039 | $3.57 \times 10^{-3}$ |
| Uninterleaved Decoder | Virtex 5 | 265 | 24,295 LUTs 204 DSP48Es | 480 | Yes | 140,371 | $3.42 \times 10^{-3}$ |
| Interleaved Decoder | Virtex 5 | 296 | 16,601 LUTs 144 DSP48Es | 502.5 | Yes | 98,537 | $5.1 \times 10^{-3}$ |

resource cost to meet the 802.11n throughput standard, in addition to being flexible to reach several lower cost solutions which [3] cannot.

The significance of these results should not be missed: not only do they show that it is possible for a softcore-processor based implementation approach to offer real-time performance for such applications, it also shows that it is possible to do so with similar cost to dedicated circuits. The ramifications of this are considerable: it is possible that for such applications, the traditional RTL-level dedicated hardware design route could be usurped by one of predominately software-based programming, to enable the dynamic behaviour that is based on the requirement for next-generation MIMO, yet enable solutions with the same performance and cost.

## 6    Conclusion

This paper has described the use of heterogeneous networks of SIMD processors for implementation of MIMO decoding algorithms, specifically in this case FSD. We have shown that such an implementation approach, despite being based on programmable processor architectures, can enable real-time solutions for cutting edge MIMO standards, achieving up to 502 Mbps throughput, well in excess of the 480 Mbps required for 802.11n MIMO. Furthermore, we have shown that by employing task interleaving to increase the efficiency of the embedded processing, we can reduce the LUT and DSP48E resources required by 31.7% and 29.4% respectively, and increase the resource efficiency by 49.1%. This enables implementations which cost 42% less than dedicated circuit architectures in terms of equivalent LUTs, and which are comparable in absolute terms. We believe the ramifications of this observation are profound and should promote serious reconsideration of architecture design approaches for FPGA-based DSP applications;

seriously predominately software-based implementation using large scale networks of high performance parallel processors, are challenging traditional RTL-level hardware design.

# References

1. Foschini, G.J.: Layered Space-Time Architecture for Wireless Communication in a Fading Environment When Using Multi-Element Antennas. Bell Labs Technical Journal 1(2), 41–59 (1996)
2. Burg, A., Borgmann, M., Wenk, M., Zellweger, M., Fichtner, W., Bolcskei, H.: VLSI Implementation of MIMO Detection Using The Sphere Decoding Algorithm. IEEE Journal of Solid-State Circuits 40, 1566–1577 (2005)
3. Barbero, L.: Rapid Prototyping of a Fixed-Complexity Sphere Decoder and its Application to Iterative Decoding of Turbo-MIMO Systems. Ph.D. Thesis, The University of Edinburgh (2006)
4. Guo, Z., Nilsson, P.: Algorithm and Implementation of the K-Best Sphere Decoding for MIMO Detection. IEEE Journal on Selected Areas in Communications 24, 491–503 (2006)
5. Bhagawat, P., Dash, R., Choi, G.: Array Like Runtime Reconfigurable MIMO Detectors for 802.11n WLAN: A Design Case Study. In: 2009 Asia and South Pacific Design Automation Conference, pp. 751–756. IEEE, Los Alamitos (2009)
6. Yu, J., Eagleston, C., Chou, C.H.-Y., Perreault, M., Lemieux, G.: Vector Processing as a Soft Processor Accelerator. ACM Transactions on Reconfigurable Technology and Systems 2(2), 1–34 (2009)
7. Yiannacouras, P., Steffan, J.G., Rose, J.: Fine-Grain Performance Scaling of Soft Vector Processors. In: International Conference on Compilers, Architecture and Synthesis for Embedded Systems (2009)
8. Huang, X., Liang, C., Ma, J.: System Architecture and Implementation of MIMO Sphere Decoders on FPGA. IEEE Transactions on Very Large Scale Integration (VLSI) Systems 16(2), 188–197 (2008)
9. Schnorr, C.P., Euchner, M.: Lattice Basis Reduction: Improved Practical Algorithms and Solving Subset Sum Problems. Mathematical Programming 66(1), 181–199 (1994)
10. Janhunen, J., Silvén, O., Juntti, M.: Programmable Processor Implementations of K-best List Sphere Detector for MIMO Receiver. Elsevier Journal of Signal Processing 90(1), 313–323 (2009)
11. Wu, M., Gupta, S., Sun, Y., Cavallaro, J.R.: A GPU Implementation of a Real-Time MIMO Detector. In: 2009 IEEE Workshop on Signal Processing Systems, pp. 303–308 (October 2009)
12. 802.11n-2009 IEEE Local and Metropolitan Area Networks–Specific Requirements Part 11: Wireless LAN Medium Access Control (MAC) and Physical Layer (PHY) Specifications Amendment 5: Enhancements for Higher Throughput (2009)
13. Xilinx, Virtex-5 FPGA User Guide (2010)
14. Sheldon, D., Kumar, R., Lysecky, R., Vahid, F., Tullsen, D.: Application-Specific Customization of Parameterized FPGA Soft-Core Processors. In: IEEE/ACM International Conference on Computer-Aided Design, pp. 261–268 (2006)

# Design, Implementation, and Verification of an Adaptable Processor in Lava HDL

Stefan Schulze[1] and Sergei Sawitzki[2]

[1] NEMONOS GmbH
Bernstorffstraße 99
22767 Hamburg, Germany
[2] FH Wedel (University of Applied Sciences)
Feldstraße 143
22880 Wedel, Germany

**Abstract.** This paper documents the development, implementation, and verification of a RISC microprocessor using the functional hardware description language Lava. Basic methods to describe hardware in Lava are introduced and extended towards implementation of instruction set and pipeline structure. Synthesis results for Cyclone II FPGA are presented and compared against a traditional VHDL-based design flow. A loosely coupled coprocessor interface used to accelerate application-specific code is introduced. To authors' best knowledge it is the first attempt to describe a complete von Neumann machine in Lava. Project experiences as well as directions for further improvement of Lava are summarized.

**Keywords:** Functional languages, Lava, reconfigurable processor.

## 1 Motivation and Previous Work

Majority of digital hardware nowadays is designed using hardware description languages (HDLs). The most prominent HDLs are Verilog and VHDL, which were introduced around 25 years ago. During the last years, languages like SystemC, Bluespec SystemVerlog and SystemVerilog aiming at higher abstraction level are gaining attention of both academia and industry. Traditional HDLs provide capabilities to describe hardware at gate, register transfer, algorithmic and even system level. Many of the new features introduced recently are targeting higher abstraction layers (e.g. by incorporating several concepts of the object-oriented languages). Still, many of the traditional HDLs have limited parameterization and verification capabilities. Some of these shortcomings are addressed by preprocessors, code generators and GUI-based development assistants.

A language domain that does not suffer from these deficits are so-called functional HDLs like $\mu FP$ [1], Ruby [2], Reflect [3] and several others. There were a couple of approaches to use functional languages to describe and model hardware, even during the time that VHDL and Verilog were emerging, but they have never gained acceptance in the industry [4]. This situation seems to change, since both academia and industry are starting to employ functional HDLs in real-world

A. Koch et al. (Eds.): ARC 2011, LNCS 6578, pp. 145–156, 2011.

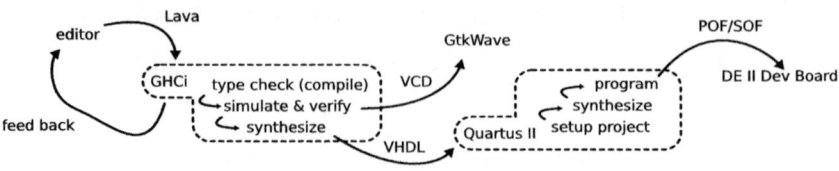

**Fig. 1.** Steps involved in the Lava build process

projects. The language used for the project described herein is based on Haskell and is called Lava HDL. Lava is known to the FPL community mostly through the work of Satnam Singh, who applied it in several designs targeting Xilinx FP-GAs [5]. Lava version he is using (referred further as *Xilinx Lava*) incorporates a lot of Xilinx-specific details like location constraints, CLB architecture etc. In addition, most of the designs in Xilinx Lava show quite regular patterns (FFT, merge sorters, etc.). The achieved results state the question if Lava can be as efficient targeting other hardware platforms and less regular designs.

In addition, our work was motivated by the results of the Reduceron project [6]. Reduceron is an application-specific processor for graph reduction described in Lava, so it can be seen as an engine for hardware based evaluation of a functional language, described in a functional language itself. Taking the results obtained with Xilinx Lava and Reduceron as a background, our aim is to build, verify and test-run a regular general-purpose microprocessor. To authors' best knowledge it is the first attempt of this kind.

The rest of this paper is organized as follows. The Section 2 gives a brief overview of Lava dialects, basic constructs and design flow. In the Section 3 the implementation of the Pipo processor together with proposed extensions to Lava library are discussed. The concept and implementation of a reconfigurable coprocessor designed to accelerate Pipo by running application-specific tasks are introduced in Section 4. Finally, Section 5 draws some conclusions.

## 2     Lava: A Functional HDL

### 2.1     A Brief History

Lava is a pure structural, higher-order language. It can be seen as a Haskell library. Quoting Mathew Naylor [7]: "*Pure structural* means that Lava does not provide any built-in constructs for behavioral description, and *higher-order* means that circuits descriptions can be passed into other descriptions like regular parameters. As a result, the approach taken in Lava differs from that taken by standard HDLs in that behavioral constructs are not built in to the language, but are provided by a small library of pure structural, higher-order components."

Lava, as domain-specific language for hardware description, had its first public appearance in the paper *Lava: Hardware Design in Haskell* [8]. It was the original version of Lava, which has later evolved to already mentioned Xilinx Lava [5]. There are two more Lava variants in the field. *Chalmers Lava* [9] introduces a library driven extension for Haskell, called *Observable Sharing* (ObS) which simplifies the detection of shared subcircuits in the design [10].

The work described herein is using *York Lava*. It has been released just recently as a part of ongoing research on the already mentioned Reduceron project [6]. It incorporates some interesting enhancements to the predominant Chalmers Lava, like freely extensible Lava primitives, the possibility to synthesize VHDL-components with multiple outputs and size restricted data types. In addition, it provides a Recipe library, which will be explained further below. In the course of our work, this version of Lava was extended.

## 2.2   Lava Environment and Design Flow

The main tool for developing circuits with Lava is a Haskell compiler or interpreter. We are using the Glasgow Haskell Compiler (GHC), that is also providing an interpreter shell to interactively work on Haskell modules. The interpreter is commonly referred to as GHCi. When simulating, synthesizing or testing Lava circuits, the desired functions are invoked from within GHCi.

Figure 1 gives an overview of the design flow. The general process of working on Lava modules is to write circuit definitions and matching functions to abbreviate the start of simulation, verification and synthesis to VHDL. These functions are called from within GHCi generating the desired output, either for manual inspection or as an input to the next step in the build process. After VHDL files have been generated, they can be incorporated into a project within a regular development framework (Altera Quartus II in our case). Since neither Chalmers nor York Lava provide an interface to Altera FPGAs we extended it in a way comparable to Xilinx Lava, so specific features of Cyclone II EP2C35 FPGA (embedded multipliers, memory etc.) can be used. A common VHDL interface for platform-independent logic synthesis is provided as well. In addition, I/O-Waveforms resulting from functional simulation are stored in VCD format.

## 2.3   Lava by Example

The Lava libraries define a number of primitive operations on netlist nodes to describe basic circuits. The most fundamental digital logic operations are formalized as follows:

```
low   :: Bit                   -- Logic 0
high  :: Bit                   -- Logic 1
inv   :: Bit -> Bit            -- Inverter
(<&>) :: Bit -> Bit -> Bit -- AND gate
(<|>) :: Bit -> Bit -> Bit -- OR gate
(<#>) :: Bit -> Bit -> Bit -- XOR gate
delay :: Bit -> Bit -> Bit -- D-flip-flop
```

Building circuits to make them available for future use is achieved by defining functions, e.g binary adder:

```
halfAdd :: (Bit, Bit) -> (Bit, Bit)
halfAdd (a, b) = (sum, cout)
  where sum  = a <#> b; cout = a <&> b
fullAdd :: (Bit, Bit, Bit) -> (Bit, Bit)
fullAdd (cin, a, b) = (sum2, cout)
  where (sum1,cout1) = halfAdd (a  , b)
        (sum2,cout2) = halfAdd (cin, sum1)
        cout = cout1 <|> cout2
binAdd :: (Bit, [Bit], [Bit]) -> [Bit]
binAdd (cin, []    , []    ) = [cin]
binAdd (cin, (a:as), (b:bs)) =
  sum : binAdd (cout, as, bs)
  where (sum, cout) = fullAdd (cin, a, b)
binAddNoCarry = init . binAdd
```

Providing `binAdd` with two equally sized lists, it will generate the output of a ripple carry adder. The second circuit in that listing — `binAddNoCarry` — is just a convenient function dropping the carry from the output, since it is usually ignored. This will allow us to construct a counter of $n$ bits width:

```
counter :: Int -> [Bit]
counter n = cnt where
  cnt  = delay (replicate n low) cnt'
  cnt' = binAddNoCarry (low, cnt, inc)
  inc  = high:replicate (n-1) low
```

In order to synthesize a circuit to VHDL files, Lava provides the function `writeVhdl`. It takes three arguments: the name of the VHDL entity to create, a circuit netlist with named input nodes and a construct naming all the output nodes. For example, to generate VHDL for the `halfAdd` circuit, with inputs named "a" and "b" and outputs named "out" and "carry", we define this synthesis function:

```
synHalfAdd :: IO ()
synHalfAdd = writeVhdl "HalfAdd"
             (halfAdd (name "a", name "b"))
             (name "sum", name "carry")
```

Upon calling this function, the directory "HalfAdd" will be created, containing the generated VHDL file(s).

### 2.4  Making Lava Behave: Recipe

The structural description is a good way to create combinatorial circuits. On the other hand, it is hard to express systems that change their function depending on a multitude of states, be it internal state or state supplied to the system. This is due to the fact, that the circuit will be speckled with multiplexers, for every signal that depends on the state. The Recipe library included with York

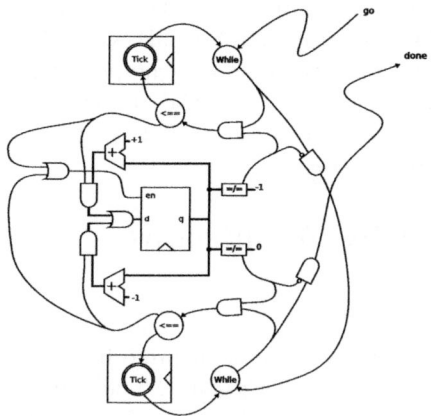

**Fig. 2.** Petri-net representation of the linSweepRecipe

Lava solves this problem by providing a set of constructs to form behavioral descriptions. Working with Recipe is divided in two steps.

*The first step* declares a type, say Circ to define access points to inputs and outputs of structural circuits. Access points are either plain Lava signals (output only), or a place holder of type Sig or Reg. The place holders act as assignable variables during behavioral description and will be implemented by simple multiplexers or a combination of multiplexers attached to registers with enable inputs, respectively. When creating a new value of type Circ, the functions newSig and newReg are used to create instances of types Sig and Reg. *The second step* is to define a function of type Circ -> Recipe, generating a description (a Recipe) of how and under what conditions the circuit parts interact. This way structural description is separated from behavioral one. The following listing gives an example of circuit generating a linear sweep (=first-count-up-then-count-down):

```
data LinSwpCirc n = LinSwpCirc
  { count :: Reg n }
newLinSwpCirc :: N n => New (LinSwpCirc n)
newLinSwpCirc=return LinSwpCirc'ap'newReg
linSwpRecipe (LinSwpCirc count) =
  Seq [ While (count!val =/= (-1)) $
    Seq [ count <== count!val +1 , Tick ]
      , While (count!val =/=   0 ) $
    Seq [ count <== count!val -1 , Tick ]]
linearSweep go = (s!count!val, done)
  where (s, done) = recipe newLinSwpCirc
            linSwpRecipe go
```

Writing a Recipe can be interpreted as writing a petri-net, which will be implemented with the help of a "one-hot" encoded state machine. Every Tick node in the petri-net will be implemented by a flip-flop, delaying the marker to be passed on for one clock cycle. On every other node, the marker will be passed by instant propagation (read: combinatorial). Conditional `Recipes` like `While` or ( `|>` ) are represented by gated edges in the petri-net, depicted in the Fig. 2, showing petri-net and attached logic for the previous example. Nodes connected by ungated edges can be combined in the petri-net representation, but this has been omitted for clarity reasons.

# 3   Designing a RISC Architecture

## 3.1   Basic Structure

The Pipo processor presented herein is inspired by MIPS RISC architecture and is loosely based on the *Plasma* design [11]. The Plasma processor provides up to three pipeline stages, and supports most of the standard MIPS instructions. The project also provides a modified gcc compiler for compiling C source code to MIPS executables. Pipo processor facilitates a five stage pipeline. This means that the *Plasma* processor is in fact only compatible to MIPS on the ISA level but it is not following the MIPS architecture.

Using the methods and language constructs described in the previous section we first describe the basic units of the processor: instruction decoder, ALU, barrel-shifter, multiplier, register set etc. The corresponding code is quite straightforward. The most complex design task is to combine the units into the pipeline structure and to describe the behavior of the processor while it is executing the instructions.

## 3.2   `PExpr` Language

When disregarding the pipelined structure, the most common actions taken by the processor are actually easy to describe: Take some values from designated resources, perform and operation on them and store the result somewhere:

```
destination := operation(op1,op2...opN)
```

The operation can be anything from simply relocating data between resources to performing a more sophisticated action in the execution stage. To model this semantic within Haskell, we defined an own language called `PExpr`. We start by defining the following data type:

```
data PExpr = PExprOp PExprOp
  -- perform operation PExprOp
| PExprID :=: PExpr
  -- assign evaluated PExpr to PExprID
| PExprPassOn PExprID -- pass on a operand
| ...
```

This allows us to express operations and assignments to `PExprID` identifiers. We continue by defining a few operations (e.g. addition and subtraction):

**Table 1.** PExpr identifiers

| Name | Description |
|------|-------------|
| RS | register bank, addressed with RS part |
| RT | register bank, addressed with RT part |
| RD | register bank, addressed with RD part |
| SAM | shift amount |
| JMP | jump target; the lower 28 bits of instruction |
| IMM | immediate part of instruction |
| MEM B W | memory access to address (B+IMM) of width W |
| (E)PC | (exception) program counter |

```
data PExprOp = PExprID :+: PExprID
  | PExprID :-: PExprID | ...
```

To make the resources of the processor accessible, we define a list of representative identifiers. Since an operation always resides within the scope of a single instruction, we use the naming convention for parts of the instruction word as an inspiration for the identifiers. These are the identifiers immediately available from the instruction word:

```
data PExprID = RS | RT | RD | SAM | JMP
  | IMM | ... deriving Eq
```

Following lines construct valid PExpr expressions and are pretty self-explanatory:

```
RD :=: PExprOp (RS :+: RT)
RD :=: PExprOp (RS :-: IMM)
RD :=: PExprPassOn RS
```

Not all syntactically correct expressions form a legal operation, as, for example, the IMM value is read-only. These limitations are taken into account, when expressions are compiled into actual hardware description. Furthermore, we need to have access to other components of the system, including memory and program counter. The program counter is modeled as an identifier as well. When accessing the memory on the other hand, we need to assert a specific memory address and an access width. Consequently, the memory identifier has two parameters, one setting the access base and the other one the width. The base parameter is resembled by any PExprID identifier and the width is either 8, 16 or 32 bit. The complete set of identifiers is listed in Table 1.

As a final beautification touch to our newly created expression language, we define a type class and fitting instances that will make the call to a specific PExpr constructor implicit, by wrapping them in the new assignment operator (.=).

```
class PExprAble a where toExpr :: a->PExpr
instance PExprAble PExprID
  where toExpr = PExprPassOn
instance PExprAble PExprOp
```

```
  where toExpr = PExprOp
instance PExprAble PExpr where toExpr = id
x .= y = x :=: toExpr y
```

This will make the previously shown expressions even more readable:

```
RD .= (RS :+: RT)
RD .= (RS :-: IMM)
RD .= RS
```

To complete the expressiveness of PExpr language and to match the abilities of our processor, a few extra semantics are introduced. This includes conditional execution of assignments and triggering of events (i.e. calling coprocessor functions as described below).

### 3.3   Verification

The correctness of circuits is verified by testing known corner cases and checking for the desired results, or even by checking every possible input state with the expected output state. While this can be accomplished manually for small circuits, it is hard to guarantee correctness when circuits are getting more complex (e.g. corner cases might remain unchecked, if the tester is unaware of them).

A significant advantage in using Lava is the fact, that Haskell community is providing several libraries for property based verification of algorithms. The basic idea is to just provide constrains — that is, properties of the algorithm under test — that should hold for any applied input data, while the library core determines the correctness. The most prominent library is *QuickCheck*, which follows the methodology to generate all test data randomly, finishing when a given number of data sets has been generated or when a contradiction has been found. For structured data *QuickCheck* tries to simplify input data after a contradiction has been found, so spotting the actual corner case is easier. The *SmallCheck* library is following a more deterministic approach of generating the test data successively, starting with simple values and building them up to more complex cases. The reasoning behind is that erroneous algorithms will in most cases fail already for simple (small) input values. This is especially true for hardware circuits: A circuit working for 2 bit input is likely to work for 32 bit or more.

There are other libraries for property base verification, that use non-Haskell back-ends. Most of them, however, have drawbacks: Either they are not supported any more, incompatible with new compilers or cannot be integrated into Lava. All subunits of the Pipo processor were verified using *SmallCheck* library. The complete core was simulated in VHDL and tested on an FPGA board.

### 3.4   Synthesis and Test-Runs

The synthesis of the processor follows two step manner of working with Recipes as explained in section 2.4. First, the structural circuitry is instantiated with the initial memory contents. In the second step the Recipe library is used to

**Table 2.** Synthesis results and comparison with *Plasma* CPU

|  | Pipo CPU | Plasma CPU | |
|---|---|---|---|
| pipeline stages | 5 | 2 | 3 |
| logic cells | 2,137 | 2,453 | 2,461 |
| register cells | 381 | 452 | 568 |
| lines of code | 1,345 | 5,341 | |
| memory bits | 2,048 | 2,048 | |
| embedded multipliers | 8 | 0 | |
| maximum clock (worst case) [MHz] | 60.26 | 19.49 | 38.68 |

compile the `pipoRecipe` and abbreviate the call to `writeVhdl`. VHDL sources are created by calling `synPipo` with the initial memory contents and passed to Quartus II. The VHDL synthesis results including a comparison with the *Plasma* processor (described completely in VHDL) are shown in Table 2. The numbers provide a rough but fair comparison. On one hand, *Plasma* CPU has some extra units, like a DMA controller, implements more MIPS instructions and has a sequential multiplier. On the other hand, Pipo has a five stage pipeline and a dedicated hardware multiplier unit. The major conclusions of the comparison are that Pipo is less complex in terms of logic resources and its description is much more compact (Lava code is around one quarter of the VHDL code). The higher clock frequency of Pipo is the consequence of a deeper pipeline.

To run the Pipo processor with some "real" software, a dedicated assembler was implemented. Every assembly language instruction calls a mnemonic function, which returns a hexadecimal instruction word. These words are sequenced in a list, which is loaded into the system memory of the processor. Upon booting the system, the processor will execute the instructions starting from memory address "0x00". Using this "developing environment" a number of simple applications ("Hello world!", image filters etc.) were developed to test the behavior of the processor. These applications were chosen in such way, that all the instructions of the Pipo processor are executed in many different combinations. For all implemented test cases Pipo behaves correctly [12].

# 4   Designing a CPU Extension

One of the major advantages of mapping a processor to programmable logic is the possibility to implement user-specific instructions accelerating the target application. This approach was well studied over last two decades [13,14,15,16]. We demonstrate its implementation using a functional HDL. There are numerous ways to attach the application specific part to the processor core. Pipo processor incorporates a loosely coupled coprocessor interface. The CPU is connected to main memory via a 32-bit bus, so it is necessary to collect data prior to a parallel execution. To achieve this, we implemented a Lava circuit acting as a common interface for parallel execution (IPE) having a single input and a single output, when viewed from the instruction set side. In the simplest case, the IPE

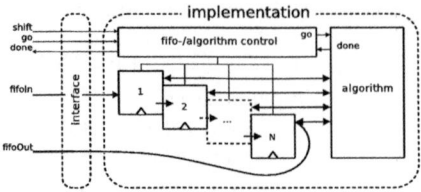

**Fig. 3.** Schematic diagram of the interface for parallel execution

**Table 3.** Pipo processor with and without FFT

|  | Pipo with radix-2 FFT | Pipo with single butterfly | Pipo CPU without FFT |
|---|---|---|---|
| logic cells | 3,325 | 2,837 | 2,137 |
| register cells | 1,396 | 794 | 381 |
| embedded multipliers | 40 | 16 | 8 |
| maximum clock [MHz] | 57.12 | 56.33 | 60.26 |

will queue the applied values into a FIFO making every value available to the parallel execution acting as a serial-parallel/parallel-serial converter (see Fig. 3).

The hardware attached to an IPE can be freely defined. For example, in case of a hardware accelerated simulation of a neural network, a set of inputs is fed into the network by applying a synaptic weight to each input in parallel for each neuron in the first layer. In this case, it makes sense to start with simulation immediately as soon as the first input is provided. There is no need to wait for more than one input value. We introduce three new instructions interfacing with the IPE: one for applying the values, one to acquire the results and another for triggering the parallel execution of the attached unit. MIPS(I) ISA specifies calls to coprocessors. We define IPEs to be the third coprocessor (CO3) and reserve a bit sequence for identifying which of the possible 8 IPEs is accessed.

To evaluate the approach, an FFT coprocessor for Pipo was developed in Lava. The structure is based on the work presented by S. Singh [17] adopted for York Lava and Pipo interface. The whole unit including all basic functions described above takes around 60 lines of Lava code. The synthesis results for a radix-2 butterfly network processing four 16-bit samples in parallel are shown in Table 3 (first column). The clock frequency is given for the complete processor core, radix-2 FFT coprocessor achieves around 180 MHz in stand-alone mode. Since communication between Pipo and FFT coprocessor is event-based, this frequency can be used in an actual design if two different clock domains are provided. An alternative FFT implementation is based upon a single butterfly circuit shared by a sequence of values and twiddle parameters. In contrast to the parallel implementation, it provides only a linear speed up over a purely software based solution. For both FFT designs, the number of samples as well as their width are parameterized and only limited by the logic capacity of the underlying hardware. Table 3 (second column) summarizes the synthesis results.

An FFT code running on Pipo consists of a main loop and an interrupt service routine. The main loop exchanges data with the service routine via a buffer. The main program waits for the FFT core to become ready, by issuing IPE FFT RDY instructions. After that, it uses IPE FFT PUSH to sequentially feed the FFT core with the signed 8-bit integers stored in the receive buffer until a complete set of samples has been pushed. Finally, the FFT calculation is initiated and the main program starts polling the core with IPE FFT RDY. The results are directly sent back over the serial line and the main loop is restarted. A test run with 32 input samples proves that Pipo with FFT coprocessor behaves as expected [12].

## 5   Conclusions

The contribution of the project introduced herein can be summarized as follows:

- first implementation of a RISC machine in Lava, competitive with comparable processor described in VHDL while requiring only 1/4 of the code size
- definition and implementation of PExpr, a language to describe CPU behavior based on its ISA
- extension of the processor with reconfigurable FFT coprocessor
- verification of processor and coprocessor using built-in Lava facilities
- extension of York Lava with three new back-ends: one generating Altera-specific VHDL code, one generating device-independent synthesizable VHDL code and one generating VCD wave-forms used for the visualization of the results of functional simulation

In general, our study has shown, that for a hardware designer familiar with functional programming, using functional HDL is as comfortable as using a conventional HDL. Advantages are more compact code, built-in verification tools and reduced complexity. The major conclusion is that Lava HDL applied to a complex design is equally suitable for description of both regular data-path and highly irregular control logic. However, there are apparently some reasons preventing functional HDLs (in our case Lava) from going mainstream:

- no proper size restricted types. Existing workarounds (e.g. Haskell extension called "functional dependencies") do not provide satisfactory results.
- infinite recursions (e.g. resulting from combinatorial loops). It should be noted, however, that VHDL netlist simulation suffers from the same problem.
- native control structures are not synthesizable. This stems from the fact, that Lava components are merely *generating* data that represents a netlist. The Haskell code itself is not a part of the netlist. For example, a multiplexer cannot be instantiated by an if x then a else b construct.
- no probing of internal circuit states. In the current form using Haskell functions to generate Lava netlists does not allow to inspect the state of internal nodes. Although it is possible for the Lava libraries to collect the state of internal nodes, there is no way to refer to a particular node.

– no proper names spaces when using Recipe. While being a genuine simple approach, the Recipe library has some shortcomings that can be denounced as a lack of abstraction and scoping. To access the variables of a Recipe, they are structured into Haskell records polluting the global name space. with functions that extract specific fields of a record data type.
– no direct synthesis of Lava to hardware. Converting Lava to synthesizable VHDL is somewhat artificial and introduces unnecessary overhead.

Some of the problems mentioned above present a considerable burden preventing fluent development cycles. It is especially true for unintentional infinite recursion, exhaustive memory consumption during simulation and the inability to inspect internal nodes. Nevertheless, all of these problems are imposed by implementation details, not by the concept of functional hardware description itself.

# References

1. Sheeran, M.: $\mu$FP, an algebraic VLSI Design Language, PhD thesis, Oxford (1983)
2. Jones, G., Sheeran, M.: Circuit Design in Ruby. In: Formal Methods for VLSI Design, pp. 13–70. Elsevier Science Publishers, Amsterdam (1994)
3. Grundy, J., Melham, T., O'Leary, J.: A Reflective Functional Language for Hardware Design and Theorem Proving. J. of Functional Programming 16(2), 157–196 (2006)
4. Sheeran, M.: Hardware Design and Functional Programming: a Perfect Match. J. of Universal Computer Science 11(7), 1135–1158 (2005)
5. Singh, S., James-Roxby, P.: Lava and JBits: From HDL to Bitstream in Seconds. In: Proc. of FCCM, pp. 91–100 (2001)
6. Naylor, M., Runcimann, C.: The Reduceron Research Project, 2008–2010, http://www.cs.york.ac.uk/fp/reduceron/
7. Naylor, M.: Hardware-Assisted and Target-Directed Evaluation of Functional Programs, PhD thesis, University of York (2008)
8. Bjeese, P., Claessen, K., Sheeran, M., Singh, S.: Lava: Hardware Design in Haskell. In: Proc. of ICFP, ACM SIGPLAN (1998)
9. Claessen, K.: An Embedded Language Approach to Hardware Description and Verification, Lic. thesis, Chalmers University of Technology (August 2000)
10. Claessen, K., Sands, D.: Observable Sharing for Functional Circuit Description. In: Thiagarajan, P.S., Yap, R.H.C. (eds.) ASIAN 1999. LNCS, vol. 1742, pp. 62–73. Springer, Heidelberg (1999)
11. Rhoads, S.: Plasma — most MIPS I(TM) opcodes, 2001–2010, http://plasmacpu.no-ip.org
12. Schulze, S.: Design, Implementation and Verification of a Processor with a Functional Hardware Description Language, Diplomarbeit, FH Wedel (March 2010)
13. Athanas, P., Silverman, H.: Processor Reconfiguration through Instruction-Set Metamorphosis. IEEE Computer 26(3), 11–18 (1993)
14. Razdan, R.: PRISC: Programmable Reduced Instruction Set Computers, PhD thesis, Harvard University, Cambridge, Massachusetts (May 1994)
15. Hauser, J., Wawrzynek, J.: Garp: A MIPS Processor with a Reconfigurable Coprocessor. In: Proc. of FCCM, pp. 24–33 (1997)
16. Moscu Panainte, E., Bertels, K.L.M., Vassiliadis, S.: The Molen Compiler for Reconfigurable Processors. ACM TECS 6(1) (February 2007)
17. Singh, S.: Xilinx Lava Hardware Description Language 1 (October 2009), http://www.raintown.org/lava

# Towards an Adaptable Multiple-ISA Reconfigurable Processor

Jair Fajardo Junior, Mateus B. Rutzig, Antonio C.S. Beck, and Luigi Carro

Universidade Federal do Rio Grande do Sul – Porto Alegre/Brazil
{jfajardoj,mbrutzig,caco,carro}@inf.ufrgs.br

**Abstract.** As technology advances, new hardware approaches are proposed to speed up software execution. However, every new added hardware feature must not change the underlying instruction set architecture (ISA), in order to avoid adaptation or recompilation of existing code. As binary translation allows the execution of binary codes of already compiled applications on different architectures, it opens new possibilities for designers, previously tied to a specific ISA and all its legacy hardware issues. The problem with binary translation is its inherent performance penalty: it will always take more cycles than the simple execution on the native machine. To address that, we propose a new mechanism based on a dynamic two-level binary translation system. While the first level is responsible for the BT de facto (in our first implemented case study, X86 to MIPS translations), the second level optimizes the already translated instructions to be executed on a dynamically adaptable reconfigurable architecture. This way, both software portability and performance are maintained.

**Keywords:** Binary Translation, Reconfigurable Architectures.

## 1 Introduction

With the constant growth of the embedded systems market, more complex applications have been developed to fulfill consumer needs. At the same time, technological development has already started to stagnate as a result of the decline in Moore's law [1], and one can observe that the processing capabilities of traditional architectures are not growing in the same pace as before [2].

In this scenario, new alternatives are necessary to minimize this problem. However, the support for binary compatibility, so that the large quantity of tools and applications already deployed can be reused, is an important requirement to introduce new processors into the market. With this in mind, companies develop their products focusing on the improvement of a given architecture that will execute the same Instruction Set Architecture (ISA) as before. Nevertheless, this need for compatibility imposes a great number of restrictions to the design team.

Binary translation systems can give back to designers the freedom previously lost, since they do not need to be tied to a specific ISA anymore. However, only the maintenance of binary compatibility is not enough to handle market needs. It is also necessary to translate code execution in a competitive fashion, when compared to native

A. Koch et al. (Eds.): ARC 2011, LNCS 6578, pp. 157–168, 2011.
© Springer-Verlag Berlin Heidelberg 2011

execution [3]. This way, the concept of binary translation must also be tightly con-nected to code optimization and acceleration [4].

This work proposes a new mechanism based on a dynamic two-level binary trans-lation system that, besides maintaining binary compatibility, amortizes its costs. An overview of the proposed system is presented in Figure 1. The first BT level is re-sponsible for translating the source code to the target code, as any conventional BT machine would do. In the case study presented in this paper, x86 to MIPS code is translated. The rest of the system comprises another BT mechanism, a MIPS proces-sor and a dynamically reconfigurable system [5] [6]. The second BT level is responsi-ble for transforming the already translated MIPS code to be executed on the dynami-cally reconfigurable array (Fig. 1a). The greatest advantage of using such proposal is that once a sequence of code has passed through the two levels (Figure 1a), the next time it is found both BT levels will be skipped (both translations will not be neces-sary), and the reconfigurable array will be directly used (Figure 1b).

This way, performance improvements are reached because:

- Both BT mechanisms are completely implemented in hardware for fast transla-tion and minimum performance overhead;
- Once the code is optimized to an array configuration, source to target machine translation is not necessary, as long as there memory available;
- A dynamic reconfigurable array is used to adapt the underlying architecture to the running software, which brings code execution speedups.

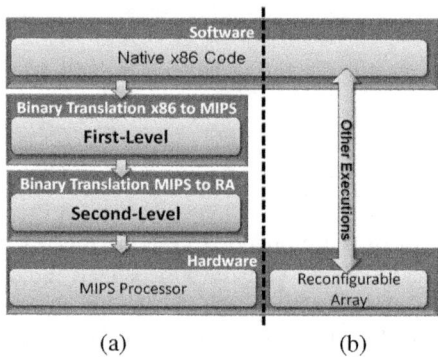

**Fig. 1.** Execution layers of proposed architecture

With the two-level BT mechanism, another advantage emerges: by only changing the first BT level it is possible to execute different ISAs in a completely transparent fashion to the second BT level, thus greatly facilitating the porting of radically differ-ent ISAs without the need for changing the underlying reconfigurable architecture. Therefore, applications compiled for other ISAs can be executed in the reconfigurable fabric as long as different first BT level layers are available. In this work, we present the first step towards this objective.

The rest of this paper is organized as follows. In section 2, we show some related binary translation architectures, with a brief explanation about their operation. In the next section, an overview about the proposed architecture is given. In section 4 we present the experimental results and a discussion on these tests. In Section 5 we conclude this article and discuss future works.

## 2  Related Work

Binary translation systems have been used mainly because companies need to reduce the time-to-market and maintain backward software compatibility. They can work at different layers in a computing architecture: as if it was another regular application, visible to the user; or yet implemented in hardware, working below the operating system [7].

One example is Rosetta [8]: used into Apple systems to maintain compatibility between the PowerPC and x86. It works in the application layer with the sole purpose of maintaining binary compatibility, causing a great overhead. Another case is the FX!32 [9] [10] that allows 32-bit programs to be installed and executed like an x86 architecture running Windows NT 4.0 on Alpha systems. The FX!32 is composed of an emulator and a binary translator system. The emulator performs code conversion, and also provides profiling information at run-time. The binary translator uses the profiling information to generate optimized images through identified hotspots into the code, saving them for future reuse and avoiding excessive run time overhead.

The Transmeta Crusoe processor [11] had the main purpose of translating x86 code to execute onto a VLIW processor, reducing power consumption and saving energy. In this case, the BT is implemented in software, but the Crusoe hardware (a VLIW processor) was designed to speed up the execution with minimum energy, which minimizes the translation overhead.

The Godson3 processor [12] has the same goal as the Transmeta Crusoe: using a software layer for binary translation (QEMU), it converts the x86 to MIPS instructions. However, it uses a different strategy to optimize the running program. Godson3 is a scalable multicore architecture, which uses a mix between a NOC (network on-chip) and a crossbar system for its communication infrastructure. This way, up to 64 cores can be used. Each core is a modified superscalar MIPS with hardware support to assist the dynamic translation. Therefore, Godson3 can achieve satisfactory execution time for applications already implemented and deployed in the field. However, the cost of having several superscalar processors is not small.

The binary translation process in software is more flexible due to the possibility to execute the BT system on other processors by recompiling the translator. However, it causes a huge overhead in execution time [13]. On the other hand, the implementation of the BT in hardware amortizes the translation overhead. In this case, the flexibility is strongly reduced: the hardware translation is hence tied to a specific ISA. Consequently, there is no opportunity to migrate to a new ISA (or a new version of the same ISA) because the hardware was specifically tailored to that system. As a meet in the middle approach considering the two aforementioned methods, some BT systems present some kind of hardware modification to give better support for the software execution of the BT system. That is the case of Godson and Crusoe. Nevertheless, these works still rely on software for the main binary translation mechanism.

Our proposed approach is different for three reasons:

- It is totally implemented in hardware, with the fastest translation speed;
- Instead of using Superscalar or VLIW processors, we use reconfigurable logic as the main optimization mechanism. Reconfigurable systems have already proven to accelerate software and reduce energy consumption, showing gains over both systems [14][15]. Moreover, it is common sense that as the more the technology shrinks, the more an important characteristic of reconfigurable systems is highlighted: regularity – since this will impact the reliability of printing the geometries employed today in 65 nanometers and below [16]. Besides being more predictable, regular circuits are also low cost, since the more customizable the circuit is, the more expensive it becomes. This way, regular fabric could solve the mask cost and many other issues such as printability, power integrity and other aspects of the near future technologies;
- ISA adaptability. Our proposal uses a two-level BT mechanism: the first level is responsible for translating binary code from the source to the target processor, while the second is responsible for the code optimization. Since there is a well defined interface between both, there is the possibility of easily ISA migration by only changing the first level of the BT system. In this way, hardware modifications can be fine tuned to several markets by the use of a reconfigurable fabric and by changing the first level of the BT mechanism.

Therefore, with the proposed approach one can achieve:

- Amortized performance overhead in the translation from the source to the target machine, because it is implemented in hardware, so it is faster than if it were implemented in software;
- Performance gains when compared to the execution of the original code in the source machine, since a dynamically reconfigurable system is used;
- Flexibility through the employment of the two-level BT system, making it easier to migrate to another ISA or update it to a new version of the family, so the system has almost the same flexibility as if it were implemented in software.

The next section details some implementation aspects of our system.

## 3  System Overview

Fig. 2 gives a general overview of the system. The first level (Fig. 2a) represents the hardware to make x86 to MIPS translations. It interfaces the memory and the rest of system, which is composed of the second-level BT mechanism, a special cache, a MIPS processor and a dynamically reconfigurable array (Fig. 2b). The BT in the second level analyzes the MIPS code at run-time and uses the reconfigurable logic to optimize and execute the hotspots found in the code. The system works like a native x86 processor, but with an additional possibility to run MIPS code too. In the future, it will be possible to execute other ISAs by only changing the first BT level (Fig. 2a).

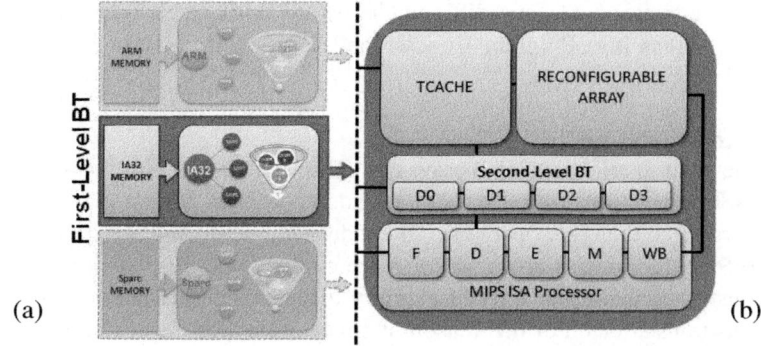

**Fig. 2.** General overview of the system

## 3.1 Architecture Operation

Let us consider an application compiled using the x86 ISA that will be executed for the first time. Initially, the first level starts to fetch instructions from memory. As the first level is translating the code, the MIPS processor actually executes the instructions. In this level there are no translations savings for future reuse: all the data is processed at run-time by the first BT level in order to maintain small storage overhead. It also must be said that the same code, but in the optimized form, will be saved by the second-level for future reuse, as we shall see next. The second BT level analyzes the interpreted code (already in MIPS ISA) during execution. When a hotspot is identified, this level generates and saves a configuration of the reconfigurable array for that hotspot in a special cache (TCache), indexed by the x86 Program Counter (PC). The next time a chuck of x86 code that has already been transformed to MIPS and been optimized to the reconfigurable array is found, the equivalent configuration if fetched from the TCache. Then, the first BT level, MIPS processor and the second level mechanism are stalled, and the reconfigurable array starts its reconfiguration and execution.

Therefore, once a sequence of x86 instructions that were translated from the x86 to MIPS ISA was found and, after that, also became a configuration for the array, none of the BT mechanisms neither the processor need to work. As sequences of instructions are executed and translated, and the TCache is being filled, the impact of the two levels of BT are amortized and the performance gains provided by the array starts to appear. In the next subsections both BT levels are explained in more details.

## 3.2 First-Level Binary Translator

In the current implementation, it is possible to translate 50 different instructions in a total of 150 considering the IA32 ISA, with all addressing modes supported. The implemented subset is enough to compile and execute all the benchmarks tested. Segmentation is emulated, but there is no support for paging. Interruptions, and other multimedia instructions, such as the MMX and SSE, are still not implemented. This

BT level is composed of four different hardware units, with two pipeline stages: Translation, Mounting, Program Counter and Control Units. They will be briefly discussed in the next sections.

### 3.2.1 Translation Unit

This is the main component of the system. The Translation Unit is responsible for fetching x86 instructions from the memory, analyzing their format in order to classify them according to the type, operators, and addressing mode and generating the equivalent MIPS instructions. It takes one or more cycles to perform such operation. This unit is constituted mainly of a ROM memory that holds all possible equivalent MIPS instructions translations. For this reason, it concentrates the major part of the BT system area. Besides that, this unit provides some information to the other auxiliary units, such as: number of generated MIPS instructions, quantity of bytes to calculate the next PC and the type of instructions (e.g. logical operation, conditional or unconditional jumps, etc).

### 3.2.2 Mounting Unit

The MIPS processor needs to fetch instructions serially from the BT mechanism, since it must behave as it was the original MIPS memory. The role of the Mounting Unit is exactly that: to simulate such behavior. It fetches all the equivalent MIPS instructions in a parallel fashion from the Translation unit and sends them to the MIPS processor, so it provides an interface between both. The Mounting Unit is composed of a queue of registers in which each MIPS instruction fetched from the Translation Unit is allocated. As instructions are processed, this unit constantly sends to the other units the number of occupied slots in its queue, in order to guarantee that it will not empty, so the MIPS processor will not stall.

### 3.2.3 Program Counter Unit

In opposite to the MIPS instructions, x86 instructions have different sizes, so the x86 and MIPS addresses translation cannot be considered on a one-to-one basis. This way, the Program Counter Unit has been developed to calculate the address of the next x86 instruction that must be fetched from memory.

### 3.2.4 Control Unit

The function of this unit is to keep the timing and consistency of information between the units. Each unit of the BT system has flags that keep its actual state. Through this information, the control unit decides the behavior for all the system, such as the fetch of new instruction from memory at the instant there are free slots in the queue in the Mounting Unit; and the calculus of the new x86 PC when the instruction (branch or regular) is fetched from memory.

## 3.3 Second-Level System

### 3.3.1 The Reconfigurable System

The reconfigurable system is a dynamic adaptable architecture [14]. It is a pure combinational logic coarse grain reconfigurable array, tightly coupled to the MIPS processor, composed of several ALUs, load/store and multiplication units, organized in rows and columns. The array does not support divisions and floating-point operations. Each functional unit is connected through multiplexers and can execute one equivalent RISC instruction. In the same cycle, many instructions can be executed in parallel depending on the level of data dependence between themselves. Fig. 3 shows the organization of the reconfigurable array.

The Second-Level BT system was extended from [5]. It runs in parallel with the MIPS processor, analyzing the execution code at run-time and checking which parts can be optimized. If a hotspot is found an array configuration for that part is generated. As configurations are generated, they are allocated into a reserved space called Translation Cache (TCache). If the same part of the code is found again, the configuration is loaded, the operands are fetched and the array starts its execution.

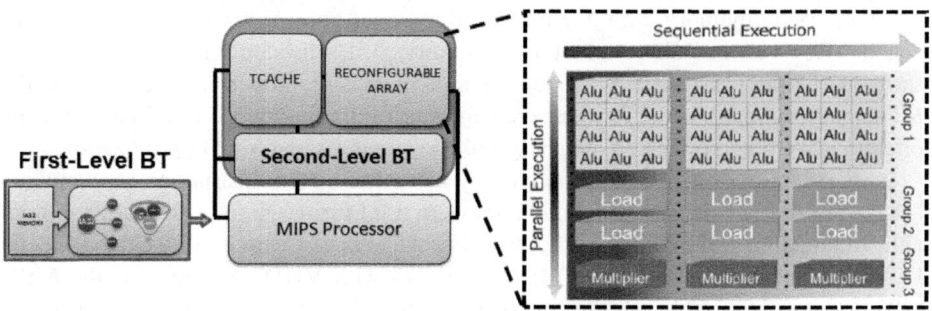

**Fig. 3.** The reconfigurable array

### 3.3.2 Extended MIPS

The great advantage of using the MIPS ISA is the regularity of code with well known behavior, making it easy to translate another ISA to this one. However, the translation of a complex ISA as such as the x86 to MIPS is inefficient, because in several times just one x86 instruction is converted to many MIPS instructions. For example, in X86 instructions it is possible to use the memory contents as operators in arithmetic instructions. Furthermore, there are flag registers, which are automatically updated in most of the arithmetic/logical operations, so these can be used in branch instructions, whereas such flags are not supported in the MIPS architecture. In this case, more than 20 instructions would be necessary per x86 instructions to correctly emulate these flags on the MIPS processor. The same can be considered for segment addressing modes and so on for several other constructs. Therefore, to lower this overhead, the MIPS processor was extended to give hardware support to these issues, but still maintaining compatibility with the standard code, as follows:

*Byte Manipulation* – Several operations that occur in x86 code are based on manipulation of variables with 8,16 and 32-bit in a register. As the MIPS processor only executes 32-bit operations, a special hardware was added to manipulate small variables the same way as x86 processors do, avoiding the need of using mask operations to insert or extract information to/from 32-bit registers.

*Address Mode* – The MIPS is a load-store architecture. In contrast to the X86 ISA, which supports several addressing modes, the MIPS supports only the Base (register) + Index (immediate) addressing mode. To reduce this gap, the MIPS was extended, so Base (register) + Index (Register) and Base + Index + Immediate (byte) operations are possible.

*EFlags–* Additional hardware that generate the flag values and store the results into a mapped register in the MIPS processor has been added.

# 4   Results

## 4.1  Simulation Environment

To perform all of the tests we used a MIPS R3000 Processor with a unified instruction/data cache memory with 32Kbytes and a reconfigurable array configuration that can be observed in Table 1. In previous works [5], this configuration has already shown to be the best tradeoff considering area overhead and performance boosts. The Mibench benchmark set [17] was executed on a Linux based OS. In all cases the applications were compiled and statically linked using GCC with -O3 optimization.

X86 execution traces were generated by using the Simics instruction set simulator [18]. After that, cycle accurate simulators were used for the first level BT, reconfigurable architecture and the MIPS processor. For the area evaluation, we used the Mentor Leonardo Spectrum [19] (TSMC 0.18u library) with VHDL versions of the MIPS [20], the reconfigurable architecture [5] and the first BT level. None of them increased the critical path of the MIPS processor, which runs at 600Mhz.

**Table 1.** Array Configuration

| | |
|---|---|
| #Columns | 48 |
| #Rows | 16 |
| **#ALU / Columns** | **8** |
| **# LD/ST / Columns** | **6** |
| **#Multipliers / Columns** | **2** |
| **#Configurations in Tcache** | **512** |

## 4.2  Binary Translation Data

In Fig. 4, we analyze the memory occupation of the generated binary code. On average, considering the whole set of benchmarks, the MIPS compiler generated a binary code 26.69% bigger than the same code for the x86 processor. Furthermore, as can be observed in Table 2, the MIPS processor executes, on average, 36,63% more instructions than the x86, to run the same algorithm.

As explained before, the MIPS processor was modified to give additional support to the binary translation process. The Fig. 5 shows the mean number of MIPS instructions generated from an x86 instruction when there is no support for the translation

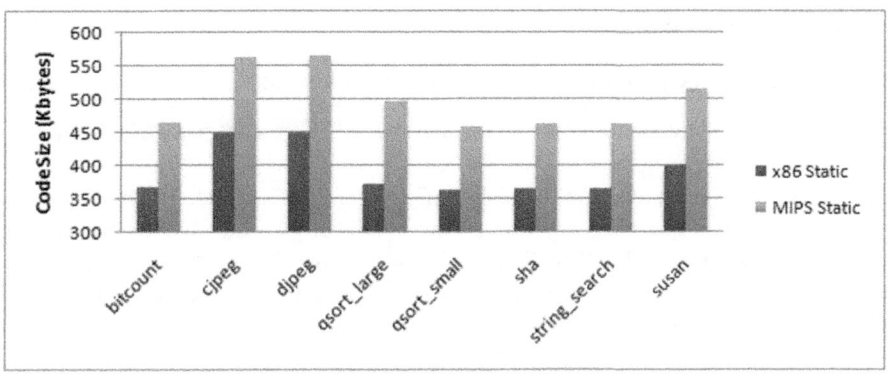

**Fig. 4.** Memory usage for different benchmarks, in Kbytes

**Table 2.** Number of executed instructions considering the two different ISAs

| Benchmark | MIPS | x86 |
|---|---|---|
| String Search | 279,725 | 199,362 |
| Sha | 15,976,677 | 12,274,689 |
| Bitcount | 59,810,191 | 41,334,546 |
| Qsort | 51,695,224 | 27,386,935 |
| Gsme | 30,578,227 | 16,975,259 |
| Gsmd | 13,896,515 | 11,038,642 |

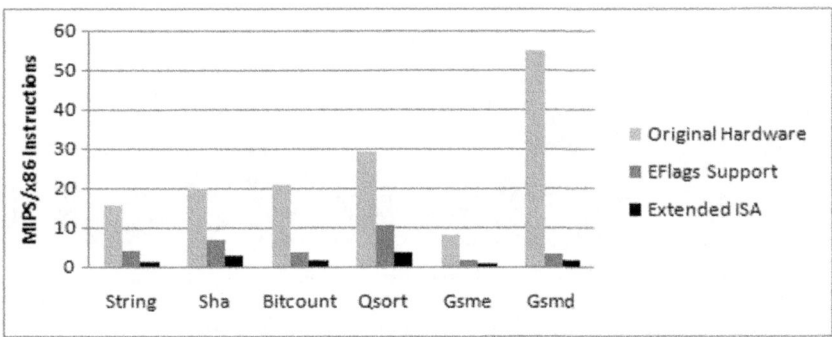

**Fig. 5.** The advantages of using hardware support for the BT process

(Original Hardware), there is support to EFlags computation only (EFlags Support) and when other hardware modifications, as explained in section 3.3.2, are also included (Extended ISA).

## 4.3 Performance Evaluation

Fig. 6 demonstrates the performance for four different setups:

- Native MIPS code execution on the standalone MIPS processor *(MIPS Code Execution)*;
- Native MIPS code execution with reconfigurable acceleration. In this case, the first BT level is bypassed: only the second BT level plus the Reconfigurable Architecture (RA) are used *(MIPS Code Execution +RA)*;
- x86 code execution without reconfigurable optimization, so only the first BT level is used *(X86 Code Execution without RA)*;
- x86 execution using the two BT mechanisms and the reconfigurable array *(X86 Code Execution – Two Levels BT)*.

The native code execution on the standalone MIPS processor was normalized to 100%. The *MIPS Code Execution + RA* presents a speedup of more than two times on average. For example, *Sha* presents a speedup of 3.43 times, *Bitcount* has gains of 2.42 times, whereas the *GSM Encoder* presents a speedup of 1.53 times, which is the worst case considering the benchmark set. Similar speedups are found when using other reconfigurable architectures [21][22].

Now, let us consider the x86 code being translated to MIPS code but not optimized by the reconfigurable system. As should be expected, there are performance losses because of the translation mechanism. In the GSMD, a slowdown of more than 2 times is presented when compared to the native execution of the same algorithm in MIPS code. However, X86 code execution on the proposed system is faster than the native MIPS code execution on the standalone MIPS processor, hence amortizing the original BT costs. The speedup over the standalone MIPS execution varies between 1.11 and 1.96 times. On average, the performance gains are of 45%.

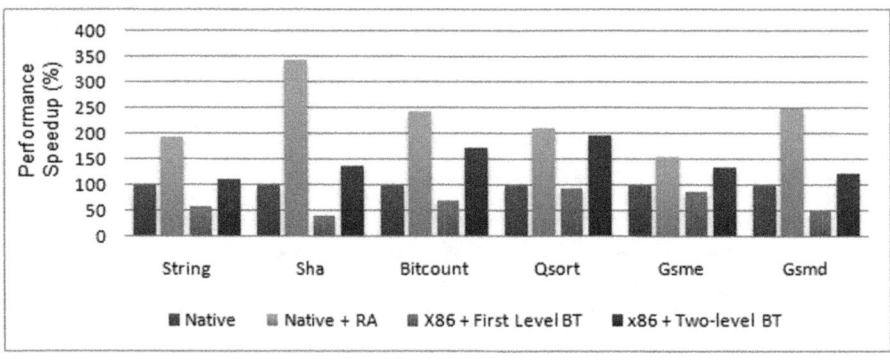

**Fig. 6.** Performance of each algorithm when there are executed in three different ways

These results can be considered very satisfactory: only the virtualization process (with no binary translation involved) of the Qemu virtual machine (VM) is 4 times slower than native execution of x86 instructions [22]. Because of such overhead, the Godson3, when translating code from X86 to MIPS using Qemu and without hardware support for the BT, is on average 6 times slower than native MIPS execution of the same software [11]. With hardware support for the BT mechanism, Godson3 performs on average 1.42 times slower than MIPS native execution. Although it is not our intent to directly compare our architecture to Godson3, since the Godson3 supports the whole X86 ISA, including interrupts and virtual memory, it gives one an idea that the translation is not an easy task to do, and that it presents significant overhead even if heavy hardware support is given.

### 4.4 Area Overhead

Table 3 demonstrates the number of gates each hardware component takes. As can be observed, the fist BT level represents only 2% of the total system area. If we consider that each gate is composed of 4 transistors, the whole system would nearly take 4,87 million of transistors to be built. It is important to note that, if one compares the proposed system, which executes X86 instructions, to the standalone MIPS processor, there is a significant reduction in the instruction memory footprint, as can be observed in Figure 4, amortizing the hardware costs. Moreover, as already stated, the Godson-3 processor uses 4-superscalar MIPS R10000 cores. According to [24], each one of them takes nearly 2.4 million gates to be implemented. Therefore, around 9.6 millions of transistors would be necessary to implement Godson, being 2 times larger than our system.

**Table 3.** Area overhead of each component into the system

| Unit | Area (Gates) |
|------|--------------|
| First-Level BT | 22,406 |
| MIPS R3000 | 26,866 |
| Second-Level BT | 15,264 |
| Rec. Array | 1,017,620 |
| **Total** | **1,219,535** |

## 5   Conclusions

In this paper, we demonstrated that it is possible to maintain code portability with no performance losses. The possibility of executing the large amount of available x86 applications using an optimizing architecture represents a great improvement in terms of code reusability. Another important factor is that, as all the optimizations are made at run-time, in a totally transparent fashion, no kind of user intervention is necessary. We intend to improve our system, by increasing the number of supported X86 instructions and by adding support for different ISAs (e.g. ARM). Moreover, we will also measure the power and energy consumption of the mechanism.

## References

1. Kim, N.S., Austin, T., Blaauw, D., Mudge, T., Flautner, K., Hu, J.S., Irwin, M.J., Kandemir, M., Narayanan, V.: Leakage current: Moore's law meets static power. Computer 36(12), 68–75 (2003)
2. Mak, J., Mycroft, A.: Limits of parallelism using dynamic data dependence graphs. WODA, Chicago, Illinois, USA (2009)

3. Sites, R.L., Chernoff, A., Kirk, M.B., Marks, M.P., Robinson, S.G.: Binary translation. Commun. ACM 36(2), 69–81 (1993)
4. Altman, E.R., Kaeli, D., Sheffer, Y.: Welcome to the opportunities of binary translation. Computer 33(3), 40–45 (2000)
5. Beck, A.C., Rutzig, M.B., Gaydjiev, G., Carro, L.: Transparent reconfigurable acceleration for heterogeneous embedded applications. In: Proceedings of DATE, pp. 1208–1213. ACM, New York (2008)
6. Rutzig, M.B., Beck, A.C.S., Carro, L.: Dynamically adapted low power ASIPs. In: Becker, J., Woods, R., Athanas, P., Morgan, F. (eds.) ARC 2009. LNCS, vol. 5453, pp. 110–122. Springer, Heidelberg (2009)
7. Altman, E.R., Ebcioglu, K., Gschwind, M., Sathaye, S.: Advances and Future Challenges in Binary Translation and Optimization. In: Proceedings of the IEEE Special Issue on Micro-processor Architecture and Compiler Technology (2001)
8. Rosetta, Apple Inc., http://www.apple.com/rosetta/
9. Chernoff, A., Herdeg, M., Hookway, R., Reeve, C., Rubin, N., Tye, T., Yadavalli, S.B., Yates, J.: FX!32: A Profile-Directed Binary Translator. IEEE Micro, 56–64 (1998)
10. Hookway, R.J.. Herdeg, M.A.: DIGITAL FX!32: combining emulation and binary translation. Digital Tech. J. 9(1), 3–12 (1997)
11. Dehnert, J.C., Grant, B.K., Banning, J.P., Johnson, R., Kistler, T., Klaiber, A., Mattson, J.: The Transmeta Code Morphing$^{TM}$ Software: using speculation, recovery, and adaptive retranslation to address real-life challenges. In: Proceedings of CGO, San Francisco, California, pp. 15–24. IEEE Computer Society, Washington, DC (2003)
12. Hu, W., Wang, J., Gao, X., Chen, Y., Liu, Q., Li, G.: Godson-3: A Scalable Multicore RISC Processor with x86 Emulation. IEEE Micro 29(2), 17–29 (2009)
13. Gschwind, M., Altman, E., Sathaye, P., Ledak, Appenzeller, D.: Dynamic and Transparent Binary Translation. IEEE Computer 3(33), 54–59 (2000)
14. Beck Filho, A.C.S., Carro, L.: Dynamic Reconfiguration with Binary Translation: Breaking the ILP barrier with Software Compatibility. In: Proceedings of 42nd DAC, Anaheim, pp. 732–737. ACM Press, New York (2005)
15. Beck Filho, A.C.S., Carro, L.: Transparent Acceleration of Data Dependent Instructions for General Purpose Processors. In: Proceedings of 15th VLSI-SOC, Atlanta, pp. 66–71. IEEE, Los Alamitos (2007)
16. Or-Bach, Z.: Panel: (when) will FPGAs kill ASICs? In: 38th DAC (2001)
17. Guthaus, M.R., Ringenberg, J.S., Ernst, D., Austin, T.M., Mudge, T., Brown, R.B.: MiBench: A free, commercially representative embedded benchmark suite. In: Proceedings of WWC, pp. 3–14. IEEE Computer Society, Washington, DC (2001)
18. Magnusson, P.S., Christensson, M., Eskilson, et al.: Simics: A Full System Simulation Platform. Computer 35(2), 50–58 (2002)
19. Leonardo Spectrum, http://www.mentor.com
20. Minimips VHDL, http://www.opencores.org
21. Goldstein, S.C., Schmit, H., Budiu, M., Cadambi, S., Moe, M., Taylor, R.R.: Piperench: A reconfigurable architecture and compiler. Computer 33(4), 70–77 (2000)
22. Clark, N., Kudlur, M., Park, H., Mahlke, S., Flautner, K.: Application-Specific Processing on a General-Purpose Core via Transparent Instruction Set Customization. In: MICRO-37, pp. 30–40 (2004)
23. Bellard, F.: QEMU, a Fast and Portable Dynamic Translator. In: USENIX 2005 Annual Technical Conference, FREENIX Track (2005)
24. Yeager, K.C.: The Mips R10000 superscalar microprocessor. IEEE Micro 16(2), 28–41 (1996)

# FPGA-Based Cherenkov Ring Recognition in Nuclear and Particle Physics Experiments

Ming Liu[1,2], Zhonghai Lu[2], Wolfgang Kuehn[1], and Axel Jantsch[2]

[1] II. Physikalisches Institut, Justus-Liebig-Universität Giessen, Germany
[2] Department of Electronic Systems, Royal Institute of Technology, Sweden
{ming.liu,wolfgang.kuehn}@physik.uni-giessen.de
{mingliu,zhonghai,axel}@kth.se

**Abstract.** Cherenkov ring is often adopted to identify particles flying through the detector systems in nuclear and particle physics experiments. In this paper, we introduce an improved ring recognition algorithm and present its FPGA implementation. Compared to the previous implementation based on VMEBus and FPGAs, our design is evaluated to outperform by several tens up to hundred times with acceptable resource utilizations on a Xilinx Virtex-4 FX60 FPGA. The design module will reside in the online data acquisition (DAQ) and trigger facilities, and contribute to significantly reduce the data rate of storage for offline analysis by retaining only interesting events and dropping the noise. Our customized FPGA cluster in one ATCA [1] shelf is foreseen to achieve an equivalent computation capability up to thousands of commodity PCs for particle recognition.

## 1 Introduction

Nuclear and particle physics is a branch of physics that studies the elementary constituents of matter and the interactions between them. It is also called high energy physics because many elementary particles do not occur under normal circumstances in nature, but can be created and detected during energetic collisions of other particles, as is done in particle colliders. Modern nuclear and particle physics experiments, for example HADES [2] and PANDA [3] at GSI Germany, BESIII [4] at IHEP China, ATLAS, CMS, LHCb, ALICE at the LHC [5] at CERN Switzerland, achieve their goals by studying the emission direction, the energy, and the mass of the produced particles when the accelerated beam hits the target. In the experimental facilities, different kinds of detectors are adopted to generate raw data which are used to recognize emitted particles after the collision and analyze their characteristics. Figure 1 shows the exploded view of the HADES detector system as an example.

The Cherenkov effect was discovered by the Russian experimentalist P. A. Cherenkov in 1934, and explained by the Russian theorists I. Y. Tamm and I. M. Frank. All three scientists recieved the Nobel prize in physics in 1958 because of this discovery. It describes the emission of light (Cherenkov radiation) that occurs in a transparent substance, when a charged particle travels through the

A. Koch et al. (Eds.): ARC 2011, LNCS 6578, pp. 169–180, 2011.
© Springer-Verlag Berlin Heidelberg 2011

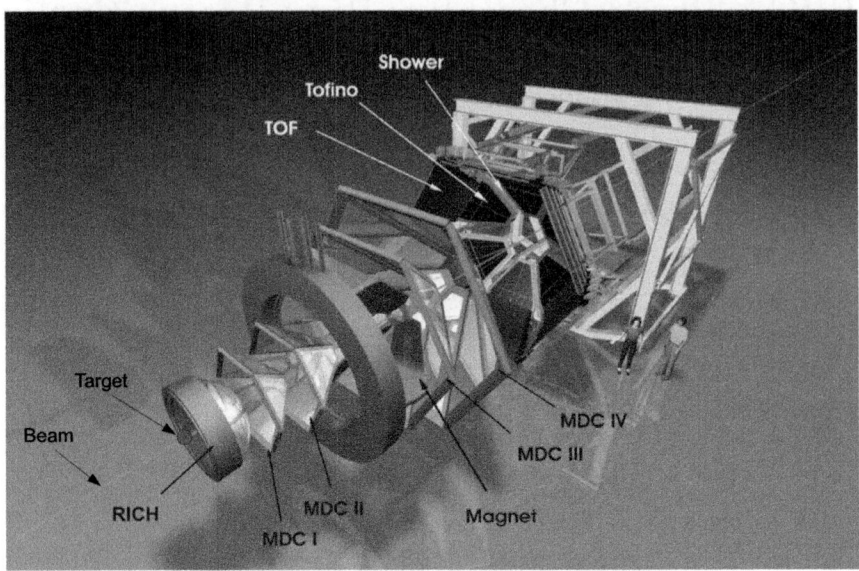

**Fig. 1.** Exploded view of the HADES detector system (RICH detector for Cherenkov ring recognition)

material with a speed faster than the speed of light in that material [6]. This process is analygous to the shock wave of sound generated by a jet flying faster than the speed of sound in air. Based on the Cherenkov effect, the Ring Imaging CHerenkov (RICH) detector is widely adopted in nuclear and particle physics experiments, to determine the velocity of charged particles and identify particle types. For instance in the HADES experiment, RICH detector together with the Cherenkov ring recognition algorithm is used to identify dilepton pairs in hadron and heavy ion induced nuclear reactions.

Taking into account the experiment time lasting for months and huge data rates ranging from $10^7$ to $10^{11}$ Bytes/s generated by detectors, it is neither realistic nor necessary to entirely record the experimental data for offline analysis. Therefore it is essential to realize an efficient online data acquisition (DAQ) and trigger system which process the events[1] and reduce the data rate by several orders of magnitude by means of rejecting background noise. In the contemporary facilities, pattern recognition algorithms [7] [8] [9] including Cherenkov ring recognition, are implemented as sophisticated criteria to select interesting events which possess expected patterns generated by certain types of particles. Uninteresting background data will be discarded on the fly.

The remainder of the paper is organized as follows: The previous implementation of Cherenkov ring recognition is addressed in Section 2. The HADES

---

[1] In high-energy physics, one "event" corresponds to a single interaction of a beam particle with a target particle. It consists of sub-events which typically represent the information from individual detector sub-systems.

detector system and the algorithm principle of Cherenkov ring recognition are explained in Section 3. In Section 4, on-FPGA hardware design is presented. Implementation and performance results will be discussed in Section 5. Finally we conclude the paper and propose our future work in Section 6.

## 2    Previous Work

The Cherenkov ring recognition computation was previously implemented on FPGAs in [10] and [11], and the design is running in the current HADES DAQ and trigger system. The designers accommodate the computation on 12 dedicated FPGA-based VMEBus cards to search for valid rings appearing on the total 6 trapezoidal sectors of the RICH detector. In their original design, ring recognition for the RICH detector works as separate modules and does not correlate with identified particle tracks from the Mini Drift Chamber (MDC) detectors: The RICH sub-event data are introduced from detectors into the VME cards. Afterwards the complete hit information of the RICH plane is reconstructed in a memory device, distinguishing hit and non-hit pixels. Next ring patterns are searched with all the pixels on the RICH plane regarded as possible ring centers. In order to obtain hardware acceleration over software, the total 96 columns are processed in parallel on 12 Xilinx FPGAs. Despite the parallel structure of the original design, we still believe it computation-inefficient due to the following reasons: Firstly, the hit information of the RICH plane has to be reconstructed before ring search, by filling all the pixels with "hit" or "non-hit"; Secondly, "blind" search considering all the pixels as possible ring centers loses computation efficiency, taking into account the fact that the interesting ring patterns do not occur very frequently; Finally, it results in an inadequate data reduction rate in heavy ion reactions for mass storage and offline analysis, due to the lack of correlation with MDC particle tracks. In the recent HADES upgrade project, we will take the advantage of the MDC track reconstruction results [9] and improve the Cherenkov ring recognition algorithm as well as its FPGA implementation for higher performance. The principle difference of the improved algorithm will be clarified in detail in Section 3.

## 3    Algorithm Description

### 3.1    RICH and MDC Detectors in HADES

As an experiment example using the RICH detector to identify particles, Figure 1 shows the exploded view of the HADES detector system and Figure 2 shows the lateral cut-away view. In the experiment, accelerated energetic beam particles collide with target particles. New types of particles are therefore emitted from the collision and fly through the detector system. With the help of the strong magnetic field generated by the superconducting coil, inner (I and II) and outer (III and IV) MDC detectors are employed to reconstruct the flying tracks of particles and further investigate their momentum [9]. When light and

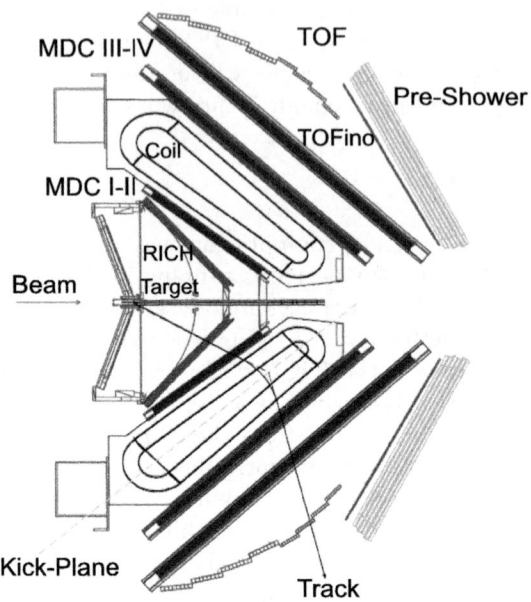

**Fig. 2.** Lateral cut-away view of the HADES detector system

fast particles (for instance dileptons in HADES) fly through the inner MDCs from the target, the generated Cherenkov light cone is reflected by the mirror and displayed on the RICH detector in the shape of a ring.

### 3.2    MDC Track Reconstruction

MDC detectors are employed to reconstruct the particle tracks entering and leaving the magnetic field, for further deriving the deflection angle inside it. The magnetic field does not penetrate into the inner or outer MDCs and exists only within the coil space. Thus particle tracks only bend in the magnetic field, and the segments before or behind the coil could be approximately described by straight lines. Detailed discussion on MDC tracking is out of the range of this paper. What we need only to understand, is that the identified particle tracks will point to the Cherenkov ring centers if they are also reflected by the mirror onto the RICH plane, because light cones are simply generated along the particle flying tracks.

### 3.3    Cherenkov Ring Recognition

As a demonstration example, Figure 3 displays the captured image frame of one sub-event on a RICH sector whose resolution is 96 × 96 pixels (pads). According to the physics principle, the Cherenkov ring from the dilepton pair features a constant diameter equivalent to the distance of 8 pixels on the RICH plane.

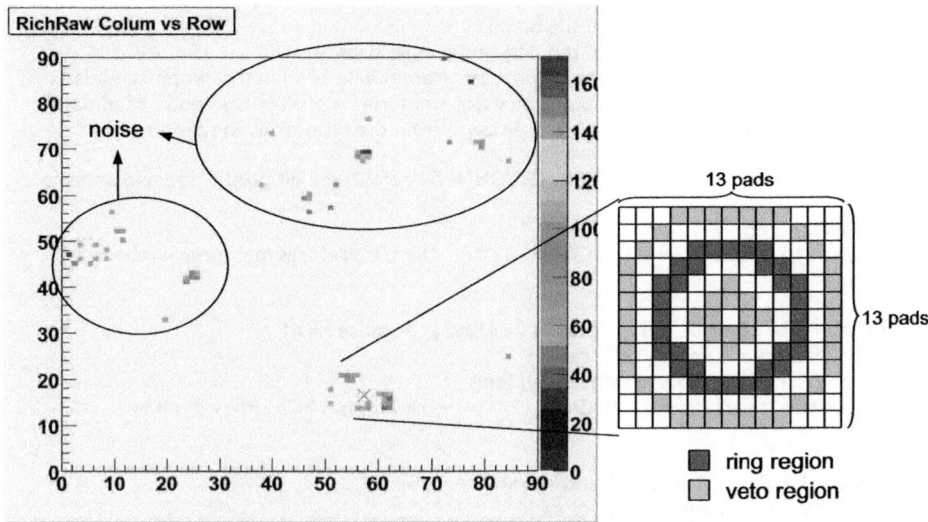

**Fig. 3.** Ring recognition on the RICH detector

For each potential ring center, the pattern search is conducted within a fixed mask region of $13 \times 13$ pixels. The hit number on the ring region with a radius of 4 pixels are counted with the value *ring_region*. In order to shape the ring pattern rather than a large piece of solid region full of hits, two veto regions inside and outside the ring region are defined with their hit pixel counts also accumulated. Therefore the ring pattern can be identified only if both the *ring_region* sum is above and the *veto_region* sums are below their respective thresholds. The thresholds are derived through physics analysis and they are expected to be programmable during the experiment.

Because of the constant diameter of ring patterns, the computation challenge falls on the position identification of ring centers. In the original design of [10] and [11], the designers treat all the $96 \times 96$ pixels on the RICH plane as potential ring centers: The system first receives RICH sub-event raw data containing the position of all hit pixels from the detector readout circuits. Then the complete hit information of the RICH plane is reconstructed in a memory device. Afterwards ring patterns are searched within respective mask regions of all the pixels regarded as possible ring centers, in parallel for all 96 columns on 12 Xilinx FPGAs [10] [11]. To treat all the pixels as ring centers is not only computation inefficient, but also resouce consuming on FPGAs. In addition, it requires extra work to further correlate the RICH results with the rest detector system (especially inner MDCs) in the offline analysis. In order to simplify ring recognition and correlate the RICH pattern with the inner MDC tracking information, identified particle tracks in inner MDCs are introduced to point out potential ring centers. The particle tracks are to be reflected by the mirror onto the RICH plane. Hence the coordinate of the track penetration points on the MDC projection plane is converted into the one of potential ring centers on the

```
-- (x1, y1) : position coordinate of the hit pixel
-- (x0, y0) : position coordinate of the ring center candidate
-- x_distance = abs(x1 – x0); : distance on x axis from the hit pixel to the center candidate
-- y_distance = abs(y1 – y0); : distance on y axis from the hit pixel to the center candidate
-- hop =  x_distance + y_distance; : hop distance from the hit pixel to the center candidate

position_result <= FARAWAY_NOISE_REGION; -- by default the hit pixel is deemed as noise

if (hop <=2) then
      position_result <= INNER_VETO_REGION; -- the hit pixel falls into inner_veto_region
end if;

if (((hop = 5 or hop = 6) and x_distance <= 4 and y_distance <= 4)
  or (y_distance = 0 and x_distance = 4)
  or (y_distance = 4 and x_distance = 0)) then
      position_result <= RING_REGION;          -- the hit pixel falls into ring_region
end if;

if ((hop = 9 and x_distance <= 6 and y_distance <= 6)
  or (y_distance = 6 and x_distance <= 2)
  or (x_distance = 6 and y_distance <= 2)) then
      position_result <= OUTER_VETO_REGION; -- the hit pixel falls into outer_veto_region
end if;
```

**Fig. 4.** Position judgment of a hit pixel to a ring center candidate

RICH plane. To avoid complex online geometrical calculation, the coordinate conversion task is done offline to arrive at a Look-Up Table (LUT). Taking into account the coordinate conversion error due to the resolution difference from MDC to RICH, normally we map a single particle track to multiple neighboured pixels in a search window (e.g. $5 \times 5$) on the RICH plane. Hence interesting ring patterns can be prevented from being ignored due to the slight coordinate conversion error.

With the small number of specified ring center candidates, we do not have to reconstruct the complete hit information for all the pixels on the RICH plane, but need only traverse all the hit pixels belonging to the same RICH sub-event to judge their positions. If they fall into the ring region of a center candidate, they may come from the valid Cherenkov light generated by flying dileptons; Otherwise they are probably the noise to be discarded. The position judgment is realized by geometrical calculation on the distance between the hit pixel and the ring center, as demonstrated by the VHDL-syntax code in Figure 4.

After the position judgment of all the hit pixels corresponding to all the potential ring centers, the hit counts in the ring region as well as in the inner/outer veto regions can be accumulated. They will be compared to the thresholds for determining whether a ring pattern is successfully identified or not. Only the data with identified patterns are to be retained. The noise will be discarded on the fly for reducing the data rate before storage.

# 4   Implementation

## 4.1   Ring Recognition Unit Design

The Cherenkov Ring Recognition Unit (RRU) is described in VHDL and implemented on our customized Compute Node (CN) based on the Advanced Telecommunications Computing Architecture (ATCA) backplane and Xilinx Virtex-4 FX60 FPGAs [12]. Figure 5 illustrates its design structure in block diagram, and Figure 6 shows the overall system design on the FPGA with RRU incorporated. The incoming event data via optical links are buffered in on-board DDR2 memory. Afterwards, RICH sub-events are supplied into the input FIFO by DMA transfers via the system PLB bus. The coordinate information of hit pixels belonging to the same event are extracted and further buffered in *single_event_buffer* in the RRU module. Meanwhile, ring center candidates are imported from the MDC tracking results [9]. The coordinates of track points are reflected onto the RICH plane, converting them into ring center candidates with an offline-built LUT. Then potential ring centers are loaded into *ring_search_units*. The number of *ring_search_unit* is configurable according to the available resources on the FPGA. Loading the ring center candidates is also in the unit of a same event: If the number of configured *ring_search_unit* is larger than or equal to the center candidate count of an event (i.e. the number of recognized particle tracks from MDCs), the hit pixel data in *single_event_buffer* can be simply read out and traversed for deciding their positions and identifying rings from the accumulated values of *ring_region*, *inner_veto_region* and *outer_veto_region*. Otherwise ring centers have to be loaded into *ring_search_unit* in multiple computation batches, and accordingly all the hit pixels belonging to this same event must be looped back and reiterated in *single_event_buffer* until all the center candidates are done. After each round computation, the coordinates of center candidates with recognized rings are shifted out and collected in the output FIFO, to be exported by Gigabit Ethernet for result mass storage in the PC farm.

In each *ring_search_unit* shown in Figure 5, not only the directly derived RICH plane pixel from an MDC particle track is loaded as a potential center candidate for ring search, but also its neighbours in a region (e.g. 24 neighbours in a search window of 5 × 5) considering the coordinate conversion error from MDC to RICH. We name the computation cores for the neighbour pixels *shadow cores*. Thus for each *ring_search_unit*, there exist in fact 25 cores (1 core for the track derived pixel and 24 shadow cores for its neighbours) working in parallel. The parallel infrastructure and the pipelined design guarantee RRU a high performance in the ring recognition computation.

In the practical experiment, the occupancy of hit pixels (the proportion of hits out of the total 96 × 96 pixels) on the RICH plane is normally rather small. Among them, valid ring patterns are even rare. Therefore in contrast to blind search scanning all the pixels on the plane, our new design traverses only the hits in a pipelined fashion. With respect to various ring centers specified by identified particle tracks, the processing is conducted in parallel *ring_search_units*. This approach will lead to significantly higher performance, as we can observe in Section 5.

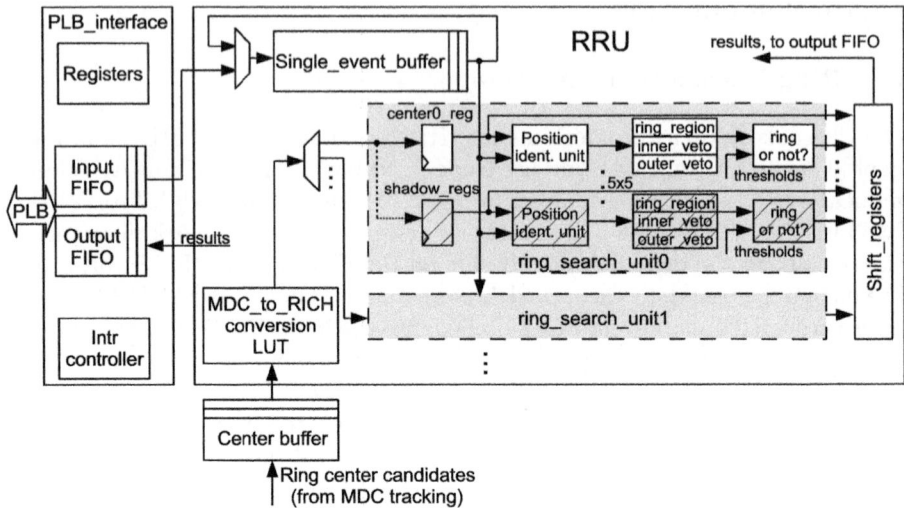

**Fig. 5.** Design structure of RRU

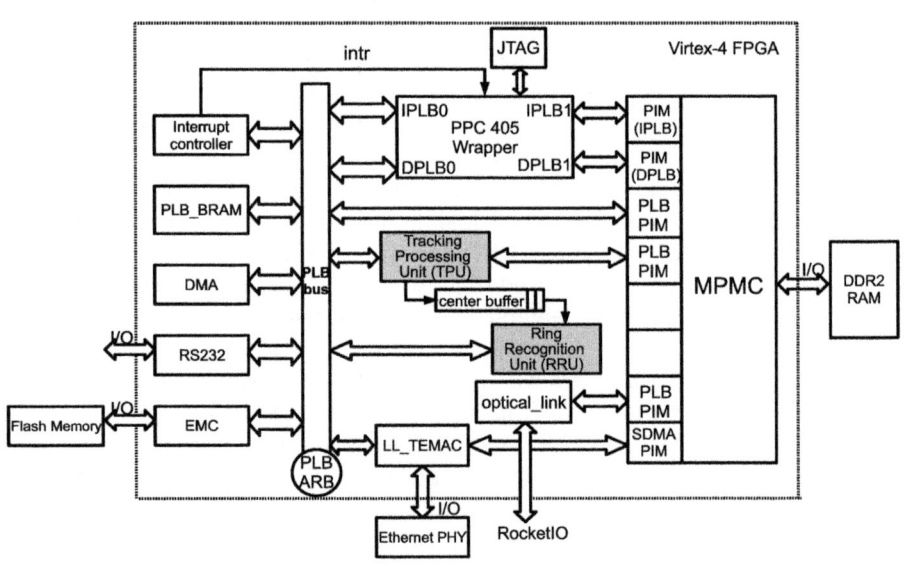

**Fig. 6.** System design with algorithm engines

### 4.2  System Integration

Together with the MDC Tracking Processing Unit (TPU) [9], RRU will be integrated in the system-on-an-FPGA as an algorithm processing engine (see Figure 6). Incoming event data are received via the optical link from detector readout circuits, and buffered in the DDR2 memory under the control of the Multi-Port Memory Controller (MPMC). Afterwards MDC and RICH data are respectively supplied by DMA transfers to TPU and RRU, which have a buffer in between to deliver identified particle tracks to RRU for pointing out ring center candidates. All the processed results will be again collected by DMA back into DDR2, and exported to the PC farm for mass storage through Gigabit Ethernet. In the system, a hardcore PowerPC 405 processor with embedded Linux OS achieves slow controls and conducts TCP/IP stack processing for Ethernet transmission.

## 5   Experimental Results

### 5.1   Implementation Results

Resource utilizations of RRU with 1 or 2 *ring_search_unit* configurations are listed in Table 1. We observe that both designs consume less than one sixth of available resources on the Xilinx Virtex-4 FX60 FPGA. The overall system design (shown in Figure 6) with a single *ring_search_unit* RRU consumes less than half of the Virtex-4 FX60 FPGA. The resource utilization is acceptable and still enables the possibility to extend the system in future designs.

**Table 1.** Resource consumption

| Resources | RRU (1 ring_search_unit) | RRU (2 ring_search_unit) | system (RRU of 1 ring_search_unit) |
|---|---|---|---|
| 4-input LUTs | 4723 out of 50560 (9.3%) | 8186 (16.2%) | 21933 (43.4%) |
| Slice Flip-Flops | 3663 out of 50560 (7.2%) | 5190 (10.3%) | 17185 (34.0%) |
| Block RAMs | 31 out of 232 (13.4%) | 31 (13.4%) | 104 (44.8%) |

The complete RRU design features two clock domains: One is the PLB interface and the other is the RRU core. Two clock domains are coupled by input and output asynchronous FIFOs. To match the system PLB bus speed, the interface runs at 100 MHz. The RRU core can run at a maximum frequency of 160 MHz, according to the timing constraints.

### 5.2   Performance Measurements

To evaluate the performance of the RRU design, we pick some RICH and MDC sub-events from the HADES experimental data and initialize them in the DDR2 memory. DMA takes charge of supplying the raw data to RRU and TPU, and collecting their results back into DDR2. According to the measurements, we observe that a typical interesting HADES event with 3 MDC particle tracks or Cherenkov rings takes a single *ring_search_unit* RRU about 2000 ns for ring recognition computation. For pure noise events without any interesting pattern, the processing time may further be reduced to hundreds of ns or even less. Pure noise events require little computation effort and result in the best-case processing speed (e.g. ~10 MSub-events/s). In the worst case when all the events contain 3 ring patterns (i.e. 3 dilepton pairs. This will never be possible in practice, because interesting events occur very rarely in experiments. ), the 2000 ns processing time implies a processing speed of about 0.5 MSub-events/s. With more practical estimation of the mixture of rare interesting events and large proportion of uninteresting noise events, the processing speed can be reasonably estimated in the order of magnitude of several MSub-events/s[1]. In [11], the authors reported a speed of 49 KSub-events/s of their system. Thus we conclude that a single *ring_search_unit* in our RRU design can outperform the previous system consisting of 2 VME cards and 12 obsolete FPGA chips for each detector sector, by several tens up to hundred times. The performance speedup mainly comes from the algorithm principle improvement of introducing MDC particle tracks to point out ring centers. In addition, the fully optimized design running at high clock frequencies also contribute to the performance enhancement. Further tests using large amount of experimental data will be scheduled in the final system verification stage.

According to the experimental results reported in [9], each single TPU core can achieve a processing speedup of about 20 times than an Intel Xeon 2.4 GHz CPU core for particle track reconstruction. Together with RRU, the system design on a single Virtex-4 FX60 FPGA is roughly estimated to achieve a computation capability equivalent to several tens up to hundred of commodity PCs for HADES particle recognition. In the customized computation platform described in [12], up to 70 FPGA chips are accommodated within one ATCA shelf. Many TPU and RRU cores can be instantiated and distributed on the FPGA cluster. They will work together to cope with the enormous raw data rate from the particle detectors, in a form of Single-Instruction-Multiple-Data (SIMD). Therefore one ATCA shelf full of 70 FPGAs implies an equivalent processing capability of about thousands of commodity PCs for the particle recognition computation in the HADES experiment.

## 6    Conclusion and Future Work

In this paper, we have presented a new Cherenkov ring recognition algorithm and its FPGA implementation. Correlated with the particle track reconstruction algorithm, the RRU module identifies flying particles with ring patterns and significantly removes the noise in the online DAQ and trigger systems of nuclear and particle physics experiments. With acceptable resource utilizations, a single RRU module can outperform the previous system design by several tens up to hundred times. The complete ATCA platform consisting of 70 Xilinx

---

[1] The exact event processing speed is heavily dependent on the data stream constitution consisting of interesting events with ring patterns and noise data. Therefore from the experimental statistics in the long run, the effective processing speed is between the best-case and the worse-case performance, but very close to the best case due to the appearance rarity of interesting events. Hence it is only feasible but meaningful to estimate the system performance within the accuracy of one order of magnitude.

Virtex-4 FX60 FPGAs, is estimated to achieve an equivalent processing capability of thousands of commodity PCs for particle recognition computation. The improved computation efficiency will largely reduce the hardware costs, increase the online data reduction rate, and focus the offline analysis on the data which most probably interest the physicists.

In our future work, various algorithm engines specifically the RRU module for Cherenkov ring recognition and the TPU module for MDC tracking, are to be dynamically reconfigured during the system run-time. They will be chosen as a real application to verify the design framework of self-aware adaptive computing [13]. Through dynamically loading or unloading different modules into or out of the same reconfigurable region, more efficient resource utilization is foreseen and higher performance/area ratio may be achieved in comparison with the conventional static design approach on FPGAs.

## Acknowledgment

This work was supported in part by BMBF under contract Nos. 06GI9107I and 06GI9108I, FZ-Juelich under contract No. COSY-099 41821475, HIC for FAIR, and WTZ: CHN 06/20.

## References

1. PCI Industrial Computers Manufactures Group (PICMG), PICMG 3.0 Advanced Telecommunications Computing Architecture (ATCA) specification (December 2002)
2. High Acceptance Di-Electron Spectrometer (HADES) @ GSI, Darmstadt, Germany (2008), http://www-hades.gsi.de
3. antiProton ANnihilations at DArmstadt (PANDA) @ GSI, Darmstadt, Germany (2008), http://www.gsi.de/panda
4. BEijing Spectrometer (BES) @ IHEP, Beijing, China (2008), http://bes.ihep.ac.cn/bes3/index.html
5. The Large Hadron Collider (LHC) @ CERN, Geneva, Switzerland (2008), http://lhc.web.cern.ch/lhc/
6. Cherenkov, P.A.: Visible Radiation Produced by Electrons Moving in a Medium with Velocities Exceeding that of Light. Physics Review 52, 378–379 (1937)
7. Froehlich, I., et al.: Pattern Recognition in the HADES Spectrometer: an Application of FPGA Technology in Nuclear and Particle Physics. In: Proc. of the IEEE International Conference on Field-Programmable Technology (December 2004)
8. Hinkelbein, C., Kugel, A., Manner, R., Muller, M., Sessler, M., Simmler, H., Singpiel, H.: Pattern Recognition Algorithms on FPGAs and CPUs for the ATLAS LVL2 Trigger. IEEE Transactions on Nuclear Science 48(3) Part 1, 296–301 (2001)
9. Liu, M., Kuehn, W., Lu, Z., Jantsch, A.: System-on-an-FPGA Design for Real-time Particle Track Recognition and Reconstruction in Physics Experiments. In: Proc. of the EUROMICRO Conference on Digital System Design (September 2008)
10. Lehnert, J., et al.: Ring Recognition in the HADES Second-level Trigger. Nuclear Instruments and Methods in Physics Research A 433, 268–273 (1999)

11. Lehnert, J., et al.: Performance of the HADES Ring Recognition Hardware. Nuclear Instruments and Methods in Physics Research A 502, 261–265 (2003)
12. Liu, M., Johannes, L., et al.: ATCA-based Computation Platform for Data Acquisition and Triggering in Particle Physics Experiments. In: Proc. of the International Conference on Field Programmable Logic and Applications (September 2008)
13. Liu, M., Lu, Z., Kuehn, W., Yang, S., Jantsch, A.: A Reconfigurable Design Framework for FPGA Adaptive Computing. In: Proc. of the International Conference on ReConFigurable Computing and FPGAs (December 2009)

# FPGA-Based Smith-Waterman Algorithm: Analysis and Novel Design

Yoshiki Yamaguchi[1], Hung Kuen Tsoi[2], and Wayne Luk[3]

[1]Graduate School of Systems and Information Engineering, University of Tsukuba,
1-1-1 Ten-ou-dai Tsukuba Ibaraki, 305-8573, Japan
[2,3]Department of Computing, Imperial College London
180 Queen's Gate London SW7 2BZ, United Kingdom
yoshiki@cs.tsukuba.ac.jp, khtsoi@doc.ic.ac.uk, wl@doc.ic.ac.uk
http://www.cs.tsukuba.ac.jp/~yoshiki/

**Abstract.** This paper analyses two methods of organizing parallelism for the Smith-Waterman algorithm, and show how they perform relative to peak performance when the amount of parallelism varies. A novel systolic design is introduced, with a processing element optimized for computing the affine gap cost function. Our FPGA design is significantly more energy-efficient than GPU designs. For example, our design for the XC5VLX330T FPGA achieves around 16 GCUPS/W, while CPUs and GPUs have a power efficiency of lower than 0.5 GCUPS/W.

**Keywords:** Performance comparison, dynamic programming.

## 1 Introduction

Database sequence comparisons are fundamental approach in bioinformatics. Each genetic database consists of a number of entries which are genetic character sequences. Basic Local Alignment Search Tool (BLAST) [1] is used extensively in comparative genomics and however this method includes the risk which sequence similarity will be overlooked because of heuristic approach [2,3]. Needleman-Wunsch algorithm [4] and Smith-Waterman algorithm [5] are based on dynamic programming specialized for comparative genomics. Dynamic programming can consider the best local alignment between a query sequence and database sequences. And therefore not BLAST but Needleman-Wunsch and Smith-Waterman algorithms are still used in bioinformatics.

In dynamic programming, high-speed parallel approaches are always important. One reason is that their computational speed is often slow. Another reason is that the increase of genomic data volume, especially by the appearance of automated sequencers, has surpassed the growth of computational performance of MPUs. In recent years, researches in FPGA [6,7,8] and in other architectures [9,10,11,12,13] start to focus on not only nucleotides but also amino-acid sequence comparison. Table 1 shows the performance comparison. While many studies have been reported on particular platforms, there is not much research on analytic treatment for parallelizing the Smith-Waterman algorithm, with novel

A. Koch et al. (Eds.): ARC 2011, LNCS 6578, pp. 181–192, 2011.

**Table 1.** Comparison of computational performance in protein sequence alignment

| ref. | year | device | freq. (MHz) | core (#) | chip (#) | performance (GCUPS) |
|------|------|--------|-------------|----------|----------|---------------------|
| [6]  | 2007 | XC2VP70-5   | 39.2  | 138 | 1 | 5.4 |
| [7]  | 2007 | EP2S180     | 66.7  | 384 | 1 | 25.6 |
| [8]  | 2009 | XC2V6000-4  | 40.0  | 168 | 1 | 6.7 |
| [9]  | 2009 | 9800GX2     | 1,500 | 128 | 2 | 9.0~14.5 |
| [10] | 2009 | GTX280      | 1,296 | 240 | 1 | 9.0~9.7 |
| [10] | 2009 | GTX295      | 1,242 | 240 | 2 | 10.7~16.1 |
| [11] | 2010 | GTX295      | 1,242 | 240 | 2 | 10.1~10.4 |
| [12] | 2010 | GTX295      | 1,242 | 240 | 2 | 9.1~12.7 |
| [12] | 2010 | GTX295      | 1,242 | 240 | 4 | 29.5~43.1 |
| [13] | 2010 | Xeon E5420  | 2,500 | 8   | 2 | 18.9~34.4 |

systolic designs and experimental comparison of various FPGA and GPU implementations. Firstly, this paper tries to evaluate how efficient FPGA is in comparative genomics through theoretical comparison of how to implement the application program. After that, this study aims to establish techniques for optimizing performance by organizing parallelism effectively and analyzing the resulting effects.

To understand how the problem can be addressed, this study starts from the basic Smith-Waterman algorithm [4,5] in Section 2. Then challenges of the sequence alignment problem are identified and performance analysis of parallel algorithms in Section 3. Novel design optimization and implementation are shown in Section 4, including efficient realization of compression techniques for score matrices and reduction techniques for affine gap cost functions, which have been proposed in bioinformatics literature [14,15,16]. Experimental results and performance comparison are discussed in Section 5. Section 6 summarizes our approach and future work.

## 2    Smith-Waterman Algorithm

This section defines the fundamental nature of Smith-Waterman algorithm. In 1982, the following recurrence formula was introduced to Smith-Waterman algorithm [16].

$$s_{i,j} = \max \begin{cases} s_{i-1,j-1} + \delta(q_i, d_i) \\ s_{i,j,\downarrow} \\ s_{i,j,\rightarrow} \\ 0 \end{cases}, \tag{1}$$

where $s_{i,j}$ is the similarity score of a node at the $(i,j)$ position, $\delta(x,y)$ is the similarity score by genetic-character comparison of $x$ and $y$, $q_i$ is the i-th character of a query sequence, $d_j$ is the j-th character of a database sequence, $\downarrow$ denotes a gap insertion in query sequence direction, and $\rightarrow$ denotes a gap insertion in database sequence direction. $s_{i,j,\downarrow}$ and $s_{i,j,\rightarrow}$ are called affine gap cost functions and they are obtained by

$$s_{i,j,\downarrow} = \max \begin{cases} s_{i-1,j,\downarrow} + \beta \\ s_{i-1,j} + \alpha \end{cases} \tag{2}$$

$$s_{i,j,\rightarrow} = \max \begin{cases} s_{i,j-1,\rightarrow} + \beta \\ s_{i,j-1} + \alpha \end{cases} \tag{3}$$

$\alpha$ is the opening-gap-penalty cost and $\beta$ is the continuous-gap-penalty cost, and generally $\alpha \leq \beta \leq 0$. These gap penalties were introduced for genetic character insertion or deletion. These genetic mutations are usually caused by the error during DNA replications. Considering that two or more DNA bases may be inserted or deleted at the same time, it is preferable to give a penalty score more gradually compared to the constant penalty [16].

Fig.1 illustrates the data movement for parallel processing involving a processing element called SWPE, Smith-Waterman Processing Element. The affine gap functions, Eqs.2 and 3, are also implemented as recursive functions in an SWPE.

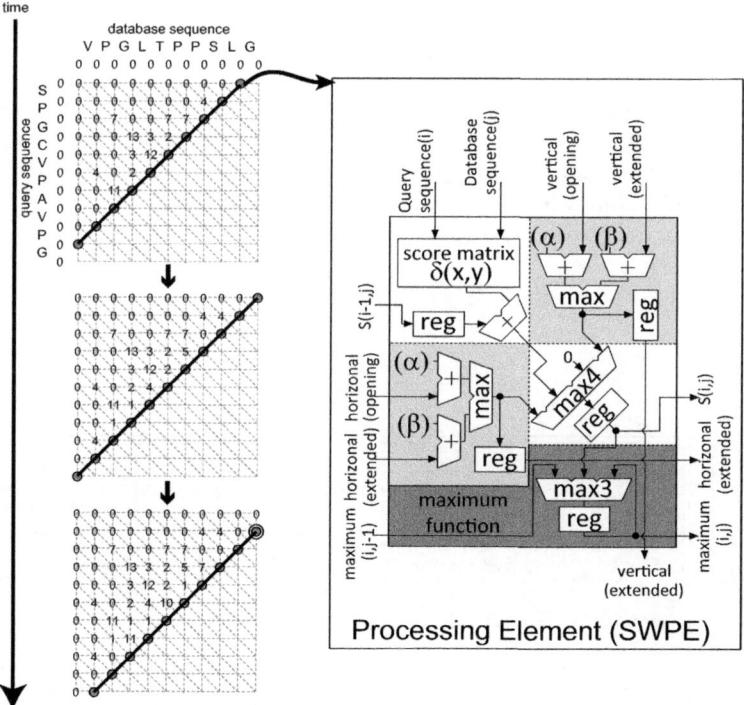

**Fig. 1.** Data movement for the parallel processing in Smith-Waterman algorithm and SWPE

Smith-Waterman algorithm is known to be computable in parallel along the oblique line shown in Fig.1. Thus, the number of SWPEs contributes to performance increase. In SWPE, it is necessary to store the maximum value used for judgement of a correlation between query and database sequences. Hence, SWPE includes circuits of not only Eq.1 but also the maximum function. Additionally, Smith-Waterman algorithm has highly data locality. This is the reason why its acceleration has been tried in ASICs and FPGAs.

## 3   Performance Analysis

This section provides an analytical estimation of the performance of our proposed design. In contrast to theoretical treatment based on parallelization of recurrences [17], our discussion focuses on a specific one-dimensional systolic array which includes: (a) multiple reconfigurable devices; (b) derivation of performance between line-based method and lattice-based method; (c) comparison of the achieved and theoretical peak performance of these methods.

Each SWPE can be regularly connected to form a systolic array. In the following discussion, we assume that Smith-Waterman algorithm is implemented on SWPEs which are arranged as an one-dimensional systolic array as shown in Fig.1. Then, the computational clock cycles becomes

$$f_{ideal}(Q, D) = Q + D - 1 \qquad (4)$$

from $QD$ when the number of SWPE, $p$, is larger than $Q$, where $Q$ and $D$ are defined as the length of a query sequence and a database sequence, respectively. When $p$ is smaller than $Q$, it is possible to compute in parallel by dividing the computational domain to multiple rows as shown in Fig.2 (i).

In this case, computational clock cycles becomes

$$f_{line}(Q, D, p) = q(p + D - 1), \qquad (5)$$

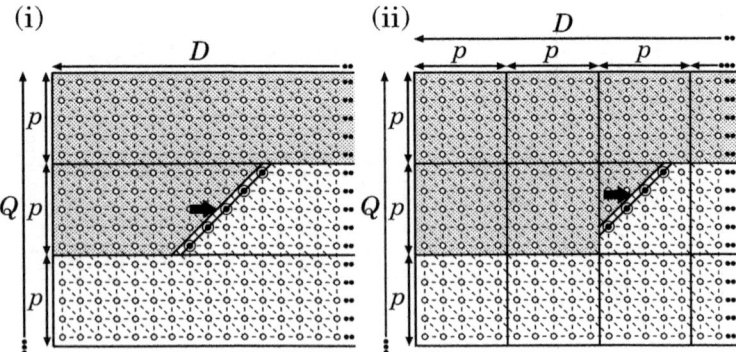

**Fig. 2.** (i) line-based parallel computation and (ii) lattice-based parallel computation

where $q = \lceil Q/p \rceil$. This computation can be extended to support multiple reconfigurable devices. Assuming that the number of devices is $k$, the computational time is obtained by the following expressions:

$$f_{line_k}(Q, D, p, k) = \frac{q(pk + D - 1)}{k} \tag{6}$$

$$\lim_{k \to q} f_{line_k}(Q, D, p, k) = pq + D - 1$$

$$\approx Q + D - 1, \tag{7}$$

where $q \geq k \geq 1$. $k$ should be sufficiently large for higher performance but the improvement stops when $kp > Q$.

Fig.2(ii) is another possibility of multiple device acceleration. In this case, the rectangular area is delimited not by $p$ but cache size on a single device, and the computation time is obtained by the following equation:

$$f_{lattice}(Q, D, p) = (2p - 1)qd, \tag{8}$$

where $d = \lceil D/p \rceil$. The computational clock cycles with $k$ devices are obtained by the following expression:

$$f_{lattice_k}(Q, D, p, k) = (2p - 1)\left(\frac{qd}{k} + k - 1\right) \tag{9}$$

$$\lim_{k \to q} f_{lattice_k}(Q, D, p, k) = (2p - 1)(q + d - 1)$$

$$\approx 2(Q + D - 1). \tag{10}$$

Fig.3 shows the ratio of line-based and lattice-based performance to theoretical peak performance obtained by Eq.4. It can be seen that line-based parallelism is always better than lattice-based parallelism since the former is closer to the ideal performance.

From Fig.3, it can also be seen that the performance efficiency will decrease when the number of SWPEs and the length of a query sequence do not match. This result is important because it enables power-performance improvement.

## 4   Systolic Array Design

This section describes a new design for SWPE for the Smith-Waterman algorithm. The novel aspect of our design concerns hardware optimisation by transforming numerical expressions in computing the affine gap cost function.

### 4.1   The Overview of an SWPE

Fig.1 describes the basic structure and internal function modules of an SWPE. A processing element is composed of 5 modules: one similarity computation with score matrix, two affine gap cost functions, one maximum detection and one maximum score-history function. The score matrix corresponds to $\delta(q_i, d_i)$ of

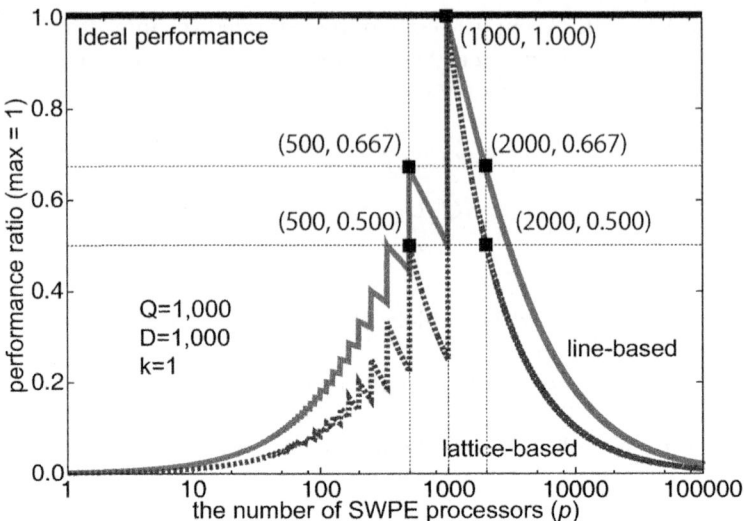

**Fig. 3.** Performance ratio of line-based and lattice-based performance to the theoretical peak performance: excessive parallelization induces the larger number of idle elements and it causes performance degradation

Eq.1 and the circuits which are placed in light-gray boxes shows the affine gap cost functions. The maximum detection function involves selecting a maximum as shown in Eq.1. The maximum score-history function is an essential function for obtaining the maximum value of Smith-Waterman algorithm though it is not shown in numerical expressions; it can be expressed by one single comparator.

## 4.2   Affine Gap Cost Function ($\alpha \leq \beta \leq 0$)

When the gene is copied, insertion and deletion of characters might take place. Gap cost functions are quantification of the gap inserted or deleted at this time. The affine gap cost function [16] is well known and is obtained by Eq.2 and Eq.3. In the numerical equations, $\alpha$ is the cost of opening gap and $\beta$ is the cost of continuous gap. In general, $\alpha$ is smaller than $\beta$.

When using this function, we must treat at least 6 values: $s_{i-1,j-1}$, $s_{i-1,j}$, $s_{i,j-1}$, $s_{i-1,j,\downarrow}$, $s_{i,j-1,\rightarrow}$, 0 for every SWPE. Therefore, at least five comparators, namely 5 branch instructions, are needed for getting the maximum of them in every SWPE. A single SWPE must require one or two additional comparators since the SWPE has a maximum value function as shown in Fig.1. Based on this, the size of a single SWPE is estimated to be around 160 LUTs in this paper which is almost the same as the size of the design in [8] which is estimated to be 85 slices, i.e. 170 LUTs, on XILINX Virtex-II architecture. This section discusses how to realize a better circuit for the SWPE.

The original numerical equations should be optimized for hardware implementation; they use signed circuits in most operations. A signed comparator is larger than an unsigned one. In general, $\alpha \leq \beta \leq 0$. We can take advantage of this relationship and further reduce the number of LUTs. Here, Eqs.1-3 are revised to produce Eqs.11-13. Each underscored term in Eqs.11-13 means a signed number. $(\beta - \alpha)$ has to be larger than 0 as a precondition to this application.

$$s_{i,j} = \max \begin{cases} s_{i-1,j-1} + \underline{\delta(q_i, d_i)} \\ s_{i,j,\downarrow} = \max \begin{cases} s_{i,j,\downarrow,\alpha} + \underline{\alpha} \\ 0 \end{cases} \\ s_{i,j,\rightarrow} = \max \begin{cases} s_{i,j,\rightarrow,\alpha} + \underline{\alpha} \\ 0 \end{cases} \end{cases} \tag{11}$$

$$s_{i,j,\downarrow,\alpha} = \max \begin{cases} s_{i-1,j,\downarrow} + (\beta - \alpha) \\ s_{i-1,j} \end{cases} \tag{12}$$

$$s_{i,j,\rightarrow,\alpha} = \max \begin{cases} s_{i,j-1,\rightarrow} + (\beta - \alpha) \\ s_{i,j-1} \end{cases}. \tag{13}$$

In Fig.4(i), each SWPE has four 15-bit comparators, one 16-bit comparator, one 16-bit adder-subtractor, two 15-bit adders, and two 15-bit positive-number discriminant adders, m+, whose details are illustrated in Fig.4(ii).

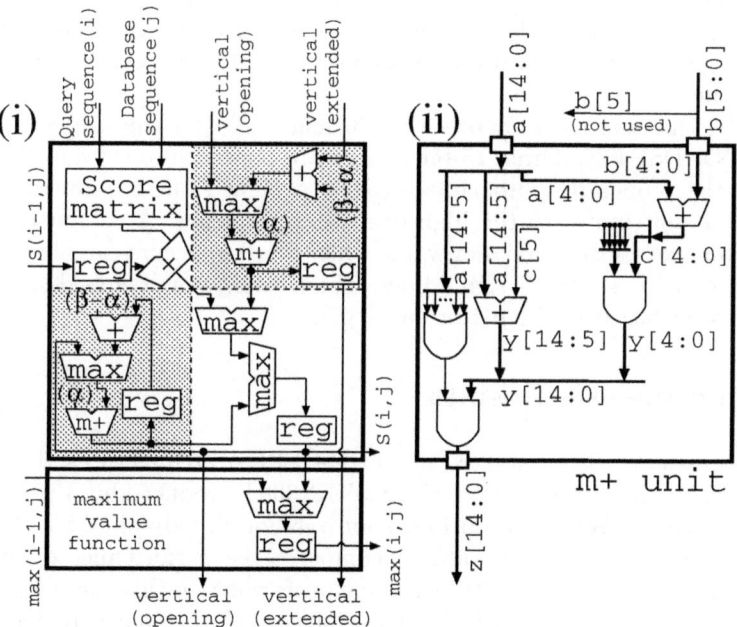

**Fig. 4.** (i) an optimized SWPE by arranging Smith-Waterman equations, (ii) a positive-number discriminated adder for SWPE

Compared to previous approach, we can reduce 243 LUTs to 219 LUTs in case of 4-input LUTs for Virtex-4 FPGAs; and from 239 LUTs to 231 LUTs in case of 4-input LUTs for Virtex-II Pro and Virtex-II FPGAs. In case of 6-input

**Table 2.** Circuit resource requirement for a single SWPE. Each SWPE includes a single embedded RAM.

| FPGA | LUT | | | regs |
|------|-----|------|------|------|
|      | total | logic | thru | |
| ideal | 152 | | | |
| Virtex5 | 177 | 138 | 39 | |
| Virtex4 | 219 | 191 | 28 | 85 |
| Virtex-II Pro | 231 | 204 | 27 | |
| Virtex-II | 231 | 204 | 27 | |

LUTs for Virtex-5 FPGAs, the number of logic LUTs decreases even though the total does not decrease, as shown in Table 2. For these experiments, ISE12.2 (ver.M.63c) is used for Virtex 4 and 5, and ISE8.2i (ver.I.31) is also used for Virtex II and II pro.

Here, a thru LUT means a 'route-through' LUT in XILINX FPGAs and the number is counted when the circuits other than LUTs drives registers, carry, and some circuits because of the composition where a minimum unit contains a LUT and other circuits. As for the thru circuit, there is a possibility of it being eliminated by the synthesis tools, which is confirmed by experiments in Section 5 for a larger circuit. Thus, this approach significantly improves the SWPE array performance.

Finally, this approach enables the efficient use of an embedded adder such as XILINX DSP48E. Three 15-bit adders are packed in one embedded adders because the proposed approach can reduce a signed bit. It reduces the use of LUTs and contributes to the high operating frequency. A compact saturation adder which keeps the maximum value when overflow occurs can also be realized by the use of 16, 32, 48 bit signal lines. The efficient use of embedded circuits is an important factor in the performance gain.

## 5  Experimental Results

SWPE arrays are also evaluated on current FPGA architectures. They are implemented on ADM-XRC-5T2 with XC5VLX330T produced by Alpha Data. We adopt Fig.4 as a SWPE and optimize not only for an individual SWPE but also for a SWPE systolic array. Table 3 compares the performance of our FPGA implementation and current FPGA implementations. In this comparison, billion cell update per second (GCUPS) is used for performance measurement and it is obtained by $QD/T_{comp} \times 10^{-9}$, where $T_{comp}$ is the computational time.

### 5.1  Background for the Performance Assessment

Our performance assessment is an evaluation based on an isolated single FPGA. We find that the estimated peak performance of our synthesized design is comparable to the performance predicted by our analytical model in Section 3.

The value for peak performance in Table 3 corresponds to the FPGA peak performance. The lowest performance is decided in consideration of the I/O interface. As for the I/O interface in a real environment, it is various according to the system though it is ideally preferable to be connected with external memory or host PC closely. Then, it is assumed that the reading/writing time from/to main memory requires hundreds of clock cycles, and the value of 70% of the FPGA peak performance is adopted as a performance in the lowest case.

Finally, the second place of the decimal point is rounded off in Table 3. High accuracy more than this is unnecessary in the application environment into which the performance changes by the condition: the length of query sequence, sequence set in a database, the combination and so on.

**Table 3.** Performance comparison with [6] and [8]

| ref. | device | freq. (MHz) | core (#) | FPGA resource utilization LUT(#) | Register(#) | performance (GCUPS) |
|------|--------|-------------|----------|-----------------------------------|-------------|---------------------|
| [6] | 2VP70-5 | 39.2 | 138 | (*3)65,964/66,176(99.7%) | no data | 5.4 |
| ours | 2VP70-5 | 59.8 | 138 | 31,790/66,176(48.0%) | 12,488/66,176(18.9%) | 5.8~8.3 |
| [8] | 2V6000-4 | 40.0 | 168 | no data | no data | (*2)6.7 |
| ours | 2V6000-4 | 59.3 | 168 | 38,720/67,584(57.3%) | 15,218/67,584(22.5%) | 7.0~10.0 |

(*1) In these three tables, the title "LUTs" means the total number of LUTs: the total number of logic LUTs and thru LUTs.

(*2) The value is obtained by 168(units) multiplied by 40(MHz) from Table 1 in [8].

(*3) The value is obtained by 138(unit) × 239(used slices/unit) × 2 (LUTs/slice), where each parameter comes from Table 1 in [6].

## 5.2 Performance Comparison with Other FPGA Designs

Before the performance assessment, preliminary experiments are performed for checking the validity of our proposed approach. The computation reported in [6] and [8] on protein-sequence alignment on an FPGA are selected for our test-bed study. For fair consideration, we implemented a one-dimensional SWPE array on the same device.

In [6], it considers not only Smith-Waterman algorithm but also the Needleman-Wunsch algorithm. Table 3 shows that the proposed SWPE array, in the same device as used in [6], can reach higher clock speed and higher performance than the design in [6], with a resource utilisation of below 50%.

Two methods, *affine3* and *affine2*, have been introduced by a figure and equations in [8], and our approach is equivalent to the method of *affine3*. The technique that we propose results in 60% or lower resource utilisation as shown in Table 3, and seems to be useful enough though only the speed and the operating frequency are comparable because there is no information on resource utilisation in [8].

It is possible that the improved performance of the proposed design is partly due to the use of more recent versions of FPGA tools from Xilinx. Such effects are impossible to quantify since we do not have access to old versions of FPGA tools. However the optimisations described in the preceding sections would also contribute to the superior performance of our designs.

### 5.3   Performance Evaluation of FPGA

In this section, we evaluate the maximum performance obtained by applying the proposed techniques to the XILINX XC5VLX330T FPGA in the Alpha Data ADM-XRC-5T2 system. Our design for XILINX XC5VLX330 has 183,416 LUTs and 86,638 registers; it contains 1,000 SWPE elements and can reach a performance of up to 129 GCUPS. It is likely to be one of the fastest single-chip implementation of the Smith-Waterman algorithm. Moreover, since systolic architectures are regular and scalable, SWPE arrays and the associated optimizations would be applicable to next-generation FPGA devices as they become available.

In power-performance evaluation, the FPGA achieves around 16 GCUPS/W when we use two DDR-II Synchronous SRAM banks in the Alpha Data ADM-XRC-5T2 system. This power-performance is better than that of CPU and GPUs; CPU, such as Xeon E5420, is less than 0.5 GCUPS/W and GPUs, such as GTX295, are less than 0.08 GCUPS/W.

### 5.4   CPU and GPUs

There is recent research on Smith-Waterman targeting GPUs [9,11,12,18] but the theoretical peak performance is not so high; for instance, the performance of four parallel GPUs hardly reaches one single XC4VLX200: about 40 GCUPS in our estimation. Moreover, a single Spartan produced by XILINX or one single Cyclone by ALTERA are comparable to the performance of a single GPU. [9] shows the bottleneck is not memory bandwidth and it implies current GPU architecture is not appropriate for this application when compared with FPGA architecture. We confirm this observation using NVIDIA GTX480; the memory bandwidth is not a bottleneck in this latest device.

Recent studies, [11] and [12], also show the discrepancy between theoretical performance of GPU and real performance of this application. It seems that this application is unsuitable for GPU even though GPU has shown remarkable progress in accelerating various algorithms. On the other hand, appropriate CPUs can achieve a decent performance compared with their theoretical performance [13]. The reason could be due to the availability of bit-level and branch instructions in CPUs which enables an optimized implementation. In our assembly code analysis, issued instructions of Intel CPU are about three times less than that of GPU, where the numbers of GPU instructions are confirmed by NVIDIA Compute Visual Profiler Version 3.2. Here, GPUs do not seems to be suitable for the application which has a lot of branch instructions and fine-grain data structures even though the peak performance of GPU is high.

# 6   Conclusion

This paper provides an analytical treatment of the SWPE systolic approach to the Smith-Waterman algorithm. The line-based and lattice-based methods for organizing parallelism are introduced; the effect of parallelism on the performance of these methods is analysed with respect to peak performance. The insights from this analysis are used in deriving a novel systolic design, which includes techniques for reducing affine gap cost functions.

The potential of our approach is demonstrated by the high performance of the resulting designs. For example, the XC5VLX330T FPGA can accommodate 1,000 SWPE cores operating at 130MHz, resulting in a performance of up to 129 GCUPS, which is 3 times faster than the fastest quad-GPU processor, GTX295. Moreover, the FPGA is far more energy efficient than GPUs: XC5VLX330T achieves around 16 GCUPS/W, while the power-performance for CPU is less than 0.5 GCUPS/W, and for GPUs is less than 0.08 GCUPS/W.

We are continuing our quest to achieve further speedup and energy efficiency for designs targeting various bioinformatics applications, and to provide effective tools for the productive automation of such designs.

**Acknowledgments.** This work was partially supported by Grant-in-Aid for Young Scientists (B) 20700044.

# References

1. Altschul, S.F., Gish, W., Miller, W., Myers, E.W., Lipman, D.J.: Basic Local Alignment Search Tool. Molecular Biology 215(3), 403–410 (1990)
2. Pearson, W.R.: Comparison of methods for searching protein sequence databases. Profein Science 4(6), 1145–1160 (1995)
3. Shpaer, E.G., Robinson, M., Yee, D., Candlin, J.D., Mines, R., Hunkapiller, T.: Sensitivity and selectivity in protein similarity searches: A comparison of Smith-Waterman in hardware to BLAST and FASTA. Genomics 38, 179–191 (1996)
4. Needleman, S.B., Wunsch, C.D.: A general method applicable to the search for similarities in the amino acid sequence of two proteins. Journal of Molecular Biology 48(3), 443–453 (1970)
5. Smith, T.F., Waterman, M.S.: Identification of common molecular subsequences. Journal of Molecular Biology 147(1), 195–197 (1981)
6. Van Court, T., Herbordt, M.C.: Families of FPGA-based accelerators for approximate string matching. Microprocessors & Microsystems 31, 135–145 (2007)
7. ALTERA. Implementation of the smith-waterman algorithm on a reconfigurable supercomputing platform (September 2007)
8. Benkrid, K., Liu, Y., Benkrid, A.: A highly parameterised and efficient FPGA-based skeleton for pairwise biological sequence alignment. IEEE Transactions on Very Large Scale Integration (VLSI Systems) 17(4), 561–570 (2009)
9. Ligowski, L., Rudnicki, W.R.: An efficient implementation of smith waterman algorithm on GPU using CUDA, for massively parallel scanning of sequence databases. In: Proceedings of the IEEE International Symposium on Parallel and Distributed Processing (appeared in HICOMB), pp. 1–8 (May 2009)

10. Liu, Y., Maskell, D.L., Schmidt, B.: CUDASW++: optimizing smith-waterman sequence database searches for CUDA-enabled graphics processing units. BMC Research Notes 2(1), 73–82 (2009)
11. Ligowski, Ł., Rudnicki, W.R.: GPU-SW sequence alignment server. In: Proceedings of International Conference on Computational Science, pp. 1–10 (June 2010)
12. Dohi, K., Benkrid, K., Ling, C., Hamada, T., Shibata, Y.: Highly efficient mapping of the smith-waterman algorithm on CUDA-compatible GPUs. In: Proceedings of the IEEE International Conference on Application-specific Systems Architectures and Processors, pp. 29–36 (July 2010)
13. Aldinucci, M., Danelutto, M., Meneghin, M., Kilpatrick, P., Torquati, M.: Efficient streaming applications on multi-core with fastflow: the biosequence alignment testbed. In: Proceedings of International Conference on Parallel Computing, pp. 273–280 (September 2009)
14. Dayhoff, M.O., Schwartz, R.M., Orcutt, B.C.: A model of evolutionary change in proteins, vol. 5. National Biomedical Research Foundation (1978)
15. Altschul, S.F.: Amino acid substitution matrices from an information theoretic perspective. Journal of Molecular Biology 219(3), 555–565 (1991)
16. Gotoh, O.: An improved algorithm for matching biological sequences. Journal of Molecular Biology 162(3), 705–708 (1982)
17. Jacob, A.C., Buhler, J.D., Chamberlain, R.D.: Design of throughput-optimized arrays from recurrence abstractions. In: Proceedings of the IEEE International Conference on Application-specific Systems Architectures and Processors, pp. 133–140 (July 2010)
18. Manavski, S.A., Valle, G.: CUDA compatible GPU cards as efficient hardware accelerators for smith-waterman sequence alignment. BMC Bioinformatics 9(suppl. 2), S10 (2008)

# Index to Constant Weight Codeword Converter

Jon T. Butler[1] and Tsutomu Sasao[2,*]

[1] Naval Postgraduate School, Monterey, CA, 93921-5121, USA
jon_butler@msn.com
[2] Kyushu Institute of Technology, Iizuka, Fukuoka, 820-8502, Japan
sasao@cse.kyutech.ac.jp

**Abstract.** A constant weight codeword is a binary $n$-tuple with exactly $r$ 1's. We show two circuits that generate constant weight codewords. The first is based on the combinatorial number system. Its input is an index to the codeword. That is, there are $\binom{n}{r}$ $n$-bit codewords with exactly $r$ 1's. The index generates a unique codeword, and is a binary number between 0 and $\binom{n}{r} - 1$. Such a circuit is useful for encoding data. If a *random* constant weight codeword is needed, as in Monte Carlo simulations, then the index is random. If a random constant weight codeword only is needed, then our other circuit is even more compact. It is based on a trellis configuration. Both designs can be pipelined to produce one constant weight codeword per clock period. We give experimental results showing the efficiency of our designs on the SRC-6 reconfigurable computer.

## 1 Introduction

The generation of an arbitrary $n$-bit binary word with a fixed weight $r$ (number of 1's) is surprisingly difficult. It is convenient to describe such a word as a *constant weight codeword*, even when discussing a non-coding application.

A constant weight code generator is useful in the enumeration of bent Boolean functions by reconfigurable computer [4,20]. Bent functions are used in cryptographic applications because they are resilient to a *linear* attack. It is known that the truth tables of $n$-variable bent functions have one of only two weights, $2^{n-1} \pm 2^{n/2-1}$ [16]. Therefore, instead of testing all $2^{2^n}$ $n$-variable truth tables for bentness, it is sufficient to enumerate only functions with these weights. Because the search space of this reduced space is still large, one seeks a Monte Carlo approach, in which random binary numbers, representing truth tables with a fixed number of 1's, are generated.

* We thank Jon Huppenthal, President and CEO of SRC Computers, Inc., Colorado Springs, CO for data used in this paper. This research is supported by a Grant-in-Aid for Scientific Research of the Japan Society for the Promotion of Science (JSPS) and a Knowledge Cluster Initiative (the second stage) of MEXT (Ministry of Education, Culture, Sports, Science and Technology). Two referees provided suggestions that improved the manuscript.

A. Koch et al. (Eds.): ARC 2011, LNCS 6578, pp. 193–205, 2011.
© Springer-Verlag Berlin Heidelberg 2011

We have used the constant weight codeword generator in the enumeration of Boolean functions by reconfigurable computer to determine their correlation immunity [6]. Correlation immunity is a cryptographic property of Boolean functions used in encryption/decryption to determine the extent to which the input values can be determined from the output value. We were able to test one function in each clock period because the index to constant weight code converters shown here can process at one constant weight code per clock period.

Such circuits have application in other areas. For example, Yamanaka, Shimizu, and Shan [23] program the lexicographical generation of constant weight codewords on a reconfigurable computer to analyze energy efficient networks. Balanced codes, in which there are as many 0's as 1's, are useful for encoding data transferred on and off VLSI chips in a way that minimizes the current fluctuation during switching [21]. In other instances of VLSI data transfer, codes with small weight are desired because they yield faster and more compact circuits [21]. Constant weight codes are a countermeasure to "side-channel" attacks [8]. Such attacks use data dependent differences in power consumption to extract secret information. Constant weight codes have been used in asynchronous logic as a means to implement delay-insensitive codes [22]. Three-out-of-six and two-out-of-seven constant weight codes have been used to build a parallel processor for neural simulation [9].

The generation of constant weight codewords in lexicographic order has received much attention spanning 40 years (c.f. [14]). One of the earliest contributions, Gosper's "Hack" [7], is an elegant sequence of basic instructions that can be easily programmed (see also Knuth's MMIX version [10]). The output is a sequence of constant weight codewords whose binary number representation increases each time a codeword is generated. Both normal and reverse lexicographical sequences are useful in heuristics for the generation of sets of codewords with large cardinality [15]. That is, the generation of codewords in either normal or reverse lexicographical order is useful in producing large sets of codewords each a minimum Hamming distance from all other codewords in the set. Interestingly, this bin-packing problem, in which one seeks the *largest* number of constant weight codewords each no less than a specified Hamming distance from another codeword, has remained unsolved for 50 years [1,13].

Unfortunately, Gosper's Hack is not able to convert an index to a constant weight code corresponding to that index. Thus, it cannot be used in an *encoding algorithm* for constant weight codewords or in a Monte Carlo simulation. In both cases, there is a need to freely choose the sequence of constant weight codewords. A software version of such an encoding algorithm was developed more than 30 years ago [2], but as far as we know, a hardware implementation has never been reported.

We correct this deficiency in this paper. For example, there are $\binom{6}{3} = 20$ 6-bit codewords with exactly three 1's. These can be indexed by a five bit index, whose value ranges from 0 to 19. The index values 20 through 31 are unused. In a coding application, the index will be determined by the plaintext message. In a Monte Carlo simulation, there is an issue related to the index value because typical random number generators produce a value from 0 to $2^n - 1$. We discuss how to deal with this mismatch. Our architecture is a LUT cascade and is simple. Yet, it produces one constant weight codeword every clock period.

In Section 2, we discuss the combinatorial number system. We show how it can be used to generate constant weight codes, and we discuss its circuit implementation. Then, in Section 3, we discuss a trellis circuit for computing *random* constant weight codewords and compare its complexity/speed with that derived from the combinatorial number system. The trellis circuit is an especially efficient way to generate random constant weight codes. Finally, in Section 4, we give concluding remarks.

## 2   The Combinatorial Number System

### 2.1   Introduction

As in the standard binary number system, in the combinatorial number system, each number is represented by a unique vector of basis values.

**Definition 1.** *In an $\binom{n}{r}$ combinatorial number system [11], integer $N <$ $\binom{n}{r}$ is represented as $N = c_r c_{r-1} \ldots c_1$, where*

$$N = \binom{c_r}{r} + \binom{c_{r-1}}{r-1} + \ldots + \binom{c_1}{1}, \tag{1}$$

*such that $c_r > c_{r-1} > \ldots > c_1 \geq 0$.*

**Example 1.** *Table 1 shows the representation of numbers in the $\binom{6}{3}$ combinatorial number system, where $0_{10} \leq N \leq 19_{10}$. The rightmost column of Table 1 shows the 6 bit constant weight code corresponding to $N$. The constant weight, in this example, is 3, as there are three 1's in each word. Note that the three elements of the vector representation of $N$ correspond to the position of the 1 in the constant weight codeword. For example, $19_{10}$ or 543 corresponds to 111000, while $0_{10}$ or 210 corresponds to 000111.*

*(End of Example)*

We can make the following observations.

1. Regardless of $N$, each representation has exactly $r$ "digits" (vector elements). For example, a $\binom{7}{3}$ combinatorial number system also has three "digits". However, the basis values are larger than those in a $\binom{6}{3}$ combinatorial number system.
2. Each set of digits, such that $c_3 > c_2 > c_1 \geq 0$, corresponds to a unique value of $N$. Each value of $N$ corresponds to a *unique* set of digits, such that $c_3 > c_2 > c_1 \geq 0$. It can be seen to be true in this example. This was proven to hold in a general $\binom{n}{r}$ combinatorial number system by Lehmer [12].

**Table 1.** The $\binom{6}{3}$ Combinatorial Number System for $0_{10} \leq N \leq 19_{10}$

| $N$ | $c_3\ c_2\ c_1$ for $k = 3$ | Value of $N$ for $k = 3$ | Constant Weight Codeword |
|---|---|---|---|
| $19_{10}$ | 5 4 3 | $\binom{5}{3} + \binom{4}{2} + \binom{3}{1} = 10 + 6 + 3$ | 111000 |
| $18_{10}$ | 5 4 2 | $\binom{5}{3} + \binom{4}{2} + \binom{2}{1} = 10 + 6 + 2$ | 110100 |
| $17_{10}$ | 5 4 1 | $\binom{5}{3} + \binom{4}{2} + \binom{1}{1} = 10 + 6 + 1$ | 110010 |
| $16_{10}$ | 5 4 0 | $\binom{5}{3} + \binom{4}{2} + \binom{0}{1} = 10 + 6 + 0$ | 110001 |
| $15_{10}$ | 5 3 2 | $\binom{5}{3} + \binom{3}{2} + \binom{2}{1} = 10 + 3 + 2$ | 101100 |
| $14_{10}$ | 5 3 1 | $\binom{5}{3} + \binom{3}{2} + \binom{1}{1} = 10 + 3 + 1$ | 101010 |
| $13_{10}$ | 5 3 0 | $\binom{5}{3} + \binom{3}{2} + \binom{0}{1} = 10 + 3 + 0$ | 101001 |
| $12_{10}$ | 5 2 1 | $\binom{5}{3} + \binom{2}{2} + \binom{1}{1} = 10 + 1 + 1$ | 100110 |
| $11_{10}$ | 5 2 0 | $\binom{5}{3} + \binom{2}{2} + \binom{0}{1} = 10 + 1 + 0$ | 100101 |
| $10_{10}$ | 5 1 0 | $\binom{5}{3} + \binom{1}{2} + \binom{0}{1} = 10 + 0 + 0$ | 100011 |
| $9_{10}$ | 4 3 2 | $\binom{4}{3} + \binom{3}{2} + \binom{2}{1} = 4 + 3 + 2$ | 011100 |
| $8_{10}$ | 4 3 1 | $\binom{4}{3} + \binom{3}{2} + \binom{1}{1} = 4 + 3 + 1$ | 011010 |
| $7_{10}$ | 4 3 0 | $\binom{4}{3} + \binom{3}{2} + \binom{0}{1} = 4 + 3 + 0$ | 011001 |
| $6_{10}$ | 4 2 1 | $\binom{4}{3} + \binom{2}{2} + \binom{1}{1} = 4 + 1 + 1$ | 010110 |
| $5_{10}$ | 4 2 0 | $\binom{4}{3} + \binom{2}{2} + \binom{0}{1} = 4 + 1 + 0$ | 010101 |
| $4_{10}$ | 4 1 0 | $\binom{4}{3} + \binom{1}{2} + \binom{0}{1} = 4 + 0 + 0$ | 010011 |
| $3_{10}$ | 3 2 1 | $\binom{3}{3} + \binom{2}{2} + \binom{1}{1} = 1 + 1 + 1$ | 001110 |
| $2_{10}$ | 3 2 0 | $\binom{3}{3} + \binom{2}{2} + \binom{0}{1} = 1 + 1 + 0$ | 001101 |
| $1_{10}$ | 3 1 0 | $\binom{3}{3} + \binom{1}{2} + \binom{0}{1} = 1 + 0 + 0$ | 001011 |
| $0_{10}$ | 2 1 0 | $\binom{2}{3} + \binom{1}{2} + \binom{0}{1} = 0 + 0 + 0$ | 000111 |

3. Given $N$, a greedy algorithm derives $c_r\ c_{r-1} \ \ldots \ c_1$. For example, in Table 1, the first digit for $19_{10}$ can be obtained by finding the largest $c_3$, such that $\binom{c_3}{3} \leq 19_{10}$. Since $\binom{2}{3} = 0_{10}$, $\binom{3}{3} = 1_{10}$, $\binom{4}{3} = 4_{10}$, $\binom{5}{3} = 10_{10}$, $\binom{6}{3} = 20_{10}$, $\ldots$, $c_3 = 5_{10}$. Similarly, we seek the largest $c_2$ such that $\binom{c_2}{2} \leq 19_{10} - 10_{10} = 9_{10}$, etc.

## 2.2   Circuit Implementation

The keystone of our contribution is a circuit that produces constant weight codewords from an index that is an implementation of an $\binom{n}{r}$ combinatorial number system. Consider, for example, the generation of 6-bit binary words with three 1's. Let *index* be a 5-bit index whose value specifies which of these codewords is produced. There are $\binom{6}{3} = 20$ codewords, which we assume are specified by $0 \leq index \leq 19$. Let *output* be a vector of six bits ordered as *output*(5) *output*(4) *output*(3) *output*(2) *output*(1) *output*(0), three of which are 1 and three of which are 0's. The pseudo-code for this circuit is as follows.

Set $output := 000000$.

IF      $index \geq \binom{5}{3} = 10$,  Set $output(5) := 1$ and $index := index - 10$.
ELSEIF $index \geq \binom{4}{3} = 4$,   Set $output(4) := 1$ and $index := index - 4$.
ELSEIF $index \geq \binom{3}{3} = 1$,   Set $output(3) := 1$ and $index := index - 1$.
ELSEIF $index \geq \binom{2}{3} = 0$,   Set $output(2) := 1$ and $index := index - 0$.

IF      $index \geq \binom{4}{2} = 6$,  Set $output(4) := 1$ and $index := index - 6$.
ELSEIF $index \geq \binom{3}{2} = 3$,   Set $output(3) := 1$ and $index := index - 3$.
ELSEIF $index \geq \binom{2}{2} = 1$,   Set $output(2) := 1$ and $index := index - 1$.
ELSEIF $index \geq \binom{1}{2} = 0$,   Set $output(1) := 1$ and $index := index - 0$.

IF      $index \geq \binom{3}{1} = 3$,  Set $output(3) := 1$ and $index := index - 3$.
ELSEIF $index \geq \binom{2}{1} = 2$,   Set $output(2) := 1$ and $index := index - 2$.
ELSEIF $index \geq \binom{1}{1} = 1$,   Set $output(1) := 1$ and $index := index - 1$.
ELSEIF $index \geq \binom{0}{1} = 0$,   Set $output(0) := 1$ and $index := index - 0$.

Each of the three IF statements corresponds to the generation of one 1 bit in the codeword, where the first generates the leftmost 1 bit, the second the middle 1 bit and the third the rightmost 1 bit. Fig. 1 shows the circuit that computes the description above. *index* comes in from the left, and *output* exits to the right. Between is a circuit that performs the four operations above. This includes testing the index against a threshold and then performing two operations. The first sets the output to an appropriate value and the second subtracts an appropriate value from the index and passes it on to the next stage, which performs a similar operation. Note that this circuit can be implemented as an $r$-stage cascade of combinational circuits [17].

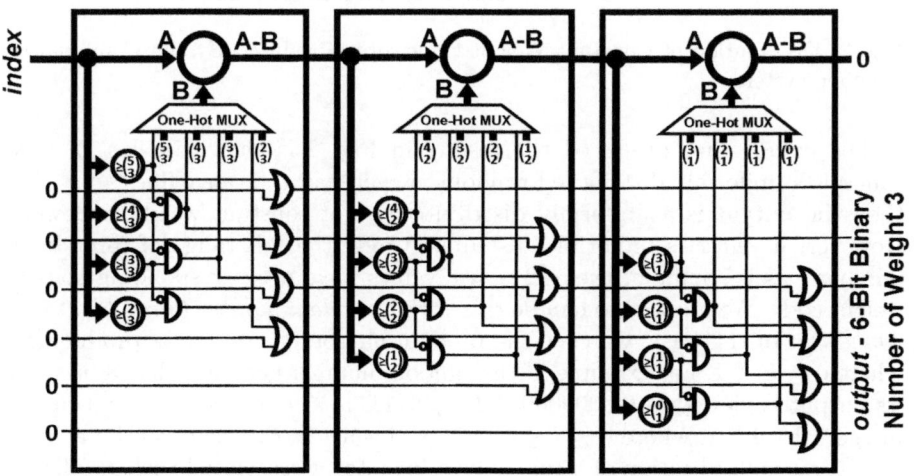

**Fig. 1.** Example of a Constant Weight Codeword Generator Circuit

At each stage, there are inputs and outputs that carry a partially completed *output*. Also, there are inputs and outputs that carry *index* reduced by the values contributed by higher order digits. The rightmost stage produces a 0 value at its *index* output, since there are no digits to the right.

Note that this is easily pipelined. Pipeline registers can simply be inserted between stages. Doing so, causes the latency to be $r$, the weight. Note that, after the first codeword emerges, a codeword emerges at each clock period.

## 2.3    Results

Fig. 2 shows the result of a program on the SRC-6 reconfigurable computer to produce random constant weight codewords. The SRC-6 uses the Xilinx Virtex2p XC2VP100 FPGA with Package FF1696 and Speed Grade -5. Here, the distribution of constant weight codes with $n = 6$ bits and $r = 3$ 1's is plotted. A total of 1,048,576 ($= 2^{20}$) 64-bit random numbers were generated and converted into random integers from 0 to 19 and applied as indices to the constant weight code generator. For example, the leftmost bar in Fig. 2 corresponds to 52,079 codewords of the form 000111 (=7), and the rightmost bar corresponds to 52,285 codewords of the form 111000 (=56).

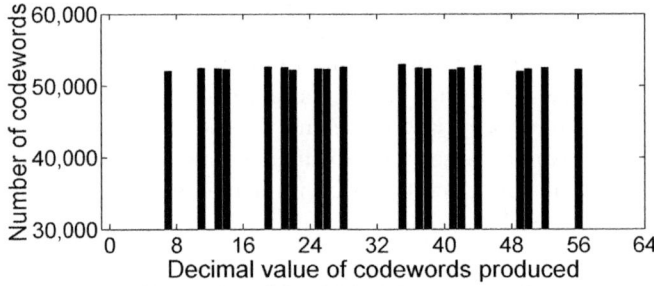

**Fig. 2.** Distribution of Constant Weight Codewords Produced By the Combinatorial Number System

The circuit that produced the results in Fig. 2 is shown in Fig. 3. If the *index* is a uniformly distributed random integer over the range $0_{10} \leq N \leq 19_{10}$, then the output is a uniformly distributed set of constant weight codewords. However, if *index* is uniformly distributed over the full range of 5-bit binary numbers, as is common, then 12 *index* values have no corresponding constant weight code. We propose to handle this with a *random number to random integer converter*. In this case, we view the random number generator as producing $R$, where $0 \leq R < 1$. For example, if the random number generator has 8 bits, then its output is viewed as $0.0000000 \leq R \leq 0.11111111 < 1$. To produce a random integer of value $i$, where $0 \leq i \leq v - 1$, we form $v \times R$, which can be achieved by integer multiplication of $v$ times the 8 bit integer associated with $R$ following by a division by 256, which corresponds to a right shift by 8 bits. The product $vR$ involves multiplication by a constant. This is done quickly by addition, shift,

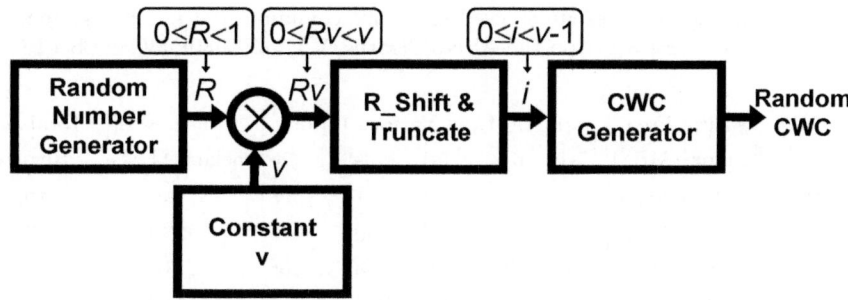

**Fig. 3.** Block Diagram of a Random Constant Weight Code Generator

and truncate. Fig. 3 shows the circuit that realizes this. Note that the random number to random integer converter (i.e. domain converter) consists of all blocks in Fig. 3 except the CWC Generator.

The complete circuit uses 2,880 out of 88,192 4-input LUTs (3%) and 3,804 out of 88,192 slice flip-flops (4%). It can run at 100.1 MHz, which is slightly greater than the SRC-6's operating frequency of 100 MHz. The random number generator is a cellular automata system proposed by Shackleford, Tanaka, Carter, and Snider [19]. As shown in Fig. 3, this is multiplied by $v$ (in this specific example, $v = 20$). The product is right shifted by 64 bits and truncated. The result is a uniformly distributed random integer from 0 to 19. This is applied to the CWC Generator in Fig. 3, which produces the corresponding constant weight code. A random constant weight codeword is produced at each clock period of the SRC-6's 100 MHz clock. This accounts for 1,048,576 clock periods. However, a total of 1,048,770 clock periods are required. This includes 194 additional clock periods for initialization, data collection, and overhead. Neglecting the overhead, this constant weight codeword generator produces 100 million codewords per second. A C code version of the circuit in Fig. 3 was written and run on the SRC-6's 2.8 GHz Xeon microprocessor. Despite its much higher clock frequency, this implementation produced only 7.6 million random constant weight codewords per second.

## 2.4   Complexity of Implementation

To understand how the complexity of a $\binom{n}{r}$ combinatorial number system constant weight code generator depends on $n$ and $r$, we programmed this system for various $n$ and $r$. Because the SRC-6, with its 130 nm Xilinx Virtex 2p XC2VP100, is a legacy system, we chose the 40 nm Altera Stratix IV EP4SE530F43C3NES FPGA. This is to be used on the SRC Company's newest version of the SRC-7. Table 2 shows the frequency obtained and the resources used in this implementation. A large codeword is achievable (128 bits using 91% of the available ALMs). Although this table shows only balanced constant weight code generators where the number of bits is a power of 2, our approach applies to any number of bits and to any weight.

**Table 2.** Frequency and resources used to realize combinatorial number system constant weight code generators on the Altera Stratix IV EP4SE530F43C3NES FPGA

| Con. Wgt. Code $\binom{n}{r}$ | #Bits index | Freq. (MHz) | # of LUTs of Various Inputs | | | | | Est. # of Packed ALMs | Total # of Registers |
|---|---|---|---|---|---|---|---|---|---|
| | | | 7- | 6- | 5- | 4- | 3- | | |
| $\binom{4}{2}$ | 3 | 406.3 | 0 | 0 | 0 | 1 | 8 | 5(0%) | 10(0%) |
| $\binom{8}{4}$ | 7 | 310.2 | 0 | 0 | 23 | 30 | 14 | 37(0%) | 47(0%) |
| $\binom{16}{8}$ | 14 | 213.9 | 0 | 40 | 112 | 153 | 66 | 211(0%) | 198(0%) |
| $\binom{32}{16}$ | 30 | 179.7 | 2 | 453 | 719 | 915 | 377 | 1,461(0%) | 842(0%) |
| $\binom{64}{32}$ | 61 | 129.5 | 45 | 880 | 983 | 2,709 | 44,873 | 25,428(11%) | 3,443(0%) |
| $\binom{128}{64}$ | 125 | 95.8 | 163 | 1,422 | 15,902 | 14,551 | 354,448 | 194,950(91%) | 430,608(3%) |

The second column in Table 2 also shows the number of bits needed to represent index. Recall that index must be sufficiently large so that all $\binom{n}{r}$ values of the index can be uniquely represented. Specifically, the number of bits needed is $\lfloor log_2\binom{n}{r} \rfloor + 1$. A naive description in which this was computed as $\lfloor log_2 \frac{n!}{r!(n-r)!} \rfloor + 1$ was not able to give correct results for the bottom half of the table because of the very large value of $n!$. Therefore, this computation was performed as $\lfloor \sum_{i=1}^{n} log_2 i - 2 \sum_{i=1}^{n/2} log_2 i \rfloor + 1$. The Verilog compiler used to implement the circuits lacks the word size to compute $n!$ for moderate $n$. Also, it is not capable of computing the $log_2$ function. Instead, a MATLAB program was used. This produced values that were written to a header file that was included in the Verilog code. Similarly, to realize the circuits represented in Table 2, it was necessary to compute $\binom{n}{r}$, which cannot be realized by 32 bits for moderate values of $n$ and $r$. Another MATLAB program was written that computed these values and printed them to a header file that was included in the Verilog code.

# 3    Trellis Generator

## 3.1    Introduction

An alternative approach for generating random constant weight binary numbers is the trellis circuit. We know of no prior work on this approach except a description in a Japanese book [18] of a program to generate random constant weight codes. A hardware implementation of this is as follows. Fig. 4 shows the trellis circuit of a random constant-weight binary number generator with 6 bits of weight 3. Each bit is generated one at a time starting at top. A complete $n$-bit number is generated after $n$ clock periods. However, this circuit is pipelined, so that thereafter, a 6-bit binary number of weight 3 is generated at every clock period.

At the top node, the left bit is 0/1 with probability 50%/50%. Depending on this bit's actual value, control goes to the node labeled $\binom{5}{3}$ (0) or the node labeled $\binom{5}{2}$ (1). At this point, a similar process takes place. In this case, the

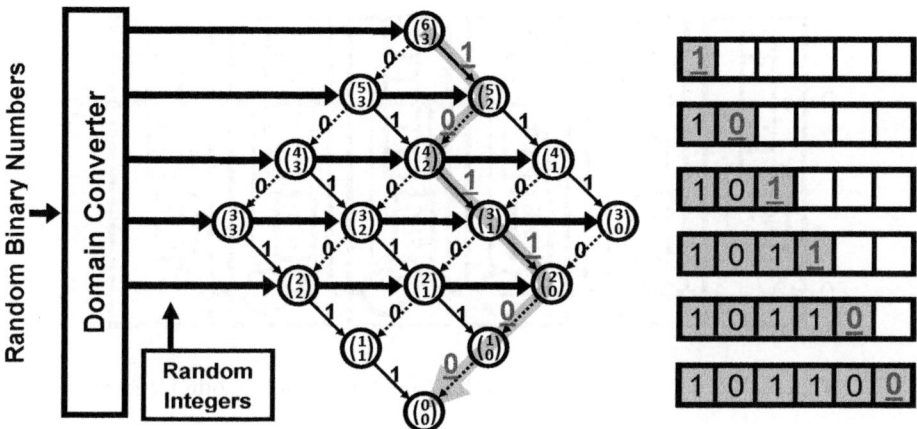

**Fig. 4.** Trellis Circuit

probability of a 0 or 1 bit adjusts so that each $n$-bit number of weight $r$ has the same probability as any other $n$-bit number of weight $r$. In the case of the node labeled $\binom{5}{3}$, 0 and 1 are generated with probability 40% and 60%, while, in the case of the node labeled $\binom{5}{2}$, 0 and 1 are generated with probability 60% and 40%.

The probabilities required for each level are generated by the circuit along the right side of Fig. 4. This circuit generates an integer between 0 and $m - 1 > 1$, where $m$ is the level. The top level corresponds to $m = n$, the next lower level to $m = n - 1$, etc.. The nodes in the trellis then convert this number into a 0 or 1, as needed at that node. For example, for $m = 4$, the right-side integer generator produces 0, 1, 2, and 3 with equal probability. For the node labeled $\binom{4}{3}$, a threshold of 1 is used to produce 0 with a probability of 25% (0) and 1 with a probability of 75% (1, 2, and 3). Similarly, the nodes labeled $\binom{4}{2}$ and $\binom{4}{1}$ use thresholds 2 and 3, respectively. We note that the generation of *one* uniformly distributed integer at level $n$ is sufficient because only one bit of a random constant-weight binary number is generated at that level.

## 3.2   Circuit Implementation

The trellis can be implemented by a pipeline with $n$ stages. In each stage, the (partially completed) constant weight code is processed and passed to the next stage, as suggested by the words shown along the right side of Fig. 4. Fig. 5 shows the pipeline implementation of the trellis circuit. The block labeled RNG (random number generator) in each stage determines exactly one bit. Whether it is a 0 or 1 is determined at random by a probability that depends on the number of 1 bits generated so far. For example, if all of the $r$ 1 bits occur in the previous stages, then the probability that a 0 is produced by RNG is 100%.

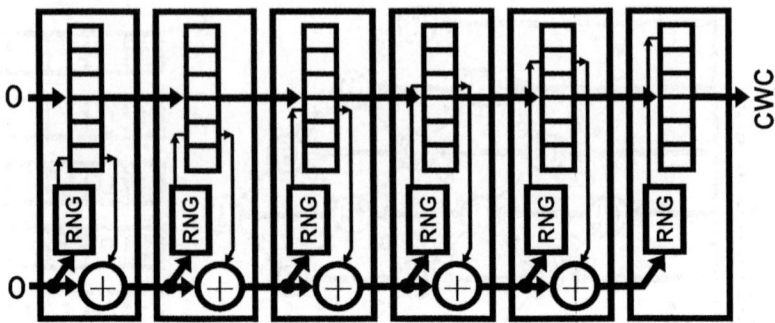

**Fig. 5.** Block Diagram of the Trellis Constant Weight Code Generator

## 3.3   Results

Fig. 6 shows the distribution of constant weight codes when 1,048,576 ($= 2^{20}$) sets of random numbers are generated and applied to the trellis circuit. This was programmed on the SRC-6. For the Xilinx Virtex2p XC2VP100 FPGA used in this system, the complete circuit uses 2,767 out of 88,192 4-input LUTs (3%) and 3,795 out of 88,192 slice flip-flops (4%). It can run at 106.2 MHz, which accommodates the SRC-6's fixed 100 MHz clock. It produces one constant weight codeword at each 100 MHz clock cycle, and takes a total of 1,048,766 clock cycles. This includes 90 clock periods in addition to those 1,048,576 clock cycles that each produce a constant weight codeword. Each level in the trellis uses a 16 bit random number generator that creates a random integer generator, as described above. Note that the resources just described include circuits needed to implement overhead functions like data collection. Neglecting the overhead, the trellis random constant weight codeword generator produces 100 million codewords per second. A C code version of the circuit in Fig. 5 was written and run on the SRC-6's 2.8 GHz Xeon microprocessor. Despite its much higher clock frequency, this implementation produced only 57.2 million random constant weight codewords per second.

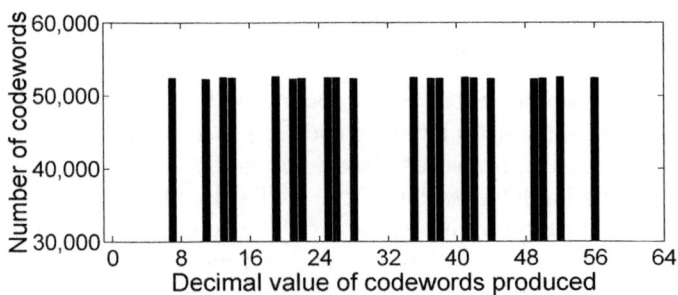

**Fig. 6.** Distribution of Constant Weight Codewords Produced by the Trellis Circuit

### 3.4 Complexity of Implementation

Like the combinatorial number system constant weight codeword generator, the trellis was programmed on the Altera Stratix IV EP4SE530F43C3NES FPGA. Table 3 shows the resource usage and frequency for various types of constant weight codewords. Unlike the combinatorial number system constant weight codeword generator, 256-bit constant weight codewords with 128 1's can be easily implemented within one FPGA. The Estimated Number of ALMs increases by a factor of more than 2 for each one line advance in Table 3. A similar statement is approximately true of the column labeled Total Number of Registers. The resources shown in Table 3 do not cover the circuits that perform the overhead functions, such as data collection; they include only the trellis circuit.

**Table 3.** Frequency and resources used to realize a trellis constant weight code generator on the Altera Stratix IV EP4SE530F43C3NES FPGA

| Con. Wgt. Code $\binom{n}{r}$ | Freq. (MHz) | # of LUTs of Various Inputs 7- | 6- | 5- | 4- | 3- | Est. # of Packed ALMs | Total # of Registers |
|---|---|---|---|---|---|---|---|---|
| $\binom{4}{2}$ | 487.6 | 0 | 0 | 1 | 24 | 83 | 42 (0%) | 65 (0%) |
| $\binom{8}{4}$ | 463.8 | 0 | 0 | 19 | 12 | 71 | 122 (0%) | 172 (0%) |
| $\binom{16}{8}$ | 344.4 | 0 | 6 | 28 | 33 | 281 | 358 (0%) | 444 (0%) |
| $\binom{32}{16}$ | 274.2 | 0 | 31 | 96 | 101 | 765 | 978 (0%) | 1,137 (0%) |
| $\binom{64}{32}$ | 250.2 | 0 | 71 | 289 | 365 | 1,994 | 2,839 (1%) | 3,387 (0%) |
| $\binom{128}{64}$ | 231.1 | 1 | 301 | 908 | 941 | 4,673 | 5,344 (2%) | 4,691 (1%) |
| $\binom{256}{128}$ | 174.9 | 1 | 2,757 | 2,363 | 10,653 | 4,673 | 11,309 (5%) | 8,011 (1%) |

## 4 Concluding Remarks

Although there is a need for a circuit that computes constant weight codewords from indices, we have not seen an implementation. Our results are useful, for example, in the encoding/decoding of data, such as between on-chip and off-chip and in asynchronous circuits. We show two approaches 1) a combinatorial number system implementation and a 2) trellis implementation. The combinatorial number system can be implemented as a pipeline producing a constant weight codeword at each clock. For a constant weight code of $n$ bits, of which $r$ are 1, the pipeline is $r$ stages long. If one only wants to produce random constant weight codewords, for example in Monte Carlo simulations, the trellis is also implemented efficiently. Its pipeline is $n$ stages long. The trellis requires less resources and operates at a higher frequency. We have implemented both designs on the SRC-6 reconfigurable computer and on an Altera Stratix IV EP4SE530F43C3NES FPGA. This has shown that both are efficiently implemented.

We remark on two extensions of our results. First, both circuits can be implemented as combinational logic. Indeed, the diagrams, Figs. 1 and 5, show them as combinational logic. Second, in both circuits, the probability of certain codewords can be controlled.

# References

1. Brouwer, A.E., Shearer, J.B., Sloane, N.J.A., Smith, W.D.: A new table of constant weight codes. IEEE Trans. Infor. Theory 36(6), 1134–1380 (1990)
2. Buckles, B.P., Lybanon, M.: Algorithm 515: Generation of a vector from the lexicographical index [G6]. ACM Transactions on Mathematical Software 3(2), 180–182 (1977)
3. Bubniak, G., Goralczyk, M., Karp, M., Kokosinski, Z.: A hardware implementation of a generator of (n,k)-combinations. In: Proc. IFAC Workshop Programmable Digital Systems, PDS 2004, Krakow, pp. 228–231 (2004)
4. Butler, J.T., Sasao, T.: Boolean functions for cryptography. In: Progress in Applications of Boolean Functions, pp. 33–54. Morgan & Claypool Publishers (2010)
5. Combinadic, http://en.wikipedia.org/wiki/Combinadic
6. Etherington, C.: An analysis of cryptographically significant functions with high correlation immunity by reconfigurable computer, M.S. Thesis (December 2010)
7. Gosper, R. W. Item 175 in Beeler, M., Gosper, R. W., and Schroeppel, R., HAKMEM, MIT Artificial Intelligence Laboratory, Memo AIM-239, Cambridge (February 1972), http://www.inwap.com/pdp10/hbaker/hakmem/hacks.html#item175
8. http://en.wikipedia.org/wiki/Side_channel_attack
9. Khan, M.M., Lester, D.R., Plana, L.A., Rast, A., Jin, X., Painkras, E., Furber, S.B.: SpiNNaker: mapping neural networks onto a massively-parallel chip multiprocessor. In: Inter. Joint Conf. on Neural Networks (IJCNN), pp. 2850–2857 (2008)
10. Knuth, D.E.: The Art of Computer Programming. Bitwise Tricks and Techniques 4(Fascicle 1), 152, ISBN 0-321-58050-8
11. Knuth, D.E.: The Art of Computer Programming. Generating All Combinations and Partitions 4(Fascicle 3), 5–6 (2009) ISBN 0-321-58050-8
12. Lehmer, D.H.: The machine tools of combinatorics. In: Beckenbach, E.F. (ed.) Applied Combinatorial Mathematics, pp. 5–30. Wiley, New York (1964)
13. MacWilliams, F.J., Sloane, N.J.A.: The Theory of Error-Correcting Codes. North-Holland, Amsterdam (1977)
14. Nijenhuis, A., Wilf, H.S.: Combinatorial Algorithms, 2nd edn. Academic Press, London (1978)
15. Montemanni, R., Smith, D.H.: Heuristic algorithms for contructing binary constant weight codes. IEEE Trans. on Inform. Theory 55(10), 4651–4656 (2010)
16. Rothaus, O.S.: On 'bent' functions. J. Combinatorial Theory, Ser. A 20, 300–305 (1976)
17. Sasao, T.: Memory Based Logic Synthesis, 1st edn. Springer, Heidelberg (2011) ISBN 978-1-4419-8103-5
18. Senba, I.: Combinatorial Algorithms (in Japanese). Science Inc., Tokyo (1989)
19. Shackleford, B., Tanaka, M., Carter, T., Snider, G.: High-performance cellular automata random number generators for embedded probabilistic computing systems. In: Proc. of 2002 NASA/DOD Conf. on Evolvable Hardware, July 2002, pp. 191–200. IEEE Computer Society, Los Alamitos (2002)

20. Shafer, J.L., Schneider, S.W., Butler, J.T., Stanica, P.: Enumeration of bent Boolean functions by reconfigurable computer. In: The 18th Annual Inter. IEEE Symp. on Field-Programmable Custom Comput. Mach. (FCCM 2010), Charlotte, NC, May 2-4, pp. 265–272 (2010)
21. Tallini, L.G., Bose, B.: Design of balanced and constant weight codes for VLSI systems. IEEE Trans. on Computers 47(5), 556–572 (1998)
22. Verhoeff, T.: Delay-insensitive codes - an overview. Distr. Comp. 3(1), 1–8 (1988)
23. Yamanaka, N., Shimizu, S., Shan, G.: Energy efficient network design tool for green IP/ethernet networks. In: ONDM 2010, Kyoto, Japan, January 31-February 3 (2010)

# On-Chip Ego-Motion Estimation Based on Optical Flow

Mauricio Vanegas[1,2], Leonardo Rubio[1], Matteo Tomasi[1],
Javier Diaz[1], and Eduardo Ros[1]

[1] Department of Computer Architecture and Technology, University of Granada,
C/ Periodista Daniel Saucedo, sn 18071 Granada, Spain
http://atc.ugr.es/atc.php?menu=personal
[2] PSPC-Group, Department of Biophysical and Electronic Engineering (DIBE),
University of Genoa, Via Opera Pia 11A, I-16145 Italy
mvanegas@atc.ugr.es

**Abstract.** A novel system on chip (SoC) is presented for estimating the
ego-motion of the vehicle based on optical flow cues. The main novelty
of the system consists in its implementation as an on-chip hybrid hard-
ware/software system. The improvements in the FPGA technology allows to have programmable logic resources accompanied by processors on
the same chip. In this way, inherently sequential tasks are implemented
as software modules executed in embedded general purpose processors
while hardware friendly modules are implemented in specific purpose
co-processing engines. The proposed SoC is capable of estimating ego-
motion by using the PowerPC available in the FPGA *XC4VFX60-10*
of Xilinx.

**Keywords:** Field programmable gate arrays; Machine vision; Real time
systems; Reconfigurable architectures.

## 1 Introduction

In recent years, accurate estimation of the ego-motion is considered one key feature for autonomous driving and driving assistance based on computer vision
[6] [8] . Here is presented a novel implementation of an ego-motion estimation
system in real time. The ego-motion estimation of a camera aims to determine
the 3D motion of that camera within the enviroment using a secuence of images
taken by the camera. The ego-motion is calculated based on optical flow cues
which are generated from a single camera as a system on chip (SoC). Ego-motion
calculation facilitates the development of other computer vision modules, such
as independent moving objects (IMOs) detection.

Most of ego-motion applications require real time implementation of a complex mathematical model. A pure software implementation can be achieved by
using GPU platforms, however these platforms are unsuitable for standalone
driving assistance. Application specific circuits (ASICs) offer the best performance in both time and power consumption, but they restrict any further design
flexibility. The FPGA technology can offer both the necessary design flexibility

A. Koch et al. (Eds.): ARC 2011, LNCS 6578, pp. 206–217, 2011.

and standalone capability regardless of its weakness compared to both GPUs and ASICs in their respective areas of interest. To construct a system suitable for being used as a standalone machine for driver assistance or for robot navigation is the motivation of the present work. The system was built on FPGA technology and was synthesized in a *Virtex4 XC4VFX60-10* of Xilinx [2].

The proposed SoC is mainly composed of two blocks. A pure hardware implementation of an optical flow model and a PowerPC in which is executed the software implementation (ANSI C) of the ego-motion algorithm. The optical flow core implements a phase-based optical flow method introduced by Gautama and Van Hulle [5]. The benefit of the proposed SoC lies in the ability to embed on-chip any ego-motion algorithm based on optical flow data. This provides a platform to run different algorithms and thus, allows us to analyze the different performances of each method.

The paper is organized as follows. Section 2 includes a brief literature review. In section 3 is briefly described the mathematical model for estimating ego-motion; in subsection 3.1 is explained the bilinear constraint equation in which is based most of the optical-flow-based ego-motion methods; also, in subsection 3.2 is depicted the Gautama and Van Hulle optical flow model. The entire system design is outlined in section 4. The section 5 contains a summary of ego-motion algorithms used for testing the system and their results over synthetic and real image sequences. Finally, section 6 presents the work conclusions and section 7 puts forward some ideas about future works.

## 2 Related Work

There is vast literature on ego-motion estimation, Bruss and Horn [3] introduced one of the first ego-motion algorithms which optimizes the squared Euclidean distance of the residual vector between the flow model and the flow estimates. The bilinear constraint derived from Bruss and Horn's study has been used by Heeger and Jepson [7] for building a linear subspace in which is eliminated the rotation and depth dependency of the bilinear constraint equation; thus, it avoids a priori estimation of these variables in the calculation of the 3D-translation variable. These two methods are examples of algorithms systematically biased which are highly susceptible of noisy-flow estimates. A more complex flow field is encountered when independent moving objects (IMOs) appear into the scenes, in this kind of environments the biased algorithms have poor performances. In the overall literature, there exist a sort of methods that can be denoted as optimal due to their unbiased behavior and minimal variance against IMOs in the scene. These algorithms have better results compared to biased algorithms when addressing complex flow estimates. Zhang and Tomasi [17] have proposed a Gauss-Newton iteration over bilinear constraint for estimating between rotation, depth, and translation. Pauwels and Van Hulle [11] used the Zhang and Tomasi's Gauss-Newton update in translation for illustrating their gradually-"unweight" method. Pauwels and Van Hulle argue a more robust method against local minima than those introduced by Bruss and Horn, Heeger and Jepson, and Zhang and Tomasi due to the non-decrease and upper-bound characteristics of the regularization parameter in which is based the gradually-"unweight" method.

A lot of optical flow models have been implemented in hardware [15,12]; also using FPGAs [10,4]; however, there are few systems related to ego-motion estimation for driving assistance. Stein and Mano [6] have proposed a method for computing the ego-motion of the vehicle by using the features of the road as a reference for the ego-motion and reduced the number of estimated parameters to a minimum of three. The method of calculation focuses on the roadway itself and assumes that it is a planar structure. All image structure above the road are considered outliers. Yamaguchi and Kato [8] proposed a method for estimating the ego-motion of the vehicle by selecting feature points using the detection results for moving objects in the previous frame. As the previous method, roadway region is segmented and used as center of interest. Our system does not use specific roadway features, which could be missing in different scenarios. Any stational object (building, bush, etc) could be used for ego-motion estimation. This facilitates the ego-motion estimation in different environments such as areas of open ground or even corridors for autonomous driving robots. Another important feature of our system is the calculation of 6 parameters for ego-motion. The system does not reduce parameters, it provides translation (3 parameters) and rotation (3 parameters), which are enough to define self-motion [9].The methods previously described in the literature [6] [8], postprocess the image sequence and do not work in real time.

## 3    Mathematical Model of the Ego-Motion Algorithm

Two optimal approaches to calculate the ego-motion are the minimization problems formulated by Pauwels and Van Hulle [11] and by Raudies and Neumann [13]. These algorithms are easily divided in two processes, the first process is responsible of the optical flow computation and the second process calculates the ego-motion estimation. The first process in charge of the optical flow, has an appropriate structure for its implementation as a pure hardware core [5]. On the other hand, the second process in charge of the ego-motion estimation has a lower computational load and is inherently iterative. Thus, the ego-motion process fits better as a software module, which is executed in the embedded PowerPC of the SoC and it allows quick development and implementation of different algorithms. In subsection 3.1 are briefly detailed the hardware approach of the optical flow model. Likewise, in subsection 3.2 is stated the mathematical process to calculate the ego-motion from optical flow data, as well as is outlined the algorithm which will be implemented in the PowerPC.

### 3.1    Phase-Based Algorithm

Among the different existing algorithms in the literature, we chose a simplified version of the phase-based optical flow method described in [5]. The original algorithm computes phase at 8 different spatial orientations and uses a multi-resolution scheme with a neural network to combine spatial scales information

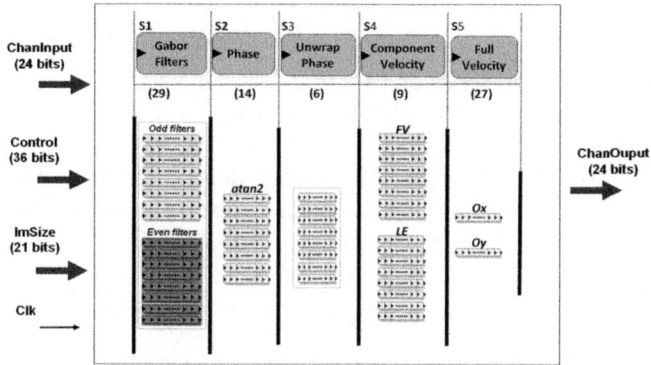

**Fig. 1.** Block diagram of the optical flow unit

and deal with large displacements. Our system can also be considered as a single-scale version of the model described in [14].

As shown in Fig. 1, the hardware architecture has different processing stages in a deep fine grain pipelined data path. The data path starts with a convolution process in which 8 quadrature pairs of Gabor filters, tuned at different phase orientations, are structured in a parallel arrangement for a maximum throughput. Then, the output of the previous stage is passed through the phase data path in which is estimated the local phase for each orientation (it includes the arctangent operation). Next, it is necessary unwrap the phase values considering their periodicity for temporal derivative estimate. Three temporal frames are used. The penultimate stage is the velocity component estimate; the velocity components are achieved from the phase at each orientation. Finally, a threshold operation based on confidence values is executed.

## 3.2  Ego-Motion Problem Statement

Longuet-Higgins and Prazdny demonstrated that an observer can determine the structure of a rigid scene and its direction of motion relative to it (ego-motion) from instantaneous retinal velocity field [9]. Their model is based on a hemispherical pinhole camera in arbitrary motion through a static environment. The camera has a focal length $f$ and it projects 3-D points $(X, Y, Z)$ onto 2-D image plane; assuming perspective projection the coordinates $(x, y)$ of the point $P$ in the image plane is defined as:

$$x = f\frac{X}{Z}, \quad y = f\frac{Y}{Z} \tag{1}$$

The motion at any instant can be described as contribution of two components: the translational velocity of the pinhole relative to the scene, and the angular velocity of the hemisphere about the pinhole, also measured relative to the scene. Thus, the ego-motion causes a 3-D instantaneous displacement that can be written as indicated in (2):

$$(\dot{X}, \dot{Y}, \dot{Z})^T = -(t_x, t_y, t_z)^T - (w_x, w_y, w_z)^T \times (X, Y, Z)^T \qquad (2)$$

where $T$ denotes the transpose of a vector, dots denote the first temporal derivative, $T = (t_x, t_y, t_z)$ is the translational velocity, and $W = (w_x, w_y, w_z)$ is the angular velocity.

The optical flow at each point in the image plane is the instantaneous velocity of the eye perception pattern at that point. Hence, the optical flow $U = (u, v)$ can be obtained differentiating in time expression (1) as follows:

$$u = \dot{x} = f\frac{\dot{X}}{Z} - f\frac{X\dot{Z}}{Z^2}, \quad v = \dot{y} = f\frac{\dot{Y}}{Z} - f\frac{Y\dot{Z}}{Z^2} \qquad (3)$$

Substituting (2) in (3) we arrive to the following expression:

$$U^T = \frac{1}{Z}AT^T + BW^T, A = \begin{bmatrix} -f & 0 & x \\ 0 & -f & y \end{bmatrix}, B = \begin{bmatrix} xy/f & -(x^2 + f^2)/f & y \\ (y^2 + f^2)/f & -xy/f & -x \end{bmatrix}$$
$$(4)$$

The matrix $A$ in (4) projects 3-D velocities onto the image plane orthogonal to the camera's optical axes. The parameter $Z$ is scene depth. Given that $T$ and $Z$ appear as a ratio in (4), their absolute magnitudes cannot be determined. The representation of the formulation was modified by Pauwels and Van Hulle and can be obtained from [11]. Raudies and Neumann [13] have introduced an accurate lineal method less computationally expensive than the proposed by Pauwels and Van Hulle. Raudies and Neumann proposed a lineal subspace from the bilinear constraint; the method is again a linear optimization problem in which, iteratively, is obtained the translation estimate and then the rotation estimate. The proposed algebraic transformation of the bilinear constraint can be obtained from [13].

To provide robustness against outliers, in the original implementation, Raudies and Neumman used RANSAC for a better adjustment in the translation estimates. RANSAC is an algorithm used to estimate iteratively parameters of a mathematical model from a set of observed data which contains outliers; since RANSAC is an iterative algorithm which is very computationally expensive, we replaced the RANSAC algorithm with a simple iterative execution; from now on, we will call it *R2-Iterative*. Just two iterations are done; in the first one it is estimated the ego-motion $(T, W)$ by using a small subset of optical flow data; this result is used to remove the wrong optical flow estimates from the optical flow data. In the second iteration, the ego-motion can be estimated by using all the remaining optical flow data, even by using a subset of these ones, obtaining high accuracy. It is important to highlight that an additional iteration does not significantly improve the accuracy of the estimates, but affects significantly the system throughput (egomotion estimations per second).

## 4    System Architecture

The performance of the proposed system (SoC) is highly dependent on the characteristics of the memory elements used. The whole system was built on

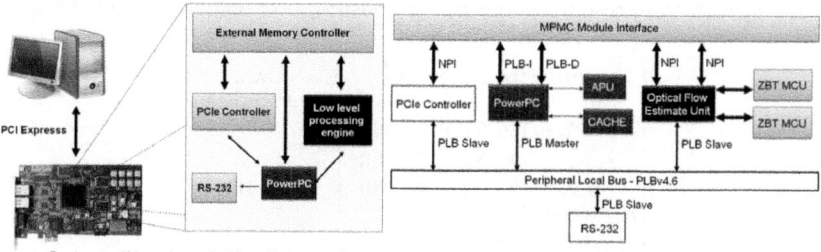

**Fig. 2.** Left Image: Block diagram of the SoC architecture. Right Image: Connection diagram of the SoC architecture.

a *XIRCA-V4* platform of the Seven Solution S.L. company [1]. The platform is equipped with one FPGA *XC4VFX60-10* of Xilinx which comprises two PowerPC processor blocks; two *DDR SDRAM* memory banks of 512Mb each one; four *ZBT SSRAM* memory chips of 72Mb (2M x 36) each one. Fig. 2 shows a scheme of the proposed SoC. The system is connected to a desktop computer through the *PCI Express* interface. Initially, a video frame is captured by using a web cam connected to the computer and then it is sent to the SoC through the *PCI Express* interface; the *PCI Express* controller writes in or reads from the *DDR SDRAM* directly. Once the video frame is processed on the FPGA chip, it sent to the host PC optical flow estimates and heading estimates. Even though the system is connected to a computer for capturing the video frames; it is easy to change the architecture for providing it with a frame grabber; in this way, both the *PCI Express* interface and the computer can be avoided.

All the processing units in the system can read from and write to the *DDR SDRAM* autonomously; however, the PowerPC is in charge of synchronizing the execution by using special registers. Also, each processing unit can manipulate its own memory space without inference of the rest of processing units. The execution starts when the PowerPC assigns the memory space which will be used by the rest of processing units; the memory space is distributed in such a way that the computer writes the video frame in current time $t_0$ while the optic flow unit is processing the video frame in time $t_{-1}$. The execution of the ego-motion algorithm in the PowerPC begins when the optical flow unit has calculated the optical flow estimates; these two processes are executed sequentially with respect to each other.

In Fig. 2 is exhibit a connection diagram of the SoC. In the system, just the PowerPC is connected as a master in the PLB and the rest ones are slaves; this entails a centralized processing scheme in which the PowerPC is the central processing unit.

In Fig. 2 are also included an auxiliary processor unit (APU) configured as a floating-point unit. This APU is connected in order to improve the performance of the PowerPC when a lot of mathematical operations need to be executed; likewise, the mathematical operations used in the estimation of ego-motion require floating-point precision. On the other hand, the optical flow unit uses fixed-point

**Table 1.** Hardware resources and power consumption on a XC4FX60-10 device

| | Hardware Resources | | Power |
|---|---|---|---|
| Entity | Used | Available | Consumption |
| *Flip-Flops* | 36.062 | 50.560 | |
| *LUTs* | 40.614 | 50.560 | |
| *Slices* | 25.090 | 25.280 | 3,5 *W* |
| *RAMB16s* | 127 | 232 | |
| *DSP48s* | 120 | 128 | |

arithmetic; the mathematical operations for estimating optical flow can be performed using fixed-point precision in such a way that the integer part uses 8 bits in signed logic and the fractional part uses 4 bits; the resultant optical flow estimate is 12 bits length for each component of the optical flow vector (see $(O_x, O_y)$ in Fig. 1). Also, the optical flow unit has a specific memory control unit (MCU) [16]. The MCU offers a solution to the problem of multiple entities needing access shared-data at maximum throughput; This is of high interest for the optical flow unit which has multiple processing data-paths needing access memory concurrently. The full system implementation within the FPGA XC4VFX60-10 has a power and resources consumption shown in table 1.

## 5    System Validation

The proposed system architecture can execute any ego-motion algorithm based on optical flow estimates. To demonstrate this, we have chosen the two methods mentioned in 3.1; these methods were described using C language and executed in the SoC yealding some interesting results. There is a huge difference in time consumption according to the computational complexity of the methods used. The linear method proposed by Raudies and Neumann does not require initialization and therefore, it is better suited for real-time applications. It is important to highlight that our test is focused in the run-time of the algorithms, but not in the accuracy of the ego-motion estimates; a detailed study about the run-time and the accuracy of different ego-motion algorithms was done in [13], the contribution presented here, shows the results of the Pauwels and Van Hulle, and the Raudies and Neumann model, both of them running in the FPGA XC4VFX60-10. In Fig. 3 is shown the SoC performance with respect to the number of optical flow vectors used for estimating the ego-motion; the algorithm was executed one time in both cases. One iteration is enough for achieve the ego-motion estimation in the Raudies and Neumann algorithm, although for the Pauwels and Van Hulle one iteration does not mean that a global minimum is reached.

The non-linear methods means that a large number of initializations must be used in order to achieve better results; Pauwels and Van Hulle demonstrated that just fifteen initializations were enough to reach an optimum value. According to the aforementioned, we gave more emphasis in the Raudies and Neumann model. We tested the Raudies and Neumann method by using two synthetic

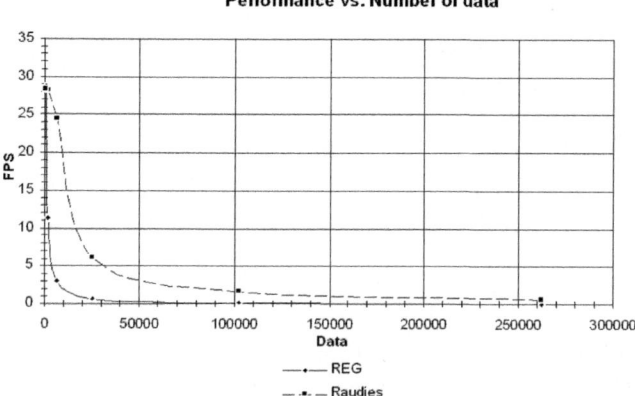

**Fig. 3.** Performance in frames per second (fps) with respect to the number of optical flow vectors used for estimating ego-motion executed in the FPGA XC4VFX60-10. *REG* corresponds to the Pauwels and Van Hulle's ego-motion estimation model [11]; this performs "only" one initialization (typically 15 are used in practical applications). *Raudies* is the lineal estimation method proposed by Raudies and Neumann [13]; no additional iterations.

optical flow field. *Flow 1* is estimated by the parameters $\alpha = 0°$ and $\beta = 0°$, and *Flow 2* is estimated by the parameters $\alpha = 30°$ and $\beta = 0°$. Also, an independent moving object (IMO) was added that corresponds to the 25% of the image size (320x240). There is also added a normal-distributed noise to the optical flow. With this data set, the SoC and the proposed *R2-Iterative* modification is validated (Fig. 4). The results are shown in the Fig. 5. In comparation with a not noise data set, this time, the *Serie 1* is quite affected by the noisy optical flow field, but even so, the *Serie 2* shows that the *R2-Iterative* variant works fine even in presence of outliers.

Fig. 6 shows how many images can be processed in the system per second according to the number of optical flow vectors used for estimating the ego-motion. Note that the optical flow is always estimated in images 320x240 size. Taking into account the results showed in Fig. 4 and in Fig. 5, the system can perform an ego-motion estimation by using down to 1200 optical flow vectors and even so it can obtain high accuracy; thus, the system can process 14 frames per second which make it suitable for real time driving assistance and robotic applications.

Finally, we test the reliability of the system with a real sequence. The video was recorded with a front view camera. The image sequence has a resolution of 320x256 pixels and 30 FPS. As we are dealing with a real world sequence, this implies that we have not ground truth for the ego-motion to be compared with our results. Therefore, we represent the heading by projecting the ego-motion vector on the image plane. Fig. 7 shows a frame of the processed sequence which represent a typical road images. On the other side of the image, is shown the optical flow generated and the projections of the three headings. We can not determine which method has the best performance, although we can conclude

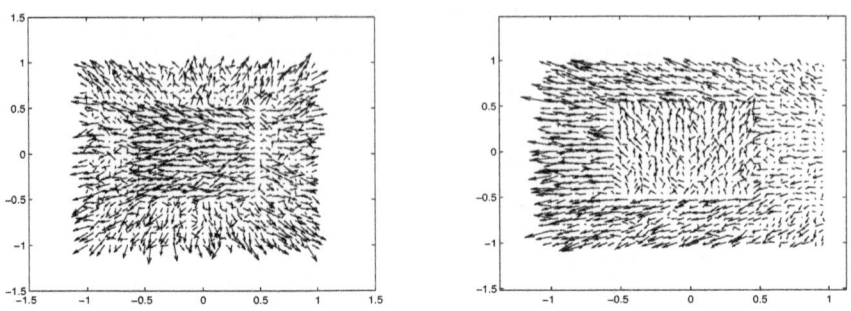

**Fig. 4.** Synthetic optical flow fields with a normal-distributed noise. The IMO is the 25% of the image size (320x240). The variance of the noise is about 10%.

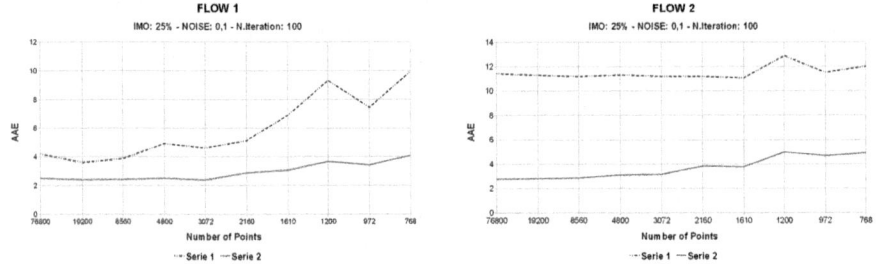

**Fig. 5.** Average absolute error measured on each iteration according to the number of optical flow vectors used in the estimation for a noisy optical flow field

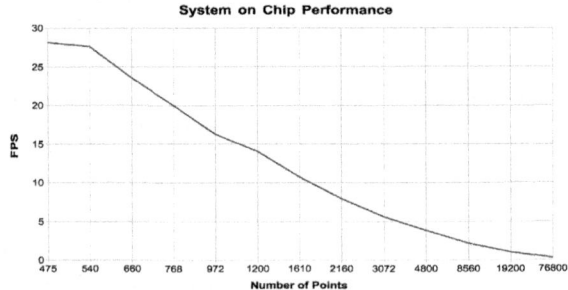

**Fig. 6.** Performance of the System on Chip according to the number of optical flow vectors used for estimating the ego-motion

that both methods produced similar results. As we can see in the figure, Raudies method and the proposed method have different outcomes despite having the same algorithm. This variation is attributed to two main factors. The first one is the implementation mechanisms that have been used in each case, MATLAB in the case of Raudies and ANSI C in the proposed method. The second factor

**Fig. 7.** A)Frame of the real sequence 320x256 pixels.B)Optical flow of the real sequence. The cross, the circle and the diamond; represent the projection on the image plane of the heading calculated by Pauwels et al [11], Raudies et al [13] and the implementation in the PPC respectively.

lies in the execution platform. In the first method the optical flow is processed in double precision, floating-point format, while for the second method, the optical flow is processed in fix point format in the hardward and transferred to the PowerPC where the format is changed again to single precision floating-point. Due all these changes and format restrictions, we can notice a difference in the final estimation of the ego-motion.

## 6   Conclusions

We have introduced a novel system on chip architecture. This system can execute any ego-motion estimation model based on optical flow estimates. Its versatility is demonstrated by using two ego-motion models namely, a non-linear method that needs several initializations for achieving good results and, a linear method that represents, a priori, the better option for real-time ego-motion applications. The proposed SoC can be easily modified in order to increase its computational capabilities. The instruction set of the PowerPC can be extended and specific image operators can be added. Even, more engines as the optical flow estimate unit can be easily connected within the SoC. The computational capabilities of the SoC cannot be compared with current CPU's and GPU's computational capabilities; however, this system has a low electrical consumption and the technology used makes it suitable for standalone application. A comprehensive analysis must be done in order to validate the *R2-Iterative* variant; nonetheless, the SoC can be customized providing it of specific processing data-paths to increase the system throughput. In this way, the system will not depend on the effectiveness of the *R2-Iterative* variant for being it used in real time applications.

   If we compare the system with the state-of-the-art, we note that the SoC is capable of processing the image in situ instead of an offline postprocessing. Our work also present a validation method based on the generation of synthetic optical flow where the ground truth is known. In terms of frames per second

(FPS), the proposed system reaches a speed of 28 FPS in situ, and performance comparison with other approaches for heading estimation in the literature is difficult, since most authors focus on the accuracy of the models, but not on the performance (in terms of frames per second) or the computational load of the proposed models.

## 7  Future Work

The ego-motion estimate can be used in autonomous navigation. In this line, the SoC needs to be standalone, that means, the current architecture must be modified in order to add a frame grabber to avoid the connection to the host computer. Besides, the ego-motion process can be accelerated by using hardware resources available in the FPGA for speeding up the processes, this means, it needs to migrate some part of the ego-motion algorithm to hardware. The system can be also used to solve the problem of accurately detecting independent moving objects (IMOs). The work will focus on the development of a SoC for the automotive sector with IMO detection capabilities.

## Acknowledgment

This work has been supported by the Programme Alβan, the European Union Programme of High Level Scholarships for Latin America, scholarship No. (E06D101749CO), the Spanish Grants DINAM-VISION (DPI2007-61683), RECVIS (TIN2008-06893-C03-02), P06-TIC-02007 and TIC-3873. The authors especially thank to Karl Pauwels for providing a MATLAB version of his ego-motion algorithm. Also thank to Florian Raudies and Heiko Neumann for online access of their ego-motion algorithm in a C version, http://www.informatik.uni-ulm.de/ni/mitarbeiter/FRaudies/ego_motion/ego_motion.htm.

## References

1. Seven solution s.l., sevensols, seven Solutions is a technology-based company specialized in design of processing systems (2006)
2. Xilinx Inc., Xilinx Datasheet Virtex4 Family Features (2007)
3. Bruss, A.R., Horn, B.K.P.: Passive navigation. Computer Vision, Graphics, and Image Processing 21(1), 3–20 (1983)
4. Díaz, J., Ros, E., Agís, R., Bernier, J.L.: Superpipelined high-performance optical flow computation architecture. CVIU (122), 262–273 (2008)
5. Gautama, T., Van Hulle, M.: A phase-based approach to the estimation of the optical flow field using spatial filtering. IEEE Trans. on Neural Networks 13(5), 1127–1136 (2002)
6. Gideon, P., Stein, O.M., Shashua, A.: A robust method for computing vehicle ego-motion. In: Intelligent Vehicles Symposium, pp. 362–368 (2000)
7. Heeger, D.J., Jepson, A.D.: Subspace methods for recovering rigid motion i: algorithm and implementation. Int. J. Comput. Vision 7(2), 95–117 (1992)

8. Koichiro Yamaguchi, T.K., Ninomiya, Y.: Vehicle ego-motion estimation and moving object detection using a monocular camera. In: 18th International Conference on Pattern Recognition, ICPR 2006, pp. 610–613 (2006)
9. Longuet-Higgins, H.C., Prazdny, K.: The interpretation of a moving retinal image. Royal Society of London Proceedings Series B 208, 385–397 (1980)
10. Martn, J.L., Zuloaga, A., Cuadrado, C., Lzaro, J., Bidarte, U.: Hardware implementation of optical flow constraint equation using fpgas. CVIU 98(3) (2005)
11. Pauwels, K., Hulle, M.M.V.: Optimal instantaneous rigid motion estimation insensitive to local minima. CVIU 104(1), 77–86 (2006)
12. Pudas, M., Viollet, S., Ruffier, F., Kruusing, A., Amic, S., Leppvuori, S., Franceschini, N.: A miniature bio-inspired optic flow sensor based on low temperature co-fired ceramics (ltcc) technology. Sensors and Actuators A: Physical (2007)
13. Raudies, F., Neumann, H.: An efficient linear method for the estimation of ego-motion from optical flow. In: Denzler, J., Notni, G., Süße, H. (eds.) DAGM 2009. LNCS, vol. 5748, pp. 11–20. Springer, Heidelberg (2009)
14. Sabatini, S.P., Gastaldi, G., Solari, F., Pauwels, K., Hulle, M.V., Daz, J., Ros, E., Pugeault, N., Krger, N.: Compact and accurate early vision processing in the harmonic space. In: In The Harmonic Space. VISAPP (2007)
15. Török, L., Zarándy, A.: Analog-vlsi, array-processor-based, bayesian, multi-scale optical flow estimation: Research articles. Int. J. Circuit Theory Appl., 49–75 (2006)
16. Vanegas, M., Tomasi, M., Díaz, J., Ros, E.: Multi-port abstraction layer for fpga intensive memory exploitation applications. Journal Sys. Arch. (56), 442–451 (2010)
17. Zhang, T., Tomasi, C.: Fast, robust, and consistent camera motion estimation. In: IEEE Comp. Society Conf. on Comp. Vision and Pattern Recog., vol. 1 (1999)

# Comparison between Heterogeneous Mesh-Based and Tree-Based Application Specific FPGA

Umer Farooq, Husain Parvez, Zied Marrakchi, and Habib Mehrez

LIP6, Université Pierre et Marie Curie
4 Place Jussieu BC 167, 75005 Paris, France
{umer.farooq,parvez.husain,zied.marrakchi,habib.mehrez}@lip6.fr

**Abstract.** An application specific FPGA (ASIF) is an FPGA with reduced flexibility and improved density. A heterogeneous ASIF is reduced from a heterogeneous FPGA for a predefined set of applications. This work presents a new tree-based heterogeneous ASIF and uses two sets of open core benchmarks to explore the effect of lookup table (LUT) and arity size on it. For tree-based ASIF, LUT size is varied from 3 to 7 while arity size is varied from 4 to 8 and 16. Experimental results show that smaller LUTs with higher arity sizes produce good area results. However, smaller LUTs produce worse results in terms of delay. Further experimental results show that for tree-based ASIF, the combination LUT 4 with arity 16 for SET I and LUT 3 with arity 16 for SET II gives best results in terms of area-delay product. Area comparison between mesh and tree-based ASIFs shows that tree-based ASIF gives 11.27% routing area gain for SET I and gives almost same area results for SET II while consuming 70.30% and 69.80% less wires for SET I and SET II benchmarks respectively. Finally the quality analysis shows that tree-based ASIF produces around 18% better results compared to mesh-based ASIF.

## 1   Introduction

Field Programmable Gate Arrays (FPGAs) offer a convenient and economical solution for low volume application production as they are easy to design and program in a short time. However the reconfigurability of FPGAs makes them unsuitable for high performance and high volume applications as they are larger, slower and more power consuming than their ASIC (Application Specific Integrated Circuits) counterparts [4]. ASICs, on the other hand, have a higher non-recurring engineering (NRE) cost and time to market. This issue is addressed by the introduction of Structured-ASICs which comprise of an array of optimized logic elements that can implement desired functionality by making changes to a few upper mask layers [14]. However, Structured-ASICs loose their flexibility once they are programmed. On the contrary, an ASIF comprises of an array of optimized logic and routing resources like Structured-ASIC but is flexible enough that it can implement a set of predetermined applications that operate at mutually exclusive times. Generalized example of an ASIF for a set of 3 applications is shown in Fig. 1. When an FPGA-based product is in its final phase of development and if the circuits being mapped on it are known, it can be reduced for the given set of circuits. These circuits can be executed on ASIF at mutually exclusive times by loading their respective bitstreams. A mesh-based heterogeneous ASIF was presented in [11]

A. Koch et al. (Eds.): ARC 2011, LNCS 6578, pp. 218–229, 2011.

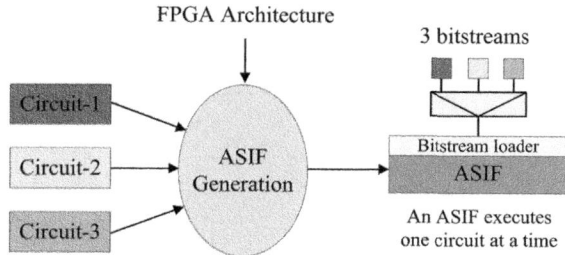

**Fig. 1.** Generalized Example of an ASIF

where authors have shown that for a set of predetermined applications an ASIF is 85% smaller than a unidirectional mesh-based FPGA.

In this work a new tree-based heterogeneous ASIF is presented and it is compared with mesh-based heterogeneous ASIF. The two architectures differ from each other on the basis of structural arrangement of logic and routing resources. In a mesh-based architecture resources are arranged in island-style while in tree-based architecture resources are arranged in a hierarchical manner. Before comparing the two architectures, a detailed exploration is performed to determine the best LUT size[1] and arity size[2] for tree-based ASIF. Usually when LUT size (K) or arity size (N) is increased, the functionality of base-cluster of the architecture is also increased which reduces overall number of base-clusters that are required to implement a certain function. But on the other hand, area of base-cluster increases with increase in K or N. So an increase in K or N may increase base-cluster functionality and decrease the total number of base-clusters that are required to implement a certain benchmark. But it can leave a bad effect on the overall area of the architecture due to increased area of base-clusters. So, in this work we explore the effect of K and N on a heterogeneous tree-based ASIF and seek the answer of following questions:**(1)**What is the effect of K and N on a tree-based ASIF? **(2)** What is the combination of K and N that gives the best results for tree-based ASIF? **(3)** What does the best combination of tree-based ASIF give when compared to mesh-based ASIF?

The remainder of the paper is organized as follows: Section 2 gives a brief overview of the mesh and tree-based heterogeneous FPGA and section 3 describes their associated software flow. Later these FPGA architectures are reduced to their respective ASIFs. Section 4 details ASIF generation technique. Section 5 presents experimental results and section 6 finally concludes this paper and presents some future work.

## 2   Reference FPGA Architectures

### 2.1   Mesh-Based FPGA Architecture

The architecture used in this work is a VPR-style (Versatile Place & Route) [7] architecture that contains configurable logic blocks (CLBs), I/Os and hard-blocks (HBs) that

---

[1] No of inputs in a lookup table (LUT).

[2] No of LUTs grouped in one cluster at the base level of a tree-based architecture. In this work, the cluster at the base level of the architecture is termed as base-cluster.

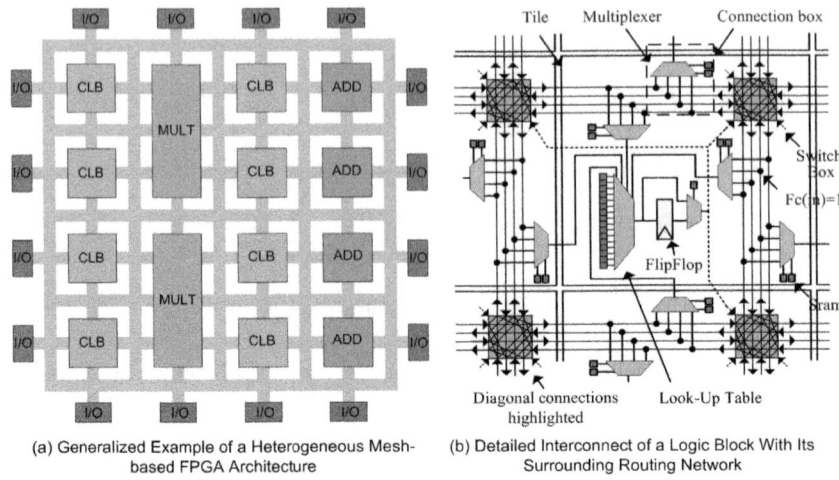

(a) Generalized Example of a Heterogeneous Mesh-based FPGA Architecture

(b) Detailed Interconnect of a Logic Block With Its Surrounding Routing Network

**Fig. 2.** Mesh-based Heterogeneous FPGA

are arranged on a two dimensional grid. In order to incorporate HBs in a mesh-based FPGA, the size of HBs is quantized with size of the smallest block of the architecture i.e. CLB. The width and height of an HB is therefore a multiple of width and height of the smallest block in the architecture. A generalized example of mesh-based heterogeneous FPGA architecture is shown in Fig. 2(a). A block (referred as CLB or HB) is surrounded by a uniform length, single driver, unidirectional routing network [6]. An example of a detailed routing interconnect of a CLB with its surrounding routing network is shown in Fig. 2(b) where CLB contains one LUT that has 4 inputs and 1 output. The routing network uses disjoint switch box to connect different routing tracks together. The connectivity of the routing channel with the input and output pins of a block, abbreviated as Fcin and Fcout, is set to be 1. The channel width is varied according to the netlist requirement but remains a multiple of 2 [6].

## 2.2   Tree-Based FPGA Architecture

A heterogeneous tree-based architecture [9] is a hierarchical architecture having unidirectional interconnect. In this architecture CLBs, I/Os and HBs are partitioned into a multilevel clustered structure where each cluster contains sub clusters and switch blocks allow to connect external signals to sub-clusters. Fig. 3(a) shows a four-level, arity-4, tree-based architecture. In a heterogenous tree-based architecture, CLBs and I/Os are placed at the bottom of hierarchy whereas HBs can be placed at any level of hierarchy to meet the best design fit.

Tree-based architecture contains two unidirectional, single length, interconnect networks: a downward network and an upward network. Downward network is based on butterfly fat tree topology and allows to connect signals coming from other clusters to its sub-clusters through a switch block. The upward network is based on hierarchy and it allows to connect sub-cluster outputs to other sub-clusters in the same cluster and

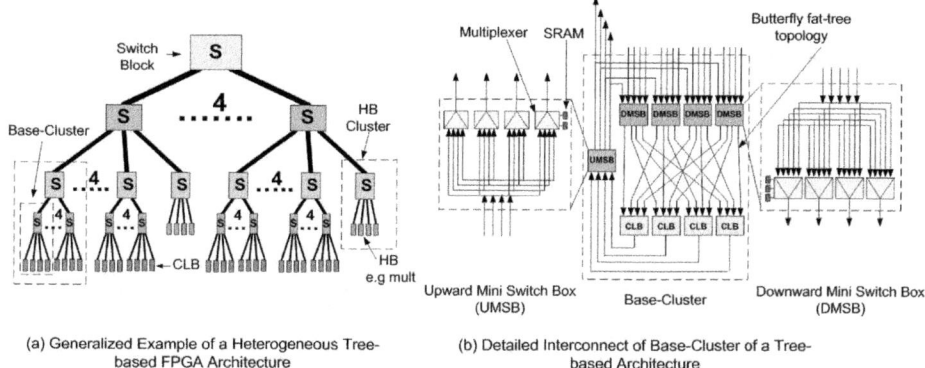

(a) Generalized Example of a Heterogeneous Tree-based FPGA Architecture

(b) Detailed Interconnect of Base-Cluster of a Tree-based Architecture

**Fig. 3.** Tree-based Heterogeneous FPGA

to clusters in other levels of hierarchy. A detailed base-cluster example of two inter-connect networks is shown in Fig. 3(b). In this figure, base-cluster contains 4 CLBs where each CLB contains one LUT with 4 inputs and one output. It can be seen from the figure that switch blocks are further divided into downward and upward mini switch boxes (DMSBs & UMSBs). These DMSBs and UMSBs are unidirectional full cross bar switches that connect signals coming into the cluster to its sub-clusters and signals going out of a cluster to other clusters of hierarchy. The number of DMSBs in a switch block of a cluster at level $\ell$ are equal to number of inputs of a cluster at level $\ell - 1$ and the number of UMSBs in a cluster at level $\ell$ are equal to number of outputs of a cluster at level $\ell - 1$. The number of signals entering into and leaving from the cluster can be varied depending upon the netlist requirement. The signal bandwidth of clusters is controlled using Rent's rule [5] which is easily adapted to tree based architecture. This rule states that

$$
IO = \left( \underbrace{k.n^{\ell}}_{L.B(p)} + \underbrace{\sum_{x=1}^{z} a_x.b_x.n^{(\ell-\ell_x)}}_{H.B(p)} \right)^{p}
\tag{1}
$$

where

$$
H.B(p) = \begin{cases} 0 & if(\ell - \ell_x < 0) \\ a_x.b_x.n^{(\ell-\ell_x)} & if(\ell - \ell_x \geq 0) \end{cases}
\tag{2}
$$

In (1) $\ell$ is a tree level, $n$ is the arity size, $k$ is the number of in/out pins of a LUT, $a_x$ is the number of in/out pins of a HB, $\ell_x$ is the level where HB is located, $b_x$ is the number of HBs at the level where it is located and $IO$ is the number of in/out pins of a cluster at level $\ell$. Since there can be more than one type of HBs, their contribution is accumulated and then added to the $L.B(p)$ part of (1) to calculate $p$. The value of $p$ is a factor that determines the cluster bandwidth at each level of the tree-based architecture and it is averaged across all the levels to determine the $p$ for the architecture.

**Fig. 4.** Software Flow

## 3   Software Flow

The software flow used to place and route different benchmarks (netlists) on the two architectures is shown in Fig. 4. The flow starts with the conversion of vst (structured vhdl) file to BLIF format [1]. The BLIF file is then passed through PARSER-1 which removes HBs from the file and passes it to SIS [12] that synthesizes it into LUT format of a given size (K). The file is then passed to T-VPACK [8] which packs and converts it into net format. A netlist in net format contains CLBs and I/O instances that are connected together using nets. The size of a CLB is defined as the number of LUTs contained in it and in this work this size is set to be 1 for both mesh and tree-based architectures. After T-VPACK the netlist is passed through PARSER-2 that adds previously removed HBs and finally it is placed and routed separately on tree-based and mesh-based FPGAs.

For tree-based architecture, the netlist obtained in net format is first partitioned using a partitioner [3]. Partitioner partitions CLBs, HBs and I/Os into clusters of given size (N) in such a way that the inter-cluster communication is minimized. Once partitioning is done, placement file is generated that contains positions of different instances of netlist on the architecture. The placement file along with netlist file is then passed to router which is responsible for the routing of netlist. Router is based on PathFinder [10] routing algorithm that uses an iterative, negotiation-based approach to successfully route all nets in a netlist.

For mesh-based architecture, the netlist file is passed to placer that uses simulated annealing algorithm [13] to place CLBs, HBs and I/Os on their respective blocks in FPGA. The main objective of the placer is to place connected instances close to each other in such a way that the sum of half-perimeters of the bounding boxes of the associated nets is minimized. The bounding box (BBX) of a net is a minimum rectangle that contains the driver instance and all receiving instances of a net. Placer moves an instance randomly from one block position to another, the BBX cost is updated and depending on cost value and annealing temperature, the operation is accepted or rejected. After placement, pathfinder [10] based router routes the netlist on the architecture.

Once the routing process is over, area of the FPGA is calculated separately for mesh and tree-based architectures using a generic area model. The area of an FPGA architecture is the sum of the logic area and routing area of the architecture. The area of all the CLBs and HBs of the architecture constitute the logic area of the architecture while the area of interconnect multiplexors and their associated programming bits is combined together to give the routing area of the architecture. Area model is based on SXLIB [2] that works on unit Lambda ($\lambda$). Since an ASIF is a reduced form of reference FPGA architecture, the area model of ASIF is also based on the area model of FPGA except that ASIF area contains only the used architecture resources.

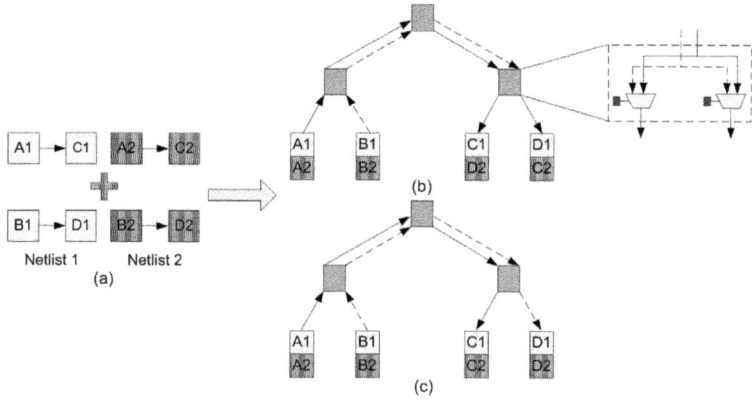

**Fig. 5.** Efficient Logic Resource Sharing

## 4    ASIF Generation

Reconfigurability of FPGAs is their biggest asset but it is also their largest drawback. Customized reconfigurable architectures like ASIF can reduce the overheads of FPGA while maintaining a certain degree of flexibility. In order to generate an ASIF, first a common FPGA architecture is defined. Netlists are then efficiently placed and routed on the architecture and later all unused resources are removed to generate an ASIF. Conventional placement/partitioning, routing algorithms do not consider the inter-netlist dependance. So these algorithms are modified to efficiently share the logic and routing resources of the architecture.

### 4.1    Efficient Logic Resource Sharing

Efficient logic sharing is mainly associated with placement/partitioning algorithms and it is achieved by simultaneously mapping a set of pre-defined netlists on the architecture in such a way that the inter-netlist dependance is optimized without compromising the intra-netlist optimization. Inter-netlist optimization can be understood with the help of Fig. 5. Fig. 5(a) shows two simple netlists, Fig. 5(b) shows mapping of two netlists on a simple tree-based ASIF where inter-netlist dependance is not considered and in Fig. 5(c) two netlists are efficiently mapped on the architecture which can eventually lead to smaller number of switches compared to the inefficient mapping.

$$\text{Cost} = ((W * BBX) + ((100 - W) * DC * \text{NormalizationFactor})) / 100$$
$$\text{Where } 0 \leq W \leq 100, \text{NormalizationFactor} = \text{Initial BBX} / \text{Initial DC} \qquad (3)$$
$$BBX = \text{Bounding Box Cost}, DC = \text{Driver Count Cost}$$

For mesh-based ASIF, efficient logic sharing is performed by simultaneously mapping multiple netlists on the architecture where the mapping of multiple instances of different netlists is allowed on each block position but, multiple instances of the same netlist are not allowed on the same block position. Inter-netlist dependance is optimized by modifying the existing cost function. In new cost function (ref Equation 3), intra-netlist placement is optimized by minimizing BBX cost and inter-netlist placement is optimized by minimizing Driver Count (DC) cost. DC cost is the sum of the driver blocks targeting the receiver blocks of the architecture over all the netlists of the group. If more driver instances of different netlists share a common position on the architecture and their respective receiver instances also share a common position then DC cost is said to be small and vice-versa. As DC cost and BBX cost are not of the same magnitude, they are made comparable by using a normalization factor. The influence of the two costs on the total cost of the function is controlled by factor "W". For our experimentation the value of "W" is set to be 80 because it gives best area results.

For tree-based ASIF, efficient partitioning is achieved by simultaneously partitioning multiple netlists. The partitioning of the netlists starts with the top level of the biggest netlist of the group. Once the top level of the netlist is partitioned, certain number of driver instances and their associated receiver instances are flagged to perform the inter-netlist optimization. Before partitioning the top level of next netlist, the corresponding instances of the netlist are fixed in the same partition as those of the flagged ones of the previous netlist while the rest of the netlist is passed to partitioner for intra-netlist optimization. In this way partitioning continues until the bottom of hierarchy is reached. Although by using this technique we are able to have same driver and receiver positions for a fixed number of instances and propagate these positions through all the netlists of the group, it can severely damage the intra-netlist optimization of the netlists and increase overall area of the ASIF. So, similar to placement function of mesh-based ASIF, 85% instances of each netlist are partitioned using intra-netlist optimization while 15% are reserved to serve the inter-netlist optimization purpose.

## 4.2   Efficient Routing Resource Sharing

Efficient routing resource sharing is associated with the routing algorithm which is modified to better utilize the architecture resources. This algorithm is common for both architectures and modification performed in it are detailed below.

Before we present the changes, a brief overview of basic routing algorithm is presented here. In the routing network, routing resources are modeled as a directed graph $G(N, E)$ where set of nodes $N$ represents the wires of the network and set of edges $E$ represents the potential connections between the nodes. Routing algorithm uses a negotiation based iterative approach to successfully route all nets of the netlist. During each iteration, individual nets of the netlist are routed using a congestion driven shortest path algorithm. However, at the end of an iteration there might be conflicts as different nets use same nodes. So congestion parameters of the nodes are updated and iteration is repeated until either the routing algorithm succeeds (i.e. there are no conflicts) or it fails. Multiple netlists are routed on the network by allowing the sharing of nodes by multiple nets of different netlists. However, nets of same netlist are not allowed to share a node.

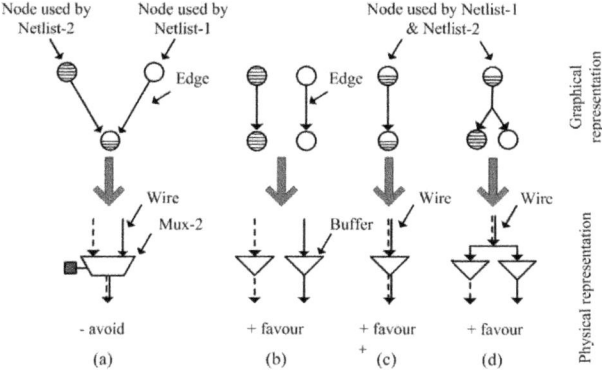

(a) Nodes use different edges to drive same node (b) Nodes use different edges to drive different nodes
(c) Node uses the same edge to drive same node (d) Node uses different edges to drive different nodes

**Fig. 6.** Efficient Routing Resource Sharing

| (Normal) | Cost(n) = CongestionCost(n) | |
|---|---|---|
| (Avoid) | Cost(n) = (1 + Factor) * CongestionCost(n) | (4) |
| (Prefer) | Cost(n) = (1 − Factor) * CongestionCost(n) | |
| | Where $0 \leq$ Factor $\leq 0.99$ | |

The efficient wire sharing can be best understood with the help of examples shown in Fig. 6. In order to reduce total number of switches, the examples in Fig. 6 suggest that while routing different nets of different netlists, case (a) must be avoided and cases (b), (c) and (d) must be supported. These cases are better exploited with abundant routing resources in the FPGA architecture. For this reason, the comparison between mesh and tree architectures is performed for a varying range of signal bandwidths. In order to avoid the undesirable cases and favor the preferred ones, the cost function of pathfinder routing algorithm is changed (ref Equation 4). In modified function a particular node is favored or avoided by decreasing or increasing the cost of a node by a constant factor whose value ranges between 0 and 0.99. For an architecture with fewer routing resources, the higher value of constant factor (i.e. 0.99) might hinder the successful routing of the netlists. So the value of constant factor is gradually reduced if the routing algorithm is unable to resolve the conflicts over a certain number of iterations. However with an increased signal bandwidth, this is not the case and higher constant factor value helps in exploiting the cases shown in Fig. 6.

## 5   Experimental Results and Analysis

Experiments are performed for 17 open core benchmark circuits (netlists). Details of these benchmarks are shown in Table 1. Based on the types of HBs used, these benchmarks are divided into two sets. Experimental results divided into two parts; first we determine the effect of K and N on tree-based ASIF and then comparison with mesh-based ASIF is performed.

**Table 1.** Benchmark Details

| Index | Circuit Name | In | Out | Mult 18x18 | Mult 16x16 | Add 20+20 | LUT-3 | LUT-7 |
|-------|--------------|----|----|-----------|-----------|-----------|-------|-------|
| | | | | SET I Benchmark Details | | | | |
| 1. | cf_fir_3_8_8 | 42 | 22 | 4 | - | - | 217 | 186 |
| 2. | diffeq_f_systemC | 66 | 99 | 4 | - | - | 2114 | 1366 |
| 3. | diffeq_paj_convert | 12 | 101 | 5 | - | - | 1013 | 471 |
| 4. | fir_scu | 10 | 27 | 17 | - | - | 2267 | 629 |
| 5. | iir | 33 | 30 | 5 | - | - | 524 | 322 |
| 6. | iir1 | 28 | 15 | 5 | - | - | 898 | 410 |
| 7. | rs_decoder_1 | 13 | 20 | 13 | - | - | 2367 | 900 |
| 8. | rs_decoder_2 | 21 | 20 | 9 | - | - | 4204 | 1835 |
| | | | | SET II Benchmark Details | | | | |
| 9. | cf_fir_3_8_8 | 42 | 18 | - | 4 | 3 | 159 | 159 |
| 10. | cf_fir_7_16_16 | 146 | 35 | - | 8 | 14 | 639 | 638 |
| 11. | cfft16x8 | 20 | 40 | - | - | 26 | 1937 | 1122 |
| 12. | cordic_p2r | 18 | 32 | - | - | 43 | 803 | 801 |
| 13. | cordi_r2p | 34 | 40 | - | - | 52 | 1497 | 1178 |
| 14. | fm | 9 | 12 | - | 1 | 19 | 1508 | 1046 |
| 15. | fm_receiver | 10 | 12 | - | 1 | 20 | 1004 | 677 |
| 16. | lms | 18 | 16 | - | 10 | 11 | 965 | 935 |
| 17. | reed_solomon | 138 | 128 | - | 16 | 16 | 537 | 537 |

## 5.1    Effect of LUT and Arity Size on Tree-Based ASIF

In order to explore the effect of K and N on a tree-based ASIF, K is varied from 3 to 7 while N is varied from 4 to 8 and 16 and value of $p$ is set to be 1. So with 5 different K values and 6 different N values, a total of 30 architectures are explored. For each architecture, benchmarks are efficiently placed and routed on an architecture which is later reduced to ASIF. The details of the exploration are shown in Table 2. It can be seen from the table that in general, for a fixed N, the total area of the architecture increases with increase in K. This is because of the fact that for a fixed N, an increase in K decreases the average number of LUTs required by the architecture but at the same time LUT area increases exponentially with its size as there are $2^k$ bits in a K-input LUT, therefore leading towards an increase in logic area of the architecture. Although the routing area of the architecture decreases with increase in K because of the decreased number of LUTs, increase in logic area overshadows the decrease in routing area.

In order to perform the timing analysis of the tree-based ASIF, an elementary timing model is implemented. This model is based on the number of switches that are crossed by critical path. The variation in the number of switches with varying K and N is shown in columns 5 and 10 for SET I and SET II benchmarks respectively. For two sets of benchmarks, average number of switches decrease with an increase in K and N. For SET I benchmarks, for a fixed N, an increase in K decreases the average number of switches because of the decreased number of LUTs . However, this trend is not as significant for SET II benchmarks. This is because of the fact that when K is varied from 3 to 7, for 5 out of 9 benchmarks of SET II, LUT requirement remains almost same (ref Table 1) and number of switches of these 5 benchmarks constitute around 88% of the average switch numbers of SET II; hence a significant decrease in the average switch numbers is not observed. Finally, it can be seen that smaller K with bigger N

**Table 2.** Effect of LUT and Arity Size on Tree-based ASIF

| Architecture Description | SET I Benchmark Results | | | | | SET II Benchmark Results | | | | |
|---|---|---|---|---|---|---|---|---|---|---|
| | Logic Area | Routing Area | Total Area | Switch Number | Area-Delay Product | Logic Area | Routing Area | Total Area | Switch Number | Area-Delay Product |
| | $\times 10^6 \lambda^2$ | | | | $10^6$ | $\times 10^6 \lambda^2$ | | | | $10^6$ |
| K=3, N=4 | 227 | 74 | 301 | 51 | 15351 | 112 | 99 | 211 | 69 | 14559 |
| K=4, N=4 | 256 | 77 | 333 | 45 | 14985 | 149 | 87 | 236 | 68 | 16048 |
| K=5, N=4 | 378 | 74 | 452 | 42 | 18984 | 236 | 83 | 319 | 67 | 21373 |
| K=6, N=4 | 610 | 66 | 676 | 38 | 25688 | 397 | 76 | 473 | 65 | 30745 |
| K=7, N=4 | 945 | 95 | 1040 | 37 | 38480 | 743 | 72 | 815 | 64 | 52160 |
| K=3, N=5 | 204 | 81 | 285 | 47 | 13395 | 115 | 90 | 205 | 59 | 12095 |
| K=4, N=5 | 245 | 78 | 323 | 39 | 12597 | 142 | 86 | 228 | 58 | 13224 |
| K=5, N=5 | 367 | 73 | 440 | 35 | 15400 | 221 | 80 | 301 | 57 | 17157 |
| K=6, N=5 | 581 | 70 | 651 | 28 | 18228 | 358 | 70 | 428 | 56 | 23968 |
| K=7, N=5 | 960 | 73 | 1033 | 31 | 32023 | 661 | 70 | 731 | 56 | 40936 |
| K=3, N=6 | 200 | 84 | 284 | 37 | 10508 | 120 | 85 | 205 | 58 | 11890 |
| K=4, N=6 | 244 | 72 | 316 | 35 | 11060 | 150 | 78 | 228 | 57 | 12996 |
| K=5, N=6 | 375 | 73 | 448 | 33 | 14784 | 233 | 74 | 307 | 56 | 17192 |
| K=6, N=6 | 600 | 66 | 666 | 29 | 19314 | 379 | 67 | 446 | 56 | 24976 |
| K=7, N=6 | 993 | 66 | 1059 | 29 | 30711 | 689 | 67 | 756 | 55 | 41580 |
| K=3, N=7 | 206 | 84 | 290 | 35 | 10150 | 116 | 86 | 202 | 48 | 9696 |
| K=4, N=7 | 270 | 66 | 336 | 33 | 11088 | 144 | 80 | 224 | 46 | 10304 |
| K=5, N=7 | 411 | 62 | 473 | 30 | 14190 | 221 | 76 | 297 | 46 | 13662 |
| K=6, N=7 | 588 | 64 | 652 | 25 | 16300 | 345 | 75 | 420 | 46 | 19320 |
| K=7, N=7 | 937 | 68 | 1050 | 25 | 26250 | 615 | 74 | 689 | 45 | 31005 |
| K=3, N=8 | 226 | 76 | 302 | 34 | 10268 | 112 | 90 | 202 | 47 | 9494 |
| K=4, N=8 | 240 | 69 | 309 | 29 | 8961 | 143 | 82 | 225 | 46 | 10350 |
| K=5, N=8 | 367 | 68 | 435 | 30 | 13050 | 232 | 78 | 310 | 48 | 14880 |
| K=6, N=8 | 590 | 62 | 652 | 24 | 15648 | 362 | 70 | 432 | 48 | 20736 |
| K=7, N=8 | 940 | 64 | 1040 | 25 | 26000 | 640 | 69 | 709 | 44 | 31196 |
| **K=3, N=16** | **201** | **72** | **273** | **27** | **7371** | **112** | **84** | **196** | **37** | **7252** |
| **K=4, N=16** | **238** | **69** | **307** | **23** | **7061** | **146** | **76** | **222** | **37** | **8214** |
| **K=5, N=16** | **373** | **65** | **438** | **23** | **10074** | **225** | **73** | **298** | **36** | **10728** |
| **K=6, N=16** | **583** | **63** | **646** | **19** | **12274** | **346** | **69** | **415** | **35** | **14525** |
| **K=7, N=16** | **949** | **63** | **1012** | **17** | **17204** | **614** | **68** | **682** | **33** | **22506** |

**Table 3.** Comparison Between Mesh and Tree-based ASIF

| Signal Bandwidth | Area Comparison | | | | | | | | Quality Analysis | | | |
|---|---|---|---|---|---|---|---|---|---|---|---|---|
| | SET I Results | | | | SET II Results | | | | | SET I | | SET II | |
| | Routing Area $\times 10^6 \lambda^2$ | | Wires Used | | Routing Area $\times 10^6 \lambda^2$ | | Wires Used | | Netlist Number | Total Area $\times 10^6 \lambda^2$ | | | |
| | Mesh | Tree | Mesh | Tree | Mesh | Tree | Mesh | Tree | | Mesh | Tree | Mesh | Tree |
| ch-width=12, $p$=1 | 107 | 69 | 88342 | 38114 | 101 | 84 | 110887 | 32838 | 1 | 218 | 218 | 75 | 75 |
| ch-width=24, $p$=1.2 | 81 | 65 | 129936 | 40627 | 69 | 67 | 154764 | 46245 | 3 | 316 | 295 | 124 | 115 |
| ch-width=36, $p$=1.4 | 73 | 65 | 138153 | 40452 | 65 | 66 | 156634 | 47340 | 6 | 467 | 390 | 210 | 173 |
| ch-width=48, $p$=1.5 | 71 | 63 | 136373 | 40500 | 65 | 66 | 156052 | 47040 | 9 | 569 | 464 | 277 | 225 |

give best area results but their performance results are poor compared to larger LUT sizes. So, to find the best K-N combination, the product of area and number of switches crossed by critical path is shown in columns 6 and 11 for SET I and SET II benchmarks respectively. For SET I, K=4 with N=16 gives best area-delay product while for SET II K=3 with N=16 gives best area-delay product and these are the combinations that will be used for two sets for the comparison with mesh-based ASIF.

## 5.2  Mesh and Tree ASIF Comparison

Comparison between mesh and tree-based ASIF is presented in Table 3. For mesh-based ASIF, for SET I benchmarks K is set to be 4 and for SET II benchmarks K is set to be 3 whereas CLB size is set to be 1 for both architectures. For both architectures, starting from minimum required, signal bandwidth is varied to the point where a further increase does not improve the area density of the architecture. These signal bandwidth values are shown in column 1 of Table 3 where 'ch-width' corresponds to signal width for mesh-based architecture and $p$ values correspond to signal width for tree-based architecture. Comparison between two architectures is presented between columns 2 and 9 of Table 3. As the logic area of the two ASIFs is same and it remains constant with an increase in the signal bandwidth, only the variation in routing area of the two architectures is presented here. The variation in the routing area of the two architectures with varying signal bandwidth is presented in columns 2, 3 and 6, 7 for SET I and SET II benchmarks respectively. As it can be seen, an increase in signal bandwidth causes a decrease in the routing area of the architecture. This is because of the phenomenon which is described in Fig. 6. This phenomenon leads to the reduction in the number of switches and ultimately leading to better area density of the architecture. For SET I benchmarks, for a maximum value of signal bandwidth, tree-based ASIF gives 11.27% routing area gain over mesh-based ASIF and for SET II benchmarks, tree-based ASIF consumes 1.5% more routing area than mesh-based ASIF. It can be seen from columns 4, 5 and 8, 9 of Table 3 that a rise in signal bandwidth increases the number of wires that are being used by both architectures and the comparison between the two architectures shows that at maximum signal bandwidth tree-based ASIF consumes 70.30%, 69.85% less wires than mesh-based ASIF for SET I and SET II benchmarks respectively. Since the two architectures might become wire dominant at higher signal bandwidths, a comparison between the two for minimum signal bandwidth shows that for SET I benchmarks tree-based ASIF gives 35% routing area gain with 57% wire count gain and for SET II benchmarks tree-based ASIF gives 17% routing area gain with 70% wire count gain.

In order to further evaluate the two architectures, the quality analysis of two architectures is also performed. Ideally, an ASIF for a group of similar netlists should contain no switches. But as the ASIF generation of the two architectures is based on heuristic placement/partitioning and routing algorithms, ideal solution is not guaranteed. So, quality analysis of the two architectures is performed by generating ASIFs for a group of similar netlists. ASIFs are generated for two sets of benchmarks where 'rs_decoder_2' is chosen from SET I and 'cfft16x8' (ref Table 1) is chosen from SET II. We start with a single netlist and then increment their number by repeatedly placing and routing same netlist to generate the ASIF. The results of quality analysis are shown in columns 11 to 14 of Table 3. As it can be seen from the table that as the count is increased, the quality of the two architectures deteriorates and for a group of 9 similar netlists, for SET I, mesh-based ASIF is 2.6 times larger and tree-based ASIF is 2.1 times larger than ideal solution. Similarly for SET II benchmarks, mesh-based ASIF is 3.7 times larger while tree-based ASIF is 3 times larger than the ideal solution. The comparison between the two architectures shows that, for a group of 9 similar netlists, tree-based ASIF is 18.4%, 18.8 % more area efficient than mesh-based ASIF for SET I and SET II benchmarks respectively.

# 6  Conclusion

In this work a new heterogeneous tree-based ASIF is presented. Exploration of LUT and arity size reveals that smaller LUTs with larger arity sizes give better area results for tree-based ASIF. However, smaller LUTs give poor performance results and architectures with LUT size 3, 4 and arity size 16 produce best area-delay results for a range of different benchmark circuits. Further, the comparison between mesh and tree-based ASIFs reveals that tree-based ASIF produces equal or better area results when compared to the mesh-based ASIF while using far less wires. Finally the quality comparison of two architecture shows that tree-based ASIF is around 18% more efficient than mesh-based ASIF. In this work only the area comparison of two architectures is presented. In future, we want to implement more accurate timing and power models for the two architectures and perform their respective comparison.

# References

1. Berkeley logic synthesis and verification group,university of california, berkeley. berkeley logic interchange format (blif), http://vlsi.colorado.edu/vis/blif.ps
2. Greiner, A., Pecheux, F.: Alliance: A complete set of cad tools for teaching vlsi design. In: 3rd Eurochip Workshop (1992)
3. Karypis, G., Kumar, V.: Multilevel k-way hypergraph partitioning. In: Proceedings of 36th Design Automation Conference, pp. 343–348 (1999)
4. Kuon, I., Rose, J.: Measuring the gap between FPGAs and ASICs. In: 14th International Symposium on Field Programmable Gate Arrays, pp. 21–30 (2006)
5. Landman, B., Russo, R.: On Pin Versus Block Relationship for Partition of Logic Circuits. IEEE Transactions on Computers 20(1469-1479) (1971)
6. Lemieux, G., Lee, E., Tom, M., Yu, A.: Directional and single-driver wires in fpga interconnect. In: IEEE Conference on FPT, pp. 41–48 (2004)
7. Luu, J., Kuon, I., Jamieson, P., Campbell, T., Ye, A., Fang, W., Rose, J.: VPR 5.0: FPGA cad and architecture exploration tools with single-driver routing, heterogeneity and process scaling. In: International Symposium on Field Programmable Gate Arrays, pp. 133–142 (2009)
8. Marquardt, A., Betz, V., Rose, J.: Using cluster based logic blocks and timing-driven packing to improve fpga speed and density. In: Proceedings of the International Symposium on Field Programmable Gate Arrays, pp. 39–46 (1999)
9. Marrakchi, Z., Farooq, U., Parvez, H., Mehrez, H.: Comparison of tree-based and mesh-based coarse-grained fpga architectures. In: 2009 International Conference on Microelectronics (ICM), pp. 248–251 (2009)
10. McMurchie, L., Ebeling, C.: Pathfinder: A Negotiation-Based Performance-Driven Router for FPGAs. In: Proc. FPGA 1995 (1995)
11. Parvez, H., Marrakchi, Z., Mehrez, H.: Application specific fpga using heterogeneous logic blocks. In: Sirisuk, P., Morgan, F., El-Ghazawi, T., Amano, H. (eds.) ARC 2010. LNCS, vol. 5992, pp. 92–109. Springer, Heidelberg (2010)
12. Sentovich, E.M., et al.: Sis: A system for sequential circuit analysis. Tech. Report No. UCB/ERL M92/41, University of California, Berkeley (1992)
13. Skiścim, C.C., Golden, B.L.: Optimization by simulated annealing: A preliminary computational study for the tsp. In: WSC 1983: Proceedings of the 15th Conference on Winter Simulation, pp. 523–535. IEEE Press, Piscataway (1983)
14. Wu, K., Tsai, Y.: Structured ASIC, Evolution or Revolution. In: Proc. ISPD, pp. 103–106 (April 2004)

# Dynamic $V_{DD}$ Switching Technique and Mapping Optimization in Dynamically Reconfigurable Processor for Efficient Energy Reduction

Tatsuya Yamamoto[1], Kazuei Hironaka[2], Yuki Hayakawa[1],
Masayuki Kimura[2], Hideharu Amano[2], and Kimiyoshi Usami[1]

[1] Graduate School of Engineering, Shibaura Institute of Technology
3-7-5 Toyosu, Koto-ku, Tokyo, 135-8548, Japan
[2] Graduate School of Fundamental Science and Technology, Keio University
3-14-1 Hiyoshi, Kohoku-ku, Yokohama city, Kanagawa, 223-0061, Japan
{m109094,m110112,usami}@shibaura-it.ac.jp,
muccra-dvdd@am.ics.keio.ac.jp

**Abstract.** This paper describes a dynamic $V_{DD}$ switching technique to reduce energy dissipation of Dynamically Reconfigurable Processors. Either high or low supply is dynamically selected at each PE at the context-by-context basis. We designed a part of a PE array and applied this technique. A test chip fabricated in 65nm technology operated successfully. Detailed simulations revealed that energy reduction is hindered by energy overhead due to supply switching when we use even lower $V_{DD}$. We propose a mapping optimization algorithm "PFCM" to minimize the overhead. PFCM reduced energy overhead by 90.8% and thereby the dynamic $V_{DD}$ switching technique reduced energy dissipation by up to 12.5% when running sepia filter, alpha blender and Laplacian filter programs.

**Keywords:** Dynamically Reconfigurable Processor, Power Reduction, Dynamic $V_{DD}$ Switching, Mapping Optimization.

## 1 Introduction

Coarse-grained Dynamically Reconfigurable Processors (DRPs) have been received an attention as flexible low power accelerators for embedded systems [1][2][3][4]. Since datapaths required for computation are dynamically formed on an array of Processing Elements (PEs), the DRP is more power-efficient compared to general purpose processors for specific processing. To enhance this advantage, various types of power reduction techniques for DRPs have been researched so far.

Power dissipation consisting of dynamic and leakage power can be reduced by lowering the supply voltage. In particular, dynamic power is reduced quadratically as the supply voltage is lowered. Meanwhile, lowering the supply voltage increases the circuit delay and hence degrades the performance. To deal with this drawback, multi-$V_{DD}$ technique to use the normal voltage $V_{DD}H$ for critical paths and the lower voltage $V_{DD}L$ for non-critical paths was proposed and is currently a well-known technique in ASICs. In contrast, approaches to apply multiple supply voltages to reconfigurable

A. Koch et al. (Eds.): ARC 2011, LNCS 6578, pp. 230–241, 2011.

devices have not been fully explored yet. An approach to apply the dual-V$_{DD}$ technique to FPGAs was proposed in [5]. However, in the dual-V$_{DD}$ techniques for either ASICs or FPGAs, assignment of V$_{DD}$H and V$_{DD}$L is completed before the chip begins to run. Such a static assignment approach cannot be used in DRPs because configuration of each PE is changed during the run time dynamically and thereby critical paths change one after another.

To solve this problem, we propose a dynamic V$_{DD}$ switching technique for DRP. In this technique, supply voltage is switched between V$_{DD}$H and V$_{DD}$L at each PE at context-by-context while the DRP is running. Voltage assignment information is included in the context data and either V$_{DD}$H or V$_{DD}$L is selected at each PE. We demonstrate effectiveness of this approach through real design and implementation of a test chip.

The contributions of the paper are as follows:

- We proposed a design technique for DRPs to dynamically switch the supply voltage of each PE at the context-by-context basis.
- We evaluated energy reduction through real design of a part of a PE array to which the dynamic V$_{DD}$ switching technique is applied. We demonstrated that the test chip fabricated in the Fujitsu 65nm CMOS technology operated successfully.
- We investigated enegy overhead caused by switching supply voltage and newly proposed a mapping optimization technique to minimize the energy overhead.

The paper is organized as follows. Section 2 describes the related work and Section 3 presents the target DRP, MuCCRA-3. Section 4 describes the dynamic V$_{DD}$ switching technique for the target DRP and Section 5 presents the mapping optimization algorithm for the proposed method. Section 6 presents evaluation results.

## 2  Related Work

Since controlling power voltage is a common low power technique, a lot of proposals have been reported for reconfigurable devices including FPGAs. Dynamic Voltage Scaling [6] and Dual-V$_{DD}$ techniques [5] were applied, then more sophisticated methods combining multiple techniques also have been tried [7][8]. However, most of them took a static approach fixed for each target application rather than run-time voltage switching. A context dependent run-time voltage scale control [9] which makes the use of the slack of hardware contexts was proposed, but it only included the idea and some theoretical studies. Practical study on the context dependent run-time power gating was also reported [10], but it mainly aimed to reduce the leakage power. Our previous work [11] shows the possibility of run-time V$_{DD}$ switching on DRP and feasibility study. However, the evaluation was done at the gate level and any energy overhead was not taken into account in [11]. In practice, the run-time V$_{DD}$ switching approach is accompanied by energy overhead occurring at the supply switching. This overhead can be evaluated only by designing power switches to switch the supply voltage and implementing a layout for a circuit with power switches. This paper demonstrates effectiveness of the proposed approach considering the actual overhead through a detailed design and implementation.

# 3 Structure of Our DRP

## 3.1 Array Structure

In this work, we use the structure proposed in the conventional DRP, MuCCRA-3 [12], as a target to apply our dynamic $V_{DD}$ switching technique. MuCCRA-3 consists of 4 X 4 PE array as shown in Fig.1. The bit width of MuCCRA-3 is 16 and the number of context is 32. As shown in Fig.2, a PE in MuCCRA-3 has Arithmetic Logic Unit (ALU) and Register File Unit (RFU) for storing intermediate data. In the port selection modules, several simple functions such as shift, bit reverse, constant generation are provided. The operations in the ALU are also simple; addition, subtract, logic operations, shift operation, comparison and data selection. RFU module is an 8-depth 2-reads/1-write register file, FIFO mode is available for functioning as an 8-entry FIFO buffer. In MuCCRA-3, a register is provided at the output of ALU and all data are stored into it after the computation. This register reduces the delay caused by directly cascaded interconnections of multiple PEs. Distributed memory (MEM) modules for storing data are provided at the top and the bottom of the array in order to relax the access conflicts. The depth of each MEM is 256 words due to the area limitation. Dual-memory-bank method is introduced to overlap the time for computation and transferring data from/to the external. A dedicated address counter is provided to each MEM module such that all PEs are used for the main part of applications. When the address computation is simple, MEM can be accessed without using any PE.

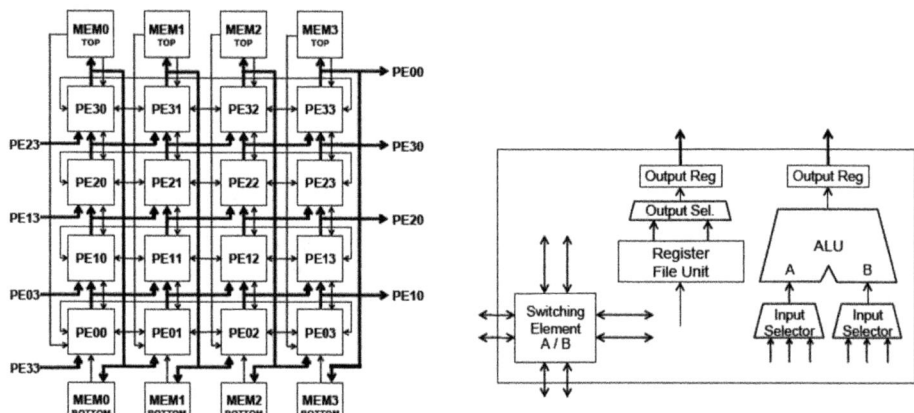

Fig. 1. An outline of MuCCRA-3                    Fig. 2. An outline of PE

## 3.2 Context Control

Like other DRPs, MuCCRA-3 is a multi-context style DRPA in which multiple sets of configurations called hardware contexts are switched. Each PE and MEM is provided with its own context memory module, and reads out the configuration data according to the context pointer in every clock cycle. The configuration data in each context memory must be transferred from the memory module outside the chip before the computation.

# 4 Design and Implemention of Dynamic V$_{DD}$ Switching Technique on DRP

## 4.1 Supply-Line Selector for Dynamic V$_{DD}$ Switching

Here, we use 65nm CMOS process with 1.2V standard supply voltage. To realize the dynamic V$_{DD}$ switching scheme, we use two pMOS power-switches; one is connected to the high-V$_{DD}$ (V$_{DD}$H:1.2V) and the other is connected to the low-V$_{DD}$ (V$_{DD}$L: 0.7V at minimum). A select signal is connected to the gate of each pMOS power-switch. When the select signal is '0', the supply voltage V$_{DD}$H is given. Otherwise, the voltage V$_{DD}$L is supplied. In this work, we apply the dynamic V$_{DD}$ switching technique only to ALU and data selectors since they are built only with combinational circuits. We did not apply this approach to memory elements such as SRAMs or flip-flops so as not to introduce unstable operation. Transistor size of the pMOS power-switch was determined while considering area and delay penalties. Simulation results showed that the delay penalty of logic circuit due to the insertion of the power-switch was less than 12%.The area penalty due to insertion of the power-switch was less than 6.5% in the circuit to which the dynamic V$_{DD}$ switching technique was applied. At the entire PE, the area penalty was less than 1%. The settling time for the supply switching was also taken into account when determining the power-switch size. The settling time is defined as the time for the virtual V$_{DD}$ voltage to reach ±0.05V of the target voltage after triggering the voltage switching. When the power lines are switched from V$_{DD}$H to V$_{DD}$L, the settling time was 1.5ns, while at the switching from V$_{DD}$L to V$_{DD}$H the settling time was 0.8ns, both at V$_{DD}$L of 0.7V. It was found that the settling time is much smaller than the cycle time 25ns at the target frequency 40MHz. Thus, the voltage switching and computation can be done in a clock cycle.

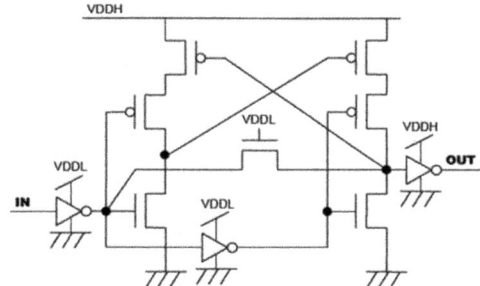

**Fig. 3.** Schematic diagram of Level Shifter

## 4.2 Level Shifter

When using multiple power domains with different supply voltages, level shifters are required at the boundary where the lower voltage signals are transmitted to the high power voltage domain Without them, the input voltage "high" is not raised high enough to fully cut off pMOS transistors in the high-V$_{DD}$ domain. This causes DC current flowing that increases power dissipation. In our approach, level shifters are inserted between ALU and its output registers. Since the ALU has 16-bits data outputs and a carry output, totally 17 level shifters are inserted. In this work, we use a simple yet fast level shifter presented in the literature [13]. The circuit diagram is shown in Fig.3. We designed this circuit in a commercial 65nm technology. Simulation results based on extracted parasitic from the layout showed that level conversion from 0.7V to 1.2V can be performed within 0.2ns. Note that the overhead of the level shifter will be counted in all evaluations here.

### 4.3 Design Flow

The design flow is almost the same as that for the conventional DRPs. From RTL description, logic synthesis is done to generate a netlist. Then, floor planning, place-and-route including clock tree synthesis, and verification are performed. For the dynamic $V_{DD}$ switching design, level shifters and supply-line selectors must be inserted. In order to insert level-shifter cells just before the output registers of ALU, we modified the netlist manually after the synthesis. Supply-line selectors are inserted during the place-and-routing step. The dynamic $V_{DD}$ switching portion is defined as a macro module and place-and-route is applied independently. Finally, the supply-line selectors are inserted into the two supply-lines ($V_{DD}H$ and $V_{DD}L$) for the macro module as shown in Fig.4.

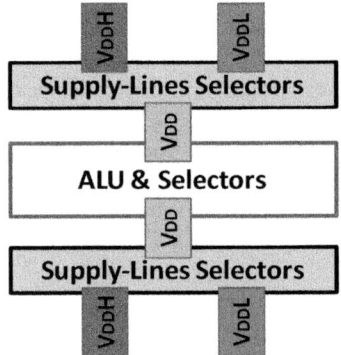

**Fig. 4.** Inserting position of the supply-lines selector

ALU & Selectors (Dynamic $V_{DD}$ Switching area)    Context memory

**Fig. 5.** Layout of a PE in MuCCRA-DVDD

## 4.4  Prototype Chip of Dynamic V$_{DD}$ Switching

We designed and implemented a prototype chip, referred to as MuCCRA-DVDD, in which cascaded two PEs and data memory modules are only provided. The dynamic V$_{DD}$ switching technique was applied to each PE. Fig.5 shows the layout of the PE used in MuCCRA-DVDD. The Fujitsu 65nm CMOS technology with 12 metal layers was used at this chip. Synopsys Design Compiler and IC Compiler were employed for logic synthesis and physical layout, respectively.

# 5  Mapping Policy

## 5.1  Optimization Algorithm "PFCM"

In order to make the best use of the power reduction by dynamic dual V$_{DD}$, we applied a mapping optimization method called Partially Fixed Configuration Mapping (PFCM). Although the fundamental concept of PFCM was proposed for reducing the frequency of dynamic reconfiguration, it is expected to suppress the overhead caused by dynamic voltage switching as the configuration of a PE is kept as possible. The PFCM is a mapping optimization policy that assigns nodes of the data flow graph (DFG) into PEs of dynamically reconfigurable processors. It is used combining compilers for coarse grain reconfigurable processors [14], and changes the assignment after the mapping. Here, the retargetable compiler Black Diamond [15] is used for DFG generation, partitioning into each context and initial assignment. The PFCM changes the assignment of nodes based on the separated DFG and initial assignment results as follows.

1. Classify the nodes in the DFG by its operation and count the number of nodes for each operation type $t$ ($n_t$).
2. At the beginning, all PEs are assumed to be empty that means no node has been assigned.
3. In the PFCM, once a node is assigned into a PE in a context, the same type of node is assigned into the PE as possible in the other contexts. Start from the first context and apply this policy for all contexts with the following steps.

   (a) Select a node of operation type $t$ whose $n_t$ is the largest, and assign it into a PE to which the same operation type was assigned in the previous context. If there are multiple candidates, follow the initial assignment.
   (b) If there are no PE which satisfies (a), assign the node into empty PEs based on the initial assignment.
   (c) If there are no PE which satisfies (a) and (b), assign it based on the initial assignment without taking care of the assignment in the previous context.
   (d) Iterate it until all nodes of the same operation type are assigned. Then, apply it for nodes in the decreasing order of $n_t$ iteratively.
   (e) When all nodes for a context are assigned, the routing is tried. If the routing is impossible, give up the optimization in the context and use the initial assignment.

The mapping examples of an edge filter with and without PFCM are shown in Fig.6. In this example, shadowed boxes represent PEs which must change its configuration in the context. Compared with the initial mapping (Fig.6(a)), the number of configuration change is suppressed as possible with some exceptions (Fig.6(b)). An example of the exceptions is shown in Context 1 in which eight PEs assigned MULT in Context 0 are changed into ADD because of the shortage of assignment possibility. Note that since the operand isolation is applied to all computational modules in a PE, unnecessary power consumption is never required just for keeping the configuration.

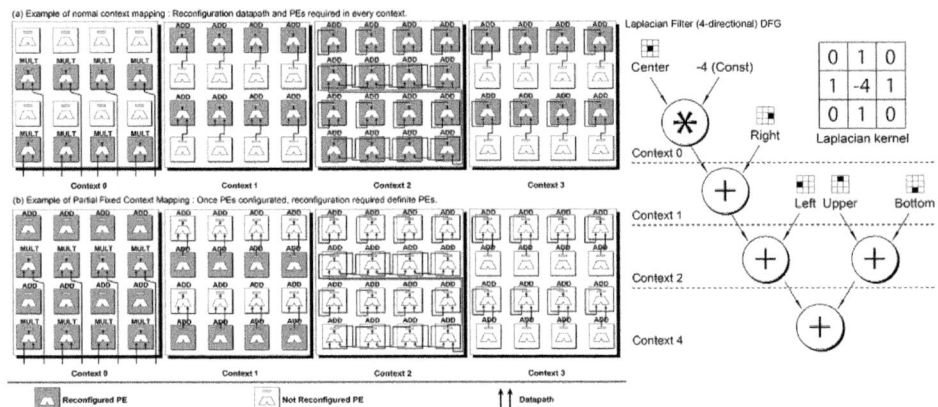

**Fig. 6.** Mapping example with/without using PFCM

The PFCM tries to assign the same operations to a PE in all contexts as possible. So, if the interconnection network of the target dynamically reconfigurable processors is not enough flexible, the assignment fails frequently and the initial assignment policy is used in the context. It means that there is a limitation of applying PFCM in the complicated context. Also, it tends to extend the communication delay between PEs. However, the PE array of MuCCRA-3 is not so large and it also provides enough network resources (two flexible island style network + direct links). Thus, this policy can be applied without degrading the operational frequency in most applications.

### 5.2 Voltage Assignment

In MuCCRA-DVDD, the voltage assignment is specified into a bit of the configuration data and can be switched for every context per each PE. However, since the unnecessary switching causes energy overhead, the voltage assignment must be done considering whether it can improve the energy or not. Here, we introduce the concept of BET (Break Even Time) which is the minimum number of clock cycles to use $V_{DD}L$ for saving the energy. If the $V_{DD}L$ is used more than BET continuously, the saved energy by running with $V_{DD}L$ becomes more than the overhead of voltage switching. If $V_{DD}L$ becomes low, saved energy becomes large while the switching overhead is also increased. So, BET must be evaluated with a circuit level simulation based on the design. We will show them in Section 6, and once the BET is fixed in each $V_{DD}L$, we can decide the voltage assignment in the following simple policy.

1. First, as the initial voltage assignment, $V_{DD}H$ is assigned into PEs executing MULT operation which requires the largest delay time in the current PE design, and $V_{DD}L$ is assigned into others in each context.
2. If the dynamically voltage switching is required and the interval is shorter than BET, the voltage switching is canceled and $V_{DD}H$ is kept.

By using the PFCM with this voltage assignment policy, the overhead of voltage switching can be reduced as well as the total number of PEs which use $V_{DD}H$.

# 6  Evaluation

We conducted evaluation using the MuCCRA-DVDD chip. The fabricated chip operated functionally and reduction in current dissipation was observed. However, we could not separate the current dissipation for the PE from that for the memory. In order to evaluate energy reduction and overhead for the PE, we extracted properties from the layout of the MuCCRA-DVDD chip and conducted circuit-level simulations.

## 6.1  Energy Dissipation of PE

The supply current both from the $V_{DD}H$ and $V_{DD}L$ are measured when the PE executes representative operations (ADD, MULT, SELECT and SHIFT are selected here). Based on the obtained current and supply voltage, we computed the total energy dissipated in a cycle. The cycle time was assumed to be 25ns because the target frequency of MuCCRA-DVDD is 40MHz. First, we investigated energy dissipation when $V_{DD}L$ is always used without switching. Results are shown in Fig.7. Here, the $V_{DD}L$ is changed from 0.7V to 1.2V, since with $V_{DD}L$ less than 0.7V, a large part of operations of PE cannot be finished within 25ns because of the increasing delay.

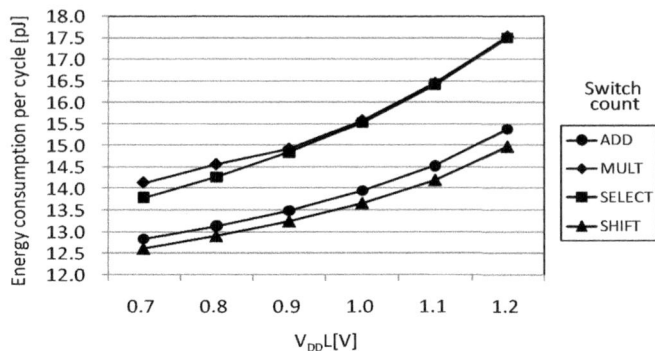

**Fig. 7.** Energy dissipation for 1PE when the supply-lines isn't switched

In all operations, the total energy dissipation reduces as the $V_{DD}L$ gets lowered as expected. For example, compared to the energy dissipation of $V_{DD}L$=1.2V (i.e. $V_{DD}H$), the energy dissipation of $V_{DD}L$=0.7V is reduced by 20% when a PE executes SELECT.

Next, the total energy dissipation including the energy overhead of voltage switching is evaluated. In this analysis, a PE executes ADD for 1000 cycles, and the supply voltage is iteratively switched with the switch count set by the parameter. Fig.8 shows the results. Since the overhead of voltage switching becomes large for lower $V_{DD}L$, the $V_{DD}L$ which achieves the minimum energy (here, referred as $V_{DD}LMIN$) becomes high with the frequent switching (thus, a large number of switching count).

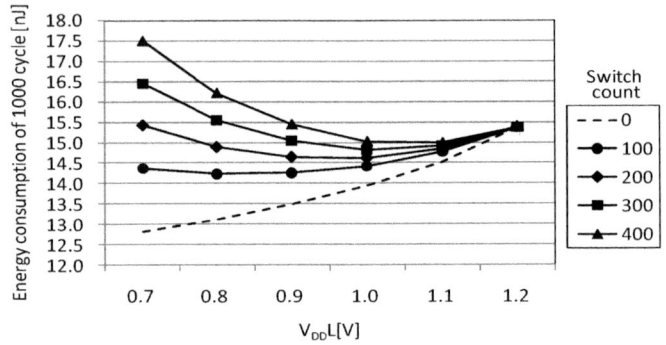

**Fig. 8.** Energy dissipation for 1PE when the supply voltage is switched

For 0.8V $V_{DD}L$, the energy cannot be reduced if the switch count is more than 100, while 1.0V $V_{DD}L$ can save with 300 times switching. From this evaluation, BET (Break Even Time) used for the voltage assignment policy in Section 5 can be calculated and shown in Table.1. Here, the results are shown in the number of clock cycles when MuCCRA-3 works in 40MHz. Tbale.1 shows that the increasing of the overhead of switching to lower $V_{DD}L$ is more than the gain by using the lower $V_{DD}L$, thus, the BET gradually increases with lower voltage.

**Table 1.** BET(Break Even Time) in each $V_{DD}L$

| $V_{DD}L(V)$ | BET(cycle) |
|:---:|:---:|
| 1.1 | 1 |
| 1.0 | 2 |
| 0.9 | 3 |
| 0.8 | 4 |
| 0.7 | 5 |

## 6.2   Evaluation of Energy Dissipation for 4×4 PE Array

Here, the energy saving effect of the 4×4 total PE array by using dynamic voltage switching with the PFCM is evaluated by the simulation. Here, we used application programs for image processing: sepia filter, alpha blender and Laplacian filter. The evaluated results with several $V_{DD}L$ voltages are shown in Fig.9.

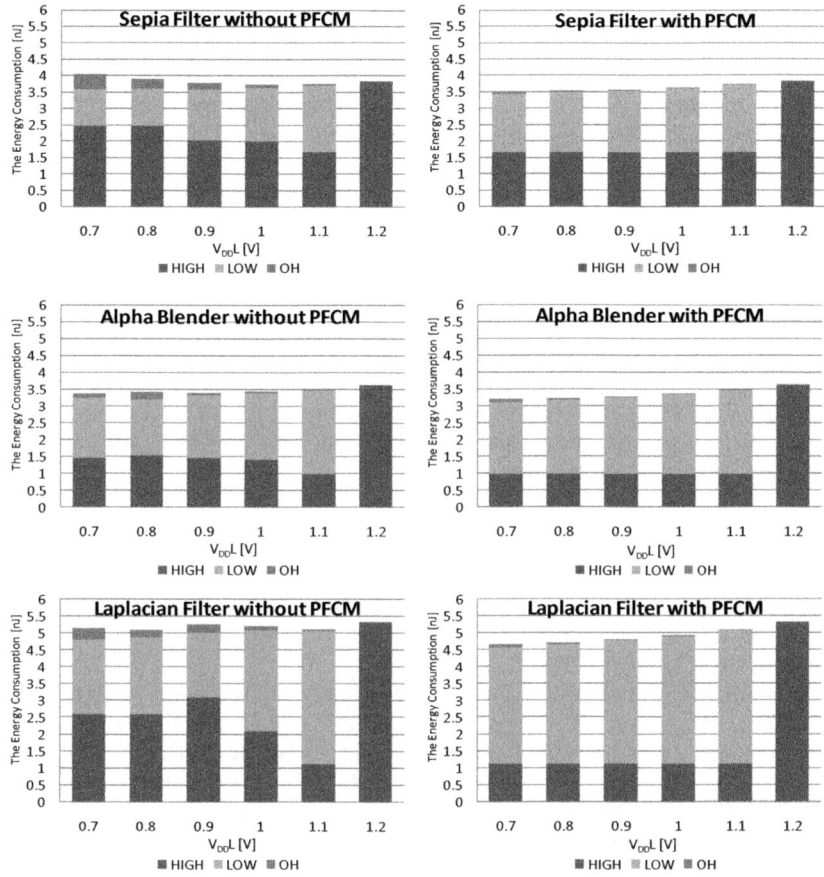

**Fig. 9.** Energy dissipation for 4×4 PE with and without PFCM when application is executed

Left side figures show the cases without the PFCM. Note that, the voltage assignment policy considering BET is used in both cases. Although the energy can be saved, the overhead of switching degrades the effect. As a result, the 2.1% energy reduction is achieved with 1.0V V$_{DD}$L for sepia filter and 4.3% achieved in 0.8V V$_{DD}$L for Laplacian filter. For alpha blender, which has a simple datapath structure, achieves 6.8% with 0.7V V$_{DD}$L. The ratio of using V$_{DD}$H tends to be increased with lower V$_{DD}$L, since the BET becomes large.

On the other hand, since the overhead can be well suppressed with PFCM, 8.1% energy reduction is achieved in sepia filter with 0.7V V$_{DD}$L, 11.8% in alpha blender with 0.7V V$_{DD}$L, and 12.5% in Laplacian filter with 0.7V V$_{DD}$L. Compared with the case without the PFCM, 90.8% of switching overhead is reduced. When we use the PFCM, the ratio of using V$_{DD}$H is not so increased with lower V$_{DD}$L in spite of the relatively large BET. It means that the frequency for switching the voltage is well suppressed by using the PFCM. Although the largest energy saving is achieved with 0.7V V$_{DD}$L, most operations of the PE cannot work with 0.6V V$_{DD}$L at 40MHz clock because of the increasing delay. Thus, further gain cannot be obtained by lowering the V$_{DD}$L.

## 7 Conclusion

In this paper, we proposed a dynamic $V_{DD}$ switching technique to reduce energy in DRP while maintaining the performance. We evaluated effectiveness of the proposed technique through real design and implementation of a test chip. Simulation results demonstrated that energy can be reduced by up to 6.8% at the 4×4 PE array. However, the results also revealed that energy overhead due to $V_{DD}$ switching hinders energy reduction. For further energy savings, we proposed a mapping optimization technique "PFCM" to minimize the energy overhead. This technique reduced energy overhead by 90.8% at the maximum and thereby energy dissipation was decreased by up to 12.5%. In this experiment, we applied the dynamic $V_{DD}$ switching technique only to ALU and data selectors. Although the design time increased for adding dynamic voltage switching mechanism is not so large, the achieved power reduction is not enough. Further energy reduction will be achieved by increasing the circuit portions to which this technique is applied. This is our future work as well as evaluating applications other than image processing.

## References

1. Motomura, M.: STP Engine, a C-based Programmable HW Core featuring Massively Parallel and Reconfigurable PE Array: its Architecture, Tool, and System Implications. In: Prof. of CoolChips XII (2009)
2. Amano, H., Hasegawa, Y., Tsutsumi, S., Nakamura, T., Nisimura, T., Tunbunheng, V., Parimala, A., Sano, T., Kato, M.: MuCCRA Chips: Configurable Dynamically-Reconfigurable Processors. In: Proc. of ASSCC, pp. 384–387 (2007)
3. Veradas, F.J., Scheppler, M., Moffat, W., Mei, B.: Custom Implementation of the Coarse-Grained Reconfigurable ADRES architecture for multimedia Purposes. In: Proc. of International Conference on Field Programmable Logic and Applications (FPL 2005), pp. 106–111 (2005)
4. Ebeling, C., Cronquist, D.C., Franklin, P.: RaPiD - Reconfigurable Pipelined Datapath. In: International Workshop on Field-Programmable Logic and Applications, pp. 126–135. Springer, Berlin (1996)
5. Vijaykrishnan, G.L., et al.: A Dual-VDD Low Power FPGA Architecture. In: Becker, J., Platzner, M., Vernalde, S. (eds.) FPL 2004. LNCS, vol. 3203, pp. 145–157. Springer, Heidelberg (2004)
6. Chow, C.T., et al.: Dynamic Voltage Scaling for Commercial FPGAs. In: IEEE Int. Conf. on Field Programmable Technology (ICFPT), pp. 173–180 (2005)
7. Li, F., et al.: Low-Power FPGA Using Pre-defined Dual-Vdd/Dual-Vt Fabrics. In: Proc. of 2004 ACM/SIGDA 12th Int. Symp. on Field Programmable Gate Arrays (FPGA), February, pp. 42–50 (2004)
8. Tran, C.Q., et al.: Low-Power Low-Leakage FPGA Design using Zigzag power-gating, dual-VTH/VDD and micro-VDD-hopping. IEICE Trans. Electron E89-C(3), 280–286 (2006)
9. Schweizer, T., et al.: Exploiting Slack Time in Dynamically Reconfigurable Processor Architectures. In: Proc. of IEEE Int. Conf. on Field Programmable Technology (ICFPT), pp. 381–384 (December 2007)

10. Saito, Y., et al.: Leakage Power Reduction for Coarse Grain Dynamically Reconfigurable Processor Arrays With Fine-Grained Power Gating Technique. In: Int. Conf. on Field Programmable Technology (ICFPT), pp. 329–332 (December 2008)
11. Umahashi, Y., et al.: Power Reduction Technique for Dynamic Reconfigurable Processors with Dynamic Assignment of Dual Supply Voltages. In: ITC-CSCC 2008 (2008)
12. Kimura, M., et al.: Low Power Image Processing using MuCCRA-3: A Dynamically Reconfigurable Processor Array. In: Proc. of Int. Conf. on Field Programmable Technology (December 2009)
13. Tran, C.Q., Kawaguchi, H., Sakurai, T.: Low-power High-speed Level Shifter Design for Block-level Dynamic Voltage Scaling Environment. In: IEEE International Conference on Integrated Circuit Design and Technology, Texas, USA, vol. 1, pp. 229–232 (May 2005)
14. Mei, B., et al.: DRESC: a retargetable compiler for coarse-grained reconfigurable architectures. In: Proc. of FPT 2002, pp. 155–173 (December 2002)
15. Tunbunheng, V., Amano, H.: Black-Diamond: a Retargetable Compiler Using Graph with Configuration Bits for Dynamically Reconfigurable Architectures. In: Proc. of The 14th Workshop on Synthesis And System Integration of Mixed Information Technologies (SASIMI), pp. 412–419 (2007)

# MEMS Interleaving Read Operation of a Holographic Memory for Optically Reconfigurable Gate Arrays

Hironobu Morita and Minoru Watanabe

Electrical and Electronic Engineering
Shizuoka University
3-5-1 Johoku, Hamamatsu, Shizuoka 432-8561, Japan
tmwatan@ipc.shizuoka.ac.jp

**Abstract.** Optically reconfigurable gate array (ORGAs) were developed to realize next-generation large-virtual gate count programmable VLSIs. An ORGA consists of an ORGA-VLSI, a holographic memory, and a laser array, which is used for addressing the holographic memory. Since many configuration contexts can be stored on a volume-type holographic memory, the corresponding number of lasers must be implemented on an ORGA. However, a laser array with numerous lasers is always expensive. Therefore, to accommodate numerous configuration contexts with fewer lasers, this paper presents a novel method using an interleaving read operation of a holographic memory for ORGAs. This method can provide an addressing capability of a billion configuration contexts along with a nanosecond-order high-speed configuration capability.

## 1 Introduction

Recent slowing of VLSI process technology progress has given rise to exploration of methods to increase VLSI performance that are independent of progress in process technology. Among those methods, high-speed dynamic reconfiguration techniques are being examined. They are expected to open a new programmable VLSI paradigm with large numbers of virtual gates. Such high-speed dynamic reconfiguration techniques not only realize large numbers of virtual gates but also increase a gate array's activity, since idle circuits on the gate array can be removed and other necessary circuits can be downloaded at that time from memory into the gate array. Currently, Field Programmable Gate Arrays (FPGAs) are widely used [1]–[3]. However, FPGA reconfiguration invariably requires more than one hundred milliseconds; FPGAs therefore can not execute such dynamic reconfiguration operations.

Up to the present day, optically reconfigurable gate arrays (ORGAs) have been developed to realize next-generation large-virtual gate count programmable VLSIs [4]–[12]. An ORGA consists of an ORGA-VLSI, a holographic memory, and a laser array. The ORGA-VLSI is a type of fine-grained gate array, as are FPGAs, meaning that its function is the same as those of currently available FPGAs [9]. However, the configuration procedure of the ORGA-VLSI is executed optically. In an ORGA, many configuration contexts can be stored on a holographic memory that is addressed by a laser array, and which can be implemented dynamically onto the ORGA-VLSI in a very short time [10][11]. By virtue of those features, the ORGA can achieve a large number of virtual

A. Koch et al. (Eds.): ARC 2011, LNCS 6578, pp. 242–252, 2011.

Table 1. Specifications of a digital mirror array device

|  | 0.55 XGA |
| --- | --- |
| Resolution | 1024 × 768 mirros |
| Mirror tilt angle | ±12° |
| Mirror size | 10.8 μm × 10.8 μm |
| Package size (inch) | 1.6 × 1.25 |

Fig. 1. Photograph of a digital micromirror device (DMD) device

gates along with a high-speed nanosecond-order context switching capability. However, although the ORGA architecture presents such advantages, an important issue is its future mass production. The salient cost problem is the laser array. Other components, such as photopolymer holographic memory materials [12] and a standard process ORGA-VLSI [9], are cheap.

In the ORGA architecture, a laser array is used for addressing a holographic memory. Although many configuration contexts can be stored on a volume-type holographic memory, the corresponding number of lasers is necessary to read them. For example, to implement a million reconfiguration contexts onto an ORGA, a million lasers must be implemented onto the ORGA. However, a laser array with numerous lasers is always expensive. Therefore, the number of lasers presents an important concern in developing ORGAs.

Recently, a useful microelectromechanical system (MEMS) technology, a digital micromirror device (DMD), was produced by Texas Instruments Inc. [13][14]. The DMD chip is a type of spatial light modulator used in many video projectors. The specifications of one DMD device are presented in Table 1. A photograph of the chip, which consists of 1,024 × 768 mirrors, is portrayed in Fig. 1. Potentially, it can address numerous reconfiguration contexts. Nevertheless, although studies using the DMD device as an electrically rewritable holographic memory have been reported [15], no study examining exploitation of many mirrors on the DMD device used for addressing a holographic memory of an ORGA has been reported. One important issue to be considered is that the

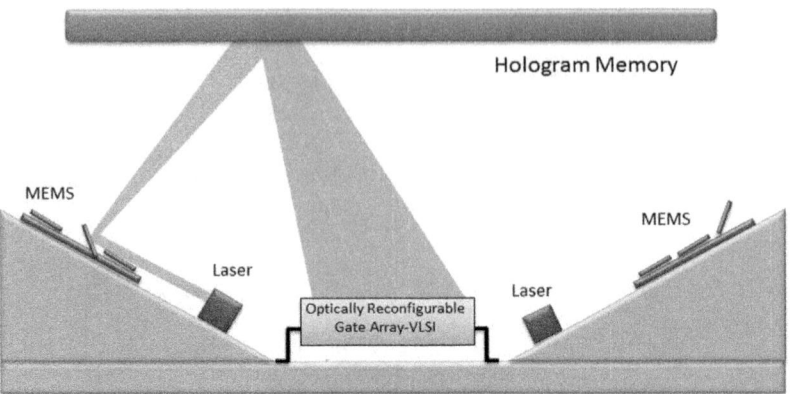

**Fig. 2.** Novel concept of an MEMS interleaving optically reconfigurable gate array (ORGA)

DMD device switching speed, which is of microsecond-order, is insufficient to provide nanosecond-order reconfiguration. However, to date, many interleaving methods have been proposed to increase the speed of slow response devices, particularly the speed of memory devices [16][17][18][19].

This paper therefore presents a proposal of an MEMS interleaving method for a holographic memory of optically reconfigurable gate arrays. In addition, this paper describes results of its demonstration.

## 2   MEMS Interleaving ORGA and Its Method

### 2.1   MEMS Device

A block diagram of a novel concept of an MEMS interleaving ORGA is shown in Fig. 2. The MEMS interleaving ORGA consists of MEMS devices, lasers, a volume holographic memory, and an ORGA-VLSI. As explained previously, the MEMS device described in Table 1 and presented in Fig. 1 has $1,024 \times 768$ tiny mirrors, each having a size of $10.8 \times 10.8 \ \mu m^2$. Therefore, a lot of mirrors of the MEMS device are useful for addressing many configuration contexts stored on a holographic memory. For example, if the DMD device described above is implemented and each mirror is used for addressing one configuration context, 786,432 configuration contexts can be addressed. Moreover, since the angle of each mirror can be moved from $-12°$ to $+12°$, angle-multiplexed reading is possible. In this case, the number of reconfiguration contexts can be increased to more than one. Currently, an MEMS device with $1,920 \times 1,200$ pixels is also available. Therefore, if 10 angle-multiplexed reading is used for each mirror's reconfiguration, then a total of 23 million addressing operation of a holographic memory can be achieved. Therefore, the MEMS is useful for addressing numerous reconfiguration contexts.

However, the microsecond-order switching speed of the MEMS device is not fast enough. Always, in an ORGA, the gate array performance can be increased dramatically by exploiting a high-speed reconfiguration. Even if the state of a circuit is idle

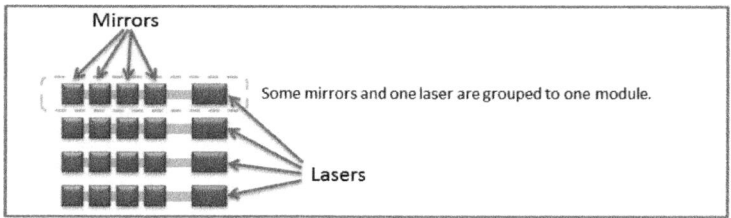

**Fig. 3.** Laser-MEMS module

for only one clock cycle, it is removed and another necessary circuit is implemented onto this area so that all gate array parts can be activated constantly. For that reason, microsecond-order switching speed is insufficient for this application.

## 2.2   Interleaving Method

This paper therefore presents a proposal of an MEMS interleaving ORGA to achieve a higher reconfiguration frequency than the MEMS switching speed. Many interleaving methods have been proposed in earlier reports of the literature [16][17][18][19]. Based on them, the concept of the MEMS - laser addressing interleaving method was produced. Using this method, some MEMS mirrors and a laser are grouped to a module, as shown in Fig. 3. In addition, many modules are implemented onto an MEMS interleaving ORGA. When a certain reconfiguration request arises, an MEMS mirror angle is changed first; then a laser in the same module turns on so that the laser beam is reflected on the MEMS mirror, incident to a holographic memory. The optical configuration context is read out from the holographic memory. Finally, the configuration context is programmed onto an ORGA-VLSI, as shown in Fig. 2. This is a normal reconfiguration procedure.

Of course, if a second configuration procedure is executed inside the same module, then the procedure must wait until the first mirror angle is changed to an off state, another mirror angle is changed to an on-state, and the laser turns on again. In this case, the wait period becomes the summation of MEMS response time and the laser switching period. As a result, the period of this reconfiguration procedure is longer than the MEMS switching period: no acceleration can be done. However, using the interleaving method, in such case, a laser of another module for which the angles of mirrors have already adjusted and a configuration has been ready, turns on. Furthermore, the lasers on the third module, the fourth module, and so on turn on, in turn. While the other modules work, modules which one configuration procedure has been completed start to prepare next-configuration mirror position. For example, it is assumed that if the switching speeds of laser and MEMS are 10 ns and 10 $\mu s$, and 1001 modules which have 1000 mirrors are implemented onto the ORGA, then the ORGA has a million configuration contexts. Each reconfiguration can be executed within 10 ns because, while another 1000 modules work for a period 1000 × 10 ns, mirrors of the idle module can be changed for 10,000 ns. Therefore, using the proposed method, even a million configuration contexts can be switched by only 1001 lasers. Results show that the number of lasers can be reduced dramatically.

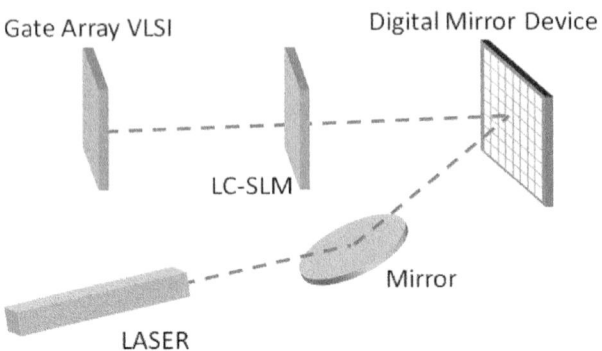

**Fig. 4.** Experimental system

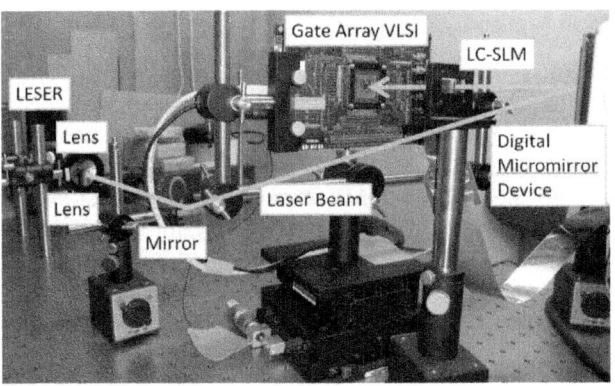

**Fig. 5.** Photograph of the experimental system

## 3   Experimental System

### 3.1   Experimental System

For this study, a single module implementation with four configuration contexts was conducted as the first step for MEMS-interleaving ORGA development. Figure 4 portrays a block diagram of a MEMS-interleaving ORGA. A photograph is shown in Fig. 5. The MEMS interleaving ORGA was constructed using a 532 nm, 300 mW laser (torus 532; Laser Quantum), a MEMS device, a liquid-crystal spatial light modulator (LC-SLM), and an ORGA-VLSI. The 1.7-mm-diameter beam from the laser source is expanded three times to 5.1 mm using two lenses of 50 mm focal length and 150 mm focal length. The expanded beam is incident to a MEMS mirror device (Digital Mirror Device). The MEMS mirror device specifications are the same as those shown in Table 1. In this case, the mirror state is controlled as with a binary state. In addition, in this experiment, $236 \times 236$ mirrors were used as one large mirror to simplify the experiments. Since each mirror size is 10.8 $\mu m$ × 10.8 $\mu m$, the total size of each mirror is

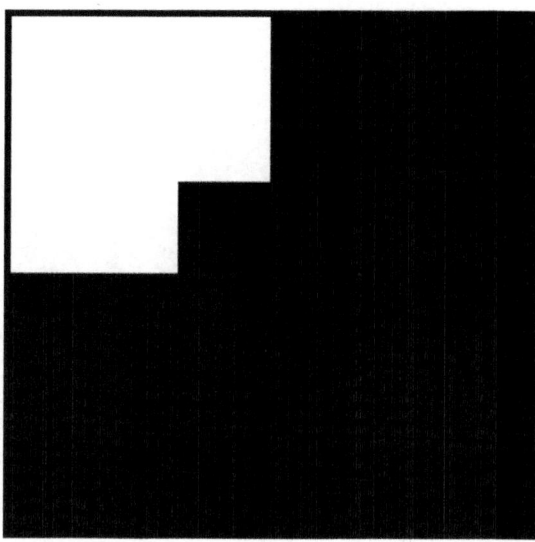

**Fig. 6.** Mirror pattern for one configuration context. The mirror set, which comprises $236 \times 236$ pixels, is used to choose a configuration context on a holographic memory. The size of each pixel is $10.8 \ \mu m \times 10.8 \ \mu m$.

$2{,}548.8 \ \mu m \times 2{,}548.8 \ \mu m$, as shown in Fig. 6. The mirror device has four large mirrors to address four configuration contexts. When the mirror is at angle $+12°$, the laser beam is reflected from it, incident to the LC-SLM, which functions as a holographic memory. Otherwise, the reflected beam is never incident to the LC-SLM. On the other hand, a holographic memory pattern is displayed on the LC-SLM. The LC-SLM is a projection TV panel (L3D07U-81G00; Seiko Epson Corp.). It is a $90°$ twisted nematic device with a thin film transistor. The panel consists of $1{,}920 \times 1{,}080$ pixels, each having a size of $8.5 \times 8.5 \ \mu m^2$. The LC-SLM is connected to an evaluation board (L3B07-E60A; Seiko Epson Corp.). The board's video input is connected to the external display terminal of a personal computer. Programming for the LC-SLM is executed by displaying a holographic memory pattern with 256 gradation levels on the personal computer display. The holographic memory pattern displayed on the LC-SLM is presented in Fig. 7. The holographic memory has four recording regions. Each region includes a configuration context. Therefore, four configuration contexts are stored on four regions of the holographic memory, where they are addressed by four large mirrors.

Here, a calculation method for two-dimensional holographic medium is introduced. An aperture plane of target lasers, a holographic plane, and a DORGA-VLSI plane are parallelized. The laser beam is collimated. The collimated reference wave from the laser propagates into the holographic plane. The holographic medium comprises rectangular pixels of $\delta_x \times \delta_y$ on the $x_1 - y_1$ holographic plane. The pixels are assumed as binary values. The input object is made up of rectangular pixels of $d_x \times d_y$ on the $x_2 - y_2$ object plane. The pixels can be modulated to be either on or off. The intensity distribution of a holographic medium is calculable using the following equation:

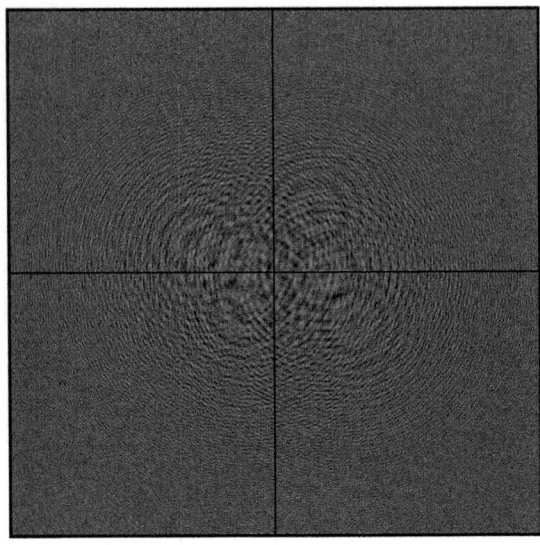

**Fig. 7.** Holographic memory pattern comprising $602 \times 602$ pixels. Each pixel is 8.5 $\mu m \times$ 8.5 $\mu m$. The holographic memory includes four configuration contexts. The distance between holographic memory regions is two pixels.

$$H(x_1, y_1) \propto \int_{-\infty}^{\infty} \int_{-\infty}^{\infty} O(x_2, y_2) \sin(kr) dx_2 dy_2,$$

$$r = \sqrt{Z_L^2 + (x_1 - x_2)^2 + (y_1 - y_2)^2}, \tag{1}$$

where $O(x_2, y_2)$ represents a binary value of a reconfiguration context, $k$ is the wave number, and $Z_L$ denotes the distance between the holographic plane and the object plane. The value $H(x_1, y_1)$ is normalized as 0–1 for the minimum intensity $H_{min}$ and maximum intensity $H_{max}$, as the following.

$$H'(x_1, y_1) = \frac{H(x_1, y_1) - H_{min}}{H_{max} - H_{min}}. \tag{2}$$

Finally, the normalized image $H'$ is used for implementing a holographic memory. Other areas on the holographic plane are opaque to the illumination.

A laser on the module is collimated. The outgoing beam can illuminate all mirror areas. The set of the four mirrors and the laser described above constitutes one module. For this implementation, an ORGA was placed 100 mm distant from the LC-SLM. The LC-SLM works as a holographic memory. The ORGA had been fabricated using a 0.35 $\mu m$ triple-metal CMOS process. Photodiodes were constructed between the N-well layer and the P-substrate. The photodiode size and distance between photodiodes were designed as $25.5 \times 25.5 \ \mu m^2$ and as 90 $\mu m$ to facilitate the optical alignment. The gate array structure is fundamentally identical to that of typical FPGAs. The ORGA-VLSI chip includes 4 logic blocks, 5 switching matrices, and 12 I/O bits. In all, 340 photodiodes were used to program the gate array.

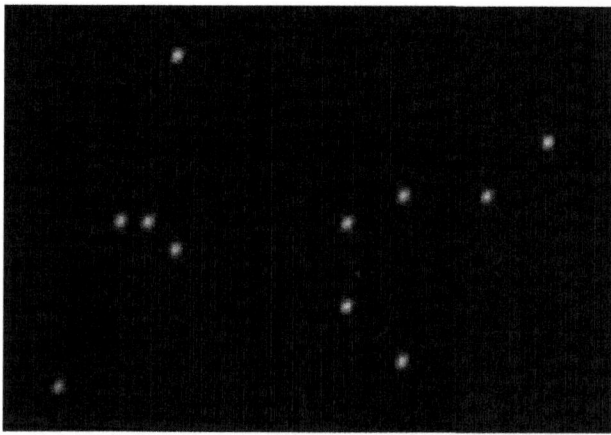

**Fig. 8.** CCD-captured image of a configuration context pattern of an XOR circuit recorded on the upper left side holographic region

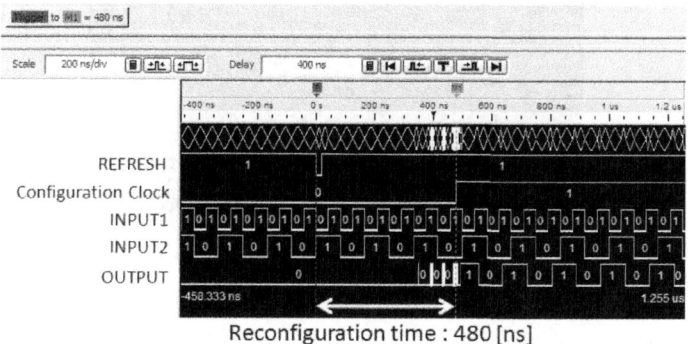

Reconfiguration time : 480 [ns]

**Fig. 9.** Timing diagram of an XOR circuit configuration procedure

Of course, to execute perfectly high-speed interleaving operation, many modules must be used. However, because of hardware resource limitations, only one module was tested in this demonstration. Based on these experimental results, the system performance was then estimated for a case having many modules.

## 4  Experimental Results

Using the optical system explained above, the MEMS-interleaving operation has been confirmed. As one of four configuration contexts, the CCD-captured configuration context pattern of an XOR circuit is presented in Fig. 8. The configuration context was stored on the upper left side holographic memory, which is addressed by the same upper left side mirror array. First, one mirror angle is adjusted to a turn-on state; then,

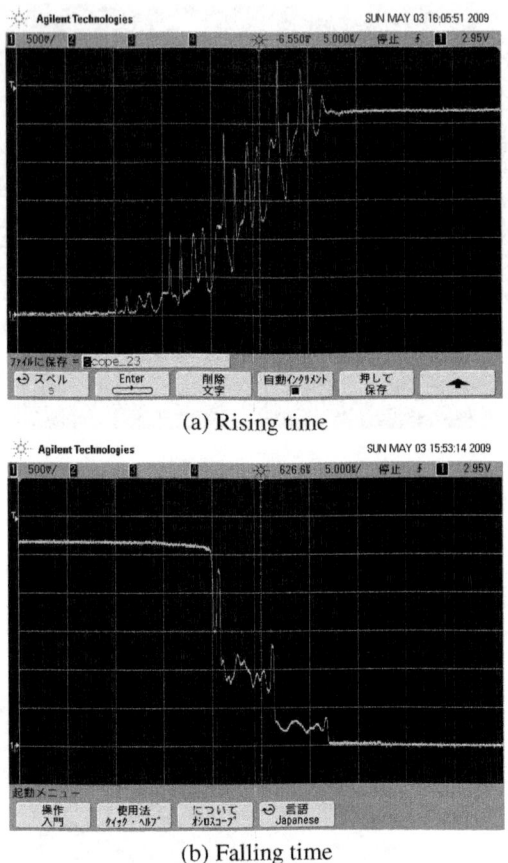

(a) Rising time

(b) Falling time

**Fig. 10.** Response time of an MEMS mirror array device. The turn-on time is 22 $\mu s$; the turn-off time is 12 $\mu s$.

a laser turns on. Subsequently, the configuration time was measured as shown in Fig. 9. The results confirmed a 480 ns reconfiguration time. The other holographic region configuration procedures were also confirmed.

## 5   Discussion

The response time of an MEMS mirror array device is shown in Fig. 10. The switching time of MEMS mirror array was estimated as 22 $\mu s$ in the worst case. In addition, the laser switching time was measured as 480 ns. In this case, if 47 experimental modules are used for the MEMS interleaving ORGA, the number of reconfiguration contexts is 47 × 4. That is, 47 × 4 reconfiguration contexts are read out constantly within 480 ns. Of course, the reconfiguration speed is independent of the number of mirrors inside a module. For example, if one module has 100 mirrors and 47 modules are used for the MEMS interleaving ORGA, although 4,700 configuration contexts are implemented onto the MEMS interleaving ORGA, the number of addressing lasers is only 47. Of course, in this case, the total number of mirrors is 4,700. Such a large number of mirrors can be fabricated easily on an MEMS mirror device.

## 6   Conclusion

To date, optically reconfigurable gate arrays (ORGAs) have been developed to realize next-generation large-virtual gate count programmable VLSI. However, conventional ORGAs require many lasers to address the configuration contexts stored on a holographic memory. Such a laser array with numerous lasers is always expensive, which has become a main concern related to their development. Therefore, to address numerous configuration contexts with fewer lasers, this paper has proposed a novel method using an MEMS-interleaving ORGA. If we can use $4,000 \times 4,000$ mirror array with 10 $\mu m$ response time, and 1,000 lasers that can generate 10 ns light pulse, then 16 million reconfiguration contexts can be achieved along with 10 ns reconfiguration speed. This method can be expected to provide an addressing capability of a billion configuration contexts along with nanosecond-order high-speed configuration capability.

## Acknowledgments

This research was supported by the Ministry of Education, Science, Sports and Culture, Grant-in-Aid for Scientific Research on Innovative Areas, No. 20200027. The VLSI chip in this study was fabricated in the chip fabrication program of VLSI Design and Education Center (VDEC), the University of Tokyo in collaboration with Rohm Co. Ltd. and Toppan Printing Co. Ltd.

## References

1. Altera Corporation, Altera Devices, http://www.altera.com
2. Xilinx Inc., Xilinx Product Data Sheets, http://www.xilinx.com
3. Lattice Semiconductor Corporation, LatticeECP and EC Family Data Sheet (2005), http://www.latticesemi.co.jp/products
4. Mumbru, J., Panotopoulos, G., Psaltis, D., An, X., Mok, F., Ay, S., Barna, S., Fossum, E.: Optically Programmable Gate Array. In: SPIE of Optics in Computing 2000, vol. 4089, pp. 763–771 (2000)
5. Mumbru, J., Zhou, G., An, X., Liu, W., Panotopoulos, G., Mok, F., Psaltis, D.: Optical memory for computing and information processing. In: SPIE on Algorithms, Devices, and Systems for Optical Information Processing III, vol. 3804, pp. 14–24 (1999)
6. Mumbru, J., Zhou, G., Ay, S., An, X., Panotopoulos, G., Mok, F., Psaltis, D.: Optically Reconfigurable Processors. In: SPIE Critical Review 1999 Euro-American Workshop on Optoelectronic Information Processing, vol. 74, pp. 265–288 (1999)
7. Yamaguchi, N., Watanabe, M.: Liquid crystal holographic configurations for ORGAs. Applied Optics 47(28), 4692–4700 (2008)
8. Seto, D., Watanabe, M.: A dynamic optically reconfigurable gate array - perfect emulation. IEEE Journal of Quantum Electronics 44(5), 493–500 (2008)

9. Watanabe, M., Kobayashi, F.: Dynamic Optically Reconfigurable Gate Array. Japanese Journal of Applied Physics 45(4B), 3510–3515 (2006)
10. Nakajima, M., Watanabe, M.: A four-context optically differential reconfigurable gate array. IEEE/OSA Journal of Lightwave Technology 27(20), 4460–4470 (2009)
11. Nakajima, M., Watanabe, M.: A 100-Context Optically Reconfigurable Gate Array. In: IEEE International Symposium on Circuits and Systems, pp. 2884–2887 (2010)
12. Ogiwara, A., Watanabe, M., Mabuchi, T., Kobayashi, F.: Formation of holographic memory for defect tolerance in optically reconfigurable gate arrays. Applied Optics 49(22), 4255–4261 (2010)
13. Texas Instruments, DLP, http://www.ti.com/
14. Texas Instruments, Discovery 4000, http://www.ti.com/
15. Morita, H., Watanabe, M.: Microelectromechanical Configuration of an Optically Reconfigurable Gate Array. IEEE Journal of Quantum Electronics 46(9), 1288–1294 (2010)
16. Khargharia, B., Hariri, S., Yousif, M.S.: An Adaptive Interleaving Technique for Memory Performance-per-Watt Management. IEEE Transactions on Parallel and Distributed Systems 20(7), 1011–1022 (2009)
17. Sohi, G.S.: High-bandwidth interleaved memories for vector processors-a simulation study. IEEE Transactions on Computers 42(1), 34–44 (1993)
18. Song, C., Postula, A.: Synthesis of custom interleaved memory systems. IEEE Transactions on Very Large Scale Integration (VLSI) Systems 8(1), 74–83 (2000)
19. VanCourt, T., Herbordt, M.C.: Application-Specific Memory Interleaving Enables High Performance in FPGA-based Grid Computations. In: IEEE Symposium on Field-Programmable Custom Computing Machines, pp. 305–306 (2006)

# FaRM: Fast Reconfiguration Manager for Reducing Reconfiguration Time Overhead on FPGA

François Duhem, Fabrice Muller, and Philippe Lorenzini

University of Nice-Sophia Antipolis - LEAT/CNRS
{Francois.Duhem,Fabrice.Muller,Philippe.Lorenzini}@unice.fr

**Abstract.** In this paper, we present a fast ICAP controller providing high-speed configuration and easy-to-use readback capabilities, reducing configuration overhead as much as possible. In order to enhance performance, FaRM uses techniques such as DMA, ICAP overclocking, bitstream pre-load into controller and bitstream compression, using an evolution of the Run Length Encoding algorithm. We also propose a reconfiguration overhead estimation model which gives a good idea of the overhead. This approach is tested with an AES encryption/decryption architecture. With proper ICAP overclocking to 200 MHz, we are able to reach the ICAP upper bound throughput of 800 MB/s.

## 1 Introduction

Partial Reconfiguration (PR) has been introduced lately in order to face the need for more and more resources on Field Programmable Gate Arrays (FPGA), allowing to change reconfigurable partitions behavior while the remaining logic is still running. Therefore, PR can be used to change the functionality of a system or to save resources and power of the FPGA [1] [2].

Recent Xilinx FPGA provide this feature via the Internal Configuration Access Port (ICAP) [3]. However, Xilinx's controller, *xps_hwicap* [4], comes with low performance. If the system performs scheduling on hardware tasks, the ratio reconfiguration time to task execution time might become unacceptable.

It is possible to overcome this issue in many ways. First, by compressing the configuration data, called bitstream. Decompression has to be done by the system, so that the resources overhead is a significant metric. We can also work on the controller's architecture, e.g. integrating a DMA (Direct Memory Access) to increase the throughput of the configuration interface [5]. Scheduling may also be able to predict the tasks to execute on a reconfigurable zone (RZ) [6], thus bitstream pre-loading could significantly improve performance.

We propose to combine those approaches in our controller, FaRM (Fast Reconfiguration Manager). We present an architecture able to provide performance reaching the ICAP limit. In order to reduce transfer time, our controller integrates its own DMA and is able to handle bitstream compression and pre-load. In addition, we want FaRM to provide an easy-to-use yet efficient readback capability (i.e. retrieving configuration data from the FPGA). This work is done within the ARDMAHN ANR project [7].

A. Koch et al. (Eds.): ARC 2011, LNCS 6578, pp. 253–260, 2011.

This paper is structured as follows. In Sect. 2, we discuss works related to the acceleration of partial reconfiguration. Section 3 introduces our approach to speed up reconfiguration. Section 4 sums up the results we obtained. Finally, we discuss some improvements we want to implement in our controller.

## 2   Related Works

In [8], the authors discuss different bitstream compression techniques. Their algorithm, based on Run Length Encoding (RLE) and LZW, is compared with algorithms such as canonic RLE or GZIP. However, [8] provides the compressed bitstream sizes but does not give their initial size nor the achieved compression ratio. It appears that RLE offers poor results and that their algorithm gives ratios slightly lower than a ZIP algorithm. Note that they use a virtual FPGA layer so that these results may not be representative for physical FPGAs bitstreams.

The work presented in [9] tends to be more exhaustive, not only considering compression ratio but also key metrics like throughput and resource overhead. Compression reduces the transfers on the bus, thus saving costly memory accesses, but the decompression part embedded in the FPGA also has to efficiently send data to the ICAP to get a good reconfiguration time.

In [10], the authors present a bitstream repository hierarchy. Their local architecture is based on a DMA writing bitstreams to ICAP through an OPB bus. A similar approach is presented in [5]: the authors present their high-speed controller, containing a BRAM dedicated to bitstream write. Even if they are close to theoritecal maximum throughput, the IP requires a large amount of BRAM (nearly half the BRAM resource of a Virtex-4 FX20 FPGA).

Authors in [11] use virtual configurations to decrease reconfiguration time. It consists of a running configuration context and another one in the background. PR may influence the background context while the foreground context is still running. The major drawback appears when working with a mono-context FPGA: there have to be as many RZs as configuration contexts, resulting in an important size overhead.

## 3   Our Approach

### 3.1   FaRM Architecture

FaRM (Fig. 1) has both master and slave interfaces, whereas Xilinx's IP only has a slave interface. The slave interface deals with the registers control of the IP while the master interface is responsible for the accesses to the memory where the bitstreams should be stored, allowing the IP to act like a DMA. The ICAP macro is driven by two FSMs and interfaced with two FIFOs, for read and write accesses, to separate clock domains. Like Xilinx's IP, the ICAP and the bus are on different clock domains in order to deal with the ICAP clock limit of 100 MHz without limiting the bus frequency. However, we were able to go past this limitation for the ICAP clock with a write access, but not with a read access (see Sect. 4), thus we also separated the read and write clocks.

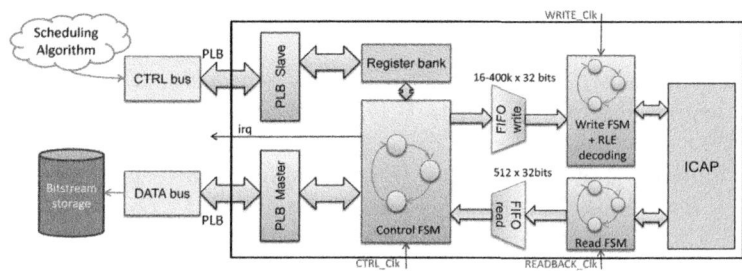

**Fig. 1.** FaRM architecture

## 3.2  Compression Technique

Run Length Encoding is a lossless data compression algorithm in which sequences of identical data are coded as the data combined with the number of times it is being repeated. Therefore, this algorithm perfectly fits to redundant data (e.g. memory initialization). As RLE principle is quite simple, it will result in an efficient hardware decompression part, fulfilling the requirements.

In the sequence presented in Fig. 3, the word 0x87654321 appears five times in a row in the original bitstream. After compression, it will appear twice to indicate a sequence of redundant data, followed by a counter representing the number of times the word is repeating again (3 times here). A clear drawback is that the repeating word still appears twice in the compressed bitstream (the word 0xaabbccdd repeats twice but is coded with three words).

As an improvement, our technique called Offset-RLE (O-RLE, see Fig. 2), aims at removing this extra word from the compressed bitstream. In order to indicate repeating data, we use a pointer mechanism. At the beginning of the compressed bitstream, we insert a word containing the offset to the next repeating data. After the data to repeat, we insert a word containing the number of times the data is repeated and the offset to the next repeating word. If it is the last repeating data of the bitstream, we use the word 0xffff as an offset. Note that the counter and the offset are coded on two bytes each. In our experience, this is a good compromise since a maximum value of 65536 is not likely to happen for the bitstreams we are working on. Figure 3 shows an example of O-RLE.

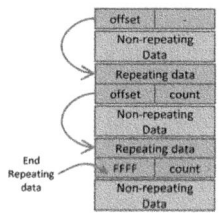

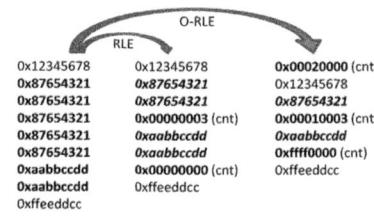

**Fig. 2.** O-RLE principle                **Fig. 3.** Canonic RLE vs. O-RLE

### 3.3   Operating Modes

We introduce a pre-load mode, which allows the user to pre-load a bitstream (or its beginning) into the write FIFO to reach ICAP theoretical throughput. The FIFO size does not need to be greater than the bitstream size (most of the time, it may not be relevant). In fact, using compression and pre-load mode significantly reduces the memory needs of the system for equivalent performance. Figure 4 shows a timing sequence with and without pre-load. With pre-load, the configuration overhead for the second IP is reduced since bitstream transfer is begun while the first IP is running. This mode is interesting if a scheduling can predict reconfigurations. If so, the overhead might be reduced to its lower bound (if all the data are present into the FIFO so that there only remains the ICAP write part of the transaction).

The major feature of FaRM is auto-readback. It provides an easy yet efficient way to read the configuration data from the FPGA. A readback is composed of three parts. First, a command part written to the ICAP prepares the readback (transfer size, frame addressing). This is step 1 in Fig. 4. Then, the ICAP fills the read FIFO and the FSM transfers it on the bus using burst transfers (step 2). Finally, there is a last command part to write to the ICAP to end the transaction (step 3). With auto-readback, the entire process is automated: after writing both command parts into memory and configuring the IP, the auto-readback can be started. Note that we can use the readback data to configure the RZ again: this is called *writeback*.

Please note that our controller may handle any readback size, in contrast of Xilinx's IP which can only read one frame at a time (which is the configuration

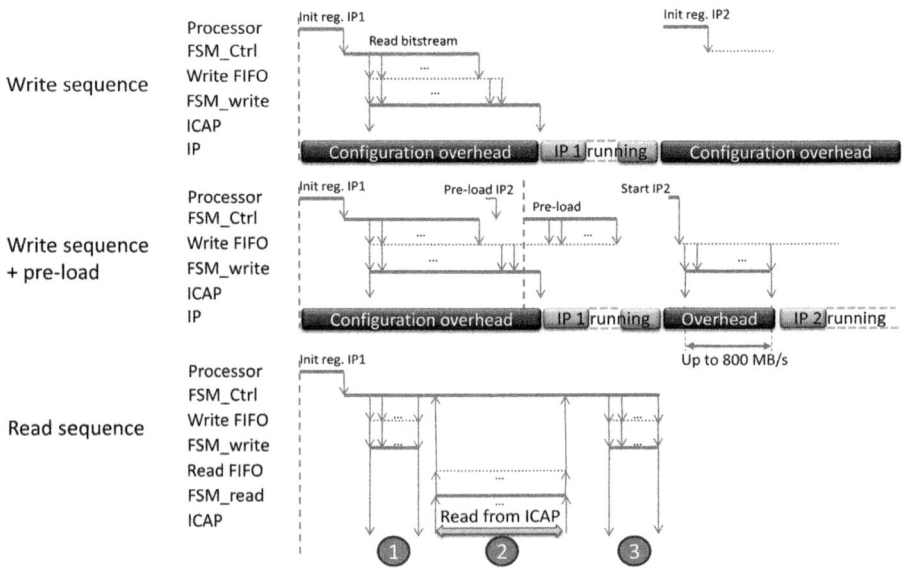

**Fig. 4.** Operating modes

granularity). Moreover, for each read operation, an extra padding frame has to be read from the ICAP. While this overhead can be neglected for large readbacks, it doubles the data read for a frame-by-frame readback and since it does not contain any relevant data, we do not transmit this frame on the bus.

Finally, note that FaRM instantiates the readback capture macro [3]. In addition to reading all configuration memory cells, this macro reads the current state of all CLB and IOB registers, allowing to capture the exact state of a reconfigurable partition.

# 4    Benchmarks

## 4.1    Bitstream Compression

Table 1 shows a comparison of different bitstream compression algorithms, tested on bitstreams with different size and complexity. O-RLE is slightly more performant than the 16 and 32 bits versions of canonic RLE. Even though we cannot compete with state-of-the-art algorithms such as ZIP and 7z, our solution does not need much resources for the decompression hardware implementation and has a throughput of one word per cycle.

**Table 1.** Compression ratios in % for different algorithms and bitstreams

| IP | Size (byte) | FaRM | RLE 16 | RLE 32 | ZIP | 7z |
|---|---|---|---|---|---|---|
| AES decoder | 97676 | 23.4 | 21.6 | 20.9 | 57 | 60.8 |
| AES encoder | 97676 | 31 | 31.6 | 26.6 | 67.6 | 69.7 |
| AES Black Box | 97676 | 90.8 | 93 | 88.1 | 97.3 | 97.5 |
| Basic DES | 24348 | 7 | 4.4 | 4.1 | 48.3 | 50.9 |
| Basic RSA | 68156 | 36.9 | 35.4 | 35.8 | 61.8 | 65.4 |
| DCT | 66844 | 41.1 | 40.5 | 38.8 | 65.3 | 67.9 |
| FFT64 | 161308 | 32.9 | 31.3 | 32.2 | 57.3 | 60.8 |
| FIR_7_16_8 | 17132 | 11.7 | 7.6 | 7.3 | 64.3 | 65 |
| FIR_7_16_16 | 23036 | 12.8 | 10.3 | 7.5 | 65.3 | 67.1 |
| Hibert | 24348 | 19.9 | 18.7 | 14.8 | 65.4 | 66.7 |
| Count 1 | 6632 | 51.2 | 48.9 | 44.8 | 78.3 | 78.5 |
| Count 2 | 6632 | 51 | 48.8 | 44.6 | 78.2 | 78.3 |
| **Geometric mean** | | **26.7** | **23.9** | **21.5** | **66.1** | **68.1** |

## 4.2    Reconfiguration Overhead Estimation

Let us estimate reconfiguration overhead for a canonic write operation. In our experience, the ICAP is not limiting the transfer: once the access is finished on the bus, the ICAP is able to process all the words before the next burst, so that the overhead only reflects the bitstream bus transfers. Let us note $N_{bitstream}$ the bitstream length in 32-bits words, $T_{bus}$ the bus period in $ns$, $latency$ the initial latency in cycles, $t_{burst}$ the average time for a burst in cycles and $N_{burst}$ the number of words in a burst. Equation (1) gives an estimation of the reconfiguration overhead for an uncompressed bitstream.

$$t_{\text{write}}(\text{ns}) = (latency + t_{\text{burst}} * \lfloor \frac{N_{\text{bitstream}}}{N_{\text{burst}}} \rfloor +$$
$$(t_{\text{burst}} - N_{\text{bitstream}} \bmod N_{\text{burst}})) * T_{\text{bus}} . \qquad (1)$$

We cannot properly estimate this overhead for a compressed bitstream since it depends on its regularity. Introducing compression into (1) gives us the lower bound. In the worst case scenario, compressed data are located at the end of the bitstream so that there is an extra ICAP write overhead. Let us note $T_{icap}$ the ICAP period in $ns$ and $ratio$ the achieved compression rate (1 if using uncompressed bitstreams). Equations (2) and (3) give a lower and an upper bound of the reconfiguration overhead for a compressed bitstream.

$$t_{\text{min}}(\text{ns}) = (latency + t_{\text{burst}} * \lfloor \frac{ratio * N_{\text{bitstream}}}{N_{\text{burst}}} \rfloor +$$
$$(t_{\text{burst}} - (ratio * N_{\text{bitstream}}) \bmod N_{\text{burst}})) * T_{\text{bus}} . \qquad (2)$$

$$t_{\text{max}}(\text{ns}) = t_{\text{min}} + N_{\text{bitstream}} * (1 - ratio) * T_{\text{icap}} . \qquad (3)$$

### 4.3   Application

FaRM was tested on a ML507 board with an AES encryption/decryption system as depicted in Fig. 5. The RZ hosts either the encoder or the decoder and has the following resources: 12 CLB columns and one BRAM column (590 frames, each one with 41x32-bits words [3]). However, it is currently impossible to correctly readback from BRAM columns. So, for readback operations, we only worked on the CLB subset of the RZ, containing 462 frames.

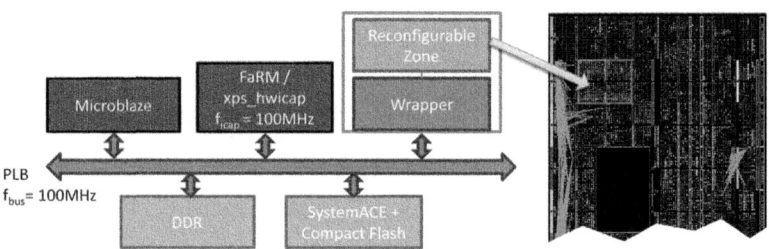

**Fig. 5.** AES test system

We used different ICAP controllers for the tests. First, we used Xilinx's controller and its drivers. In this case, the microprocessor performs all the operations by itself. We enhanced a little bit this controller by coupling it to a DMA taking care of data transfers. Finally, we used our controller, with and without bitstream compression.

**Table 2.** Reconfiguration and readback times

| $f_{bus} = 100MHz$ $f_{icap} = 100MHz$ | xps_hwicap | | | xps_hwicap + DMA | | |
|---|---|---|---|---|---|---|
| | Time ($\mu s$) | COM BW (MB/s) | ICAP BW (MB/s) | Time ($\mu s$) | COM BW (MB/s) | ICAP BW (MB/s) |
| Reconfiguration | 72800 | 1.29 | 1.29 | 1550 | 60.5 | **60.5** |
| Frame/frame readback | 159000 | 0.92 | 0.92 | 49200 | 2.97 | 2.97 |
| | FaRM | | | FaRM + RLE | | |
| Reconfiguration | 731 | 128 | **128** | 538 | 127 | **174** |
| Frame/frame readback | 1536 | 47 | 95 | 1600 | 45 | 91 |
| Global readback | 560 | 129 | 129 | 560 | 129 | 129 |

Results are listed in Table 2. We measured the overhead and calculated the bandwidth (BW) for a reconfiguration, a frame-by-frame readback and a global readback (reading all frames at once) corresponding to the AES encoder bitstream from Table 1. We differentiate communication throughput (on the bus) and ICAP throughput since in readback mode, FaRM does not transmit the extra padding frame and in write mode, we have to consider compression rate.

It is now possible to verify our time estimation model. Let us take a latency of 10 cycles, 16 words per burst, 48 cycles per burst access (obtained with ChipScope Analyzer) and a period of 10 ns. We estimate the overhead without compression to $733\mu s$ (actual value $731\mu s$). We estimate the overhead with compression between $506\mu s$ and $581\mu s$ (the average is $544\mu s$, and the actual value $538\mu s$).

Pre-load mode was tested along with ICAP overclocking, the bus running at 125 MHz and ICAP at 200 MHz. The bitstreams used were Count1 and Count2 from Table 1). Reconfiguration took 8304 ns while the ICAP needs at least 8290 ns (1658 ICAP cycles needed to write 6632 bytes), meaning that we achieved the maximum ICAP throughput of 800 MB/s.

## 5   Future Works

We are currently studying dynamic reconfiguration power footprint. We want to infer consumption models as we made for the time overhead.

In order to complete our approach, we also want our reconfiguration manager to provide the user with services at a higher level of abstraction. It may gather informations about the FPGA and the RZs and use it to perform on line placement and scheduling regarding some pre-defined strategies (e.g. favouring power consumption or performance). Among other things, scheduling will use the models we presented for the reconfiguration overhead estimation and also the power models we are working on.

## 6   Conclusion

In order to reduce reconfiguration overhead, we proposed an approach based on a high-speed architecture combined with an evolved compression technique,

Offset-RLE. We were able to obtain a huge speedup compared to Xilinx's controller, obtaining a thoughput of 800 MB/s for a write operation to the ICAP working at 200 MHz using the pre-load mode. We also proposed an accurate reconfiguration overhead calculation model, verified for our test architecture, which will be used for developing scheduling strategies. The controller has also an high speed auto-readback capability to retrieve configuration data from the FPGA.

# References

1. Kao, C.: Benefits of Partial Reconfiguration. Xcell Journal 55, 65–67 (2005)
2. Paulsson, K., Hübner, M., Bayar, S., Becker, J.: Exploitation of Run-Time Partial Reconfiguration for Dynamic Power Management in Xilinx Spartan III-based Systems. In: International Conference on Field Programmable Logic and Applications, FPL 2008, pp. 699–700 (2008)
3. Xilinx Inc.: Virtex-5 Configuration User Guide (2010)
4. Xilinx Inc.: LogiCORE IP XPS HWICAP datasheet (2010)
5. Liu, M., Kuehn, W., Lu, Z., Jantsch, A.: Run-time Partial Reconfiguration Speed Investigation and Architectural Design Space Exploration. In: International Conference on Field Programmable Logic and Applications, FPL 2009 (2009)
6. Belaid, I., Muller, F., Benjemaa, M.: New Three-level Resource Management Enhancing Quality of Off-line Hardware Task Placement on FPGA. International Journal of Reconfigurable Computing (IJRC), 65–67 (2010)
7. ARDMAHN consortium: ARDMAHN project, http://ARDMAHN.org/
8. Siozios, K., Koutroumpezis, G., Tatas, K., Soudris, D., Thanailakis, A.: DAGGER: A Novel Generic Methodology for FPGA Bitstream Generation and Its Software Tool Implementation. In: Proceedings of 19th IEEE International Parallel and Distributed Processing Symposium, p. 165b (2005)
9. Koch, D., Beckhoff, C., Teich, J.: Bitstream Decompression for High Speed FPGA Configuration from Slow Memories. In: International Conference on Field-Programmable Technology, ICFPT 2007, pp. 161–168 (2007)
10. Bomel, P., Crenne, J., Ye, L., Diguet, J.P., Gogniat, G.: Ultra-Fast Downloading of Partial Bitstreams through Ethernet. In: Berekovic, M., Müller-Schloer, C., Hochberger, C., Wong, S. (eds.) ARCS 2009. LNCS, vol. 5455, pp. 72–83. Springer, Heidelberg (2009)
11. Liu, M., Lu, Z., Kuehn, W., Jantsch, A.: Reducing FPGA Reconfiguration Time Overhead using Virtual Configurations. ReCoSoC (2010)

# Feasibility Analysis of Reconfigurable Computing in Low-Power Wireless Sensor Applications

Andreas Engel[1], Björn Liebig[1], and Andreas Koch[2]

[1] LOEWE Research Center AdRIA, Darmstadt
[2] Embedded Systems and Applications Group, Technische Universität Darmstadt

**Abstract.** With increasing complexity of sensor network applications, the trade-off between node-local processing and transmission of data to a central node for handling becomes more significant. For distributed structural health monitoring applications (SHM), we consider different realization choices of the underlying wireless sensor network and implement a key part of the application (a high-order filter) on the novel *HaLoMote* architecture, a reconfigurable wireless sensor node (rWSN) with FPGA-based processing capability. We compare different tool flows supporting development of algorithms above the RTL regarding to achievable area and energy efficiency and outline the advantage of rWSN over traditional MCU- and DSP-based sensor systems in this scenario.

**Keywords:** reconfigurable computing, wireless sensor network, high-level synthesis, wordlength optimization, low-power mode.

## 1   Introduction

Networks of wireless sensor nodes (WSN) have been used in numerous practical applications [1]. Those applications require data acquisition, some kind of processing for data aggregation, and finally the dissemination of results through the network.

In general the small compute power of the WSN allows only limited local preprocessing, restricting it to simple data logging and communication tasks. This approach is not suitable for all applications, though. If data has to be sent to the central node(s) at shorter intervals, a significant amount of energy will be required for the radio transmissions [2].

Motivated by adaptive vibration control and structural health monitoring applications in the context of the LOEWE Research Center for Adaptronics (AdRIA) [3], we have investigated the use of energy-efficient reconfigurable computing in the nodes to allow for more intelligent local processing, thus saving energy by reducing transmission data volumes. The first focus of this work will be the evaluation of real-world applications on different platforms. To ease this comparison, we concentrated on a high-order filter (384-tap FIR), a key operation in most AdRIA applications.

A. Koch et al. (Eds.): ARC 2011, LNCS 6578, pp. 261–268, 2011.

Since our work in context of AdRIA is performed in close collaboration with non-hardware designers, we also require our rWSN architecture, named *HaLo-Mote* (for Hardware-Accelerated Low-power Mote), to be easily "programmable". Thus, the second focus of this work is the support of automatic tool flows from descriptions in Simulink and Matlab onto the target platform. We will characterize the solutions examined in terms of computing performance, energy requirements and area required.

To this end, we will briefly survey related work in Section 2. Section 3 gives an overview of the *HaLoMote* architecture, concentrating on the processing elements. A number of tool flows for programming the *HaLoMote* from high-level descriptions will be examined in Section 4. We evaluate our benchmark kernel, the 384-tap FIR filter, implemented on the *HaLoMote* and on three traditional low-power micro-controllers and DSPs in Section 5. Finally, Section 6 concludes and looks forward to future work.

## 2   Related Work

### 2.1   Reconfigurable WSN Computing

Popular microprocessor-based WSN platforms are the Mica2 motes [4], which use an 8 bit Atmel ATmega128L [5] MCU, the TelosB motes [6] and the T-Mote sky [7], both of which are based on 16 bit MSP430 [8] MCU. A more detailed summary about conventional WSN technologies and services can be found at [1].

While many FPGA vendors claim to offer energy-efficient devices, only few devices are actually aimed at very low-power operation (e.g., in mobile devices). The key to extreme energy conservation are deep sleep modes, that can be both quickly entered and exited. While some suggestions have been made on how to extend the conventional Xilinx Spartan-3 FPGA series with this capability [9], devices which natively support such operations are preferable. Examples include the SiliconBlue iCE65 family [10] and the Actel Igloo series [11], the latter of which will be used in our *HaLoMote*.

Reconfigurable processing has been considered before for WSNs, specifically for image processing applications in a Wireless Visual Sensor Network (WVSN) [12,13]. The combination of an 8051-based MCU and a Xilinx Spartan-3 (XC3S200) FPGA was presented in [14]. However, these prior attempts have not examined power consumption in detail and do not describe active power saving measures (e.g., managing deep sleep modes) or do not consider low-power implementation alternatives.

### 2.2   Automatic Mapping of High-Level Descriptions to RTL

Our use-cases require mostly control engineering and signal processing applications to be executed in the WSN. Since these algorithms are often developed in Matlab and Simulink, it is worthwhile to examine the current state of tool flows supporting the automatic mapping of these high-level descriptions to reconfigurable processing units.

A number of commercial tools allow the translation of Matlab/Simulink models into RTL HDL netlists suitable for mapping onto FPGAs [15,16,17]. For Simulink, this is generally achieved by restricting models to the subset of blocks supported by the high-level synthesis tool (for which underlying hardware implementations have been developed manually). Translating Matlab, which allows greater freedom of expression than just composing blocks, is supported by fewer tools [15,17] and more severely restricted: Only very limited constructs can be automatically translated into hardware (and then often not very efficiently).

An alternative is an indirect approach by first exporting the Matlab/Simulink description as a C program using a tool such as the Real-Time Workshop Toolbox [18]. Then, the many academic (e.g., [23]) or commercial (e.g., [24,25,26]) C-to-HDL synthesis systems can be applied to hardware mapping problem. This approach is not entirely seamless, as the generated C code contains unsupported constructs (e.g., pointers, floating-point computation). We will examine later in this paper how the gap between the Matlab-exported C and the subsets accepted by the C-to-HDL tools can be closed.

Both approaches require predetermination of fixed-point word length, which should be done for each signal individually [20]. While an analytic approach exists for signal to noise ratio (SQNR) [21], other quality functions often have to be calculated by simulation.

## 3 HaLoMote Architecture and Prototype Implementation

Fig. 1 gives a high-level overview of the *HaLoMote* platform architecture. Some of the aspects, e.g., the sensor interfaces, memory system and power supply lie outside the scope of this work and will not be discussed further. Instead, this work will mainly deal with the actual processing elements: An 8-bit MCU is integrated into the Radio Communications SoC for low-performance tasks (e.g., running the wireless networking protocols). The FPGA can be used both to realize a software-programmable 32 bit soft-core CPU as well as dedicated accelerators directly implementing an algorithm in hardware.

For our first *HaLoMote* implementation, we selected the following devices for the platform components: 2.4 GHz IEEE 802.15.4 compliant radio communications are provided by a TI CC2530 RF-SoC [27], which includes an 8051-compatible MCU. Software running on the 8051 implements the Zigbee protocol

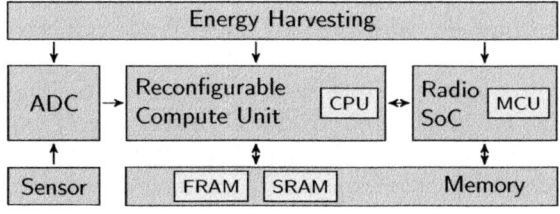

**Fig. 1.** Simplified overview of the *HaLoMote* platform

stack and support services. The RF-SoC consumes about 24 mW when operating at 32 MHz with radio disabled, about 92 mW when receiving data and between 86 mW and 118 mW when transmitting data. The 8051 starts operations on the RCU, implemented by an Actel M1AGL1000 Igloo FPGA [11], which was chosen for to its ultra low-power "Flash Freeze" sleep-mode, that can be entered and exited in ≈ 1 μs, saving all outputs and register content while lowering power draw to 52 μW.

## 4     High-Level Synthesis Tool Flows

For evaluating the high-level programmability of our architecture, specifically the RCU, we first consider the fixed-point word-length optimization, then two ways to generate hardware: One going from Simulink directly to RTL HDL, the second one exporting C and translating that to RTL HDL.

### 4.1     Word-Length Optimization

Due to the inefficiency (both area and energy-wise) of floating-point computations on FPGAs, we convert the computations to word-length optimized fixed-point form, allowing for separate word-lengths for each operator to achieve even smaller logic. As a quality measure, we use the mean square error over the filter response. Using a heuristic word-length approach we can generate an entire set of possible realizations (targeting different mean square error bounds) in 80 seconds on a Core 2 Duo E8500 PC. Assuming that an error bound of 0.5 dB suffices for this application, the resulting computation will have a 16 bit datapath, 14 bit coefficients and 7 bit data width on the multipliers.

### 4.2     Hardware Synthesis

The first approach is the direct conversion from Matlab/Simulink to VHDL. This is especially easy for our 384-tap FIR benchmark, which can directly map to a specialized block, generally also giving additional implementation options such as resource sharing (folding) or optimized constant coefficient multiplication. In the first alternative, we directly translate this model to RTL HDL for implementation on the FPGA.

The indirect approach using C based synthesis, is also applicable to models containing blocks not available in the tool vendors hardware libraries. The C code generated for the Simulink model by Real Time Workshop has to be transformed to become suitable for C-to-Hardware compilation. This includes pointer and file operations, computations split into several functions which need to be merged, and floating-point arithmetic re-introduced during the C export. For discrete single-rate Simulink models, we developed a software tool that automatically removes or rewrites the problematic constructs, ending up with C code amenable to hardware compilation.

# 5   Experimental Evaluation

After annotating word-lengths into the Simulink model, we translate it to hardware suitable for execution on the *HaLoMote*-RCU. We will have to refer to the design tools used for this step just by S1/S2 for direct Simulink-HDL translation, and C1/C2 for Simulink-C-HDL translation, since the tool license terms prohibit direct benchmarking. However, this approach is sufficient to evaluate the applicability of our architecture and design methodology.

## 5.1   High-Level Synthesis: Latency vs. RCU Area Trade-Off

Fig. 2 compares the latency required to process a single sample, and area required on the M1AGL1000-FPGA, for different implementations achievable using the different tool flows. While the Simulink-HDL tools support a very finely granular setting of resource sharing, the flows involving C-to-HDL translation are more restricted in that they support only the extremes; in the case of C2, actually only the (very small, high latency) design point. This is due to C2 not recognizing how often the loops in the FIR would be executed, and thus only allowing full sequentially executing on a single multiplier. The two RTL models generated by C1 differ in their internal storage scheme: In the small (slow) implementation, BRAMs are used to store the filter state while in the large (fast) implementation registers are used for this purpose.

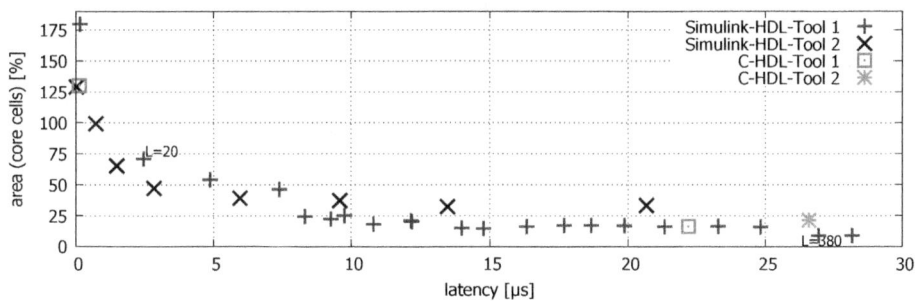

**Fig. 2.** Area vs. latency for final synthesis results

## 5.2   Latency and Area vs. RCU Power Draw Trade-Off

Fig. 2 does not consider the power drawn by the different realizations. For further analysis, two extremal solutions generated by S1 are examined: L=20 is the fastest one fitting on the FPGA and uses 19 multiplier in parallel, L=380 is the smallest one generated by all tools containing only a single multiplier. The first filter needs 20 clock cycles at a maximum frequency of 8.2 MHz for one sample, which results in a minimum execution time of 2.44 μs. The second filter has a latency of 380 clock cycles at 14.1 MHz, resulting in a minimum execution time of 26.95 μs.

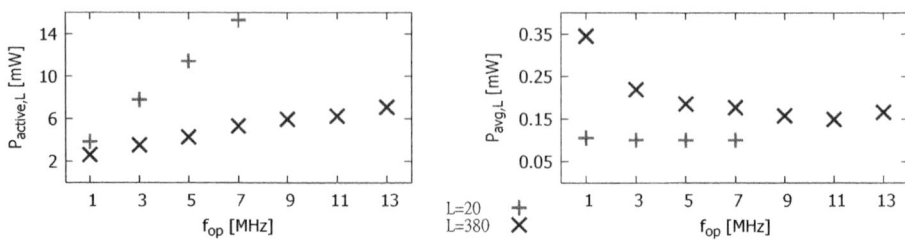

**Fig. 3.** Measured active and average M1AGL1000 power draw; computation of duty cycle for 384-FIR at different operating clock frequencies

To determine the power draw, each of these filters was mapped onto the M1AGL1000-FPGA and measured their core current (at 1.2 V) when operating them at a range of clock frequencies $f_{op}$. The left graph in Fig. 3 gives the resulting measurements as $P_{active,L}$, which show the expected result of increasing power drawn for larger logic areas toggling at higher speeds.

In a second scenario, which is typical for our vibration control application, the filter is not running continuously. Instead, the M1AGL1000-RCU is just woken up from Flash-Freeze by the RF-SoC at a rate of $f_s = 400$ Hz to process a single sample. Note that the filter hardware still executes for $L$ cycles at the higher clock frequency $f_{op}$. Thus, the duty cycle of the RCU actually operating relative to the entire sample time is $\mathrm{duty}_L(f_{op}) = \frac{f_s}{f_{op}} \cdot L$.

As the right part of Fig. 3 indicates, the average power $P_{avg,L}$ drawn in this scenario is at least an order of magnitude below $P_{active,L}$, and is actually *decreasing* with larger $f_{op}$. This demonstrates, that, given the availability of an ultra-low power sleep mode, it is energy-efficient to compute as quickly as possible, even accepting faster clock speeds to maximize time in deep sleep mode. It can also be seen that the power savings of L=380 due to smaller area in the first graph can not compensate the effect of faster runtime which results in a higher average power consumption of the smaller design.

### 5.3   RCU Performance Evaluation

Fig. 4 shows the power draw of the best design points generated by the different tool flows. S2 outperforms S1 due to its lower latency, allowing longer sleep times.

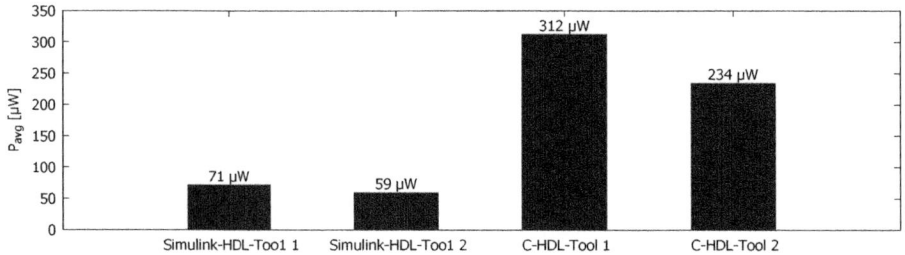

**Fig. 4.** Best results of different Toolflows

The two Simulink-C-HDL flows fare worse, because only their (small, slow) fully resource-shared designs actually fit on the M1AGL1000 device. These designs have long latencies and thus poor power efficiency, despite their small area.

In Fig. 5 energy efficiency of the M1AGL1000 implementation, is compared to low-power MCUs and DSPs. The 8 bit 8051 MCU could not reach the desired sampling frequency of 400 Hz, even when running at a maximum of 32 MHz. In practice, this would require radio transmission of the sample to a central node for computation. When ignoring protocol overhead, a lower bound for the duty cycle of transmission of a 16 bit value over a 250 kbps IEEE 802.15.4 channel each 2.5 ms can be calculated to draw 2.2 mW of average power.

For the 16 bit MSP430 MCU [28] an operating frequency of 9 MHz was sufficient to run the filter at $f_s = 400$ Hz. At this operating frequency, the MSP430 draws 5.6 mW, but has to run continuously (no sleeping). Stepping up the MSP430 clock frequency would allow sleeping between the samples, but also requires higher supply voltage which annihilates the power savings of sleeping.

The 16 bit ultra-low-power DSP TMS320C5515 [29] running at 3 MHz fulfilled the required sampling rate while drawing 0.75 mW.

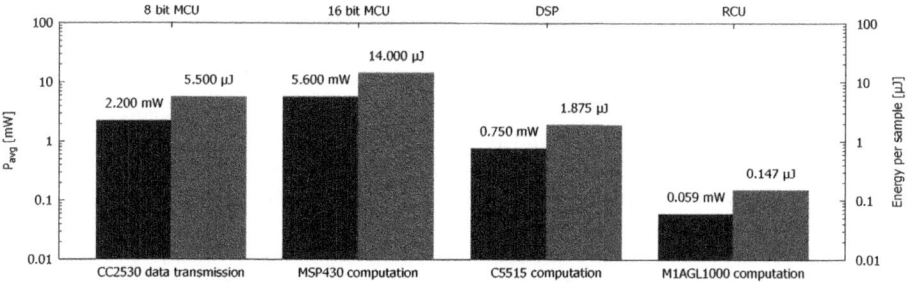

**Fig. 5.** Comparison of MCU- and RCU-based FIR implementations

# 6   Conclusion

We have shown that, with current design tools, even domain experts not proficient in hardware design can implement performance-critical parts of common algorithms on the RCU directly from their high-level Simulink descriptions.

Given a reconfigurable device capable of quickly entering and leaving an ultalow power sleep mode, we have determined that tools should aim for the fastest possible realization, even if that requires higher clock frequencies or larger chip areas (due to limited resource sharing). The energy gains of waking up from deep sleep only briefly for computation dominate the additional power required for these faster designs.

Our "run to idle" strategy is only applicable, however, if the RCU is not used to continuously perform traditional WSN middle-ware services (e.g., communication protocols, timekeeping, synchronization). To this end, our *HaLoMote* platform, being a heterogeneous multi-processor, can leave these tasks on the low-power MCU and use the RCU just for brief bursts of computation.

# References

1. Yick, J., Mukherjee, B., et al.: Wireless sensor network survey. Comput. Netw. 52, 2292–2330 (2008)
2. Sadler, C.M., Martonosi, M.: Data Compression Algorithms for Energy-Constrained Devices in Delay Tolerant Networks. In: Proc. Fourth ACM Conf. Embedded Networked Sensor Systems (2006)
3. LOEWE-Zentrum AdRIA, http://www.loewe-adria.de/
4. MICA2 WIRELESS MEASUREMENT SYSTEM, http://www.memsic.com
5. 8-bit Microcontroller with 128K Bytes In-System Programmable Flash, http://www.atmel.com
6. TELOSB MOTE PLATFORM, http://www.memsic.com
7. Ultra low power IEEE 802.15.4 compliant wireless sensor module, http://www.sentilla.com
8. MSP430x1xx User's Guide
9. Tuan, T., Rahman, A., et al.: A 90-nm Low-Power FPGA for Battery-Powered Applications. IEEE Transactions on Computer-Aided Design of Integrated Circuits and Systems 26(2), 296–300 (2007)
10. iCE65 Ultra Low-Power mobileFPGA Family, http://www.siliconbluetech.com/
11. IGLOO Handbook, http://www.actel.com
12. Latha, P., Bhagyaveni, M.A.: Reconfigurable FPGA based architecture for surveillance systems in WSN. In: Intl. Conf. on Wireless Communication and Sensor Computing, pp. 1–6 (2010)
13. Zhiyong, C.H., Pan, L.Y., et al.: A novel FPGA-based wireless vision sensor node. In: IEEE Intl. Conf. on Automation and Logistics, pp. 841–846 (2009)
14. Portilla, J., Riesgo, T., et al.: A Reconfigurable Fpga-Based Architecture for Modular Nodes in Wireless Sensor Networks. In: 3rd Southern Conference on Programmable Logic, pp. 203–206 (2007)
15. Synopsys Synphony Model Compiler, http://www.synopsys.com
16. Xilinx System Generator for DSP, http://www.xilinx.com
17. Simulink HDL Coder, http://www.mathworks.com/products/slhdlcoder/
18. Real-Time Workshop, http://www.mathworks.com/products/rtw/
19. Akyildiz, I.F., Su, W., et al.: A survey on sensor networks. Communications Magazine 40(8), 102–114 (2002)
20. Constantinides, G.A., Cheung, P.Y.K., et al.: Multiple Precision for Resource Minimization. In: IEEE Symp. on Field-Programmable Custom Computing Machines (2000)
21. Constantinides, G.A., Cheung, P.Y.K., et al.: Synthesis and Optimization of DSP Algorithms, pp. 27–38 (2004)
22. Sbarcea, B., Nicula, D.: Automatic Conversion of MatLab/Simulink Models to HDL. In: Intl. Conf. on Optimization of Electrical and Electronic Equipment (2004)
23. Kasprzyk, N., Koch, A.: High-Level-Language Compilation for Reconfigurable Computers. In: Intl. Conf. on Reconfigurable Communication-centric SoCs (2005)
24. Synopsys Synphony C Compiler, http://www.synopsys.com
25. Mentor Graphics CatapultC, http://www.mentor.com/esl/catapult/
26. AutoESL AutoPilot, http://www.autoesl.com/
27. CC253x SoC Solution for 2.4 GHz IEEE 802.15.4 and ZigBee® Applications, http://www.ti.com
28. CC430F613x MSP430 SoC, http://www.ti.com
29. TMS320C5515 Fixed-Point Digital Signal Processor, http://www.ti.com

# Hierarchical Optical Flow Estimation Architecture Using Color Cues

Francisco Barranco, Matteo Tomasi, Javier Diaz, and Eduardo Ros

Dept. Technology and Computer Architecture, University of Granada,
C/P. Daniel Saucedo Aranda s/n, 18074 Granada, Spain
{fbarranco,mtomasi,jdiaz,eduardo}@atc.ugr.es

**Abstract.** This work presents an FPGA implementation of a highly parallel architecture for color motion estimation. It implements the well-known Lucas & Kanade algorithm with a multiscale extension for an accurate computation. Our system fulfills real-time requirements estimating 32 frames per second with 512x512 resolution. It presents our architecture based on fine pipelines and the benchmark of the alternatives analyzing the accuracy and the hardware resource requirements.

**Keywords:** FPGA; Real-time systems; Reconfigurable architectures.

## 1 Introduction

The optical flow estimation consists on the computation of a 2D motion field (projection of the 3D real motion onto the image plane) of the scene at different instants [1]. A lot of methods for its estimation are available but their real-time computation is still an open issue.

Some previous works estimated color optical flow: initially with multispectral images [2]; Ohta proposed the estimation with color information [3]; Golland proposed the color conservation concept looking for robustness under illumination variations [4]; Andrews and Barron benchmark different methods [5][6].

Our implementation is based on the Lucas & Kanade (L&K) algorithm, particularly the model described in [7][1]. We add a hierarchical extension to deal with higher motion ranges. We select an FPGA to exploit the algorithm maximum parallelization. Real-time computation is one of our objectives: the monoscale core reaches 270 fps and the multiscale one 32 fps (VGA resolution).

## 2 Lucas and Kanade Optical Flow Estimation

The optical flow estimation is based on the brightness constancy: is the so called *Optical Flow Constraint* (1) and defines the optical flow as a vector $(u, v)$. The resolution is performed using the first-order Taylor expansion. For the color implementation we extend it from intensity to color channel values. As in [4] we use a two channel representation ($R = \{F_1, F_2\}$) instead of three. Its authors assume the color conservation rather than the intensity conservation. This work

A. Koch et al. (Eds.): ARC 2011, LNCS 6578, pp. 269–274, 2011.

points out that: for the normalized RGB representation we could select any two different channels because it presents the color as ratios; for the HSV we use $H$ and $S$ channels. It concludes that this implementation achieves more stable and accurate results.

The new overdetermined system is solved using the least-squares method (using 5x5 neighborhoods) as is shown in (2) and (3). We have simplified the notation for the next equations, e.g. $F_{1x}$ stands for the $F_1$ derivative for the $x$ direction. In (3), the $W_i$ stands for the weights for the neighborhood ($\Omega$).

$$I(x, y, t) = I(x + u, y + v, t + 1), \qquad \frac{\delta I}{\delta x}u + \frac{\delta I}{\delta y}v + \frac{\delta I}{\delta t} = 0 \qquad (1)$$

$$A = \begin{bmatrix} F_{1x} & F_{1y} \\ F_{2x} & F_{2y} \end{bmatrix}, b = \begin{bmatrix} -F_{1t} \\ -F_{2t} \end{bmatrix}, (u, v) = (A^T W^2 A)^{-1} A^T W^2 b. \qquad (2)$$

$$(A^T W^2 A) = \begin{bmatrix} \sum_{i \in \Omega} W_i^2 I_{xi}^2 & \sum_{i \in \Omega} W_i^2 I_{xi} I_{yi} \\ \sum_{i \in \Omega} W_i^2 I_{xi} I_{yi} & \sum_{i \in \Omega} W_i^2 I_{yi}^2 \end{bmatrix}, (A^T W^2 b) = \begin{bmatrix} \sum_{i \in \Omega} W_i^2 I_{xi} I_{ti} \\ \sum_{i \in \Omega} W_i^2 I_{yi} I_{ti} \end{bmatrix}.$$
$$(3)$$

With the multiscale extension we achieve a working range 30x higher (with 5 scales) which helps us improving considerably the accuracy. This extension is explained in Section 4.

## 3   Benchmarking

The benchmark is composed by the sequences (available at the Middlebury database [8]): Grove2, Grove3, Hydrangea, RubberWhale, Urban2 and Urban3 ($s1$ to $s6$ respectively).

We compare the monoscale implementation results using gray values and color information (RGBN results). The left graphic of Fig. 1 shows how the color algorithm leads us to more accurate (although in this version the improvements are not very significant) and denser results. We have to remark the growing of the density that reaches in $s3$ almost a 40-point increment.

The AAEs are still high in this stage (as mentioned, the monoscale version has a restricted dynamic range) although we appreciate a slight difference (and for $s1$ and $s2$ the accuracy improves). Furthermore, we have to take into account the significant increment in the density.

For benchmarking the algorithm we compare the results using three and two component representations: RGB, HS and RGN. RGB is the same than in the monoscale case; taking only the H and S channels from the HSV representation; taking the R and G channel of the normalized RGB (RGN presents the best results between all the options). The right graphic in Fig. 1 shows that RGB results are the best obtaining the highest densities and the lowest AAE (although in $s5$ and $s6$ the HS is revealed as the best choice). Fig. 1 also shows us that

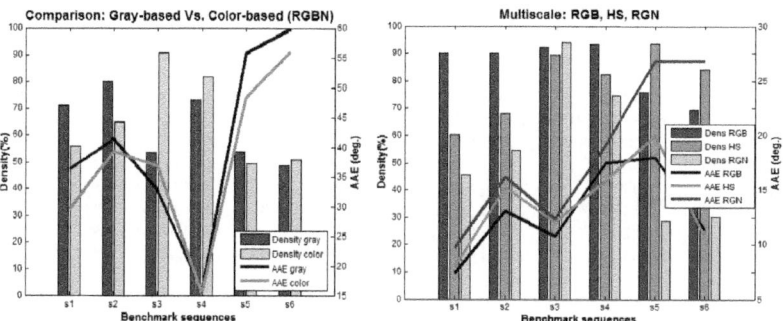

**Fig. 1.** Left: Gray Vs. RGBN-based algorithms. Right: Multiscale color alternatives: RGB, HS and RGN. The left axis shows density (lines) and the right AAE (bars).

the normalized RGB representation is not a good choice for this benchmark (it achieves the worst results). In general, comparing the mono and the multiscale version the density keeps almost constant but, for the best case, the accuracy is improved by a factor of 3x. The problem of the sequences is their lack of the proper noise due to the capture devices (they are synthetic). In such cases, the RGB representation achieves the best results.

## 4    Hardware Implementation

The device we decided to use is an FPGA (a Xilinx Virtex4 XC4vfx100). In our work as in previous [9], we do not propose just an implementation for a specific architecture but a methodology to implement this kind of algorithms. The selected device provides us the possibility of taking advantage of the high-performance massive parallelization inherent to local vision algorithms. We used a fine-pipeline based architecture whose aim is to achieve a throughput of one pixel per clock cycle. The Memory Controller Unit [10] and the interface with the PCI were developed using VHDL, the motion estimation algorithm was implemented using the high level Handel-C language. This tool allows us a simpler algorithmic description without a significant lost of performances [11].

### 4.1    Lucas and Kanade Optical Flow Core

Our implementation is based on previous approaches [9]. Our multiscale extension with warping is the most significant distinction. This approach is usually avoided due to its architectural complexity and cost. The core is implemented as a pipeline with 5 stages:

- $St_0$: This stage filters the input using a Gaussian smoothing kernel of 3 taps $K = [1\ 2\ 1]/4$.
    - $St_1$: Temporal derivative and smoothing (3 frames).
    - $St_2$: Spatial derivatives from the $St_1$ (partial derivatives $I_{xi}$, $I_{yi}$, $I_{ti}$).

**Table 1.** Hardware resource utilization and frame rate (resolution of 640 x 480) for the presented alternatives using a Xilinx Virtex-4 FX100 FPGA

| | 4 input LUTs (out of 84352) | Slice Flip Flops (out of 84352) | Slices (out of 42716) | DSP (160) | Block RAMs (376) | Freq (MHz) | Frame Rate (fps) |
|---|---|---|---|---|---|---|---|
| Fixed Gray | 5039 (5%) | 6622 (7%) | 4224 (10%) | 30 (18%) | 48 (12%) | 83 | 270 |
| Float Gray | 8865 (10%) | 4715 (5%) | 6551 (13%) | 12 (7%) | 48 (12%) | 76 | 247 |
| Fixed 2 Ch | 7939 (9%) | 9068 (10%) | 6562 (15%) | 35 (21%) | 92 (24%) | 83 | 270 |
| Float 2 Ch | 11773 (13%) | 7124 (8%) | 8829 (20%) | 17 (10%) | 92 (24%) | 71 | 231 |
| Fixed 3 Ch | 10837 (12%) | 11519 (12%) | 9274 (21%) | 40 (25%) | 136 (36%) | 83 | 270 |
| Float 3 Ch | 14665 (17%) | 9575 (11%) | 11262 (26%) | 22 (13%) | 136 (36%) | 71 | 231 |

- $St_3$: This stage computes the coefficients of the linear system of (3). The weights $W_i$ for the neighborhood $\Omega$ are set by the 5-by-5 separable kernel used in [1] [9]: $W = [1\ 4\ 6\ 4\ 1]/16$.
- $St_4$: The last stage solves the 2-by-2 system and uses the determinant of the matrix as a confidence measure.

For this system we use 523 parallel processing units: $St_0$ has 9 paths (3 frames) for Gaussian filtering, $St_1$ has 6 paths (for temporal derivative and smoothing), $St_2$ has 9 paths (for each derivative $I_x$, $I_y$, $I_t$), $St_3$ has 18 paths (for each coefficient of (3))) and finally $St_4$ has only one path. We have implemented two alternatives for this last stage: using fixed-point or floating-point arithmetic. This effort is done because we need a good accuracy at the coarsest scales because they drive the estimations of the finest scales along the multiscale approach. Table 1 shows the resources and the reached frame rate for each alternative. In the best case we reach 83 MHz which means 270 fps (VGA resolution) with an occupation of 10% for the monoscale approach. Using 3 or 2 channel cores does not mean a 3x or 2x increment, the optimization process and the resource sharing allow us in the worst case (3 channels) an increment of 2,195x. The use of only 2 color channels help us saving a 6% of the resources (we duplicate warping and pyramid modules) without a significant lost of accuracy and keeping frequency.

### 4.2  Multiscale Architecture and System Performances

The interactions between our system and memory are performed by the MCU that multiplexes data our system has to read/store [10]. The main modules of the system are (see Fig. 2):

- Pyramid: Consisted on a smoothing and a sub-sampling circuit (see Fig. 2). The 2D convolution is done with Gaussian filters with 5-by-5 kernel decomposed in two arrays $K = [1\ 4\ 6\ 4\ 1]/16$ as suggested in [12].
- Warping: It consists on a bilinear interpolation of the input images with the previous optical flow estimation. It requires the read of a pair ($\Delta x$, $\Delta y$) whose integer part is used for retrieving from memory the four pixels of the original image. The warped pixel is calculated with the fractional part performing the interpolation. This and the previous modules are replicated for each channel.
- Merging and median filtering: This module computes the addition of the previous optical flow estimation and the current one. The non-valid values are

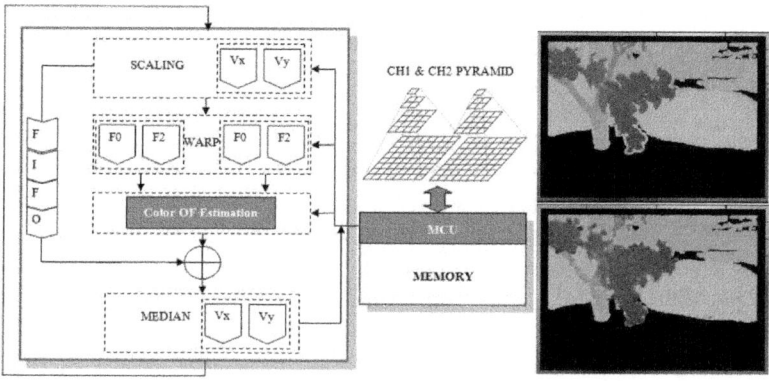

**Fig. 2.** Left: Hardware system architecture. Right: Captures of the ground-truth (top) and hardware result (bottom) for *Grove2* sequence. The color indicates the direction of the motion according with the frame.

**Table 2.** Resource utilization for the multiscale implementation

|  | 4 input LUTs | Slice Flip Flops | Slices | DSP | Block RAMs | Freq |
|---|---|---|---|---|---|---|
| Gray-based | 31796 (37%) | 24694 (29%) | 26036 (61%) | 62 (38%) | 112 (29%) | 44 |
| Color-based | 44239 (52%) | 37916 (44%) | 34630 (82%) | 98 (61%) | 220 (58%) | 44 |
| Scaling | 413 (1%) | 270 (1%) | 367 (1%) | 0 | 1 (1%) | 86 |
| Warping + Int. | 9943 (11%) | 9097 (10%) | 9894 (23%) | 32 (20%) | 43 (11%) | 51 |
| Merging | 364 (1%) | 244 (1%) | 235 (1%) | 0 | 4 (1%) | 107 |

propagated from the coarsest scales to the finest ones. Then, we filter the output and the intermediate estimations with a 3-by-3 median filter.

Table 2 shows the resource utilization for the multiscale implementation. In the table are also listed the most important modules of the multiscale implementation as scaling, merging the warping modules and it is also showed information about the interface with the board. The most important fact is that, the color-based implementation does not utilize the double of resources of the gray-based architecture, although it replicates some of the components with the highest costs as the warping module. Our complete system use the 64% - 80% of the available resources. Therefore, it is possible to add more cores to the multi-scale architecture to build new on-chip engines based on color information. Derived from the performance study, the best representation is the HSV (taking the $H$ and the $S$ channels) and it achieves an AAE of 7.3 with a density of 57.5% for Grove2. The qualitative results are also shown in Fig. 2.

# 5   Conclusions

We have designed an embedded system for the multiscalar color motion estimation implementing the L&K method. Our main issue is the development of an architecture to perform its real-time computation: we obtain 270 fps for the monoscale core and 32 fps for the multiscale system with 512x512 resolution. Moreover, we also achieve good accuracy rates. We also analyze the color implementation using two or three channels for the color representation. The implementation with two channels allows us to save hardware resources without a substantial accuracy lost. The best results are obtained with the HSV. Our monoscale implementation corresponds to the 15% of the resources and the multiscale to the 80% of a Xilinx Virtex4 XC4vfx100 chip. Our design strategy allows easy sharing of hardware resources (varying the number of pipelined stages and superscalar units), allowing us the implementation of new cores. Moreover, the fine-pipeline architecture benefits high system performances and low power consumption [9], crucial for industrial applications. Finally, the implemented architecture could be the low-level layer for future implementations such as segmentation, 3D reconstruction or attention on chip.

**Acknowledgments.** This work has been supported by the Spanish project DINAM-VISION (DPI2007-61683), the Spanish Grant (AP2007-00275), and the regional projects MULTIVISION (TIC-3873) and ITREBA (TIC-5060).

# References

1. Barron, J.L., Fleet, D.J., Beauchemin, S.S.: Performance of optical flow techniques. Int. Jl. of Comp. Vis. 12, 43–77 (1994)
2. Markandey, V., Flinchbaugh, B.: Multispectral constraints for optical flow computation. In: Proc. 3 Int. Conf. on Comp. Vis., pp. 38–41 (1990)
3. Ohta, N.: Optical flow detection by color images, pp. 801–805 (1989)
4. Golland, P., Bruckstein, A.M.: Motion from color (1995)
5. Andrews, R.J., Lovell, B.C.: Color optical flow. In: Proc. Work on Digital Image Computing, vol. 1, pp. 135–139 (2003)
6. Barron, J., Klette, R.: Quantitative color optical flow. In: Int. Conf. on Pattern Recognitioin, vol. 4, pp. 251–255 (2002)
7. Beauchemin, S.S., Barron, J.L.: The computation of optical flow. ACM Computing Surveys 27(3), 433–466 (1995)
8. Middlebury: Middlebury computer vision, http://vision.middlebury.edu/flow/
9. Diaz, J., Ros, E., Agis, R., Bernier, J.: Superpipelined high-performance optical-flow computation architecture. Int. J. CVIU 112(3), 262–273 (2008)
10. Vanegas, M., Tomasi, M., Daz, J., Ros, E.: Multi-port abstraction layer for FPGA intensive memory exploitation applications. JSA 56(9), 442–451 (2010)
11. Ortigosa, E., Caas, A., Ros, E., Ortigosa, P., Mota, S., Daz, J.: Hardware description of multi-layer perceptrons with different abstraction levels. Microprocessors and Microsystems 30(7), 435–444 (2006)
12. Burt, P.J., Adelson, E.H.: The laplacian pyramid as a compact image code. IEEE Transactions on Communications 31, 532–540 (1983)

# Magnetic Look-Up Table (MLUT) Featuring Radiation Hardness, High Performance and Low Power

Yahya Lakys, Weisheng Zhao, Jacques-Olivier Klein, and Claude Chappert

IEF, Univ. Paris-Sud, UMR8622, Orsay, F-91405, France
CNRS, Orsay, F-91405, France
{yahya.lakys,weisheng.zhao,jacques-olivier.klein,
claude.chappert}@u-psud.fr

**Abstract.** Thanks to its non-volatility, high write/sense speed and small size, Magnetic Tunnel Junction (MTJ) is under investigation to be integrated in the future reconfigurable computing circuits offering higher power efficiency and performance. Another advantage of MTJ is that it provides good radiation hardness compared with other storage technologies used in reconfigurable computing circuits. In this paper, we present a design of Magnetic Look-Up-Table (MLUT) performing radiation hardness and keeping high reconfiguration /computing speed, high reliability and low power. Simulation results using an accurate model of MTJ and CMOS 130nm design kit confirm its expected performances in terms of reliability, power and speed.

**Keywords:** Hybrid Design, High Reliability, MLUT, Radiation Hardness.

## 1 Introduction

Look-Up Table (LUT) is one of the important building blocks for reconfigurable computing devices [1]. This element requires memory points currently based on SRAM or flash technologies [2]. Recently, Magnetic Tunnel Junction (MTJ) [3] has demonstrated a great potential for integration as memory elements into embedded and reconfigurable systems such as FPGA [4-6]. This new memory intends to replace SRAM that need high standby power and relatively slow flash memory. In addition, 3D integration of MTJs is easily achieved because their fabrication is compatible with CMOS process [7]. Their high switching/sensing speed and non-volatility are exploited to overcome the major limitations of conventional devices such as high standby power and long delay for (re)configuration [5]. Moreover, the radiations hardness characteristic of MTJs enables the design of radiation tolerant circuits. Usually, hardening techniques are implemented by either technological solution (i.e. silicon on insulator SOI etc.) or by adding redundant blocks [8-9].

In this paper, we present a new design of Magnetic Look-Up-Table (MLUT). Based on a Pre-Charged Sense Amplifier (PCSA) [10], it features radiation hardness, high computing speed and low power. As MTJs are arranged in cross-point array structure [11], multi-context configuration can be easily implemented providing dynamic reconfiguration capability.

A. Koch et al. (Eds.): ARC 2011, LNCS 6578, pp. 275–280, 2011.

By using an accurate Thermally Assisted Switching (TAS) MTJ model [12-13] and CMOS 130nm technology [14], simulations have been performed to confirm the behaviour of this MLUT and demonstrate its expected performances.

## 2   Architecture of Magnetic Look-Up Table (MLUT)

Figure 1-a shows a simplified diagram of conventional Magnetic Look-Up-Table (MLUT) [5-6]. A Sense Amplifier (SA) reads the binary information stored is a couple of MTJs [15]. Both play the role of one SRAM/flash memory point to save configuration data.

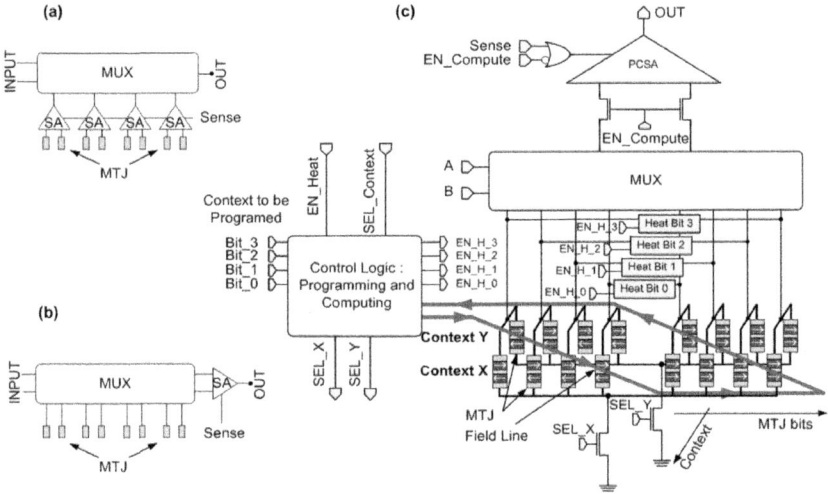

**Fig. 1.** Circuit and architecture implementation: (a) Architecture of conventional MLUT (b) New architecture of MLUT (c) Detailed schematic of new MLUT

A simplified diagram of the new MLUT is presented on Fig. 1-b. The SA is shifted to the output of a two branches MUX. Hence, only one SA is shared for all memory points. The detailed schematic is presented on Fig. 1-c, which is composed of three main parts:

1. A Pre-Charged Sense Amplifier (PCSA) shown on Fig. 2, [10]. Formed by transistors P1 to P4 and N3 to N5, it senses the LUT data stored in couples of MTJs by the falling edge of signal "Sense". The frequency of "Sense" is equal to the frequency of data A and B in normal mode but it could be improved up to the chip clock in highest computing speed mode. As we previously demonstrated, the PCSA features high reliability and low power compared to state-of-the-art SA [10].
2. A cross-point MTJ array, organized in $M$ contexts addressed by selection signals such as "SEL_X/Y" (see Fig. 1- c). Each context is composed of $2^N$ couples of MTJs (i.e. $2^N$ bits) to implement $N$-input logic functions. As there is only one additional selection transistor per context, multiple contexts can be easily implemented without any footprint overhead.

3. A logic block generates the control signals required for the operation of MLUT: "Sense", "SEL_Context" and "EN_Compute" for logic computation and dynamic reconfiguration; "Bit_0 to 3" and "EN_Heat" generate the signals "EN_H_0 to 3" for context programming through TAS-MTJ switching approach [13].

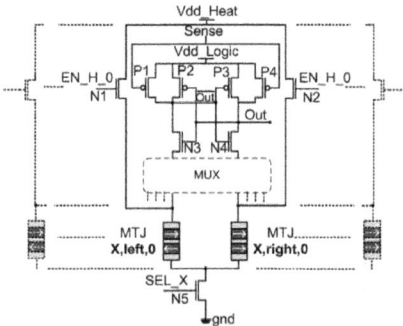

**Fig. 2.** Detail circuit of Pre-Charged Sense Amplifier (PCSA). There are four PMOS transistors (P1-P4) and three NMOS transistors (N3-N5). By using the MUX, the couple of MTJs for sensing can be selected, for example, (X, left, 0) and (X, right, 0) refers to the couple of MTJs presenting bit number 0 in the context X.

## 3  Simulated Performances

The functional behaviour of the MLUT is studied through transient simulations by using CMOS 130nm design kit [14] and an accurate TAS-MTJ model [12]. The default MTJ nanopillar is BiFe(10)/IrMn(6)/CoFe(1)/MgO(1.2)/CoFe(3)/PtMn(6). Fig. 3 shows a representative cycle that includes three operations:

1. Logic computation: As contexts X or Y are selected for reading (from 0 to 200ns and from 400ns to 600ns), MLUT begins logic computation (Fig. 3-a). The data stored in the configuration memory of context X/Y is available on the output of the MLUT. This simulates two different logical functions according to the value of inputs A & B (Fig. 3-d & e) and to the data stored in different contexts ($X_1 = A$, $Y_1 = \overline{A}+B$, $X_2 = \overline{A}$ and $Y_2 = A\overline{B}$. The whole logic delay for the calculated data to be available on the output is as low as 300ps including a rise time of (~100ps) for "Sense" signal. This corresponds to a maximum operating frequency of 3.3 GHz.
2. Dynamic reconfiguration between different configuration contexts: This operation means that the MLUT changes dynamically its logical function. This occurs when the control signal "Select X/Y" switches from Read X to Read Y (see Fig. 3-c). The reconfiguration of MLUT between two contexts $X_1 = A$ and $Y_1 = \overline{A}+B$ could be very fast, lower than 1ns.
3. Context programming: The two contexts can be dynamically (re)-programmed to $X_2 = \overline{A}$ and $Y_2 = A\overline{B}$ in about 200ns while the previous calculated result logic '1' remains latched (see Fig. 3-a).

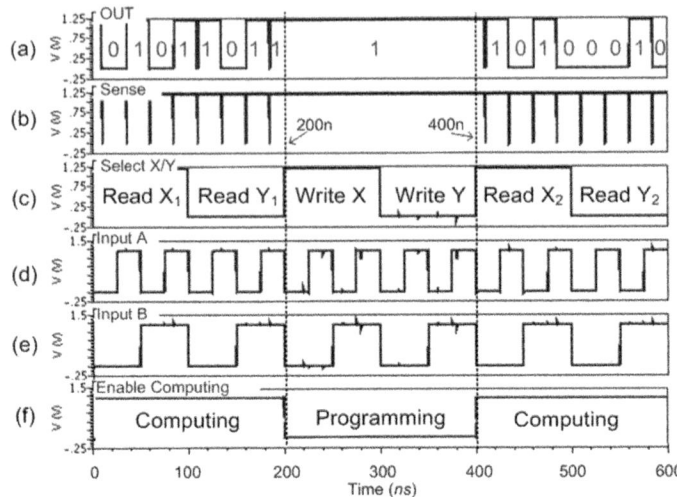

**Fig. 3.** Transient simulation of 2-input MLUT with 2 contexts (X/Y): (a) Output of MLUT (b) Sequence control signal "Sense" (c) Select context X and Y (d) Input data "A" (e) Input data "B" (f) Control signal "EN_Compute"

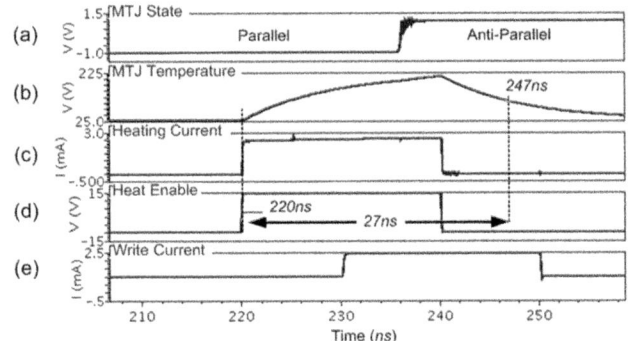

**Fig. 4.** Transient simulation TAS Writing operation: (a) State of an MTJ (b) Temperature of the same MTJ (c) Current flowing through MTJ during heating operation (d) Control signal "En_Heat" (e) Switching current, triggered when the MTJ temperature reaches ~150°C

The programming operation is show on Fig. 4. We use the Thermally Assisted Switching (TAS) approach [13]. The programming starts as the control signal "En_Heat" is active; a current passes through the selected MTJ and heats it. when its local temperature reaches up to the blocking temperature (~150°C) of anti-ferromagnetic IrMn layer associated with the free layer [12-13], a magnetic field is generated to align the magnetization of the free layer of MTJ and thus change its state (Fig. 4-a) from P to AP or vice-versa. The programming is accomplished when the MTJs cool down to about 100°C. Benefiting from a parallel programming architecture [16], the whole operation requires only 27ns to program all the bits of a context.

The simulation shows also low power dissipation of MLUT. Firstly, its static power is reduced down to nearly zero as MTJ does not require power to keep data in standby mode. Secondly, during logic computation, PCSA consumes only low dynamic energy. It dissipates ~3 fJ/bit in computing mode and ~72 pJ/bit in context programming mode. The latter comes mainly from the heating/switching currents of TAS operation. It is important to note that new switching technologies under investigation such as Spin Transfer Torque (STT) allow the switching power to be minimized in the future [3].

## 4  Radiation Hardness

In microelectronic circuits, the sensitive nodes presenting logic value with charge can be struck by ions or electro-magnetic radiation and this leads to state change from logic '0' to '1' or vice-versa at a relatively low frequency, [8-9]. This effect is called Single Event Upset (SEU) or soft error, which happens more frequently as the altitude increases. In order to resist to radiation, logic circuits need special design with the sacrifice of power, die area or speed. For example, flash and anti-fuse based reconfigurable logic circuits are often used in space applications with lower computing speed and the loss of reconfigurability [9].

Conventional MLUT structure use nearly the same number of sensitive nodes as SRAM based LUT (see Fig. 1-a), which limits its hardness during circuit computing. The new architecture of the MLUT enhances the immunity to radiations thanks to the reduction of sensitive points. The tolerance to radiation could also be improved by increasing the frequency of "Sense" in order to operate more sensing actions. Thus, if a disturbance occurs during the MLUT computing, the correct value is available after another sensing operation.

## 5  Conclusion

In this paper, we presented a new design of MLUT. Its architecture with one sensitive point per logic gate and PCSA allows better radiation hardness, higher reliability and lower power consumption compared with previous MLUT designs while keeping high reconfiguration/computing speed. A cross-point array of MTJ sharing many peripheral circuits is used to store the multi-context configuration. This provides high-speed dynamic reconfiguration, enhances the fault tolerance capacity and increases greatly the embedded logic density. By using an accurate MTJ model and CMOS 130nm design kit, hybrid simulations of this MLUT confirm its functional behaviour and demonstrate its interesting performances in terms of power and computing/reconfiguration speed etc. High-speed performance and high power efficiency make MLUT become one of the most promising candidates to replace conventional LUT in the future and this new design opens the door for MLUT based reconfigurable circuits to be developed for aerospace, security and defense applications.

## Acknowledgment

The authors wish to acknowledge the support from the French national projects CILOMAG and NANOINNOV SPIN. We thank also G. PRENAT, B. DIENY from

SPINTEC laboratory for decisive inputs scientific discussions and crucial help, O. REDON from CEA LETI, K. TORKI and G. DIPENDINA from CMP.

# References

1. Brown, S., Francis, R., Rose, J., Vranesic, Z.: Field-programmable gate arrays. Kluwer Academic Publishers, Dordrecht (1992)
2. Virtex-III data sheet, http://www.xilinx.com
3. Chappert, C., Fert, A., Nguyen Van Dau, F.: The emergence of spin electronics in data storage. Nature Materials 6, 813–823 (2007)
4. Lakys, Y., Zhao, W.S., Klein, J.O., Chappert, C.: Low Power, High Reliablity Magnetic Flip-Flop. Electronics Letters 46(22), 1493–1494 (2010)
5. Zhao, W.S., Belhaire, E., Chappert, C., Mazoyer, P.: Spin Transfer Torque (STT)-MRAM based Run Time Reconfiguration FPGA circuit. ACM Transactions on Embedded Computing Systems 9(2), article 14 (2009)
6. Guillemenet, Y., et al.: Non-volatile run-time field-programmable gate arrays structures using thermally assisted switching magnetic random access memories. Computers & Digital Techniques, IET 4(3), 211–226 (2010)
7. Matsunaga, S., et al.: Fabrication of a Nonvolatile Full Adder Based on Logic-in-Memory Architecture Using Magnetic Tunnel Junctions. Appl. Phys. Express (APEX) 1(9), 091301-1–091301-3 (2008)
8. Yu, F.X., Liu, J.R., Huang, Z.L., Luo, H., Lu, Z.M.: Overview of radiation hardening techniques for IC design. Inform. Technol. J. 6, 1068–1080 (2010)
9. Dupont, E., et al.: Radiation Results of the SER Test of Actel, Xilinx and Altera FPGA instances, http://www.actel.com/documents/RadResultsIROCreport.pdf
10. Zhao, W.S., Chappert, C., Javerliac, V., Noziere, J.P.: High Speed, High Stability and Low Power Sensing Amplifier for MTJ/CMOS Hybrid Logic Circuits. IEEE Transactions on Magnetic 45(10), 3784–3787 (2009)
11. Chaudhuri, S., Zhao, W.S., Klein, J.O., Chappert, C., Mazoyer, P.: Design of TAS-MRAM Prototype for NV Embedded memory Applications. In: Proc. of International Memory Workshop, Korea, pp. 152–155 (2010)
12. Elbaraji, M., Javerliac, V., Guo, W., Prenat, G., Dieny, B.: Dynamic compact model of thermally assisted switching magnetic tunnel junctions. Journal of Applied Physics, 123906 (2010)
13. TAS MRAM technology, http://www.crocus-technology.com
14. STMicroelectronics, Manual of design kit for CMOS 130nm (2006)
15. Zhao, W.S., Belhaire, E., Chappert, C., Jacquet, F., Mazoyer, P.: New non-volatile logic based on Spin-MTJ. Physica Status Solidi-a: Applications and Material Science 205(6), 1373–1377 (2008)
16. Zhao, W.S., Belhaire, E., Dieny, B., Prenat, G., Chappert, C.: TAS-MRAM based Nonvolatile FPGA logic circuit. In: IEEE International Conference on Field-Programmable Technology (IEEE-ICFPT), Kitakyushu, Japan, pp. 153–161 (2007)

# Reconfigurable Stream-Processing Architecture for Sparse Linear Solvers

Kevin Cunningham and Prawat Nagvajara

Electrical and Computer Engineering
Drexel University
Philadelphia, PA
kac89@drexel.edu, nagvajara@ece.drexel.edu

**Abstract.** Applications such as electrical power grid operation and planning rely on high-performance linear solvers involving large sparse matrices. Previous custom sparse solver hardware implemented on a Field Programmable Gate Array (FPGA) has shown an 8-fold performance gain over state-of-the-art sparse software packages. Generally, the drawback of hardware solvers lies in their design complexity. This paper presents an alternative architecture in which the host CPU software computes the main program and caches data that are streamed to a pipelined hardware, implemented on an FPGA, for part of the computation. With the lower-upper triangular decomposition solver, the hardware computes the sparse matrix row addition operation, called merging. The prototype merge core processes data at the optimum rate, i.e., the FPGA clock frequency. With the proposed triple-buffer bus architecture, the core is projected to attain a data rate of 250 MHz on the Virtex 6 FPGA in comparison to the average 200MHz for the merge software subroutine on a general-purpose processor.

**Keywords:** FPGA, Sparse LU Decomposition, Stream Processing.

## 1 Introduction

High-performance sparse linear algebra computation impacts applications such as electrical power grid operation and planning. Due to sparse grid interconnection, the analyses involves large sparse matrices. Direct-method linear solvers based on Lower-Upper (LU) triangular decomposition as part of the Newton-Raphson technique in solving power equations, is used for calculating power flow between the nodes in the grid. The reliability of the grid, i.e., prevention of blackouts, relies on real-time contingency analysis of single failures where power flow is computed for each contingency. Based on the flow solution of each contingency, the grid operators determine whether the system will be in the secure state, i.e., the system is operating within its generation and transmission capability, or whether precaution actions must be taken to prevent the system from going to an unsecure state if such failure occurs [1].

A. Koch et al. (Eds.): ARC 2011, LNCS 6578, pp. 281–286, 2011.
© Springer-Verlag Berlin Heidelberg 2011

Previous custom sparse LU hardware implemented on a Field Programmable Gate Array (FPGA), has shown an 8-fold performance gain over the UMF-PACK sparse LU software package [2]. The sizes of the square matrices used in the performance benchmark were 2,982, 14,508 and 19,285, with 0.24%, 0.05% and 0.079% of non-zero elements, respectively. The LU hardware comprised a custom computation unit and an FPGA Block-RAM (BRAM) custom cache unit interfaced with external DDR memory. The host CPU downloaded the matrix data to the DDR and afterward uploaded, from the DDR, the result matrices computed by the hardware.

Generally, the drawback of hardware solvers lies in their design complexity. This paper presents stream processing as an alternative architecture where the host CPU software computes the main program and caches the data that are streamed to the pipelined hardware implemented on the FPGA. Proof of concept includes an implementation of an optimal pipeline-rate merge unit for performing sparse row addition of the LU decomposition and a prototype of steam computing based on the proposed triple-buffer bus architecture emulated by FPGA BRAM. The projected data rate of the merge unit is 250 MHz, whereas a benchmark study on the merge software subroutine shows an average data processing rate of 200 MHz [3].

## 2   Sparse Row Addition - Merge Algorithm

The LU decompostion factorizes a matrix into a lower triangular matrix and an upper triangular matrix. In each step, a pivot row is chosen to eliminate elements below the diagonal in a column. By scaling and adding the pivot row to each row being elimnated, the elements in a column are zeroed. Row v of a sparse matrix with N columns is represented as $v = v_i$: $i = 1, ..., NNZ(v)$, $v_i = (v_i.col, v_i.val)$, $v_i.col \in 1, ..., N$, $v_i.col < v_{i+1}.col$; $v_i.val \in \mathbb{R}$, $v_i.val \neq 0$; where NNZ(v) denotes the Number of Non-Zero elements and $v_i.val$ is the value at the column number $v_i.col$. This row-compressed representation enumerates only the non-zero elements of a sparse row-vector; moreover, v is an ordered set. The row addition is the equivalent of merging two sorted, variable-length arrays, which comprises a large portion of the computation in the LU algorithm.

**if** $(u_i.col == v_j.col)$ **then** $output \leftarrow (u_i.col, u_i.val + v_j.val)$;
**else if** $(u_i.col < v_j.col)$ **then** $output \leftarrow u_i$;
**else** $output \leftarrow v_j$;

The data-dependent branching of the merge algorithm performs poorly on general-purpose processors, because the column numbers must be retrieved and compared to determine the outcome of the branch. Branch prediction does not provide any consistent benefit since branch outcomes are dependent on data and not previous branches. The performance of the merge step in software is highly dependent on the structure of the rows it is processing.

Analysis of the merge performance on an Intel Q9300 at 2.5GHz, with a variety of input rows, reveals that the software outputs the merged row elements at an average rate of about 200MHz. However, there is a large variation in results with the lowest rate at 35MHz and the highest at 920MHz. Merging that alternates between elements in the two rows performs the worst, while cases with long streams of elements from a row perform the best [3].

## 3  Streaming Merge Core and Proposed Architecture

Analysis of LU software, identifies the merge (sparse row addition) step of the LU algorithm as a bottleneck for general-purpose processors. Because of this, custom merge hardware has a potential advantage over software [3].

### 3.1  Merge Hardware Design

The design of a custom hardware core to combine two sorted rows, u and v, is presented. First, each input row is loaded into a First-In-First-Out (FIFO) memory structure. The core reads the rows from the FIFOs and compares the column numbers to put the elements into sorted order. If both rows have an element with the same column number, the two values are summed with a pipelined, floating-point adder.

The elements of the two input rows are compared in a two-stage process pictured in Fig. 1. A single comparison is done on each cycle between the two elements that will reside in the Stage-2 registers on the next cycle. This look-ahead comparison is necessary to account for the one cycle read latency of the input FIFOs. The FIFOs receive read requests in advance, so that a new input element is available as soon as another element moves into the output row. Preventing gaps in the inputs enables the core to output an element on every

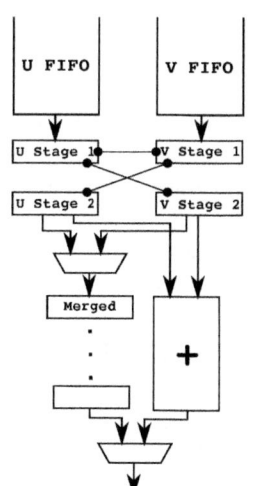

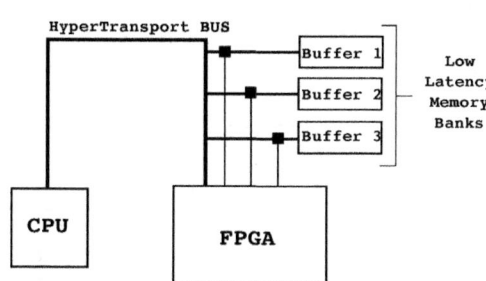

**Fig. 1.** Merge Core Design          **Fig. 2.** Triple-Buffer Bus Architecture

cycle, meaning that the data rate matches the clock rate of the FPGA. The compare stages account for 2 cycles of latency in the merge core, while the remaining latency depends on the implementation of the floating point adder.

The total number of clock cycles needed to merge two rows is dependent on the size of the input rows. The maximum number of clock cycles occurs when the two input rows do not have any elements with the same column numbers, requiring all input elements to be in the output row. The minimum number of clock cycles occurs when all of the column numbers in one row exist in the other input row, so that all elements in one row are merged with the other row.

## 3.2   Streaming Platform

In order to take full advantage of a stream-processing core, such as the merge core, it is necessary to have a continuous stream of inputs for the hardware core. Currently, many FPGA platforms have limited architectural support for continuously streaming data between a CPU and FPGA, since they need to send and receive data at the same time. This requires the bus to be shared between both directions. While this architecture is sufficient for sending a batch of data from the CPU to the FPGA to process, it does not work well for streaming. The CPU will be attempting to read results and send new inputs while the FPGA is attempting to reads inputs and write results all across the same memory bus. To allow for successful streaming of data, a simple extension of existing architectures is proposed.

The proposed architecture is based off the design of the DRC Coprocessor Unit [5]. It consists of a CPU connected to an FPGA by a HyperTransport(HT) bus, which is a high-bandwidth, low-latency interconnect bus[6]. The proposed streaming platform uses a triple-buffer bus architecture, shown in Fig. 2, to allow for continuous streaming of data through the reconfigurable hardware core. Each of the three buffers is a bank of single port, low-latency memory that is accessible to both the FPGA and CPU. The CPU is able to send data across the HT bus to the memory, while the FPGA has a bridge into the memory bus.

The triple-buffer scheme allows the CPU to communicate with one buffer at a time, while the FPGA communicates with the other two buffers. The CPU is responsible for uploading results and downloading new inputs into a buffer. The FPGA streams inputs from one of the buffers and streams the resulting outputs to the remaining buffer. This arrangement removes any competition on the memory bus for each bank. Figure 3 shows the schedule of data transfer.

| CPU | Send Inputs Buffer 1 | | Send Inputs Buffer 2 | Receive Outputs Buffer 3 | Send Inputs Buffer 3 | Receive Outputs Buffer 1 | Send Inputs Buffer 1 |
|---|---|---|---|---|---|---|---|
| FPGA | | Compute Results Buffer 1 to Buffer 3 | | Compute Results Buffer 2 to Buffer 1 | | Compute Results Buffer 3 to Buffer 2 | |

Fig. 3. Streaming Data Schedule

The FPGA and CPU can also communicate over the HT bus to synchronize the streaming operation. Since the CPU and the HT bus operate at higher rates than the FPGA, the CPU is able to transfer the results and the new inputs in the time that the FPGA takes to compute the next set of results.

## 4   Results

A prototype design of the triple-buffer scheme is implemented on a DRC board with a Virtex 4 FPGA[5]. Because the DRC board does not have the architectural support for three blocks of memory to serve as buffers, the buffers were emulated with FIFOs in BRAM on the FPGA. The BRAM operates at the FPGA clock frequency, so the CPU is not able to send and receive data within one compute cycle. This limits the theoretical data rate of the prototype to one-half the clock frequency. However, given architectural support, the design can be modified to use banks of memory instead of BRAM, as described in Section 3.

A streaming merge core is implemented as a core within the streaming platform. The merge core is able to process streams of row data sent from the software and return the merged rows. The small design only occupies 1% of the available slices on the Virtex 4 and is able to run at 200MHz, the maximum clock frequency of the Virtex 4 on the DRC board. The projected clock frequencies from synthesis estimates for the Virtex 6 and Spartan 6 FPGAs are reported in Table 1 along with the projected data rates, estimated from measurements of the prototype.

**Table 1.** Merge Core Frequencies

| FPGA Device | Clock Frequency | Projected Data Rate |
|-------------|-----------------|---------------------|
| Virtex 4    | 200MHz          | 142.8MHz            |
| Virtex 6    | 355MHz          | 253.5MHz            |
| Spartan 6   | 186MHz          | 132.8MHz            |

Measurements of the prototype at a 200MHz clock frequency yielded an average data rate of 71.4MHz. By using BRAM buffers, the theoretical data rate is 100MHz for the 200MHz clock, since the hardware is only processing for half of the time. Given the proposed stream architecture, the projected rate doubles to 142.8MHz. Ideally, the data rate will approach the clock frequency of the FPGA. The test system uses the first version of the HT bus, which is much slower than the newest HT v3.1, capable of a maximum transfer rate of 51.2 GB/s [6]. A faster bus transfer would increase the rate above the estimates in Table 1. In addition, the use of multiple parallel cores, can help to increase the hardware throughput.

The custom merge hardware has an advantage over software, because it merges two rows at a constant rate, regardless of the row structures. Although the FPGA operates at a much lower rate than a general purpose processor, estimates for higher performance platforms show that the FPGA is capable of matching or exceeding the software rate in most cases.

## 5   Conclusion

Designing complex hardware systems can be a tedious and time-consuming process. In addition, the lower clock rate of many reconfigurable computing platforms makes it difficult for a hardware design to compete with general-purpose processors in all aspects of an algorithm. For these reasons, designing less complex hardware that focuses on aspects where an FPGA can outperform a general processor is appealing. While the overhead of transferring data to off-chip hardware can be expensive, using a streaming platform allows the hardware to continually process data and hide much of the transfer latency by overlapping it with computation.

The proposed streaming platform uses three buffers of memory to supply the hardware with a constant stream of data. The streaming schedule ensures there is no competition between the CPU and FPGA on the memory buses.

A stream-processing core that performs the sparse row addition in the LU decomposition algorithm was implemented on a prototype of the streaming platform using a DRC board with a Virtex 4 FPGA and BRAM as buffers. The merge core processes rows at a consistent data rate, while the data rate for a general-purpose CPU is data dependent.

The presented work explores the benefits of reconfigurable stream-processing cores with reduced design complexity and time compared to the previous custom hardware system approach. Future work will integrate the merge core into the full LU computation. This task requires additional hardware to retain rows for the next iteration, so the CPU does not have to wait for updated rows. Additional work includes the development of a library of sparse linear algebra cores for Givens rotation [7], Householder reflection, singular value decomposition [8] and sparse matrix-vector multiplication to be used in a streaming environment.

## References

1. Albur, A., Expsito, A.: Power System State Estimation: Theory and Implementation. Marcel Dekker, New York (2004)
2. Chagnon, T., Johnson, J., Vachranukunkiet, P., Nagvajara, P., Nwankpa, C.: Sparse LU Decomposition Using FPGA. In: PARA 2008: 9th International Workshop on State-of-the-Art in Scientific and Parallel Computing, Trondheim, Norway (May 2008)
3. Chagnon, T.: Architectural Support for Direct Sparse LU Algorithms. Masters Thesis, Drexel University (2010)
4. Vachranukunkiet, P.: Power Flow Computation using Field Programmable Gate Arrays. PhD Thesis, Drexel University (2007)
5. DRC Computer Corporation. DRC Coprocessor System Users Guide (July 2007)
6. HyperTransport Consortium. HyperTransport I/O Link Specification: Revision 3.10C (May 2010)
7. Nagvajara, P., Lin, Z., Nwankpa, C., Johnson, J.: State Estimation Using Sparse Givens Rotation Field Programmable Gate Array. In: Proc. IEEE North America Power System Symposium (September 2007)
8. Wang, Y., Cunningham, K., Johnson, J., Nagvajara, P.: Singular Value Decomposition Hardware for MIMO: State of the Art and Custom Design. In: Proc. IEEE Reconfigurable Computing and FPGA Conference, December 13-15 (2010)

# The Krawczyk Algorithm:
# Rigorous Bounds for Linear Equation Solution on an FPGA

Christophe Le Lann, David Boland, and George Constantinides

Electrical and Electronic Engineering, Imperial College London,
London, SW7 2AZ, UK

**Abstract.** In the majority of scientific computing applications, values are represented using a floating point number system. However, this number system only considers an approximate value without any indication of the approximation's accuracy. Interval arithmetic provides a means to ensure that the solution is bounded with absolute certainty.

However, whilst interval arithmetic can be applied to any algorithm to ensure bounds on a solution, the limitations of interval arithmetic can lead to bounds that are not always tight and hence not particularly useful. As a result, some algorithms are specifically designed with interval arithmetic in mind to find high quality bounds on a solution; the Krawczyk algorithm is one such algorithm. The Krawczyk algorithm is targeted towards solving systems of linear equations, which is a common problem in scientific computing and has drawn a wide interest in the FPGA community. We show that by accelerating this algorithm in hardware, developing specialised arithmetic units, it is possible to gain orders of magnitude improvement in execution time over a C implementation.

**Keywords:** FPGA, Interval Arithmetic, Krawczyk Algorithm.

## 1 Introduction

On any modern processor, real numbers are usually represented using a floating point number system. However, due to their finite precision, only a subset of real numbers can be accurately represented, meaning most values are approximated to the nearest floating point number. Over the course of an algorithm, errors arising from these approximations accumulate and can cause a significant deviation from the nominal result, and unfortunately it is impossible to directly gain any insight into the size of this deviation, or the accuracy of the output data.

Interval arithmetic is a simple method to obtain a bound on the accuracy, where every number is defined by an interval bounding all possible values it may have taken due to previous approximations. However, any software implementation of interval arithmetic for an algorithm will result in significantly lower performance than the equivalent algorithm in floating point arithmetic [1]. Instead, in this work, we maintain high performance by creating an algorithm-specific hardware implementation using interval arithmetic operators.

A. Koch et al. (Eds.): ARC 2011, LNCS 6578, pp. 287–295, 2011.

In order to satisfy this aim, we first needed the relevant hardware blocks for basic operators $(+, -, \times, \div, \sqrt{\ })$ operating on intervals, themselves using operators and comparators $(=, >, <)$ operating on floating point numbers. While hardware implementations for general purpose interval arithmetic processors have previously been created [2, 3], we have created a customisable library of operators, notably in terms of rounding mode, exponent and mantissa size, so as to exploit the full freedom offered by FPGAs in creating a fully-custom datapath.

We then create such a custom datapath to accelerate the Krawczyk algorithm, which is an algorithm to find the solution of a system of linear equations that is specifically tailored towards interval arithmetic. We show that through exploiting the parallelism inherent in these new operators, as well as parallelising the algorithm itself, we gain a significant speed up over software. Though in this work we have only reported results for single precision, we note our customisable library of operators will also be of use for the acceleration of alternative algorithms or to facilitate future exploration into the trade-offs between performance and error for the Krawczyk algorithm in variable precision.

## 2   Background

### 2.1   Interval Arithmetic

Interval arithmetic [4] is based upon defining a closed interval as the set of all real numbers lying between its bounds, then propagating these intervals through any operation to ensure that the resulting interval encloses all real numbers that are the result of the operator applied to any two real numbers taken from the respective input operand intervals. We note here that interval arithmetic is an important tool when searching for rigorous results because while it is not possible to represent all reals in floating point, it is possible to create an interval of two floating point values which bound the desired real number.

### 2.2   Ensuring Correct Rounding

The IEEE-754 standard defines four rounding modes: "round to nearest even", "round to zero" (truncate) [5], "round towards $+\infty$" (ceil), and "round towards $-\infty$" (floor). Whilst most software is written using the first mode, interval arithmetic requires latter two in order to entirely enclose the solution interval.

In order to ensure correct rounding such that safe bounds are achieved at the output, the floating point unit requires a higher precision in its inner working than that seen at the input and output of a floating point unit. The need for this can easily be seen in the case of subtraction: with a three bit mantissa (plus the leading 1.), one might try to compute the result of $16 - 15 = 1.000 \cdot 2^4 - 1.111 \cdot 2^3$. After normalisation, this becomes $(1.000 - 0.111) \cdot 2^4 = 0.001 \cdot 2^4 = 1.000 \cdot 2^1$. Even though the correct result is representable with three bits $(1.000 \cdot 2^0)$, the result returned is incorrect because a bit was lost during normalisation.

The IEEE-754 standard defines three additional bits to avoid such errors: the "guard", "round" and "sticky" bits [6]. The guard and round bits are used as classic bits to locally increase the mantissa precision, while the sticky bit represents whether the result is exact or not, to ensure correct rounding.

### 2.3 The Solution of a System of Linear Equations

The solution to a system of linear equations of the form $Ax = b$ (where $A$ is an $N \times N$ matrix, while $x$ and $b$ are $N \times 1$ vectors) forms the basis of a large number of problems, most notably in the realm of scientific computing. As such, there is a large interest in accelerating algorithms to find this solution using hardware. Some examples include Cholesky [7]; Gauss-Jordan [8]; and Conjugate Gradients [9]. Whilst it is possible to replace every operator with its interval arithmetic equivalent in any of these algorithms to obtain a bounded solution, this may not be the tightest possible bound because interval arithmetic suffers from the so-called "Dependency Problem", where wide bounds arise due to the fact every interval for a given variable is treated independently [4]. A trivial example is the following: for a variable $x$ which lies in the interval $[0, 1]$, perform the operation $x - x$. The interval should be $[0, 0]$, but the result using interval arithmetic would be $[-1, 1]$. Whilst these algorithms contain dependencies and will suffer from this effect, the Krawczyk method, described in Figure 1, attempts to mitigate this problem by iteratively refining the interval solution vector $x$ over a finite number of iterations to get tight bounds for $x$ which satisfy $A \cdot x \supseteq b$ [4].

We define additional interval operations, as in [4], for the absolute value of an interval (1), the mid-point of an interval (2) and the norm of an interval matrix (3).

$$|[\,x\,;\,y\,]| = \max\left(|x|\,,|y|\right) \tag{1}$$

$$\mathrm{mid}\left([\,x\,;\,y\,]\right) = \frac{x+y}{2} \tag{2}$$

$$\|M\| = \max_i \sum_j |M_{ij}| \tag{3}$$

1. $Y = [\mathrm{mid}(A)]^{-1}$ (in floating point arithmetic).
2. $E = I - YA$ (in floating point arithmetic). If $\|E\| \geq 1$ exit with fail
3. $X_0 = \left[ -\frac{\|Yb\|}{1-\|E\|} \,;\, \frac{\|Yb\|}{1-\|E\|} \right]$ (in interval arithmetic).
4. Repeat Until Convergence
   $X_{n+1} = (Yb + EX_n) \cap X_n$ (in interval arithmetic).

**Fig. 1.** Pseudo code for the Krawczyk method to solve $Ax = b$

The Krawczyk method initially finds an approximate solution by a non interval method $Y$. Moore then showed that under specified conditions, this can be used to create an interval $X_0$ which both contains the answer and could be refined using Krawczyk's interval version of Newton's method [4].

## 3 Parameterisable Interval Arithmetic Units

To create interval arithmetic components, we need the relevant floating point operators with parameterisable rounding modes. While many IP cores which implement floating point arithmetic, including Xilinx LogiCores [10], FloPoCo [11] and Northeastern University's cores [12,13], none of these libraries directly meet our requirements. In this work, we modify the Northeastern University library, because it is open source and easy to use, with our add rounding mode selection.

## 3.1  Enabling Correct Rounding

In order to ensure correct rounding, we need to add and handle the guard, round and sticky bits. This is relatively straightforward for addition, subtraction and multiplication. For the first two, we retain the guard and round bits, calculate the sticky bits after denormalisation of the two input operands, perform the operation and re-normalise. As multiplication is simply an integer addition of the exponents and an integer multiplication of the mantissas, we just retain the most significant bits for the desired precision along with the extra guard and round bits, and calculate the sticky bit from the remaining least significant bits.

Division and square root operations, however, are more complex. This is because the Northeastern library, as described in [13], accelerates these operations using Taylor series approximations with table look-up. Unfortunately, this means the sticky bit cannot be determined. We decided to always set the sticky bit to one because while such an approximation may lead to an inaccurate result for a single floating point value, it guarantees safe rounding with respect to interval arithmetic such that the derived bounds will still contain the true solution - albeit bounds that may be slightly wider than the bounds if the correct value for the sticky bit were used. We adopt a similar approach for the square root.

## 3.2  Parameterizable Interval Unit Implementation

**Addition and subtraction.** Implementing an ALU on intervals according to interval arithmetic rules [4] is quite straightforward the basic floating point operators, in our work, to maximise the speed, we use separate adders for the lower and upper bound, resulting in the operators shown in Figures 2 and 3.

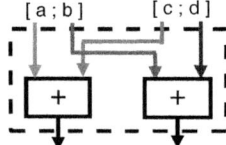    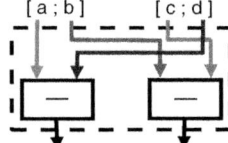

**Fig. 2.** Interval Adder          **Fig. 3.** Interval Subtractor

**Multiplication and Division.** Unlike addition and subtraction, a direct interval arithmetic implementation of multiplication, requires the calculation and comparison of several possible solutions to find the extremes. However, by examining the input operands' sign, it is possible eliminate several candidate bounds without even computing them. In the most complex case, we require two multipliers per bound, such that the hardware given in Figure 4 is sufficient. For division, we applied a similar process results in only two parallel dividers.

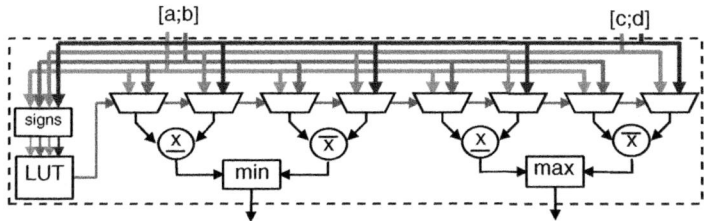

**Fig. 4.** Interval multiplier

**Other operators.** To simplify our implementation of the Krawczyk algorithm, we created three additional specialist interval operators: magnitude (1), mid-point (2) and intersection. Interval magnitude is calculated by forcing the sign bit to zero, so that we only need to compare the mantissas and exponents of the two inputs. A mid-point component was made, because this is just an addition and a divide by 2, with the latter operation being just a subtraction of one from the exponent which is cheaper than normal division. Intersecting two intervals is nothing more than selecting the highest lower bound and the lowest upper bound, though we added a check for the case of the null interval for completeness.

## 4   Krawczyk Algorithm Implementation

**Memory Architecture.** We decided to initially load and store the entire matrix on-chip and to make use of the large memory bandwidth available on an FPGA. This is a reasonable choice for applications consisting of small to medium size matrices, such as MIMO computation [14], or control system design [15]. Furthermore, as this algorithm consists of many stages, including an iterative refinement stage, we believe it is easily possible to interleave the I/O communication with computation, as discussed in Section 5.1. Furthermore, we also store intermediate matrices in on chip RAM to maintain high performance. Though this comes at a cost of high RAM use, we wish to take advantage of the growing size of the FPGAs, and note that if necessary we could examine RAM saving techniques from existing literature to improve scalability or trade it with performance [16].

Our RAMs are organised such that matrix rows are stored in individual RAMs, allowing us to perform operations for matrix cloumns in parallel.

**Computation of $Y = [\mathbf{mid}(A)]^{-1}$.** In this block, the mid-point can be computed for each column in parallel by using $n$ instances of our mid-point operator. This operator can be fully pipelined for maximum speed. We then invert this matrix, using the Cholesky decomposition algorithm followed by a lower triangular inversion. We note that this stage does not require interval operators, meaning alternative existing optimised hardware implementations, such as [7], could easily replace our implementation. However, we adopted a simple approach where any operations that are common to any column, such as the division or the subtraction are parallelised.

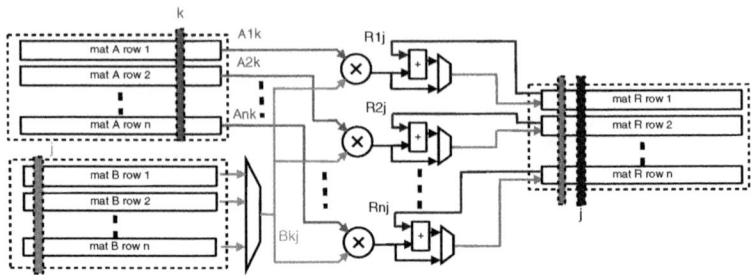

**Fig. 5.** Matrix multiplication – simplified view

**Computation of $E = I - YA$.** For the matrix multiplication, we perform parallel multiplication of a column of the $Y$ matrix with the first associated element of the $A$ matrix and store the $n$ temporary results in $n$ RAMs. We then repeat this for all the columns of $Y$. After this step, the initial values for every element of the result matrix are created, meaning we can the repeat the column multiplication of $Y$ with the next associated element of $A$ and sum this with the temporary results from the RAMs. Provided the system order is greater than the ALU pipeline latency, there will be no data hazards and the system will be fully pipelined; otherwise, we simply stall the pipeline to avoid any problems. This process is summarised in Figure 5. Finally to compute $E$ we then compute the subtraction for each column in parallel, using interval components.

**Computation of $X_0 = \left[ -\frac{\|Yb\|}{1-\|E\|} ; \frac{\|Yb\|}{1-\|E\|} \right]$.** The matrix-vector multiplication of $Yb$, is achieved with an architecture similar to Figure 5, but using only one vector column in the second operand. Pipeline stalls are added between column multiplications if necessary for the accumulator. The matrix norm $\|E\|$ is calculated with a similar component that replaces the multiplier with an absolute operation. The maximum of a vector $\|Yb\|$ is an absolute operation and serial comparison of elements over a vector. Finally, as the bounds of $X_0$ are created by simply changing the sign bit of the result.

**Computation of $X_{n+1} = (Yb + EX_n) \cap X_n$.** The value $EX_n$ is computed by re-using the matrix-vector multiplier in the previous step. As the matrix-vector multiplier outputs each vector element in series, the summations and intersections are performed serially as results are produced.

## 5   Results

All these components were written in VHDL and synthesized using Xilinx XST M.63c (Xilinx ISE 12.2) targetted towards a Xilinx Virtex6 XC6VLX760-1. Results for the components of the Krawczyk algorithm in Section 4 for a matrix order of 16 in IEEE single precision floating point are shown in Table 1.

**Table 1.** Hardware Implementation Results

| Description | Regs | LUTs | DSPs | BRAMs | $f_{max}(MHz)$ |
|---|---|---|---|---|---|
| Middle matrix | 5233 | 0 | 0 | 0 | 301.42 |
| Cholesky decomposition | 12798 | 17990 | 73 | 17 | 154.76 |
| Triangular inversion | 8582 | 16364 | 40 | 4 | 111.14 |
| Matrix by matrix FP multiplier | 27105 | 44284 | 128 | 0 | 154.76 |
| Matrix by vector interval multiplier | 28058 | 45166 | 128 | 0 | 154.76 |
| Matrix sum of magnitudes | 6355 | 10632 | 0 | 0 | 231.75 |
| Vector norm | 141 | 332 | 0 | 0 | 239.26 |
| Krawczyk initialization | 1250 | 1090 | 8 | 4 | 266.81 |
| Krawczyk iteration | 1742 | 2765 | 0 | 0 | 285.39 |

## 5.1   Comparison against an MPFR C Simulator

**Validation.** We first validated both the individual components, and the complete design against the result given by the MPFR C simulator [17] for several different linear systems. We chose the MPFR library as it is directly comparable to our hardware components as it contains parameterisable precision and rounding modes. The design met the expectations, albeit with the small caveat that the $Y$ matrix slightly differs from the one given by the C simulator because of the non IEEE-754 compliance of the floating point dividers and square root operators, as stated in Section 3.2, which in some cases lead to bounds that where slightly wider, although still valid, than the software counterpart.

**Performance Comparison.** The different latencies corresponding to the different sub-components composing the whole Krawczyk algorithm implementation were used to calculate the total latency of $10.5n^2 + 28.5n + 106$ clock cycles for the data preparation (until completion of the Krawczyk initialization, computing $x_0$), plus $7n + 15$ clock cycles per iteration of the Krawczyk loop.

For a main clock operating at 100 MHz, a 16$^{th}$ order linear solver completes within less than 4000 clock cycles, or less than 40 μs (assuming the convergence is reached within five iterations). A 100$^{th}$ order linear solver would complete within approximately 1.1 ms. In comparison, the C simulator on a AMD Turion 64 X2 requires around 20 ms for a 16$^{th}$ order system, and 2.1 seconds for a 100$^{th}$ order system: that is 500 to 2000 times slower than the FPGA-based solution. This large speed up is a result of parallelism of the algorithm – we have reduced the computational complexity from $\Theta(n^3)$ to $\Theta(n^2)$, and the efficiency of our specialist parallel interval arithmetic operators in contrast to the software approach of using MPFR. Computing bounds in variable precision with MPFR – as well as with any software capable of finding robust solutions in interval arithmetic with variable precision - is significantly slower than computing in standard single or double precision floating point because all the operations to compute floating point values (ordering the operands, computing the exponent difference, shifting the mantissa if necessary, performing the operation and renormalising) must be simulated in software instead of making use of the floating point hardware components on a computer [1, 17].

Our result estimates are based on a sustained performance, assuming that I/O is interleaved with computation, which we believe is a realistic assumption, given that the amount of data that must be transferred is $\Theta(n^2)$, and the computation time is also $\Theta(n^2)$. However, we do acknowledge that interleaving I/O with computation does increase our RAM requirements to store the $A$ matrix for a subsequent problem whilst computing the current problem.

# 6   Conclusions

Interval arithmetic constitutes an original method for representing and computing numbers on digital systems that circumvents the inability of floating point to track data inaccuracy by considering an interval bounding a real value with an absolute certainty instead of an approximate value without any indication of the approximation accuracy. In this work, we have modified a pre-existing library of floating point operators to develop a library of interval operators.

We have then applied these to the Krawczyk algorithm, which is specifically designed to solve linear systems of equations based on interval arithmetic, and shown that a dedicated hardware operator which conforms to the computer C simulations to be very efficient: the algorithm optimizations and parallelizations led to a speed-up in orders of magnitude in comparison with a C implementation on modern computers for system orders up to a few dozen. Though we are limited to small orders, we believe by integrating existing techniques which trade performance with scalability from relevant literature for the various operations in the Krawczyk algorithm with our interval components and still gain significant improvements over software. Altogether, we believe that we have both demonstrated the potential for FPGA acceleration of the Krawczyk algorithm and created a library of parameterisable floating point and interval operators that could result in significantly superior performance in many further applications.

# References

1. Schulte, M.J., Swartzlander Jr., E.E.: Software and hardware techniques for accurate, self-validating arithmetic. Applications of Interval Computations, 381–404 (1996)
2. Schulte, M.J., Swartzlander Jr., E.E.: A family of variable-precision interval arithmetic processors. IEEE Trans. Comput. 49(5), 387–397 (2000)
3. Kirchner, R., Kulisch, U.: Hardware support for interval arithmetic. Reliable Computing 12, 225–237 (2006), 10.1007/s11155-006-7220-9
4. Moore, R.E., Kearfott, R.B., Cloud, M.J.: Introduction to Interval Analysis. SIAM, Philadelphia (2009)
5. IEEE Computer society, IEEE standard for floating-point arithmetic, IEEE Std 754-2008, pp. 1 –58 (August 2008)
6. Koren, I.: Computer arithmetic algorithms. Prentice-Hall, Inc., Upper Saddle River (1993)
7. Salmela, P., Happonen, A., Burian, A., Takala, J.: Several approaches to fixed-point implementation of matrix inversion. In: Proc. Int. Symp. Signals, Circuits and Systems, vol. 2, pp. 497–500 (July 2005)

8. de Matos, G., Neto, H.: On reconfigurable architectures for efficient matrix inversion. In: Proc. Int. Conf. Field Programmable Logic and Applications, pp. 369–374 (August 2006)
9. Roldao, A., Constantinides, G.A.: A high throughput fpga-based floating point conjugate gradient implementation for dense matrices. ACM Trans. Reconfigurable Technol. Syst. 3, 1:1–1:19 (2010)
10. Xilinx, Xilinx logicore, http://www.xilinx.com/ipcenter/
11. de Dinechin, F., Detrey, J., Cret, O., Tudoran, R.: When FPGAs are better at floating-point than microprocessors. In: Proc. Int. Symp. Field Programmable Gate Arrays, p. 260 (2008)
12. Belanovic, P., Leeser, M.: A library of parameterized floating point modules and their use. In: Proc. Int Conf. Field Programmable Logic and Applications, pp. 657–666 (2002)
13. Wang, X., Leeser, M.: Variable precision floating point division and square root. In: Workshop on High Performance Embedded Computing, pp. 47–48 (2004)
14. Biglieri, E., Calderbank, R., Constantinides, A., Goldsmith, A., Paulraj, A., Poor, H.V.: MIMO Wireless Communications. Cambridge University Press, Cambridge (2007)
15. Maciejowski, J.M.: Predictive control with constraints. Prentice Hall, Essex (2002)
16. Boland, D., Constantinides, G.: Optimising memory bandwidth use for matrix-vector multiplication in iterative methods. In: Sirisuk, P., Morgan, F., El-Ghazawi, T., Amano, H. (eds.) ARC 2010. LNCS, vol. 5992, pp. 169–181. Springer, Heidelberg (2010)
17. Fousse, L., Hanrot, G., Lefèvre, V., Pélissier, P., Zimmermann, P.: MPFR: A multiple-precision binary floating-point library with correct rounding. ACM Trans. Math. Softw. 33(2), 13 (2007)

# A Dynamic Reconfigurable CPLD Architecture for Structured ASIC Technology

Traian Tulbure

Dept. of Electronics and Computers, Transilvania University
29 Eroilor, 500036, Brasov, Romania
tulbure@vega.unitbv.ro

**Abstract.** This paper describes the architecture of a reconfigurable Complex Programmable Logic Device (CPLD) designed for structured ASIC technology. The proposed architecture adds the feature of reconfiguration to structured ASIC with both static and dynamic reconfiguration options. Static reconfiguration is realized using the possibility to reprogram the SRAM based look-up tables at power-up while dynamic reconfiguration uses embedded memory to implement a multi-context device. Dynamic reconfiguration is realized by storing sixteen CPLD configurations in on-chip memory. This inactive on-chip memory is distributed around the chip allowing single cycle configuration change and it can be accessed either from offchip or from internal logic. Implementation results on structured ASIC validated the solution from both area and timing perspective.

**Keywords:** structured ASIC, reconfigurable computing, programmable logic.

## 1 Introduction

Reconfigurable computing need a reconfigurable fabric to implement a portion of a dataflow component of an application. For a runtime reconfiguration the overhead of serial configuration can be prohibitive, an alternative is to provide storage for multiple configurations and ability to overlap the computation and reconfiguration stages. Previous work in this area was mainly focused in dynamic reconfiguration of FPGA. Several different multi-context architectures have been proposed such as the Dynamically Programmable Gate Array [1], Time Multiplexed FPGA [2] and the Time Switched FPGA [3] that use distributed SRAM to permit overlapping of computation and configuration stages. CPLDs are devices with lower complexity than FPGA, a CPLD generator for SoC is proposed in [4], while [5] introduces a architecture for structured ASIC.

First dynamic reconfigurable circuits for structured ASIC came in a form of simple PAL and PLA [6]. Because in the PLA structure the programmable logic plane structure grows too quickly as the number of inputs increases, we are introducing a dynamic reconfigurable CPLD with higher logic capacity.

Structured ASIC technologies, also called standard metal and lately zero-NRE technologies, appeared as an alternative to the standard cells technology

A. Koch et al. (Eds.): ARC 2011, LNCS 6578, pp. 296–301, 2011.

for the designs that want to reduce costs and for FPGA designs that want to improve performances for middle volume production. Such a solution is developed by eASIC [7] in Nextreme platforms. The solution is to use predefined, pre-characterized logic structures containing LUTs and NAND logic gates with predefined routes that can be programmed through upper metal via structures. The advantage of via programmed circuits is that the circuit can be manufactured up to the last metallization layer and based on the design features customize this via layer to implement the desired operations.

In structured ASIC programming the interconnect with single via metallization has great benefit in improving speed, area and power but it practically eliminates re-programmability, a feature so needed to implement multiple design revisions on same sillicon or for reconfigurable computing. The solution to add back re-programmability for structured ASIC is to define PLD architectures that use the SRAM based LUTs, distributed and block memories to model the interconnect. These architectures can have complexity from PAL to FPGA and can have either static or dynamic configurability option. Dynamic reconfiguration is the only solution for the latest structured ASIC families [8], because there the LUT can be only implemented with via metallization.

## 2   eCPLD Architecture

A complex programmable logic device (CPLD) is a programmable logic device with complexity between that of PALs and FPGAs, and architectural features of both. There are many different types of CPLD architectures but they all have few elements in common:

- the larger members of the families have an interconnect matrix between smaller blocks
- the smaller blocks have AND-OR PLD structures with some feedback
- the PLD structures also drive flip-flops which feedback into both the PLD structure and interconnect structures.

A diagram of such structure is presented in Fig. 1a. The PLD structure is usually 8 to 32 bits wide with more inputs than outputs, the outputs are usually from flip-flops but maybe combinatorial. Based on those features of comercial CPLDs, we chose that the number of inputs is double then the number of outputs and both are multiple of 8 to be able to model byte wide interconnect buses. Usually all the inputs connect to all the product terms for all the PLD structures with some feedback and structures available for routing or expansion terms. We can model in two ways configuration for the proposed CPLD architecture:

- static single context configuration - configuration data is stored in LUTs and can be changed only at power-up
- dynamic multi-context configuration - configuration data is stored in SRAM and can be changed at any time during application execution

The proposed dynamic reconfigurable architecture, called eCPLD, is built from multiple dynamic-reconfigurable AND-OR arrays (ePLD) and one dynamic reconfigurable interconnect (eConnect).

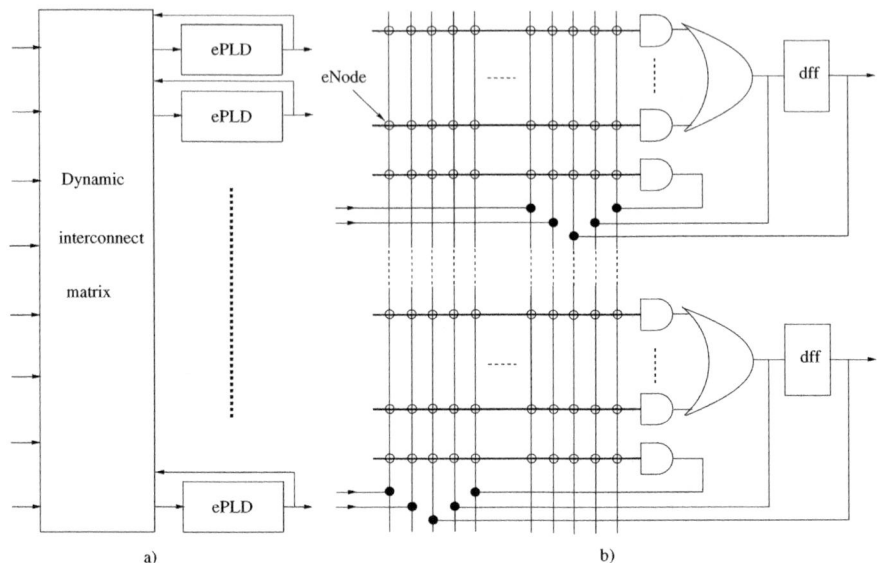

**Fig. 1.** a) eCPLD architecture b) ePLD structure

## 2.1  ePLD - Dynamic Programmable AND-OR Structure

This section describes the dynamic programmable AND-OR structure. ePLD is a dynamic reconfigurable structure which use the neutral element for AND logic functions. Fig. 1b show a simple ePLD structure with programming nodes controlled by memory elements for AND array. The dynamic reconfigurable node, called eNode, is implemented with a multiplexer, a XOR gate for programmable inversion and a 2 bit memory element that store the active configuration.

Assuming that we want to implement multiple functions at different time moments, when using the ePLD structure we must control the eNodes using small size distributed memories. In this paper we also propose to use block RAM to implement context memory with the advantage of less area and less congestion and disadvantage that context change cannot be realized in single cycle. A small logic context controller was designed to perform sequential context change and provide read/write arbitration for block RAM memory. Because the context memory organization is basically changed from a wide memory size to the size of block RAM the dynamic reprogrammable node described in Fig. 2a need to be modified to include a memory elements (flip-flops). Fig. 2b presents the modified structure for eNode with possibility to store the configuration bits that can be loaded from on-chip memory.

The configuration change for the modified structure cannot be done in single cycle as in the structure that uses small distributed memory blocks, multiple cycles are needed to transfer a new configuration in all eNodes.

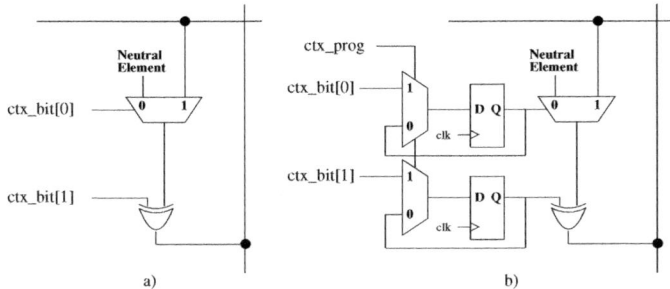

**Fig. 2.** a) eNode b) Modified eNode for block RAM configuration

## 2.2   eConnect - Dynamic Programmable Interconnect Matrix

The interconnect matrix must take all outputs from all ePLD macrocells and external circuit inputs and connect them to all ePLD inputs and circuit outputs. It is more difficult to layout a full size interconnect matrix so we decided to model a interconnect at byte level. The proposed interconnect require a smaller configuration memory than a full size interconnect but it can complicate the CAD tools for proposed architecture.

## 3   Implementation

Described using Verilog 2001, the CPLD is highly parametrizable. We did implementation for both static and dynamic reprogrammable eCPLD with 16 contexts for a medium-small sized CPLD with 64 macrocells grouped in 8 ePLD structures. Thus the ePLD structure is configured as 16 inputs and 8 outputs with 3 pterms and one expansion term per output. There are 5 inputs and feedbacks per output which would mean 40 inputs if product terms are fully populated.

### 3.1   Results

The implementation was performed on eASIC Nextreme NX5000 device with Magma Design Automation environment for structured ASIC 90 nm process. Two versions of dynamic reconfigurable CPLD were implemented, eCPLD_v1 uses distributed memory while eCPLD_v2 uses block RAM. Table 1 presents area results for the implementation of the three versions of eCPLD.

As presented in [7] the basic logic cell, called eCell, is built from 2 three input LUTs, 2 NAND gates, a flip-flop, a multiplexer and 3 buffers. It can also be configured to implement distributed memory, called eRAM, while bRAM is the available 32 kbit block RAM.

We can see that the dynamic reconfigurable eCPLD that uses distributed memory is difficult to layout because of the big number of eRAM instances and can fit only on the biggest array. This is caused by a limitation of Nextreme that does not allow configuring the eRAM to size up to 16x256. Fig. 3 present

**Table 1.** Area results

| Design name | eCell no. | eRAM no. | bRAM no. | $NX750$ % | $NX1500$ % | $NX2500$ % | $NX4000$ % | $NX5000$ % |
|---|---|---|---|---|---|---|---|---|
| eCPLD_st | 3680 | 0 | 0 | 6.65 | 3.66 | 2.06 | 1.33 | 1.02 |
| eCPLD_v1 | 50546 | 1248 | 0 | NA | NA | NA | NA | 14.10 |
| eCPLD_v2 | 30052 | 32 | 8 | 54.31 | 29.94 | 17.66 | 10.86 | 8.38 |

**Table 2.** Timing results

| Design name | Intra ePLD timing [ns] | Inter ePLD timing [ns] | Context timing [ns] | Context change [ns] |
|---|---|---|---|---|
| eCPLD_st | 2.886 | 3.771 | NA | NA |
| eCPLD_v1 | 9.844 | 11.172 | 14.275 | 14.275 |
| eCPLD_v2 | 3.574 | 4.781 | 4.933 | 374.908 |

comparative layout of the eCPLD_v1 and eCPLD_v2, showing how the eRAM limitation affects the placement.

The final placed and routed netlist was analyzed with a static time analysis tool - Synopsys PrimeTime. Table 2 present timing results. It shows improvement of the critical paths through CPLD when using block RAM, with increased time for configuration change, because context change requires 76 clock cycles.

A static reconfigurable CPLD is possible with advantages of low area utilization and high performance. A configuration change is done by reprogramming

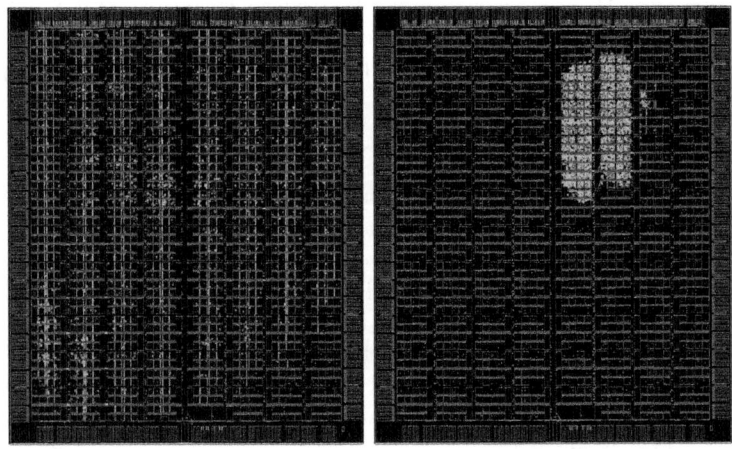

**Fig. 3.** Comparative layout for dynamic reconfigurable eCPLD (eCPLD_v1 on left, eCPLD_v2 on right)

LUT data for entire structured ASIC device, process that takes hundreds of milliseconds depending on the selected structured ASIC platform.

A dynamic reconfigurable CPLD with single clock configuration change is not really an option without a very wide distributed memory, that is not possible in existing structured ASIC layout. This CPLD architecture can be implemented for small configurations but probably a simple PLA will be the preferred option in these cases.

A dynamic reconfigurable CPLD that uses block RAM and has multicycle context change is a good tradeoff between the first two options with good area overhead and performance. The reconfiguration can be done quite fast, in few hundreds of nanoseconds, with the possibility to reduce this time further by doing only partial reconfiguration.

## 4  Conclusions

This paper described a CPLD architectures that allows reconfiguration for structured ASIC. Static reconfiguration is done using flexibility of SRAM based LUT. For dynamic reconfiguration dedicated on-chip memories are used to hold multiple configurations that allows logic resource to implement different functionality in time. The proposed solution can be used for high speed reconfigurable computing or can be embedded in designs implemented on structured ASIC allowing easy, in system reprogramming.

## References

1. DeHon, A.: DPGA Utilization and Application. In: Proceedings of the ACM fourth international symposium on FPGAs, Monterey, pp. 115–121 (1996)
2. Trimberger, S., Carberry, D., Johnson, A., Wong, J.: A Time Multiplexed FPGA. In: Proceedings of the 5th Annual IEEE Symposium on FPGAs for Custom Computing Machines, Napa Valley, pp. 22–28 (1997)
3. Chang, D., Marek-Sadowska, M.: Partitioning Sequestial Circuits on Dynamically Reconfigurable FPGAs. IEEE Trans. Computers 48(6), 565–579 (1999)
4. Holland, M., Hauck, S.: Automatic Creation of Domain-Specific Reconfigurable CPLDs for SoC. IEEE Trans. on Computer-Aided Design of Integrated Circuits and Systems 26(2), 291–295 (2007)
5. Cooke, L.: gCPLD Architecture, unpublished paper (2001)
6. Tulbure, T.: A Time Multiplexed Programmable Array for Structured ASIC Technology. In: Proceedings of the 9th International Symposium on Electronics and Telecommunications, Timisoara, pp. 25–28 (2010)
7. Nextreme Zero Mask-Change ASIC Handbook (2009), http://www.easic.com
8. Nextreme 2 Device Handbook (2010), http://www.easic.com

# FPGA Accelerated Parallel Sparse Matrix Factorization for Circuit Simulations*

Wei Wu, Yi Shan, Xiaoming Chen, Yu Wang, and Huazhong Yang

Department of Electronic Engineering, Tsinghua National Laboratory for Information Science and Technology, Tsinghua University
100084, Beijing, China
wwnigel@gmail.com,
{shany08,chenxm05}@mails.tsinghua.edu.cn,
{yu-wang,yanghz}@mail.tsinghua.edu.cn

**Abstract.** Sparse matrix factorization is a critical step for the circuit simulation problem, since it is time consuming and computed repeatedly in the flow of circuit simulation. To accelerate the factorization of sparse matrices, a parallel CPU+FPGA based architecture is proposed in this paper. While the pre-processing of the matrix is implemented on CPU, the parallelism of numeric factorization is explored by processing several columns of the sparse matrix simultaneously on a set of processing elements (PE) in FPGA. To cater for the requirements of circuit simulation, we also modified the Gilbert/Peierls (G/P) algorithm and considered the scalability of our architecture. Experimental results on circuit matrices from the University of Florida Sparse Matrix Collection show that our architecture achieves speedup of 0.5x-5.36x compared with the CPU KLU results.

**Keywords:** Circuit Simulation, Sparse Matrix, LU Factorization, FPGA, Parallelism.

## 1 Introduction

With the growing complexity of integrated circuits, manual approaches of circuit test, such as breadboard probing, are not applicable. Those approaches were substituted by circuit simulation software such as SPICE from 1975, when the SPICE2 was delivered and became really popular[1]. Currently, there are many circuit simulation software packages designed based on SPICE, such as HSPICE owned by Synopsys[3] and PSPICE owned by Cadence Design Systems[3]. In the flowchart of circuit simulation, as drafted in Figure 1, a significant and time consuming step is repeatedly solving an equation set $Ax = b$ generated from targeted circuits according to Kirchhoff's circuit laws in Newton-Raphson Iterations[4]. In the very large scale integrated circuit (VLSI), the dimension of the matrix $A$, in equation set $Ax = b$, can reach up to tens of thousands or even million, which brings great challenges to the computations.

There are two methods of solving the equation set $Ax = b$, iterative methods and direct methods. The former approach attempts to solve the problem by successive

---

* This work was supported by National Key Technological Program of China No. 2008ZX01035-001 and NSFC No. 60870001.

A. Koch et al. (Eds.): ARC 2011, LNCS 6578, pp. 302–315, 2011.

approximations to the solution from an initial assumption. However, this approach is not applicable for all of the matrices, since its data stability greatly depends on the convergence of the matrix $A$. Distinguished from the iterative methods, the direct methods, such as factorizing the matrix $A$ into a lower matrix $L$ and an upper matrix $U$, deliver the exact solution by a finite sequence of computations in the absence of rounding error. In these methods, the LU factorization are widely utilized in circuit simulation because it is universal and irrelevant to the convergence of the matrix $A$. There are usually two steps of the LU factorization: 1) the pre-processing, which reorders the matrix to maintain data stability and sparsity, 2) the numeric factorization to compute $L$ and $U$.

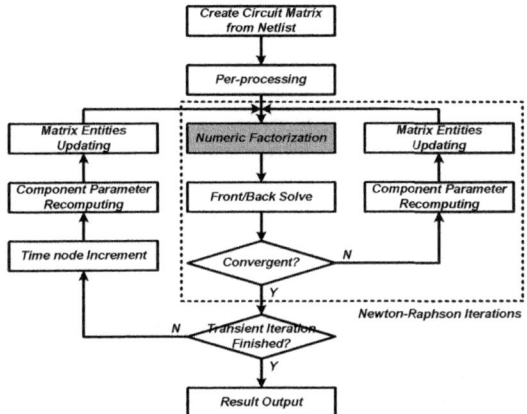

**Fig. 1.** Flowchart of Circuit Simulation

Several characters of circuit simulation make the LU factorization of circuit matrices very different from other matrices.

Firstly, the circuit matrices are extremely sparse[13]. Therefore the algorithms designed to factorize circuit matrices shall be targeted for sparse matrix.

Secondly, during the update of nonlinear components, values of entities in matrix $A$ vary during the simulation while the nonzero structure remains unchanged. Therefore, as shown in Figure 1, the pre-processing is only required to be carried out for once, while the numeric factorization, which is marked as gray in Figure 1, needs to be performed for many times. Consequently, the acceleration of the numeric factorization is critical to the performance of circuit simulation.

Currently, there are already many approaches to accelerate the LU factorization, by means of developing sophisticated algorithm on CPU and exploiting the parallelism on hardware, such as FPGA. Comparatively, the FPGA designs hold higher performance compared with the CPU implementations. However, most of the FPGA designs are with deficiencies on scalability and performance, and some of them can only be applied to special matrix patterns such as the *bordered diagonal block* (BDB) forms.

In this paper, a CPU+FPGA architecture for LU factorization is proposed. While the pre-processing is fulfilled on CPU, FPGA performs the numeric factorization of the matrix. The key contribution of this paper includes:

- Modified the G/P algorithm by extracting the symbolic analysis from the numeric factorization.
- Designing a CPU+FPGA architecture for LU factorization to accelerate the circuit simulation, with the pre-processing and numeric analysis implemented on CPU and the numeric factorization realized on FPGA. This architecture explore the parallelism by processing several columns of the matrix simultaneously on a set of PEs in FPGA.
- Modified the G/P algorithm again to consider the scalability to matrix size, a potential scalable version of current architecture is also introduce.
- Quantitative comparison between CPU KLU and our CPU+FPGA based implementation by a variety of circuit matrices from *the University of Florida Sparse Matrix Collection*[5].

The rest of this paper is organized in five parts. Section 2 introduces the preliminary algorithms and the related work. In section 3, the dataflow and complexity of both left-looking and right-looking algorithm are studied and our modification on G/P algorithm is introduced. Section 4 proposed our FPGA architecture, the detail implementation and its scalability. In section 5, the experimental results and its comparison with CPU implementation are provided. Section 6 concludes the paper and provides the future directions.

## 2  Preliminary Algorithms and Related Work

In this section, firstly, a typical data structure of sparse matrix, Compressed Column Storage (CCS) format, is introduced. Then a brief overview of the algorithms of direct LU factorization and its implementations on CPU and FPGA are provided.

### 2.1  Compressed Column Storage (CCS) Format [23]

A typical data structure, CCS format, is introduced to minimize the memory usage. The space requirement of the CCS format grows linearly with the number of nonzero entities (nnz) in the sparse matrix $A$. In the column-wise CCS format, all the row indexes and values of nnzs are stored in vector $A_v$ column by column, while starting indexes of every column are stored in vector $A_p$. An example of column-wise CCS is provided as below. In $A_v$, (0 3) represents the nonzero entities in the $0^{th}$ row of the $1^{st}$ column, whose value is 3.

$$A = \begin{matrix} 2 & 3 & 0 \\ 0 & 1 & 0 \\ 0 & 0 & 1 \end{matrix}$$
$$A_v = [0\ 2\ \ 0\ 3\ 1\ 1\ 2\ 1], A_p = [0\ 1\ 3\ 4]$$

The algorithm and architecture in following of this paper are based on CCS format.

### 2.2  Algorithms of Direct LU Factorization

*Pre-processing*
As discussed in Section 1, the direct LU factorization includes 2 steps, the pre-processing and numeric factorization. The pre-processing part, which only needs to be

executed once, performs the row/column pivoting to maintain data stability and to preserve sparsity. There are several different algorithms of pre-processing, which can be categorized into 2 groups: the static pivoting[11] and partial pivoting[12]. The static pivoting computes all the row/column permutation during pre-processing, while the partial pivoting just carries out part of the pivoting operations during pre-processing, some pivoting operations have to be carried out during the numeric factorization.

It is memory access intensive for the pivoting of rows in a column wise formatted matrix, because it is required to search for the entities of the targeted row in every column. To avoid the intensive irregular memory accesses during the numeric factorization, the static pivoting algorithm, which is used in SuperLU-DIST[10], is implemented on CPU, while the repeated numeric factorization is implemented on FPGA.

### Numeric Factorization

The numeric factorization approaches are categorized into mainly two kinds of algorithms, the left-looking[6] and right-looking[6] algorithms, whose pseudo-codes are illustrated in Figure 2 and Figure 3 respectively. Other algorithms such as the G/P algorithm[24] and the left-right-looking[7] algorithm are derived from the basic left-looking algorithm. The multifrontal algorithm[8] [9] is evolved from the right-looking algorithm.

```
1  for k = 1 to n do
2        f = A(:, k)
3        for r = 1 to k - 1 do
4                f = f - f(r) * L(r + 1 : n, r)
5        end for
6        U(1 : k) = f(1 : k)
7        L(k : n) = f(k : n) / U(k, k)
8  end for
```

**Fig. 2.** Left-looking Algorithm

```
1  for k = 1 to n - 1 do
2        L(k : n, :) = A(k : n, :)
3        U(:, k : n) = A(:, k : n) / L(k, k)
4        A(k + 1 : n, k + 1 : n)
            = A(k + 1 : n, k + 1 : n) - L(k + 1 : n, :) × U(:, k + 1 : n)
5  end for
```

**Fig. 3.** Right-looking Algorithm

In Figure 2, the left-looking algorithm updates matrix $A$ column by column to calculated the $L$ and $U$. While updating the current column of $A$, it goes leftwards to fetch the result of $L$. In right-looking, updating of the sub-matrix is carried out rightwards, since the sub-matrices are located at the bottom right corner.

The G/P algorithm is designed for sparse matrices factorization with the complexity proportional to arithmetic operations. The left-right-looking algorithm updates several columns are updated simultaneously in different processors or threads. In this algorithm, it is required to look leftwards to fetch data, and rightwards to notify other processors or threads that the data of current column are ready. The multifrontal algorithm is different from the former three algorithms. It reorganizes the factorization of original sparse matrix into a sequence of partial factorizations of dense smaller matrices according to *assembly tree*[8].

## 2.3 Related Work

### CPU implementations
Currently, there are several CPU based implementations of sparse matrix factorization algorithms, such as SuperLU[10], KLU[13], PARDISO[14], UMFPACK[15] and MA41 in HSL Mathematical Software Library[16]. The sequential SuperLU[10] used the G/P algorithm with supernode involved, while the KLU does not consider supernode, but uses block triangular form (BTF) to fit circuit simulation matrices [13]. A multithread version of sequential SuperLU, SuperLU-MT, parallelizes the computation by means of multithreads[10]. For the right-looking algorithm, the SuperLU-DIST is a typical implementation on distributed memory systems[10]. PARDISO implements the left-right-looking algorithm on shared memory parallel machines[14]. In UMFPACK and MA41 of HSL Mathematical Software Library, the multifrontal algorithm is utilized[15] [16]. In this paper, we will mainly compare the performance of our implementation with KLU since it is the only CPU implementation targeted for circuit simulation problems.

### FPGA implementations
The FPGA implementations of direct LU factorization appeared after 2000, which were much later than the CPU implementations. In 2004, V. Daga et al. introduced an architecture for direct LU factorization[17]. Later in 2006, they proposed a modified architecture with parameterized resource consumption[18]. However, these architectures are not designed for the sparse matrix. It is not applicable for large sparse matrices whose size may reach hundreds of thousands or even million. Xiaofang Wang et al. proposed an FPGA architecture for circuit matrices factorization in 2003[19]. Their work was limited to BDB matrix, but, actually, not all the circuits can be represented by BDB matrix. In 2008, Jeremy Johnson et al. implemented a row-wise right-looking algorithm in FPGA[20]. Their architecture depends on the data pattern, in which two copies of the matrix data are required, one in row-wise compressed format and the other in column-wise. Moreover, the performance of their architecture does not overcome the CPU implementations[21]. In 2010, Tarek Nechma et al. proposed a medium-grained paralleled architecture by means of column-dependency tree[23]. While all the data are loaded from DDR to on-chip BRAM before the computation, the problem size that can be processed is limited, since the size of on-chip memory cannot be too large. N Kapre et al. proposed a fine-grained sparse matrix solver based on a dataflow compute graph in 2009[22]. This architecture is a fine-grained one and greatly depends on the dataflow compute graph.

To be more useful for the circuit simulation, the FPGA architecture shall be scalable or at least have scalable potential, and compatible with all the form of sparse matrix and with a high performance. In the following two sections, the factorization algorithms and their suitable architecture will be analysed, and then we will propose our FPGA architecture.

## 3   Algorithm Complexity

In this section, the dataflow and complexity of both left-looking and right-looking algorithms for direct LU factorization are evaluated. Also a slight modification on G/P algorithm is proposed to reduce the overall complexity for circuit simulation problem.

### 3.1   Complexity of Left-Looking Algorithm

In this subsection, we will analyse the dataflow of both left-looking and right-looking algorithms. During studying the left-looking algorithm, we will consider the G/P algorithm since it targets for sparse matrices.

*Left-looking algorithm*
According to the pseudo-codes shown in Figure 2, the left-looking algorithm performs the factorization of the sparse matrix column by column. While updating the $k^{th}$ column, the complexity can be denoted as:

$$P_{left}(Col\ k) = n + (2 * \textstyle\sum_{i \forall\ U_{ik} \neq 0} L_i) + L_k$$

In this expression, $n$ stands for the matrix demension, the $L_i$ denotes the number of nnz in the $i^{th}$ column of matrix $L$. The first $n$ in this expression stands for the complexity spends on searching for the nnzs in current column, because only nnzs are required to be processed. The second part, $2 * \sum_{i \forall\ U_{ik} \neq 0} L_i$, stands for the complexity of updating current column by $1^{st} \sim (k-1)^{th}$ columns, while the third part, $L_k$, denotes the complexity of normalizing current column.

The second part and the third part of the complexity expression are proportional to arithmetic operations. However, the first part in the complexity grows with $n^2$, which will become the dominant part of the complexity when the matrix dimension $n$ is large.

*Modification on G/P algorithm*
The G/P algorithm, as shown in Figure 4(a) and Figure 4(b), is designed to solve this problem[24], while Figure 4(b) is the solution for the $3^{rd}$ line in Figure 4(a). Before updating every column of $A$, it analysis the potential nnz structure in $L$ and $U$ by the information of nnz structure in the matrix $L$ and current column of $A$. Moreover, the complexity of nnz analysis for a column is also proportional to the arithmetic operations rather than $n$.

| (a) G/P Algorithm, Overview | (b) G/P algorithm, Solve x = L \ b |
|---|---|
| 1  *for* $k = 1\ to\ n$  *do* | 1  *Analysis for potential nonzero structure of L,U* |
| 2      $b = A(:,k)$ | 2  *for* $i = 1\ to\ k-1\ in\ the\ predicted\ structure$  *do* |
| 3      $x = L \backslash b$ | 3      $x(j+1:n) = x(j+1:n) - L(j+1:n,j)x(j)$ |
| 4      $U(1:k) = f(1:k)$ | 4  *end for* |
| 5      $L(k:n) = f(k:n)/U(k,k)$ | |
| 6  *end for* | |

**Fig. 4.** G/P Algorithm

Since the symbolic analysis of potential nonzero structure is independent to other arithmetic operations, this step can be performed before the factorization. Furthermore, as mentioned before, the nonzero structure remains unchanged during the flow of circuit simulation. the symbolic predicting can even be performed during the preprocessing before entering the inner loop of circuit simulation. After this modification on G/P algorithm, the complexity of updating a column is almost minimized and illustrated as below, with the complexity of symbolic analysis totally ruled out.

$$P_{Modified}(Col\ k) = (2 * \sum_{i\forall\ U_{ik}\neq 0} L_i) + L_k$$

It is also straightforward to conclude that the complexity of factorizing a sparse matrix with modified G/P algorithm as below:

$$P_{Modified} = \sum_{k=1}^{n}((2 * \sum_{i\forall U(i,k)\neq 0} L_i) + L_k)$$

The matrix data are stored in CCS format, which means the nnz in a column are stored one by one. During the processing of a column, we first create an index for the nnz in this column. Then, we can refer to the index to find the address of nnz in this column. The index of a column consumes $n$ words of memory. Fortunately, the left-looking algorithm only factorizes the matrix column by column, so only the index of one column is required for this algorithm.

## 3.2  Complexity of Right-Looking Algorithm

When it comes to the right-looking algorithm, the matrix is processed by sub-matrix. Not like the left-looking algorithm, we cannot create the index for the entire sub-matrix since it may consume $n^2$ words of memory. Without the index information, it may be required to search in every column to find the data to be accessed. Although the arithmetic complexity of right-looking algorithm is the same as the left-looking algorithm, it may consume more time on data manipulation.

According to the analysis in this section, the modified G/P algorithm is the most suitable algorithm for circuit simulation problem.

# 4  Proposed Architecture

In this section, the architecture and implementation detail supporting modified G/P algorithm is proposed. Also the potential parallelism is analysed and corresponding parallel architecture is proposed. Then, the scalability of this architecture is also discussed.

## 4.1  Architecture for the Modified G/P Algorithm

To fulfill the function of modified G/P algorithm, a hardware architecture is proposed and illustrated in Figure 5.

This architecture is constructed of the following parts: the Processing Controller, the Arithmetic Logic, the Content Address Memory (CAM) and the Cache, including both the inner on and external one.

The Processing Controller controls the flow of factorizing a matrix and the state of this architecture. The CAM fulfills the function as an index. If the row ID $i$ of $A(i,j)$ is inputted, the address of the nnz will be returned in one cycle. The Arithmetic Logic is

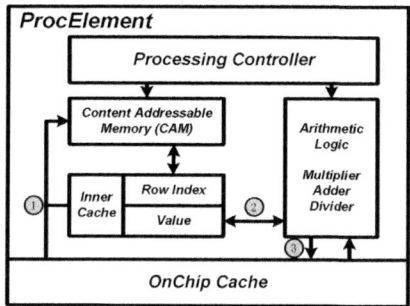

**Fig. 5.** Architecture for Modified G/P Algorithm

constructed of three units, a subtracter, a multiplier, and a divider. The Caches are construct of two parts, the inner part and the external part. Actually, the cache is implemented by a Tri-Port RAM (TPRAM). In these three ports, one write port and one read port are connected to local PE, while the rest read port is connected outwards for external access. The inner cache can be a virtual memory mapped on the On chip cache.

In this architecture, before the factorization, data are loaded to cache from CPU. When the factorization starts, the processing of every column in a matrix is performed in three steps, under the control of Processing Controller according to the state switching diagram in Figure 6.

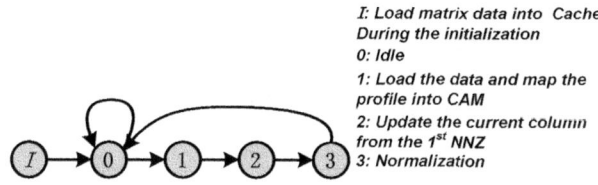

**Fig. 6.** State Switching Diagram of Processing Controller

In Figure 6, the first step is to load the data from on chip cache and to map the position of every nnz in CCS format into CAM. The second step is to update this column by the former columns of $L$, according to the nnz in current column of $U$. The third step is to normalize the entities in current column of $L$ and dump them back to the on chip cache.

## 4.2 Parallelized Architecture

### Potential parallelism
The architecture in the former subsection factorizes the matrix almost sequentially, except a few cycle level parallelism between the arithmetic operations. It seems that the G/P algorithm is a sequential algorithm because the processing of a column may require the data of former columns. However, three parallelism strategies can still be explored in this algorithm.

Firstly, the different column of the matrix can be processed simultaneously according to the elimination tree[7] in the parallel hardware such as multi-core GPP and FPGA. Secondly, to reduce the time on memory accessing and processing the dense block of matrix with optimized algorithm, the supernode is proposed to accelerate the processing. This approach is adopted in SuperLU[10] and PARDISO[14], but the supernode is not suitable for circuit matrices because they are extremely sparse[13]. The third parallelism is the fine-grained parallelism between the dataflow of every operations. N. Kapre et al. explored this parallelism in their FPGA architecture. However, the generation and optimization of the dataflow is required before the factorization.

Therefore, we only pursue the first parallelism by implementing a group of PEs in FPGA, while every PE process a column of the matrix independently.

***Parallelized architecture***

We introduce the module that factorizes a column in the sparse matrix in the former subsection. In this subsection, that module is referred as a PE. To achieve parallel processing, we implemented an architecture with several PEs. While processing a column in the matrix, all the column of matrix $L$ might be accessed. Therefore, the data of matrix $L$ are required to be shared to all PEs for accessing.

Our first attempt on the shared memory is an external DDR2 memory with an arbitrator to decide which PE holds the bus of the memory. That trial failed because the memory bandwidth is always the bottleneck of the system. To increase the bandwidth, we adopt a distributed shared memory to replace the original shared memory. The multi-PE architecture with distributed shared memory is shown in Figure 7.

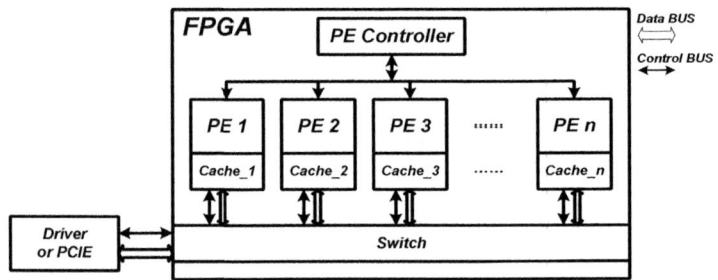

**Fig. 7.** Parallelized Architecture

In Figure 7, data are located at the cache distributed in every PE. To be easily realized, all the PEs are connected to a switch to construct a on chip network, in which a PE can access the data in its own cache directly and access the data stored in other cache via a switch. Since data need to be prepared in caches before the factorization, a Driver interface is also reserved on the switch for the loading matrix data from PC to FPGA, corresponding to state I in Figure 6. By replacing a single shared memory to a set of distributed shared memory, the peak bandwidth is increased by $n$ times, in which the $n$ stands for the number of PEs, also the number of caches in the distributed memory. In our prototype, we use 16 PEs. Under this configuration, the performance of our hardware exceeds KLU on most circuit matrices.

## 4.3  Scalability

As mentioned in subsection 2.2, many related designs suffer from the scalability problem[17] [18] [23]. In this subsection, we will discuss the scalability of our architecture on both the architecture and the algorithm aspects.

Firstly, we need consider how to make full use of the on-chip memory to enable our architecture to process matrices as large as possible, in other words, the scalability to matrix size. As discussed in subsection 4.1, a CAM is required in every PE to facilitate the indexing of nnzs in the column processed by PE. To index a whole column, the CAM will consume $n$ words of memory, in which $n$ stand for the matrix dimension. In an $m*$PE system, it will take m*n words of memory for the CAM. Since there may be only average 4-5 nnzs in a column of circuit matrices, a matrix will only consume 4-5*$n$ words of memory to store. Comparatively, the memory consumption of CAM is very considerable.

To alleviate the memory consumption on CAM, we need to reduce the size of the CAM without influencing the performance. Therefore, we modified the G/P algorithm again by divide a column of the matrix into several sections. Then we processing a column in the matrix section by section, rather than row by row. The pseudo-code of section based G/P algorithm consideration is shown in Figure 8.

```
1   for k = 1 to n do
2       for r = 1 to j do
3           f = A(SecStart : SecEnd, k)
4           for x = 1 to min(SecStart - 1, r - 1) and U(x, k) ≠ 0
5               f = f - U(x, k) * L(SecStart : SecEnd, x)
6           end for
7           if (SecStart ≤ r)
8               for x = SecStart to r - 1 and U(x, k) ≠ 0
9                   f = f - f(x) * L(SecStart : SecEnd, x)
10              end for
11          end if
12          U(SecStart : k) = f(SecStart : k)
13          L(k : SecEnd) = f(k : SecEnd) / U(k, k)
14      end for
15  end for
```

**Fig. 8.** Section Based G/P Algorithm for Scalability

In the pseudo-code, if the length of a section is $m$, there will be $j$ sections in current column, while $j = floor(\frac{n-1}{m}) + 1$. *SecStart* and *SecEnd* in the inner for loop refer to the first and the last row indexes in a section.

An example of section based left-looking algorithm, in which a column is divided into 2 sections, is illustrated in Figure 9. The lines in Figure 9 indicate the update steps. In the original algorithm, the $k^{th}$ column is updated by the 3 nonzero entities from top to bottom, whereas, in the modified version, the yellow line is updated section by section. The solid lines stand for the steps of updating the first section, which

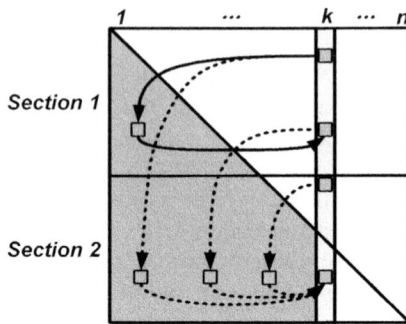

**Fig. 9.** Dataflow of Section Based G/P Algorithm for Scalability

is same as the original left-looking algorithm, while the steps of updating the second section are marked in dotted line. The second section is firstly updated by the nonzero entities of $U$, which are computed in the $1^{st}$ section, and then by the nonzero entities in current section until the last nnz in this column of $U$ is reached.

Besides considering the scalability of matrix size, we should also consider the extension of the architecture itself. As mentioned in subsection 4.2, we increase the memory bandwidth by means of the distributed memory. In this architecture, all the inter-PE communication are performed by the fully connected switch, and the total connection in this switch is proportional to $n^2$. Therefore the design of the switch becomes increasingly difficult when the quantity of PE mounts up.

This scalability problem can be solved by replacing the switch based network of PEs and the mesh network is adopted to connect the PEs, which is also introduced in [22]. In the mesh network, the communication burden is not mounted on a switch anymore, but distributed to the nodes in the network. The communication overhead will be replaced by inserting more network interfaces and designing more sophisticated communication strategy using meshed network. Moreover, the communication time between two PEs should be a variant and may influence the overall performance when the mesh becomes larger. It is also possible to create a multi-FPGA version with the mesh network architecture. In this paper, we do not implement the hardware prototype of mesh network based architecture, but list it as a solution for scalability of the hardware architecture.

## 5  Experimental Result

In this section, we discussed the resource consumption of with parallelized architecture and the performance compared with the software implementation.

### 5.1  Resource Consumption

In our implementation, we used the floating point divider generated in Altera MegaWizard, the floating point subtracter and multiplier in the proposed architecture are designed by ourselves, which is faster and more efficient compared with the standard IP. The resources consumption of these arithmetic units and PEs are considered based on Altera Stratix III FPGA, EP3SL340, with Quartus II 10.1. The detail resource consumption is given in Table 1 as below.

**Table 1.** Resource Utilization

|  | Logic Utilization (%) | BRAM Utilization (%) | DSP Utilization (%) | Clocks (MHz) |
|---|---|---|---|---|
| Subtracter | <1% | 0 | 0 | 203 |
| Multiplier | <1% | 0 | 4(<1%) | 248 |
| Divider | <1% | <1% | 16 (3%) | 125 |
| PE | 1% | 3% | 20(4%) | 125 |
| 16PEs | 36% | 48% | 240(56%) | 83 |

In this Stratix III FPGA chip, only about 50% resource is consumed in the 16-PE architecture. We can notice that the resource utilization increases quickly along with PE numbers due to the resource consumed by the switch. With the 32-PE architecture, Quartus II can even not fulfill the Place & Route step. Meanwhile the maximum frequency is lower when the number of PE increase, which is also resulted from the bottleneck of the switch based PE interconnection. Fortunately, the 16-PE architecture is enough to achieve the acceleration compared with CPU implementation such as KLU. If more PE is needed, the mesh network based multi-PE architecture can be adopted to reduce the resource consumed by PE interconnection. The transmission latency of mesh network should not be a big problem because the number of PE does not need to be too large. 16~32 PE is enough to achieve acceleration on CPU implementations.

## 5.2 Performance

In this subsection, we compared the performance of the parallel architecture with KLU on a set of circuit matrices from *the University of Florida Sparse Matrix Collection*, as illustrated in Table 2.

**Table 2.** Test Sets and Results

| Matrix | Matrix size | Non-Zeros | Sparsity (%) | KLU runtime (ms) | FPGA runtime (ms) | Acceleration |
|---|---|---|---|---|---|---|
| rajat19 | 1157 | 5399 | 0.403 | 0.466 | 0.208 | 2.24 |
| circuit_1 | 2624 | 35823 | 0.520 | 2.269 | 0.719 | 3.15 |
| circuit_2 | 4510 | 21199 | 0.104 | 1.868 | 0.694 | 2.69 |
| add32 | 4960 | 23884 | 0.097 | 1.841 | 0.343 | 5.36 |
| meg4 | 5860 | 26324 | 0.077 | 0.338 | 0.687 | 0.5 |

In Table 2, the KLU runtime is tested on an Intel i7 930 platform. To the FPGA platform, we test the performance by counting the cycles of factorization in Modelsim. Since it is not necessary to use switch to construct the network, we used the max frequency of PE (125MHz) to evaluate the performance. From the result acquired, we learnt that our architecture can achieve 0.5x-5.36x acceleration compared with KLU. The geometric average acceleration is about 2.19x. The acceleration varies because

KLU employ the partial pivoting during numeric factorization, while static pivoting is utilized in our system. The difference in pivoting strategy may result in different non-zero structure, which means different complexity in factorization.

In the switch based architecture, the matrix size is limited by the on-chip memory size of FPGA. Therefore we just test several small matrices in this experiment. Since the architecture can process matrices by section, large matrices can be factorized by employing larger FPGA or ASIC with more on-chip memory, especially the ASIC with 3D-stacked memory architecture.

## 6  Conclusions and Future Work

In this paper, a parallel CPU+FPGA based architecture for sparse matrix LU factorization is proposed. Not only the pre-processing is carried out on CPU, the symbolic analysis in G/P algorithm is also extracted from the numeric factorization of G/P algorithm and executed in CPU. The parallelism in the numeric factorization is explored by processing columns of sparse matrix simultaneously in different PEs of our architecture.

The proposed architecture is not only configurable on the scale of hardware by extending PEs, but also it is scalable to the matrix size, by dividing large matrix into small sections and processing them in PEs. The performance of our architecture exceeds the latest available KLU on a variety of circuit matrices from *the University of Florida Sparse Matrix Collection,* and achieves average 2.19x acceleration on KLU.

A few potential changes are identified as future work to improve upon current architecture. First, additional logic can be implemented in current architecture to reuse the PE for front/back solver. Second, computational burden can be further reduced by partially factorization: since only part of the entities change their value during the circuit simulation, we can only carry out computations that related to modified entities and leave constant entities alone.

## References

1. Nagel, L.: Spice 2: A computer program to stimulate semiconductor circuits. University of California, Berkeley (1975)
2. Nagel, L.W., Pederson, D.O.: SPICE (Simulation Program with Integrated Circuit Emphasis), Memorandum No. ERL-M382. University of California, Berkeley (April 1973)
3. Vladimirescu, A.: SPICE – The Third Decade. In: Proc. 1990 IEEE Bipolar Circuits and Technology Meeting, Minneapolis (September 1990)
4. Warwick, C.: Everything you always wanted to know about SPICE* (*But were afraid to ask) (PDF). EMC Journal (Nutwood UK Limited) (82), 27–29 (2009)
5. Davis, T.A., Hu, Y.: University of Florida sparse matrix collection. ACM Trans. Math. Software (2010) (to be appeared),
   http://www.cise.ufl.edu/sparse/matrices
6. Sparse Gaussian Elimination on High Performance Computers, Computer Science Division, UC Berkeley, UCB//CSD-96-919 (LAPACK Working Note #127) (September 1996)
7. Schenk, O., Gartner, K., Fichtner, W.: Efficient sparse LU factorization with left-right looking strategy on shared memory multiprocessors. BIT 40(1), 158–176 (2000)

8. Amestoy, P.R., Duff, I.S.: Vectorization of a multiprocessor multifrontal code. The International Journal of Supercomputer Applications 3, 41–59 (1989)
9. Rothberg, E., Gupta, A.: An evaluation of left-looking, right-looking and multifrontal approaches to sparse Cholesky factorization on hierarchical-memory machines. Int. J. High Speed Computing 5, 537–593 (1993)
10. Li, X.S.: An Overview of SuperLU: Algorithms, Implementation, and User Interface. ACM Trans. on Math. Software 31(3), 302–325 (2005)
11. Li, X.S., Demmel, J.W.: Making Sparse Gaussian Elimination Scalable by Static Pivoting. In: Proceedings of Supercomputing (1998)
12. Demmel, J.W., et al.: A Supernodal Approach to Sparse Partial Pivoting. SIAM J. Matrix Analysis and Applications 20(3), 720–755 (1999)
13. Natarajan, E.: KLU: A high performance sparse linear solver for circuit simulation problems. Master's Thesis, University of Florida (2005)
14. Schenk, O., et al.: PARDISO: a high performance serial and parallel sparse linear solver in semiconductor device simulation. Future Generation Computer Systems 789(1), 1–9 (2001)
15. Davis, T.A.: Algorithm 8xx: UMFPACK V4.1, an unsymmetric-pattern multifrontal method with a column preordering strategy. University of Florida, Tech. Rep. TR-03-007, submitted to ACM Trans. Math. Software (2003)
16. Amestoy, P.R., Puglisi, C.: An unsymmetrized multifrontal LU factorization. SIAM J. Matrix Anal. Appl. 24(2), 553–569 (2002)
17. Daga, V., Govindu, G., Gangadharpalli, S.: Efficient Floating-point based Block LU Decomposition on FPGAs. In: Proc. of ERSA 2004 (June 2004)
18. Zhuo, L., Prasanna, V.K.: High-performance and parameterized matrix factorization on FPGAs. In: International Conference on Field Programmable Logic and Applications (2006)
19. Wang, X., Ziavras, S.G.: Parallel direct solution of linear equations on FPGA-based machines. In: International Parallel and Distributed Processing Symposium (2003)
20. Johnson, J., Chagnon, T., Vachranukunkiet, P., Nagvajara, P., Nwankpa, C.: Sparse LU decomposition using FPGA. In: International Workshop on PARA (2008)
21. Chagnon, T.: Architectural support for direct sparse LU algorithms. Master Dissertation paper (March 2010)
22. Kapre, N., DeHon, A.: Parallelizing sparse Matrix Solve for SPICE circuit simulation using FPGAs. In: International Conference on Field-Programmable Technology (2009)
23. Nechma, T., et al.: Parallel Sparse Matrix Solver for Direct Circuit Simulations on FPGAs. In: Proceedings of 2010 ISCAS (2010)
24. Gilbert, J.R., Peierls, T.: Sparse partial pivoting in time proportional to arithmetic operations. SIAM J. Sci. Statist. Comput. 9, 862–874 (1988)

# FPGA Optimizations for a Pipelined Floating-Point Exponential Unit

Nikolaos Alachiotis and Alexandros Stamatakis

The Exelixis Lab, Scientific Computing Group
Heidelberg Institute for Theoretical Studies
{Nikolaos.Alachiotis,Alexandros.Stamatakis}@h-its.org

**Abstract.** The large number of available DSP slices on new-generation FPGAs allows for efficient mapping and acceleration of floating-point intensive codes. Numerous scientific codes heavily rely on executing the exponential function. To this end, we present the design and implementation of a pipelined CORDIC/TD-based (COordinate Rotation DIgital Computer/Table Driven) Exponential Approximation Unit (EAU) that will be made freely available for download (including the hardware description). The EAU supports single and double precision arithmetics and we provide appropriate configurations for Virtex2, Virtex4, and Virtex5 FPGAs. The architecture has been verified via simulations and by testing on a real FPGA. The implementation achieves the highest clock frequency reported in literature to date. Moreover, the EAU only occupies 5% of hardware resources on a medium-size FPGA such as the Virtex 5 SX95T. In addition, a general framework for safely conducting application-specific optimizations of floating-point operators on FPGAs is presented. We apply this framework to a bioinformatics application and optimize the EAU architecture using width-reduced floating-point operators and application-specific performance tuning. The optimized application-specific EAU occupies approximately 70% less hardware resources than the initial single precision implementation.

**Keywords:** floating point, exponential, FPGA, CORDIC, Table-Driven.

## 1 Introduction

Field Programmable Gate Arrays (FPGAs) are increasingly being used as accelerators for floating-point intensive scientific applications which suffer from long execution times. Furthermore, the unprecedented growth of FPGAs in terms of reconfigurable resources, in particular with respect to the number DSP slices and memory blocks available, has facilitated their deployment as accelerator devices for floating-point intensive codes. Because of their inherent complexity, widely used functions such as the exponential function require an excessive amount of reconfigurable resources when both good performance *and* high accuracy are desired.

Our research focuses on developing a reconfigurable phylogenetic co-processor [1,2] for RAxML [3], a Bioinformatics program, which evaluates the Maximum

A. Koch et al. (Eds.): ARC 2011, LNCS 6578, pp. 316–327, 2011.

Likelihood function on evolutionary trees. The likelihood computations require frequent evaluation of the exponential function.

There already exist several implementations of the exponential function on FPGAs [4,5,6,7,8,9,10]. While most of these implementations provide high numerical accuracy—that may however not always be required—only one is freely available for download. This open-source exponential unit can be generated using the FloPoCo tool suite [9].

Here, we present and make available http://wwwkramer.in.tum.de/exelixis/expFPGA.tar.bz2 a single precision pipelined floating-point Exponential Approximation Unit (EAU) that is based on similar design principles as our recently released Logarithm Approximation Unit (LAU) [11]. Moreover, we apply a RAxML-specific optimization/adaptation process to further improve the performance of the EAU co-processor and to reduce the amount of hardware resources that are required for the calculation of the exponential function. Based upon this optimized single precision EAU configuration, we have developed a double precision EAU that will also become available for download.

The EAU architecture is based on a TD (Table-Driven) implementation of the CORDIC (COordinate Rotation DIgital Computer) algorithm. CORDIC (also known as Volder's algorithm [12]) is a digit-by-digit method that relies on additions, shift operations, and read-only memory. The original algorithm that focused on calculating trigonometric functions was later extended by Walther [13] to compute functions like the logarithm and the exponential. This iterative algorithm generally requires resource-intensive hardware implementations to attain sufficient accuracy levels coupled with high performance. However, accuracy and performance requirements are determined by the application at hand. Thus, it may be desirable to sacrifice a certain amount of accuracy and/or speed for saving hardware resources and thereby make more resources available to the larger, potentially slower, and more complex overall hardware design (e.g., RAxML) into which an exponential unit is embedded.

Based upon this rationale, the EAU, can be optimized and adapted with respect to the architecture that will be using it, in our specific case, the phylogenetic co-processor. Design and optimization decisions have thus been made to generate a unit that is both resource-efficient and does not decrease the average performance of the entire co-processor.

The remainder of this paper is organized as follows: In Section 2 we review previous work on FPGA-based exponential units. Section 3 introduces the EAU architecture. The application-specific optimization framework that was applied to the single precision EAU is described in Section 4. In Section 5 we assess EAU performance and conduct a performance comparison with competing implementations. We conclude in Section 6.

## 2   Related Work

There already exist various alternative implementations of floating-point exponential units for FPGAs [4,5,6,7,8,9,10,16].

Boudabous [16] presented a CORDIC algorithm on a Xilinx VirtexE FPGA. However, as discussed in the evaluation section of [16] this implementation suffers from a comparatively high relative error rate.

The implementations presented in [8] and [9,10] only address SP (single precision) exponential units, while those presented in [6,7] and [4,5] focus on DP (double precision). Our EAU architecture can accomodate both SP (SP-EAU) and DP (DP-EAU). The number of DSP slices and memory blocks used is slightly higher for the DP-EAU. Since the amount of DSP slices and memory blocks increases significantly with each FPGA generation, the EAU architecture is thus well-suited for new-generation FPGAs (e.g., Virtex 5 and 6 families).

With respect to SP, Doss *et. al* [8] presented a pipelined table-driven approach that occupies as much as 5,564 slices on a Virtex II FPGA and operates at a maximum clock frequency of 85MHz. Detrey *et. al* [10,9] presented an alternative table-driven approach which is significantly more efficient than the implementation by Doss [8] in terms of resources (only 948 slices are required). At the same time the implementation by Detrey exhibits a higher clock frequency (100MHz) when mapped to a FPGA of the same family (Virtex II). While it is not entirely clear from the paper what the accuracy of the implementation by Doss is, the core by Detrey *et. al* offers last-bit accuracy. The SP-EAU does not attain this level of accuracy, since the optimization stategy (see Section 4) that has been adopted for the design of the EAU targets a specific application (RAxML), that does not require such a high degree of accuracy for numerical stability. Furthermore, the SP-EAU occupies less resources than [8] but is not as resource-efficient as [10,9]. Nonetheless, the SP-EAU clearly outperforms both aforementioned implementations in terms of maximum clock frequency (168 MHz on a Virtex II).

Regarding DP, Jamro *et. al* [6,7] also presented a table-driven implementation that occupies approximately 5,000 slices on a Virtex 4 FPGA. It exhibits a very low latency (27 clock cycles), high accuracy (to meet precision requirements of a quantum chemistry application), and has the second-highest clock frequency (166MHz) after the DP-EAU. Pottathuparambil *et. al* [5] presented, and recently improved [4], a CORDIC implementation which was also mapped to a Virtex 4 FPGA. The most recent paper [4] introduced a more efficient implementation than [6,7] in terms of resources, a latency of 258 cycles, and a clock frequency of 100 MHz. The implementation is partially pipelined, but due to the iterative procedure, the pipeline needs to be flushed after every iteration. In every iteration the computation of 5 DP values can be accomodated since this corresponds to the pipeline length of the iterative part. The RAxML-optimized DP-EAU architecture is partially pipelined as well and the computation of 11 DP values can be accomodated during each iteration. To allow for a fair performance comparison, the DP-EAU was also mapped to a Virtex 4 FPGA. The implementations by Jamro [6,7] occupy more FPGA slices than the DP-EAU, while the one presented in [4,5] is more resource-efficient than both the Jamro as well as the DP-EAU implementations.

The EAU significantly outperforms both [6,7] and [5,4] implementations in terms of maximum clock frequency (252 MHz). The EAU architecture can support both SP and DP and has been designed for applications that do not require maximum accuracy. It offers a fully pipelined and also a partially pipelined mechanism and represents a sufficiently accurate implementation at the highest maximum clock frequency reported in literature to date.

## 3   The EAU Architecture

The EAU architecture represents a one-to-one transformation into VHDL of the exponential function implemenetation in C which forms part of the most recent release of RAxML (v7.2.8, `http://wwwkramer.in.tum.de/exelixis/software.html`). The RAxML C exponential function implementation is based on the CORDIC C++ library by Burkardt [14].

Throughout the paper, we denote the C++ exponential function of the CORDIC library [14] as *EXP_CORDIC*. The TD extension of *EXP_CORDIC* that was integrated into the RAxML C code is denoted as *EXP_FPGA*. It also represents an *exact* software model of the EAU hardware architecture. Furthermore, by SP, DP, and FP we denote IEEE-754 single precision arithmetics, IEEE-754 double precision arithmetics, and floating-point representations respectively.

The *EXP_CORDIC* code performs 4 operations denoted by the author as: *Determine Weights, Calculate Products, Perform Residual Multiplication*, and *Account for factor EXP (X_INP)*, where $X\_INP = floor\ (INPUT)$. The first two operations execute *for-loops* that perform a predetermined—fixed—number of iterations. The third operation is a static mathematical function that combines the results of the first two fields. The last operation, which calculates the factor *EXP(X_INP)*, is implemented as an iterative process using multiplications/divisions. The number of iterations and hence the execution time for this operation are not known *a priori*, since they are determined by the absolute value of *X_INP*. Such an unpredictable behavior is problematic for a pipelined hardware architecture, since results can be produced at unexpected clock cycles. In order to overcome this drawback of *EXP_CORDIC* in the EAU, the respective *Account for factor EXP(X_INP)* operation of *EXP_FPGA* deploys a lookup table.

Figure 1 depicts the fully pipelined general EAU architecture (left) and the optimized application-specific unit for RAxML (right). The design consists of three components denoted as *PRE_ITER, ITER* and *AFT_ITER*.

The *PRE_ITER* component splits the input value into respective integer and decimal values. The *floor()* function (see above) has been implemented using a subtracter and a Xilinx Floating-Point Operator (FPO) [15] configured for float-to-fixed operations. The subtracter is used to execute the operation: *input_number* − 0.5. This is necessary because the default (and sole available) rounding mode of the Xilinx FPO is "Round to Nearest", as defined by the IEEE-754 Standard.

The *ITER* component corresponds to the *Determine Weights* operation of *EXP_CORDIC*. This component calculates an array of FP values and reduces the decimal part of the input argument by using a parameter that is divided by

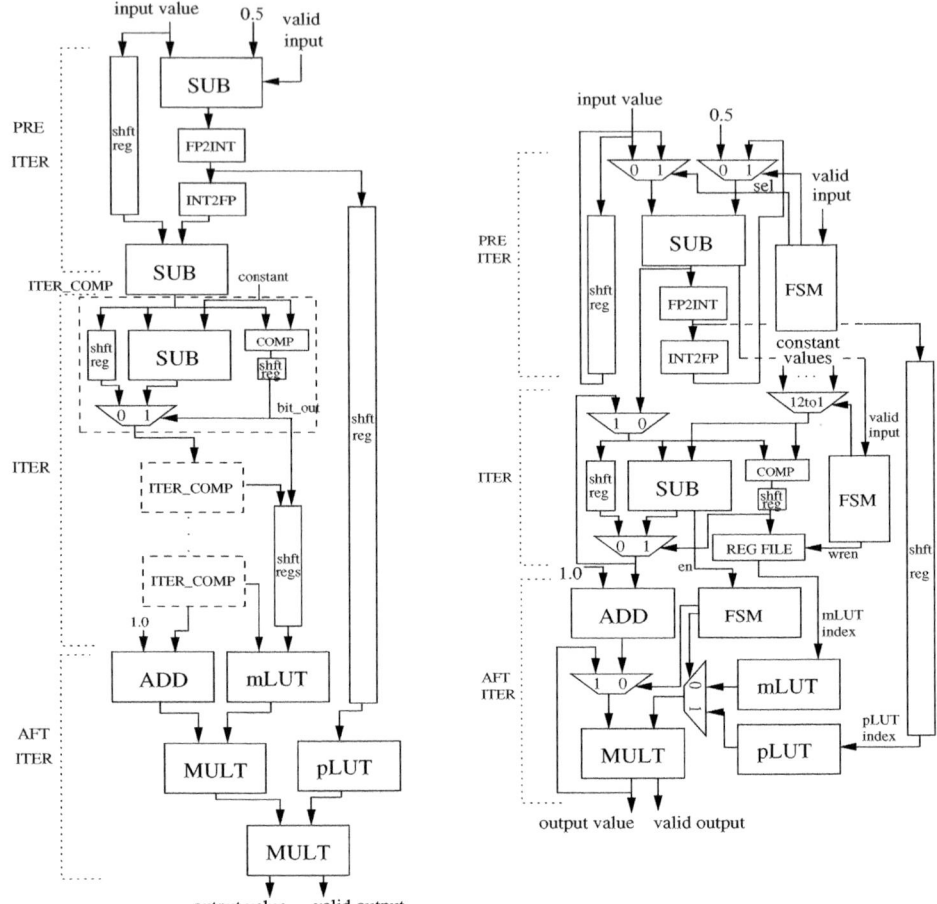

**Fig. 1.** Block diagram of the general EAU architecture (left) and the optimized, application-specific EAU architecture (right)

two in each iteration. The array of FP values is used by the iterative *Calculate Products* operation to compute a base value which is then provided as input to the *Perform Residual Multiplication* field. In order to further optimize this part of the algorithm, *EXP_FPGA* (the C code as well as the hardware implementation) calculates a bit-vector (instead of a FP array) during the iterative part. This bit-vector is then used as an index for a second lookup table that contains values that would otherwise need to be calculated by the *Calculate Products* field.

Finally, the *AFT_ITER* component implements the remaining operations: *Calculate Products*, *Perform Residual Multiplication*, and *Account for factor EXP(X_INP)*. As already mentioned, the *Calculate Products* and *Account for factor EXP(X_INP)* fields are calculated via lookup-tables (*m_LUT* and *p_LUT* in Figure 1) while the *Perform Residual Multiplication* operation only requires an addition and a multiplication.

# 4   Application-Specific Optimization

The EAU architecture has been extensively optimized. The optimizations aim to reduce the hardware resources occupied by the unit, while not affecting the overall accuracy of the phylogenetic coprocessor into which the EAU is embedded. In order to identify the type of optimizations that can be applied, a set of experiments were conducted. We tested the behavior of RAxML in software for various accuracy levels of the exponential function and analyzed the exponential function call pattern, that is, at what frequency the specific function is invoked and with which *load* each time. Here, the term *load* refers to the number of consecutive exponentials the program needs to calculate without other intervening arithmetic operations, that is, *for-loops* that only contain calls to the exponential function can be used for determining the (maximum) exponential function *load* of RAxML.

The accuracy required by the exponential function in the application allowed for further reducing the number of iterations in *EXP_CORDIC. EXP_FPGA* only executes 12 iterations without significantly (in a statistical sense) affecting the behavior of RAxML. The next step consists of quantifying the maximum relative error of *EXP_FPGA* versus the GNU DP EXP (GNU C Library [17]) function that is used by RAxML. This information allowed to safely apply the reduce-width technique [6,7] for floating-point operators, that is, the use of FP operators that do not comply with the IEEE-754 standard for SP/DP representations. When the width is reduced, the exponent and mantissa fields only contain as many bits as necessary to attain the required arithmetic range and precision. Furthermore, we also appropriately decreased the width of the floating-point representations in the lookup tables to reduce the number of required memory blocks.

The application of the reduce-width technique alone was not sufficient to decrease the EAU hardware resource requirements to an acceptable level, since not all operators of the EAU can be width-reduced. In order to determine if an operator can be reduced or not, we simulated the behavior of width-reduced operators in *EXP_FPGA* by reducing the width of the input and output arguments of the operator.

Finally, the largest reduction in EAU resource utilization was achieved by analyzing the exponential function call pattern and respective *load* in RAxML. A thorough analysis of the source code revealed that the exponential function is called a specific number of times that is determined by the *load*. In between such sequences of exponential invocations, a huge number of multiplications and additions is carried out that perform other parts of the likelihood calculation.

The time window, during which only multiplications and additions are carried out, allows for further optimization of the EAU with respect to hardware resource utilization, by reducing the unit's pipelining capability. The rationale is that, a pipelined EAU architecture which can accomodate more exponential calls than the maximum *load* of the application using it, will exhibt exactly the same performance as an EAU whose pipeline matches the *load*.

Thus, the limit-pipeline optimization approach allowed us to further reduce the hardware footprint of the EAU by utilizing only a single width-reduced subtracter for the *ITER* component. As already mentioned in Section 2 the latency of the iterative part of the EAU determines the maximum number of input values that can be accomodated at each invocation of the exponential function. The current EAU configuration utilizes a minimal amount of hardware by occupying only one subtracter in the respective *ITER* component. Thus, only 11 exponentials can be calculated between pipeline-flushes. Note that, this configuration is not sufficient to accomodate the maximum exponential *load* of RAxML, which can amount to 40 consecutive exponential calculations when protein data is analyzed. It can fully accomodate the *load* of DNA analyses though. Therefore, further tuning is required to determine the optimal number of input values that the EAU should be able to accomodate at each call and/or whether two or more partially pipelined EAUs are more efficient than a single, fully pipelined, one.

## 5   Evaluation and Performance

Initially, we verified the functionality of the EAU architecture (Section 5.1) and examined the overall behavior of the application (Section 5.2). A detailed resource usage, accuracy, and performance analysis on the same FPGA device that was used for verification can be found in Section 5.3. Section 5.4 describes how each step of the optimization process affected the efficiency of the architecture. Finally, Section 5.5 provides a comparison with other hardware and software implementations.

**Table 1.** Log-likelihood score deviation of RAxML with EXP_FPGA

| Dataset | RAxML with GNU EXP | RAxML with EXP_FPGA |
|---|---|---|
| 44-355 | -11231.33 | -11231.32 |
| 90-1524 | -54074.89 | -54077.97 |
| 150-1130 | -39606.93 | -39611.42 |
| 218-1846 | -134160.35 | -134166.02 |
| 140-1041 | -120849.31 | -120849.41 |

### 5.1   Hardware Verification

The EAU was implemented in VHDL, using the Xilinx ISE Suite 10.1 for synthesis and post place and route. In order to verify correctness of the proposed architecture, we conducted extensive post place and route simulations as well as tests on an actual FPGA. As simulation tool we used Modelsim 6.3f by Mentor Graphics. For hardware verification we used the HTG-V5-PCIE development platform equipped with a Xilinx Virtex 5 SX95T-1 FPGA. The advanced verification tool Chipscope Pro Analyzer was used to monitor the output port of the SP- and DP-EAUs and the expected signals for given input numbers were tracked.

**Table 2.** Resource Usage, Accuracy and Performance of the SP-/DP-EAUs on a Virtex 5 SX95T-2 FPGA. (* Relative Error).

|  | SP-EAU | DP-EAU |
|---|---|---|
| RESOURCES-Total | | |
| slice registers-58,800 | 1792 | 3131 |
| slice LUTs-58,800 | 1669 | 2909 |
| occupied slices-14,720 | 724 | 1085 |
| # 36k blockRAM-244 | 2 | 6 |
| # DSP48Es-640 | 6 | 15 |
| ACCURACY | | |
| Max RE* | $0.83 * 2^{-17}$ | $0.86 * 2^{-23}$ |
| Mean RE* | $0.66 * 2^{-19}$ | $0.59 * 2^{-24}$ |
| PERFORMANCE | | |
| Clock Frequency(MHz) | 317,6 | 307,9 |
| Latency(# clock cycles) | 212 | 222 |

## 5.2 Application-Level Error Analysis

Due to the application-specific optimization process described in Section 4, the accuracy of the EAU is inferior compared to other existing implementations. Nonetheless, the accuracy is sufficient for our target application. Table 1 shows the log-likelihood score deviation of RAxML with and without using the EAU for the exponential on various real-world biological datasets. Based on standard statistical significance tests (as implemented in the CONSEL package [21]), that are commonly used in phylogenetics (see [20] for a review), the differences (induced by the approximation of the exponential function) of log-likelihood scores between trees is not statistically significant. Therefore, an EAU with 12 iterations in the *ITER* component provides sufficient accuracy for RAxML.

## 5.3 EAU Architecture Evaluation

Table 2 contains the resource utilization report for the EAU after the post place and route process. Accuracy results (maximum and mean relative error) as well as performance (maximum clock frequency and latency) for the SP and DP configurations are also provided. Benchmarks with $10^8$ random numbers were used to measure the maximum and mean relative error of the implementations.

## 5.4 Optimization Techniques Evaluation

The initial SP-EAU implementation executes 12 iterations and is fully pipelined. The optimization techniques described in Section 4 were then applied step-by-step to this basic design. Table 3 shows the effect of each application-specific optimization step on hardware resources, clock frequency, and latency.

The reduce-width optimization yielded a significant reduction of DSP slices, while slightly increasing reconfigurable resource utilization (slice registers, slice

**Table 3.** The effect of each optimization step on the SP-EAU when mapped on a Virtex 5 SX95T-2 FPGA

|  | initial | width-reduced | pipeline-limited |
|---|---|---|---|
| slice registers-58,800 | 5964 | 6853 | 1792 |
| slice LUTs-58,800 | 5396 | 6433 | 1669 |
| occupied slices-14,720 | 2020 | 2274 | 724 |
| # 36k blockRAMs-244 | 2 | 2 | 2 |
| # DSP48Es-640 | 34 | 10 | 6 |
| max frequency(MHz) | 305,9 | 325,4 | 317,6 |
| latency(# clock cycles) | 194 | 194 | 212 |

LUTs, occupied slices). This redistribution of resources, that is, less DSPs and more slices, is due to different implementation decisions made by the Xilinx FPO operator, when custom-sized floating-point operators are generated (i.e., reconfigurable resources are used instead of DSPs).

The limit-pipeline optimization further reduced the number of DSP slices as well as all other reconfigurable resources used. Clock frequency and latency slightly increased after application of all optimization steps. The increased latency is caused by the width-reduced floating-point operators, that are reconfigured after the second optimization step (limit-pipeline) to obtain a final maximum clock frequency that is roughly equivalent to the initial clock frequency of the EAU.

## 5.5    Comparison with Other Implementations

As explained in Section 2 the SP-EAU was also mapped to a Virtex II device in order to conduct a fair comparison between our implementation and those presented in [8] and [10]. Accordingly, the DP-EAU was also mapped to a Virtex 4 device and compared to the respective DP implementations [6,5]. Tables 4 and 5 provide a summary of these comparisons.

Furthermore, we assessed the performance of the EAU architecture with respect to software implementations: SP-/DP-GNU exponential functions [17] and SP-/DP-MKL (Intel Math Kernel Library [19]) exponential functions. In order

**Table 4.** Resource Usage, Accuracy and Performance comparison of SP implementations. (* Not Available in [8]).

| Details | SP-EAU | Doss [8] | Detrey [10] |
|---|---|---|---|
| Style | CORDIC + TD | TD | TD |
| Error (Max) | $0.83 * 2^{-17}$ | NA* | $2^{-23}$ |
| Slices | 2483 | 5564 | 948 |
| Max Frequency | 168 MHz | 85 MHz | 100 MHz |
| Latency | 212 cycles | NA* | 85ns |

**Table 5.** Resource Usage, Accuracy and Performance comparison of DP implementations. (* This value is *mean* absolute error measured in ULP (Unit in the last place [18])).

| Details | DP-EAU | Pottathuparabil [5] | Jamro [6] |
|---|---|---|---|
| Style | CORDIC + TD | CORDIC | TD |
| Error (Max) | $0.86 * 2^{-23}$ | $2^{-53}$ | 0.4708 * |
| Slices | 3407 | 2024 | 5000 |
| Max Frequency | 252 MHz | 100 MHz | 161 MHz |
| Latency | 224 cycles | 258 cycles | 27 cycles |

to take full advantage of the Intel Core2 Duo T9600 processor@2.8GHz that was used for the comparisons, we used the Intel icc compiler with appropriate optimization flags.

Table 6 provides the execution times of the SP/DP GNU functions (expf,exp) and SP/DP MKL functions (vsExp,vdExp) for $10^8$ invocations of the functions. The SP GNU function (expf) is known to be slower than the DP GNU function (exp; see comments in the expf source code).

The fully pipelined SP-EAU implementation is 94 times faster than the GNU expf function and as fast as the MKL vsExp function. As expected, the optimized (width-reduced and pipeline-limited) SP and DP EAUs are slower than the MKL implementations. Nonetheless, the SP-EAU is 7 times faster than the SP GNU function and the DP GNU function is only 1.34 times faster than the DP-EAU.

**Table 6.** Execution times (in seconds) of the GNU, MKL and EAU implementations for $10^8$ invocations

| Implementation | Execution Time | Clock Frequency |
|---|---|---|
| expf (gcc) | 29,408 | 2,8 GHz |
| vsExp (icc) | 0,312 | 2,8 GHz |
| exp (gcc) | 3,268 | 2,8 GHz |
| vdExp (icc) | 0,632 | 2,8 GHz |
| Initial SP-EAU | 0,31 | 305 MHz |
| Pipeline-Limited SP-EAU | 4,2 | 317 MHz |
| Pipeline-Limited DP-EAU | 4,4 | 307 MHz |

# 6 Conclusion and Future Work

A new architecture to calculate an approximation of the exponential function in reconfigurable logic under SP and DP was presented. The SP-/DP-EAU configurations for several FPGA families (Virtex2, Virtex4 and Virtex5) will be made freely available for download. The functionality of the EAU architecture was verified on real hardware and both (SP/DP) configurations occupy less than 5% of overall hardware resources on a medium-sized new-generation FPGA like the Virtex5 SX95T.

326 N. Alachiotis and A. Stamatakis

Furthermore, the EAU component was optimized for being used as an embedded component in a larger and more complex reconfigurable phylogenetic co-processor that is currently under development. We provide a detailed description of this application-specific optimization process and individually assess the effects of every optimization step.

Future work will focus on the integration of the EAU into the phylogenetic co-processor and on further tuning after integration, that is, to determine the optimal number and EAU(s) configuration in terms of performance, resources, and number of units deployed.

# References

1. Alachiotis, N., Sotiriades, E., Dollas, A., Stamatakis, A.: Exploring FPGAs for Accelerating the Phylogenetic Likelihood Function. In: Proceedings of HICOMB 2009, Rome, Italy, pp. 1–8 (2009)
2. Alachiotis, N., Stamatakis, A., Sotiriades, E., Dollas, A.: A Reconfigurable Architecture for the Phylogenetic Likelihood Function. In: Proceedings of FPL 2009, Prague, pp. 674–678 (September 2009)
3. Stamatakis, A.: RAxML-VI-HPC: maximum likelihood-based phylogenetic analyses with thousands of taxa and mixed models. Bioinformatics 22(21), 2688–2690 (2006)
4. Pottathuparambil, R., Sass, R.: A Parallel/Vectorized Double-Precision Exponential Core to Accelerate Computational Science Applications. In: Proceedings of FPGA 2009, Monterey, California, USA, pp. 285–285 (2009)
5. Pottathuparambil, R., Sass, R.: Implementation of a CORDIC-based Double-Precision Exponential Core on an FPGA. In: Proceedings of RSSI 2008, Urbana, Illinois, USA (2008)
6. Jamro, E., Wiatr, K., Wielgosz, M.: FPGA Implementation of 64-bit Exponential Function for HPC. In: Proceedings of FPL 2007, pp. 718–721 (2007)
7. Wielgosz, M., Jamro, E., Wiatr, K.: Highly Efficient Structure of 64-bit Exponential Function Implemented in FPGAs. In: Woods, R., Compton, K., Bouganis, C., Diniz, P.C. (eds.) ARC 2008. LNCS, vol. 4943, pp. 274–279. Springer, Heidelberg (2008)
8. Doss, C.C., Robert, J., Riley, L.: FPGA-based Implementation of a Robust IEEE-754 Exponential Unit. In: Proceedings of FCCM 2004, pp. 229–238 (2004)
9. de Dinechin, F., Klein, C., Pasca, B.: Generating High-Performance Custom Floating-Point Pipelines. In: Proceedings of FPL 2009, Prague (2009)
10. Detrey, J., de Dinechin, F.: Parameterized Floating-Point Logarithm and Exponential Functions for FPGAs. In: Proceedings of Microprocess. Microsyst., pp. 537–545 (2007)
11. Alachiotis, N., Stamatakis, A.: Efficient Floating-Point Logarithm Unit for FPGAs. In: Proceedings of RAW 2010, Atlanta, GA, USA, pp. 1–8 (2010)
12. Volder, J.E.: The CORDIC trigonometric computing technique. Proceedings of IRE Transactions on Electronic Computers, 330–334 (1959)
13. Walther, J.S.: A Unified Algorithm for Elementary Functions. In: Spring Joint Computer Conference, pp. 379–385 (1971)
14. Burkardt, J.: CORDCIC Approximation of Elementary Functions, http://people.sc.fsu.edu/~burkardt/cpp_src/cordic/cordic.html (last visited: 17-05-2010)

15. Xilinx: Floating Point Operator v.4.0,
    http://www.xilinx.com/support/documentation/ip_documentation/
    floating_point_ds335.pdf (last visited: 17-05-2010)
16. Boudabous, A., Ghozzi, F., Kharrat, M., Masmoudi, N.: Implementation of Hyperbolic Functions using CORDIC Algorithm. In: Proceedings of ICM 2001, pp. 738–741 (2004)
17. McGrath, R.: GNU C Library, http://www.gnu.org/software/libc (last visited: 17-05-2010)
18. Goldberg, D.: What every computer scientist should know about floating-point arithmetic. ACM Comput. Surv., 5–48 (1991)
19. Intel: Intel Math Kernel Library Reference Manual,
    http://www.intel.com/software/products/mkl/docs/WebHelp/mkl.htm
20. Goldman, N., Anderson, J.P., Rodrigo, A.G.: Likelihood-based tests of topologies in phylogenetics. Systematic Biology 49(4), 652–670 (2000)
21. Shimodaira, H., Hasegawa, M.: CONSEL: for assessing the confidence of phylogenetic tree selection. Bioinformatics 17(12), 1246 (2001)

# NetStage/DPR: A Self-adaptable FPGA Platform for Application-Level Network Security

Sascha Mühlbach[1] and Andreas Koch[2]

[1] Secure Things Group, Center for Advanced Security Research Darmstadt (CASED), Germany
[2] Embedded Systems and Applications Group, Dept. of Computer Science, Technische Universität Darmstadt, Germany

**Abstract.** Increasing transmission speeds in high-performance networks pose significant challenges to protecting the systems and networking infrastructure. Reconfigurable devices have already been used with great success to implement lower-levels of appropriate security measures (e.g., deep-packet inspection). We present a reconfigurable processing architecture capable of handling even application-level tasks, and also able to autonomously adapt itself to varying traffic patterns using dynamic partial reconfiguration. As a first use-case, we examine the collection of Malware by emulating an entire honeynet of potentially hundreds of thousands of hosts using a single-chip implementation of the architecture.

## 1 Introduction

With the growing reliance of business, government, as well as private users on the Internet, the demand for high-speed data transfer has ballooned. On a technical level, this has been achieved by improved transmission technologies: 10 Gb/s Ethernet is already in widespread practical use at the ISP and data-center levels, standards for 40 Gb/s and 100 Gb/s speeds have already been formulated.

The data volume transferred at these speeds presents a significant challenge to current security measures, especially when going beyond simple firewalls and also considering payload inspection, or even application-level protocols. Conventional software-programmable processors are sorely pressed to keep up with these speeds. A recent evaluation of the popular network intrusion detection system Snort showed that such a software system can scan only up to 200 Mb/s without noticeable packet loss on a standard CPU [1].

As an alternative, both software-programmed dedicated network processing units (NPUs), as well as hardware accelerators for these operations have been proposed. The use of reconfigurable logic for the latter allows greater flexibility than hardwiring the functionality, while still allowing full-speed operation [4,11]. Our own research has demonstrated that modern FPGAs can also go beyond these traditional packet-processing tasks by also handling application-level protocols in hardware. As a first use-case of our architecture, we implemented a low-interaction honeypot, which emulates entire networks of hosts with vulnerable applications, entirely in hardware (the "MalCoBox") [8].

A. Koch et al. (Eds.): ARC 2011, LNCS 6578, pp. 328–339, 2011.

In contrast to related work such as [10], which mainly interpreted RAM-based state transition tables at run-time, our approach fully exploits hardware features such as parallel FSMs and pattern matchers to actually keep-up with data rates of 10 Gb/s and beyond. We thus achieve not only high-performance, but also harden the honeypot itself against hijacking: No general-purpose processor exists that could be subverted to actually execute attack code.

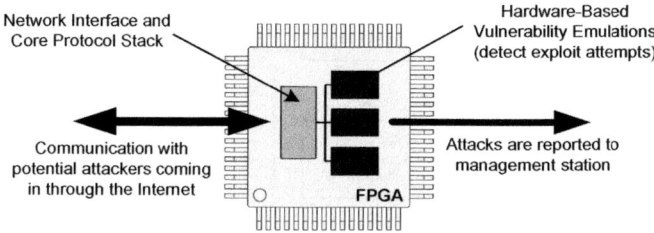

**Fig. 1.** Honeypot as use-case for FPGA-based network processing

We have since improved our initial architecture by adding networking capabilities such as a domain-specific highly optimized TCP/IP processing in hardware, restructured into a very modular architecture that allows the addition of new application-level services in hardware analogously to setting up software servers, and have added partial dynamic reconfiguration to hot-swap service modules (called *Handlers*) while keeping the rest of the system running [9]. In the honeypot scenario (see Figure 1) these Handlers are named Vulnerability Emulation Handlers (VEHs) to reflect their intended purpose.

Here, we present a refined architecture not only capable of dynamic partial reconfiguration (DPR), but able to autonomously adapt itself to react to varying traffic characteristics: The base architecture is described in Section 2, followed by details on the self-adaptation strategy in Section 3. The honey-pot application is a good use-case for our approach, since a large library of VEHs will not completely fit on the FPGA, and it should operate independently without user intervention. Implementation details and results for the honeypot are presented in Sections 4 and 5. Finally, we close with a conclusion and an outlook towards further research in the last Section.

## 2   Architecture

Figure 2 shows the architecture of our dynamically partially reconfigurable high-level network platform, called NetStage/DPR. The application-independent core (Fig. 2-a) can process IP, UDP and TCP protocols as well as ARP and ICMP messages. It has an easily extensible hierarchical design [8] that allows the quick addition of new protocols in dedicated modules at all layers of the networking model.

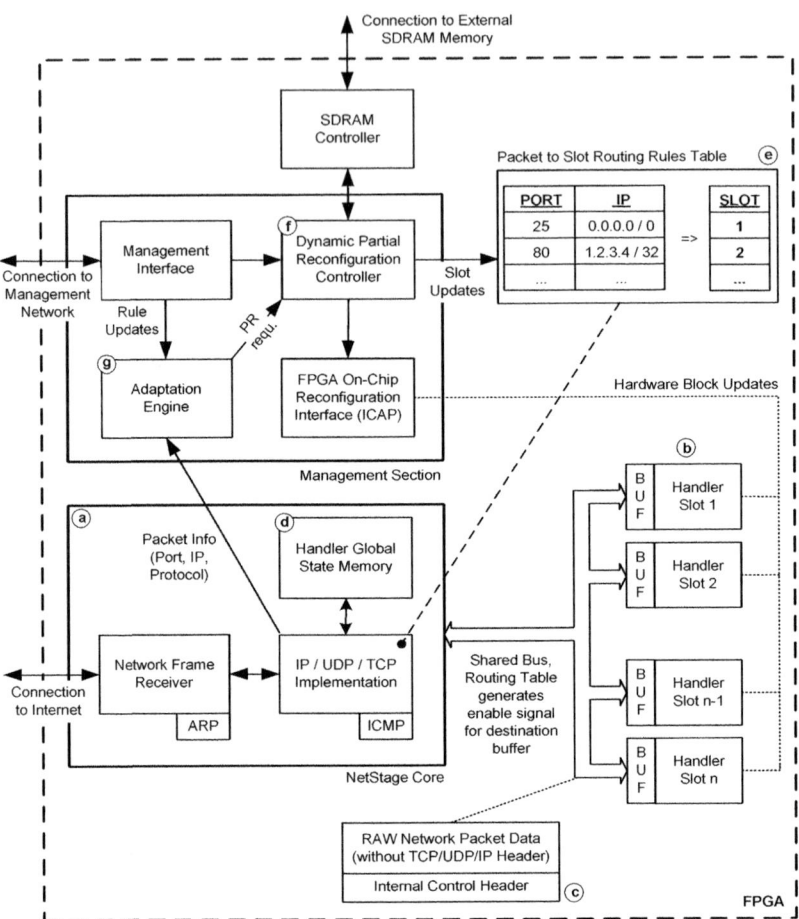

**Fig. 2.** NetStage/DPR self-adaptable network platform

The Handlers (Fig. 2-b) are connected to the core by using two separate shared buses with a throughput of 20 Gb/s each, one for the transmit and one for the receive side. Buffers decouple the different processing stages and limit the impact of Handler-local stalls in the processing flow. The interface between the buffers and the actual handlers forms a natural boundary for using dynamic partial reconfiguration to swap the handlers in and out as required.

## 2.1   Handler Interface

All handlers share the same logical and physical interfaces to the core system. The physical interface consists of the connection to the ingress and egress buffer and logistical signals such as clock and reset. However, the handlers actually communicate with the rest of the system purely by sending and receiving messages (not necessarily corresponding to actual network packets). These messages

(Fig. 2-c) consist of an internal control header (containing, e.g., commands or state data) and (optionally) the payload of a network packet. In this fashion, the physical interface can remain identical across all handlers, which considerably simplifies DPR. For the same reason, handlers should also be stateless and use the Global State Memory service (Fig. 2-d), provided by the NetStage/DPR core instead (state data will then just become part of the messages). This approach avoids the need to explicitly save/restore state when handlers are reconfigured.

## 2.2   Packet Forwarding

Incoming packets must be routed to the appropriate Handler. However, using DPR, the Handler may actually be configured onto different parts of the FPGA. Thus, we need a dynamic routing table (Fig. 2-e) that directs the message-encapsulated payloads to the appropriate service module. Our routing table has the usual structure of matching protocol, socket, and address/netmask data of an incoming packet to find the associated Handler. Note that a single Handler can thus receive data for an entire subnet. On the sending side, handlers deposit outgoing messages into their egress buffers, where they will be picked up by the core for forwarding (and possible transmission to the network). This is currently done using a simple round-robin approach, but more complex schemes (e.g., QoS-based) could, of course, be added as needed.

If packets are destined for a Handler with a full ingress buffer, they will be discarded. However, since all of our current handlers can operate at least at the line rate, this should not occur during regular operation. Packets for which a Handler is available off-line (not yet configured onto the device) will be counted before being discarded, eventually resulting in configuring the Handler onto the FPGA (bringing it on-line) if enough demand has been detected (see Section 3). Note that this strategy does not guarantee the reception of *all* packets (which is acceptable for the honeypot), but represents a good compromise between speed and complexity. If no appropriate Handler exists (either off-line or on-line on the device), packets will be discarded right away.

## 2.3   Handler Reconfiguration

Our system can perform the actual DPR operation autonomously of a host PC. A dedicated hardware unit (Fig. 2-f) is used as DPR Controller (DPRC) instead of an embedded soft-core processor, since the latter would not be able to achieve the high reconfiguration speeds we aim for (see Section 5.2 and [7]). Because of the storage requirements the Handler bitstreams are stored in an external SDRAM memory, and fed into the on-chip configuration access port (ICAP) by the DPRC using fast DMA transfers.

The DPRC is also responsible for selecting the specific bitstream to load: For simplicity, our initial implementation requires separate bitstreams for each Handler, corresponding to the physical location of the partially reconfigurable areas (which we call a *Slot*). To this end, the SDRAM is organized in clusters, which hold multiple versions of each Handler, addressed by the Handler ID and the target Slot number (see Figure 3). Again, for simplicity, we set the cluster size to the average size of each Handler's bitstream. In a more refined implementation, we could use a single bitstream for each Handler, which would then be relocated to the target Slot at run-time [2], and bitstream compression techniques [5] to further reduce its size.

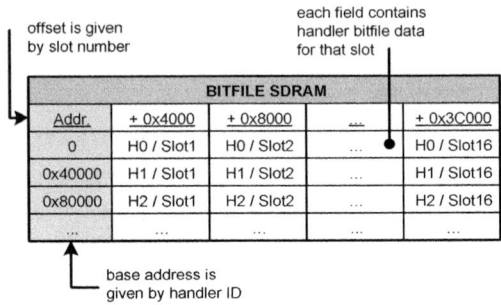

**Fig. 3.** Addressing of Handler bitstreams in SDRAM

Note that the actual decision when and which slot to reconfigure with which Handler is not made by the DPRC, but by another subsystem (see next Section).

## 3    Self-adaptation Strategy

We use a rule-based adaptation strategy, implemented in the Adaptation Engine (Fig. 2-g), that interprets packet statistics. Specifically, we consider packets at the socket level (destination protocol, port, and IP address), received in a time interval (currently set to 1s). These statistics are only kept for packets for which a Handler is actually available (either on-line or off-line).

### 3.1    Rule Representation

Our architecture (see Figure 4) aims for fast rule lookups and statistics updates (few cycles) even for high packet rates (10 Gb/s, packet size $< 100$ B). It is characterized by the following underlying Assumptions: A) We will have $100 \ldots 200$ handlers, with $5 \ldots 10$ packet matching rules each, and B) the most distinctive criterion of a rule is the port number.

Since the Packet Matching Rules for the counter updates themselves are very similar in nature to the Packet Forwarding Rules (see Section 2.2), we combine both representations into a single Rule Table (Fig. 4-a) that has the Forwarding Rules (to on-line handlers) as a subset of the Matching Rules (encompassing both on-line and off-line handlers). In addition to the socket-level specifications, the Rule Table also holds the ID of the Handler responsible for the rule, and a field for linking rules that should be matched in order. Furthermore, multiple rules can also be aggregated into a Rule Group, which structures the packet counters in the Counter Table (Fig. 4-b): We keep packet counts per Rule Group (instead

| (c) PORT LOOKUP CAM | |
| --- | --- |
| Port | Rule Base Addr. |
| (16b) | (8b) |
| 80 | 0 |
| 23 | 1 |
| ... | ... |

| (b) PACKET COUNTER TABLE (BRAM) | | | | |
| --- | --- | --- | --- | --- |
| Addr. | TTL | Slot | Handler ID | Value |
| (10b) | (16b) | (8b) | (16b) | (24b) |
| 0 | 0 | 0 | 4 | 125 |
| 1 | 36 | 4 | 7 | 1890 |
| ... | ... | ... | ... | ... |

| (a) MATCHING RULE TABLE (BRAM) | | | | | | | |
| --- | --- | --- | --- | --- | --- | --- | --- |
| Addr. | Protocol | Rule Group | Port | Netmask | IP Addr. | Handler ID | Next Rule |
| (10b) | (8b) | (16b) | (16b) | (32b) | (32b) | (16b) | (16b) |
| 0 | 0x06 | 3 | 80 | 0x00000000 | 0x00000000 | 0 | 0 |
| 1 | 0x06 | 1 | 23 | 0xFFFFFFFF | 0x10100501 | 7 | 256 |
| ... | ... | ... | ... | ... | ... | ... | ... |
| 256 | 0x11 | 0 | 23 | 0xFFFFFF00 | 0xA0AE2300 | 4 | 257 |
| 257 | 0x06 | 1 | 23 | 0xFFFFFF00 | 0x10100600 | 7 | 0 |
| ... | ... | ... | ... | ... | ... | ... | ... |

➤ Example Packet Info for Lookup: Protocol = 0x11, IP = 0xA0AE2301, Port = 23 (d)

**Fig. 4.** Rule and Counter Tables, First-level CAM

of per individual rule), thus reducing storage needs for complex Rule Tables. Off-line, but available handlers are indicated by a Target Slot value of zero. For efficiency, we keep a copy of the Handler ID in both Rule and Counter Tables (see Section 3.4). To keep the architecture flexible, we set the size for the fields Rule Group and Next Rule to 16b, even as the current implementation uses a lower number of rules and counter entries.

## 3.2  Fast Hierarchical Rule Matching

To speed-up look-ups, we exploit our Assumption B to realize a hierarchical matching beginning with the destination port of a packet (see Figure 5): Using a CAM (Fig. 4-c), we can quickly determine the start of the rule chain for this port, which is then processed in order. The linked list allows us to match rules

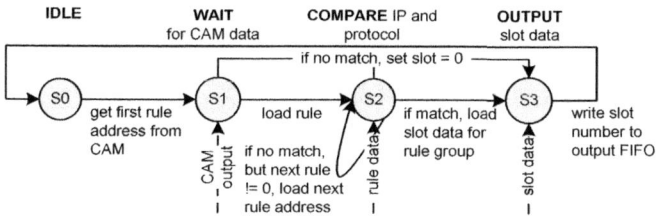

**Fig. 5.** Look-up of destination slot for a packet

in an explicit priority ordering, normally considering more specific rules (having a longer netmask) before more general ones. Rules will be inserted into the table at the correct position depending on the length of their netmask. For efficiency, the chain starts are all located in the lower 256 entries of the Rule Table (to be directly addressable by an 8b CAM entry), succeeding elements of chains begin at address 256 of the Rule Table. As only the port numbers of existing rules are stored in the CAM, we assume that 256 entries suffice for the current implementation. The arcs in Figure 5 show the lookup path for the given example input tuple (Fig. 4-d).

### 3.3    Packet Counter

The Counter Table is indexed by the Rule Group that matched an incoming packet to increment its corresponding counter value. The counters are reset after a parametrized time interval (currently: 1 s) to begin the next sampling window.

### 3.4    Reconfiguration Candidate Selection

The Counter Table (Fig. 4-b) is scanned periodically (every 1 ms in the current implementation, this interval may not be shorter than the Handler reconfiguration time, see Section 5.2) to make adaptation decisions (configuring a new Handler, possibly replacing an existing Handler). To this end, we select as candidate for the *new* Handler the offline one with the highest packet count, as candidate to be *replaced* the online one with the lowest packet count. If the new candidate has a higher count than the replacement candidate, the replacement will occur. If the system still has free Slots available, the new candidate will just be configured in without displacing an existing Handler. This approach can miss some attack patterns (e.g., if the network data contains many *different high-volume* attacks), but is a very resource efficient algorithm, with acceptable trade-offs for the honeypot scenario (which needs to collect each malware just once).

The decision reached will be used to update the Counter Table (which also keeps track of the Handler-Slot associations) and to inform the DPRC (Section 2.3) to perform the actual reconfiguration operation. Having all information for the adaptation decision available within the Counter Table simplifies the process implementation and justifies the redundant storage of values in both Tables (Fig. 4-a) and (Fig. 4-b).

To avoid reconfiguration thrashing (immediately replacing handlers just brought on-line), an optional time-to-live (TTL) value can be associated with a Counter Table entry. For this number of rule evaluation scans, that Handler will be exempt from replacement. The TTL value will be decremented during each scan, once it reaches zero, that Handler can become a replacement candidate again.

## 4    Implementation Details

We have implemented a NetStage/DPR prototype on a Xilinx Virtex 5 FPGA on the BeeCube BEE3 platform. Xilinx XAUI and 10G MAC IP cores provide the network connectivity at 10 Gb/s line speed, while the NetStage core datapath can handle 20 Gb/s by having a 128b processing width. This allows the core to catch-up with momentary stalls by burst-processing buffered data at the higher rate. These parts of the architecture run at a clock frequency of 156.25 MHz.

The ICAP is fed at its specified limit of 400 MB/s (32b@100 MHz), with the configuration data read from BEE3's DDR2-SDRAM using a dedicated Xilinx MIG block able to supply at least the required 400 MB/s. The core and ICAP clock domains are decoupled using FIFOs.

For fast lookups, the Global State Memory (Section 2.1) is implemented as on-chip BlockRAM. For the honeypot use-case, only very few handlers will actually need to keep state. Even then, data will also need to be retained for only a few seconds. Thus, 64k x 32b = 256 kB of Global State Memory suffices for this application.

Management functions (e.g., updating the Matching Rule Table, loading the bitstream memory, retrieving malware) are performed through a separate network interface. For simplicity, we trust the management network and do not perform security checks on the incoming bitstreams. However, such functionality could be easily added [3].

### 4.1   Packet Forwarder and Adaptation Engine

Since they rely on the same data structures, the Packet Forwarder and the Adaptation Engine are realized in a common hardware module (Figure 6). It contains the logic for tracking statistics, interpreting rules, and managing Handler-Slot assignments. Dual-port BlockRAMs are used to realize the 1024-entry Rule and 512-entry Counter Tables. Thus, lookups to determine the Slot of the destination Handler for an incoming packet can be performed in parallel to the rule management and counter processes. For area efficiency, the CAM (see Section 3) is shared between the functions. But since the throughput of the system is directly affected by the Packet Forwarding performance, the corresponding slot-routing lookups will always have priority when accessing the CAM. Since the CAM is used only briefly for each process, it will not become a bottleneck.

The Packet Forwarder logic (Fig. 6-a) puts the destination Handler slot for an incoming packet in the output queue. The forwarding look-up is pipelined: by starting the process as soon as protocol, IP address and port number have been received, the looked-up destination slot will generally be available when it is actually required (once the packet has passed through the complete core protocol processing). Since packets will be neither reordered nor dropped before the Handler stage, simple queues suffice for buffering look-up results here.

Since not all incoming packets should be counted (e.g., TCP ACKs should be ignored), the Adaptation Engine uses a separate port (Fig. 6-c) to update the Counter Table only for specific packets.

The Rule Management subsystem (Fig. 6-b) accepts commands from the management network interface through a separate FIFO, and has an internal FIFO that keeps track of available row addresses in the Rule Table. In a similar fashion, a separate FIFO also keeps track of available Slots, so new handlers are preferentially configured into empty slots before replacing existing handlers.

Reconfiguration requests are passed to the DPRC using the DPR Request FIFO as Handler ID and target Slot pairs.

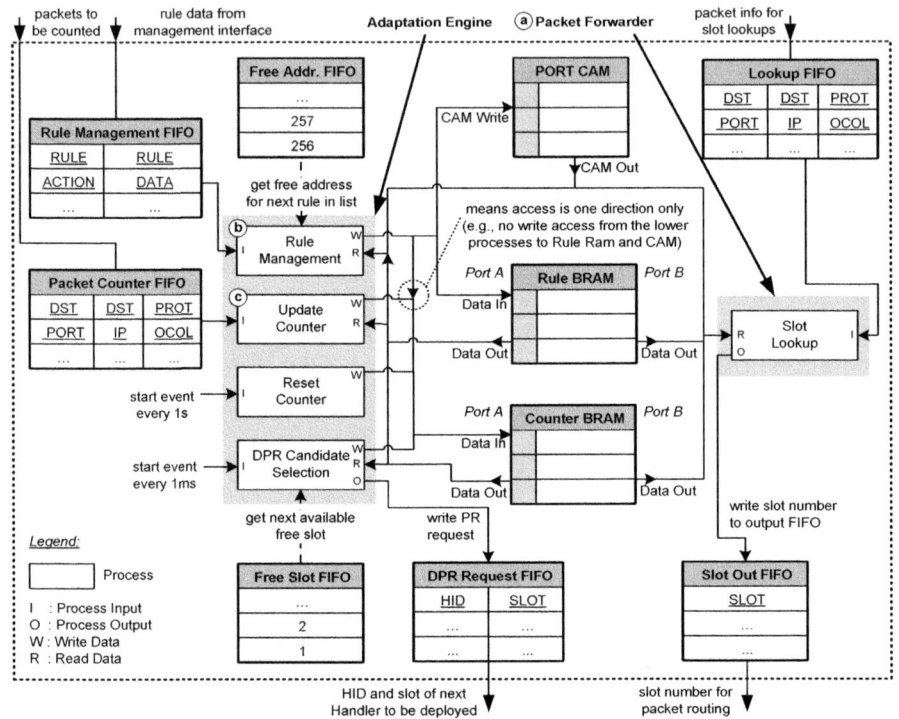

**Fig. 6.** Packet Forwarder and Adaptation Engine

## 5    Experimental Evaluation

For testing, we have connected the BEE3 with the MalCoBox application running on the NetStage/DPR architecture by a 10 Gb/s Ethernet point-to-point CX4 link to a dedicated eight-core Linux server for traffic generation.

### 5.1    Synthesis Results

Table 1 shows the results when implementing the design with Xilinx ISE 12.3. The complete system with management logic for 16 Handler Slots requires roughly one third of the FPGA capacity, the rest is available for the Slots themselves. The critical resource are the BlockRAMs, of which five are required per Slot for ingress and egress buffers. The Packet Forwarding and Adaptation Engine (PF&AE) block is relatively small compared to the overall design.

**Table 1.** Synthesis results for components and emulation modules

| Module | LUT | Reg. Bits | BRAM |
|---|---|---|---|
| NetStage Core System incl. TCP / UDP | 9,064 | 5,804 | 68 |
| Interfaces for 16 Slots w/o Slot Contents | 8,656 | 3,968 | 80 |
| Management Section w/o PF&AE | 890 | 1,271 | 9 |
| Packet Forwarder & Adaptation Engine | 3,343 | 1,647 | 14 |
| **NetStage/DPR Total** | **21,953** | **12,690** | **171** |
| **Mapped incl. MIG and MAC/XAUI** | **33,208** | **18,788** | **192** |
| in % of LX155T resources | 34 | 19 | 90 |
| SIP Emulation Handler [9] | 1,082 | 358 | 0 |
| MSSQL Emulation Handler [9] | 875 | 562 | 0 |
| Web Server Emulation Handler [9] | 1,026 | 586 | 0 |
| Mail Server Emulation Handler [9] | 741 | 362 | 0 |

For our tests, we chose four Handlers, each emphasizing a different implementation aspect: vulnerability emulations of a SIP application (focus on pattern matching) [12] and the MSSQL server (focus on byte matching and response generation) [6], as well as emulations of a simple Web Server (focus on large response packets) and Mail Server (focus on multiple protocol steps). The Handler implementations have been taken from [9]. Their characteristics are presented in the second part of the table.

### 5.2 Dynamic Partial Reconfiguration Results

The 16 Handler Slots have been distributed across the FPGA using PlanAhead 12.3 (see Figure 7). The FPGA regions for each Slot have been sized to 1920 LUTs (just twice as the average module size). All slots have equal area, as the results show that module sizes are relatively close. This simplifies the adaptation process, since otherwise we would need to perform multiple scans when selecting on-line/off-line candidates (one for each different Slot size class).

Table 2 gives the dynamic partial reconfiguration times and the resulting number of possible reconfigurations per second for the ICAP frequency of 100 MHz we use. We show the times not only for the 1920 LUT Slots we have used for the MalCoBox (indicated by *), but also for both smaller and larger choices (the best size is application-dependent). In general, LUTs are not scarce when realizing larger Slots, but the limited number of available BlockRAMs can constrain a design to less than 16 Slots if a Slot requires dedicated BlockRAMs.

Considering the complete adaptation operation, the time required is dominated by the actual reconfiguration time, as ICAP throughput is the limiting factor. All other processes are significantly faster. For example, the process to scan over all 512 Counter Table entries to find the next candidates (see Section 3.4) requires only about $3\mu s$ at 156.25 MHz clock speed, a negligible time relative to the reconfiguration time.

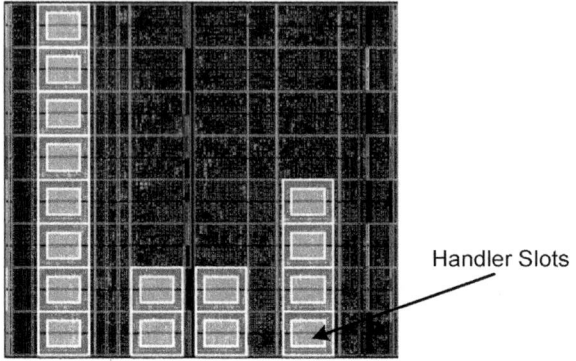

**Fig. 7.** FPGA Layout and Distribution of Handler Slots

**Table 2.** Reconfiguration time for different slot sizes

| LUT/ BRAM | Bitfile Size | % of LUTs LX155T | Reconfig. Time | # Reconfigs/ second |
|---|---|---|---|---|
| 1064/0 | 41 KB | 1.09% | 106$\mu s$ | 9438 |
| (*) 1920/0 | 70 KB | 1.97% | 180$\mu s$ | 5563 |
| 1920/4 | 96 KB | 1.97% | 245$\mu s$ | 4081 |
| 4144/0 | 162 KB | 4.26% | 416$\mu s$ | 2401 |

However, as the remaining slots can continue to process packets while one slot is being reconfigured, the DPR performance is more than sufficient for the honeypot scenario. Here, we assume a traffic distribution with a high volume of similar requests trying to exploit well known security flaws (initiated by worms, etc.). Only a small number of packets distributed over time will be attacking (possibly older) vulnerabilities that are not that common, and that will actually need to be reconfigured.

## 6   Conclusion and Future Work

NetStage/DPR has demonstrated that it is not only feasible to perform application-level (instead of just the packet-level) network processing in FP-GAs, but also actively exploit the dynamic partial reconfiguration capabilities of modern devices to build self-adapting architectures.

The base architecture of separate processing stages that allows the flexible integration of new functionality based on a hardware-based network protocol stack is suited to a wide number of domains. Our use-case of malware collection using the MalCoBox application is just one example scenario.

In the next research steps, we will improve the current state of the Net-Stage/DPR platform by partitioning the system to support multiple FPGAs to further increase the number of Handler slots, and by experiments with dynamic bitstream relocation. Furthermore, the MalCoBox application will be evaluated in a production environment using true real-time Internet traffic to refine the NetStage/DPR adaptation strategy.

**Acknowledgments.** This work was supported by CASED and Xilinx, Inc.

# References

1. Alserhani, F., Akhlaq, M., Awan, I.U., Mellor, J., Cullen, A.J., Mirchandani, P.: Evaluating Intrusion Detection Systems in High Speed Networks. In: Proc. of the 5th. Intl. Conf. on Information Assurance and Security, vol. 02, pp. 454–459 (2009)
2. Flynn, A., Gordon-Ross, A., George, A.D.: Bitstream relocation with local clock domains for partially reconfigurable FPGAs. In: Proc. of the Conference on Design, Automation and Test in Europe, pp. 300–303 (2009)
3. Hori, Y., Satoh, A., Sakane, H., Toda, K.: Bitstream Encryption and Authentication Using AES-GCM in Dynamically Reconfigurable Systems. In: Proc. of the 3rd Intl. Workshop on Security, pp. 261–278 (2008)
4. Katashita, T., Yamaguchi, Y., Maeda, A., Toda, K.: FPGA-Based Intrusion Detection System for 10 Gigabit Ethernet. IEICE - Trans. Inf. Syst. E90-D, 1923–1931 (2007)
5. Koch, D., Beckhoff, C., Teich, J.: Bitstream Decompression for High Speed FPGA Configuration from Slow Memories. In: Proc. of the Intl. Conference on Field-Programmable Technology (2007)
6. Litchfield, D.: Microsoft SQL Server 2000 Unauthenticated System Compromise (2000), http://marc.info/?l=bugtraq&m=102760196931518&w=2
7. Liu, M., Kuehn, W., Lu, Z., Jantsch, A.: Run-time Partial Reconfiguration Speed Investigation and Architectural Design Space Exploration. In: Proc. of the Intl. Conference on Field Programmable Logic and Applications (2009)
8. Mühlbach, S., Brunner, M., Roblee, C., Koch, A.: Malcobox: Designing a 10 gb/s malware collection honeypot using reconfigurable technology. In: Proc. of the 20th Intl. Conf. on Field Programmable Logic and Applications, pp. 592–595 (2010)
9. Mühlbach, S., Koch, A.: A dynamically reconfigured network platform for high-speed malware collection. In: Proc. of the Intl. Conf. on ReConFigurable Computing and FPGAs (2010)
10. Pejovic, V., Kovacevic, I., Bojanic, S., Leita, C., Popovic, J., Nieto-Taladriz, O.: Migrating a Honeypot to Hardware. In: Proc. of the Intl. Conf. on Emerging Security Information, Systems, and Technologies, pp. 151–156 (2007)
11. Singaraju, J., Chandy, J.A.: FPGA based string matching for network processing applications. Microprocessors and Microsystems 32(4), 210–222 (2008)
12. Thumann, M.: Buffer Overflow in SIP Foundry's SipXtapi (2006), http://www.securityfocus.com/archive/1/439617

# A Correlation Power Analysis Attack against Tate Pairing on FPGA*

Weibo Pan and William P. Marnane

Dept. of Electrical and Electronic Engineering
University College Cork, Cork, Ireland
{weibop,liam}@rennes.ucc.ie

**Abstract.** Pairings on elliptic curves are deeply researched and used in applications such as identity based schemes. Recently there have been several hardware implementations of the Tate Pairing. Along with the algorithms, their security has to be considered. This paper presents a correlation power analysis (CPA) attack against a Tate pairing implementation. Real power traces are taken from the FPGA implementation. The experimental result shows a successful attack.

**Keywords:** Tate pairing, CPA, FPGA.

## 1 Introduction

Pairing based cryptography is a new type of public-key cryptographic scheme based on Elliptic Curve Cryptography (ECC). ECC is efficient because it achieves the same security level as 1024 bit key RSA cryptography, with only a 163 bit key [8]. Pairings have the properties of bilinearity and non-degeneracy which is of interest for many applications. Cryptographic schemes based on the bilinear pairings have been developed to exploit Miller's algorithm [9]. Among the popular pairings, the Tate pairing has proved to be the most efficient in all fields for frequently used key sizes [10]. There have been many algorithms implementing the Tate pairing [12,15]. Barreto et al. [12] developed a fast algorithm of the Tate pairing on supersingular elliptic curve over finite fields of characteristic two ($GF(2)$). Shu et al. [7] developed a fast hardware implementation of the algorithm, while our work [6] discussed different hardware designs for implementing the algorithm on a Xilinx FPGA.

In implementating a cryptosystem, security as well as efficiency is a factor that has to be considered. An attacker can recover the secret information by monitoring the side channel informations such as power consumption[1]. Thus along with the pairing algorithms, side channel analysis (SCA) has become popular. The implementations of cryptosystems might be insecure against SCAs if not implemented carefully. Whelan et al. [4] and Kim et al. [5] investigated the possibility of SCA, including simple, differential and correlation power analysis

---

* This material is based upon works supported by the Science Foundation Ireland under Grant No. [SFI/ 08/RFP/ENE1643].

A. Koch et al. (Eds.): ARC 2011, LNCS 6578, pp. 340–349, 2011.

(SPA, DPA and CPA) against practical pairing algorithm. In 2005, Page and Vercauteren [14] presented the first side channel analysis of Duursma-Lee's algorithm [15] for characteristic three. This paper presents an implementation of a CPA attack on an FPGA implementation of the Tate pairing [6] using the pairing algorithm developed by Shu et al. [7].

## 2    Tate Pairing Algorithm

### 2.1    Tate Pairing Over $GF(2^m)$

Let $E$ be an elliptic curve over a finite field of characteristic two: $E(GF(2^m))$ : $Y^2 + Y = X^3 + X + g$, where $g \in \{0, 1\}$. A point on this elliptic curve is represented as a pair of elements $(x, y) \in GF(2^m)$ which satisfy the curve equation.

The Tate pairing in cryptosystems, is generally represented by $e_l(P; Q)$, where $P$ and $Q$ are points of order $l$ on curve $E(GF(2^m))$, $m{=}163$ in this work. It evaluates to a point over the extended field $GF(2^{4m})$. A closed formula of the Tate pairing[7] implemented in [6] is given in Algorithm 1.

**Algorithm 1.** Algorithm for computing Tate pairing
**Input**: $P = (\alpha, \beta), Q = (x, y)$     **Output**: $C = e_l(P; Q)$
1: $C \leftarrow 1$
2: $u \leftarrow x^2 + y^2 + g + \frac{m-1}{2}, v \leftarrow x^2 + 1, \alpha \leftarrow \alpha^4, \beta \leftarrow \beta^4, \gamma \leftarrow \alpha v$
3: **for** $i = 0$ to $m - 1$
4:     $A(t) \leftarrow \gamma + u + \beta + (\alpha + v + 1)t + (\alpha + v)t^2$
5:     $C \leftarrow C^2 * A(t)$
6:     $u \leftarrow u + v, v \leftarrow v + 1, \alpha \leftarrow \alpha^4, \beta \leftarrow \beta^4, \gamma \leftarrow \alpha v$
7: **endfor**
8: $C(x) = C(x)^{2^{2m}-1}$
9: **return** $C(x)$

### 2.2    Design of Tate Pairing Components Over $GF(2^m)$

As shown in Algorithm 1, there are additions, squarings, multiplications and division in the algorithm, among which the division appears only once in the final exponentiation in step 8.

**Addition** is the most basic operation in the algorithm, performed as per $c(x) = a(x) + b(x)$. It adds two elements on $GF(2^m)$ through an XOR chain, taking only one clock cycle. Thus addition and subtraction are equivalent in $GF(2^m)$, and it is noted that there exists $a + a = 0$ in $GF(2^m)$.

**Squaring** in $GF(2^m)$ is represented by $c(x) = a^2(x) \bmod f(x)$ where $f(x)$ is the irreducible polynomial of $GF(2^m)$. A bit-parallel squaring architecture introduced in [17] is applied in this design. Rather than inputing two same elements into a multiplier, the specific squarer simply interleaves the input with zeroes, followed by a $2m - 1$ to $m$ bit reduction block. It takes only one clock cycle to compute a squaring.

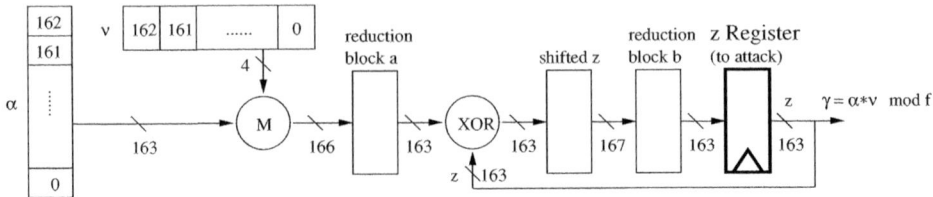

**Fig. 1.** $GF(2^m)$ Digit Serial Multiplier applied in Tate pairing

**Division** in $GF(2^m)$ is represented by $c(x) = a(x)/b(x) \bmod f(x)$. A field division using an architecture based on the Extended Euclidean Algorithm introduced in [18] is applied in the design of this paper. It takes $2m$ clock cycles to compute a division. Such time consuming operation appears only once in the final exponentiation of the Tate pairing in step 8 of Algorithm 1.

**Multiplication** in $GF(2^m)$ is represented as per
$$c(x) = (a(x) * b(x)) \bmod f(x) = \left( \sum_{i=0}^{m-1} a_i x^i * \sum_{j=0}^{m-1} b_j x^j \right) \bmod f(x). \text{ There are}$$
7 multiplications in step 4-5 in Algorithm 1. These multiplications take most of the operation time of the Tate pairing algorithm. The architecture of Digit-Serial Multiplication (DSM) applied in the Tate pairing design introduced by Hankerson et al. [16] is shown as in Fig.1.

The DSM takes elements $\alpha$ and $v$ as input, and outputs the products modulo the fixed irreducible polynomial $f(x)$. It deals with $d$ bits of the input element in every iteration and takes $n = \frac{m}{d}$ clock cycles to finish the operation. A larger digit size $d$ makes the multiplier larger while reduces the calculation time in the same time. The trade-offs between area and computation time was discussed in [6].In this paper, we pick digit size $d = 4$ as an example.

## 2.3   Tate Pairing Architecture Over $GF(2^m)$

There are 7 multipliers in step 4-6. A designer can schedule these 7 multiplications by putting in different number of multipliers [6]. A simplest way is to use only 1 multiplier, and have all the 7 multiplications operated in serial. The architecture of this design is shown in Fig.2. While putting in more multipliers, the multiplications can be operated in parallel. As there are 7 multiplications in each iteration of the *for* loop of Algorithm 1, applying 7 multipliers pipelined in the design and have all the multiplications operated in parallel is the fastest design, with maximum area as shown in Fig.3. In this paper, we present the minimum area design using only 1 multiplier and the maximum area design using 7 multipliers. The attack and correlation result will be presented in section 4.

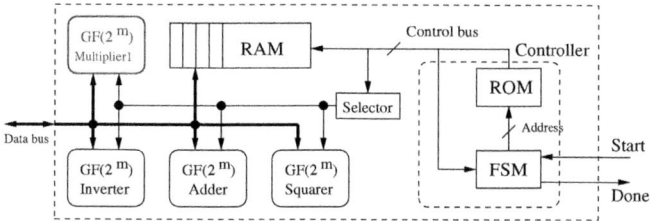

**Fig. 2.** Tate pairing implementation architecture over $GF(2^m)$, 1 multiplier

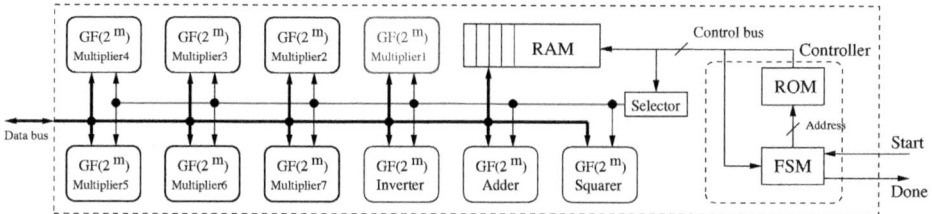

**Fig. 3.** Tate pairing implementation architecture over $GF(2^m)$, 7 multipliers

### 2.4 Tate Pairing in Identity Based Encryption

Pairings are used in Identity Based Encryption (IBE)[11] as a public key scheme. In IBE the Tate pairing $e_l(P;Q)$ is used to generate cypher text $C$ with two inputs: a public key and a secret text. Since Tate pairing has the property that $C = e_l(P;Q) = e_l(Q;P)$, either $P$ or $Q$ can be input as the secret text. This means that the attacker can choose which input to be the secret text[4]. In the design of this paper, we assume that $P$ is public and $Q$ is the secret text to attack. Due to point compression, the Elliptic Curve $E(GF(2^m))$ restricts the two coordinates of a point $Q(x, y)$, knowing one coordinate leads to knowing the other. Thus we only need to focus on the $x$ coordinate of the secret input $Q(x, y)$. The detail of how the coordinate $x$ is revealed is introduced in Section 4.

## 3 CPA Model and Attack

Based on Hamming Distance (HD) model, CPA reveals the relationship between hardware power consumption and the intermediate values of the operations.

### 3.1 Hamming Distance Model

HD model is based on Hamming Weight (HW)[1] model. In a hardware implementation of a cryptosystem, an $m$-bit binary data word $D$ is represented as $D = \sum_{j=0}^{m-1} d_j 2^j$, where $d_j \in \{0, 1\}$. Its HW is the number of elements that are equal to 1, i.e. $H(D) = \sum_{j=0}^{m-1} d_j$. This is the HW model based upon which many power analyses attacks on software implementations are built. Since $H$ is an integer between 0 and $m$, if the data words $D$ are independent and uniformly distributed, $D$ has an average HW $\mu_H = m/2$ and a variance $\sigma_H^2 = m/4$.

The HD model [2] assumes that the side channel information leaked from a system depends on the number of bits switching from one state to the other and is more appropriate for hardware implementations. The basic HD model is:

$$W = aH(D \oplus R) + noise, \tag{1}$$

where $noise$ encloses switching and electrical noise, $D$ is the current state and $R$ is next state, $a$ is a scalar gain between $W$ the power consumption and $H$ the HW of $(D \oplus R)$. $H(D \oplus R)$ here represents the number of bits switched between register states $D$ and $R$. This is called the HD between $D$ and $R$. In this model, $R$ is usually targeted by the attacker.

### 3.2  Correlation Power Analysis

The basic principle of CPA [2] is that there exists a relationship between HD of two register states and the measurable power consumption. The correlation factor between HD and consumed power, is used to tell whether the HD model fits the real power consumption or not. It is the covariance between the two variables $H$ and $W$ normalized by the product of their standard deviations. Assuming the noise is of Gaussian distribution, with the HD model, we have:

$$\rho_{WH} = \frac{cov(W, H)}{\sigma_W \sigma_H} \tag{2}$$

This relationship shows that $\rho_{WH}$ helps determine the next state $R$. Assuming the variance of noise tends to 0, if the hypothetical value of $R$ is correct, the value $\rho_{WH}$ tends to $\pm 1$ at the correlated point. In experiments, if an attacker predicts the correct secret value at the target clock cycle, there will be a high correlation value at the related point, otherwise the correlation values tend to 0.

## 4    CPA against Tate Pairing and Result Analysis

In this paper, the design in [6] is implemented on a SASEBO-GII board [13] which was designed for side channel attacks. The algorithm is running at speed of 24 MHz. A number $N = 1000$ of power traces of the operation are taken, measured using a $1\Omega$ resistor at the $V_{CC}$ side. By putting in different number of multipliers, there are several different schedules of designing the architecture of the Tate pairing algorithm. Here we implement two different design architectures. The simple design contains only 1 multiplier in the architecture and the most complicated design has 7 multipliers in parallel in the architecture.

As mentioned in Section 2, the $x$ coordinate of secret input $Q$ tells the secret. To reveal $x$, we pick the multiplication $\gamma \leftarrow \alpha v$ in step 6 of Algorithm 1. It involves the coordinates $\alpha$ and $v$, where $v$ relates closely with secret coordinate value $x$. Once the secret value $v$ is known, the coordinate values $x$ can be achieve by XOR "1" $\in GF(2^m)$ followed by a square root operation [3], and thus the secret text $Q$.

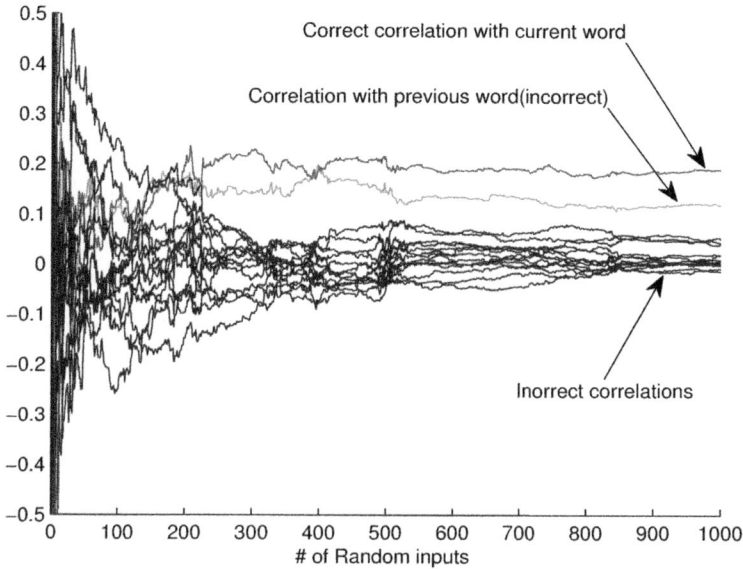

**Fig. 4.** CPA against Tate pairing at target time point, 1 mult

### 4.1 CPA against Single Multiplier Design

In the architecture of Fig.2 only one digit serial multiplier [16] is used. All multiplications in the Pairing algorithm are operated in serial using the only multiplier. The structure of the multiplier is shown in Fig.1. With two inputs $\alpha$ and $v$, the multiplier calculates the product of $\alpha$ and $d=4$ bits of $v$, called a 4-bit word of $v$, in every iteration. The targeted register "z Register" stores the product of $\alpha$ and a 4-bit word of $v$ and is updated in every iteration. The multiplication $\gamma \leftarrow \alpha v$ finishes in $n = \lceil \frac{m}{d} \rceil = \lceil \frac{163}{4} \rceil = 41$ clock cycles.

Since $v$ contains the secret and $\alpha$ is known by the attacker, we input $N = 1000$ random plaintexts as $\alpha$, and collect the power traces of the operations. The most significant bits (MSBs) are first dealt with in the multiplication. The multiplier deals with 4 bits of input $v$ in most iterations except for the first iteration. In the first iteration, since the targeted field size is $m = 163$, the multiplier deals with one bit '0' as the most significant bit and the first 3 bits of $v$ as the least significant bits.

For each clock cycle of the attack, we do the following steps:

1. for each of the $N = 1000$ public inputs, generate $2^4$ hypothetical values of the 4 bits of input $v$ by traversing all possible values from "0000" to "1111".
2. generate hypothetical values of the target register "z Register" in last and the current clock cycle.
3. calculate the Hamming Distance of the value in "z Register" between last and the current clock cycle.
4. calculate the correlations between the hypothetical values and the measured power traces.

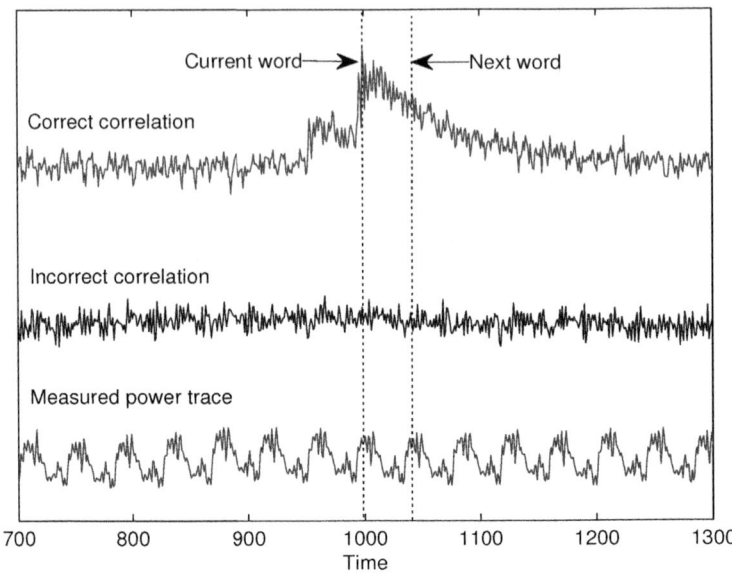

**Fig. 5.** CPA against Tate pairing power traces, 1 mult

Fig.4 shows the correlation attack against the target multiplication in the Tate pairing algorithm. Assume the previous 4-bit words of $v$ "(0)101 0111 1000" are correctly guessed. The hypothetical values of the next 4-bit word is between "0000" - "1111". Fig.4 shows the correlation of all $2^4$ predictions at the target time point. It is obvious that a correlation value comes much higher than others, which indicates the correct prediction "1001" of current 4-bit word of $v$. The second highest correlation value, which is about half the highest, indicates the effect remained from the previous 4-bit word of $v$ (1000).

For better analysis, we pick traces of all time points rather than the target time point. Fig.5 shows the correct correlation and an incorrect correlation, compared with the real measured power trace sample. In the correct correlation trace, there is a peak at the target time point. While the incorrect correlation trace corresponds to noise. The correct correlation peak doesn't drop instantly after the target time point, but decays in the next 2 clock cycles. Thus every correct prediction of the input affects the next clock cycle's prediction, with a correlation value of about half its peak value. By doing the same attack shown in Fig.5 $n = \lceil \frac{m}{d} \rceil = \lceil \frac{163}{4} \rceil = 41$ times, the secret text $v$ is determined, and thus the secret input $Q(x, y)$. The architecture of the complicated design with 7 multipliers is shown in

## 4.2   CPA against Maximum Area Design of Tate Pairing

The architecture of the 7 multiplier design is shown as in Fig.3. In this design, all the 7 multipliers are parallel and pipelined in each iterations of the $for$ loop of Algorithm 1. What's different from the single multiplier design is that all the

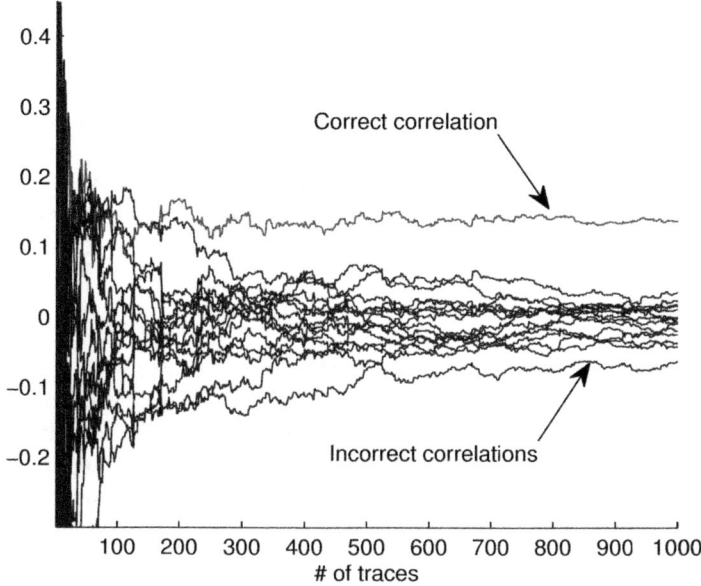

**Fig. 6.** CPA against Tate pairing at target time point, 7 mults

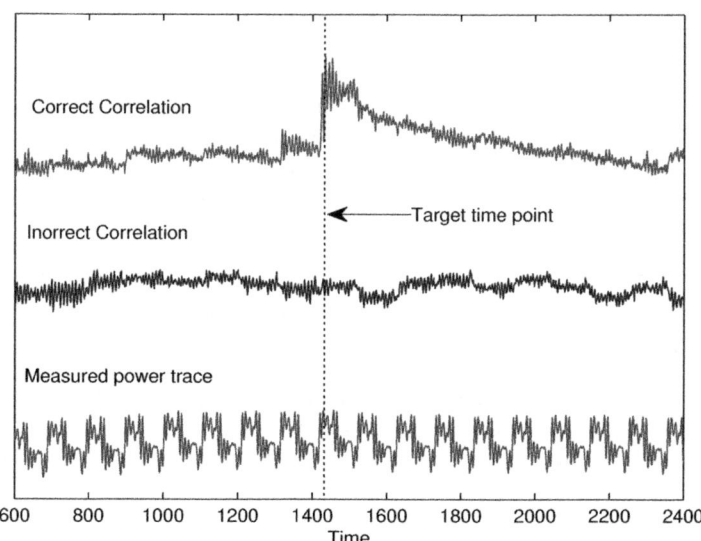

**Fig. 7.** CPA against Tate pairing power traces, 7 mults

7 multiplications in each iteration of the *for* loop are operated in the same time. So the FPGA consumes more power in each clock cycle, and thus more noise. However the effect of such noise will be removed in the power analysis because its correlation value tends to 0 after taking N=1000 power trace samples.

For the multiple multipliers design, we do the same as what we did to the single multiplier design. Fig.6 shows the correlation attack against the target multiplication in the Tate pairing algorithm. As can be seen from Fig.6, at the target time point, it is obvious that the correct correlation value is higher than the incorrect ones. The target time point is different from the single multiplier design because all 7 multiplications are operated in the same time. From Fig.7 we see that the correlation peak is still sharp which means the noise introduced by putting in 6 more multipliers doesn't affect the correlation result.

## 5    Conclusion

In this paper we presented the first correlation power analysis attack against an FPGA implementation of the Tate pairing. The multiplication over $GF(2^m)$ in the pre-computation step was targeted. We performed this attack by correlating the predicted value (i.e. the hypothetical value of an intermediate value in the multiplication generated by partial input) with the real measured power traces. A single multiplier and a maximum area design with 7 multipliers of the Tate pairing have been targeted. The result shows a peak in the trace of the correct hypothesis value at the corresponding period. Hence the design of the pairing algorithms should be carefully considered.

## References

1. Kocher, P.C., Jaffe, J., Jun, B.: Differential Power Analysis. In: Wiener, M. (ed.) CRYPTO 1999. LNCS, vol. 1666, pp. 388–397. Springer, Heidelberg (1999)
2. Brier, E., Clavier, C., Olivier, F.: Correlation Power Analysis with a Leakage Model. In: Joye, M., Quisquater, J.-J. (eds.) CHES 2004. LNCS, vol. 3156, pp. 135–152. Springer, Heidelberg (2004)
3. Fong, K., Hankerson, D., López, J., Menezes, A.: Field inversion and point halving revisited. IEEE Transactions on Computers 2004 53, 1047–1059 (2004)
4. Whelan, C., Scott, M.: Side channel analysis of practical pairing implementations: Which path is more secure? In: Nguyên, P.Q. (ed.) VIETCRYPT 2006. LNCS, vol. 4341, pp. 99–114. Springer, Heidelberg (2006)
5. Kim, T.H., Takagi, T., Han, D.-G., Kim, H.W., Lim, J.: Side Channel Attacks and Countermeasures on Pairing Based Cryptosystems over Binary Fields. In: Pointcheval, D., Mu, Y., Chen, K. (eds.) CANS 2006. LNCS, vol. 4301, pp. 168–181. Springer, Heidelberg (2006)
6. Pan, W., Marnane, W.: A Reconfigurable Implementation of the Tate Pairing Computation over $GF(2^m)$. In: Sirisuk, P., Morgan, F., El-Ghazawi, T., Amano, H. (eds.) ARC 2010. LNCS, vol. 5992, pp. 80–91. Springer, Heidelberg (2010)
7. Shu, C., Kwon, S., Gaj, K.: FPGA Accelerated Tate Pairing Based Cryptosystems over Binary Fields. In: Proceedings of the IEEE International Conference on Field Programmable Technology 2006, pp. 173–180. IEEE, Los Alamitos (2006)
8. Gupta, V., Gupta, S., Chang, S.: Performance analysis of elliptic curve cryptography for SSL. In: Proceedings of the 1st ACM Workshop on Wireless Security, pp. 87–94. ACM Press, New York (2002)

9. Miller, V.S.: Short Programs for functions on Curves. unpublished manuscript (1986)
10. Granger, R., Page, D., Smart, N.P.: High Security Pairing-Based Cryptography Revisited. In: Hess, F., Pauli, S., Pohst, M. (eds.) ANTS 2006. LNCS, vol. 4076, pp. 480–494. Springer, Heidelberg (2006)
11. Shamir, A.: Identity-based cryptosystems and signature schemes. In: Blakely, G.R., Chaum, D. (eds.) CRYPTO 1984. LNCS, vol. 196, pp. 47–53. Springer, Heidelberg (1985)
12. Barreto, P.S.L.M., Kim, H.Y., Lynn, B., Scott, M.: Efficient algorithms for pairing-based cryptosystems. In: Yung, M. (ed.) CRYPTO 2002. LNCS, vol. 2442, pp. 354–369. Springer, Heidelberg (2002)
13. Research Center for Information Security, National Institute of Advanced Industrial Science and Technoloty. Side-channel Attack Standard Evaluation Board SASEBO-GII Specification. Version 1.0 (2009)
14. Page, D., Vercauteren, F.: Fault and Side-Channel Attacks on Pairing Based Cryptography. IEEE Transactions on Computers 55(9), 1075–1080 (2006)
15. Duursma, I.M., Lee, H.-S.: Tate pairing implementation for hyperelliptic curves $y^2 = x^p - x + d$. In: Laih, C.-S. (ed.) ASIACRYPT 2003. LNCS, vol. 2894, pp. 111–123. Springer, Heidelberg (2003)
16. Hankerson, D., Menezes, A., Vanstone, S.: Guide to Elliptic Curve Cryptography. Springer, Heidelberg (2004)
17. Mastrovito, E.D.: VLSI Architectures for Computation in Galois Fields. PhD thesis, Dept. Electrical Engineering, Linkoping University, Linkoping, Sweden (1991)
18. Shantz, S.C.: From Euclids GCD to Montgomery Multiplication to the Great Divide. Tech. Rep. SMLI TR-2001-95, Sun Microsystems, pp. 1–10 (2001)

# From Plasma to BeeFarm: Design Experience of an FPGA-Based Multicore Prototype

Nehir Sonmez[1,2], Oriol Arcas[1,2], Gokhan Sayilar[3], Osman S. Unsal[1],
Adrián Cristal[1,4], Ibrahim Hur[1], Satnam Singh[5], and Mateo Valero[1,2]

[1] Barcelona Supercomputing Center, Spain
[2] Computer Architecture Department, Universitat Politècnica de Catalunya
[3] Faculty of Engineering and Natural Sciences, Sabanci University, Turkey
[4] IIIA - Artif. Intelligence Research Inst. CSIC - Spanish National Research Council
[5] Microsoft Research Cambridge, United Kingdom

**Abstract.** In this paper, we take a MIPS-based open-source uniprocessor soft core, Plasma, and extend it to obtain the Beefarm infrastructure for FPGA-based multiprocessor emulation, a popular research topic of the last few years both in the FPGA and the computer architecture communities. We discuss various design tradeoffs and we demonstrate superior scalability through experimental results compared to traditional software instruction set simulators. Based on our experience of designing and building a complete FPGA-based multiprocessor emulation system that supports run-time and compiler infrastructure and on the actual executions of our experiments running Software Transactional Memory (STM) benchmarks, we comment on the pros, cons and future trends of using hardware-based emulation for research.

## 1 Introduction

This paper reports on our experience of designing and building an eight core cache-coherent shared-memory multiprocessor system on FPGA called BeeFarm to help investigate support for Transactional Memory [11, 17, 23]. The primary reason for using an FPGA-based simulator is to achieve a significantly faster simulation speed for multicore architecture research compared to the performance of software instruction set simulators. A secondary reason is that a system that uses only the FPGA fabric to model a processor may have a higher degree of fidelity since no functionality is implemented by a magical software routine. Another way to use FPGA-based emulation is to offload infrequent or slow running instructions and I/O operations to a software simulator but retain the core functionality in FPGA hardware [7]. In our work we model the entire multiprocessor system on reconfigurable logic, although commercial simulator accelerators like Palladium and automated simulator parallelization efforts also take advantage of reconfigurable technology [19].

Recent advances in multicore computer architecture research are being hindered by the inadequate performance of software-based instruction set simulators which has led many researchers to consider the use of FPGA-based emulation.

A. Koch et al. (Eds.): ARC 2011, LNCS 6578, pp. 350–362, 2011.

Although sequential software-based simulators are mature and it is relatively fast to make changes to the system in a high-level environment, they turn out to be slow for the simultaneous simulation of the cores of a typical multiprocessor.

The inherent advantages of using today's FPGA systems are clear: multiple hard/soft processor cores, fast SRAM blocks, DSP units, more configurable logic cells each generation on a more rapidly growing process technology than ASIC and already-tested Intellectual Property (IP) cores. There are various synthesizable open-source Register Transfer Level (RTL) models of x86, MIPS, PowerPC, SPARC, Alpha architectures which are excellent resources to start building a credible multicore system for any kind of architectural research. Furthermore, various IPs for incorporating UART, SD, Floating Point Unit (FPU), Ethernet or DDR controllers are easily accessible [1]. Although FPGA-based multiprocessor emulation has received considerable attention in the recent years, the experience and tradeoffs of building such an infrastructure from these available resources has not yet been considered. Indeed, most infrastructures developed were either (i) written from scratch using higher level HDLs, such as Bluespec, (ii) using hard cores such as PowerPC, or (iii) using proprietary cores e.g. Microblaze.

Therefore, in this work we choose a new approach: We take an existing MIPS uniprocessor core called Plasma [2] and we heavily modify and extend that to build a full multiprocessor system designed for multicore research. To obtain the Honeycomb core, the basic building block for the BeeFarm, we designed and implemented two coprocessors, one providing support for virtual memory using a Translation Lookaside Buffer (TLB), and another one encapsulating an FPU; we optimized the Plasma to make better use of the resources on our Virtex-5 FPGAs; we modified the memory architecture to enable addressing for 4 GB; we implemented extra instructions to better support exceptions and thread synchronization and we developed the BeelibC system library to support the BeeFarm system. Additionally, we designed coherent caches and developed a parameterizable system bus that accesses off-chip RAM through a DDR2 memory controller [21]. Finally, we developed a run-time system and compiler tools to support a programming environment rich enough to conduct experiments on Software Transactional Memory (STM) workloads. A hypothesis we wish to investigate is the belief that an FPGA-based emulator for multicore systems will have better scalability compared to software-based instruction set simulators. We check this hypothesis on 1–8 cores using our flexible BeeFarm infrastructure, obtaining performance speedups of up to 8x. The key contributions of this paper are:

- A description of extending Plasma for implementing the BeeFarm multiprocessor system on the BEE3 platform [9] and discussions on the tradeoffs and an analysis of the FPGA resource utilization of our approach.
- Experimental results for three benchmarks investigating support for Transactional Memory and an analysis of the performance and scalability of software simulators versus the BeeFarm system.
- An experience reporting the pros and cons of using FPGA-based multicore emulation and identification of specific challenges that need to be overcome to better support FPGA-based emulation in the future.

## 2     The BeeFarm System

The synthesizable MIPS R2000-compatible soft processor core Plasma was designed for embedded systems and written in VHDL. It has a configurable 2-3 stage pipeline (no hazards), a 4 KB direct-mapped L1 cache, and can address up to 64 MB of RAM. It was designed to run at a clock speed of 25 MHz, and it includes UART and Ethernet cores. It also has its own real-time operating system with some support for tasks, semaphores, timers etc. Although the original Plasma core is suitable for working with diverse research topics, it has some limitations that makes it unsuitable as the processing element of the BeeFarm system, such as the lack of virtual memory (MIPS CoProcessor 0), exceptions and floating point arithmetic (MIPS CoProcessor 1). Furthermore, the design only infers optional on-chip resources for the register file, and there is no support for multiprocessing or coherent caches.

The BEE3 platform contains four Virtex5-155T FPGAs, where each FPGA controls four DDR2 DIMMs, organized in two channels of up to 4 GB each. The DDR2 controller [21] manages one of the two channels, performs calibration and serves requests, occupying a small portion of the FPGA (around 2%). Using one controller provides sequential consistency for our multicore since there is only one address bus, reads are blocking and stall the processor pipeline.

### 2.1     The Honeycomb Core: Extending Plasma

On Honeycomb processor (Figure 1) is implemented in a 3-stage pipeline with an optional stage for data accesses. Instructions and data words are 32-bit wide, and data can be accessed in bytes, half words (2 bytes) or words (4 bytes). In a typical ALU instruction, the program counter passes the program counter to the memory control unit, which fetches the 32-bit opcode from memory. In the next stage, the memory returns the opcode which is passed to the control unit that converts it to a 60-bit control word and forwards it to the appropriate entities through a central multiplexer (bus-mux). Cache accesses pause the CPU and can take various cycles in case of a miss.

**The MMU (CP0):** In order to support virtual memory, precise exceptions and operating modes, we implemented a MIPS R3000-compatible 64-entry TLB, effectively upgrading the R2000 core to an R3000, which we named Honeycomb. It provides memory management and exception handling intercepting the memory control unit datapath. There exist various approaches to implement an efficient Content Addressable Memory (CAM) on FPGAs, with configurable read/write access times, resource usage, and the technology utilized, where general-purpose LUTs or on-chip block memories can be used[5]. The use of LUT logic for medium and large CAMs and multi-cycle access are inappropriate since the TLB must translate addresses each cycle on our design. We implemented this unit with on-chip BRAM configured as a 64-entry CAM and a small 64-entry LUTRAM. Virtual patterns that are stored in the CAM give access to an index to the RAM that contains the physical value. It is driven by a half-cycle shifted clock that performs the translation in the middle of the

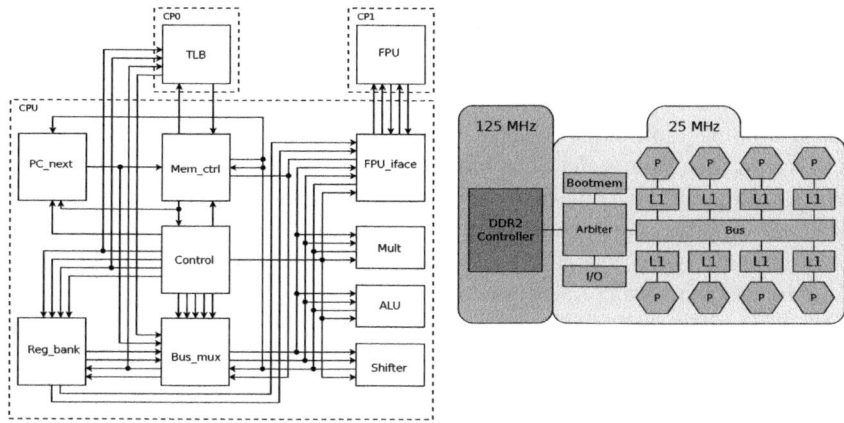

**Fig. 1.** Left: the Honeycomb processor. Right: the BeeFarm multiprocessor system.

memory access stage so a dedicated pipeline stage is not needed. This 6-bit deep by 20-bit wide CAM occupies four BRAMs and 263 LUTs.

**Double-Precision FPU (CP1):** The MIPS 3010 FPU implemented in Coprocessor 1, which was designed using Xilinx Coregen, can perform IEEE 754-compatible single and double precision floating point operations. It takes up 5520 LUTs and 14 DSP units, performing FP operations and conversions in variable number of cycles (4–59). We used only 4 of the 6 integer-double-float conversion cores to save space. This optional MIPS CP1 has 32x32-bit FP registers and a parallel pipeline. The integer register file was extended to include FP registers implemented as LUTRAM. For double precision, two registers represent the low and high part of the 64-bit number and the register file was replicated to allow 64-bit (double precision) read/write access each cycle.

**Memory Map and ISA Extensions:** We redesigned the memory subsystem which could originally only map 64 MB of RAM, to use up to 4 GB with configurable memory segments for the stack, bootloader, cache, debug registers, performance counters and memory-mapped I/O ports. Furthermore, we extended the Honeycomb ISA with three extra instructions borrowed from the MIPS R4000: **ERET** (Exception RETurn), to implement precise exception returns that avoid branch slot issues, **LL** (Load-Linked) and **SC** (Store Conditional), which provide hardware support for synchronization mechanisms such as Compare and Swap (CAS) or Fetch and Add (FAA). This is useful for Software TM support, as we detail in Section 2.4.

## 2.2   The BeeFarm Architecture

Honeycomb's 8 KB write-through L1 cache design that supports the MSI cache coherency for both data and instructions in 16-byte, direct-mapped blocks, uses 2+1 BRAMs for storing data and cache tags. The BRAM's dual-port access enables serving both CPU and bus requests in a single cycle. Reads and writes are blocking, and coherence is guaranteed by the snoopy cache invalidation protocol that we implemented. The caches designed are interconnected with a central split-bus controlled by an arbiter, as shown in Figure 1. They snoop on the system bus to invalidate entries that match the current write address, where write accesses are processed in an absolute order. This protocol can perform invalidations as soon as the writes are issued on the write FIFOs of the DDR and it serves to find an adequate balance between efficiency and resource usage. More complex caches that demand more resources would make it difficult to implement a large multiprocessor given the limited resources present on chip. We are not interested in using large, multithreaded soft cores like OpenSPARC and Leon3 because we concentrate on designing our own TM-capable manycore emulator by upgrading a popular soft core, and reflecting on such experience.

The bus arbiter implemented interfaces the FIFOs of the DDR controller, serving requests from all processors following a round-robin scheme. The boot-up code is stored in a BRAM next to the arbiter and mapped to a configurable region of the address space. I/O ports are also mapped, and the lowest 8 KB of physical memory give access to the cache memory, becoming a useful resource during boot-up when the DDR is not yet initialized. Furthermore, the cache can be used as stack thanks to the uncached execution mode of MIPS. Such direct access to cache memory is useful for debugging, letting privileged software to read and even modify the contents of the cache.

The arbiter, the bus, caches and processors can run at a quarter of the DDR frequency (25 - 31.25 MHz), the CPU's shallow pipeline being the main cause of this upper bound on the clock. Although bus and cache frequencies could be pushed to work at 125 MHz or at an intermediate frequency, it was not desirable to decouple this subsystem from the processor because partitioning the system in many clock domains can generate tougher timing constraints, extra use of BRAM to implement asynchronous FIFOs or additional circuitry for signals that cross different clock domains. Further optimizations to the Honeycomb are possible by clocking faster all special on-chip units and including such extra circuitry.

We can fit 8 Honeycomb cores without FPUs or 4 cores with FPUs on one Virtex5-155T FPGA. The system bus can become a bottleneck not only during system execution, but also when placing and routing the design. To use all four FPGAs on the BEE3 and to support up to 40 Honeycomb cores, a distributed directory scheme that will provide system-wide memory coherency is being designed and implemented. Each FPGA will have a quarter of the memory space and a directory that is responsible for local locations and a proxy directory with information about lines from the local memory that are cached on remote nodes.

## 2.3   FPGA Resource Utilization

One of the objectives of the design is to fit the maximum number of cores while supporting a reasonable number of features.The Honeycomb core without an FPU occupies 5712 LUTs (Figure 2) on a Virtex-5 FPGA including the ALU, MULT/DIV and Shifter units, the coherent L1 cache, the TLB and the UART controller, a comparable size to the Microblaze core. The functional blocks on Honeycomb can be categorized in three groups:

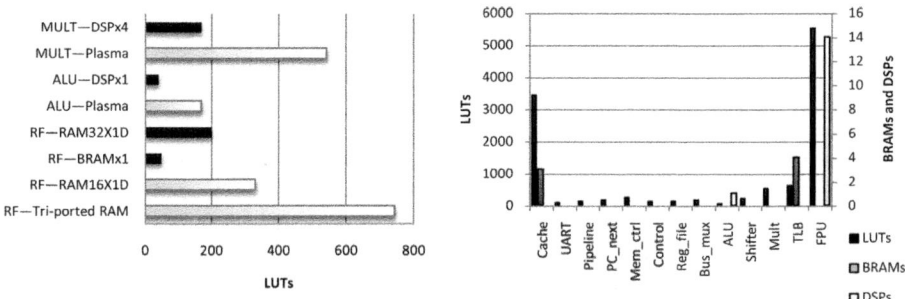

**Fig. 2.** Left chart: some of the available options (in 5-LUTs) to implement the Register File, the ALU and the Multiplier unit. The lighter bars indicate the choices in the original Plasma design. Right chart: LUT and BRAM usage of Honeycomb components.

**Compute-intensive (DSP):** Eg. ALU, MULT/DIV, Shifter, FPU can take advantage of hard DSP units. In the original Plasma core these units fit the third category, since the ALU is a combinatorial circuit, while the MULT/DIV take 32 cycles to iterate and compute. The ALU can be mapped directly on a DSP block while a MULT can be generated with Xilinx Coregen in a 35x35 multiplier utilizing an acceptable 4 DSPs and 160 LUTs. The shifter can also benefit from these 4 DSPs thanks to dynamic opmodes, however, a 32-bit divider can take anywhere between 1100 LUTs to 14 DSP units: The optimal way of combining all these operations to have a minimal design is not yet clear, we leave this as future work.

**Memory-intensive (BRAM/LUTRAM):** Eg. Reg_Bank, Cache, TLB. The TLB is designed in a CAM, the cache and tags in BRAMs. The Reg_Bank in Plasma selects between using 4-LUT RAMs (RAM16), behaviorally describing a tri-ported RAM, or using a BRAM. The use of a large BRAM is inefficient, and the tri-ported RAM infers too many LUTs, as seen in Figure 2. When distributed LUTRAM is inferred, each 5-LUT can act as a 32-bit register on the Virtex-5, enabling two reads and one write per cycle assuming one of the read addresses is the write address. Few options to enable two reads and a write to distinct addresses on each CPU cycle are: (i) to do the accesses in two cycles, using one of the address inputs for reading or writing, (ii) to clock the register file twice as fast and do the reads and writes separately, or (iii) to duplicate the register file. Although we currently use the third approach, our design accepts either configuration. Other groups have proposed latency insensitive circuits which save resources by accessing the register file in a few cycles[25].

**LUT-intensive:** Eg. implementing irregular if/case structures or state machines: PC_next, Mem_ctrl, control, bus_mux, TLB logic, system bus and cache coherency logic. This category demands a high LUT utilization; one striking result in Figure 2 is that providing cache coherency occupies roughly half of the LUT resources used by the Honeycomb. Such complex state machines do not map well on FPGAs, however synthesis results show that our core would perform 43.7% faster on a Virtex-6 FPGA, so such irregular behavioral descriptions can still be expected to perform faster as FPGA technology advances.

Unlike the cache coherence protocol and the shared system bus that map poorly, compute-intensive units and the register bank are good matches for distributed memory that use 5-LUTs, although one still can not do a single cycle 3-ported access. BRAMs and DSP units must be used carefully, to match better the underlying FPGA architecture. Regular units that match a compute-and-store template rather than complex state machines must be fashioned. In general, we believe that caches are a bottleneck and a good research topic for multicore prototyping. There is little capacity for larger or multi-level caches on our FPGA, and it would not be easy at all to provide high levels of cache associativity.

### 2.4   The BeeFarm Software

Since we are not running a full Linux with all system calls implemented, we can not use the standard C library libC, so we developed a set of system libraries called BeelibC for memory allocation, I/O and string functions. Other groups process system calls and exceptions falling back to a host machine or a nearby on-chip hard processor core [20, 7]. A MIPS cross-compiler with GCC 4.3.2 and Binutils 2.19 is used to compile the programs with statically linked libraries. The cores initially boot from the read-only Bootmem that initializes the cores and the stack and then loads the RTOS kernel code into memory.One of the most attractive proposals for shared-memory CMPs has been the use of atomic instructions in Transactional Memory (TM), a new programming paradigm for deadlock-free execution of parallel code without using locks, providing optimistic concurrency by executing atomic transactions in an all-or-none manner. In case of a data inconsistency, a confict occurs and one of the transactions has to be aborted without committing its changes, and restarted. Transactional Memory can be implemented in hardware (HTM) [11], which is fast but resource-bounded while requiring changes to the caches and the ISA, or software (STM) [10] that can be flexible at the expense of weaker performance. Specifically, we are interested in the intermediate approaches, or Hardware-assisted STM (HaSTM) which aims to accelerate an STM implementation for which we provide a framework that could be easier for conducting architectural studies. Towards this goal, we have successfully ported TinySTM [10], a lightweight and efficient word-based STM library implementation, and ran TM benchmarks on the BeeFarm, we present these results in Section 3.

## 3   Comparison with SW Simulators

The multiprocessor system presented in this work was designed to speed up multiprocessor architecture research, to be faster, more reliable and more scalable than software-based simulators. Its primary objective is to execute real applications in less time than popular full-system simulators. Our tests: (i) Measure the performance of the simulator platform, and not of the system simulated. (ii) Abstract away from library or OS implementation details, so that external functions like system calls would not significantly affect the results of the benchmark. (iii) Can be easily ported to different architectures, avoiding architecture-specific implementations like synchronization primitives. (iv) Pay special attention to the scalability of the emulation, a key weakness of software multiprocessor simulators. Our emulations are not affected by the number of processors in other ways than the usual eg. memory bandwidth, contention, cache protocols.

M5 [4] is an easily modifiable "full-system simulator" that can simulate Alpha processors with cache and bus details. We believe that despite the fact that MIPS and Alpha are distinct architectures, this can be a fair comparison: Both architectures are 32 register 32-bit RISC, operate on fixed-size opcodes and the only operations that access the memory are load and store. We executed the test in M5 fast mode (with optimizations, minimum timing and profiling options), and additionally for ScalParC in a slower profiling mode with timing. The compilers used to obtain the test programs for the BeeFarm and the M5 both use GCC version 4.2, compiled with the -O2 optimization level or -O3 when possible on a 64-bit Intel Xeon E5520 server with 2x quad-core processors running at 2.26 GHz with 64 GB of DDR3 RAM and 8 MB of L3 cache memory. All results were obtained using Xilinx ISE 12.2 running on RHEL5.

### 3.1   BeeFarm Multicore Performance of STM Benchmarks

To test multicore performance with STM benchmarks running on the BeeFarm, we have run ScalParC from RMS-TM [13], Intruder and SSCA2 TM benchmarks from STAMP [16] which are very commonly used for TM research. We modified ScalParC with explicit calls to use TinySTM. In our experiments, ScalParC was run with a dataset with 125K records, 32 attributes and 2 classes, SSCA2 was run with problem scale 13 and Intruder with 1024 flows.

The results that are normalized to the single-core M5 executions show that while the BeeFarm can scale in a near-linear way, the M5 simulator fails to scale and the performance rapidly degrades as the core counts are increased. Figure 3 shows that the gap opens with more cores and with only four, the BeeFarm with FPU just needs fifteen minutes to run the ScalParC benchmark, an eightfold difference. The scalability of our hardware is more obvious when the abort ratio between the transactions are low and little work is repeated, so the benchmark itself is scalable. SSCA2 also benefits from the inherent parallelism of the FPGA infrastructure and the good performance of the FPU: The two-core BeeFarm takes about half of the runtime of the M5 and it shows better scalability with more cores. In this sense our FPU which takes roughly the space of a single CPU core is clearly a worthy investment for the case of this particular benchmark. Other available hardware kernels such as a quicksort core [6] would be a very useful accelerator for this particular benchmark, and such specialized cores/execution kernels could further push the advantages of multicore emulation on reconfigurable platforms.

Intruder is a very high abort rate integer-only benchmark that scales poorly, and this can be seen on both M5 and BeeFarm results. We are able to run Intruder with 8 CPUs because this design does not use FP. It performs worse on the BeeFarm for single processor runs, however for more than two cores, it runs faster than the M5, whose scalability again degrades rapidly. Certain benchmarks with

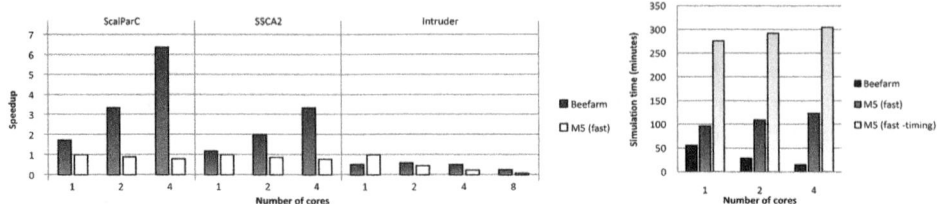

**Fig. 3.** BeeFarm vs M5 (fast). Left: Speedups for ScalParC, SSCA2 and Intruder (normalized to 1 core M5 run). Right: ScalParC simulation time.

certain configurations (eg. without an FPU) for a small number of cores could result in software simulators performing faster than FPGA devices. Mature simulators that take advantage of the superior host resources could still have advantages over FPGA emulators for simulations of a small number of cores.

## 4   The Experience and Trade-Offs in Hardware Emulation

Although we achieved good scalability for our simulations with respect to the number of processor cores, we have observed several challenges that still face the architecture researcher that adopts FPGA-based emulation.

Place and route times can be prohibitively long, although newer synthesis tool versions have started to make use of the host multithreading capabilities. In the case of adding a simple counter to the design for observing the occurrence of some event, the resynthesis, mapping, placing and routing of an 8-core BeeFarm takes 2-3 hours on our 8-core server.

Another issue is the low level of observability of online debugging tools like ChipScope plus the resource overhead. This problem could be mitigated by an application specific debug framework that is tailored to capturing information about multiprocessor systems. Furthermore, in the example of working with a DDR controller that resides outside of the FPGA, a precise simulation model of the controller should be developed. While in its absence, a fully-working simulation of a design can fail to run when loaded onto the actual FPGA. For such cases, certain 'extra' versions (eg. one that substitutes the DDR with an on-chip memory of BRAMs to separate away all possible problems interfacing the DDR controller) prove to be extremely useful. We also observe an impedance mismatch between the speed of the off-chip DDR memory which runs much faster than the internal processing elements. This mismatch could be exploited by using the fast external memory to model multiple independent smaller memories which would better support architecture research where each core has its own local memory. Alternatively, one controller on each FPGA can be dedicated to model secondary-level caches.

Although the Virtex-5 FPGAs that we use in this work do not allow for implementing a greater number of cores or large multi-level caches, new FPGAs that support 6-LUTs on 28 nm technology double the total number of gates available on chip while allowing the designer to have access to up to six MB of BRAM capacity and thousands of DSP units. Such abundance of resources might be more suitable for building larger and faster prototypes on reconfigurable infrastructures.

Finally, other researchers have advocated the use of higher level HDLs to improve programmer productivity. We undertook our design in VHDL/Verilog and based on our experience, we would also consider moving to a higher level representation because the design effort and debug difficulty of working with a lower level language when producing a system for emulation rather than production is probably not worthwhile compared to a system that offers rapid design space exploration, e.g. Bluespec.

## 5   Related Work

Some of the recent multicore prototyping proposals such as RAMP Blue [14] implement full ISA on RTL and require access to large FPGA infrastructures, while others such as the Protoflex [7] can use single-FPGA boards with SMT-like execution engines for simulator acceleration. Although multithreading leads to a better utilization on FPGAs, our focus is architectural emulation where it is generally desirable to keep as close to the original architecture that we are emulating. There is a wide variation of ISAs such as larger SMP soft cores [8], hard cores [26] and smaller ones like the Beehive [22], for prototyping shared memory as well as message-passing schemes [3]. Our work differs from these approaches in the sense that we model the cores only on reconfigurable logic and we effectively upgrade a full ISA open source soft processor core to better fit the architecture of modern FPGAs and to be able to closely examine STM applications and implementations. The only previous study on adapting an available soft core onto a commercial FPGA platform has been the LEON-3 core on the BEE2 [27]. Similar work that involves building a cache coherent MP with MIPS cores was presented in [24]. As for comparison of hardware emulation with software simulators, RAMP Gold [20] compares a SPARC V8 ISA design with three different Simics configurations: Functional, cache, and timing, reporting up to 250x speedup for 64 cores while the ATLAS design compares 8 on-chip 100 MHz PowerPC hard cores with HTM support on five TM applications with a execution-driven simulator at 2 GHz to show 40-200x speedup, also concluding that higher level caches and high associativity were problematic to implement on current FPGAs[26].

Transactional Memory has already drawn a lot of attention in the research community as a new easy-to-use programming paradigm for shared-memory multicores. However, so far mostly preliminary work has been published in the context of studying TM on FPGA-based multicore prototypes. The ATLAS emulator has read/write set buffers and caches augmented with transactional read-write bits and TCC-type TM support, and a ninth core for running Linux [26, 18]. A TM implementation that targets embedded systems which can work without caches, using a central transactional controller interconnecting four Microblaze cores was explained in [12].

Recent work that also utilizes MIPS soft cores focuses on the design of a conflict detection mechanism that uses Bloom filters for a 2-core FPGA-based HTM, however they do not consider/detail any design aspects on their infrastructure. They derive application-specific signatures that are used for detecting conflicts in a single pipeline stage. The design takes little area, reducing false conflicts, and this approach is a good match for FPGAs because of the underlying bit-level parallelism used for signatures[15].

## 6    Conclusions and Future Work

In this work, we have described a different roadmap in building a full multicore emulator: By heavily modifying and extending a readily available soft processor core. We have justified our design decisions in that the processor core must be small enough to fit many on a single FPGA while using the on-chip resources appropriately, flexible enough to easily accept changes in the ISA, and mature enough to run system libraries and a well-known STM library. We've presented an 8-core prototype on a modern FPGA prototyping platform and compared performance and scalability to software simulators for three benchmarks written to explore tradeoffs in Transactional Memory.

The BeeFarm architecture shows very encouraging scalability results which helps to support the hypothesis that an FPGA-based emulator would have a simulation speed that scaled better with more modelled processor cores than a software-based instruction set simulator. For small numbers of cores we find that software simulators are still competitive, however the gap widens dramatically as more cores are used as ScalParC runs suggest, where for 4 cores the BeeFarm system outperforms the M5 simulator in fast mode by 8x.

Our experience showed us that place and route times, timing problems and debugging cores are problematic issues working with FPGAs. We have also identified components of a typical multiprocessor emulator that map well on FPGAs, such as processing elements, and others that map poorly and consume a lot of resources, such as a cache coherency protocol or a large system bus. We are working on a ring bus that can substantially reduce routing congestion to fit more cores on an FPGA and a memory directory design to extend our infrastructure to use all four FPGAs on the BEE3.

## Acknowledgements

We would like to thank Roberto Hexsel, Miquel Pericàs, Gokcen Kestor, Vasileios Karakostas, Steve Rhoads and all anonymous reviewers for their comments and valuable feedback. This work is supported by the cooperation agreement between the Barcelona Supercomputing Center and Microsoft Research, by the Ministry of Science and Technology of Spain and the European Union (FEDER funds) under contracts TIN2007-60625 and TIN2008-02055-E, by the European Network of Excellence on High-Performance Embedded Architecture and Compilation (HiPEAC) and by the European Commission FP7 project VELOX (216852). The BeeFarm is available at http://www.velox-project.eu/releases

# References

[1] OpenCores Website, http://www.opencores.org
[2] Plasma soft core, http://opencores.org/project,plasma
[3] Angepat, H., Sunwoo, D., Chiou, D.: RAMP-White: An FPGA-Based Coherent Shared Memory Parallel Computer Emulator. In: Austin CAS (March 2007)
[4] Binkert, N.L., et al.: The M5 simulator: Modeling networked systems. In: MICRO 2006 (2006)
[5] Brelet, J.-L.: XAPP201: Multiple CAM Designs in Virtex Family Devices (1999), http://www.xilinx.com/support/documentation/application_notes/xapp201.pdf
[6] Calazans, N.L.V., et al.: Accelerating sorting with reconfigurable hardware, http://www.inf.pucrs.br/~gaph/Projects/Quicksort/Quicksort.html
[7] Chung, E.S., et al.: A complexity-effective architecture for accelerating full-system multiprocessor simulations using FPGAs. In: FPGA 2008, pp. 77–86 (2008)
[8] Dave, N., Pellauer, M., Emer, J.: Implementing a functional/timing partitioned microprocessor simulator with an FPGA. In: WARFP (2006)
[9] Davis, J., Thacker, C., Chang, C.: BEE3: Revitalizing computer architecture research. Microsoft Research (2009)
[10] Felber, P., Fetzer, C., Riegel, T.: Dynamic performance tuning of word-based software transactional memory. In: PPoPP, pp. 237–246 (2008)
[11] Hammond, L., et al.: Programming with transactional coherence and consistency (TCC). In: ASPLOS-XI, pp. 1–13 (2004)
[12] Kachris, C., Kulkarni, C.: Configurable transactional memory. In: FCCM 2007, pp. 65–72 (2007)
[13] Kestor, G., Stipic, S., Unsal, O., Cristal, A., Valero, M.: RMS-TM:a tm benchmark for recognition, mining and synthesis applications. In: TRANSACT 2009 (2009)
[14] Krasnov, A., et al.: Ramp Blue: A message-passing manycore system in FPGAs. In: FPL 2007, pp. 27–29 (2007)
[15] Labrecque, M., Jeffrey, M., Steffan, J.: Application-specific signatures for transactional memory in soft processors. In: Sirisuk, P., Morgan, F., El-Ghazawi, T., Amano, H. (eds.) ARC 2010. LNCS, vol. 5992, pp. 42–54. Springer, Heidelberg (2010)
[16] Minh, C.C., Chung, J.W., Kozyrakis, C., Olukotun, K.: STAMP: Stanford transactional applications for multi-processing. In: IISWC, pp. 35–46 (2008)
[17] Moore, K.E., Bobba, J., Moravan, M.J., Hill, M.D., Wood, D.A.: LogTM: Log-based transactional memory. In: HPCA 2006, pp. 254–265 (2006)
[18] Njoroge, N., Casper, J., Wee, S., Teslyar, Y., Ge, D., Kozyrakis, C., Olukotun, K.: ATLAS: A chip-multiprocessor with TM support. In: DATE 2007, pp. 3–8 (2007)
[19] Penry, D.A., et al.: Exploiting parallelism and structure to accelerate the simulation of chip multi-processors. In: HPCA, pp. 29–40 (2006)
[20] Tan, Z., et al.: RAMP gold: an FPGA-based architecture simulator for multiprocessors. In: DAC 2010, pp. 463–468 (2010)
[21] Thacker, C.: A DDR2 controller for BEE3. Microsoft Research (2009)
[22] Thacker, C.: Beehive: A many-core computer for FPGAs (v5). In: MSR Silicon Valley (2010), http://projects.csail.mit.edu/beehive/BeehiveV5.pdf
[23] Tomic, S., Perfumo, C., Armejach, A., Cristal, A., Unsal, O., Harris, T., Valero, M.: EazyHTM: Eager-lazy hardware transactional memory. In: MICRO 42 (2009)
[24] Tortato Jr., J., Hexsel, R.: A minimalist cache coherent mpsoc designed for fpgas. Int. J. High Performance Systems Architecture (2011)

[25] Vijayaraghavan, M., Arvind, M.A.: Bounded dataflow networks and latency-insensitive circuits. In: MEMOCODE, pp. 171–180 (2009)
[26] Wee, S., Casper, J., Njoroge, N., Tesylar, Y., Ge, D., Kozyrakis, C., Olukotun, K.: A practical FPGA-based framework for novel CMP research. In: FPGA 2007 (2007)
[27] Wong, T.: LEON3 port for BEE2 and ASIC implementation,
     http://cadlab.cs.ucla.edu/software_release/bee2leon3port/

# Architectural Support for Multithreading on Reconfigurable Hardware

Pavel G. Zaykov and Georgi Kuzmanov

Computer Engineering Department,
Delft University of Technology
Delft, The Netherlands
{P.G.Zaykov,G.K.Kuzmanov}@tudelft.nl

**Abstract.** In this paper, we address organization and management of threads on a multithreading custom computing machine composed by a General Purpose Processor (GPP) and Reconfigurable Co-Processors. Our proposal to improve overall system performance is twofold. First, we provide architectural mechanisms to accelerate applications by supporting computationally intensive kernels with reconfigurable hardware accelerators. Second, we propose an infrastructure capable to facilitate thread management. The latter can be employed by, e.g., RTOS kernel services. Besides the architectural and microarchitecural extensions of the reconfigurable computing system, we also propose a hierarchical programming model. The model supports balanced and performance efficient SW/ HW co-execution of multithreading applications. Our experimental results based on real applications suggest average system speedups between 1.2 and 19.6 times and based on synthetic benchmarks, the achieved speedups are between 1.3 and 29.8 times compared to software only implementations.

## 1 Introduction

Reconfigurable embedded devices often require multiple applications to be executed concurrently. A common strategy to encapsulate various application functionalities in a conventional software system environment is to use multithreading. Typically, an Operating System (OS) is employed to manage the dynamic creation, execution and termination of multiple threads. If the hardware platform is composed of a reconfigurable logic and a General Purpose Processor (GPP), the OS should be capable to efficiently map the running threads on the available reconfigurable hardware resources.Due to its heterogeneity, the platform complexity and respectively OS service overhead has grown rapidly. As a result, some of the conventional OS kernel services should be optimized to be able to fully exploit the new high performance system capabilities.

The objective of this work is to improve the overall performance of the heterogeneous reconfigurable systems following the multithreading execution paradigm. We provide architectural and microarchitectural mechanisms to accelerate OS kernels and applications in hardware as an extension to the Molen processor [17]. The programming code is organized in a new programming model, which efficiently exploits the proposed hardware architectural and micro-architectural augmentations. The introduced architectural model is not entailed neither to a specific GPP architecture, nor to any

A. Koch et al. (Eds.): ARC 2011, LNCS 6578, pp. 363–374, 2011.

reconfigurable fabrication technology. More specifically, the main contributions of this paper are:

- Architectural extensions that allow multithreading applications and RTOS to co-execute in software and in reconfigurable hardware are proposed. More specifically, we extend the processor interrupt system, the register file organization and we modify hardware task synchronization at the instruction level.
- Microarchitectural extensions which support newly introduced Thread Interrupt State Controller (TISC) are provided.
- A hierarchical programming model capable to provide flexible task migration from software to hardware, exploiting inter- and intra-thread parallelism is provided.
- Proposed A Real-Time Interrupt Service Routine (ISR) to support the new Interrupt system is proposed.

Depending on the experimental scenario, results with real applications suggest average system speedups between 1.2 and 19.6 times. Based on synthetic benchmarks, the average speedup is between 1.3 and 29.8 times compared to SW only implementation.

The remainder of the paper is organized as follows. The related work is presented in Section 2. Section 3 describes the architecture and microarchitecture in details - hardware components and interfaces, including XREGs, polymorphic instructions implementation, TISC controller and Interrupt management are presented. Section 4 covers the software prospectives of our proposal, which includes the programming model description. Section 5 provides some specific implementation details and the obtained experimental results. Finally, Section 6 concludes the paper and outlines some future research directions.

## 2   Related Work

The problem of efficient sharing of hardware computing resources among multiple threads or processes could be solved statically or dynamically. The former involves the usage of advanced compiler techniques and the latter employs an Operating System or a sort of dynamic resource scheduler. The compiler approach solves the resource management problem by performing different optimizations on the application control dataflow graph. Examples of such embedded architectures with static resource management are: MT-ADRES [20] and UltraSonic [7]. In our work, we focus on the infrastructure for dynamic run-time approaches for resource management, therefore we do not address any Compiler related optimizations.

In the dynamic scheduling approach, assuming an RTOS is employed, parts of the programming code, both from the Operating System and/ or the applications, can be transferred onto reconfigurable logic. A detailed classification of the existing reconfigurable multithreading architectures is presented in [21]. Based on it, in the category of dynamic approaches, we identify projects such as [10], [19] and [22]. There, the designers improve the system performance and lower the energy consumption by transferring parts of the OS kernels to hardware. Similar approach is followed by other authors, e.g. [9], [8], where a dedicated hardware resource manager is proposed. The manager takes the decisions using heuristic scheduling and placement algorithms. In contrast to the

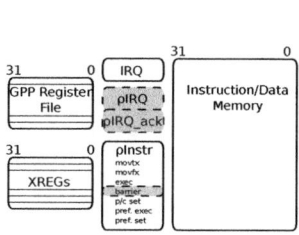

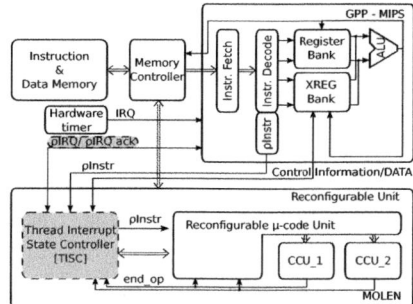

**Fig. 1.** The Architectural Extensions          **Fig. 2.** The Microarchitecture

above cited related works, we propose a system capable to accommodate on reconfigurable logic parts of the user applications, as well as parts of the OS. These OS services could be responsible for the scheduling of hardware tasks but also for the management of software tasks. The idea of accelerating OS routines on reconfigurable logic, such as the scheduling of software tasks only, has been already presented in several research projects, e.g. [6]. Our architectural proposal, however, allows to co-execute the management routines for both software and hardware tasks on reconfigurable hardware.

To our best knowledge, the Hthreads [12] is the most relevant project to our current research. The authors use a programming model [1] to distribute the running threads among GPP and reconfigurable logic. The major difference between [12] and our proposal is: We migrate either user application or RTOS thread functions (the concept is described in Section 4) while only complete application threads are moved to hardware in [12]. In [12], the authors use dedicated RTOS modules for communication and synchronization procedures among hardware threads. We believe that our model is more flexible, since it supports migration of parts of the user thread and RTOS kernels in hardware.

There are also projects such as Silicon OS [11], where the Operating System is completely transferred into hardware. Such an approach is not flexible enough and is limited for future improvements, because the RTOS is represented by a complex Finite State Machine (FSM).

**The Molen prototype:** The Molen Polymorphic Processor [18] consists of a GPP and a Reconfigurable Processor (RP) operating under the processor - co-processor paradigm. The GPP architecture is extended with up to 8 additional instructions, which can support an arbitrary application functionality. Six of these instructions are related to the RP and two - to the parameters transferred between the GPP and the RP through exchange registers (XREGs). The RP related instructions, support different variations of the set-execute paradigm, described in details in [17]. The set-execute model can be supported by an additional "break" instruction, providing synchronization in a sequential consistency programming paradigm. In this paper, we extend the "break" instruction to support synchronization in a multithreading scenario and we call it a "barrier" instruction. In the Molen context, the implementations of application specific functionalities in

**Table 1.** Original Molen XREGs

| XREG#31 | 0 |
|---------|---|
| 0 | CCU Offset |
| 1 | Input params, CCU#1 |
| ... | ... |
| m | Output param, CCU#1 |
| m+1 | Input params, CCU#2 |
| ... | ... |
| n | Output param, CCU#2 |

**Table 2.** XREGs in Molen TISC Design

| XREG#31 | 24 | 23 | 16 | 15 | 8 | 7 | 0 |
|---------|-----|-----|------|-----|-----|------|---|
| 0 | Input Thread CCU Offset | | | | | | |
| 1 | PID_OUT | | TID_OUT | | –FREE– | | |
| ... | ... | | | | | | |
| m | PID_IN | | TID_IN | | FID | Priority | |
| m+1 | Input parameter#1 CCU#1 | | | | | | |
| m+2 | Input parameter#2 CCU#1 | | | | | | |
| m+3 | Output parameter CCU#1 | | | | | | |

reconfigurable hardware are called Custom Computing Units (CCUs) and we assumed the same terminology.

In the original Molen design [18] , multithreading was not considered, but in [16], interleaved multithreading (IMT) was addressed and a Hardware scheduler was used instead of Operating System. The achieved simulation performance speedup reported in [16], with an MJPEG benchmark was 2.75, having a theoretical maximum of 2.78. Since these results were quite appealing, we decided to design a system with an RTOS managing multiple user applications executed concurrently. Moreover, we provide the infrastructure to partition the RTOS and transfer parts of its functionality on reconfigurable logic.

## 3   Architectural and Microarchitectural Extensions

The proposed **architectural** extensions with respect to [17] are visualized in Figure 1 by shaded blocks. More specifically, they are: 1) new XREG file organization; 2) modified interrupt system, extended with two software accessible registers - $\rho$IRQ/ $\rho$IRQ-ack; 3) modified 'break' instruction, called 'barrier'.

**XREG Organization:** In Table 1, the original Molen XREG organization is presented. The XREG#0 stores an offset, interpreted as a starting XREG address of the input parameters to the corresponding CCU. In our design, the XREGs are integrated into the GPP core as an extension of the existing register file.

Because of the fact that an RTOS is running concurrently with hardware tasks, some of the CCUs might finish at a time when a different thread has started on the GPP. Therefore, a mechanism is needed that allows the CCU to inform the OS which thread it corresponds to. Another problem occurs, if a context switching is performed after the CCU input parameters and XREG#0 offset are loaded, just before the "execute" instruction is fetched. Later, when the hardware task starts, it might read wrong offset value at XREG#0, if it has been changed by another thread. We solve these problems by: 1) modifying the XREG organization, as suggested by Table 2; and 2) pushing and popping the contents of XREG#0 to/ from the program stack during context switching.

The interpretation of the XREG parameter abbreviations in Table 2 is as follows: Process Identifier (PID_IN), Thread Identifier (TID_IN), Function Identifier (FID) and Priority. Note, the Priority might be equal to the Thread Priority or custom set by the programmer. The FID is used to differentiate multiple hardware tasks executed in task-parallel mode and having the same $\rho\mu$-code address. An example illustrating intra-thread and inter-thread communication is depicted in Figure 5. Tasks f_21 and f_22 are

**Table 3.** Barrier instruction and its OS interpretation

| Barrier instruction | | | | OS interpretation |
|---|---|---|---|---|
| 31          26&#124;25          16&#124;15          8&#124;7          0 | | | | |
| Opcode | FID_Num | FID_1 | FID_2 | OS_Semaphore_Send |
| ... | ... | ... | ... | OS_Semaphore_Post |
| FID_N | FID_N+1 | FID_N+2 | FID_N+3 | |

executed on CCU_2, therefore they need to have unique FID. Since both are using the same CCU, they will be consecutively executed according to their assigned Priority. After the CCU computation completes, it writes back the result to an XREG address calculated as the sum of the offset address and the number of input parameters. It also writes back its PID and TID to the PID_OUT and TID_OUT fields of XREG#1. They are used by the RTOS to identify which one of the threads is ready for execution.

There is a possibility that multiple CCUs simultaneously acquire read/ write access to the XREGs. The requests are granted according to task Priorities through an XREG Controller, designed as part of the exchange register file. Similarly, we also design an appropriate Memory Controller.

**Barrier Instruction:** The "barrier" instruction provides synchronization mechanism used by the OS to manage the CCUs execution. It is an extended version of the Molen "break" instruction. In task-sequential execution mode, the barrier instruction participates in each CCU invocation. In task-parallel mode, one barrier instruction corresponds to multiple CCU invocations indicating which of them will be executed in parallel. In Figure 5, the barrier instruction is placed after f_11 in Thread 1, executing it in task-sequential mode and after f_21, f_22 and f_23 in Thread 2 indicating task-parallel mode. An exemplary instruction format of the barrier instruction is presented to the left in Table 3. It has two components - hardware and software representation. The "barrier" instruction is encoded by the "Opcode". The "FID_Num" field corresponds to the number of CCUs synchronized by the current barrier instruction. The multiple "FID_*" fields indicate the Function IDs of the corresponding blocked hardware task. The FID is the unique identifier of the hardware task, as multiple tasks might use the same hardware computing unit. The OS interpretation of the barrier is done by blocking a thread by semaphore. The thread is unblocked only after all CCUs, marked by the barrier, have finished their execution.

**Interrupt Handling:** In task-sequential execution mode, after a hardware task has completed, it acquires access to the XREGs. When such access is granted, the CCU writes back the computed result in the corresponding XREG. Next, an Interrupt is issued to the RTOS indicating that a task has completed. In task-parallel execution mode, depending on the position of the barrier instruction, CCU could be marked as finished and possibly reused by another task without generating any Interrupt. After an Interrupt is asserted by a CCU, the Interrupt Service Routine (ISR) fetches the content of XREG#1 and un-blocks the corresponding thread or Kernel service. Then, the thread is placed in the OS Ready queue and an $\rho$IRQ-ack is send back to signal the TISC.

**Microarchitecture:** We assume that the GPP has been already extended with the original Molen architecture features and our microarchitectural augmentations are denoted as shaded blocks in Figure 2. The "$\rho$Instr. unit" is a Molen style Arbiter/ Decoder [17], integrated in the GPP Decode stage.

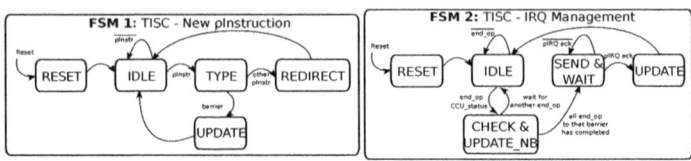

**Fig. 3.** TISC Finite State Machines

Our main contribution at microarchitecture level is the Thread Interrupt State Controller (TISC). This unit allows concurrent execution of multiple threads having tasks co-executed in software and in hardware. The TISC controller, illustrated in Figure 3, has two finite state machines (FSMs) responsible for instruction predecoding, synchronization and interrupt management of multiple CCUs. The TISC executes the "barrier" instruction at FSM 1: "TISC - New $\rho$-instruction" in state "Update". The rest of the $\rho$-instructions are redirected to the Molen Style Coprocessor at FSM 1 in state "Redirect". When a CCU completes, it uses "end_op" signal to inform FSM 2:"TISC - IRQ Management", which switches to "Check & Update_NB" state. The TISC checks whether all "end_op" signals assigned to the corresponding barrier instruction have been activated. If it is the case, FSM 2 asserts Interrupt and jumps to "Send & Wait" state to wait for an '$\rho$IRQ-ack' signal. When a hardware task completes execution, it generates an interrupt to the processor. The interrupts are consecutively dispatched to the GPP by the TISC Controller according to their priority. Contrary to other approaches found in literature, e.g. [15], which connect each hardware kernel to a separate interrupt vector, we decided to use only one interrupt vector for all active kernels (CCUs). Thus, the achieved system portability is at the cost of minimal time overhead - no more than six additional clock cycles are necessary for the FSMs (see Figure 3). It must be noted that the proposed interrupt mechanism is applicable both in preemptive and non-preemptive execution modes of the CCUs.

## 4   Software Support

Up to date, there are several widespread multithreading paradigms, such as POSIX Threads [4] and OPENMP [5]. Because of the fact that any of the existing multithreading paradigms for GPP needs to be modified in order to accommodate management for reconfigurable resources, we propose a new hierarchical programming model. The proposed programming model is applicable as an extension to any of the existing standards.

**Hierarchical Programming Model:** We currently address an embedded system with one GPP core. In order to simplify the software complexity, we partitioned the executed programming code in three abstraction layers - application, thread and task. A small example is illustrated in Figure 4. The application layer accommodates multiple user applications, running independently from each other. Each one of the applications could be composed by one or multiple threads, dynamically created and terminated.

The second level of this abstraction model is the thread layer, where user threads and OS kernel service threads co-exist. At this level only, we positioned control and data dependencies between the threads. In the example of Figure 4, we assume that

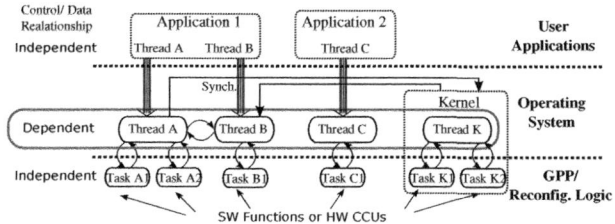

**Fig. 4.** The proposed Hierarchical Programming Model: An Example

Application 1 has two threads - Thread A and B, which are communicating between each other. In our programming model, the communication/ synchronization channel is established through the OS, encapsulated in tasks K1 and K2.

The source code of a user thread contains one or multiple tasks. These tasks are the building blocks of the third layer. Depending on where a task is executed, we distinguish two types of the tasks: a function and a CCU. When a task is executed in software, we refer to it as to a function; when a task is executed in reconfigurable hardware, we refer to it as to a CCU. All tasks have the following property - when started, they do not communicate with each other, i.e., they do not contain neither control nor data dependencies. In software, a task, being a function, receives a set of input parameters, performs computations and returns a result. These input parameters are transferred through the GPP Registers and the program stack. In hardware, the task input parameters are transferred through a preassigned exchange registers, described in Section 3, and a special "execute" instruction is invoked to start the execution. When the CCU completes, it writes back the computed result to a dedicated exchange register or in a designated location in shared memory.

**Intra-thread and Inter-thread parallelism:** To simplify the scenario, we assume that the RTOS is running only on the GPP, scheduling two user threads - Thread 1 and Thread 2, depicted in Figure 5. Each thread is composed by multiple tasks, some executed on CCUs. In Thread 1, it is f_11 running on CCU_1 and in Thread 2, tasks f_21, f_22 are executed on CCU_2 and f_23 is running on CCU_3. An example of software executed task/ function is f_12 from Thread 1. The time slots during which the thread is running on reconfigurable logic are marked by solid lines. The thread execution time on the GPP is denoted by a dashed line. The thick solid line marks the time when Thread 1 is blocked during synchronization/ communication period with Thread 2.

The programming model supports two levels of parallelism - intra- and inter-thread parallelism corresponding to two execution modes - task-sequential and task-parallel. The type of the execution mode is corresponding to the location of the special "barrier" instruction in the programming code.

*Task-sequential mode* addresses Inter-thread parallelism - In this mode, each CCU is executed sequentially. When it is finished - it signals back the processor, and the next thread continues its execution. An example is task f_11 from Thread 1 in Figure 5.

*Task-parallel mode* addresses Intra-thread parallelism - In this mode, multiple hardware CCUs and/ or software functions could be co-executed in parallel. In Figure 5, such tasks are f_21, f_22 and f_23 from Thread 2. The concurrent execution of CCUs inside of a single thread mimics the traditional out-of-order execution. The CCU

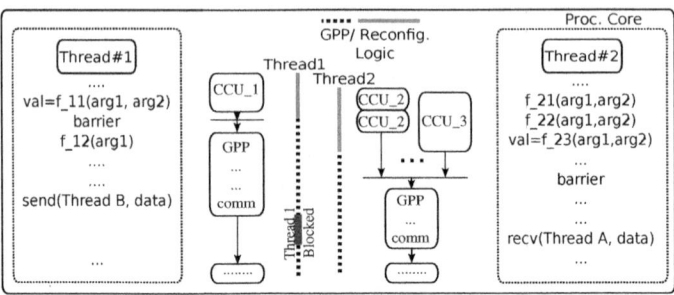

**Fig. 5.** Inter- and Intra-thread Parallelism: An Example

synchronization is controller at the software level by a dedicated barrier instruction, described in more details in Section 3.

Figure 5 also visualizes a scenario when the system has to execute CCUs acquiring more reconfigurable resources than the available ones. For example, in Thread 2 - tasks f_21 and f_22 are using the same hardware representations (CCUs). The only differences are the values of their input parameters. As it is assumed, multiple CCUs can be consequently executed over the same hardware. In current implementation, we assumed that all CCU resource requests will be always fulfilled.

## 5  Experimental Setup and Results

We have developed an experimental platform based on Xilinx Virtex II XC2VP30 FPGA chip using the XUPV2P Prototyping Board. In the following, we briefly discuss our experimental setup.

**GPP Core:** The GPP, used to obtain the experiments, has a traditional RISC architecture. It is based on the MIPS R3000 [13] implemented as a soft-core on the FPGA chip.

**RTOS:** The RTOS running on the GPP is a light-weight version of [13], which we named $\rho$RTOS. It has a tiny memory footprint, less than 20 KBytes, with a support of multithreading, memory management, synchronization and round-robin (RR) scheduling.

To satisfy our RTOS requirements, we made the following modifications to [13]: 1) improve the ISR that services the hardware timer - the XREG#0 value is pushed and popped to/ from the program stack; 2) a new ISR is designed, managing thread semaphores; 3) a Molen programming library is used to emulate the Molen instructions.

**Compiler Support:** We do not address any static scheduling techniques by the Compiler. We create the MIPS compatible binary code, by using a standard version of the GCC compiler. Instead of modifying the compiler to consider Molen polymorphic instructions, we create a Molen programming library which emulates them. In our experimental implementation, the FIDs are statically generated by the system programmer, but ultimately they should be managed by an appropriately designed Compiler.

**Evaluation Methodology:** We run several real streaming applications and we design our own synthetic benchmark suite to evaluate the impact of the RTOS and the Interrupt

**Table 4.** Evaluation Results with Floyd Algorithms

| Applic. Type: | Pure SW | | Scenarios Reconfig. HW | | SW + Reconfig. HW | | |
|---|---|---|---|---|---|---|---|
| | 1SW1T | 4SW4T | 1C1T | 4C4T | 3C1SW4T | 2C2SW4T | 1C3SW4T |
| FL25 | 47 650 | 120 483 | 46 520 | 112 079 | 116 497 | 116 981 | 119 382 |
| FL400 | 158 082 | 568 505 | 50 830 | 126 787 | 240 635 | 346 849 | 454 976 |
| FL1600 | 914 349 | 3 591 126 | 65 470 | 187 630 | 1 032 139 | 1 886 204 | 2 739 194 |
| $S_{av}$(Var. Floyd) | 1 | 1 | 6.1 | 8.2 | 2.3 | 1.5 | 1.2 |

Controller on the thread and task performance. Each one of the experiments includes: thread creation, thread termination, interrupt handling and an OS scheduling policy algorithm. To evaluate the system performance in scenario $k$, we use average speedup, denoted by $S_{av}(k)$:

$$S_{av}(k) = \sum_{i=1}^{n\_exp} \frac{T_{SWe}(i)}{T_{HWe}(i) * n\_exp} \tag{1}$$

$T_{SWe}(i)$ corresponds to the computation time of the software only implementation and $T_{HWe}(i)$ is the computation time in each one of the other scenarios, containing reconfigurable hardware executions. The $n\_exp$ variable represents the number of performed simulations in each one of the scenarios.

We employ the following nomenclature to structure the Scenario names($S_N$): $S_N$= $\{S_N,(DL)\}$ where D=$\{1,2,3,4\}$ and L=$\{C,SW,T\}$. $S_N$ is composed by multiple (DL) couples, where $L$ are interpreted as follows: $C$ corresponds to CCU, $SW$ is Software task and $T$ is Thread. For example: 4C1T should be interpreted as 4 CCUs running in parallel in 1 thread; 1C3SW4T means 4 threads, one executing CCU, the others - running in software. Note, that in the 4C1T scenario, the TISC Unit shall assert an interrupt to signal the GPP only after all four hardware tasks (CCUs) are finished.

The streaming package includes three popular applications: *Floyd-Warshall* algorithm, *Conjugate Gradient* and *MJPEG* Encoder. We choose them, because they present three different application domains: graph analysis, linear equation systems and multimedia domain. The results, in terms of clock cycles, are presented in Table 4. Note, that in any other scenario than 1C1T/ 1SW1T, there are four CCUs, identical to the one used in 1C1T/ 1SW1T. The CCUs (e.g 4C4T) are executed in four different threads, each one working on dataset sizes equal to the one from 1C1T/1SW1T.

**Real Benchmarks:** The *Floyd-Warshall* algorithm (FL) finds all shortest paths in a weighted graph. In Table 4, it is marked as FL25, FL400 and FL1600, where the numbers are the count of nodes in the graph. Working with small data-sets - FL25, the execution time of the system among all scenarios is almost equal to the pure software execution time - 1SW1T and 4SW4T. The reason for such a behaviour is caused by the OS overhead in terms of thread_creation and scheduling routines. Working with larger datasets, FL400 and FL1600, the execution time of 1C1T/4C4T remains relatively constant compared to pure software. The experiments composed by software functions and hardware CCU threads such as 2C2SW4T, mimics the behaviour of 4SW4T due to the software tasks. The FL CCU is designed following the implementation details given in [3].

The second experimental application is based on the *Conjugate Gradient* (CG) benchmark, part of the *NAS* Parallel Benchmark Suite [2]. The most computation

**Table 5.** Evaluation Results with CG and MJPEG applications

| Applic. Type: | Scenarios | | $S_{av}$ |
|---|---|---|---|
| | Pure SW<br>1SW1T | Reconfig. HW<br>1C1T | |
| CG14 | 72 251 488 | 3 684 817 | 19.6 |
| MJPEG64 | 4 030 275 | 1 269 830 | 3.2 |

intensive parts of this application are the floating point arithmetic operations. As results suggest, even with small number of trails - 14, running such applications on a simple RISC core without floating point unit using software math library only, consumes tremendous amount of time. This is the reason that we do not perform any experiments with larger datasets and we do not run more than one thread. The purpose of this benchmark is to indicate the potential portability of our ideas in application domains traditionally positioned outside of embedded world. On the other side, we demonstrate that we can port such complex applications in embedded systems, that have not been considered before. The experimental results, reported in Table 5, suggest acceleration of more than 19 times compared to the pure software implementation. The experiments are produced, using a dedicated memory hierarchy which efficiently feeds the CCUs with data. The description of such a new hierarchy is outside the scope of this paper. The reason of such high acceleration ratio is the fact that more than 95% of the application computation time is spend in a simple function. More implementation details of the CG CCU could be found in [14].

The most time intensive function of the *MJPEG* Encoder, we considered, is the Discrete cosine transformation (DCT), which we implemented in a CCU. The experimental results, reported in Table 5, suggest that the overall application execution time drops more than 3 times for a tiny video stream with 64 pixels ($8 \times 8$) per frame.

**Synthetic Benchmarks:** Last but not least, we have designed a synthetic benchmark suite, which covers more use-cases than the previously described real applications. The suite is predominantly composed by arithmetic and/or logical operations with limited number of memory accesses. The experimental results of our synthetic benchmarks are visualized in Table 6. They include two basic scenarios: 1) software functions are executed 10 times slower than their corresponding hardware implementations; and 2) when software functions are 100 times slower than the corresponding CCUs. The execution time of the CCU, modelled as number of iterations in a single loop, varies from 100 cycles upto 12000 clock cycles. Depending on the hardware acceleration ratio (10 times or 100 times), the number of software executions varies from $10 \times 100$ upto $10 \times 12000$ and from $100 \times 100$ upto $100 \times 12000$. All synthetic simulations are implemented with four tasks, executed over variable number of software threads with equal priorities.

The experimental results in 4C4T and 4C1T have almost constant execution time while the dataset size has been scaled. The execution time difference of almost four times between 4C4T and 4C1T is caused by an OS overhead. In use-cases such as 3C1SW4T and 2C2SW4T with dataset size equal to 200 elements, the system performance is even lower than pure software implementation - 4SW4T. The performance degradation is caused by the applied Round Robin scheduling policy which further delays ready for execution software threads composed by hardware tasks. An appropriate dynamic priority scheme could potentially solve this problem.

**Table 6.** Experimental Results with our Synthetic Benchmark Suite

| Dataset | SW tasks are running 10x slower than HW implementation | | | | | | SW tasks are running 100x slower than HW implementation | | | | | |
|---|---|---|---|---|---|---|---|---|---|---|---|---|
| | 4C1T | 4C4T | 3C1SW4T | 2C2SW4T | 1C3SW4T | 4SW4T | 4C1T | 4C4T | 3C1SW4T | 2C2SW4T | 1C3SW4T | 4SW4T |
| 100 | 22 865 | 90 951 | 92 449 | 92 538 | 96 532 | 197 852 | 22 865 | 90 951 | 112 035 | 133 891 | 155 597 | 177 229 |
| 200 | 22 965 | 90 940 | 93 114 | 97 136 | 101 382 | 167 335 | 22 965 | 90 940 | 439 304 | 314 000 | 241 231 | 297 986 |
| 500 | 23 015 | 92 469 | 97 461 | 113 940 | 121 646 | 133 243 | 23 015 | 92 469 | 210 234 | 297 342 | 425 868 | 530 231 |
| 1000 | 23 226 | 92 035 | 111 874 | 133 857 | 155 597 | 178 239 | 23 226 | 92 035 | 306 114 | 538 857 | 764 621 | 990 551 |
| 2000 | 24 312 | 93 982 | 436 304 | 314 000 | 234 015 | 297 986 | 24 312 | 93 982 | 479 348 | 1 323 123 | 1 122 233 | 1 893 149 |
| 4000 | 25 807 | 94 625 | 176 648 | 269 143 | 358 575 | 448 696 | 25 807 | 94 625 | 953 265 | 1 884 584 | 2 033 432 | 3 698 131 |
| 8000 | 26 968 | 96 541 | 263 322 | 312 540 | 689 630 | 810 119 | 26 968 | 96 541 | 1 544 811 | 2 382 857 | 3 523 423 | 7 223 112 |
| 10000 | 27 465 | 98 135 | 306 037 | 538 857 | 764 132 | 990 551 | 27 465 | 98 135 | 1 629 822 | 3 383 123 | 4 128 654 | 9 123 232 |
| 12000 | 29 969 | 100 112 | 354 556 | 618 788 | 867 546 | 1 170 848 | 29 969 | 100 112 | 1 796 858 | 3 996 828 | 4 696 858 | 11 488 934 |
| $S_{av}$ | 11.5 | 2.7 | 1.7 | 1.6 | 1.3 | 1 | 29.8 | 7.3 | 2.3 | 1.7 | 1.5 | 1 |

# 6 Conclusions and Future Work

In this paper, we proposed a holistic architectural support for performance efficient multithreading execution on reconfigurable hardware. More specifically, a new programming model for inter- and intra-thread parallelism was introduced and several architectural and microarchitectural improvements were proposed. The system was verified by means of synthetic benchmarks as well as by real applications. In order to benefit from our Custom Computing Machine model, a system programmer should consider the following recommendations: First, restructure the programming code and employ CCUs in task-parallel execution mode whenever possible - especially with tasks having short execution times. Second, carefully select the number and type of threads working on CCUs, since such an action can even decrease the system performance if applied improperly. If the system has hard realtime requirements, more advanced scheduling algorithms should be employed. In our future works, we shall focus on transferring parts of the RTOS on hardware. Looking at further prospective, we believe that our ideas are widely applicable on heterogeneous and homogeneous multiprocessor platforms, as well.

## Acknowledgement

This work is carried out under the COMCAS project (CA501), a project labelled within the framework of CATRENE, the EUREKA cluster for Application and Technology Research in Europe on NanoElectronics, the HiPEAC European Network of Excellence - cluster 1200 (FP6-Contract number IST-004408) and the Dutch Technology Foundation STW, applied science division of NWO (project DSC.7533).

## References

[1] Andrews, D., Niehaus, D., Jidin, R., Finley, M., Peck, W., Frisbie, M., Ortiz, J., Komp, E., Ashenden, P.: Programming models for hybrid FPGA-CPU computational components: a missing link. IEEE Micro 24, 42–53 (2004)

[2] Bailey, D.H., Barszcz, E., Barton, J.T., Browning, D.S., Carter, R.L., Fatoohi, R.A., Frederickson, P.O., Lasinski, T.A., Simon, H.D., Venkatakrishnan, V., Weeratunga, S.K.: The NAS parallel benchmarks. Tech. rep., The International Journal of Supercomputer Applications (1991)

[3] Bondhugula, U., Devulapalli, A., Fernando, J., Wyckoff, P., Sadayappan, P.: Parallel fpga-based all-pairs shortest-paths in a directed graph. In: IPDPS (2006)

[4] Buttlar, D., Farrell, J., Nichols, B.: PThreads Programming: A POSIX Standard for Better Multiprocessing. O'Reilly Media, Sebastopol (1996)

[5] Chandra, R., Dagum, L., Kohr, D., Maydan, D., McDonald, J., Menon, R.: Parallel programming in OpenMP. Morgan Kaufmann Publishers Inc., San Francisco (2001)

[6] Chandra, S., Regazzoni, F., Lajolo, M.: Hardware/software partitioning of operating systems: a behavioral synthesis approach. In: GLSVLSI 2006, pp. 324–329. ACM, New York (2006)

[7] Haynes, S.D., Epsom, H.G., Cooper, R.J., McAlpine, P.L.: UltraSONIC: A reconfigurable architecture for video image processing. In: Glesner, M., Zipf, P., Renovell, M. (eds.) FPL 2002. LNCS, vol. 2438, pp. 482–491. Springer, Heidelberg (2002)

[8] Cui, J., Deng, Q., He, X., Gu, Z.: An efficient algorithm for online management of 2D area of partially reconfigurable FPGAs. In: DATE, pp. 129–134 (2007)

[9] Marconi, T., Lu, Y., Bertels, K., Gaydadjiev, G.N.: Online hardware task scheduling and placement algorithm on partially reconfigurable devices. In: Woods, R., Compton, K., Bouganis, C., Diniz, P.C. (eds.) ARC 2008. LNCS, vol. 4943, pp. 306–311. Springer, Heidelberg (2008)

[10] Marescaux, T., Nollet, V., Mignolet, J.Y., Bartic, A., Moffat, W., Avasare, P., Coene, P., Verkest, D., Vernalde, S., Lauwereins, R.: Run-time support for heterogeneous multitasking on reconfigurable SoCs. Integration 38(1), 107–130 (2004)

[11] Nakano, T., Utama, A., Itabashi, M., Shiomi, A., Imai, M.: Harware implementation of a real-time operating system. In: 12th TRON Project International Symposium, pp. 34–42 (1995)

[12] Peck, W., Anderson, E., Agron, J., Stevens, J., Baijot, F., Andrews, D.: HTHREADS: a computational model for reconfigurable devices. In: FPL, pp. 885–888 (2006)

[13] Rhoads, S.: http://www.opencores.org/project,plasma

[14] Roldao, A., Constantinides, G.A.: A high throughput fpga-based floating point conjugate gradient implementation for dense matrices. ACM Trans. Reconfigurable Technol. Syst. 3(1), 1–19 (2010)

[15] Tumeo, A., Branca, M., Camerini, L., Monchiero, M., Palermo, G., Ferrandi, F., Sciuto, D.: An interrupt controller for fpga-based multiprocessors. In: ICSAMOS, pp. 82–87 (2007)

[16] Uhrig, S., Maier, S., Kuzmanov, G.K., Ungerer, T.: Coupling of a reconfigurable architecture and a multithreaded processor core with integrated real-time scheduling. In: RAW, pp. 209–217 (2006)

[17] Vassiliadis, S., Wong, S., Cotofana, S.D.: The MOLEN $\rho\mu$-coded processor. In: Brebner, G., Woods, R. (eds.) FPL 2001. LNCS, vol. 2147, pp. 275–285. Springer, Heidelberg (2001)

[18] Vassiliadis, S., Wong, S., Gaydadjiev, G.N., Bertels, K., Kuzmanov, G.K., Panainte, E.M.: The Molen polymorphic processor. IEEE Transactions on Computers 53, 1363–1375 (2004)

[19] Walder, H., Platzner, M.: Reconfigurable hardware Operating Systems: From design concepts to realizations. In: Engineering of Reconfigurable Systems and Algorithms, pp. 284–287. CSREA Press (2003)

[20] Wu, K., Kanstein, A., Madsen, J., Berekovic, M.: MT-ADRES: Multithreading on coarse-grained reconfigurable architecture. In: Diniz, P.C., Marques, E., Bertels, K., Fernandes, M.M., Cardoso, J.M.P. (eds.) ARC 2007. LNCS, vol. 4419, pp. 26–38. Springer, Heidelberg (2007)

[21] Zaykov, P.G., Kuzmanov, G.K., Gaydadjiev, G.N.: Reconfigurable multithreading architectures: A survey. In: SAMOS-IW, pp. 263–274 (July 2009)

[22] Zhou, B., Qui, W., Peng, C.L.: An operating system framework for reconfigurable systems. In: CIT, pp. 781–787 (2005)

# High Performance Programmable FPGA Overlay for Digital Signal Processing

Séamas McGettrick, Kunjan Patel, and Chris Bleakley

UCD Complex and Adaptive Systems Laboratory,
UCD School of Computer Science and Informatics,
University College Dublin, Belfield, Dublin 4, Ireland
{seamas.mcgettrick,kunjan.patel,chris.bleakley}@ucd.ie
http://www.ucc.ie/en/eedsp/

**Abstract.** In this paper we investigate the use of a programmable overlay to increase the performance of variable DSP workloads executing on FPGAs. The overlay approach reduces reconfiguration time and provides fast processing. The overlay was implemented on a Virtex-5 110Lx FPGA and its performance was compared with that of a conventional GPP, DSP processor and custom FPGA implementation. It is found that both FPGA based architectures outperform the GPP and DSP processor implementations. Taking into account reconfiguration the programmable overlay was found to outperform the custom FPGA implementation for small and medium data sets. On a 255 FIR filter it was shown that the programmable overlay performed better than the custom hardware on all data sets below 40 million entries.

**Keywords:** Coarse Grained Reconfigurable Arrays (CGRA), Field Programmable Gate Array (FPGA) overlay, Reconfigurable computing, Fixed point.

## 1 Introduction

Applications involving multiple task Digital-Signal Processing (DSP) workloads are common in areas such as DSP system development [4]. These workloads typically require processing of multiple sequential tasks at high speed. Tasks include filtering, Fast Fourier Transforms, matrix operations, downsampling and other filter banks. The order and quantity of these tasks varies depending on the particular application. These workloads require flexible systems in which the order of task execution and the task parameters can be changed quickly and easily while maintaining high speed processing.

Traditionally, these DSP workloads were computed on General propose processors or DSP processors. These systems are highly flexible and easily programmed but have limited parallelism. Recently, a great deal of research has been carried out showing the advantages of using FPGAs as reconfigurable DSP accelerators [4] [5] [6] [7] [8]. These papers cite the FPGA's reconfigurablility, parallel processing capability and large memory bandwidth as making it a very

A. Koch et al. (Eds.): ARC 2011, LNCS 6578, pp. 375–384, 2011.

**Table 1.** Reprogramming Time for Xilinx FPGAs using Platform Flash XL

| Devices | Slices | Bit file size (bits) | Reprogramming time (sec) |
|---|---|---|---|
| Virtex 5 LX30 | 4,800 | 8,374,016 | 0.01 |
| Virtex 5 LX110 | 17,280 | 29,124,608 | 0.04 |
| Virtex 5 LX330 | 34,560 | 79,704,832 | 0.10 |
| Virtex 6 LX75T | 11,640 | 26,239,328 | 0.03 |
| Virtex 6 LX760 | 118,560 | 184,823,072 | 0.23 |

good match to the flexibility and speed requirements of DSP workloads. The reconfigurability of the FPGA does allow the optimal hardware for these DSP workloads to be implemented. However, if the system is being used to accelerate variable workloads or if the workload cannot be entirely mapped onto the FPGA resources available, then the reconfiguration time of the FPGA soon becomes a major factor in limiting overall performance. Table 1 shows the time taken to reconfigure a number of Xilinx Virtex 5 and 6 devices using Xilinx Platform Flash XL which claims to be the fastest way to program the devices [9].

It is clear from Table 1 that reconfiguring the FPGA takes a significant amount of time and it can greatly decrease the performance of a FPGA accelerator if the device is being reconfigured frequently. The reconfiguration time is equivalent to between 2 million and 46 million clock cycles for an accelerator running at 200 MHz. This problem is becoming increasingly significant for FPGAs since configuration bit file sizes are growing and so too is the time needed to reconfigure. FPGA vendors have attempted to reduce this problem by adding partial reconfigurability to their FPGAs. However, this reduces the overall performance of FPGA as the logic being reconfigured is not available to be used by the FPGA accelerator. Partial reconfigurability is limited in its usefulness when used on a streaming data architecture. Therefore, systems where frequent reconfiguration is required, due to large workload size or task variability, would benefit from a reduction in reconfiguration time.

Coarse Grained Reconfigurable Arrays (CGRA) have been developed that allow for fast reconfiguration [2] [3]. CGRAs consist of a two dimensional array of simple Processing Elements (PE) which are individually programmed to carry out a single simple operation (e.g. Multiply, ADD). The routing of the data between PE is also reprogrammable from a limited list of options (often nearest neighbour PEs). CGRAs are therefore reprogrammable at the data-word and operator level, unlike FPGAs which are programmable on the bit and logic level. Reconfiguration of a CGRA is orders of magnitude faster than for a FPGA.

Herein we investigate using a CGRA-like programmable overlay to increase FPGA performance for variable DSP workloads. The programmable overlay implements a CGRA-like architecture with associated input - output blocks, data caches and configuration caches . The architecture can be reprogrammed at the data-word and operator level and thus reduces the need for FPGA reconfiguration. The overlay architecture proposed herein is specifically designed to support systolic mapping of regular DSP functions. This significantly improves the performance of the overlay approach. Although not investigated herein implementation of the overlay on FPGA allows for application-specific custom design of the PE level operations to further improve performance. The rest of this paper is structured as follows. The paper continues with a discussion of related work in section 2. Details of the programmable overlay are given in section 3. The performance of the overlay is compared with the performance of a CPU, DSP processor and custom FPGA implementation in section 4. Finally the paper concludes with a breif discussion of the results in section 5.

## 2   Related Work

The idea of using a programmable overlay on FPGA was previously studied by Shukla et al. in a series of papers on the QUKU architecture [10] [11] [12] [13]. The Quku architecture consists of a memory interface, a microblaze controller and a 4x4 CGRA. That is to say that the CGRA consists of 16 Processing Elements (PE). Although it is not explicitly stated, each PE appears to be able to carry out a single addition or a single multiplication. The PE has 3 inputs and a single output which is routed to four other PEs (The PE to the east, south, north-east and south-east). In [11], the performance of a FIR filter implemented on the QUKU architecture is compared with the same FIR filter implemented on a Microblaze softcore processor and in FPGA logic. The area of the resulting architectures and the number of clock cycles needed to complete the FIR filter were compared. It is unclear from the results if the reconfiguration time was taken into account. In these results the programmable overlay architecture achieved a middle ground between the microblaze soft processor which has the smallest area but the greatest number of clock cycles and the custom implementation which had the largest area and lowest number of clock cycles.

The major benefit of the QUKU architecture is its two tiered reconfiguration, namely fine grain reconfiguration and coarse grained reprogramming [13]. Fine grained reconfiguration is intended to be infrequent but can be used to make major changes to the programmable overlay architecture such as changing the data width, customising programmable overlay connections for a given type of application class. Coarse grained reprogramming changes the PE operations or routing between the PEs. This can be done very quickly since the configuration words are very short. This dynamic reconfiguration does not change the hardware on the FPGA but simply changes the order or operation performed by an individual PE.

The programmable overlay proposed in this paper builds on the foundation of the QUKU legacy. The proposed programmable overlay allows two tiered reconfiguration similar to the QUKU architecture. However, the proposed programmable overlay differs from the QUKU architecture in the following ways. The proposed programmable overlay is designed to support systolic mapping of DSP algorithms. The CGRA-like array, caches and DMA have all been designed for systolic mapping which reduces the number of memory reads required and thus the proposed architecture can utilise more PEs than the QUKU architecture, increasing the performance of the architecture. The PE in the proposed programmable overlay can carry out a multiply and add in each PE. The PE can also route data and operate on data in the same clock cycle. This is better suited to the DSP algorithms than the QUKU proposal. This paper also provides results comparing the proposed design to the GPP, DSP and FPGA implementations of the algorithms presented.

## 3    Programmable Overlay

Figure 1 shows a block diagram of the proposed programmable overlay. The architecture contains a 16x16 CGRA array (256 PE), three memory interfaces, four DMAs, four 16kB data caches and the system is controlled by a Finite State Machine controller. The current version of this hardware is implemented as a slave device to a DSP processor. The DSP processor sets up the calculations by writing instructions to the slave memory interface. The DSP processor then starts the calculation by writing a command word to the FPGA accelerator. Once the command word is written the Finite State Machine on the FPGA controls the programming of the CGRA and execution of the function. An interrupt is sent to the DSP processor when the calculation has finished. An integrated power-PC or a soft-core processor could also be used as the master controller for the calculation. This would increase the area of the design but it would allow the FPGA to be a standalone solution which would not require an external processor.

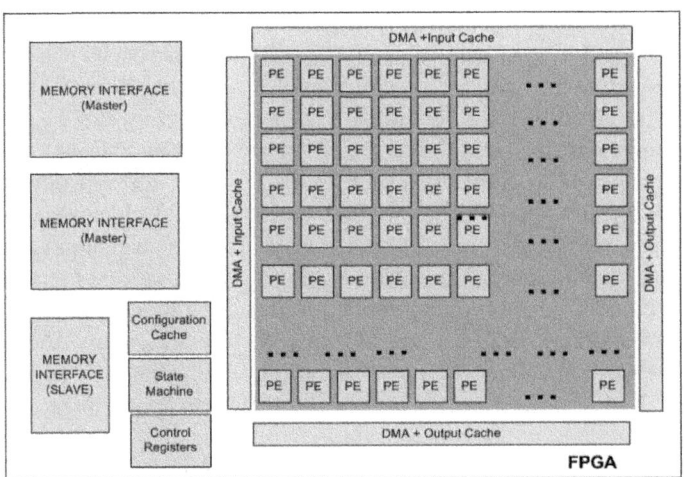

**Fig. 1.** Block diagram of the CGRA Overlay system with 256 PE

### 3.1    Communication with Memory

The programmable overlay has three memory interfaces. The first of these memory interfaces is a slave interface which is used by the host processor to connect to and program the Finite State Machine in the programmable overlay. This interface contains a number of registers which can be used to set up calculations. The registers available include address registers for data in memory, a status register and a command register. The programmable overlay carries out the command as soon as it is written to the command register.

The other two memory interfaces are master memory interfaces and are used by the DMAs to access data during the calculations. Two of the DMAs in the design are used to read data from memory into the programmable overlay and two are used to write back the result to memory. Each of the DMAs has a large memory buffer which can be used to store data to facilitate shared use of the memory interfaces. If the data stream is short the result and data can be stored in these memory buffers and written out at the end of the calculation. The current implementation of the DMA can be programmed to work using three different protocols. The first protocol is to distribute/retrieve data in a round robin fashion between all activated columns and rows of the CGRA. The second protocol is to pump data into the first CFU on the top left of the array and retrieve it from the last CFU at the bottom right of the array. This allows the overlay to stream data through all 256 CFU which can be used to implement large filters etc. Finally in the third protocol the DMA is programmed to feed all the inputs of the array with the same piece of data. The DMAs all work independently and so it is possible to program the top DMA to distribute data in a round robin fashion and left DMA to apply identical inputs to all inputs. Likewise the right side and bottom DMAs can be independently programmed to return the data in whatever format is needed.

This implementation of the programmable overlay for FPGA uses a 16 bit memory interface. This format was chosen to match the DSP host processor and memory being used. However, any memory interface width can be used.

## 3.2   The Array

The programmable array consists of a 16x16 array of processing elements as shown in Figure 1. The array has a 24 bit data path. Each of these processing elements contains a multiplier and adder, four registers and switching logic which is controlled by a control register. Figure 2 shows a block diagram of a processing element in the proposed programmable array. Each processing element has four inputs and two outputs. The PE can perform an add/sub, Multiply, MAC, Multiply subtract or a Nop using any of the inputs or internal registers. The outputs can be programmed to be any of the four internal registers. Figure 3 shows how the configuration word is used to reprogram the PE.

The array is programmed using the data lines and a configuration signal. When the configuration signal is high the data on the $input0$ data path is routed to the configuration register, see Figure 3. The data on the $input1$ data path is routed to the internal register two. This feature can be used to program filter coefficents or other constants that might be needed during the calculation. Both $input0$ and $input1$ are routed through to the outputs during configuration. In this way the array can be programmed in 16 clock cycles. Using the data line to reprogram the PE ensures that very little extra hardware is needed for configuration.

Global_en
Input port 0
Input port 1
Input port 2
Input port 3
Reg0
Reg1
Reg2
Output port 0
Output port 1
ALU
ALU reg
Flush_en
Config_en
Configuration Register (32 bits)

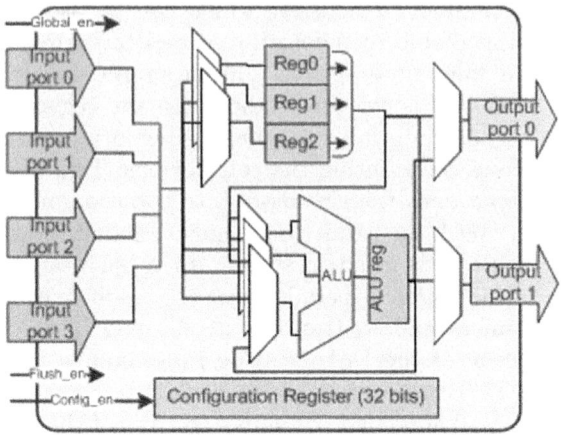

**Fig. 2.** Block diagram of Processing Element

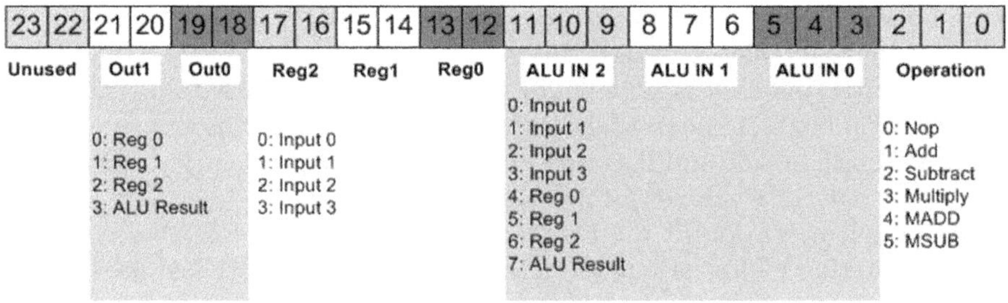

23 22 21 20 19 18 17 16 15 14 13 12 11 10 9 8 7 6 5 4 3 2 1 0
Unused
Out1
Out0
Reg2
Reg1
Reg0
ALU IN 2
ALU IN 1
ALU IN 0
Operation
0: Reg 0
1: Reg 1
2: Reg 2
3: ALU Result
0: Input 0
1: Input 1
2: Input 2
3: Input 3
0: Input 0
1: Input 1
2: Input 2
3: Input 3
4: Reg 0
5: Reg 1
6: Reg 2
7: ALU Result
0: Nop
1: Add
2: Subtract
3: Multiply
4: MADD
5: MSUB

**Fig. 3.** Configuration word for processing element

The configuration cache can be used to store a number of commonly used configurations. This allows the user to switch between configurations with a minimum of overhead. Data for configuration can also be taken from memory via the memory interfaces.

One final feature of the PE is the flush signal. This can be used flush the contents of the ALU register to memory at the end of a calculation. When this signal is set high the data in the ALU register is passed to the right until it reaches the DMA and is written to memory.

### 3.3 Mapping

Currently, mapping of calculations to the proposed programmable overlay is done manually. An API of functions for the programmable overlay is available, currently the FIR, IIR, Wavelet, Matrix Multiply, Matrix Vector Multiply and Discrete Fourier Transform have been mapped and is currently being expanded. A user would therefore simply call the function they wished to have implemented and the API takes care of loading the correct configuration to the programmable overlay.

**Table 2.** Programmable Overlay device Utilisation on a V5 Lx110 FPGA

| Logic Name | Utilisation (available) | % used |
|---|---|---|
| Slice Registers | 44,462 (69,120) | 64% |
| Slice LUTs | 57,726 (69,120) | 82% |
| Occupied Slices | 61,090 (69,120) | 88% |

# 4 Results

The proposed design was implemented in Verilog and targetted at a Virtex-5 Lx110 FPGA [14]. Two of the proposed overlays fit on the device. Table 2 shows the device utilisation for the proposed design. The current design utilises approximately 88% of the overall device and can be clocked at up to 196MHz. The overall design has an equivalent gate count of 2,872,116 gates. The average equivalent gates per PE is 5600.

The design has 512 PEs each of which can carry out two arithmetic operations per clock cycle at 196 MHz. Since we are comparing multiple platforms we have normalised a MAC operation to be two operations (a multiply and an add) This gives the current design a peak performance of 200 GOps. Table 3 compares the current architecture against a GPP, DSP processor and custom hardware on FPGA. The GPP used in this calculation is an Intel Core i7-950 Processor with four cores and a 3 GHz clock [15]. Each core can carry out eight 32bit integer operations per clock cycle. The results for a single core are presented as well as for the overlay processor chip (i.e. all four cores). A Texas Instruments TMS320c6457-1200 is used as the DSP processor in this comparison [16]. The TMS320c6457-1200 has a clock rate of 1.2 GHz and can perform eight 32 bit MACs. Each MAC is normalised to two operations for comparisons in the table.

It is only possible to compare custom hardware on a case by case bases with the programmable overlay. Therefore, the custom hardware figures have been calculated using a 255 tap FIR filter. The design is replicated to increase performance. The custom FPGA FIR filter can achieve a clock rate of 200MHz and the three 255 tap FIR filters fitted on the device with associated memory interfaces, data buffers and a controlling state machine.

**Table 3.** Peak performance comparison of programmable overlay with DSP processor, GPP and custom hardware on FPGA

| Device | Clock | Op/clock | GOP | Speed-up |
|---|---|---|---|---|
| TMS320c6457-1200 | 1.2GHz | 16 | 19.2 | 1 |
| Intel Core i7-950-Single Core | 3GHz | 8 | 24 | 1.2x |
| Intel Core i7-950- Quad Core | 3GHz | 32 | 96 | 5x |
| Programmable Overlay | 196MHz | 1024 | 200 | 10x |
| Custom | 200MHz | 1536 | 307 | 16x |

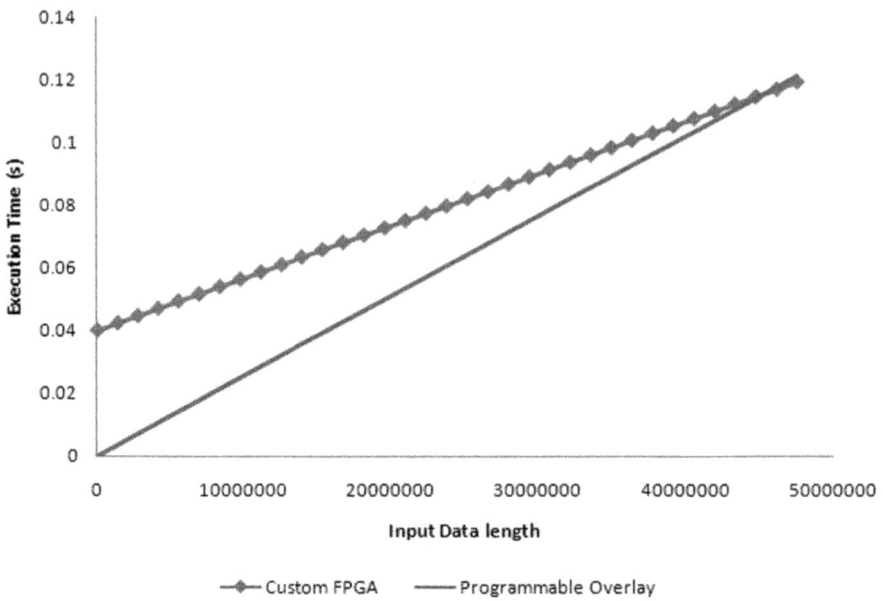

**Fig. 4.** Configuration time + Execution time vs Input data length for programmable overlay and custom FIR filter. Taking configuration time into account. Lower is better.

Table 3 shows the peak Giga-Operations (GOP) achievable on all the architecture as well as the result normalised to a multiple speed up over the slowest architecture which is the DSP processor. It can be seen from Table 3 that using an FPGA based solution in the form of custom hardware or programmable overlay will lead to the greatest overall performance. The custom hardware and programmable overlay have a peak performance of 10 and 16 times greater than the baseline DSP processor performance. They also have 2 and 3 times greater peak performance respectively than the intel i7 quad core processor. The custom FPGA solution has the highest overall performance.

However, if reconfiguration time is taken to account performance is greatly impacted. In Table 1 the reconfiguration time for the Virtex-5 Lx110 FPGA was given as 0.4 sec. The programmable overlay can be programmed in 16 clock cycles from the configuration cache. This is equivalent to 81ns. Figure 4 shows the execution time summed with the configuration time for a 255 FIR on the FPGA custom hardware and the programmable overlay for various input data vector sizes. Initially for small vectors of input data the executing time of the FIR filter is dominated by the configuration time of the FPGA for the custom FPGA solution. The Programmable overlay is affected less from this initial configuration overhead and so outperforms the custom FPGA implementation for all input vectors less than 40 million words long, despite the custom FPGA hardware having a peak performance of 1.5 times that of the programmable overlay. The point on Figure 4 where the two line intersect indicates the point where both architectures have the same execution time. This is referred to as the

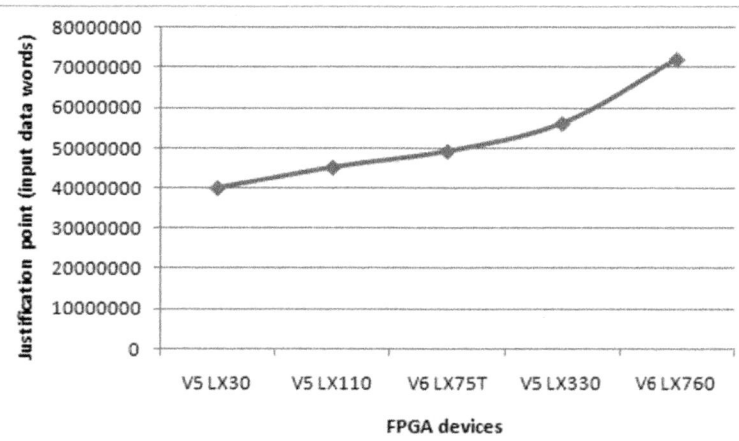

**Fig. 5.** Justifcation point of Virtex5 and Virtex 6 devices shown in Table 1

justification point. Before this point the Programmable overlay performs better than the FPGA hardware. After the justification point the greater peak performance of the custom FPGA implementation makes up for the longer configuration time and so the custom FPGA solution performs better than the programmable overlay.

Figure 5 show the justification point for a FIR Filter on the FPGA devices given in Table 1. It is clear from these results that as FPGA get bigger and their reconfiguration time increases the justification point also increases. Larger devices therefore benefit more from a programmable overlay than smaller devices.

## 5   Conclusions

In this paper a programmable overlay for FPGA was discussed for DSP algorithms with variable workloads. Traditional FPGA accelerators are hampered by long configuration time. Using a programmable overlay for the FPGA can cut this configuration time substantially and leads to overall performance increases. It was shown that these performance increases were mainly beneficial for small and medium sized data sets.

This work has further demonstrated the benefits of using a programmable overlay to increase performance in DSP algorithm. Over the coming months it is hoped to map more functions on the programmable overlay and ultimately to create an API of functions for use in the DSP realm.

**Acknowledgments.** This research was funded as a part of the Efficient Embedded Digital Signal Processing for Mobile Digital Health (EEDSP) cluster, 07/SRC/I1169 by Science Foundation Ireland (SFI).

# References

1. Baas, B., Zhiyi, Y., Meeuwsen, M., Sattari, O., Apperson, R., Work, E., Webb, J., Lai, M., Mohsenin, T., Truong, D., Cheung, J.: AsAP: A Fine-Grained Many-Core Platform for DSP Applications. IEEE Micro 27(2), 34–45 (2007)
2. Singh, H., Lee, M., Lu, G., Kurdahi, F., Bagherzadeh, N., Chaves Filho, E.: MorphoSys: an integrated recongurable system for data-parallel and computation-intensive applications. IEEE Transactions on Computers 49(5), 465–481 (2000)
3. Liang, C., Huang, X.: SmartCell: An Energy Efficient Coarse-Grained Reconfigurable Architecture for Stream-Based Applications. EURASIP Journal on Embedded Systems, 15 pages (2009); Article ID 518659, doi:10.1155/2009/518659
4. Chang, C., Wawrzynek, J., Brodersen, R.W.: BEE2: A high-end reconfigurable computing system. Design Test of Computers 22(2), 114–125 (2005)
5. Mohamed Junaid, K.A., Ravindrann, G.: FPGA accelerator for Medical Image Compression System. In: IFMBE Proceedings, vol. 15, part 10, 396-399 (2007)
6. Nallatech - FPGA accelerators, http://www.nallatech.com (accessed November 2010)
7. Altera: FPGAs provide reconfigurable DSP Solutions, white paper (2002)
8. Rubin, G., Omieljanowicz, M., Petrovsky, A.: Reconfigurable FPGA-based Hardware Accelerators for Embedded DSP. In: 14th International Conference on Mixed Design of Integrated Circuits and Systems, pp. 147–151 (2007)
9. Xilinx: Platform Flash XL, http://www.xilinx.com/products/config_mem/pfxl.htm (accessed Novemeber 2010)
10. Shukla, S., Bergmann, N.W., Becker, J.: QUKU: A fast run time reconfigurable platform for image edge detection. In: Bertels, K., Cardoso, J.M.P., Vassiliadis, S. (eds.) ARC 2006. LNCS, vol. 3985, pp. 93–98. Springer, Heidelberg (2006)
11. Shukla, S., Bergmann, N.W., Becker, J.: QUKU: A Two Level reconfigurable architecture. In: IEEE Computer Society Annual Symposium on Emerging VLSI Technologies and Architectures (2006)
12. Shukla, S., Bergmann, N.W., Becker, J.: QUKU: A Coarse Grained Paradigm for FPGA. In: Proc. Dagstuhl Seminar (2006)
13. Shukla, S., Bergmann, N.W., Becker, J.: QUKU: A FPGA Based Flexible Coarse Grain Architecture design paradigm using process networks. In: IEEE International Parallel and Distributed Processing Symposium, IPDPS 2007 (2007)
14. Xilinx. Virtex-5 Family Overview DS100 (v5), http://www.xilinx.com/support/documentation/data_sheets/ds100pdf (accessed November 2010)
15. Intel Core i7-950 Processor (8M Cache, 3.06 GHz, 4.80 GT/s Intel QPI), http://ark.intel.com/Product.aspx?id=37150 (accessed November 2010)
16. Texas Instruments TMS320C6457 -1200, http://focus.ti.com/docs/prod/folders/print/tms320c6457.html (accessed November 2010)

# Secure Virtualization within a Multi-processor Soft-Core System-on-Chip Architecture

Alexander Biedermann, Marc Stöttinger, Lijing Chen, and Sorin A. Huss

Technische Universität Darmstadt,
Department of Computer Science,
Integrated Circuits and Systems Lab,
64289 Darmstadt, Germany
{biedermann,stoettinger,chen,huss}@iss.tu-darmstadt.de
http://www.iss.tu-darmstadt.de

**Abstract.** This work aims to extend the concept of virtualization, which is known from the context of operating systems, for embedded multi-processor system-on-chip architectures. Thus, by introducing a Virtualization Middleware, we abstract from static bindings between soft-core processors and operation system kernels running on them. Using the proposed Virtualization Middleware, it is possible to remap kernels during run-time to different instances of soft-core processors. Our approach guarantees by design both privacy and integrity of virtualized data. In addition, no modifications to the employed kernels have to be done in order to be used within this approach. Therefore, it automatically secures context sensitive information against any access by unauthorized users. Therefore, the proposed hardware-based virtualization scheme is best suitable for embedded multi-processor systems with multiple users working on transparently and securely shared resource instances.

**Keywords:** virtualization, middleware, system-on-chip, processor virtualization, self-healing systems, transparent memory management.

## 1 Introduction

Virtualization is a fundamental concept in many operating systems and applications in the area of mainframes, servers, and personal computers. This concept provides transparent resource management on encapsulated environments for applications or for whole operating systems. Furthermore, virtualized environments may also share the same resources of the physical system, despite believing to be the sole user of these resources.

The advocated virtualization concept is aimed to embedded computing, needs and constraints of this field of application. Nowadays, embedded HW/SW architectures may consist of several processors and dedicated hardware modules on a single chip, delivering powerful systems-on-chip. We use the virtualization to abstract from the in general static binding between processors and the operation system kernels executed on them. Thereby, we provide arbitrary bindings during run-time without any loss of data integrity.

A. Koch et al. (Eds.): ARC 2011, LNCS 6578, pp. 385–396, 2011.

Reconfigurable devices, for instance FPGAs, may consist of hardware components as well as of soft-core processors. Both may be instantiated up to an arbitrary number, only limited by the device's logic and routing capacity. Thus, FPGA designs may employ several soft-core processors with different kernels to execute their application software, whereas fault-tolerant concepts: If parts of a processor are either detected as defective or as being attacked by a malicious application, the kernel running on this processor may be transferred to another processor. Depending on the current design architecture, this processor might be either as spare module provided for redundancy reason or might be an already running processor which then has to transparently handle two different kernels and their application code. Furthermore, we want to guarantee that despite virtualization, no mix between different kernel contexts may ever occur. Since FPGAs being increasingly used for security relevant applications, e.g., to accelerate cryptographic calculations, one has to ensure that sensitive data may never be revealed during virtualization. To follow the idea of virtualization as a transparent process, we provide in the sequel a solution, where no adaption of the kernels and related application code is necessary in a secured and reliable environment. Since virtualized environments have no knowledge about other possible virtualized environments running concurrently, virtualization disables unintentional or malicious communication between them. Therefore, our main contribution is the introduction of a generic virtualization concept for a multi-processor based embedded system, which features an intermediate layer, called *Virtualization Middleware*, between processors and allocated kernels. This middleware copes to virtualize kernels on a multi-processor architecture with respect to the already mentioned issues of reliability and security.

The paper is structured as follows: In Section 2, we introduce the related work on virtualization approaches in embedded systems, especially on FPGAs. Then, we introduce the proposed virtualization concept and discuss its properties in Section 3. Section 4 demonstrates a practical realization of the approach by means of a SoC multi-processor system instantiated on a Virtex-V FPGA,. Cryptographic algorithms are being executed on three Xilinx "MicroBlaze" soft-core processors, which are then virtualized during run-time. Finally, Section 5 subsumes the achieved benefits of this approach and lists some advanced aspects, which will be addressed in future research work.

## 2    Related Work

Common operating systems are able to provide basic functionality to virtualize system resources, cf. [3]. Multi-tasking on one or several processing resources may be seen as a important predecessor of virtualization. Brebner was the first to describe a scheme for hardware multi-tasks for FPGA, in [1]. Since then, a lot of research aimed to task handling on partial reconfigurable platforms has been done [2,4,5]. In conjunction with partial reconfiguration methods on FPGA platforms, the task handling on FPGA has to improve in order to handle fault tolerance. Examples of fault tolerant schemes using partial reconfiguration techniques are reported in [6,8]. Both, the works in [6] and [8], consider

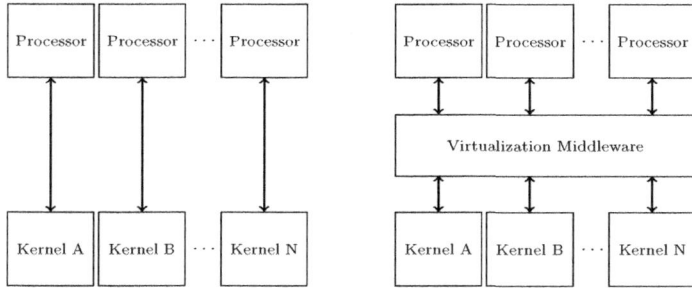

**Fig. 1.** Fixed Bindings between Programs and Processors on the left and resolved Bindings by Virtualization Middleware on the right

virtualization in designs with multiple instances of processing resources as countermeasure against faults by sharing resources to accomplish the task of the defective unit.

But none of the related work of virtualization schemes on FPGAs consider privacy issues during the virtualization phase. Apparently, a system which shares resources has to handle the privacy and integrity of data to be trustworthy even in case of virtualization. A related work which tends to the direction of a hardware-based secure virtualization scheme is quoted in [7]. Compared to our approach, the virtualization functionality is provided by a software-based operation system, therefore, the connection between the disjunct memory areas is always physically existing. In contrast, the proposed Virtualization Middleware physically separates disjunct memory data. Additionally, during virtualization, current kernel and application status values extracted from processors are stored securely and are inaccessible for any user.

## 3    Soft-Core Virtualization by a Dedicated Middleware

The trend of continuously increasing logic resources allows multiple processors to be instantiated on a single chip. Complex system-on-chip designs with several processors running independent kernels can be constructed in this way. Usually, an unique and static binding between a processor and a kernel running on it exists, cf. Figure 1, left hand side. In this scenario, a kernel cannot access data of another kernel due to physical separation. Therefore, such a structure is suited, e.g., to run applications relevant to security by isolating them from potentially malicious applications. However, a strict binding has several disadvantages. In case of a fault of a processor, the application running on it cannot be executed any further. If an attack on a processor is detected, then applications running on this processor have to be stopped to prevent information leakage. Furthermore, because of the strict binding to one kernel, no other kernel is able to use any of the resources of this processor.

Thus, our main goal is to remove any strict binding between kernels, the applications running on them, and processors but, in addition, keep the memory

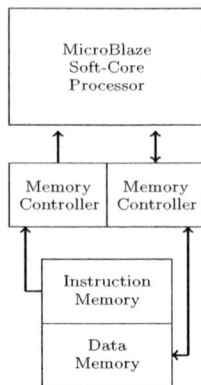

**Fig. 2.** A MicroBlaze Soft-Core Processor System

areas of different kernels strictly disjoint. We reach this goal by introducing a *Virtualization Middleware* between kernels and processors. For example, Figure 1, right hand side, shows a set of kernels, which are unchained from an explicit processor binding by the Virtualization Middleware. The approach presented in [6] proposes a virtualization middleware, too. However, this is done only for application specific hardware modules. We, therefore, generalize the approach in [6] by supporting established general-purpose soft-core processor architectures. We demonstrate the approach on top of the Xilinx MicroBlaze processor. The resulting advantages compared to [6] are the exploitation of a common processor system as well as the full transparency of virtualization: Kernels running on a multi-processor system-on-chip, cf. Figure 1, can be used within this approach without any further software adaption. As a result, the Virtualization Middleware supports a migration of applications during run-time. Besides data path rerouting, current states of kernels, which are stored in the processors, have to be migrated, too. In the following section, we discuss in detail, how to preserve disjoint memory consistency despite run-time virtualization.

### 3.1   Structure of the Virtualization Middleware

Figure 2 depicts a MicroBlaze processor system in its default configuration. This structure is being frequently used in embedded designs for Xilinx devices. A MicroBlaze processor set consists of the soft-core processor itself, two memory controllers, and independent memory areas for data and instructions, respectively. The memory controllers are connected to the MicroBlaze via *Local Memory Busses*. By taking into consideration the Virtualization Middleware, a set of several MicroBlaze processor units may now be virtualized. The Virtualization Middleware is being inserted between the processors and their data/instruction memories. An exemple for a virtualizable multi-processor system consisting of three MicroBlaze processor systems and the Virtualization Middleware is highlighted in Figure 3. In doing so, the middleware encapsulates the Memory Controllers. Thus, the Xilinx design environment treats the middleware just as a

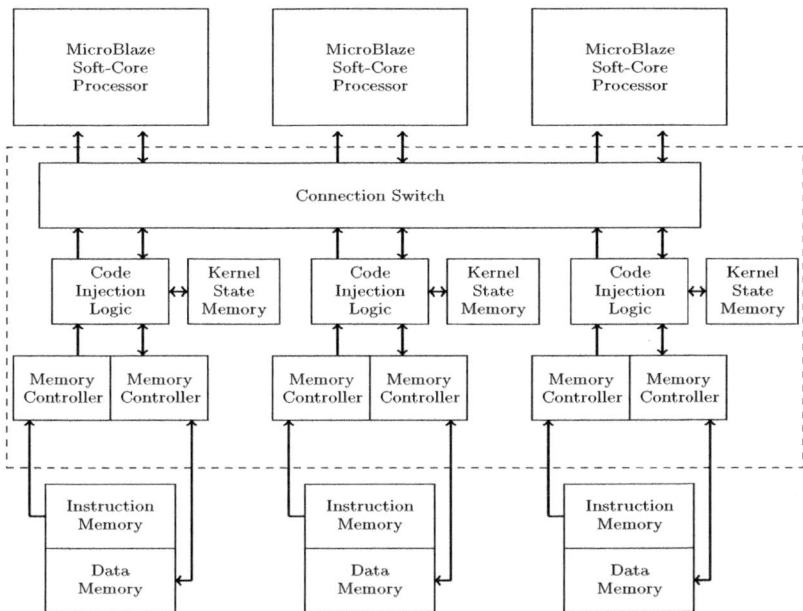

**Fig. 3.** The Virtualization Middleware for three MicroBlaze Processor Systems shown by a dashed Rectangle

set of memory controllers. As an important consequence, we achieve a smooth integration of virtualization services into the Xilinx design flow.

As mentioned before, in general each kernel, which consists of data and instruction memory, is linked to a MicroBlaze processor. This strict binding is now relieved by the Virtualization Middleware. A module called *Communication Switch* dynamically reroutes data transfers between kernels and their corresponding processors. However, by rerouting data transfers, serious side effects may arise. During the execution of applications in a kernel, the corresponding processor contains current state information of both the kernel and the application software: The *Machine Status Register* of a MicroBlaze contains both status bits of processing results as well as the current configuration of the processor. The *Program Counter Register* stores the memory address of the next instruction which has to be fetched from the instruction memory. Several *General Purpose Registers* hold intermediate data or data, which were loaded from the data memory or wait to be written back to it. The values of all these registers are necessary to ensure the correct function of the kernel. Therefore, if the Virtualization Middleware just reroutes the data transfers using the Connection Switch, the contexts of different kernels would be mixed-up. Thus, after a rerouting, an application might access data of applications of another kernel, because this data still exists in the allocated processor. Furthermore, the kernel may have lost all its current state information stored in the processor, which was assigned to the kernel before the rerouting. This situation will certainly lead

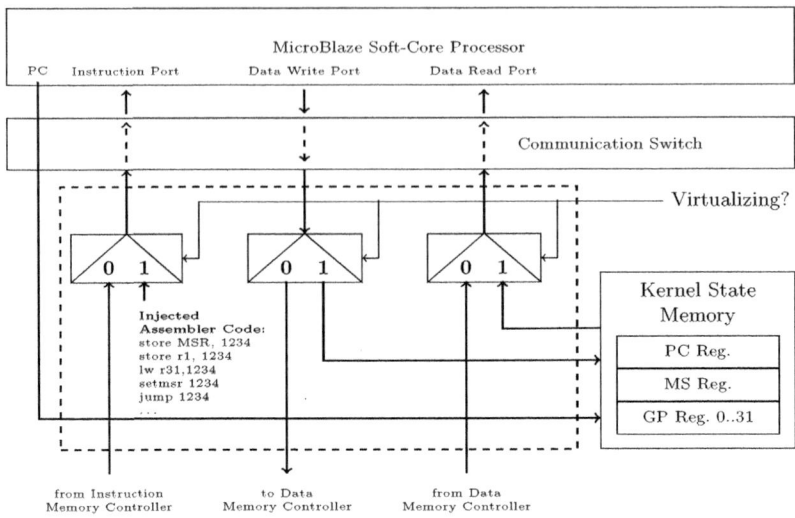

**Fig. 4.** The Code Injection Logic shown by a dashed Rectangle and connected to the Kernel State Memory

to inconsistencies in the program flow. For this reason, we address and resolve these side effects by means of the advocated virtualization concept.

### 3.2    Virtualization Procedure Using the Middleware

As the proposed Virtualization Middleware is located between instruction memories and the processors, we are able to inject instructions into the processors instead of just loading instructions from the related memories. The module named *Code Injection Logic* in Figure 3 accomplishs this task. A *Kernel State Memory* is attached to each Code Injection Logic. During a virtualization process, it saves the current state of an kernel, as it is represented by the register values of the corresponding processor. A simplified structure of the Code Injection Logic with an attached Kernel State Memory is depicted in Figure 4. To clarify the virtualization process, we introduce the following definitions:

**Definition 1.** *m is a list of processors.*

**Definition 2.** *n is a list of kernels.*

**Definition 3.** *A binding b is a mapping between a kernel and a processor.*

**Definition 4.** *A binding set B is a group of bindings for all processors. If #n ≤ #m, each kernel is bound to a dedicated processor. If #n > #m, some kernels remain unbound in the current binding set.*

**Definition 5.** *A binding set array BSA is a group of binding sets B.*

**Algorithm 1.** Virtualization Process within Virtualization Middleware
**Require:** Design running with current binding set $B \in BSA$
    $n =$ list of processors, $m =$ list of kernels, with $\#m \leq \#n$
**Ensure:** Design running with binding set $B' \in BSA$
    **for** all kernels in $m$ **do**
        **while** current processor instruction is atomic **do**
            Execute instruction.
        **end while**
        Execute instructions in pipeline of corresponding processor.
        Decouple data memory and instruction memory.
        Save Program Counter Register in Kernel State Memory.
        Save Machine Status Register in Kernel State Memory.
        Save General Purpose Registers in Kernel State Memory.
    **end for**
    $B' =$ determineNewBinding(BSA);
    **for** all kernels in $m$ **do**
        Load saved General Purpose Registers into now attached processor.
        Load saved Machine Status Register into now attached processor.
        Jump to Address from saved Program Counter Register.
        Couple data memory and instruction memory.
    **end for**

We now discuss the virtualization process for a scenario, where there are as many processors as kernels. The corresponding pseudo code algorithm is depicted in Algorithm 1. First, the design runs with a binding set $B$, where each processor is connected to a kernel. A binding set array $BSA$ contains several binding sets; in its extreme cases it either contains one binding set or binding sets covering all possible permutations of bindings. If a virtualization process is triggered, then the Code Injection Modules check for each processor in case that a non-atomic instruction sequence is the next to be fetched. Some instructions demand other instructions to follow directly without any interruption. In case that an atomic sequence is detected, the corresponding Code Injection Module waits until a non-atomic instruction follows. Only a few instructions out of the MicroBlaze instruction set are atomic and take between one and three clock cycles each. Therefore, in most cases, the virtualization process may immediately commence.

As an example, the following process is visualised in Figure 5 in a simplified illustration. No-operation instructions are first fed into each MicroBlaze processor, until each of the five-stage pipelines are emptied. Afterwards, the connections to both data and instruction memories are decoupled from the processors. Herby, we ensure that no inconsistencies in the memory contents may occur while virtualizing. We now inject a instruction into the processor which actually should write the content of the Program Counter Register into the data memory. The destination address is given in the instruction. However, one may chose an arbitrary destination address, because the Code Injection Logic redirects the data path, which originally was connected to a data memory, to the Kernel State Memory. This situation can be seen in Figure 4, where we save the content of the Program Counter Register. It contains the address of the

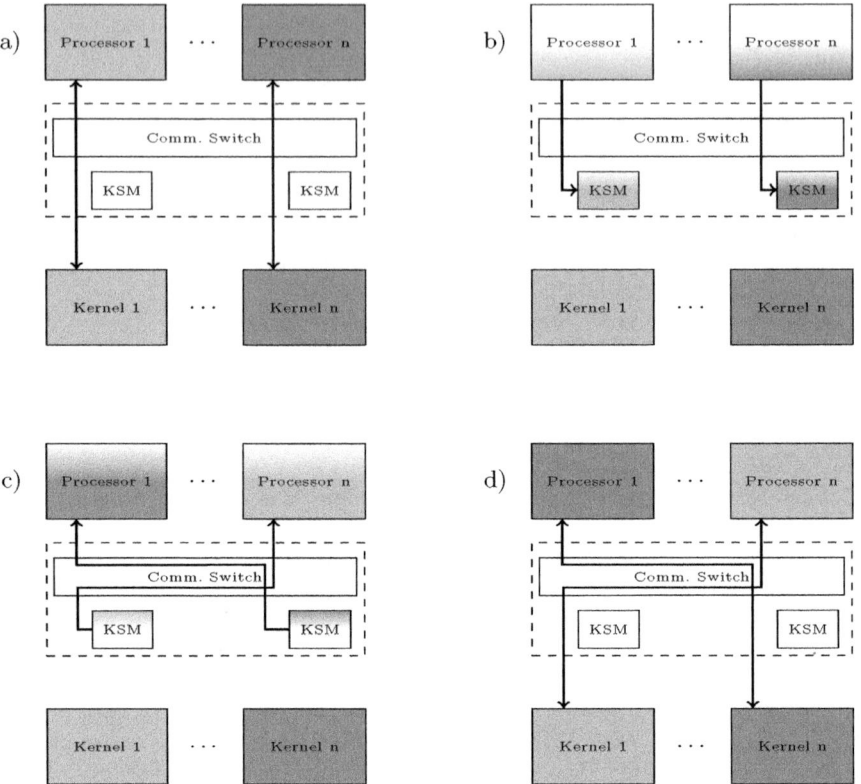

**Fig. 5.** Steps of the Virtualization Process: a) Normal Operation, b) Saving of States in the Kernel State Memories, c) Rerouting in the Communication Switch and State Restore, d) Normal Operation with virtualized Processors

module, where the execution of the kernel's applications will continue after the virtualization process has finished. In the same manner, we inject additional instructions in order to save the Machine Status Register as well as the General Purpose Registers to the data memory. Again, we redirect the data path leading to the data memory to the Kernel State Memory. After this procedure, the current states of all kernels are now stored in the corresponding Kernel State Memories. For demonstration purposes, MicroBlaze processors in their default configuration were exploited. As the MicroBlaze is a soft-core processor, several components may be added by the designer, such as floating point units. If such additional components are used, their special purpose registers also have to be saved within the Kernel State Memories. After having all internal states saved, the Communication Switch now permutes the data paths between the applications and the processors. In the pseduo code denoted in Algorithm 1, this is done by the function *determineNewBinding()*. The selection of a new binding set $B'$ out of $BSA$ is performed by this function according to the field of application at hand. For fault tolerant scenarios, for example, bindings which compensate for a failed processor might be chosen. In scenarios, where there are more kernels than processors, a scheduler arranges for the assignmend of processing resources to kernels, e.g., in a round robin scheme. After having selected a new binding, the internal state of its newly assigned kernel has to be loaded to each processor. Thus, the sequence above is executed in reversed order: Instructions are injected so that the MicroBlaze loads values from the data memory into its registers. However, instead of accessing the data memory, the MicroBlaze transparently accesses the Kernel State Memory. In that manner, all the previously saved registers of the program are restored. Then, data and instruction memory modules are linked to the processor. Finally, a unconditioned jump is injected. Its target address is the value of the Program Counter Register. Despite the dynamic context switch, the internal state of the kernel in its newly assigned processor is identical to the one previously assigned. Thus, the normal process sequence is continued. After the completion of the virtualization process, all involved processors continue the execution of their attached applications at the point of their interruption.

### 3.3   Benefits of the Virtualization Process

We apply instruction injection to save and to restore internal state information of kernels while switching between processors. Thereby, we assure the correct continuation of program execution after the virtualization process. At no point in time a mix up between program contexts can occur. This is guaranteed by the Kernel State Memories, of which each is bound to a kernel. When initializing a virtualization process, these memories save the current states of kernels, which are represented by the register values within the processors. Data memories and instruction memories are separated during virtualization. Thus, they remain untouched by the virtualization process. These memories are not reconnected before the internal kernel states are being restored in the newly assigned processors. Therefore, data memories and instruction memories of different kernels remain strictly disjoint all the time. This is an important aspect, especially for applications relevant to security. Typical security critical problems arising from a shared use of a processing resource are thus avoided. Using common multitasking systems, much effort has to be spent to guarantee that code relevant to security may not operate on the same memory as potential malicious code. Our Middelware precludes this problem by keeping the memories of different applications strictly disjoint.

Furthermore, by virtualizing on instruction set layer, the approach is independent of the contexts running on the attached processors. Therefore, different kernels or operating systems, as for the MicroBlaze, e.g., the *Xilkernel* or an embedded Linux Kernel, may be virtualized. Here, in the parallel set of processors, it makes no difference, if one processor runs the Xilkernel and another Linux. An integral aspect is that the programmer of applications does not need to adapt his code to the virtualization architecture. Arbitrary code, which is able to run on a MicroBlaze, can be directly used with this virtualization approach. Therefore, this approach is feasible to be integrated into already existing systems.

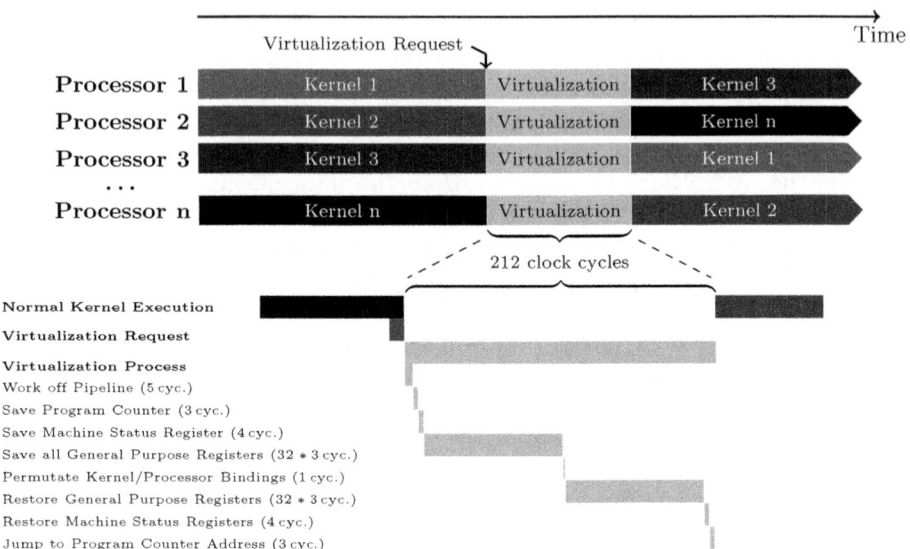

**Fig. 6.** Virtualization due to a Request within a Multi-Processor Design seen over Time

In addition, the Virtualization Middleware may be taylored such that several kernels share a single processor. A scheduler may then trigger the virtualization process to grant each application access to the processing resource. As defined for virtualization, each application seems to be the sole user of the resource.

## 4    Application Example and Discussion

In order to demonstrate the proposed virtualization concept and its ability to cope with privacy, we implemented a SoC on a Virtex-V FPGA consisting of three processors of which two run cryptographic algorithms. On two of the three MicroBlazes soft-core processors, an *Advanced Encryption Standard* (AES) cipher C-program is running with two unique keys. In this application scenario, we assume an attacker who wants to read out parts of the secret key or plaintext stored inside the general purpose register of a MicroBlaze. To avoid the success of this attack, we virtualize the attacked processor with the available third processor which runs a normal, i.e., non-security sensitive application. Via a push button, we simulate an attack detection and, therefore, change the binding set using the presented virtualization scheme. Furthermore, a blinking sequence of LEDs indicates, whether the execution of a program delivered a result which fits to pre-calculated results, i.e. whether the execution of the cryptographic algorithms was successful and correct. The correct execution despite arbitrary triggered virtualization events shows that there is no mixing of applications contents. Therefore, neither the plaintexts nor the employed keys nor the resulting ciphertexts of an application can be accessed by another application or by an attacker within this design.

**Table 1.** Resource Consumption and Timing Properties of the Virtualization Middleware

| | |
|---|---|
| LUTs | 771 |
| Registers | 293 |
| RAM32M | 16 |
| Max. Design Frequency | 96 MHz |
| Duration of Virtualization | 212 clock cycles |

Independent of the execution content of the attached kernels, the virtualization process takes just 212 clock cycles, if virtualization is being triggered when no atomic instruction occurs, cf. Figure 6. At first, emptying the five stages pipeline of each processor takes 5 clock cycles. After that, saving the Program Counter needs 3 more clock cycles. Saving the Machine Status Register in the Kernel State Memory consumes 4 clock cycles. Accessing the Kernel State Memory, saving and restoring the 32 General Purpose registers, which takes 3 clock cycles for each register, consumes 99 clock cycles. Rerouting the data paths within the Communication switch only takes one clock cycle. After the rerouting of the processor/program binding in the Communication Switch the registers have to be restored and a jump to the saved Program Counter Address is performed. This takes $99 + 3$ clock cycles. Therefore, for each virtualization process, the execution of applications is suspended for a total of 212 clock cycles.

An overview about resource consumption of the Middleware and timing properties of this exemplary design is given in Table 1. A frequency of 96 MHz is achievable, which lays slightly below usual clocking frequencies for Microblaze processors on a Virtex-V. As we used generic statements in VHDL, the current implementation is easily expandable to support more processors and memories thus featuring the important property of scalability. With an increasing number of MicroBlazes and memories, however, the routing complexity may also increase considerably.

## 5   Conclusion and Further Work

In this paper, we presented an approach to securely virtualize embedded soft-core processors on instruction level. Hereby, we abstract from a fixed application/processor binding. Therefore, applications or even whole operating system kernels may be virtualized onto another processor during run-time. The affected applications and kernels are completely unaware of this virtualization process. Applications and kernels, which are intended to run via the Virtualization Middleware need not to be reworked to fit into this architecture. All memory contents and processor states of a the active kernels remain consistent during the virtualization, in order to continue the normal execution after the virtualization step. We have demonstrated that this virtualization scheme may be employed without any dedicated design of application programs. Furthermore, we have detailed how we guarantee disjoint memory contents at any time and, therefore, allow for a dynamic yet secure context switch during run-time. In addition, this concept is able to cope with privacy issues of the memory and context content during virtualization. For future work, we will extend the virtualization concept to easily support virtualization of communication components adjacent to processors. This is an important aspect, since components need to be further accessible, even if the kernel using them has been virtualized onto another processor. We currently working on generic solution to allow the programmer to easily connect such components via the Virtualization resulting in fully virtualizable System-on-Chip environments.

## Acknowledgment

This work was supported by CASED (http://www.cased.de).

## References

1. Brebner, G.J.: A virtual hardware operating system for the xilinx xc6200. In: Glesner, M., Hartenstein, R.W. (eds.) FPL 1996. LNCS, vol. 1142, pp. 327–336. Springer, Heidelberg (1996)
2. Brebner, G.J., Diessel, O.: Chip-based reconfigurable task management. In: Brebner, G., Woods, R. (eds.) FPL 2001. LNCS, vol. 2147, pp. 182–191. Springer, Heidelberg (2001)
3. Chun-Hsian Huang, P.A.H.: Hardware resource virtualization for dynamically partially reconfigurable systems. IEEE Embedded Systems Letters 1, 19–23 (2009)
4. Huang, M., Simmler, H., Serres, O., El-Ghazawi, T.A.: Rdms: A hardware task scheduling algorithm for reconfigurable computing. In: IPDPS 2009, pp. 1–8. IEEE, Los Alamitos (2009)
5. Simmler, H., Levinson, L., Männer, R.: Multitasking on fpga coprocessors. In: Grünbacher, H., Hartenstein, R.W. (eds.) FPL 2000. LNCS, vol. 1896, pp. 121–130. Springer, Heidelberg (2000)
6. Stöttinger, M., Biedermann, A., Huss, S.A.: Virtualization within a parallel array of homogeneous processing units. In: Sirisuk, P., Morgan, F., El-Ghazawi, T., Amano, H. (eds.) ARC 2010. LNCS, vol. 5992, pp. 17–28. Springer, Heidelberg (2010)
7. Stumpf, F., Eckert, C.: Enhancing trusted platform modules with hardware-based virtualization techniques. In: SECURWARE 2008, pp. 1–9. IEEE, Cap Esterel (2008),
   http://www.sec.in.tum.de/assets/staff/stumpf/SECURWARE2008RE1.pdf
8. Yeh, C.-H.: The robust middleware approach for transparent and systematic fault tolerance in parallel and distributed systems. In: ICPP 2003, pp. 61–68. IEEE, Los Alamitos (2003)

# Author Index